T0340163

Population Issues in Social Choice Theory, Welfare Economics, and Ethics

This book presents an exploration of the idea of the common or social good, extended so that alternatives with different populations can be ranked. The approach is, in the main, welfarist, basing rankings on the well-being, broadly conceived, of those who are alive (or ever lived). The axiomatic method is employed, and topics investigated include the measurement of individual well-being, social attitudes toward inequality of well-being, the main classes of population principles, principles that provide incomplete rankings, principles that rank uncertain alternatives, best choices from feasible sets, and applications. The chapters are divided, with mathematical arguments confined to the second part. The first part is intended to make the arguments accessible to a more general readership. Although the book can be read as a defense of the critical-level generalized utilitarian class of principles, comprehensive examinations of other classes are included.

Charles Blackorby is Professor of Economics, University of Warwick, UK. He is a coauthor of *Duality, Separability and Functional Structure* and has published articles in social choice theory and welfare economics. Professor Blackorby is a Fellow of the Econometric Society and has received awards for his research. His current research interests are social choice theory, population ethics, welfare economics, and optimal taxation issues in public economics.

Walter Bossert is Professor of Economics and CIREQ Research Fellow at the University of Montreal, Canada. He has published articles on social choice theory, bargaining theory, and cooperative game theory. Professor Bossert's current research interests are the theory of individual and collective choice, population ethics, bargaining theory, and cooperative game theory. He is a member of the editorial board of *Social Choice and Welfare*.

David Donaldson is Professor Emeritus of Economics, University of British Columbia, Canada. He has received awards for teaching and research and has published articles on social choice theory and welfare economics. Professor Donaldson's current research interests include social choice theory, population ethics, and interpersonal comparisons of well-being using equivalence scales in welfare economics.

Econometric Society Monographs No. 39

Editors:
Andrew Chesher, University College London
Matthew Jackson, California Institute of Technology

The Econometric Society is an international society for the advancement of economic theory in relation to statistics and mathematics. The Econometric Society Monograph Series is designed to promote the publication of original research contributions of high quality in mathematical economics and theoretical and applied econometrics.

Population Issues in Social Choice Theory, Welfare Economics, and Ethics

Charles Blackorby
University of Warwick

Walter Bossert
University of Montreal

David Donaldson
University of British Columbia

CAMBRIDGE
UNIVERSITY PRESS

CAMBRIDGE
UNIVERSITY PRESS

32 Avenue of the Americas, New York NY 10013-2473, USA

Cambridge University Press is part of the University of Cambridge.

It furthers the University's mission by disseminating knowledge in the pursuit of education, learning and research at the highest international levels of excellence.

www.cambridge.org
Information on this title: www.cambridge.org/9780521532587

First published 2005

A catalogue record for this publication is available from the British Library

Library of Congress Cataloguing in Publication data

Blackorby, Charles, 1937–
Population issues in social choice theory, welfare economics and ethics /
Charles Blackorby, Walter Bossert, David Donaldson.
    p.   cm. – (Econometric Society monographs ; no. 39)
Includes bibliographical references and index.
ISBN 0-521-82551-2 (hardback) – ISBN 0-521-53258-2 (pbk.)
1. Population policy.   2. Population–Econometric models.   3. Quality of life.
4. Welfare economics.   5. Social choice.   I. Bossert, Walter.   II. Donaldson,
David, 1938–   III. Title.   IV. Series.
HB883.5.B55   2005
304.6'01–dc22   2005004349

ISBN 978-0-521-53258-7 Paperback

Contents

Preface

Because the subject matter of this book belongs to economics, philosophy, and political science, we have attempted to make it accessible to people who do not want to spend time with complex mathematical arguments. Following the example of Amartya Sen's *Collective Choice and Social Welfare* (1970a), each chapter after the first is divided into two parts. Readers familiar with the mathematics of social choice can read both parts, but those who are less accustomed to the technical aspects of the subject can read Part A alone, consulting Part B as needed. Our intention is to provide some motivation for the questions asked, explanations of the intuitions that lie behind the proofs, and discussions of the theorems and their importance. In all chapters except 5 and 6, almost all the unsupported assertions in Part A are proved in Part B and citations are given there for the rest. Chapter 6 offers characterizations of the principles presented and discussed in Chapter 5. As a consequence, some results discussed in Chapter 5 are proved in Chapter 6.

We have not attempted to provide a survey of all the work that has been done in the area. Rather, we focused on our view of the subject, drawing from the work of others when it harmonized with our overall plan of investigation.

When preparing the book, we benefited greatly from the comments of many colleagues, but two people deserve special mention. John Broome helped us with philosophical difficulties, and we thank him for his inspiration and encouragement. We were able to read his book *Weighing Lives* (2004a) and we found it extremely valuable. In many ways, it complements this book, offering a detailed treatment of the philosophical issues that we pass over. John Weymark has read a large part of the book and his detailed comments have made our presentation and proofs substantially better than they otherwise would be.

Many other people have given us comments and criticisms and we know the book is better for their help. They include Gustaf Arrhenius, Nick Baigent, Paul Beaudry, Donald G. Brown, Sam Bucovetsky, Erik Carlson, Peter Danielson, Marc Fleurbaey, Alan Gibbard, Walter Glannon, James Griffin, Peter Hammond, Thomas Hurka, Frank Jackson, Matthew Jackson, Serge-Christophe Kolm, Ashok Kotwal, Guy Laroque, Jean-François Laslier, Michel Le Breton, Rosa Matzkin, Stephan Michelson, Philippe Mongin, Adam Morton, Hervé

Moulin, Gordon Myers, Klaus Nehring, Marc Nerlove, Lars Osberg, Hans Peters, Wlodek Rabinowicz, El Rand, James Redekop, John Roemer, Amartya Sen, Richard Sikora, Kotaro Suzumura, William Thomson, Peter Vallentyne, Gary Wedeking, Catherine Wilson, and participants at numerous conferences, workshops, and seminars.

We thank Matthew Jackson, the editor of this series; Scott Parris, Senior Editor, Economics and Finance, Cambridge University Press; Simina Calin and Helen Lee of Cambridge University Press; and Susan Detwiler and her team at TechBooks. Research support through grants from the Social Sciences and Humanities Research Council of Canada is gratefully acknowledged.

C.B., W.B., D.D.   February 2005

CHAPTER 1

Introduction

In discussions of environmental problems, descriptions of histories of the world over the next century or two are often linked to policy alternatives. In these histories, standards of living as well as the size and composition of populations may differ at different times. It might be said, for example, that, if present policies continue, we can expect a large population, low average standards of living, environmental degradation, and wars as the relative scarcity of land increases. On the other hand, if responsible environmental and population policies are adopted, we might be told to expect a smaller population with higher average standards of living and a world with more resources and less environmental damage for subsequent generations.

Other policy decisions have population consequences as well. Examples include the allocation of public funds to prenatal care, the design of aid packages to developing countries, public funding of education, legalization of birth-control devices, resource conservation, expenditures on public health, and the design of social security systems. In addition, individual fertility decisions affect population composition and size both directly and indirectly, as the children have children. In each of these cases, history will depend, to some extent, on actions taken.

It is important to ask what it means to say that one of these histories is better than another. Because population size and individual identities may be different, this is not a straightforward question. To attempt to provide an answer, we investigate principles for social evaluation that can be used, together with factual information, to rank histories. Such an exercise requires examining the idea of the common good, extended so that it can take account of differences in population composition and size. We call principles that make comparisons of alternative histories with respect to their social goodness population principles.

Because changes in policies rarely lead to gains for everyone, principles must be able to balance gains and losses. In addition, one policy might result in a larger population with a lower standard of living than another does. Principles therefore have an ethical dimension. The idea of the common or social good provides the needed trade-offs by means of a social goodness relation. Instead of using two relations – one for betterness and one for equal goodness – we focus on a single at-least-as-good-as relation, which combines the two. Two histories are equally good if and only if each is at least as good as the other, and one is better than another if and only if it is at least as good as the other and it is not the case that the other is at least as good as it. Goodness relations may or may not be complete. If they are, every pair of histories is ranked.

Our main focus is on principles for social evaluation that are commonly called welfarist (Sen 1979). These principles use information about individual well-being to rank histories, disregarding all other information. Welfarism rests, in the main, on the idea that any two histories with the same population in which everyone is equally well off are equally good, a condition commonly called the Pareto-indifference axiom.

Welfarist principles regard values such as individual liberty and autonomy as instrumental: valuable because of their contribution to well-being. In addition, virtues and fair procedures may have instrumental value. Because of this, it is important to employ a comprehensive notion of well-being such as that of Griffin (1986) or Sumner (1996). We focus on lifetime well-being and include enjoyment, pleasure and the absence of pain, good health, length of life, autonomy, liberty, understanding, accomplishment, and good human relationships as aspects of it. Individuals who are autonomous and fully informed may have self-regarding preferences that accord with their well-being, but we do not assume that they do. In addition, sentient nonhuman animals have experiences, and it is possible to take account of their interests. We reserve our discussion of that possibility for Chapter 11, however, and focus on human beings in the rest of the book.

Most principles are impartial in the sense that individual identities do not matter. Because impartiality is ethically fundamental, all the principles that we investigate satisfy it.

In a large part of the book, we require the social at-least-as-good-as relation to be complete. We are not committed to this, but we see the exercise as important. We want to know whether there are reasonable principles that provide complete orderings of alternative histories. Some principles, however, fail to rank some of them. This may occur for one of two reasons: it may be impossible to obtain enough information, or there may be no fact of the matter. In the first case, it is possible to generate an incomplete ranking by using several principles that generate complete rankings when information is perfect. In the second case, principles must be able to take account of the incommensurabilities directly. See Chapter 7 for a discussion.

Although the idea of the common good plays an important role in discussions of government policies and consequentialist moral theories, we do not consider the normative status of actions. In situations in which actions lead with certainty to particular histories, we use population principles to rank actions according to their goodness but do not provide a link with obligations. As a result, our work is consistent with rule consequentialism, which assesses moral rules by estimating their probable consequences, and with supererogation, the idea that some actions that have very good consequences but require great sacrifices by the agents taking them are beyond the call of duty.

1.1 FRAMEWORK AND METHOD OF INVESTIGATION

We use the term *alternative* as a label for a complete history of the universe. Each alternative is associated with a list of the identities of all those individuals who ever live. Information about the well-being of each person on the list (welfare information) is available for each alternative. In addition, social nonwelfare information together with individual nonwelfare information is known for each person on the list. Nonwelfare information may include individual information such as dates of birth, lengths of life, and character traits. Social nonwelfare information may include information about individual liberties, freedom of the press, and so on.

We distinguish several cases. In the simplest one – the single-profile case – the information associated with each alternative is fixed. The other cases allow some of the information to vary and, in that case, we say that there are multiple information profiles.

A goodness relation for an individual ranks alternatives according to their goodness for that person. Individual lifetime well-being is measured by an index called a utility function, which is a representation of an individual goodness relation. If the value of the index is greater for one alternative than for another, the individual's life is better, for him or her, in that alternative. Similarly, equal utility values correspond to alternatives that are equally good for the person. Uniqueness properties of utility functions are discussed in Chapter 2.

If a person's life, taken as a whole, is worth living, we say that the level of well-being associated with his or her life is above neutrality, and, if it is not, the lifetime well-being of the individual is below neutrality. If lifetime well-being is at neutrality, it is not the case that, as a whole, the life is worth living and it is not the case that it is not worth living. We adopt the standard convention that neutrality is associated with a utility value of zero. We do not believe a person can be made better off by being born into a life above neutrality (see Chapter 2): well-being requires being.

Population principles, welfarist or not, can be captured in a formal model by employing social-evaluation functionals. A social-evaluation functional associates an ordering of the alternatives with every profile of information.[1] Welfarism obtains if and only if there is a single ordering of vectors of individual utilities that can be used, together with the information about well-being in a profile, to order the alternatives. Some welfarist principles, such as classical and average utilitarianism and all members of the critical-level utilitarian class, rank some alternatives with different population sizes differently but coincide when ranking alternatives with the same population size.

Most of the principles we investigate require interpersonal comparisons of well-being. Statements such as "person 10's life is better, as a whole, in

---

[1] Orderings are at-least-as-good-as relations that are reflexive (every alternative is as good as itself), complete, and transitive (if x is at least as good as y and y is at least as good as z, x is at least as good as z). See Chapter 2, Sections 2.2 and 2.6, for discussions.

alternative x than person 25's life is in alternative y" are assumed to be meaningful, provided that 10 is alive in x and 25 is alive in y.

Our focus is, for the most part, on welfarist principles, but we also investigate other principles. An example is a principle that uses information about individual birth dates to discount future utilities. In addition, we consider principles that can rank uncertain alternatives: lists of possible alternatives with probabilities assigned to each component. Such principles can be used to rank actions of individuals or governments according to their goodness when the consequences of actions are uncertain.

Throughout the book, we use axioms to examine a large collection of problems. Axioms for population principles, for example, isolate hypothetical situations and impose simple properties on the behavior of the principles in these situations (Thomson 2001). One such axiom is minimal individual goodness. If two alternatives have the same population and one is ranked as better than the other, the axiom requires it to be better for at least one person. The underlying idea is that our intuitions are reliable in such situations.

Population principles make two kinds of trade-offs: those that determine the relative weight assigned to the interests of different individuals, and those that trade off inequality-adjusted per-capita well-being against population size. Axioms place conditions on those trade-offs and allow us to discover and formulate classes of population principles.

Many of the theorems that we prove are characterizations of classes of principles such as critical-level generalized utilitarianism or number-dampened generalized utilitarianism. Such theorems show that each member of the class satisfies all the axioms used and that no other principle does. Some collections of axioms are inconsistent, however. Formal statements of inconsistencies are called impossibility theorems and they provide important tests of the intuitions that motivate the axioms, calling for the assignment of priorities. Consequently, some of the discussion of axioms necessarily involves assessments of their relative worth.

Our aim in using the axiomatic method is to contribute to readers' understanding of the various classes of principles. An additional contribution is provided, we believe, by applying the principles to simple choice situations. For that reason, we examine several examples. Some of these focus on choices in a certain universe and others deal with choices when consequences are uncertain.

Anonymity axioms capture the idea of impartiality in social evaluation. One version applies to pairs of alternatives in which the same number of people live and requires two alternatives to be ranked as equally good if the social nonwelfare information is the same in both, and individual welfare *and* nonwelfare information is the same but attached to different individuals. As a special case, anonymity also applies to comparisons of alternatives with the same population.

A principle implies the repugnant conclusion (Parfit 1976, 1982, 1984, Chapter 19) if every alternative in which each person experiences a utility level above neutrality is ranked as worse than some alternative in which each member of a larger population has a utility level that is above neutrality but arbitrarily close to it. In that case, population size can always be used as a substitute for quality of life as long as lives are (possibly barely) worth living. Avoidance of the repugnant conclusion is an important axiom that ethically acceptable principles should satisfy. Although classical utilitarianism leads to the repugnant conclusion, many principles avoid it but some of these have other undesirable features. To make further progress in finding the class of acceptable principles, therefore, additional axioms are needed.

It is possible to rank alternatives by using information in a single period of time only. If that is done and information in other periods is the same, it is important that the resulting rankings coincide with those obtained from a timeless point of view, using lifetime utilities. In Chapter 9, we find that such a consistency requirement, when combined with a few standard axioms, results in principles that lead to the repugnant conclusion. The reason is that the shortening of a life may appear to be a population change if viewed from within a single period. We conclude that history must matter to some extent. The critical-level generalized utilitarian principles allow the existence of every person whose life is over to be ignored but require that we take account of the well-being of any person whose life may extend into the present or future. In addition, these principles can be applied consistently to any group of people, such as a nation or a particular generation, if its members are the only ones affected by a change.

If each member of a set of feasible actions is associated with an alternative (without uncertainty), a possibility for rational action is to choose the action that leads to the best alternative. (If more than one alternative is best, an action that leads to any one of them will do.) Such choices are said to be rationalized by an ordering of the alternatives. To investigate choices directly, we use axioms that specify various conditions on the choices themselves. Two issues arise. The first is whether observed choices can be rationalized by an ordering of the alternatives. The second is conditional on the existence of such an ordering and is concerned with its properties.

For any alternative, consider another with one additional person alive and suppose, hypothetically, that each member of the common population has the same level of well-being in both. A critical level for the utility vector that corresponds to the first alternative is a level of utility for the added person that makes the two alternatives equally good. In general, critical levels may depend on utility levels of those who are alive and their number. Critical levels exist for all the principles considered here.

Most of the principles that we discuss rank alternatives with the same population size by using generalized utilitarianism. It ranks these alternatives with the sum of transformed utilities, where the transformation is increasing and continuous. Same-number utilitarian principles are also same-number generalized utilitarian, but the converse is not true. Same-number generalized utilitarian principles can be averse to inequality of well-being or, equivalently, give priority to the interests of people with low levels of well-being.

The best-known welfarist principles are classical utilitarianism, which uses the sum of utilities to rank alternatives, and average utilitarianism, which uses average utility. Because classical utilitarianism leads to the repugnant conclusion and average utilitarianism sometimes declares the ceteris paribus addition of a person whose life is not worth living to be good, these principles typically are rejected. There are, however, many principles that avoid both of these properties. Our inquiry groups principles into the following classes: critical-level generalized utilitarianism, restricted critical-level generalized utilitarianism, number-sensitive critical-level generalized utilitarianism, restricted number-sensitive critical-level generalized utilitarianism, number-dampened generalized utilitarianism (Ng 1986), and restricted number-dampened generalized utilitarianism (Hurka 2000). The classical-utilitarian and average-utilitarian principles belong to some of these classes. In addition to the above classes of principles, we consider variable-population extensions of maximin and leximin as well as principles that have been suggested by Carlson (1998) and Sider (1991). Members of the critical-level generalized utilitarian class have critical levels that are independent of utilities and population size. In the number-sensitive class, critical levels may depend on the number of people alive but not on their utilities.

Because the above principles provide complete orderings of alternatives, every pair of alternatives is ranked. In Chapter 7, we study a class of principles that rank some, but not all, pairs. It is closely related to the critical-level generalized utilitarian class and is called critical-band utilitarianism. The band is an interval of critical levels and each principle in the class ranks one alternative as at least as good as another if and only it is at least as good according to critical-level generalized utilitarianism for all critical levels in the band.

The book can be read as a defense of various classes of principles. The strongest case is made for the number-sensitive generalized utilitarian principles with nonnegative critical levels that are positive above some population size. An important part of the case for those principles is that their generalizations to principles that rank uncertain alternatives satisfy the most important axioms for that environment (see Chapter 7). A consistency axiom has the effect of ruling out all restricted principles. Additional axioms, which apply to environments with certainty (Chapter 5) or uncertainty (Chapter 7), provide support for various subclasses: the critical-level generalized utilitarian principles with positive critical levels, the number-sensitive critical-level utilitarian class, and the critical-level utilitarian principles with positive critical levels.

A good case, without considerations of uncertainty, can be made for the critical-level generalized utilitarian principles. If critical levels depend on population size, ethical significance must be attached to absolute numbers. If the axiom existence independence is employed, this problem vanishes because critical levels, if they exist, must be constant. Alternatively, the axiom extended replication invariance requires only relative population sizes to matter for social evaluation, and the only number-sensitive principles that satisfy it have constant critical levels.

In our view, the best class of principles consists of the critical-level utilitarian principles with positive critical levels. Our best defense of same-number utilitarianism (rather than same-number generalized utilitarianism) rests on acceptance of a property formulated in a model that accommodates uncertain consequences (Chapter 7). The crucial feature of the argument we use is the hypothesis that actual utility is given by one of the functions that can be used to compare uncertain outcomes. If this hypothesis is replaced by a condition that requires individual attitudes toward uncertainty about well-being to coincide across individuals and with the social attitude toward inequality of well-being, it is possible to make a case for critical-level generalized utilitarian principles that have positive critical levels and are weakly inequality averse.

To use a critical-level principle, the critical level must be chosen. The critical level must be positive to avoid the repugnant conclusion, but it must not be so large as to exclude lives that are reasonably good. For that reason, the critical-band principles may be an acceptable alternative. However, their application requires abandoning the requirement that all alternatives can be compared.

Although we offer defenses of these principles, we attempt to do more. The axiomatic investigation, if done well, should provide an understanding of the properties that are necessary for other classes, such as the restricted critical-level utilitarian and restricted number-dampened utilitarian classes. In addition, we expect our analysis will interest readers who are not welfarists, because they typically believe that considerations of well-being have some relevance for social evaluation.

1.2 ORGANIZATION

Each chapter after this one is divided into two parts, with mathematically advanced material relegated to Part B. Chapter 6 offers characterizations of the principles that are presented and discussed in Chapter 5. As a consequence, some results discussed in Chapter 5 are proved in Chapter 6.

Because the measurability and interpersonal comparability of well-being is a fundamental issue in our framework, we begin in Chapter 2 with an examination of the most important informational bases of individual well-being. If the number of alternatives is finite or countably infinite, there is a utility function for each person that ranks alternatives in the same way that the individual's goodness relation does. If there is an uncountable infinity of alternatives, goodness relations that satisfy a continuity axiom also have representations. These representations are ordinally measurable: unique up to increasing transformations.

An individual might be able to make comparisons such as "the gain to me in moving from y to x is greater than the gain in moving from z to w." If individual utility functions are cardinally measurable – unique up to increasing affine transformations – such comparisons are meaningful. In some environments, the ability to compare utility differences is sufficient to ensure cardinal measurability.

The measurement of well-being by means of utility functions is not, by itself, sufficient for interpersonal comparisons of well-being. Without such comparisons, however, there are no social-evaluation functionals based on ordinally or cardinally measurable individual utility functions that satisfy a few basic axioms (Arrow 1951, 1963; Blackorby, Donaldson, and Weymark 1984). If, however, individual utility functions are cardinally measurable, interpersonal comparisons of well-being at two (or more) levels, which we call norms, are sufficient to provide enough information for any social-evaluation functional. Temperature measurement, which employs a cardinal scale, is analogous. If the freezing and boiling temperatures for water are set at 0° and 100°, the Celsius scale is defined. Once the norms have been chosen, temperature is numerically measurable, and comparisons of temperature levels and temperature differences at different times and places are meaningful.

In addition to the measurement of lifetime well-being, we also investigate the measurement of well-being in periods of time. Because people have integrated lives, such measures may depend on experiences in other periods. Lifetime well-being may be thought of as functionally dependent on levels of well-being in all the periods of life. We take account, explicitly, of the possibility of different lengths of life in different alternatives.

In Chapter 3, we turn to welfarist social evaluation. In both the single-profile and multiprofile environments, welfarism depends critically on the Pareto-indifference axiom. This axiom can be motivated by the requirement that the principle satisfy minimal individual goodness (Goodin 1991), which implies Pareto indifference. An important aspect of the population principles we investigate is that they are impartial. The anonymity axioms that we employ guarantee that, and they take account of differences in nonwelfare characteristics.

Each population principle has subprinciples that can be applied to fixed populations and they are presented and discussed in Chapter 4. Such subprinciples are a necessary part of population principles but, by themselves, are not capable of ranking alternatives with different populations. Although the fixed-population utilitarian principle is indifferent to inequality of well-being, other principles do exhibit aversion to utility inequality. Among these are the generalized utilitarian principles that use strictly concave transformations. They give priority to the interests of people whose well-being is low (Parfit 1997). There are many other inequality-averse principles, such as the social-evaluation ordering corresponding to the Gini index of inequality.

Fixed-population principles can be extended to comparisons of alternatives with the same population size (but possibly different identities of those alive) by using an anonymity axiom. Inequality-averse fixed-population principles can be used to generate ethical indexes of inequality of well-being for each population size. In Chapter 4, the best-known ways of doing this are discussed. An important axiom in this environment is called replication invariance. It requires inequality to be unchanged if a population is replicated. Thus, inequality in a population of two with utility levels of 20 and 40 is the same as inequality in a population of four with utility levels of 20, 20, 40, and 40. An important consequence of this axiom is that, if the same-number principle for each population size is generalized utilitarian, a single transformation may be chosen for all population sizes.

In Chapters 5 and 6, we turn to population principles themselves. Although the average-utilitarian and classical-utilitarian principles have unfortunate properties, that is not true of all principles. All the classes of principles are examined in light of a set of axioms in an attempt to discover which are ethically attractive and which are not. Because some of the principles lead to the repugnant conclusion or declare the ceteris paribus addition of an individual who is below neutrality to be good, some of the classes can be eliminated easily. Of those that remain, some, such as the critical-level generalized utilitarian principles with positive critical levels, satisfy an axiom called existence independence. That axiom requires the ranking of any two alternatives to be independent of the utilities and number of people whose utility levels are the same in both. A weaker axiom called utility independence, which allows rankings to depend on the number but not the utility levels of those whose utilities are the same in two alternatives, is satisfied by the number-sensitive generalized utilitarian principles.

Critical-level generalized utilitarian principles with positive critical levels fail to satisfy an axiom that we call priority for lives worth living, which requires all alternatives in which each person is above neutrality to be ranked as better than all those in which each person is below neutrality. That axiom is satisfied by all restricted principles, but neither existence independence nor utility independence is satisfied. In Chapter 5, we find a set of axioms that the members of each class or subclass of principles satisfies. In addition, we explore the informational requirements of the various classes. We examine several examples to illustrate various principles at work.

In Chapter 6, we provide some characterization results and an important impossibility theorem, which demonstrates that there are no principles that satisfy all the axioms that we consider. In our view, the two chapters together provide a defense of the critical-level generalized utilitarian principles with positive critical levels.

Welfarist principles can be used to rank actions if they lead with certainty to particular alternatives. Because the consequences of actions are often uncertain, however, we consider uncertain alternatives in Chapter 7. Probabilities are assumed to be best-information probabilities and are used for individuals and society alike. Because principles that are capable of ranking such alternatives can also deal with the case of certainty, such principles are extensions of ordinary population principles.

Uncertain alternatives can be ranked from a social or individual point of view. We follow Harsanyi (1955, 1977) and require both social and individual rankings to be consistent with the same standard of rationality. In that case, when some additional axioms are used, we show that same-number subprinciples must be utilitarian. If a consistency requirement for critical levels is added, all restricted principles are ruled out and only the number-sensitive critical-level utilitarian principles remain. If, instead, individual preferences are required to reflect a single attitude toward utility uncertainty, social rankings must be made with a number-sensitive critical-level generalized utilitarian principle in which social inequality aversion matches each individual attitude. This suggests that all the restricted principles should be rejected.

Chapter 7 also contains a characterization of the critical-band generalized utilitarian class of principles. It employs a formalization of a suggestion of Parfit (1976, 1982, 1984) concerning additions of individuals to a utility-unaffected population.

Because people have different birth dates and life spans, an investigation of population principles would be incomplete without an explicit consideration of those facts. Indeed, natural justifications for independence axioms involve populations that are long dead, an observation that strengthens the case for an intertemporal model. In Chapters 8 and 9, we employ an intertemporal framework in which nonwelfare information includes dates of birth and lengths of life. In it, we first use the Pareto-indifference axiom and an anonymity axiom that is, as in Chapter 3, conditional on nonwelfare information. The axiom independence of the existence of the dead requires the ranking of any two alternatives to be independent of the existence of those whose lives are over. The effect of Pareto indifference is to rule out discounting, and the social-evaluation problem becomes equivalent to the timeless problem of Chapters 5 and 6, with existence independence replaced by independence of the existence of the dead. Consequently, a characterization of the critical-level generalized utilitarian class is proved.

If Pareto indifference is replaced with the weaker axiom conditional Pareto indifference, whose application is conditional on birth dates and lengths of life being the same in two alternatives, discounting or upcounting based on people's birth dates is permitted. In addition, lengths of life may matter in social evaluation. When this weaker Pareto-indifference axiom is combined with some standard requirements and birth-date-conditional strong Pareto, which rules out the influence of lengths of life, a very general kind of critical-level principle with discounting results. The stationarity axiom requires only relative dates to matter, and its effect is to make critical levels constant and independent of the birth date of the added person. In addition, with the same axioms as in the characterization of the intertemporal critical-level generalized utilitarian class in the earlier part of the chapter, a class of principles called geometric birth-date-dependent critical-level generalized utilitarianism is characterized. A few arguments against discounting are provided in the chapter, but we find the fact that principles that discount necessarily violate Pareto indifference the most convincing.

Our model allows birth dates to be different in different alternatives. It might be argued, however, that birth dates are linked to identity and, therefore, fixed. Consequently, we address that issue directly and sketch a model that yields the same results.

Chapter 9 continues the exploration of the dynamic environment introduced in Chapter 8, and we ask whether it is possible to apply population principles to a single period in a consistent way. If the information about two alternatives differs in one period only, we require their ranking to be independent of information outside the period. We use a model that makes lifetime well-being a function of well-being in the various periods of life. Using an axiom that requires an additional period at neutrality to lead to an alternative that is equally good for the individual, Pareto indifference or birth-date-conditional Pareto indifference, and several other axioms, we show that consistency leads to the repugnant conclusion in each period and overall. In addition, the functions aggregating per-period well-being into lifetime well-being must take a significantly restrictive functional form. A similar result applies to principles that allow information from any period forward to be used to rank alternatives with a common history before that time.

These results reinforce our view that population problems require a longer view. Because some individuals may die before a particular time in one alternative and after it in another, some attention must be paid to the past if ethically unattractive properties of population principles are to be avoided.

In Chapter 10, we investigate choices from feasible sets of actions, assuming that each action is associated with a single alternative. Two problems are considered. The first is the pure population problem in which the number of identical individuals who share a single resource is chosen, and the second is a general choice problem. In both, we examine axioms that ensure that choices are rationalized by an ordering of alternatives and provide characterizations of choice rules based on critical-level generalized utilitarian principles. In addition, we investigate the properties of rational choices when the critical-band generalized utilitarian principles are used.

In Chapter 11, we examine two applied problems, both of which are described by stylized economic models. In both cases, we use the maximizing approach to choice. In the first model, we assume that aid to a developing country can take the form of food aid or funding for a population-control program and employ the critical-level utilitarian principles to determine the optimal composition of an aid package. In the second, we investigate two cases in which animals provide benefits to humans in the form of food or knowledge obtained from research. A population dimension results from the fact that raising animals for food or using them in research changes the number of animals that ever live. Animals have moral standing and the population principle takes account of their well-being. We argue that critical levels are needed for each species, and we discuss ways of setting them. This results in a multispecies variant of critical-level utilitarianism.

Although based on previous work, large parts of the book are new. A list of articles that are linked to the various chapters follows.

- Chapter 2: Blackorby, Bossert, and Donaldson (1999b, 2001a, 2001b).
- Chapter 3: Blackorby, Bossert, and Donaldson (1999b, 2002b, 2004a); Blackorby and Donaldson (1984a).
- Chapter 4: Blackorby, Bossert, and Donaldson (1999e, 2002b).
- Chapter 5: Blackorby, Bossert, and Donaldson (1996b, 1997b, 1999b, 2001a, 2002b, 2002c, 2003a, 2004b); Blackorby and Donaldson (1984a).

- Chapter 6: Blackorby, Bossert, and Donaldson (1996b, 1997b, 1999b, 2001a, 2002b, 2002c, 2003a); Blackorby and Donaldson (1984a); Bossert (1990b).
- Chapter 7: Blackorby, Bossert, and Donaldson (1996a, 1998, 2002b, 2003b).
- Chapter 8: Blackorby, Bossert, and Donaldson (1995b, 1997c, 1999a).
- Chapter 9: Blackorby, Bossert, and Donaldson (1996d, 1997a).
- Chapter 10: Blackorby, Bossert, and Donaldson (1996a, 1999c, 2002a).
- Chapter 11: Blackorby, Bossert, and Donaldson (1999d); Blackorby and Donaldson (1992).

CHAPTER 2

Measurement of Individual Well-Being

Part A

Consider a set of possible worlds, each of which is a history of the universe from remote past to distant future. At any particular time, the set of possible worlds is restricted to those whose past corresponds to the actual history of the universe. In this sense, history exhibits a branching structure. Individual or collective actions taken in the present determine the immediate branch along which history travels. Alternatives are labels or names for the worlds (histories), and principles for social evaluation rank them according to their goodness.[1] For any two alternatives, one may be better than the other, the two may be equally good, or they may not be ranked at all, in which case we say they are incommensurable.

Welfarist principles rank alternatives on the basis of the well-being of the individuals that are alive in them without using other information. The approach we follow in this book is welfarist, and we provide a discussion in Chapter 3. Even in nonwelfarist approaches that employ other information, however, information about well-being also may be (and generally is) used to establish social rankings. Because it is of great importance to social evaluation in general, therefore, we devote this chapter to a discussion of individual well-being and its measurement.

2.1 INDIVIDUAL WELL-BEING

We begin with a discussion of several accounts of individual well-being. Although welfarist principles regard individual well-being as the only entity with intrinsic value, they regard things such as good health and liberty as having instrumental value – valuable because of their contribution to well-being. The account of well-being that is used in a welfarist principle, therefore, should

---

[1] In Chapters 3 and 7, we allow the histories associated with the alternatives to change and, in that case, we say there are multiple information profiles. This allows us to use axioms without assuming the existence of a large number of alternatives.

be comprehensive enough to capture all aspects of the good life. Such accounts are provided by Griffin (1986) and Sumner (1996).

Bentham (1789, 1973) understands individual well-being in terms of pleasure and pain. Life is seen as a series of pleasurable or painful experiences, differing only in intensity and duration, and well-being or utility is seen as an aggregate that measures overall hedonic value. Although this view has been rejected as too narrow, it contains the important idea that well-being is mediated by experience (Griffin 1986, Chapter 1). If someone's experiences are identical in two alternatives, therefore, he or she must be equally well off in both. We find this view attractive, but it is not needed for welfarism. As an example, it has been suggested that events that occur after a person's death may influence his or her well-being. Although it is not our own, this view can be made consistent with an account of individual well-being. Note that events that take place after someone's death are very different from that person's expectations about the events that may occur after her or his life is over.

Bentham's theory implies that individual well-being is subjective: if one alternative is better than another for someone, it must be better for the person who is the subject of the life and not better by some external standard. A theory treats well-being as subjective if it makes it depend, at least in part, on some actual or hypothetical attitude on the part of the person (Sumner 1996, Chapter 2). Our view is that subjective theories are best, but objective accounts of well-being exist and, as long as they generate individual goodness relations (see the following section), can be used with principles for social evaluation.

It is difficult to maintain that all the elements of the good life are reducible to pleasure and pain. Both pleasure and pain are complex, multifaceted experiences. In addition, enjoyment, freedom from anxiety, good health, limbs and senses that work well, length of life (when it is worth living), autonomy, liberty, understanding, accomplishment, satisfying work, and good human relationships also make significant contributions to well-being. Moreover, there is a moral dimension to well-being. Most people value being moral agents and they want to contribute to a better world.

A list view of well-being (Griffin 1986) enumerates basic elements of the good life such as the one above. A ceteris-paribus increase in any element on the list increases well-being. But individual people may differ in the way the items on the list contribute to their welfare. It may be best for a person not to be autonomous, for example, if he or she is plagued by anxiety. In addition, the importance of an ability depends on the skills a person has and intends to use. A musician might place great value on the ability to move his or her fingers quickly.

Sumner (1996) presents an account of well-being that focuses on happiness. Happiness is equated with life satisfaction "which has both an affective component (experiencing the conditions of your life as fulfilling and rewarding) and a cognitive component (judging that your life is going well for you)" (p. 172). Like Griffin, Sumner allows for many determinants of well-being but sees their importance in their contribution to happiness. Self-evaluations are useful as long as the person is informed and autonomous. In addition,

Sumner investigates the importance of attitudes toward one's past life. Suppose, for example, a man who has been happily married for many years discovers his wife has had a series of affairs. They divorce, but his attitude toward his marriage can be one of bitterness or he can accept that he was happy despite his wife's behavior and move on. His decision almost certainly will affect his future well-being.

Desire and preference accounts identify well-being with the satisfaction of self-interested individual wants.[2] The (hypothetical) person must be fully informed and, for that reason, the preferences thus identified do not, in general, coincide with actual preferences. People often want things such as a better environment a century from now. Because individual experiences are not affected, the experience requirement implies that well-being is also not affected.

When a person expresses a desire to climb a mountain or to witness his or her child's graduation, it is not the experience that is desired but the thing itself. That suggests that experiences are not the only basic components of well-being. If the experience requirement is satisfied, however, it must be granted that perfect illusions may produce as much well-being as the real thing. According to this view, however, it would be irrational for someone to choose an illusory experience if the distinction can be made.[3]

Economists have been able to describe complex preferences. Single-period preferences can change with time, as a result of either past experiences (a preference for chocolate may weaken after a binge) or aging. In addition, the value of personal investments such as learning to play the violin can be accommodated along with the changes in future preferences they cause. By contrast, preferences concerning intertemporal allocations may change over a person's lifetime. As an example, a young person might place little weight on her or his consumption in old age relative to consumption at age 50. At age 40, retirement becomes more visible, and the relative importance of retirement consumption may then increase. Overall preferences therefore can vary over time and full information may not eradicate the differences. For the purpose of social evaluation, it is necessary, in such circumstances, to assume there is a set of preferences that accords with lifetime well-being. A single set of actual preferences may or may not be one of the candidates.

There are several difficulties with preference and desire accounts. One of them is a consequence of the problems associated with the separation of preferences into those that are self-interested and those that are not. Consider, for example, a woman who lives with and takes care of her aged mother. She cares about her mother and her mother's well-being influences her own. But she also feels a moral obligation and it requires her to do more than self-interest alone requires. Because her desires and preferences take account of the dictates of both well-being and morality, it may be difficult to distinguish the self-interested part.

---

[2] See Broome (1991), Griffin (1986, 1996), Mongin and d'Aspremont (1998), Roemer (1996), and Sumner (1996) for discussions.

[3] See Griffin (1986, pp. 93–95) for a discussion of the problems with mental-state theories.

A second problem arises with "anti-social preferences, such as sadism, resentment and malice" (Harsanyi 1982, p. 56).[4] Harsanyi asserts that these preferences "must be altogether excluded from our social-utility function." Some of these preferences may be eliminated by the full-information requirement, but some may also remain. It is possible, therefore, that someone's life may be improved by harm done to others. Our view is that we should not attempt to remove such preferences. The intuition that lies behind Harsanyi's view is that actions that result from antisocial preferences are wrong. In a welfarist context, such a judgment must follow from a fact: it must be the case that the harm that such actions do outweighs any possible benefit. If we exclude such a calculation on the basis of our prior intuitions, the requisite comparison cannot be made. There is a danger, as well, that the labeling of some preferences and desires as antisocial may be completely unjustified. The sexual practices of homosexuals have been called disgusting and unnatural, for example, and these claims have been used to deny them civil rights.

Sen (1987, p. 11) criticizes preference and desire accounts of well-being on the grounds that "the battered slave, the broken unemployed, the hopeless destitute, the tamed housewife, may have the courage to desire little." This observation points to the need for full information and, possibly, autonomy qualifications of desire and preference accounts. With those qualifications, the attenuated desires can be corrected.

An individual's actual preferences may be quite different from a notion of goodness that makes comparisons of well-being. Sumner argues, however, that if people are autonomous and fully informed, it is reasonable to think the best way of determining people's well-being is to ask them. "An individual's report will accurately reflect his perceived happiness only if it is relevant (focused on the prudential dimension of the value of his life), sincere (uninfluenced by the desire to maintain a particular social image), and considered (uncolored by transitory feelings of elation or depression)" (Sumner 1996, p. 172).

Sumner's autonomy requirement may cause trouble: if it applies, people who are not completely autonomous may not be able to make accurate estimates of their own well-being. However, it is possible to think of comparisons of well-being across alternatives as being made, hypothetically, by an autonomous self. But the requirement may be too strong. In Sumner's account, informed people are not seen as forming desires that can lead to actions; instead, they are seen as assessing alternatives from the point of view of their own happiness or well-being. Rather than autonomy, what is needed is that people must be able to imagine themselves in other circumstances – something that almost everyone can do to some degree – and make comparisons of their own good. It does not follow, therefore, that the evaluations of people who are not completely autonomous are worthless: the battered slave knows that freedom would be better, for example. Children present a special case. They may not possess the requisite imagination needed to compare their lifetime well-being in different

---

[4] See also Kolm (1996, pp. 114–115) and Roemer (1996, p. 128).

alternatives. When things affect them immediately, however, they often make compelling judgments about their own interests.

A theory of functionings and capabilities, presented by Sen (1985), is similar to a list view of well-being with an added dimension. Functionings are the "doings and beings" a person achieves. Refining the list of possible functions to the list actually used is seen as a valuational exercise, and aggregation of the items on the resulting list is influenced by individual differences. As a consequence, Sen's view is similar to Griffin's list view. But Sen adds another dimension. Capabilities are opportunities to achieve various functionings and they are seen as valuable in themselves.[5] The presence of capabilities on Sen's list gives him a way to value individual liberty.

It is possible to employ Sen's theory in a welfarist context, nevertheless. What is needed is an individual goodness relation that ranks all the possible combinations of functionings and capabilities. Although the resulting view of well-being would be more objective than the ones considered above, there would be no difficulty in using it with welfarist principles.

Kolm (1972, 1996) presents a theory of individual well-being in which preferences, which represent happiness, are completely determined by individual characteristics. The resulting goodness relation is called a fundamental preference relation for the individual. Because there is no place for the influence of individual attitudes, Kolm's theory is completely objective.[6]

Although it is not necessary for the employment of most welfarist principles, it is sometimes important to discuss well-being in a particular period of time. There are no serious difficulties with this provided we realize that well-being in a period may be influenced by experiences in the past and expectations about the future. There are significant difficulties with the application of welfarist principles to single periods, however, and they are discussed in Chapter 9.

Our view is that theories of well-being such as the ones of Griffin and Sumner capture the complexities of individual well-being best. Both are subjective and provide the comprehensive accounts needed if welfarist social rankings are to assign value to objects such as liberty, freedom, and good human relationships.

2.2 INDIVIDUAL GOODNESS RELATIONS AND UTILITY REPRESENTATIONS

Our approach is based on the idea that it is meaningful to compare a single individual's lifetime well-being in the alternatives in which he or she ever lives. The individual ranking of these alternatives can be summarized by an at-least-as-good-as binary relation. Alternative x is as good as alternative y if and only if x is at least as good as y and y is at least as good as x, and x is better than y if and only if x is at least as good as y and it is not the case that y is at least

---

[5] Nussbaum (2000a, 2000b) focuses almost exclusively on capabilities. For a discussion of Sen's approach, see Sumner (1996, pp. 60–68).

[6] See also Harsanyi (1955).

as good as x. Defined this way, the as-good-as relation is symmetric (if x is as good as y, then y is as good as x) and the better-than relation is asymmetric (if x is better than y, y is not better than x). In addition, x and y are not ranked if and only if it is not the case that x is at least as good as y and it is not the case that y is at least as good as x. We also call an at-least-as-good-as relation a goodness relation. Note that the idea that an alternative is associated with a certain amount of a real measurable quantity called goodness is not needed.

We assume, throughout the book, that individual goodness relations are (i) reflexive: any alternative is at least as good as itself; (ii) transitive: if x is at least as good as y and y is at least as good as z, then x is at least as good as z; and (iii) complete: every pair of distinct alternatives is ranked. A binary relation that is reflexive, transitive, and complete is called an ordering. Transitivity of the goodness relation implies that the better-than and as-good-as relations are also transitive.[7] In addition, transitivity implies that, if x is better than y and y is at least as good as z or if x is at least as good as y and y is better than z, then x is better than z.

Sometimes quasi-orderings are considered in the literature. A quasi-ordering is a reflexive and transitive (but not necessarily complete) relation. We maintain the completeness assumption for individual goodness relations throughout but we consider incomplete social rankings in Chapter 7. Incommensurabilities may occur for two reasons. First, it may be the case that the requisite information for establishing a ranking is not available. This does not apply to the environment we have described previously, however; each possible world is a complete history and, as a consequence, information is complete. Second, it may be the case that it does not make sense to make the comparison.

Our approach is welfarist and, thus, the goodness relations we employ rank any two alternatives exclusively on the basis of the levels of individual well-being attained in them. However, the notion of a goodness relation is compatible with any conception of well-being that generates social orderings of alternatives.

A utility function measures well-being by assigning numbers to alternatives in accordance with an individual goodness relation. Suppose, for example, there are four alternatives – x, y, z, and w – and, for a single individual, z is best, x and w are equally good, and both x and w are better than y. We say that a utility function represents this ordering if it assigns the highest number to z, the same, lower number to each of x and w, and the lowest number to y. Three representing utility functions are illustrated in Table 2.1.

For any ordering, all that is required is that, for all pairs of alternatives, one is at least as good as the other if and only if the value of the representing utility function at the first is at least as great as the value at the second. This implies that two alternatives are equally good if and only if they receive the same utility number and that one alternative is better than another if and only if it receives a higher utility number.

---

[7] Broome (1991, 1993, 2004a) argues that better-than relations are necessarily transitive.

Table 2.1. *Representations*

Alternative	Function A	Function B	Function C
x	20	40	10
y	−20	10	−40
z	60	50	60
w	20	40	10

It is well known that, if two utility functions represent the same ordering, each must be an increasing transformation of the other. For the three utility functions of Table 2.1, this is illustrated in Figure 2.1. u_A, u_B, and u_C are values of the three functions. The solid line expresses the relationship between utility functions A and B: when u_A is −20, u_B is 10, and so on. The dashed line represents the relationship between utility functions A and C. Note that both transformations represented by these lines are increasing. Because any increasing transformation can be chosen, if an ordering has a representing utility function, it has infinitely many.

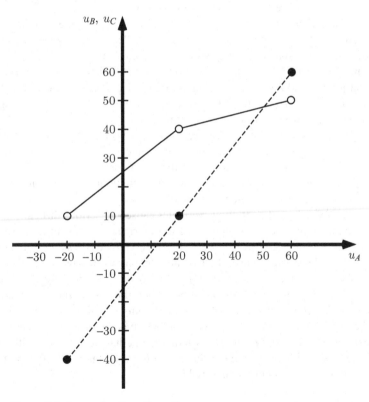

Figure 2.1. Increasing Transformations.

In general, not every ordering has a representation. But, if the total number of alternatives is either finite or countably infinite,[8] every ordering has one.

Difficulties with the existence of representations occur when alternatives are multidimensional. We may think of alternatives as vectors of indexes of the different items on a list as in Griffin's account of well-being and the individual goodness relation ranks the resulting vectors. If each of the individual items can take on a finite or countably infinite number of values at most, a representation exists. However, some or all of the elements of the vectors may be continuous variables, able to take on real values including irrational numbers. This is the case, for example, if an element is beer consumption in a particular period of time. Consumption is measured in pints or liters and it is a continuous variable.

There are well-known examples in which orderings on sets of combinations of two or more continuous variables do not have utility representations. One is a lexicographic ordering of vectors of two continuous variables. x is ranked as better than y if and only if the value of the first variable in x is higher than the corresponding value in y or the values of the first variables are the same and the value of the second variable is higher in x.

If all alternatives are vectors of continuous variables, the existence of a representation can be guaranteed by an axiom called continuity. It requires trade-offs to be gradual, without sudden jumps from better to worse. To illustrate, suppose alternative x is better than y and y is better than z. Now consider a path that joins x and z without passing through y. Continuity requires that there is an alternative on the path such that it and y are equally good. The lexicographic ordering mentioned above is not continuous.

If the set of possible alternatives consists of vectors of continuous variables only and a standard technical condition on the set itself is met, the goodness ordering is continuous if and only if there is a continuous utility function that represents it. Because the utility function is continuous, it exhibits no sudden jumps in value as the variables change.

The existence of continuous variables causes no serious difficulty if all the elements of the vectors that comprise the alternatives are continuous variables. But the various views of well-being discussed previously suggest that some of the variables are discrete and others are continuous. In this case, it is possible to fix the discrete variables and ask the conditional ordering of the continuous variables to be continuous. Even when this requirement is satisfied for each subvector of discrete variables, an axiom we call conditional continuity, the existence of a representing utility function is not guaranteed. However, an extended version of the continuity requirement that we call unconditional continuity is sufficient for the existence of a representing utility function that is continuous in the continuous variables.

---

[8] The number of elements in a set is countably infinite if and only if the members of the set can be matched, one to one, with the positive integers.

2.3 MEASURABILITY AND NORMS

Each utility function that represents an individual goodness relation contains more information than the relation itself. According to utility functions A and C in Table 2.1, for example, the utility level for y is negative and the utility gain in moving from y to x or w is equal to the utility gain from x or w to z.

It is possible to restrict the meaningful information in representing utility functions by using the idea of informational equivalence. If, for example, the goodness relation itself is all that is meaningful, all the representing utility functions are informationally equivalent and meaningful information is restricted to that which all those functions have in common. When information is restricted in this way, utility functions are said to be ordinally measurable and any two representing utility functions are said to be ordinally equivalent. Formally, two utility functions are ordinally equivalent if and only if one is an increasing transformation of the other.

This can be illustrated by the three utility functions of Table 2.1. Because each is an increasing transformation of any other, the three functions are ordinally equivalent. It is not meaningful to say that the utility level for y is negative because, although that is true of utility functions A and C, it is not true of utility function B. In addition, it is not meaningful to say that the utility gain in moving from y to x is the same as the utility gain in moving from x to z: that statement is true according to utility functions A and C but it is not true according to utility function B. All that is left is the relative size of the utility levels: all three functions (and all the other ordinally equivalent representations) agree that the utility level for z is greater than the utility levels for x and w, and the utility levels for x and w are equal and greater than the utility level for y. Consequently, meaningful information is restricted to the goodness relation itself.

Suppose that, in alternatives a, b, and c, a single individual has a constant level of consumption of goods and services over his or her lifetime, all other determinants of well-being are the same in all three alternatives, and the increase in consumption in moving from c to b is equal to the increase in moving from b to a. In this example, the person is better off in a than in b and better off in b than in c. He or she might claim, however, that the increase in well-being in moving from c to b is greater than the increase in moving from b to a. Although judgments such as this are common, they are not meaningful if utility is ordinally measurable.

Cardinal measurability does permit such comparisons. Two utility functions are cardinally equivalent if and only if one is an increasing affine transformation of the other. One utility function is an increasing affine transformation of another if it can be obtained by multiplying by a positive number and adding a constant (positive, zero, or negative).[9] Two utility functions are, therefore, cardinally

---

[9] Because all increasing affine transformations are increasing transformations, cardinal equivalence implies ordinal equivalence. Affine transformations are often called linear transformations in the literature. We prefer to use affine and reserve the term linear for those affine transformations in which the added constant is equal to zero.

equivalent if the relationship between the representing utility functions in a diagram such as Figure 2.1 is a straight line. Figure 2.1 makes it clear that utility functions A and B are not cardinally equivalent because the solid line in the figure is not straight, but utility functions A and C are cardinally equivalent because the dotted line is.

Utility is cardinally measurable if and only if the set of informationally equivalent functions associated with a particular function is the set of all cardinally equivalent functions. In addition, the meaningful information contained in a particular utility function is restricted to the information that it and all the cardinally equivalent functions have in common. For any particular utility function, the set of cardinally equivalent utility functions is a strict subset of the set of ordinally equivalent functions if there are at least three alternatives.

In the example of Table 2.1, suppose utility is cardinally measurable and that well-being is measured by utility function A. Then utility differences can be compared: the utility gain in moving from y to x or w is equal to the utility gain in moving from x or w to z. This is true of utility function C and all other functions that are cardinally equivalent to A but not of utility function B, which is not cardinally equivalent to A.

It is interesting to ask whether the ability to make comparisons of utility differences (in addition to levels) is sufficient to imply cardinal measurability. In general it is not, because there may be some ordinally equivalent but not cardinally equivalent functions in addition to the set of cardinally equivalent functions that make the same comparisons of utility gains and losses. If, however, the set of utility numbers is restricted to an interval of real numbers (which may be the whole set of real numbers), sufficiency is guaranteed. A detailed discussion of the difference between information assumptions expressed in terms of admissible transformations and in terms of meaningful statements (for example, statements regarding the comparison of utility levels, differences, or ratios) is provided in Part B.

A familiar example of cardinal measurability is the measurement of temperature. The three most commonly used scales are Fahrenheit, Celsius, and Kelvin. Temperature in one is an increasing affine transformation of temperature in any other, and temperature differences are comparable. Suppose that, without knowing which scale is in use, you were told that Wednesday was hotter than Tuesday, which in turn was hotter than Monday, and that the temperature increase from Monday to Tuesday was greater than the increase from Tuesday to Wednesday. Because each of these statements is either true or false according to all three scales (and all other cardinally equivalent ones), all of them are meaningful. On the other hand, a report that claims that a temperature increase was $2°$ is not meaningful unless we know which scale is in use.

For a particular utility function, ratio-scale measurability further restricts the set of utility functions that are informationally equivalent to the set of all those functions that are positive multiples. Consequently, if two utility functions are ratio-scale equivalent, they are also cardinally and ordinally equivalent. Table 2.2 adds another function – utility function D – to the three functions of

Table 2.2. *Ratio-Scale Measurability*

Alternative	Function A	Function D
x	20	40
y	−20	−40
z	60	120
w	20	40

Table 2.1. Its values are twice those of utility function A and they are equal to 40 at x and w, −40 at y, and 120 at z. Although utility function D is ratio-scale equivalent to utility function A, neither utility function B nor utility function C is.

Moving from cardinal measurability to ratio-scale measurability enlarges the class of meaningful statements about utilities. If well-being is measured by utility function A, all difference comparisons are meaningful but statements that utility is positive, negative, or zero and statements about utility ratios are also meaningful. Both utility functions A and D agree that utility is positive in x, z, and w and negative in y. In addition, both agree that the utility level in z is three times the utility level in w.

To complete this survey of the main ways of measuring individual well-being, we consider the case of numerical measurability. It assigns meaningful numbers to alternatives and the only utility function that is informationally equivalent to a particular utility function is the function itself. This can be done if a way can be found to choose a single utility function out of the set of ordinally equivalent utility functions. In the temperature example, such a choice is made when a political jurisdiction adopts a particular temperature scale. If we know, for example, that the Celsius scale is in use, the statement that the temperature is 25° is meaningful. In temperature measurement, this is accomplished by the use of norms: the Celsius scale sets the freezing and boiling points of water to 0° and 100°, respectively.

Sometimes people make claims such as "it would be better for me if I were to die now rather than live the rest of my life as I expect it will unfold" or "my life is, as a whole, worth living." The first of these claims is easily understood in terms of the individual's goodness relation. Let x be an alternative in which the individual's life continues as expected and let y be an alternative that coincides with x until the present time but in which he or she dies now. If x is better than y, the rest of his or her life is worth living and if y is better than x, it is not. If x and y are equally good, we say that the rest of the person's life is, as a whole, neutral. This does not mean that, at each future date, the same judgment would be made: it might be true that it would be best to live for a few more years and then die.

Consider a court case in which an adult sues his or her mother for "wrongful life." The claim is that harm was done by the parent in her refusal to have an abortion (in the early stages of pregnancy) because the person's life is not, nor could it be, worth living. This claim is problematic. In general, if a harm has been done, it must be true that the alternative that would obtain if the action in question had not been performed is better for the individual than the alternative that did obtain as a consequence of the action.[10] Many people believe, however, that an embryo or early fetus is not a sentient individual and, in that case, the claim that harm is done by allowing the pregnancy to continue cannot be true because the person does not exist in one of the alternatives.[11]

Because people who do not exist do not have interests, it does not make sense to say that an individual gains or loses by being brought into existence. Someone might have an attitude, such as a desire or preference, toward a world in which he or she does not exist but could not reasonably think that this world would be better or worse for him or her. Similarly, a person who expresses satisfaction with having been born cannot be claiming that existence is better (for him or her) than nonexistence. It makes perfect sense, of course, to say that an individual gains or loses by continuing to live because of surviving a life-threatening illness, for example. Such a change affects length of life, not existence itself.[12]

Parfit (1984, p. 489) says, "Causing someone to exist is a special case because the alternative would not have been worse for this person. We may admit that, for this reason, causing someone to exist cannot be *better* for this person. But it may be *good* for this person." In this passage, Parfit denies that a person can be benefited or harmed by being brought into existence. His assertion that the same act can be good for a person can only mean that, having been born, the individual's life is worth living.

If we believe the idea of a life worth living is meaningful, we must give an account of it. One possibility is to see it as information that supplements the individual goodness relation. In the spirit of Sumner's account of well-being, we can ask a fully informed person whether his or her life, taken as a whole, is worth living or not. If it is, we say that the level of well-being associated with this life is above neutrality, and, if it is not, the lifetime well-being of the individual is below neutrality. If lifetime well-being is at neutrality, it is not the case that, as a whole, the life is worth living and it is not the case that it is not worth living.

Broome (1993, 2004a) takes a different approach and asks whether judgments about neutrality can be derived from an individual's goodness relation. Suppose a person lives for ℓ years in alternative x and that, for every length of life t less than ℓ, there is another alternative x_t in which the person lives for exactly t years and, in addition, histories in x and x_t are identical until the individual is t years old. Now suppose that, at each age, x and x_t are equally

---

[10] See Heyd (1992) for a discussion of wrongful-life cases.

[11] This view was expressed in a joke told by Orson Welles and Groucho Marx on an old radio program (The Orson Welles Almanac Number 1, January 26, 1944). Orson said, "Did you know, Groucho, that Professor Ungerdunger of the Harvard University Sociology Department just turned in a Ph.D. thesis proving that most people would be better off if they hadn't been born?" Groucho replied, "Yes, but that seldom happens to anybody."

[12] For discussions, see Heyd (1992, Chapter 1), McMahan (1996), and Parfit (1984, Appendix G).

good. Broome (2004a) calls such a life a borderline life and x is used as a reference alternative: if the person is alive in alternative y and y is better for him or her than x, the individual's life, as a whole, is worth living; if x is better for him or her than y, the individual's life is not worth living; and if x and y are equally good, the individual's life, as a whole, is neutral.

A second possibility dispenses with the borderline requirement. Consider any alternative x in which the person is alive and define x_t as above. Now suppose there is a utility function that represents the individual's goodness relation and consider the value of the utility function as the individual's length of life approaches zero. If early experiences are good, we can expect utility to diminish as length of life approaches zero and, if early experiences are bad, we can expect utility to increase as length of life approaches zero. In addition, the value of the utility function should approach the same number for all alternatives in which the individual is alive. In that case, the limit is independent of the starting alternative and we call it u_0. We can now define a neutral life to be one for which utility is equal to u_0, a life worth living as one for which utility is greater than u_0, and a life not worth living as one for which utility is below u_0.

Our approach to the representation of a neutral life is the following. We assign a specific level of well-being to a neutral life and consider all lives with a level of well-being above neutrality as lives that are worth living and those with well-being below neutrality as lives that are not.

Neutrality can be regarded as a norm and we may, without loss of generality, set its utility level to zero. To do this, suppose a particular utility function represents an individual's goodness relation. Now consider the whole set of informationally equivalent utility functions and select all those such that the utility value associated with neutrality is zero. This procedure is common in population ethics, and we follow it in this book.[13]

A normalization such as this changes the measurability of the normalized utility functions. The most important case is the one in which, before normalization, utility is cardinally measurable. If neutrality is represented by a utility value of zero, normalized utility is ratio-scale measurable. The reason is that, if one of the normalized utility functions gives an alternative a value of zero, all the informationally equivalent functions do.

Neutrality may not be the only norm one might want to use. Suppose that, for an individual with a particular utility function, an excellent life (which is above neutrality but not the best possible life) is defined. Its value can be normalized to any positive number such as 100. Again, the normalization procedure requires the selection of all informationally equivalent utility functions that assign the normalized value to an excellent life.

If utility is cardinally measurable, the effect of both these (or similar) normalizations is to select a single utility function, resulting in numerical measurability. As an example, consider again utility function A in the example of Table 2.1 and suppose x and w are alternatives in which the person has a neutral life and z is one in which the person has an excellent life. We know that any transformation

---

[13] Dasgupta (1993) normalizes neutrality to a negative utility level.

Table 2.3. *Norms and Measurability*

Alternative	Function A	Function E	Function F
x	20	0	0
y	−20	−40	−100
z	60	40	100
w	20	0	0

in which utility function A is multiplied by a positive number and any constant (positive, zero, or negative) is added is cardinally equivalent. Utility function A therefore can be replaced by one that is obtained by subtracting 20. The result is utility function E in Table 2.3. If merely the neutrality normalization is to be preserved, utility function E is not unique: any positive multiple of it will do as well, so utility has become ratio-scale measurable.

Now suppose that, in addition to the zero normalization for neutrality, we want to normalize the value of an excellent life to 100. Because the person's life is excellent in alternative z, all that is needed is to choose a multiple of utility function E so that the utility level for z is 100. The requisite multiple is $5/2$ and utility function F results. It is unique and, as a consequence, utility is numerically measurable.

2.4 WELL-BEING IN A SINGLE PERIOD

An individual goodness relation also can be interpreted as a relation that compares alternatives with respect to individual well-being in a single period. In this case, only those alternatives in which the person is alive in the period in question can be compared. Such a ranking may depend on the events and experiences of the person's past life and on his or her expectations about the future, including expected length of life. We can then find a utility function that measures the person's well-being for all alternatives in which he or she is alive in the period.

In each alternative in which the person is alive, there is a vector of utilities: one for each period of life. If a person has an overall goodness relation, there must be a ranking of these vectors. If, for example, alternative x is better than alternative y, the vector of per-period utilities associated with x is ranked as better than the corresponding vector for y. Note that, because length of life can differ across alternatives, the vectors can be of different dimensions.

An interesting question to ask is whether, given utility representations for the per-period orderings, we can find a utility function that depends on the per-period utilities and represents the overall goodness relation. To do this, we use a continuity axiom called extended continuity that is similar to unrestricted continuity.

It is a plausible requirement that such a utility function respond positively to an increase in utility in any period. This ensures that a ceteris-paribus increase in well-being in any period is good overall. In addition, neutrality can be defined for a single period and normalized to zero. We can then require that (i) a life with an additional period at neutrality (other things equal) is neither better nor worse than the original life; and (ii) lifetime utility for a life that lasts for one period is equal to the utility level in that period. These conditions are used in Chapter 9.

Part B

We now discuss some fundamental concepts for the measurement of individual well-being. In Section 2.5, we introduce our notation and basic definitions. In Section 2.6, we define individual goodness relations and use utility as a measure of individual well-being. Furthermore, we present several representation theorems. Assumptions about the measurability of individual utilities and their consequences are discussed in Section 2.7. Section 2.8 extends this framework to an intertemporal setting.

2.5 BASIC DEFINITIONS

We begin by introducing some notation that will be used throughout the book. The set of all (positive, nonnegative) integers is denoted by $\mathcal{Z}$ ($\mathcal{Z}_{++}$, $\mathcal{Z}_+$). Let $\mathcal{R}$ ($\mathcal{R}_{++}$, $\mathcal{R}_+$, $\mathcal{R}_{--}$) be the set of all (positive, nonnegative, negative) real numbers. $\emptyset$ is the empty set. For any nonempty set Y, 2^Y is the set of all nonempty subsets of Y and, for $n \in \mathcal{Z}_{++}$, Y^n is the n-fold Cartesian product of Y. In particular, $\mathcal{R}^n$ is Euclidean n-space – that is, the set of all n-dimensional vectors composed of real numbers. $\mathbf{1}_n$ is the vector consisting of n ones. We use the following notation for vector inequalities. For all $x, y \in \mathcal{R}^n$,

$$x \geq y \Leftrightarrow x_i \geq y_i \text{ for all } i \in \{1, \ldots, n\},$$
$$x > y \Leftrightarrow x \geq y \text{ and } x \neq y,$$
$$x \gg y \Leftrightarrow x_i > y_i \text{ for all } i \in \{1, \ldots, n\}.$$

A function $f: Y \to \mathcal{R}$ with $\emptyset \neq Y \subseteq \mathcal{R}$ is affine if and only if there exist $a, b \in \mathcal{R}$ such that $f(x) = ax + b$ for all $x \in Y$. The function f is linear if and only if it is affine with $b = 0$. Furthermore, f is increasing if and only if $x > y$ implies $f(x) > f(y)$ for all $x, y \in Y$. Hence, f is increasing affine (increasing linear) if and only if it is affine (linear) with $a > 0$. Geometrically, an affine function is a function whose graph is a straight line, and a linear function is a function whose graph is a straight line passing through the origin. Increasing affine (increasing linear) functions have positively sloped straight lines (passing through the origin) as graphs.

A function $f^n: Y^n \to \mathcal{R}$ with $n \in \mathcal{Z}_{++}$ and $\emptyset \neq Y^n \subseteq \mathcal{R}^n$ is weakly increasing if and only if $x_i > y_i$ for all $i \in \{1, \ldots, n\}$ implies $f^n(x) > f^n(y)$ for all $x, y \in Y^n$. f^n is increasing if and only if $x_i \geq y_i$ for all $i \in \{1, \ldots, n\}$ with at least one strict inequality implies $f^n(x) > f^n(y)$ for all $x, y \in Y^n$.

A binary relation B on a nonempty set Y is a subset of $Y \times Y$. For convenience, we write $x B y$ instead of $(x, y) \in B$ to indicate that $x \in Y$ is in the relation B to $y \in Y$. The relation B is reflexive if and only if xBx for all $x \in Y$; B is transitive if and only if $(xBy$ and $yBz)$ implies xBz for all $x, y, z \in Y$; and B is complete if and only if xBy or yBx for all $x, y \in Y$ such that $x \neq y$. A reflexive and transitive relation is called a quasi-ordering, and an ordering is a complete quasi-ordering. B is symmetric if and only if xBy implies yBx for all $x, y \in Y$, and B is asymmetric if and only if xBy implies not yBx for all $x, y \in Y$. An equivalence relation is a reflexive, transitive, and symmetric binary relation. The relations that are of particular interest in this chapter are interpreted as individual goodness relations – that is, if x and y are alternatives, xBy means that, from the viewpoint of the individual under consideration, x is at least as good as y. See the following section for details.

The symmetric factor S and the asymmetric factor A of B are defined as follows. For all $x, y \in Y$, xSy if and only if xBy and yBx, and xAy if and only if xBy and not yBx. Clearly, it follows immediately from the definition of those relations that S is symmetric and A is asymmetric for any binary relation B. Of course, S and A depend on B but, for notational simplicity, we suppress this dependence. The interpretation of S and A in the context of individual goodness relations is such that xSy means x and y are equally good for the individual, and xAy means x is better than y.

If B is transitive, it follows that S and A are transitive and, furthermore, transitivity requirements regarding combinations of S and A are satisfied. These results are summarized in the following theorem. Note that no properties of B other than transitivity are required. In particular, B need not be reflexive or complete.

Theorem 2.1. *If B is transitive, then*

    (i) S is transitive;
    (ii) for all $x, y, z \in Y$, xAy and $yBz \Rightarrow xAz$;
    (iii) for all $x, y, z \in Y$, xBy and $yAz \Rightarrow xAz$;
    (iv) A is transitive.

Proof. (i) Suppose xSy and ySz. By definition, xBy and yBx, and yBz and zBy. Therefore, by the transitivity of B, xBz and zBx – that is, xSz.

(ii) Suppose xAy and yBz. By definition, xBy and not yBx, and yBz. Therefore, by the transitivity of B, we obtain xBz. By way of contradiction, suppose zBx. Then, using the transitivity of B again, it follows that yBx, a contradiction. Therefore, xAz.

The proof of (iii) is analogous to the proof of (ii), and (iv) is an immediate corollary of (ii) and of (iii). ∎

2.6 INDIVIDUAL GOODNESS AND UTILITY

Let X be a nonempty set of alternatives. X may have a finite or countably infinite number of elements, or it may be a nonempty and connected subset of

$\mathcal{R}^n$. Furthermore, it is possible that the elements in X can be described by a combination of continuous and discrete variables. For $x \in X$, $N = \mathbf{N}(x) \in 2^{\mathcal{Z}_{++}}$ is the set of people alive in x, and $n = \mathbf{n}(x) \in \mathcal{Z}_{++}$ is their number. Although the set of potential people $\mathcal{Z}_{++}$ is countably infinite, we consider only alternatives with a finite number of actual people.

For $i \in \mathcal{Z}_{++}$, $X_i \subseteq X$ is the set of alternatives in which individual i is alive – that is, $X_i = \{x \in X \mid i \in \mathbf{N}(x)\}$. We assume that X_i is nonempty. Each element of X_i is assumed to contain a full description of everything that may be relevant to the well-being of individual i.

A goodness relation for individual i is a binary relation $\succeq_i$ on X_i such that, for all $x, y \in X_i$, $x \succeq_i y$ if and only if x is at least as good as y for individual i. The better-than relation corresponding to $\succeq_i$ is the asymmetric factor of $\succeq_i$, and it is denoted by $\succ_i$. The symmetric factor of $\succeq_i$ is $\sim_i$, and we refer to it as the equally-good relation or the as-good-as relation corresponding to $\succeq_i$.

To define most of the principles for social evaluation discussed in this book, we require more information about individual well-being than the ordinal information contained in a goodness relation. To obtain informationally richer environments, we use utility functions that are interpreted as indicators of individual well-being. A minimal requirement imposed on such an index of individual well-being is that all goodness comparisons according to the goodness relation are preserved; that is, a utility function assigns real numbers (utility values) to alternatives in a way such that better alternatives obtain higher numbers. We say that a function $U_i: X_i \to \mathcal{R}$ is a representing utility function for the goodness relation $\succeq_i$ if and only if, for all $x, y \in X_i$,

$$x \succeq_i y \Leftrightarrow U_i(x) \geq U_i(y). \tag{2.1}$$

Thus, the ranking of alternatives according to $\succeq_i$ is the same as the ranking according to the utility numbers assigned by U_i. If (2.1) is satisfied, we call U_i a representation of $\succeq_i$.

Not every goodness relation has a representation. First, note that $\succeq_i$ must be an ordering for a representing utility function to exist. This is a consequence of (2.1) together with the observation that the relation $\geq$ on $\mathcal{R}$ is an ordering. To prove this assertion, suppose a representation exists for $\succeq_i$. For all $x \in X_i$, it follows that $U_i(x) \geq U_i(x)$ because $U_i(x)$ is a number. By (2.1), $x \succeq_i x$ and, therefore, $\succeq_i$ is reflexive. Furthermore, if $U_i(x) \geq U_i(y)$ and $U_i(y) \geq U_i(z)$, the transitivity of the relation $\geq$ on $\mathcal{R}$ implies $U_i(x) \geq U_i(z)$. Therefore, (2.1) implies that, whenever $x \succeq_i y$ and $y \succeq_i z$, $x \succeq_i z$ must be true as well. Finally, note that, for any $x, y \in X_i$ such that $x \neq y$, we must have $U_i(x) \geq U_i(y)$ or $U_i(y) \geq U_i(x)$ because $U_i(x)$ and $U_i(y)$ are numbers and the relation $\geq$ on $\mathcal{R}$ is complete. Therefore, by (2.1), $x \succeq_i y$ or $y \succeq_i x$, which shows that $\succeq_i$ must be complete.

The above argument shows that, to have a representing utility function, it is necessary that $\succeq_i$ be an ordering. If the set X_i is finite or countably infinite, this is also sufficient. We state and prove this result in the following theorem.

Theorem 2.2. *Let* X_i *be a nonempty finite or countably infinite set.* $\succeq_i$ *has a representation if and only if* $\succeq_i$ *is an ordering.*

Proof. That $\succeq_i$ must be an ordering if it is representable has been established in the remarks preceding the theorem statement. Suppose X_i is countably infinite – that is, we can write this set as $X_i = \{x_1, x_2, \ldots\}$. We construct a representing utility function $U_i \colon X_i \to \mathcal{R}$ recursively.

Let $U_i(x_1) = 0$.

For all $k \in \mathcal{Z}_{++} \setminus \{1\}$ such that $\{U_i(x_j) \mid j \in \{1, \ldots, k-1\}$ and $x_j \succ_i x_k\} \neq \emptyset$, let

$$u_{\min}(x_k) = \min\{U_i(x_j) \mid j \in \{1, \ldots, k-1\} \text{ and } x_j \succ_i x_k\}$$

and for all $k \in \mathcal{Z}_{++} \setminus \{1\}$ such that $\{U_i(x_j) \mid j \in \{1, \ldots, k-1\}$ and $x_k \succ_i x_j\} \neq \emptyset$, let

$$u_{\max}(x_k) = \max\{U_i(x_j) \mid j \in \{1, \ldots, k-1\} \text{ and } x_k \succ_i x_j\},$$

and define

$$U_i(x_k) = \begin{cases} U_i(x_j) & \text{if } \exists j \in \{1, \ldots, k-1\} \text{ such that } x_j \sim_i x_k, \\ u_{\max}(x_k) + 1 & \text{if } x_k \succ_i x_j \; \forall j \in \{1, \ldots, k-1\}, \\ u_{\min}(x_k) - 1 & \text{if } x_j \succ_i x_k \; \forall j \in \{1, \ldots, k-1\}, \\ \frac{1}{2}\left[u_{\min}(x_k) + u_{\max}(x_k)\right] & \text{otherwise.} \end{cases}$$

Clearly, this utility function is well-defined and represents $\succeq_i$. The proof for the case where X_i is finite is a simplified version of the above proof. ∎

If X_i is not countable, reflexivity, transitivity, and completeness are not sufficient for the existence of a representation. Let, for example, $X_i = \mathcal{R}^2$, and consider the lexicographic ordering on X_i defined as follows. For all $x, y \in \mathcal{R}^2$,

$$x \succeq_i y \Leftrightarrow x_1 > y_1 \text{ or } [x_1 = y_1 \text{ and } x_2 \geq y_2].$$

It can be shown that this relation is an ordering, but it does not have a representation – see, for example, Debreu (1959, pp. 72–73).

If X_i is a nonempty and connected subset of $\mathcal{R}^n$, a continuity property is sufficient for the existence of a representing utility function for an ordering. Continuity of $\succeq_i$ is defined as follows.

Continuity. For all $x \in X_i$, the sets $\{y \in X_i \mid y \succeq_i x\}$ and $\{y \in X_i \mid x \succeq_i y\}$ are closed in X_i.

This definition implies that if alternative x is better than alternative y and z is worse than y, then there exists an alternative that is as good as y on any path joining x and z.

The following theorem is due to Debreu (1959, pp. 56–59).[14]

---

[14] Debreu's original version states the "if" part of the theorem only. However, it is clear that the "only if" part is true as well.

Theorem 2.3. *Let X_i be a nonempty and connected subset of $\mathcal{R}^n$ for some $n \in \mathcal{Z}_{++}$. $\succeq_i$ has a continuous representation if and only if $\succeq_i$ is a continuous ordering.*

We now turn to the case in which the elements of X_i have both discrete and continuous components, a plausible possibility given that we employ a comprehensive notion of individual well-being. Suppose X_i is given by a Cartesian product $\mathcal{D} \times \mathcal{C}$, where $\mathcal{D} \subseteq \mathcal{Z}^d$ and $\mathcal{C} \subseteq \mathcal{R}^c$ for some $d, c \in \mathcal{Z}_{++}$. We assume that $\mathcal{D}$ and $\mathcal{C}$ are nonempty and $\mathcal{C}$ is connected. For $x \in X_i = \mathcal{D} \times \mathcal{C}$, we write $x = (x^D, x^C)$ where $x^D \in \mathcal{D}$ and $x^C \in \mathcal{C}$. The natural definition of continuity in this setting is to formulate this property conditional on fixed values of the discrete components. This leads to the following conditional-continuity axiom.

Conditional Continuity. For all $x \in X_i$, the sets $\{y^C \in \mathcal{C} \mid (x^D, y^C) \succeq_i (x^D, x^C)\}$ and $\{y^C \in \mathcal{C} \mid (x^D, x^C) \succeq_i (x^D, y^C)\}$ are closed in $\mathcal{C}$.

Conditional continuity is not sufficient to guarantee the existence of a representation. Consider, for example, the relation $\succeq_i$ on $X_i = \mathcal{Z}^d \times \mathcal{R}^c$ defined as follows. For all $x, y \in X_i$,

$$x \succeq_i y \Leftrightarrow f(x^C) > f(y^C) \text{ or } [f(x^C) = f(y^C) \text{ and } g(x^D) \geq g(y^D)]$$

where $f: \mathcal{R}^c \to \mathcal{R}$ is an arbitrary continuous and increasing function, and $g: \mathcal{Z}^d \to \mathcal{Z}$ is an arbitrary injective (one-to-one) function. This relation is an ordering satisfying conditional continuity, but it does not have a representation. See Blackorby, Bossert, and Donaldson (2001a) for a discussion of this example. The following axiom is a strengthening of conditional continuity.

Unconditional Continuity. For all $x \in X_i$ and for all $y^D \in \mathcal{D}$, the sets $\{y^C \in \mathcal{C} \mid (y^D, y^C) \succeq_i (x^D, x^C)\}$ and $\{y^C \in \mathcal{C} \mid (x^D, x^C) \succeq_i (y^D, y^C)\}$ are closed in $\mathcal{C}$.

Note that unconditional continuity also applies across different values of the discrete variables. Suppose x is better than y, y is better than z, and the discrete parts of the vectors associated with x and z are the same but, unlike in the definition of conditional continuity, they may be different from the discrete part of the vector associated with y. Consider a path connecting x and z with the subvector of discrete variables held constant along the path. Unconditional continuity requires the existence of an alternative on this path that is as good as y.

Clearly, any ordering that satisfies unconditional continuity also satisfies conditional continuity. However, unconditional continuity is stronger. To illustrate this observation, consider again the example presented after the definition of conditional continuity. For simplicity, let $c = d = 1$ – that is, there is one discrete variable and one continuous variable. As already mentioned, this ordering satisfies conditional continuity. Unconditional continuity is violated because, for example, the set $\{y^C \in \mathcal{C} \mid (1, y^C) \succeq_i (2, 0)\}$ is equal to $\mathcal{R}_{++}$, which is not closed in $\mathcal{C}$.

Unconditional continuity is sufficient for the existence of a representation of an ordering on the mixed domain $X_i = \mathcal{D} \times \mathcal{C}$. We conclude this section with a formal statement of this result. A proof of the following theorem is given by Blackorby, Bossert, and Donaldson (2001b).

Theorem 2.4. *Let $X_i = \mathcal{D} \times \mathcal{C}$ with $\mathcal{D} \subseteq \mathcal{Z}^d$ and $\mathcal{C} \subseteq \mathcal{R}^c$ for some $d, c \in \mathcal{Z}_{++}$, and suppose $\mathcal{D}$ and $\mathcal{C}$ are nonempty and $\mathcal{C}$ is connected. $\succeq_i$ has a representation that is continuous in x^C if and only if $\succeq_i$ is an ordering on X_i that satisfies unconditional continuity.*

2.7 MEASURABILITY

As illustrated in the previous section, utility functions can be used to translate the individual goodness relation $\succeq_i$ on X_i into the ordering $\geq$ on the set of real numbers. If the only purpose of using a utility function is this representation of the ordering $\succeq_i$, any utility function that preserves the ranking of the alternatives established by $\succeq_i$ will do. In that case, the utility function U_i has an ordinal interpretation. However, when employing utility functions, there are situations in which one might want to use more than ordinal information, such as information about utility gains and losses. In this section, we discuss assumptions about the measurability of individual utilities and illustrate how they can be used to obtain an informationally richer framework.

These information assumptions can be expressed by partitioning the set of all possible utility functions into subsets of informationally equivalent functions called information sets. Suppose $\mathcal{U}_i$ is the set of all possible functions $U_i \colon X_i \to \mathcal{R}$. A partition of $\mathcal{U}_i$ into information sets can be defined by using an equivalence relation on $\mathcal{U}_i$ with an information set given by an equivalence class of the relation. The approach we use to formalize measurement assumptions identifies the relevant equivalence relation by specifying, for each utility function U_i, the set of utility functions that are informationally equivalent.[15] Therefore, for information assumption A, we define a function $\Psi_i^A \colon \mathcal{U}_i \to 2^{\mathcal{U}_i}$ where, for all $U_i \in \mathcal{U}_i$,

$$\Psi_i^A(U_i) = \{V_i \in \mathcal{U}_i \mid V_i \text{ is informationally equivalent to } U_i \text{ given } A\}.$$

We consider only information assumptions A such that Ψ_i^A is obtained from an equivalence relation. See Bossert and Weymark (2004) for a discussion.

In the case of ordinal measurability, the function Ψ_i^A is given by Ψ_i^{OM}, which assigns to every utility function $U_i \in \mathcal{U}_i$ all increasing transformations of U_i.

---

[15] See Basu (1983); Bossert (1991); Bossert and Stehling (1994); Falmagne (1981); Fishburn, Marcus-Roberts, and Roberts (1988); Fishburn and Roberts (1989); and Krantz, Luce, Suppes, and Tversky (1971) for discussions of information assumptions in terms of meaningful statements and their relations to uniqueness properties of measurement scales.

Ordinal Measurability. For all $U_i \in \mathcal{U}_i$,

$$\Psi_i^{OM}(U_i) = \{V_i \in \mathcal{U}_i \mid \text{there exists an increasing function}$$
$$\phi_i \colon U_i(X_i) \to \mathcal{R} \text{ such that } V_i(x) = \phi_i[U_i(x)] \text{ for all } x \in X_i\}.$$

Ordinal measurability is equivalent to the intrapersonal comparability of utility levels. First, note that statements such as "agent i's utility in alternative $x \in X_i$ is greater than or equal to agent i's utility in $y \in X_i$" are preserved for all informationally equivalent utility functions according to ordinal measurability. This is the case because a utility-level comparison such as $U_i(x) \geq U_i(y)$ is preserved whenever an increasing transformation is applied to both sides of the inequality. Conversely, increasing transformations are the only transformations that preserve level comparisons. To provide a statement and proof of this observation, we define the information assumption of intrapersonal level comparability. It is expressed in terms of the corresponding function Ψ_i^{IALC}.

Intrapersonal Level Comparability. For all $U_i \in \mathcal{U}_i$,

$$\Psi_i^{IALC}(U_i)$$
$$= \{V_i \in \mathcal{U}_i \mid U_i(x) \geq U_i(y) \Leftrightarrow V_i(x) \geq V_i(y) \text{ for all } x, y \in X_i\}.$$

The equivalence of ordinal measurability and intrapersonal level comparability is stated in the following theorem (Krantz, Luce, Suppes, and Tversky 1971, p. 42).

Theorem 2.5. *For all $U_i \in \mathcal{U}_i$, $\Psi_i^{OM}(U_i) = \Psi_i^{IALC}(U_i)$.*

Proof. Let $U_i, V_i \in \mathcal{U}_i$. Suppose first that $V_i \in \Psi_i^{OM}(U_i)$ – that is, $V_i = \phi_i \circ U_i$ where ϕ_i is increasing and $\circ$ denotes function composition. This immediately implies $U_i(x) \geq U_i(y)$ if and only if $V_i(x) \geq V_i(y)$ for all $x, y \in X_i$ and, hence, $V_i \in \Psi_i^{IALC}(U_i)$.

Now suppose $V_i \in \Psi_i^{IALC}(U_i)$. Therefore,

$$U_i(x) \geq U_i(y) \Leftrightarrow V_i(x) \geq V_i(y) \tag{2.2}$$

for all $x, y \in X_i$, which implies, in particular,

$$U_i(x) = U_i(y) \Leftrightarrow V_i(x) = V_i(y)$$

for all $x, y \in X_i$. Hence, there is a unique value of V_i for each value of U_i. This implies that there exists a function $\phi_i \colon U_i(X_i) \to \mathcal{R}$ such that $V_i(x) = \phi_i[U_i(x)]$ for all $x \in X_i$. Furthermore, (2.2) implies

$$U_i(x) > U_i(y) \Rightarrow \phi_i(U_i(x)) > \phi_i(U_i(y))$$

for all $x, y \in X_i$, which means that ϕ_i is increasing. Therefore, $V_i \in \Psi_i^{OM}(U_i)$. ■

Next, we turn to what is commonly referred to as a cardinal interpretation of individual utility. Cardinal utility functions are unique up to increasing affine transformations only and thus carry more information than ordinal utility functions.[16] This informational environment enables us to make statements not only about intrapersonal comparisons of utility levels but also about comparisons of utility differences. However, as we demonstrate later, a cardinal interpretation of individual utility is not equivalent to the possibility of performing comparisons of utility differences – in some circumstances, transformations other than increasing affine functions may preserve difference comparisons as well.

Cardinal measurability of individual utilities is defined in terms of the function Ψ_i^{CM}.

Cardinal Measurability. For all $U_i \in \mathcal{U}_i$,

$$\Psi_i^{CM}(U_i) = \{V_i \in \mathcal{U}_i \mid \text{there exist } a_i \in \mathcal{R}_{++} \text{ and } b_i \in \mathcal{R} \text{ such that}$$
$$V_i(x) = a_i U_i(x) + b_i \text{ for all } x \in X_i\}.$$

The following definition employs the function Ψ_i^{IADC} to express the intrapersonal comparability of utility differences.

Intrapersonal Difference Comparability. For all $U_i \in \mathcal{U}_i$,

$$\Psi_i^{IADC}(U_i) = \{V_i \in \mathcal{U}_i \mid U_i(x) - U_i(y) \geq U_i(z) - U_i(w)$$
$$\Leftrightarrow V_i(x) - V_i(y) \geq V_i(z) - V_i(w) \text{ for all } x, y, z, w \in X_i\}.$$

The following result establishes that intrapersonal comparisons of utility differences are preserved by all increasing affine transformations, but there exist examples where increasing affine transformations are not the only transformations with this property. See also Basu (1983), Bossert (1991), and Bossert and Stehling (1994) for this and related observations.

Theorem 2.6.
   (i) *For all* $U_i \in \mathcal{U}_i$, $\Psi_i^{CM}(U_i) \subseteq \Psi_i^{IADC}(U_i)$.
   (ii) *If* X_i *contains at least three elements, there exists* $U_i \in \mathcal{U}_i$ *such that the set inclusion in (i) is strict.*

---

[16] The term "cardinal" is sometimes used with an interpretation that is different from ours. Although most contributions in social choice theory follow the convention we have chosen here, the term cardinality on occasion is interpreted to cover all information assumptions other than ordinal measurability. Our taxonomy of information assumptions is more precise and less likely to lead to misunderstandings.

Proof. The proof of part (i) is straightforward; see the first part of the proof of Theorem 2.5. An example is sufficient to prove part (ii). Let $X_i = \{x, y, z\}$ and define the utility functions U_i and V_i by letting $U_i(x) = 4$, $U_i(y) = 2$, $U_i(z) = 1$, and $V_i(x) = 5$, $V_i(y) = 2$, $V_i(z) = 1$. Clearly, $V_i \in \Psi_i^{IADC}(U_i)$ and $V_i \notin \Psi_i^{CM}(U_i)$. ∎

For some specific sets X_i and utility functions U_i, the sets $\Psi_i^{CM}(U_i)$ and $\Psi_i^{IADC}(U_i)$ coincide. If we amend the example used in the proof of Theorem 2.6 by letting $U_i(x) = 3$, $U_i(y) = 2$, and $U_i(z) = 1$, the only functions V_i preserving all difference comparisons are all those V_i that can be written as increasing affine transformations of U_i.

The characterization of all domains X_i and utility functions $U_i: X_i \to \mathcal{R}$ such that cardinal measurability and intrapersonal difference comparability are equivalent is an open question. To illustrate the problems involved in finding a complete characterization of these domains, we provide a formal discussion along the lines of Bossert and Stehling (1994).

Suppose $U_i \in \mathcal{U}_i$. By setting $y = w$ in the definition of Ψ_i^{IADC}, it follows that any $V_i \in \Psi_i^{IADC}(U_i)$ must preserve all utility-level comparisons according to U_i. By Theorem 2.5, $\Psi_i^{IADC}(U_i) \subseteq \Psi_i^{IALC}(U_i) = \Psi_i^{OM}(U_i)$. Therefore, any $V_i \in \Psi_i^{IADC}(U_i)$ must be such that there exists an increasing function $\phi_i: U_i(X_i) \to \mathcal{R}$ with $V_i = \phi_i \circ U_i$. Hence, using intrapersonal difference comparability, ϕ_i must satisfy

$$U_i(x) - U_i(y) \geq U_i(z) - U_i(w) \Leftrightarrow$$
$$\phi_i(U_i(x)) - \phi_i(U_i(y)) \geq \phi_i[U_i(z)] - \phi_i[U_i(w)]$$

for all $x, y, z, w \in X_i$ or, equivalently,

$$u_i - v_i \geq q_i - s_i \Leftrightarrow \phi_i(u_i) - \phi_i(v_i) \geq \phi_i(q_i) - \phi_i(s_i) \tag{2.3}$$

for all $u_i, v_i, q_i, s_i \in U_i(X_i)$. This implies

$$u_i - v_i = q_i - s_i \Leftrightarrow \phi_i(u_i) - \phi_i(v_i) = \phi_i(q_i) - \phi_i(s_i)$$

for all $u_i, v_i, q_i, s_i \in U_i(X_i)$. Hence, there is a unique value of the difference $\phi_i(u_i) - \phi_i(v_i)$ for each value of the difference $u_i - v_i$, where $u_i, v_i \in U_i(X_i)$. Letting $D_i[U_i(X_i)] = \{d_i \in \mathcal{R} \mid \text{there exist } u_i, v_i \in U_i(X_i) \text{ such that } d_i = u_i - v_i\}$ be the set of possible utility differences given U_i, this implies that there exists a function $f_i: D_i[U_i(X_i)] \to \mathcal{R}$ such that

$$\phi_i(u_i) - \phi_i(v_i) = f_i(u_i - v_i) \tag{2.4}$$

for all $u_i, v_i \in U_i(X_i)$. Furthermore, by (2.3), $u_i - v_i > q_i - s_i$ implies

$$f_i(u_i - v_i) = \phi_i(u_i) - \phi_i(v_i) > \phi_i(q_i) - \phi_i(s_i) = f_i(q_i - s_i)$$

for all $u_i, v_i, q_i, s_i \in U_i(X_i)$. Therefore, f_i is increasing. Conversely, it is clear that the existence of an increasing function f_i satisfying (2.4) is sufficient for the preservation of utility-difference comparisons. Therefore, $\phi_i \circ U_i$ is in Ψ_i^{IADC} if and only if there exists an increasing function $f_i: D_i[U_i(X_i)] \rightarrow \mathcal{R}$ such that (2.4) is satisfied.

The function ϕ_i is increasing affine if and only if f_i is increasing linear and, thus, it follows that Ψ_i^{CM} is equal to Ψ_i^{IADC} if and only if the only solutions to the Pexider equation (2.4) (Aczél 1966, pp. 141–142; Eichhorn 1978, pp. 50–52) are such that ϕ_i is affine and f_i is linear. Unless specific restrictions are imposed on $U_i(X_i)$, solutions other than those exist; see, for example, Falmagne (1981).

A sufficient condition for the relevant Pexider equation to have only solutions where ϕ_i is affine is that $U_i(X_i)$ is a nondegenerate interval.[17] This result is stated in the following theorem. Its proof follows from combining the observation that (2.4) is necessary and sufficient for the equivalence of cardinal measurability and intrapersonal difference comparability with the fact that if the domain of ϕ_i is a nondegenerate interval, then the only solutions to the functional equation (2.4) are such that ϕ_i is affine (Aczél 1987, p. 20).

Theorem 2.7. *For all $U_i \in \mathcal{U}_i$, if $U_i(X_i)$ is a nondegenerate interval, then* $\Psi_i^{CM}(U_i) = \Psi_i^{IADC}(U_i)$.

The next informational assumption we discuss is ratio-scale measurability. It requires the uniqueness of a utility function up to increasing linear transformations. The corresponding function Ψ_i^{RM} is defined as follows.

Ratio-Scale Measurability. For all $U_i \in \mathcal{U}_i$,

$$\Psi_i^{RM}(U_i) = \{V_i \in \mathcal{U}_i \mid \text{ there exists } a_i \in \mathcal{R}_{++} \text{ such that}$$
$$V_i(x) = a_i U_i(x) \text{ for all } x \in X_i\}.$$

Ratio-scale measurability is related to (but, in general, not equivalent to) the numerical significance of utility ratios. We call the corresponding information assumption intrapersonal ratio significance, and we express it by means of the function Ψ_i^{IARS}.

Intrapersonal Ratio Significance. For all $U_i \in \mathcal{U}_i$,

$$\Psi_i^{IARS}(U_i) = \{V_i \in \mathcal{U}_i \mid U_i(x)/U_i(y) = V_i(x)/V_i(y)$$
$$\text{for all } x, y \in X_i \text{ such that } U_i(y) \neq 0 \text{ and } V_i(y) \neq 0\}.$$

Analogously to the relationship between cardinal measurability and intrapersonal difference comparability, ratio-scale measurability implies that intrapersonal utility ratios are significant but the reverse implication is, in general,

---

[17] Alternative sufficient conditions can be found elsewhere (Bossert and Stehling 1994; Fishburn, Marcus-Roberts, and Roberts 1988; and Fishburn and Roberts 1989).

not true. Moreover, the two concepts are equivalent only in degenerate cases. We obtain

Theorem 2.8.
(i) For all $U_i \in \mathcal{U}_i$, $\Psi_i^{RM}(U_i) \subseteq \Psi_i^{IARS}(U_i)$.
(ii) If $U_i(X_i) \neq \{0\}$, then the set inclusion in (a) is strict.

Proof. Again, the result of part (i) is straightforward to verify. To prove part (ii), suppose $U_i(X_i) \neq \{0\}$. Therefore, there exists $y \in X_i$ such that $U_i(y) \neq 0$. Let $x \in X_i$. By intrapersonal ratio significance,

$$U_i(x)/U_i(y) = V_i(x)/V_i(y).$$

Letting $a_i \in \mathcal{R} \setminus \{0\}$ and $V_i(y) = a_i U_i(y)$, it follows that $V_i(x) = a_i U_i(x)$ for all $x \in X_i$. Choosing a_i to be negative, it follows that $V_i \in \Psi_i^{IARS}(U_i)$ and $V_i \notin \Psi_i^{RM}(U_i)$. ∎

As is apparent from the proof of Theorem 2.8, the reason why individual ratio significance does not imply ratio-scale measurability is that the scaling factor a_i may be negative. To preserve the significance of utility ratios, it is necessary that a utility function V_i that is informationally equivalent to U_i is a linear transformation of U_i, but this transformation may be decreasing rather than increasing. This suggests that, in the nondegenerate cases covered by Theorem 2.8, adding intrapersonal level comparability to ratio significance leads to an information assumption that is equivalent to ratio-scale measurability. This is indeed the case, as demonstrated in the following theorem.

Theorem 2.9. *For all* $U_i \in \mathcal{U}_i$, *if* $U_i(X_i) \neq \{0\}$, *then* $\Psi_i^{RM}(U_i) = \Psi_i^{IARS}(U_i) \cap \Psi_i^{IALC}(U_i)$.

Proof. Clearly, $\Psi_i^{RM}(U_i) \subseteq \Psi_i^{IARS}(U_i) \cap \Psi_i^{IALC}(U_i)$. To prove the reverse set inclusion, suppose $U_i(X_i) \neq \{0\}$ and $V_i \in \Psi_i^{IARS}(U_i) \cap \Psi_i^{IALC}(U_i)$. As in the proof of Theorem 2.8, it follows that $V_i(x) = a_i U_i(x)$ for some $a_i \in \mathcal{R} \setminus \{0\}$. By Theorem 2.5, it follows that V_i must be an increasing transformation of U_i, which implies $a_i \in \mathcal{R}_{++}$. Therefore, $V_i \in \Psi_i^{RM}(U_i)$. ∎

There is an interesting way to link cardinal measurability and ratio-scale measurability. In many circumstances, especially in a variable-population context, it is useful to employ norms that restrict the set of utility functions that can be employed for the purposes of social evaluation; see, for instance, Blackorby, Bossert, and Donaldson (1999b) and Tungodden (1998). For example, it is often convenient to identify a lifetime-utility level of zero with neutrality. To respect this zero normalization, any two utility functions that are informationally equivalent must coincide at zero. We call the function representing this assumption Ψ_i^{ZN}.

Zero Normalization. For all $U_i \in \mathcal{U}_i$,

$$\Psi_i^{ZN}(U_i) = \{V_i \in \mathcal{U}_i \mid U_i(x) = 0 \Leftrightarrow V_i(x) = 0 \text{ for all } x \in X_i\}.$$

We obtain the following equivalence result, which requires the nondegeneracy assumption that the zero utility level is actually attained. The discussion in Part A implicitly assumes that this is the case.

Theorem 2.10. *For all* $U_i \in \mathcal{U}_i$, *if* $0 \in U_i(X_i)$, *then* $\Psi_i^{RM}(U_i) = \Psi_i^{CM}(U_i) \cap \Psi_i^{ZN}(U_i)$.

Proof. That $\Psi_i^{RM}(U_i) \subseteq \Psi_i^{CM}(U_i) \cap \Psi_i^{ZN}(U_i)$ is straightforward to verify. Now suppose $0 \in U_i(X_i)$ and $V_i \in \Psi_i^{CM}(U_i) \cap \Psi_i^{ZN}(U_i)$. Let $y \in X_i$ be such that $U_i(y) = 0$. Therefore, there exist $a_i \in \mathcal{R}_{++}$ and $b_i \in \mathcal{R}$ such that $V_i(x) = a_i U_i(x) + b_i$ for all $x \in X_i$ and $V_i(y) = U_i(y) = 0$. Hence, $b_i = 0$, which implies $V_i \in \Psi_i^{RM}(U_i)$. ∎

Finally, we discuss the measurability assumption that assigns the maximal possible information to individual utilities – numerical significance. Utilities are numerically significant if and only if each utility function forms an information set by itself. The corresponding function is Ψ_i^{NS}.

Numerical Significance. For all $U_i \in \mathcal{U}_i$,

$$\Psi_i^{NS}(U_i) = \{U_i\}.$$

It is unlikely that information as detailed as that described in this definition is available. However, norms again can be used to obtain numerical significance from weaker informational assumptions. In particular, if there are two norms (for example, neutrality and a particular standard of living above neutrality), adding cardinal measurability makes utilities numerically significant. The information assumption representing two norms – 0 and 100 – is represented by the function Ψ_i^{ZON}.

Zero – One-Hundred Normalization. For all $U_i \in \mathcal{U}_i$,

$$\Psi_i^{ZON}(U_i) = \{V_i \in \mathcal{U}_i \mid [U_i(x) = 0 \Leftrightarrow V_i(x) = 0] \text{ and}$$
$$[U_i(x) = 100 \Leftrightarrow V_i(x) = 100] \text{ for all } x \in X_i\}.$$

Provided that the utility values 0 and 100 are actually attained, numerical significance is equivalent to the conjunction of cardinal measurability and the zero – one-hundred normalization. We conclude this section with a proof of this result.

Theorem 2.11. *For all* $U_i \in \mathcal{U}_i$, *if* $\{0, 100\} \subseteq U_i(X_i)$, *then* $\Psi_i^{NS}(U_i) = \Psi_i^{CM}(U_i) \cap \Psi_i^{ZON}(U_i)$.

Proof. Again, that $\Psi_i^{NS}(U_i) \subseteq \Psi_i^{CM}(U_i) \cap \Psi_i^{ZON}(U_i)$ is obvious. Now suppose $\{0, 100\} \subseteq U_i(X_i)$ and $V_i \in \Psi_i^{CM}(U_i) \cap \Psi_i^{ZON}(U_i)$. Let $y, z \in X_i$ be such that $U_i(y) = 0$ and $U_i(z) = 100$. Therefore, there exist $a_i \in \mathcal{R}_{++}$ and $b_i \in \mathcal{R}$ such that $V_i(x) = a_i U_i(x) + b_i$ for all $x \in X_i$. Furthermore, we have $V_i(y) = U_i(y) = 0$ and $V_i(z) = U_i(z) = 100$. Hence, $b_i = 0$ and, consequently, $V_i(z) = a_i U_i(z) = U_i(z)$, which implies $a_i = 1$ and thus $V_i \in \Psi_i^{NS}(U_i)$. ∎

2.8 MULTIPERIOD WELL-BEING

In some of our models, the intertemporal structure of individual lives is explicitly taken into consideration. It is then possible to analyze the special case in which individual lifetime well-being is an aggregate of the levels of well-being experienced in each period of the individual's lifetime. As mentioned in Part A, an individual's per-period well-being may depend on experiences in other periods of her or his life.

We treat time as a discrete variable and assume that the duration of individual lives is bounded by a maximal lifetime $\bar{L} \in \mathcal{Z}_{++}$. For $x \in X_i$, let $s_i = S_i(x) \in \mathcal{Z}_+$ be the period before individual i is born, and let $\ell_i = L_i(x) \in \{1, \ldots, \bar{L}\}$ be i's lifetime. Thus, individual i is alive from period $s_i + 1$ to period $s_i + \ell_i$. For an alternative $x \in X_i$ and a period $t \in \{s_i + 1, \ldots, s_i + \ell_i\}$, $w_i^t = W_i^t(x) \in \mathcal{R}$ is the utility of individual i in period t. The utility vector representing i's per-period utilities over her or his lifetime is $(w_i^{s_i+1}, \ldots, w_i^{s_i+\ell_i}) \in \mathcal{R}^{\ell_i}$. From the viewpoint of individual i, it is irrelevant whether we label the periods of his or her life $s_i + 1, \ldots, s_i + \ell_i$ or $1, \ldots, \ell_i$. Although keeping track of individual birth dates may be of relevance once several individuals are considered, we use the labels $1, \ldots, \ell_i$ in the remainder of this section on individual well-being to simplify notation.

Individual i ranks possible vectors of per-period utilities by means of a goodness relation R_i defined on $\cup_{\ell_i=1}^{\bar{L}} \mathcal{R}^{\ell_i}$. The better-than relation and the as-good-as relation corresponding to R_i are P_i and I_i. We use a continuity assumption analogous to that employed in Section 2.6, suitably adapted to the intertemporal framework discussed here.

Extended Continuity. For all $\ell_i, \ell_i' \in \{1, \ldots, \bar{L}\}$ and for all $(w_i^1, \ldots, w_i^{\ell_i}) \in \mathcal{R}^{\ell_i}$, the sets

$$\left\{ (v_i^1, \ldots, v_i^{\ell_i'}) \in \mathcal{R}^{\ell_i'} \mid (v_i^1, \ldots, v_i^{\ell_i'}) R_i (w_i^1, \ldots, w_i^{\ell_i}) \right\}$$

and

$$\left\{ (v_i^1, \ldots, v_i^{\ell_i'}) \in \mathcal{R}^{\ell_i'} \mid (w_i^1, \ldots, w_i^{\ell_i}) R_i (v_i^1, \ldots, v_i^{\ell_i'}) \right\}$$

are closed in $\mathcal{R}^{\ell_i'}$.

The above continuity property is analogous to the unconditional-continuity axiom discussed in Section 2.6. The domain considered here, a union of connected sets of different dimensions, is different from the domains considered in Section 2.6, but it is possible to establish a representation theorem on the above domain by employing extended continuity. The resulting representation theorem is a special case of Theorem 5 of Blackorby, Bossert, and Donaldson (2001b), and we conclude this chapter by stating it without a proof.

Theorem 2.12. *Let $\bar{L} \in \mathcal{Z}_{++}$. R_i has a representation that is continuous on $\mathcal{R}^{\ell_i}$ for all $\ell_i \in \{1, \ldots, \bar{L}\}$ if and only if R_i is an ordering on $\cup_{\ell_i=1}^{\bar{L}} \mathcal{R}^{\ell_i}$ that satisfies extended continuity.*

CHAPTER 3

Welfarist Social Evaluation

Part A

An alternative is associated with three distinct pieces of information. The first is a list of the identities of those who ever live, the second consists of information about individual well-being as represented by a collection of utility functions, and the third is all the remaining information, which we call nonwelfare information. A principle for social evaluation uses some or all of this information to generate a social goodness relation that ranks the alternatives. For any two alternatives, one may be better than the other, the two may be equally good, or they may not be ranked at all, in which case we say they are incommensurable. In this chapter, however, we focus on complete social rankings and assume that principles provide orderings – reflexive, transitive, and complete rankings – of the alternatives (see Chapter 2, Sections 2.2 and 2.6, for a discussion). Incomplete social goodness relations (quasi-orderings) are investigated in Chapter 7.

In some of the arguments in this chapter, we allow the histories associated with the alternatives to change. In that case, we say there are multiple information profiles. This allows us to investigate important properties of principles for social evaluation without assuming the existence of a large number of alternatives.

Welfarist principles rank alternatives on the basis of the well-being of the individuals that are alive (ever live) in them without using nonwelfare information. Some, but not all, also disregard information about individual identities. We say that such principles are anonymous.

Because some nonhumans are sentient (capable of having experiences), welfarist principles have often been extended "to the whole sentient creation" (Mill 1861, 1979b, p. 263) by taking account of animal well-being. We focus on humans in this chapter, however, and discuss the extension of welfarist principles to sentient nonhumans in Chapter 11.

The utilitarian principle ranks alternatives with the same population by adding or averaging the utilities of those alive. One alternative is (socially) at least as good as another if and only if the sum or average is at least as great in the first as in the second. This implies that the two are equally good if and only if the sum or average is the same in both and that the first is better than the second if and only if the sum or average is greater in the first. Many principles for social evaluation are consistent with the utilitarian principle for fixed-population comparisons. Principles that can rank all the alternatives are called population principles.

Fixed-population utilitarianism is not the only anonymous welfarist principle. One other possibility is the Gini principle, which exhibits aversion to inequality of well-being. In addition, there are nonanonymous welfarist principles such as those that use a weighted sum of utilities to rank alternatives, with higher (positive) weights attached to the utility levels of certain individuals. The most important fixed-population welfarist principles are presented in Chapter 4 and welfarist population principles are presented in Chapter 5.

Most welfarist principles require interpersonal comparisons of well-being. In some circumstances, all that is needed is the ability to make comparisons such as "person 12 is better off in alternative x than person 200 is in alternative y." These comparisons are made regularly by most people but, as is well-known, cannot be derived from individual wants or preferences without additional assumptions.[1]

In this chapter, we investigate the arguments in favor of welfarist principles. We employ several compelling axioms and show that they imply welfarism. Furthermore, we respond to some common criticisms of welfarist social evaluation.

3.1 POPULATION PRINCIPLES AND SOCIAL-EVALUATION FUNCTIONALS

A social-evaluation functional is a mathematical description of a principle for social evaluation. There are two types: fixed-population social-evaluation functionals, which correspond to fixed-population principles, and variable-population social-evaluation functionals, which correspond to population principles. Functionals of both types associate an ordering of the alternatives with each possible profile of information. Fixed-population principles rank only those alternatives with a given population, and population principles rank all the alternatives. We assume there are at least three alternatives with each possible population.

We assume, in addition, that there is a list of the identities of potential people, which is indexed by the positive integers. The identities of those who ever live in an alternative therefore can be described by a vector of positive integers. As an example, suppose that, in alternative x, there are three people who ever live and their names correspond to identity numbers 1, 2,000, and 40. The identity vector for an alternative consists of the identity numbers of those who are alive arranged from smallest to largest. Thus, the identity vector for alternative x is (1, 40, 2,000).

---

[1] For an example, see Blackorby and Donaldson (1993).

Table 3.1. *Welfare and Nonwelfare Information*

	Individual Well-Being	Nonwelfare Information
Person 1	20	hardworking
Person 2000	12	not hardworking
Person 40	22	hardworking

Information about individual lifetime well-being is provided by a profile of utility functions. In the fixed-population case, a utility profile consists of a vector of utility functions, one for each person and, in the general case, a utility profile consists of a vector of utility functions, one for each potential person. Each of these functions assigns a utility number to each alternative for each person in the identity vector.

Nonwelfare information for an alternative can take two forms: social information and individual-specific information. The first category refers to social characteristics such as whether social institutions are democratic or provide freedom of the press. The second consists of all information that applies to individuals, such as sex, length of life, whether the person has a propensity to work hard or likes classical music, and so on. To describe nonwelfare information, we use a vector of nonwelfare information functions. There is one such function for society as a whole and one for each person. Nonwelfare information can differ across alternatives.

Because nonwelfare information can include characteristics, such as being hardworking, economic preferences may differ across alternatives. Those preferences are not included in the utility profile, however. Utility functions measure the actual level of well-being that is achieved in the various alternatives.

Welfare (utility) and nonwelfare information for the alternative x in the above example is displayed in Table 3.1. Nonwelfare information is restricted to whether each person is hardworking.

A fixed-population principle for social evaluation (a fixed-population social-evaluation functional) is welfarist if and only if there is a single ordering of utility vectors so that, for all possible profiles and all pairs of alternatives x and y, x is at least as good as y if and only if the utility vector associated with x is at least as good as the utility vector associated with y according to the single ordering. We call such an ordering a social-evaluation ordering. In the maximin case, for example, one utility vector is at least as good as another if and only if the smallest utility in the first is greater than or equal to the smallest in the second.

A population principle is welfarist if and only if there is a single social-evaluation ordering of compound vectors, each of which consists of an identity vector and a utility vector of the same dimension. Alternative x is at least as good as alternative y if and only if the identity-utility vector for x is at least as good as the identity-utility vector for y. If individuals 4 and 7 are alive in alternative x with utility levels 10 and 20 and individuals 4, 7, and 60 are alive in y with utility levels of 5, 20, and −4, x is at least as good as y if and only if identity-utility vector [(4, 7), (10, 20)] is ranked as better than identity-utility vector [(4, 7, 60), (5, 20, −4)] by the social-evaluation ordering.

We consider three cases. The first is the single-profile case, and it associates a single social-evaluation ordering of the alternatives with the actual information profile. The other cases are concerned with the behavior of principles when information profiles are allowed to vary. In the second case, the nonwelfare information profile is fixed and there are multiple utility profiles. In the third case, multiple welfare and nonwelfare information profiles are considered. Although the second case is the standard one in social-choice theory, the third increases the power of the welfarism theorems, especially when anonymous principles are considered.

3.2   FIXED-POPULATION PRINCIPLES

Suppose attention is restricted to alternatives with the same population. The number of people who ever live is n and, without loss of generality, we choose their identity numbers to be $1, \ldots, n$.

The basic intuition that lies behind welfarist social evaluation is the view that, if one alternative is ranked as better than another, it must be better for at least one person (Goodin 1991). Without this requirement, we run the risk of recommending social changes that are empty gestures, benefiting no one and, perhaps, harming some or all. We use it as an axiom, which we call minimal individual goodness.

If, in any two alternatives, each person is equally well off, the Pareto-indifference axiom requires the two alternatives to be ranked as equally good. Note that the axiom refers not to preferences but to goodness; we retain the standard name from social choice theory. This axiom, which is central to welfarism, is implied by minimal individual goodness. To see this, note that, for any two alternatives x and y, minimal individual goodness is equivalent to the requirement that, if it is not the case that at least one person is better off in x, it is not the case that x is better than y. If everyone is equally well off in both, it follows that it is not the case that x is better than y and it is not the case that y is better than x. Because the social goodness relation is an ordering, it must be true that x and y are equally good. Rather than using minimal individual goodness, we employ Pareto indifference in our theorems because the stronger axiom is not needed.

First, consider the single-profile case. Because there is only one profile of information, there is only one social ordering. In this case, Pareto indifference is sufficient for welfarism. Consider the example of Table 3.2. In it, there are two people and four alternatives. Utility levels are 20 and 5 in each alternative, person 1 is hardworking in x and y only, and person 2 is hardworking in z and w only. There is no other nonwelfare information.

Suppose the principle for social evaluation ranks pairs of alternatives with the same distribution of utilities [(20, 5) or (5, 20)] by favoring the hardworking

Table 3.2. *Single-Profile Welfarism*

	Welfare Information		Nonwelfare Information	
	Person 1	Person 2	Person 1	Person 2
x	20	5	hardworking	not hardworking
y	5	20	hardworking	not hardworking
z	20	5	not hardworking	hardworking
w	5	20	not hardworking	hardworking

person. That requires x to be ranked as better than y and w to be ranked as better than z. This ranking, however, is inconsistent with Pareto indifference, which requires x and z to be ranked as equally good and y and w to be ranked as equally good. Consequently, by transitivity, if x is better than y, z is better than w. Nonwelfare information must be disregarded when making comparisons of this type.

In the single-profile case, any principle that satisfies Pareto indifference must be welfarist. A social-evaluation ordering of all attainable utility vectors can be constructed as follows. For any pair of such vectors u and v, let u be at least as good as v if and only if there is some alternative x whose utility vector is u and some alternative y whose utility vector is v with x ranked as at least as good as y. The above argument shows that, if x or y is not unique, the ranking of u and v is the same for all possibilities. Consequently, the ranking of utility vectors is well-defined. It is clearly reflexive and complete, and transitivity follows from Pareto indifference and transitivity of the ordering of alternatives.

Suppose, now, there are no pairs of alternatives that have the same utility vectors. In that case, Pareto indifference imposes no restriction and, although there is a social-evaluation ordering of utility vectors that can be used to rank alternatives, the spirit of welfarism does not appear to be captured. It may be the case that nonwelfare information has an effect but, because there is only a single information profile, we cannot separate the influences of the welfare and nonwelfare components. If it is possible to observe, hypothetically, the rankings that a principle would make given different information profiles, the separate influences of the welfare and nonwelfare components can be discerned.

Because Pareto indifference applies separately to each information profile, we need a way to require the principle to be consistent across different profiles. Such a condition is provided by the axiom binary independence of irrelevant alternatives. If two profiles coincide on any pair of alternatives, the independence axiom requires the social ranking of that pair to be the same for both profiles. Note that both welfare and nonwelfare information must be the same.

The standard domain in social-choice theory consists of all possible utility profiles linked to a single nonwelfare information profile. It is well known that, on this domain, a social-evaluation functional satisfies Pareto indifference and binary independence of irrelevant alternatives if and only if it is welfarist.

Table 3.3. *Multi-Profile Welfarism*

	Welfare Information				Nonwelfare Information			
	x	y	z	w	x	y	z	w
Profile A	(20, 5)	(15, 10)			NW_1	NW_2		
Profile B	(20, 5)	(15, 10)	(20, 5)	(15, 10)	NW_1	NW_2	NW_1'	NW_2'
Profile C	(20, 5)	(15, 10)	(20, 5)	(15, 10)	NW_1'	NW_2'	NW_1'	NW_2'
Profile D	(20, 5)	(15, 10)			NW_1'	NW_2'		

In the multiple nonwelfare profile case, we assume that utility information can be any possible utility profile. The sets of realizable nonwelfare information can be different for different individuals, and we consider all possible nonwelfare information profiles with those realizations. Together, these conditions constitute our unlimited-domain assumption. As an example, consider a society of two individuals and four alternatives in which there is no social nonwelfare information and individual nonwelfare information consists of specifying whether the person is fat (f) or thin (t). Person 1 can be fat or thin so his or her set of possible nonwelfare information values is $\{f, t\}$. Person 2 is thin in all profiles so her or his set of possible nonwelfare information values is $\{t\}$. The possibilities for the two individuals are, therefore, (f, t) and (t, t) and, by suitable choice of a nonwelfare profile domain, they can be assigned independently to the four alternatives. Consequently, there are 16 possible nonwelfare information profiles. The standard fixed nonwelfare information profile is not a special case.

Pareto indifference and binary independence together require the principle to disregard nonwelfare information. An example for four distinct alternatives and two individuals is given in Table 3.3.

In the table, entries under the welfare information heading are utility levels of the two people. In profile A, person 1's utility levels are 20 in x and 15 in y, and person 2's utility levels are 5 in x and 10 in y; utility levels for the other two alternatives are unspecified and can take on any values. In addition, in profile A, nonwelfare information is denoted as NW_1 for alternative x and as NW_2 for alternative y. In profile D, utility levels for x and y are the same as those in profile A, but nonwelfare information for the two alternatives is NW_1' and NW_2', which can be different from the nonwelfare information in profile A.

If a principle satisfies Pareto indifference and binary independence of irrelevant alternatives, the ranking of x and y by the social orderings for profiles A and D must be the same. To demonstrate that claim, we construct several other profiles. In profile B, utility levels are 20 and 5 for alternatives x and z and 15 and 10 for alternatives y and w. Nonwelfare information is NW_1 for x, NW_2 for y, NW_1' for z, and NW_2' for w. Profile C coincides with profile B on alternatives z and w and with profile D on x and y. Let the social ordering corresponding to profile A be called ordering A with similar names for the orderings that correspond to the other profiles.

Because both welfare and nonwelfare information for x and y is the same in profiles A and B, binary independence implies that the rankings of x and y by orderings A and B are the same. In profile B, Pareto indifference implies that x and z are equally good and that y and w are equally good. Consequently, ordering B ranks z and w in the same way it ranks x and y. Because profiles B and C coincide on z and w, binary independence implies that ordering C ranks z and w in the same way that ordering B does. Pareto indifference implies that ordering C ranks x and z as equally good and y and w as equally good. It follows that ordering C ranks x and y in the same way that it ranks z and w. Because profiles C and D coincide on x and y, binary independence implies that orderings C and D rank x and y in the same way. Together, these observations imply that orderings A and D rank x and y in the same way.

The above example is an instance of a general theorem. As long as there are at least three alternatives and attention is restricted to principles that satisfy our unlimited-domain assumption, any fixed-population principle that satisfies Pareto indifference and binary independence of irrelevant alternatives must disregard all nonwelfare information. It follows that principles that make use of nonwelfare information either must behave inconsistently as information changes or must fail to satisfy Pareto indifference and, therefore, minimal individual goodness.

Because any social-evaluation functional with an unlimited domain that satisfies Pareto indifference and binary independence must disregard nonwelfare information, it is equivalent to one that associates one social ordering with each *welfare* profile. The multiple nonwelfare profile case is, therefore, equivalent to the single nonwelfare profile case. Given that, here is how one can proceed to show that the principle is welfarist. First, the principle is shown to satisfy strong neutrality, defined as follows. If utility vectors for x and y in profile A are the same as utility vectors for z and w in profile B, strong neutrality requires the ranking of x and y by ordering A and the ranking of z and w by ordering B to be the same. Note that nonwelfare information contained in the profiles is not restricted by this condition. To construct a social-evaluation ordering of utility vectors, choose any two vectors u and v with n components and let u be at least as good as v if and only if there exists a profile and a pair of alternatives x and y so that u and v are the vectors of utilities for x and y, respectively, and x is at least as good as y according to the social ordering for that profile. Strong neutrality ensures that, if there are other profiles and alternatives with the same property, the social ranking is the same, so the ranking of utility vectors is well-defined. In addition, it is clearly reflexive and complete, and transitivity of the social orderings of alternatives ensures that the ranking of utility vectors is transitive. Consequently, there is a social-evaluation ordering of utility vectors with the requisite property and welfarism obtains.

There are characterizations of principles that are partially welfarist. Sen (1979) and Roberts (1980b) used the weak Pareto axiom to characterize strict-ranking welfarism. If each person is better off in x than in y, weak Pareto requires x to be ranked as better. Strict-ranking welfarism applies to comparisons of alternatives in which the individual utility rankings are strict and, in that case, the alternatives are ranked entirely on the basis of utility levels. Most principles that are not welfarist are also not strict-ranking welfarist. Sen's theorem shows that they do not satisfy weak Pareto.

3.3 POPULATION PRINCIPLES

The set of all alternatives includes some with different populations and population sizes. Consequently, it must be possible to rank alternatives in which some or all of the individuals who are alive in one are not alive in the other. Each individual utility function must be defined only for alternatives in which the person is alive. Because Pareto indifference applies to same-population comparisons only, no change, other than requiring it to apply to all populations, is needed. Binary independence is changed to an axiom that we call extended binary independence of irrelevant alternatives. It restates the fixed-population axiom so that it applies to the full set of alternatives.

The argument of the previous section following the example of Table 3.3 can be extended to cover alternatives with different populations and population sizes. Suppose, for example, that, in alternative x, only persons 1 and 2 are alive and that, in alternative y, persons 2, 4, and 6 are alive. All that is needed to generalize the argument is to choose z and w so that the populations coincide with those of x and y. The rest of the argument is the same. It follows that population principles with an unlimited domain that satisfy the two axioms must disregard all nonwelfare information. As in the fixed-population case, it follows that principles that make use of nonwelfare information either must behave inconsistently as information changes or must fail to satisfy Pareto indifference and, therefore, minimal individual goodness.

Any population principle with an unlimited domain that satisfies Pareto indifference and extended independence of irrelevant alternatives must satisfy extended strong neutrality, which is defined analogously to its fixed-population counterpart: if identities and corresponding utilities for x and y in profile A are the same as identities and corresponding utilities for z and w in profile B, extended strong neutrality requires the ranking of x and y by ordering A and the ranking of z and w by ordering B to be the same. Given extended strong neutrality, the construction of a social-evaluation ordering of identity-utility vectors is analogous to that in the fixed-population case. Consequently, any population principle with an unlimited domain that satisfies Pareto indifference and extended binary independence of irrelevant alternatives is welfarist.

3.4 IMPARTIALITY AND ANONYMITY

A principle for social evaluation may be welfarist and, at the same time, fail to be impartial. This would be the case, for example, if a weighted sum of utilities

Table 3.4. *Anonymous Welfarism*

	Welfare Information		Nonwelfare Information	
	x	y	x	y
Profile A	(20, 0)	(0, 20)	1 is hardworking	1 is hardworking
Profile B	(20, 0)	(0, 20)	2 is hardworking	2 is hardworking
Profile C	(20, 0)	(0, 20)	1 is hardworking	2 is hardworking

of those who are alive is used to rank alternatives with a weight of 2 for the utility of person 1 and a weight of 1 for all other utilities. If there is a single nonwelfare profile, such a principle might be justified by the fact that person 1 is hardworking in every alternative in which she or he is alive.

An example is provided by Table 3.4 for a fixed population of persons 1 and 2. In all profiles, utilities in x and y are 20 and 0 for person 1 and 0 and 20 for person 2. In each alternative, one person is hardworking and the other is not. If alternatives are ranked by a weighted sum of utilities with weights of 2 for person 1 and 1 for person 2, then, given profile A, x is ranked as better than y. In this example, individual interests are not given equal consideration: the principle is not impartial.

Principles can be impartial without ignoring inequalities of well-being. In single nonwelfare profile social choice theory, such principles satisfy the axiom welfare anonymity, which requires any two alternatives to be ranked as equally good if the utility vector for one is a permutation of the utility vector for the other. In the example of Table 3.4, welfare anonymity requires x and y to be ranked as equally good when either profile A or profile B obtains. In one case, however, person 1 is hardworking and person 2 is not and, in the other case person 2 is hardworking and person 1 is not. Because of this, it is possible to argue that welfare anonymity is an inappropriate axiom.

Welfare anonymity can be relaxed to an axiom that we call anonymity. It requires any two alternatives to be ranked as equally good if social nonwelfare information is the same in both and the utility *and* individual nonwelfare information vectors for one are the same permutation of the corresponding vectors for the other. In the table, this calls for x and y to be ranked as equally good by ordering C: both the welfare and nonwelfare vectors for x are the same permutations of their counterparts in y. In order to apply this axiom, it must be possible to make such permutations of nonwelfare information. That requires the sets of possible nonwelfare information to be the same for all individuals.

Anonymity is weaker than welfare anonymity and it is easily defended. The only reasons that can be given for rejecting welfare anonymity must make the claim that nonwelfare information matters and justifies principles that are not impartial. Anonymity allows for such views; all that is ruled out is the claim that an individual's identity justifies special treatment, no matter what nonwelfare information obtains. In Table 3.4, welfare anonymity requires ordering C to rank x and y as equally good but allows orderings A and B to rank one as better than the other.

When combined with the axioms Pareto indifference and binary independence of irrelevant alternatives, however, the stronger axiom welfare anonymity is implied. Anonymity requires x and y to be equally good according to ordering C. Because the utility components of profiles A and B are the same as the utility component of profile C, the argument of Section 3.2 shows that nonwelfare information is irrelevant and, thus, all three orderings rank x and y in the same way. Consequently, welfare anonymity is satisfied.

In the variable-population case, it is possible to use extended versions of welfare anonymity and anonymity. Extended anonymity extends the fixed-population axiom to cover pairs of alternatives in which the number of people alive is the same but some or all individual identities may be different. If the utility and nonwelfare-information vectors in two alternatives are the same but are assigned to different individuals, the axiom requires the two alternatives to be ranked as equally good.

In conjunction with unlimited domain, Pareto indifference and extended binary independence of irrelevant alternatives, extended anonymity implies that the social-evaluation ordering of utility vectors is anonymous: a utility vector and any permutation are equally good. As in the fixed-population case, extended anonymity is easily defended because it requires nonwelfare information to be permuted along with welfare information. The result is the same in both cases, however: the social-evaluation ordering is independent of individual identities and is anonymous.

Extended anonymity can be used in the single-profile case as well. Suppose the information vectors associated with the set of all alternatives exhaust all possibilities, a condition that is the single-profile analogue of extended unlimited domain. In that case, Pareto indifference and extended anonymity imply that there is a single anonymous ordering of all possible utility vectors that can be used to rank the alternatives.

Parfit (1984, p. 360) suggests an axiom that he calls the same-number quality claim, which is stated as follows. "If, in either of two possible outcomes the same number of people would ever live, it would be worse if those who live are worse off, or have a lower quality of life, than those who would have lived." Our axioms imply that the social-evaluation ordering is anonymous. Consequently, in same-number comparisons in which utilities are permutations of each other, the alternatives are equally good. Parfit's axiom is implied if weak Pareto is added.

Notions of desert based on nonwelfare considerations are sometimes used to construct principles for social evaluation that are not impartial and, thus, violate welfare anonymity. If the weaker property anonymity is satisfied by these principles and they are defined for all possible profiles, the above argument illustrates that they must violate Pareto indifference (and, therefore, minimal individual goodness) or behave inconsistently as information changes.[2]

3.5 CHALLENGES TO WELFARIST SOCIAL EVALUATION

In recent years, several challenges to welfarism have appeared. Some of these are challenges to consequentialist morality, and they deal with the way different theories derive the moral status of actions from knowledge of their consequences. Although those challenges are beyond the scope of this book, there are others that deal directly with welfarist principles for social evaluation, and we comment briefly on a few of them here.

Before dealing with welfarism in general, we mention a criticism directed to utilitarianism in particular. Although this is not a challenge to welfarism as a whole (it is straightforward to show that there are many welfarist principles other than utilitarianism to which the criticism does not apply), we think it should be addressed because it is a commonly used argument. Fixed-population utilitarianism exhibits indifference to inequality of well-being, and this has prompted the complaint that "persons do not count as individuals in this any more than individual petrol tanks do in the analysis of the national consumption of petroleum" (Sen and Williams 1982, p. 4). Although utilitarianism exhibits no aversion to utility inequality, it *is* averse to inequality of consumption. We can be reasonably sure that, for people in good health, the value of an additional dollar's worth of consumption declines as consumption increases. For that reason, a transfer of consumption from rich to poor (without indirect effects) increases total utility and is seen as good by utilitarianism. Similarly, the utilitarian principle expresses concern for the needs of the sick and disabled. Moreover, the criticism of Sen and Williams does not apply to welfarist principles that are averse to utility inequality: they rank more equal distributions of utility as better than less equal ones.

Welfarist principles for social evaluation are sometimes criticized as taking a narrow view of being a person, seeing individuals as "locations of their respective utilities" only (Sen and Williams 1982, p. 4). The use of comprehensive accounts of lifetime well-being, such as those of Griffin (1986) and Sumner (1996), which attempt to take account of everything in which individual people have an interest, is, in our view at least, sufficient to respond to this criticism.

An interesting challenge to welfarism that uses widely held moral intuitions has been offered by Sen (1979), and it is summarized in Table 3.5.[3] In x, person 1 is poor and hungry and person 2 is rich and has plenty of food. Alternative y results from a transfer of food from person 2 to person 1. In it, both total utility

---

[2] For discussions of desert and modifications of utilitarian principles to accommodate it, see Feldman (1997, Part III).

[3] See also Roemer (1996, p. 30).

Table 3.5. *Torture Example*

	x	y	z
Person 1	40	70	70
Person 2	100	80	80

and minimum utility rise and, as long as other people are unaffected, any weakly inequality-averse welfarist principle declares y to be better than x. In alternative z, person 1, who is a sadist, receives no transfer of food, but is allowed to torture person 2. The utility levels are not based on poorly informed or nonautonomous preferences but are supposed to represent well-being accurately.

Because utility levels are the same in y and z, Pareto indifference requires them to be ranked as equally good. Consequently, z and x must be ranked in the same way that y and x are. It follows that, if food redistribution is good, torture is also good. Sen's conclusion is that we should abandon the Pareto indifference axiom along with welfarist social evaluation.

Sen's example appeals to a moral intuition that sees torture as bad. That intuition rests on beliefs about the welfare consequences of torture, however. People who are tortured suffer terribly at the time of their ordeal and for many years afterward if they survive. The intuition is linked, in the example, to two implausible claims of fact: that torture can be a substitute for decent nutrition and that a loss of food to the rich person is just as bad as being tortured. In addition, we are rightly suspicious about the implicit assumption that there are no indirect effects of the torture. No reasonable government would pass a law that allows one named person to torture another. Rather, a change in law that applies more widely would be required. Such a legal change is likely to raise the level of bad behavior substantially, with disastrous consequences for present and future generations. A more moderate example could be constructed by using sexual harassment or something similar instead of torture, however. It would appeal to the intuition that harassment is bad and our response again would be that the intuition is based on beliefs about the consequences of harassment for well-being.

Sen's example provides an illustration of the connection between welfarism and minimal individual goodness. If y (food redistribution) is ranked above z (torture), no one is better off in y and minimal individual goodness is not satisfied. Now suppose that, in z, utility levels were 71 and 81 instead of 70 and 80. If y is ranked as better than z, the weak Pareto principle is also violated.

Those who object to welfarist social evaluation therefore might argue that the minimal individual goodness axiom is too strong because it implies Pareto indifference. A weaker version of the axiom exempts the case in which each person's well-being is the same in both alternatives: for all pairs of alternatives, x and y, if x is judged to be better than y, either each person is equally well off

Table 3.6. *Weakening Minimal Individual Goodness*

	x	y	z
Person 1	40	40	$40 - \varepsilon$
Person 2	30	30	30
Nonwelfare information	$\bar{k}$	$\hat{k}$	$\bar{k}$

in both or there is some person who is better off in x. It is straightforward to see that Pareto indifference is not implied. However, the axiom is equivalent to Pareto weak preference, which requires that if everyone's well-being is at least as great in x as in y with at least one strict inequality, then x is at least as good as y.

Consider the single-profile example illustrated in Table 3.6. Each person is equally well off in alternatives x and y but nonwelfare information is different.

Suppose that, because $\bar{k}$, the nonwelfare information in x, is regarded as more desirable (other things equal) than $\hat{k}$, the nonwelfare information in y, x is ranked as better than y. Because of this, we might expect that a move from $\hat{k}$ to $\bar{k}$ would justify a small sacrifice of well-being. This is illustrated by alternative z in which nonwelfare information coincides with that of x but person 1's well-being is reduced by the positive amount ε. If this intuition applies, there must be some value of ε so that z is ranked as better than y. This ranking conflicts with Pareto weak preference and, therefore, with weak minimal individual goodness: both require y to be ranked as no worse than z. In addition, any distribution of ε across the two individuals yields the same result. This suggests that those who object to welfarist social evaluation are likely to advocate abandoning both Pareto indifference and Pareto weak preference.

A recently introduced alternative to welfarism replaces concern for well-being with concern for *opportunities* for well-being on the grounds that individual people are responsible for their choices (in certain circumstances they may be thought to be responsible for their preferences as well).[4] In practice, welfarists often agree that providing opportunities is socially warranted, but their concern is with actual well-being. If autonomy is a significant aspect of well-being, people should be free to make important choices for themselves, and this provides a constraint that restricts the feasible set of social possibilities: some alternatives are not feasible because they conflict with decisions made by individuals regarding their autonomous spheres. By way of analogy, parents typically provide opportunities to their children, but that does not mean that opportunities are what they care about.

Although welfarist principles are consistent with rights (Mill 1859, 1979a, Chapter 4), they are not consistent with unconditional rights. An example of

---

[4] See, for example, Arneson (1989, 2000a, 2000b), Roemer (1996), and, for an unsympathetic critique, Anderson (1999); see also Fleurbaey and Maniquet (2004).

this is Sen's (1970a, Chapter 6, 1970b) Paretian liberal paradox.[5] It requires rights assignments to be independent of the utility profile and Sen shows that they are incompatible with welfarism, given an unlimited domain. But should such rights be unconditional, applying to all possible profiles?

Rights of the type Sen discusses typically are justified, in part, on the grounds that the choices under consideration affect the individual with the right much more than they affect others, a condition that is met in some, but not all, profiles. This suggests that rights assignments should be, to some extent, profile dependent. If this view is accepted, Sen's paradox can be avoided.

Welfarism does not, by itself, have conservative implications for economic policy. As an example, there are many objections, consistent with welfarism, to markets for body parts (such as kidneys) for transplantation: sellers may favor short-term gain over their own long-term well-being; sellers may be poorly informed; buyers may have monopsony power over desperate sellers; inequality of well-being may be increased; and criminal acquisition of body parts may increase. The desirability of such markets therefore depends on factual information in addition to the principle for social evaluation, welfarist or not, that is employed.

Part B

We now state and prove new versions of the welfarism theorems for fixed and for variable populations. Unlike the statements that can be found in the earlier literature, we explicitly allow for multiple profiles of nonwelfare information. In Section 3.6, we define social-evaluation functionals that may depend on individual utility functions as well as on nonwelfare information. In Section 3.7, we state and prove our fixed-population versions of the welfarism theorems. The case of a variable population is treated in Section 3.8, and we conclude in Section 3.9 with a discussion of the consequences of adding anonymity conditions to the welfarism axioms.

3.6 SOCIAL-EVALUATION FUNCTIONALS

A social-evaluation functional assigns a social ordering of the alternatives to each profile in its domain. In contrast to the framework traditionally employed in social-choice theory, we explicitly include the possibility of taking into account nonwelfare information. Thus, our notion of a profile includes both welfare information and nonwelfare information. Welfare information consists of a profile of utility functions, one function for each individual. Nonwelfare information has two components: a profile of functions, each of which assigns individual

---

[5] See Gaertner, Pattanaik, and Suzumura (1992); see also Kelly (1976) for an alternative to Sen's formulation and Austen-Smith (1979), Gaertner (1982), and Suzumura (1982) for possibility results with no-envy restrictions on rights assignments.

nonwelfare information to each alternative, and a social nonwelfare information function that assigns nonwelfare information relevant for the society as a whole to each alternative. Individual nonwelfare information, for instance, could specify whether an individual is hardworking and what kinds of food he or she likes, whereas social nonwelfare information may include features of a society such as whether there is freedom of the press.

We begin by introducing the relevant definitions for the fixed-population case and conclude this section by extending the model to a variable-population environment. Suppose the fixed population is $\bar{N} \subseteq \mathcal{Z}_{++}$. For simplicity of presentation, we let, without loss of generality, $\bar{N} = \{1, \ldots, n\}$, where $n = |\bar{N}| \in \mathcal{Z}_{++}$ and, correspondingly, we consider the set of alternatives $X^n = \{x \in X \mid \mathbf{N}(x) = \{1, \ldots, n\}\}$. We assume that X^n contains at least three elements.[6]

A utility profile is an n-tuple $U^n = (U_1^n, \ldots, U_n^n)$, where $U_i^n \colon X^n \to \mathcal{R}$ is the utility function of individual $i \in \{1, \ldots, n\}$. Because $X^n \subseteq X_i$ (X_i is the set of alternatives in which person i is alive), U_i^n is the restriction of U_i to X^n. The set of all possible utility profiles is $\mathcal{U}^n$ and we write $U^n(x) = (U_1^n(x), \ldots, U_n^n(x))$ for all $x \in X^n$ and for all $U^n \in \mathcal{U}^n$.

Social and individual nonwelfare information for the fixed population $\{1, \ldots, n\}$ is described by an $(n + 1)$-tuple $K^n = (K_0^n, K_1^n, \ldots, K_n^n)$, where $K_0^n \colon X^n \to \mathcal{S}_0$ and $K_i^n \colon X^n \to \mathcal{S}_i$ for all $i \in \{1, \ldots, n\}$. For $x \in X^n$, $K_0^n(x)$ is social nonwelfare information in alternative x and, for all $i \in \{1, \ldots, n\}$, $K_i^n(x)$ is nonwelfare information for person i in alternative x. $\mathcal{S}_0 \neq \emptyset$ and $\mathcal{S}_i \neq \emptyset$ are the sets of possible values of nonwelfare information for society and individual i, respectively. The set of all possible profiles of nonwelfare information is $\mathcal{K}^n$ and, for all $x \in X^n$ and for all $K^n \in \mathcal{K}^n$, $K^n(x) = (K_0^n(x), K_1^n(x), \ldots, K_n^n(x))$. Nonwelfare information is also modeled by Kelsey (1987), who provides a formulation of Arrow's theorem that incorporates nonwelfare criteria; see also Sen (1981). The approach presented here is that of Blackorby, Bossert, and Donaldson (2004a).

The set of all orderings on X^n is denoted by $\mathcal{O}^n$. A social-evaluation functional is a mapping $F^n \colon \mathcal{D}^n \to \mathcal{O}^n$, where $\mathcal{D}^n \subseteq \mathcal{U}^n \times \mathcal{K}^n$ is the domain of F^n, assumed to be nonempty. For convenience, we use the notation $\Upsilon^n = (U^n, K^n)$ and $R_{\Upsilon^n}^n = F^n(\Upsilon^n)$ for all $\Upsilon^n \in \mathcal{D}^n$. Furthermore, we define $\Upsilon^n(x) = (U^n(x), K^n(x))$ for all $x \in X^n$. The asymmetric factor and the symmetric factor of $R_{\Upsilon^n}^n$ are denoted by $P_{\Upsilon^n}^n$ and $I_{\Upsilon^n}^n$.

Now consider the variable-population case. A variable-population utility profile has a countably infinite number of components (one for each potential person), and we write it as $U = (U_i)_{i \in \mathcal{Z}_{++}}$ where $U_i \colon X_i \to \mathcal{R}$ for all $i \in \mathcal{Z}_{++}$.[7] The set of all logically possible utility profiles is $\mathcal{U}$. A profile of nonwelfare information functions is denoted by $K = (K_i)_{i \in \mathcal{Z}_+}$. Nonwelfare information for society is described by the function $K_0 \colon X \to \mathcal{S}_0$, and nonwelfare information

---

[6] Although we use superscripts to indicate population size in addition to using them to denote Cartesian products, it should be clear from the context what is meant.

[7] Recall that U_i is defined on X_i – that is, the set of alternatives in which i is alive – only.

for $i \in \mathcal{Z}_{++}$ is described by $K_i \colon X_i \to \mathcal{S}_i$. The set of all possible nonwelfare profiles is $\mathcal{K}$.

Let $\mathcal{O}$ denote the set of all orderings on X. We assume that, for all nonempty and finite $\bar{N} \subseteq \mathcal{Z}_{++}$, the set $X^{\bar{N}} = \{x \in X \mid \mathbf{N}(x) = \bar{N}\}$ contains at least three elements. A social-evaluation functional for the variable-population case is a mapping $F \colon \mathcal{D} \to \mathcal{O}$, where $\emptyset \neq \mathcal{D} \subseteq \mathcal{U} \times \mathcal{K}$. Again, we write $\Upsilon = (U, K)$ and $R_\Upsilon = F(\Upsilon)$ for all $\Upsilon \in \mathcal{D}$. We denote the asymmetric factor and the symmetric factor of R_Υ by P_Υ and I_Υ.

As in Chapter 2, $\mathbf{N}(x)$ is the set of people alive in alternative x and $\mathbf{n}(x) = |\mathbf{N}(x)|$ is their number. For all $n \in \mathcal{Z}_{++}$, let $\mathbf{Z}^n \subset \mathcal{Z}^n_{++}$ be the set of all $\pi \in \mathcal{Z}^n_{++}$ with distinct components ordered from smallest to largest. To illustrate this definition, consider the case $n = 3$. We obtain $\mathbf{Z}^3 = \{(i, j, k) \in \mathcal{Z}^3_{++} \mid i < j < k\}$. For any $x \in X$, let $\Pi(x) = (\Pi_1(x), \ldots, \Pi_{\mathbf{n}(x)}(x)) \in \mathbf{Z}^{\mathbf{n}(x)}$ be the vector of identities of the individuals alive in x – that is, $\{\Pi_1(x), \ldots, \Pi_{\mathbf{n}(x)}(x)\} = \mathbf{N}(x)$. For example, if individuals $1, 2{,}000$, and 40 are alive in alternative x, we obtain $\Pi(x) = (1, 40, 2{,}000)$.

Utilities for those alive in $x \in X$ are

$$\mathbf{U}(x) = (\mathbf{U}_1(x), \ldots, \mathbf{U}_{\mathbf{n}(x)}(x)) = (U_{\Pi_1(x)}(x), \ldots, U_{\Pi_{\mathbf{n}(x)}(x)}(x)) \in \mathcal{R}^{\mathbf{n}(x)}.$$

Nonutility information for x is given by

$$\begin{aligned}
\mathbf{K}(x) &= (\mathbf{K}_0(x), \mathbf{K}_1(x), \ldots, \mathbf{K}_{\mathbf{n}(x)}(x)) \\
&= (K_0(x), K_{\Pi_1(x)}(x), \ldots, K_{\Pi_{\mathbf{n}(x)}(x)}(x)) \in \mathcal{S}_0 \times \mathcal{S}_1 \times \ldots \times \mathcal{S}_{\mathbf{n}(x)}.
\end{aligned}$$

Furthermore, we define $\Upsilon(x) = (\mathbf{U}(x), \mathbf{K}(x))$.

3.7 FIXED-POPULATION WELFARISM

We discuss two versions of welfarism in the fixed-population setting. The first is a somewhat degenerate result because it operates in a single-profile environment, which makes it difficult to identify the role played by the (fixed) profile. The same criticism applies to the standard multiprofile version of welfarism because, although multiple utility profiles are permitted, nonwelfare information is fixed and, thus, it is implicitly assumed that there is only a single nonwelfare profile. Our multiprofile formulation allows for multiple profiles of nonwelfare information as well and, as a consequence, the formulations of our multiprofile results differ from those in the earlier literature.

We begin with an axiom proposed by Goodin (1991) that has been used by Blackorby, Bossert, and Donaldson (2002b) to provide a justification for welfarism. The axiom, which we call minimal individual goodness, requires that if alternative x is declared better than alternative y according to profile Υ^n, then there must be at least one individual whose level of well-being in the profile Υ^n is higher in x than in y. This is an essential property because it prevents the social-evaluation functional from recommending empty gestures that benefit no one and may even harm some or all.

Minimal Individual Goodness. For all $x, y \in X^n$ and for all $\Upsilon^n \in \mathcal{D}^n$, if $x P^n_{\Upsilon^n} y$, then there exists $j \in \{1, \ldots, n\}$ such that $U^n_j(x) > U^n_j(y)$.

Minimal individual goodness is equivalent to the conjunction of two Pareto conditions. The first of these is Pareto indifference, an axiom that is central to welfarism. It requires that if, in a profile Υ^n, all individuals are equally well off in two alternatives x and y, then x and y must be declared equally good by the social ranking corresponding to Υ^n.

Pareto Indifference. For all $x, y \in X^n$ and for all $\Upsilon^n \in \mathcal{D}^n$, if $U^n(x) = U^n(y)$, then $x I^n_{\Upsilon^n} y$.

Pareto weak preference applies the same reasoning to comparisons in which everyone's utility according to profile Υ^n in alternative x is at least as high as that in alternative y with at least one strict inequality. The axiom demands that, in these circumstances, x is at least as good as y according to the social ordering generated by Υ^n.

Pareto Weak Preference. For all $x, y \in X^n$ and for all $\Upsilon^n \in \mathcal{D}^n$, if $U^n(x) > U^n(y)$, then $x R^n_{\Upsilon^n} y$.

The above-mentioned equivalence between minimal individual goodness and the two Pareto conditions is stated in the following theorem.

Theorem 3.1. *F^n satisfies minimal individual goodness if and only if F^n satisfies Pareto indifference and Pareto weak preference.*

Proof. Suppose F^n satisfies minimal individual goodness. We first prove by contradiction that Pareto indifference is satisfied. Suppose not. Then there exist $x, y \in X^n$ and $\Upsilon^n \in \mathcal{D}^n$ such that $U^n(x) = U^n(y)$ and not $x I^n_{\Upsilon^n} y$. Because $R^n_{\Upsilon^n}$ is complete, we must have either $x P^n_{\Upsilon^n} y$ or $y P^n_{\Upsilon^n} x$. In each case, we obtain a contradiction to minimal individual goodness.

Now suppose F^n violates Pareto weak preference. Then there exist $x, y \in X^n$ and $\Upsilon^n \in \mathcal{D}^n$ such that $U^n(x) > U^n(y)$ and not $x R^n_{\Upsilon^n} y$. By the completeness of $R^n_{\Upsilon^n}$, we must have $y P^n_{\Upsilon^n} x$, again contradicting minimal individual goodness.

Finally, suppose F^n satisfies Pareto indifference and Pareto weak preference but violates minimal individual goodness. Then there exist $x, y \in X^n$ and $\Upsilon^n \in \mathcal{D}^n$ such that $x P^n_{\Upsilon^n} y$ and $U^n(y) \geq U^n(x)$. If $U^n(y) = U^n(x)$, we obtain a contradiction to Pareto indifference, and if there exists $j \in \{1, \ldots, n\}$ such that $U^n_j(y) > U^n_j(x)$, we obtain a contradiction to Pareto weak preference. ∎

If there is a single profile only, Pareto indifference alone implies that social evaluation must be welfarist: there exists an ordering of all attainable utility vectors [that is, an ordering defined on the set $U^n(X^n)$] such that any two alternatives can be ranked by ranking their associated utility vectors. We first state and prove the following preliminary result.

Theorem 3.2. *Suppose there exists a profile* Υ^n *such that* $\mathcal{D}^n = \{\Upsilon^n\}$. *If* F^n *satisfies Pareto indifference, then, for all* $x, y, z, w \in X^n$ *such that* $U^n(x) = U^n(z)$ *and* $U^n(y) = U^n(w)$,

$$x R^n_{\Upsilon^n} y \Leftrightarrow z R^n_{\Upsilon^n} w.$$

Proof. Because $U^n(x) = U^n(z)$ and $U^n(y) = U^n(w)$, Pareto indifference implies $x I^n_{\Upsilon^n} z$ and $y I^n_{\Upsilon^n} w$. Because $R^n_{\Upsilon^n}$ is transitive, the result follows immediately. ∎

Now we obtain the single-profile welfarism theorem (Blackorby, Donaldson, and Weymark 1990).

Theorem 3.3. *Suppose there exists a profile* Υ^n *such that* $\mathcal{D}^n = \{\Upsilon^n\}$. F^n *satisfies Pareto indifference if and only if there exists a social-evaluation ordering* R^n *on* $U^n(X^n)$ *such that, for all* $x, y \in X^n$,

$$x R^n_{\Upsilon^n} y \Leftrightarrow U^n(x) R^n U^n(y). \tag{3.1}$$

Proof. Define the relation R^n on $U^n(X^n)$ by $u R^n v$ if and only if there exist $x, y \in X^n$ such that $U^n(x) = u$, $U^n(y) = v$ and $x R^n_{\Upsilon^n} y$ for all $u, v \in U^n(X^n)$. Theorem 3.2 implies that R^n is well-defined. That (3.1) is satisfied is straightforward to verify. We show that R^n is an ordering. For all $u \in U^n(X^n)$, there exists $x \in X^n$ such that $U^n(x) = u$. Because $R^n_{\Upsilon^n}$ is reflexive, we have $x R^n_{\Upsilon^n} x$ and thus $u R^n u$. Hence R^n is reflexive.

To show that R^n is complete, let $u, v \in U^n(X^n)$ be such that $u \neq v$. There exist $x, y \in X^n$ such that $U^n(x) = u$ and $U^n(y) = v$. Because $u \neq v$, $x \neq y$ and, because $R^n_{\Upsilon^n}$ is complete, $x R^n_{\Upsilon^n} y$ or $y R^n_{\Upsilon^n} x$. Consequently, $u R^n v$ or $v R^n u$.

Finally, let $u, v, q \in U^n(X^n)$ be such that $u R^n v$ and $v R^n q$. Because there is a single profile, there exist $x, y, z \in X^n$ such that $U^n(x) = u$, $U^n(y) = v$, $U^n(z) = q$, $x R^n_{\Upsilon^n} y$ and $y R^n_{\Upsilon^n} z$. By the transitivity of $R^n_{\Upsilon^n}$, $x R^n_{\Upsilon^n} z$. Consequently, $u R^n q$.

That Pareto indifference is implied by (3.1) follows immediately from the reflexivity of R^n. ∎

We now move to a multiprofile setting. That is, we assume the domain $\mathcal{D}^n$ may contain more than one element. Note that, in contrast to the traditional multiprofile social choice model, multiple nonwelfare-information profiles are permitted as well. In particular, we make an unlimited-domain assumption, which requires that all possible information profiles are admissible.

Unlimited Domain. $\mathcal{D}^n = \mathcal{U}^n \times \mathcal{K}^n$.

Binary independence of irrelevant alternatives requires the social ranking of any two alternatives to depend on the utility information and nonwelfare information associated with those two alternatives only. Note that nonwelfare information is allowed to matter, which distinguishes this axiom from its counterpart in the literature where nonwelfare information is fixed.

Binary Independence of Irrelevant Alternatives. For all $x, y \in X^n$ and for all $\Upsilon^n, \bar{\Upsilon}^n \in \mathcal{D}^n$, if $\Upsilon^n(x) = \bar{\Upsilon}^n(x)$ and $\Upsilon^n(y) = \bar{\Upsilon}^n(y)$, then

$$x R^n_{\Upsilon^n} y \Leftrightarrow x R^n_{\bar{\Upsilon}^n} y.$$

Unlimited domain, Pareto indifference, and binary independence of irrelevant alternatives together imply that the social ordering does not depend on nonwelfare information. This is a fundamental result that will be employed in the proof of our multiprofile welfarism theorems.

Theorem 3.4. *If F^n satisfies unlimited domain, Pareto indifference, and binary independence of irrelevant alternatives, then, for all $x, y \in X^n$ and for all $\Upsilon^n, \bar{\Upsilon}^n \in \mathcal{D}^n$ such that $U^n(x) = \bar{U}^n(x)$ and $U^n(y) = \bar{U}^n(y)$,*

$$x R^n_{\Upsilon^n} y \Leftrightarrow x R^n_{\bar{\Upsilon}^n} y. \tag{3.2}$$

Proof. Let $x, y \in X^n$ and $\Upsilon^n, \bar{\Upsilon}^n \in \mathcal{D}^n$ be such that $U^n(x) = \bar{U}^n(x)$ and $U^n(y) = \bar{U}^n(y)$. Let $u = U^n(x) = \bar{U}^n(x)$, $v = U^n(y) = \bar{U}^n(y)$, $k = K^n(x)$, $\ell = K^n(y)$, $\bar{k} = \bar{K}^n(x)$, and $\bar{\ell} = \bar{K}^n(y)$. Because X^n contains at least three alternatives, there exists $z \in X^n \setminus \{x, y\}$. By unlimited domain, we can find profiles $\Upsilon^n_a, \Upsilon^n_b, \Upsilon^n_c,$ and Υ^n_d with the following properties. Let $\Upsilon^n_a(x) = (u, k)$, $\Upsilon^n_a(y) = (v, \ell)$, $\Upsilon^n_a(z) = (v, \bar{\ell})$, $\Upsilon^n_b(x) = (u, k)$, $\Upsilon^n_b(y) = (v, \bar{\ell})$, $\Upsilon^n_b(z) = (v, \bar{\ell})$, $\Upsilon^n_c(x) = (u, k)$, $\Upsilon^n_c(y) = (v, \bar{\ell})$, $\Upsilon^n_c(z) = (u, \bar{k})$, $\Upsilon^n_d(x) = (u, \bar{k})$, $\Upsilon^n_d(y) = (v, \bar{\ell})$, and $\Upsilon^n_d(z) = (u, \bar{k})$.

By binary independence of irrelevant alternatives, we have

$$x R^n_{\Upsilon^n} y \Leftrightarrow x R^n_{\Upsilon^n_a} y.$$

By Pareto indifference, $y I^n_{\Upsilon^n_a} z$ and it follows that

$$x R^n_{\Upsilon^n_a} y \Leftrightarrow x R^n_{\Upsilon^n_a} z.$$

Using binary independence again, we obtain

$$x R^n_{\Upsilon^n_a} z \Leftrightarrow x R^n_{\Upsilon^n_b} z.$$

By Pareto indifference, $z I^n_{\Upsilon^n_b} y$ and, therefore,

$$x R^n_{\Upsilon^n_b} z \Leftrightarrow x R^n_{\Upsilon^n_b} y.$$

Now binary independence implies

$$x R^n_{\Upsilon^n_b} y \Leftrightarrow x R^n_{\Upsilon^n_c} y.$$

By Pareto indifference, $x I_{\Upsilon_c^n}^n z$ and it follows that

$$x R_{\Upsilon_c^n}^n y \Leftrightarrow z R_{\Upsilon_c^n}^n y.$$

Using binary independence again, we obtain

$$z R_{\Upsilon_c^n}^n y \Leftrightarrow z R_{\Upsilon_d^n}^n y.$$

By Pareto indifference, $z I_{\Upsilon_d^n}^n x$ and it follows that

$$z R_{\Upsilon_d^n}^n y \Leftrightarrow x R_{\Upsilon_d^n}^n y.$$

Using binary independence once more, we obtain

$$x R_{\Upsilon_d^n}^n y \Leftrightarrow x R_{\bar{\Upsilon}^n}^n y.$$

Combining the above equivalences, (3.2) results. ∎

The following theorem is an immediate consequence of Theorem 3.4.

Theorem 3.5. *If F^n satisfies unlimited domain, Pareto indifference, and binary independence of irrelevant alternatives, then there exists a functional $f^n: \mathcal{U}^n \to \mathcal{O}^n$ such that, for all $\Upsilon^n \in \mathcal{D}^n$, $F^n(\Upsilon^n) = f^n(U^n)$.*

Given unlimited domain, Pareto indifference and binary independence of irrelevant alternatives together are equivalent to a property called strong neutrality.

Strong Neutrality. For all x, y, z, $w \in X^n$ and for all Υ^n, $\bar{\Upsilon}^n \in \mathcal{D}^n$, if $U^n(x) = \bar{U}^n(z)$ and $U^n(y) = \bar{U}^n(w)$, then

$$x R_{\Upsilon^n}^n y \Leftrightarrow z R_{\bar{\Upsilon}^n}^n w.$$

Note that, in the formulation of strong neutrality, nonwelfare information is allowed to be different in x and z and in y and w. In contrast, this is not the case in the axiom binary independence of irrelevant alternatives. Thus, adding Pareto indifference to the independence condition produces a remarkably strong result by eliminating the possible influence of nonwelfare information altogether.

The following theorem states the above-mentioned equivalence result; see, for example, Blau (1976), d'Aspremont and Gevers (1977), Guha (1972), and Sen (1977a) for versions with a single nonwelfare profile.

Theorem 3.6. *Suppose F^n satisfies unlimited domain. F^n satisfies Pareto indifference and binary independence of irrelevant alternatives if and only if F^n satisfies strong neutrality.*

Proof. First, suppose that F^n satisfies strong neutrality. That binary independence of irrelevant alternatives is satisfied follows from setting $x = z$, $y = w$, $K^n(x) = \bar{K}^n(x)$ and $K^n(y) = \bar{K}^n(y)$ in the definition of strong neutrality. To show that Pareto indifference is implied, let $U^n = \bar{U}^n$ and $y = z = w$. Strong neutrality implies that $x R^n_{\Upsilon^n} y$ if and only if $y R^n_{\Upsilon^n} y$ whenever $U^n(x) = U^n(y)$. Because $R^n_{\Upsilon^n}$ is reflexive, this implies $x I^n_{\Upsilon^n} y$.

Now suppose F^n satisfies unlimited domain, Pareto indifference, and binary independence of irrelevant alternatives. By Theorem 3.4, we know that nonwelfare information is irrelevant. Consider two profiles Υ^n, $\bar{\Upsilon}^n \in \mathcal{D}^n$ and four (not necessarily distinct) alternatives $x, y, z, w \in X^n$ such that $U^n(x) = \bar{U}^n(z) = u$ and $U^n(y) = \bar{U}^n(w) = v$.

By unlimited domain, there exist profiles Υ^n_a, Υ^n_b, Υ^n_c, $\Upsilon^n_d \in \mathcal{D}^n$ such that $U^n_a(x) = u$, $U^n_a(y) = v$, $U^n_a(w) = v$, $U^n_b(x) = u$, $U^n_b(y) = v$, $U^n_b(w) = v$, $U^n_c(x) = u$, $U^n_c(y) = v$, $U^n_c(z) = u$, $U^n_d(y) = v$, $U^n_d(z) = u$, and $U^n_d(w) = v$.

By binary independence of irrelevant alternatives,

$$x R^n_{\Upsilon^n} y \Leftrightarrow x R^n_{\Upsilon^n_a} y.$$

By Pareto indifference, $y I^n_{\Upsilon^n_a} w$ and, therefore,

$$x R^n_{\Upsilon^n_a} y \Leftrightarrow x R^n_{\Upsilon^n_a} w.$$

Using binary independence of irrelevant alternatives again, we obtain

$$x R^n_{\Upsilon^n_a} w \Leftrightarrow x R^n_{\Upsilon^n_b} w.$$

By Pareto indifference, $y I^n_{\Upsilon^n_b} w$ and, therefore,

$$x R^n_{\Upsilon^n_b} w \Leftrightarrow x R^n_{\Upsilon^n_b} y.$$

By binary independence of irrelevant alternatives,

$$x R^n_{\Upsilon^n_b} y \Leftrightarrow x R^n_{\Upsilon^n_c} y.$$

By Pareto indifference, $x I^n_{\Upsilon^n_c} z$ and, therefore,

$$x R^n_{\Upsilon^n_c} y \Leftrightarrow z R^n_{\Upsilon^n_c} y.$$

By binary independence of irrelevant alternatives,

$$z R^n_{\Upsilon^n_c} y \Leftrightarrow z R^n_{\Upsilon^n_d} y.$$

By Pareto indifference, $y I^n_{\Upsilon^n_d} w$ and, therefore,

$$z R^n_{\Upsilon^n_d} y \Leftrightarrow z R^n_{\Upsilon^n_d} w$$

and, using binary independence of irrelevant alternatives once more, we obtain

$$z R^n_{\Upsilon^n_d} w \Leftrightarrow z R^n_{\bar{\Upsilon}^n} w.$$

Combining the above equivalences, we obtain

$$x R^n_{\Upsilon^n} y \Leftrightarrow z R^n_{\bar{\Upsilon}^n} w,$$

and strong neutrality is satisfied. ∎

Given unlimited domain and our assumption that X^n contains at least three elements, strong neutrality is equivalent to the existence of an ordering R^n on $\mathcal{R}^n$, which can be used to rank the alternatives in X^n for any profile $\Upsilon^n \in \mathcal{D}^n$. The asymmetric factor and the symmetric factor of R^n are denoted by P^n and I^n. We call R^n a social-evaluation ordering.[8] Combined with Theorem 3.6, this observation yields the following version of the welfarism theorem (see d'Aspremont and Gevers 1977 and Hammond 1979 for a version with a single nonwelfare profile).[9]

Theorem 3.7. *Suppose F^n satisfies unlimited domain. F^n satisfies Pareto indifference and binary independence of irrelevant alternatives if and only if there exists a social-evaluation ordering R^n on $\mathcal{R}^n$ such that, for all $x, y \in X^n$ and for all $\Upsilon^n \in \mathcal{D}^n$,*

$$x R^n_{\Upsilon^n} y \Leftrightarrow U^n(x) R^n U^n(y). \tag{3.3}$$

Proof. Clearly, the existence of a social-evaluation ordering R^n such that, for all $x, y \in X^n$ and for all $\Upsilon^n \in \mathcal{D}^n$, (3.3) is satisfied implies Pareto indifference and binary independence of irrelevant alternatives.

Now suppose F^n satisfies unlimited domain, Pareto indifference, and binary independence of irrelevant alternatives. By Theorem 3.6, F^n satisfies strong neutrality. We complete the proof by constructing the social-evaluation ordering R^n. For all $u, v \in \mathcal{R}^n$, let $u R^n v$ if and only if there exist a profile $\Upsilon^n \in \mathcal{D}^n$ and two alternatives $x, y \in X^n$ such that $U^n(x) = u$, $U^n(y) = v$ and $x R^n_{\Upsilon^n} y$ (the existence of the profile Υ^n and the alternatives x and y is guaranteed by unlimited domain). Strong neutrality implies that nonwelfare information is irrelevant and that the ranking of any two utility vectors u and v does not depend on the profile Υ^n or on the alternatives x and y used to generate u and v. Therefore, R^n is well-defined. That R^n is reflexive and complete follows immediately because $R^n_{\Upsilon^n}$ is reflexive and complete for all $\Upsilon^n \in \mathcal{D}^n$. We have to show that R^n is transitive. Suppose $u, v, q \in \mathcal{R}^n$ are such that $u R^n v$ and $v R^n q$. By unlimited domain and the assumption that X^n contains at least three alternatives, there exist a profile $\Upsilon^n \in \mathcal{D}^n$ and three alternatives $x, y, z \in X^n$ such that $U^n(x) = u$, $U^n(y) = v$ and $U^n(z) = q$. Because $U^n(x) R^n U^n(y)$ and $U^n(y) R^n U^n(z)$, it follows that $x R^n_{\Upsilon^n} y$ and $y R^n_{\Upsilon^n} z$ by definition of R^n. Because $R^n_{\Upsilon^n}$ is transitive, we have $x R^n_{\Upsilon^n} z$. Hence, $U^n(x) R^n U^n(z)$ or, equivalently, $u R^n q$. ∎

The unlimited-domain axiom is crucial for this result. There are some nonwelfare-information domains that permit nonwelfarist social evaluation. This occurs because, on those domains, the constructions used in the proofs are not possible. Consider the fat-thin example of Part A in which there are four

---

[8] Gevers (1979) used the term social-welfare ordering for R^n.

[9] Bordes, Hammond, and Le Breton (1997) and Weymark (1998) proved variants of this theorem with specific domain restrictions, again in the single-nonwelfare-profile case.

alternatives, two individuals, $\mathcal{S}_1 = \{f, t\}$ and $\mathcal{S}_2 = \{t\}$. Suppose that, instead of the unlimited domain, the domain of the social-evaluation functional is $\mathcal{U}^2 \times \{\bar{K}^2, \hat{K}^2\}$, where $\bar{K}^2$ assigns (f, t, t, f) to the four alternatives for person 1 and (t, t, t, t) for person 2 and $\hat{K}^2$ assigns (t, f, f, t) to the four alternatives for person 1 and again (t, t, t, t) for person 2. This means that nonwelfare information for the four alternatives is (f, t), (t, t), (t, t), and (f, t) in $\bar{K}^2$ and (t, t), (f, t), (f, t), and (t, t) in $\hat{K}^2$. Note that there is no pair of alternatives with the same nonwelfare information. Consequently, binary independence does not apply.

Now consider the following social-evaluation functional. For all $x, y \in X$ and for all $U^2 \in \mathcal{U}^2$,

$$x R^2_{(U^2, \bar{K}^2)} y \Leftrightarrow U^2_1(x) + U^2_2(x) \geq U^2_1(y) + U^2_2(y)$$

and

$$x R^2_{(U^2, \hat{K}^2)} y \Leftrightarrow U^2_{(1)}(x) + 3U^2_{(2)}(x) \geq U^2_{(1)}(y) + 3U^2_{(2)}(y)$$

where $(U^2_{(1)}(x), U^2_{(2)}(x))$ and $(U^2_{(1)}(y), U^2_{(2)}(y))$ are rank-ordered permutations of $U^2(x)$ and $U^2(y)$ such that $U^2_{(1)}(x) \geq U^2_{(2)}(x)$ and $U^2_{(1)}(y) \geq U^2_{(2)}(y)$. Thus, for all utility profiles, alternatives are ranked with utilitarianism when the nonwelfare profile is $\bar{K}^2$ and with the Gini social-evaluation ordering when the nonwelfare profile is $\hat{K}^2$. All our axioms (except for unlimited domain) are satisfied but the principle is not welfarist because there is no profile-independent (single) ordering of utility vectors that can be used to rank the alternatives.

Theorem 3.5 and the proofs of Theorems 3.6 and 3.7 together provide a proof of the standard single nonwelfare-information-profile welfarism theorem. On that domain, any fixed-population social-evaluation functional that satisfies Pareto indifference and binary independence of irrelevant alternatives is welfarist (see, for example, Blackorby, Bossert, and Donaldson 2002b; Bossert and Weymark 2004; d'Aspremont and Gevers 1977; Guha 1972; Hammond 1979, Sen 1977a, 1979; and Weymark 1998). We conclude this section with a formal statement of this observation.

Theorem 3.8. *Let $\bar{K}^n \in \mathcal{K}^n$ and suppose $\mathcal{D}^n = \mathcal{U}^n \times \{\bar{K}^n\}$. F^n satisfies Pareto indifference and binary independence of irrelevant alternatives if and only if there exists a social-evaluation ordering R^n on $\mathcal{R}^n$ such that, for all $x, y \in X^n$ and for all $\Upsilon^n \in \mathcal{D}^n$,*

$$x R^n_{\Upsilon^n} y \Leftrightarrow U^n(x) R^n U^n(y).$$

3.8 VARIABLE-POPULATION WELFARISM

The welfarism theorems can be generalized to the case of a variable population. In this case, the axioms binary independence of irrelevant alternatives and strong neutrality must be extended to cover comparisons involving different populations. By contrast, Pareto indifference must be satisfied for fixed-population comparisons only. We therefore label the resulting axioms extended binary independence of irrelevant alternatives and extended strong neutrality but retain the name Pareto indifference. Moreover, we use the term extended unlimited domain for our domain condition because profiles now cover all potential individuals and, thus, the resulting axiom is a condition that extends the fixed-population version defined earlier. The interpretation of the axioms is the same as that for their fixed-population counterparts and we now state them formally.

Pareto Indifference. For all x, $y \in X$ such that $\mathbf{N}(x) = \mathbf{N}(y)$ and for all $\Upsilon \in \mathcal{D}$, if $U_i(x) = U_i(y)$ for all $i \in \mathbf{N}(x)$, then $x I_\Upsilon y$.

Extended Unlimited Domain. $\mathcal{D} = \mathcal{U} \times \mathcal{K}$.

Extended Binary Independence of Irrelevant Alternatives. For all x, $y \in X$ and for all $\Upsilon, \tilde{\Upsilon} \in \mathcal{D}$, if $\Upsilon(x) = \tilde{\Upsilon}(x)$ and $\Upsilon(y) = \tilde{\Upsilon}(y)$, then

$$x R_\Upsilon y \Leftrightarrow x R_{\tilde{\Upsilon}} y.$$

Extended Strong Neutrality. For all x, y, z, $w \in X$ such that $\mathbf{N}(x) = \mathbf{N}(z)$ and $\mathbf{N}(y) = \mathbf{N}(w)$ and for all $\Upsilon, \tilde{\Upsilon} \in \mathcal{D}$, if $U_i(x) = \bar{U}_i(z)$ for all $i \in \mathbf{N}(x)$ and $U_i(y) = \bar{U}_i(w)$ for all $i \in \mathbf{N}(y)$, then

$$x R_\Upsilon y \Leftrightarrow z R_{\tilde{\Upsilon}} w.$$

As mentioned earlier, extended binary independence of irrelevant alternatives and extended strong neutrality apply to variable-population comparisons in addition to fixed-population comparisons. However, note that extended strong neutrality only applies when x and z as well as y and w have the same population.

Analogously to Theorems 3.4, 3.6, 3.7, and 3.8, we state the following results. We omit the proofs because they are straightforward variations of the proofs of the earlier results. A direct proof of Theorem 3.12, the formulation with a single profile of nonwelfare information, can be found elsewhere (Blackorby, Bossert, and Donaldson 1999b; Blackorby and Donaldson 1984a). Again, the same interpretation of the results as in the fixed-population case applies. Thus, we do not provide a detailed discussion at this point because it would only repeat that of Part A and the previous section.

Theorem 3.9. *If F satisfies extended unlimited domain, Pareto indifference, and extended binary independence of irrelevant alternatives, then, for all x, $y \in X$ and for all $\Upsilon, \tilde{\Upsilon} \in \mathcal{D}$ such that $\mathbf{U}(x) = \bar{\mathbf{U}}(x)$ and $\mathbf{U}(y) = \bar{\mathbf{U}}(y)$,*

$$x R_\Upsilon y \Leftrightarrow x R_{\tilde{\Upsilon}} y.$$

Theorem 3.10. *Suppose F satisfies extended unlimited domain. F satisfies Pareto indifference and extended binary independence of irrelevant alternatives if and only if F satisfies extended strong neutrality.*

Theorem 3.11. *Suppose F satisfies extended unlimited domain. F satisfies Pareto indifference and extended binary independence of irrelevant alternatives if and only if there exists an ordering* $\overset{*}{R}$ *on* $\cup_{n \in Z_{++}}(\mathbf{Z}^n \times \mathcal{R}^n)$ *such that, for all* $x, y \in X$ *and for all* $\Upsilon \in \mathcal{D}$,

$$x R_\Upsilon y \Leftrightarrow \big(\Pi(x), \mathbf{U}(x)\big) \overset{*}{R} \big(\Pi(y), \mathbf{U}(y)\big).$$

Theorem 3.12. *Let* $\bar{K} \in \mathcal{K}$ *and suppose* $\mathcal{D} = \mathcal{U} \times \{\bar{K}\}$. *F satisfies Pareto indifference and extended binary independence of irrelevant alternatives if and only if there exists an ordering* $\overset{*}{R}$ *on* $\cup_{n \in Z_{++}}(\mathbf{Z}^n \times \mathcal{R}^n)$ *such that, for all* $x, y \in X$ *and for all* $\Upsilon \in \mathcal{D}$,

$$x R_\Upsilon y \Leftrightarrow \big(\Pi(x), \mathbf{U}(x)\big) \overset{*}{R} \big(\Pi(y), \mathbf{U}(y)\big).$$

In Theorems 3.11 and 3.12, the identity vectors in $\mathbf{Z}^n$ appear because the social-evaluation ordering is not necessarily anonymous and the identities of the individuals alive may matter. We discuss anonymous social evaluation, both in the fixed-population case and in the case of a variable population, in the following section.

3.9 WELFARISM AND ANONYMITY

If an anonymity axiom is added to the axioms generating welfarism, utility vectors are sufficient to establish the social ordering of the alternatives: the identities of the individuals alive are irrelevant. Moreover, fixed-population comparisons must be carried out anonymously. The axiom commonly employed requires the social goodness relation to be unchanged if utility functions are permuted across individuals (Blackorby, Bossert, and Donaldson 2004a; Sen 1970a). Although it is possible to use this axiom along with several generalizations of it, its application in the variable-population case requires the sets X_i to be profile dependent. This is the case because a permutation of all potential individuals may change the set of those alive. For simplicity of presentation, therefore, we employ simpler and more direct anonymity axioms, which, together with our other axioms, imply that social goodness relations are independent of individual identities.

We begin with the fixed-population case. The standard formulation of anonymity requires that, if individual utilities in an alternative x are obtained by permuting the utilities in an alternative y for a given profile Υ^n, then x and y must be equally good according to the social ranking obtained for Υ^n. We call this axiom welfare anonymity because it does not require nonwelfare information to be permuted.

Welfare Anonymity. For all $x, y \in X^n$ and for all $\Upsilon^n \in \mathcal{D}^n$, if there exists a bijection $\rho^n: \{1, \ldots, n\} \to \{1, \ldots, n\}$ such that $U_i^n(x) = U_{\rho^n(i)}^n(y)$ for all $i \in \{1, \ldots, n\}$, then $x I_{\Upsilon^n} y$.

In a multi-nonwelfare-profile setting, the welfare-anonymity axiom is very strong because it applies when nonwelfare information is not permuted. An alternative to this axiom requires nonwelfare information to be permuted as well. Thus, welfare anonymity can be weakened to the following condition.

Anonymity. For all $x, y \in X^n$ and for all $\Upsilon^n \in \mathcal{D}^n$, if $K_0^n(x) = K_0^n(y)$ and there exists a bijection $\rho^n: \{1, \ldots, n\} \to \{1, \ldots, n\}$ such that $U_i^n(x) = U_{\rho^n(i)}^n(y)$ and $K_i^n(x) = K_{\rho^n(i)}^n(y)$ for all $i \in \{1, \ldots, n\}$, then $x I_{\Upsilon^n} y$.

Together with the welfarism axioms unlimited domain, Pareto indifference, and binary independence of irrelevant alternatives, anonymity implies that R^n must be anonymous. An ordering R^n on $\mathcal{R}^n$ is anonymous if and only if, for all $u \in \mathcal{R}^n$ and for all bijections $\rho^n: \{1, \ldots, n\} \to \{1, \ldots, n\}$, $u I^n(u_{\rho^n(1)}, \ldots, u_{\rho^n(n)})$. We obtain the following theorem as an immediate consequence of Theorem 3.7 and the definition of anonymity and unlimited domain. Note that the weakening of welfare anonymity to anonymity requires the sets $\mathcal{S}_1, \ldots, \mathcal{S}_n$ to be identical to make it possible to permute nonwelfare information and, thus, to apply the axiom. For this reason, the assumption that the sets of possible values of nonwelfare information are equal across individuals must be added to the theorem statement.

Theorem 3.13. *Suppose $\mathcal{S}_i = \mathcal{S}_j$ for all $i, j \in \{1, \ldots, n\}$ and F^n satisfies unlimited domain. F^n satisfies Pareto indifference, binary independence of irrelevant alternatives, and anonymity if and only if there exists an anonymous social-evaluation ordering R^n on $\mathcal{R}^n$ such that, for all $x, y \in X^n$ and for all $\Upsilon^n \in \mathcal{D}^n$,*

$$x R_{\Upsilon^n}^n y \Leftrightarrow U^n(x) R^n U^n(y). \tag{3.4}$$

Proof. Clearly, if there exists an anonymous ordering R^n such that (3.4) is satisfied, then F^n satisfies Pareto indifference, binary independence of irrelevant alternatives, and anonymity.

Now suppose F^n satisfies the required axioms. By Theorem 3.7, there exists a social-evaluation ordering R^n satisfying (3.3). It remains to show that R^n is anonymous. Let $u, v \in \mathcal{R}^n$ be such that $u = (v_{\rho^n(1)}, \ldots, v_{\rho^n(n)})$ where $\rho^n: \{1, \ldots, n\} \to \{1, \ldots, n\}$ is a bijection. Similarly, let $k_0, \ell_0 \in \mathcal{S}_0$ and $k, \ell \in \mathcal{S}^n$ be such that $k_0 = \ell_0$ and $k = (\ell_{\rho^n(1)}, \ldots, \ell_{\rho^n(n)})$. By unlimited domain, there exist $x, y \in X^n$ and $\Upsilon^n = (U^n, K^n) \in \mathcal{D}^n$ such that $U^n(x) = u$, $U^n(y) = v$, $K^n(x) = (k_0, k)$, and $K^n(y) = (\ell_0, \ell)$. By anonymity, $x I_{\Upsilon^n}^n y$. By Theorem 3.7, $x R_{\Upsilon}^n y$ if and only if $u R^n v$. Consequently, $u I^n v$ and R^n is anonymous. ∎

We conclude this section with a discussion of anonymity axioms in a variable-population setting. Extended welfare anonymity is defined as follows.

Extended Welfare Anonymity. For all $x, y \in X$ and for all $\Upsilon \in \mathcal{D}$, if there exists a bijection $\rho: \mathbf{N}(x) \to \mathbf{N}(y)$ such that $\mathbf{U}_i(x) = \mathbf{U}_{\rho(i)}(y)$ for all $i \in \mathbf{N}(x)$, then $x I_\Upsilon y$.

As is the case for its fixed-population counterpart, extended welfare anonymity appears to be too strong if there are multiple nonwelfare profiles because nonwelfare information is not required to be permuted and, therefore, the scope of the axiom is too large. Thus, we weaken it analogous to the weakening introduced in the fixed-population framework. We obtain the axiom extended anonymity, which requires two alternatives x and y to be equally good according to a profile Υ if the only difference between the two is the identities of the individuals alive. Extended anonymity implies anonymity for every fixed population and, in addition, applies to pairs of alternatives in which the same number of people are alive.

Extended Anonymity. For all $x, y \in X$ and for all $\Upsilon \in \mathcal{D}$, if $K_0(x) = K_0(y)$ and there exists a bijection $\rho: \mathbf{N}(x) \to \mathbf{N}(y)$ such that $\mathbf{U}_i(x) = \mathbf{U}_{\rho(i)}(y)$ and $\mathbf{K}_i(x) = \mathbf{K}_{\rho(i)}(y)$ for all $i \in \mathbf{N}(x)$, then $x I_\Upsilon y$.

To state an anonymous version of the variable-population welfarism theorem, we need the following definitions. Let $\Omega = \cup_{n \in \mathcal{Z}_{++}} \mathcal{R}^n$. An ordering R (with asymmetric factor P and symmetric factor I) on Ω is anonymous if and only if, for all $n \in \mathcal{Z}_{++}$, the restriction of R to $\mathcal{R}^n$ is anonymous. The proof of the following theorem is straightforward given Theorem 3.11 and is thus omitted.

Theorem 3.14. *Suppose $\mathcal{S}_i = \mathcal{S}_j$ for all $i, j \in \mathcal{Z}_{++}$ and F satisfies extended unlimited domain. F satisfies Pareto indifference, extended binary independence of irrelevant alternatives, and extended anonymity if and only if there exists an anonymous social-evaluation ordering R on Ω such that, for all $x, y \in X$ and for all $\Upsilon \in \mathcal{D}$,*

$$x R_\Upsilon y \Leftrightarrow \mathbf{U}(x) R \mathbf{U}(y).$$

In the rest of the book, we use the anonymous social-evaluation ordering R. That is, we implicitly assume welfarism and extended anonymity of F. Consequently, anonymity of R does not have to be imposed explicitly.

CHAPTER 4

Fixed-Population Principles

Part A

In this chapter, we present the most commonly used anonymous social-evaluation orderings for fixed populations. Many of the social-evaluation orderings discussed in this chapter have been proposed or investigated in the literature on the measurement of income inequality. We have modified those orderings so that they rank vectors of well-being. Each of the modified orderings can be used to define a welfarist principle for social evaluation.

Although we focus mainly on the properties of social-evaluation orderings, we also investigate the relationship between these orderings and indexes of utility inequality. We show that all social-evaluation orderings that satisfy a few basic assumptions provide a trade-off between average utility and inequality as measured by an index. In addition, we show that orderings of average-utility–inequality pairs, where inequality is measured by an index applied to utility levels, are equivalent to social-evaluation orderings.

The utilitarian ordering is insensitive to inequality of well-being (but not to inequality of income or consumption) and, for that reason, it has been rejected by some. There are several classes of inequality-averse social-evaluation orderings, however, that give priority to the interests of people with low levels of well-being. Some members of the generalized utilitarian and generalized Gini classes as well as the maximin and leximin (lexicographic maximin) orderings have this property.

To apply most welfarist principles, utilities must satisfy certain measurability requirements; in addition, they must be interpersonally comparable to some extent. We identify the information requirements of the various orderings and, in Part B, prove several theorems whose purpose is to discover all the orderings that satisfy particular information assumptions.

Any anonymous fixed-population ordering can be applied to all fixed populations of the same size. If this is done, a sequence of anonymous social-evaluation orderings, one for each population size, can be produced. We investigate various consistency requirements on these sequences and show that those conditions can be used to make selections from all the sequences that satisfy our other axioms.

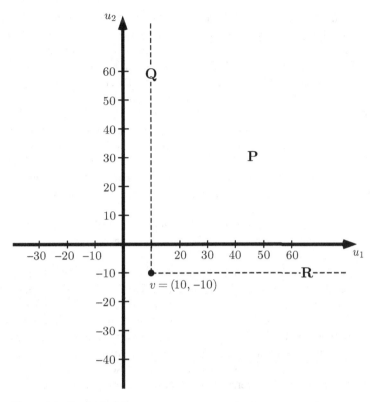

Figure 4.1. Pareto Axioms.

4.1 BASIC PROPERTIES OF SOCIAL-EVALUATION ORDERINGS

First, we present a set of basic axioms that are satisfied by most, but not all, of the principles discussed in the following section.

If each person's utility level is greater in one utility vector than in another, the weak-Pareto axiom requires the first vector to be ranked as better than the second. This axiom is illustrated for a population of two in Figure 4.1. In utility vector $v = (10, -10)$, person 1's utility is 10, person 2's utility is -10, and the set of vectors with larger values for both people is the set of points that lie to the northeast of v labeled **P**. Weak Pareto requires all these vectors to be ranked as better than v. The strong Pareto axiom requires one utility vector to be ranked as better than another whenever each person's utility level is no less in the first and at least one person's utility level is greater. In Figure 4.1, this requires all the vectors in the set **P** to be ranked as better than v and, in addition, extends betterness to the sets **Q** (vertical dashed line), in which person 1's utility is equal to 10 and person 2's utility is greater than -10, and **R** (horizontal dashed line), in which person 1's utility is greater than 10 and person

2's utility is equal to -10. If no one is worse off in one utility vector than in another, Pareto weak preference, which is a consequence of minimal individual goodness, requires the first to be ranked as no worse. In Figure 4.1, that axiom requires all the vectors in **P**, **Q**, and **R** to be ranked as no worse than v. Any social-evaluation ordering that satisfies strong Pareto satisfies weak Pareto and Pareto weak preference. In addition, any continuous social-evaluation ordering that satisfies weak Pareto also satisfies Pareto weak preference.[1]

The axiom minimal increasingness applies only to utility vectors in which all utility levels are equal and ranks increases in the common level as better. Any social-evaluation ordering that satisfies weak Pareto also satisfies minimal increasingness and, for that reason, minimal increasingness is not needed unless Pareto weak preference is the only Pareto condition employed or no Pareto axiom is imposed at all.

Because there are cases in which each person's utility level is greater in one vector than in another when, at the same time, inequality is much greater, an objection to any of these axioms might be that, in some situations, it should be possible for the increase in inequality to overturn the ranking prescribed by the Pareto condition. As long as utilities take account of all the determinants of well-being, including feelings of deprivation, envy, and the harm done by unfair treatment, however, the objection is weakened. The objection provides no criticism of minimal increasingness and, because Pareto weak preference is implied by minimal individual goodness, that axiom is easily defended. We believe, therefore, that it is reasonable to ask all social-evaluation orderings to satisfy Pareto weak preference and minimal increasingness at least.

Continuity is an axiom that prevents a social-evaluation ordering from exhibiting "large" changes in the social ranking in response to "small" changes in individual utilities. Consider any three utility vectors a, b, and c such that a is better than b and b is better than c. An illustration is provided for a two-person society in Figure 4.2 with $a = (40, 50)$, $b = (40, 10)$, and $c = (10, 20)$. Now consider any path that joins a and c. Continuity requires that there exists at least one utility vector in the path that is as good as b. In the figure, such a vector is $d = (20, 30)$. Without such a vector, there must be a sudden "jump" from better to worse without passing through equal goodness. That would occur, for example, if all the vectors in the segment joining a and d, including d, were better than b and all the vectors in the rest of the path were worse. An ordering is continuous if and only if the property illustrated in Figure 4.2 holds for all such triples of utility vectors and all paths joining a and c.

An iso-value set is a set of all the utility vectors that are as good as a particular vector. In Figure 4.2, both b and d are in the same iso-value set and, because the path between a and c can be chosen arbitrarily, many other utility vectors are in it as well. One possibility for the iso-value set that contains b and d is the dashed line that joins them. There are many possibilities, however, one of which is a curved line similar to the curves in Figure 4.3.

---

[1] Continuity is defined below, following our discussion of various Pareto conditions.

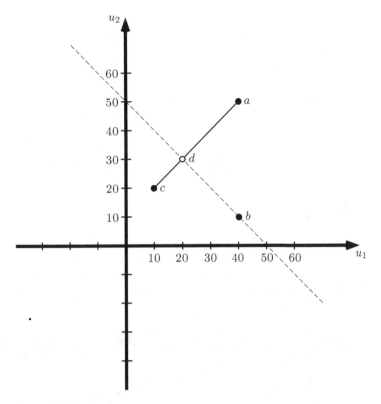

Figure 4.2. Continuity.

Although most commonly used social-evaluation orderings are continuous, a few – such as the leximin ordering – are not. As another example, suppose a social-evaluation ordering ranks one utility vector as better than another whenever total utility is greater and, when total utility is equal in both, the two are ranked by an index of (utility) equality. This ordering is not continuous and it makes stark trade-offs: equality is valued, but any increase in inequality, no matter how large, is tolerated as long as it is accompanied by an increase in total utility, no matter how small. The leximin ordering possesses a similar characteristic. Any decrease in a utility level that is higher than another is accepted if it is accompanied by an increase in the lower level, no matter how small.

We find continuity to be an ethically attractive axiom, but it is possible to defend social-evaluation orderings such as leximin. Kolm (1972) advocates leximin applied to "fundamental preferences" as his notion of "practical justice." Fundamental preferences are analogous to fully informed preferences and can be thought of as depending on individual characteristics.[2]

---

[2] Kolm does not advocate practical justice as the unique and universal criterion for social evaluation. See also Kolm (1992).

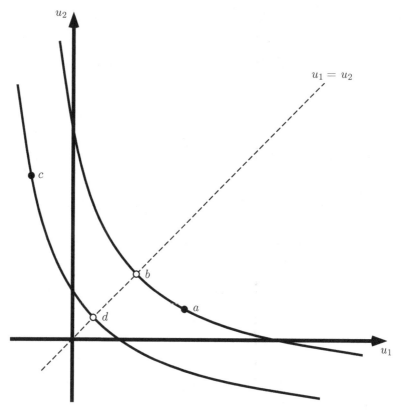

Figure 4.3. Representative Utility.

Continuity is sufficient to ensure that a social-evaluation ordering has a representation (Debreu 1959), which is called a social-evaluation function. In addition, if a social-evaluation ordering has a continuous representation, the ordering is continuous. It follows that, if representations exist for an ordering that is not continuous, none of them is continuous.

The representative utility for any utility vector is a utility level that, if assigned to every individual, produces a utility vector that is as good as the original one. This is illustrated for a society of two people in Figure 4.3. Point a is the utility vector in question and the curved line through it is the iso-value set to which it belongs. The dashed line through the origin is the ray of equality on which all utilities are equal. Point b is the vector of representative utilities because it is in the iso-value set for a (the curve through a) and also on the ray of equality. As an example, a might be $(40, 10)$ and b might be $(23, 23)$. If so, the representative utility for $(40, 10)$ is 23.

Representative utilities may not exist for some or all utility vectors. If, however, a social-evaluation ordering is continuous and satisfies Pareto weak preference and minimal increasingness, representative utilities exist for all utility vectors and are unique. In addition, representative utilities can be used to rank utility vectors. In Figure 4.3, b is the vector of representative utilities for a, and d is the vector of representative utilities for c (because d and c are in the same iso-value set and d is on the ray of equality). Because b lies to the northeast of d on the ray of equality, minimal increasingness requires b to be ranked as better than d. By definition, a and b are equally good, and c and d are equally good. Consequently, b and d are ranked in the same way that a and c are. It follows that a, with the higher representative utility, is better than c. In addition, if two utility vectors are equally good, they must belong to the same iso-value set and, therefore, have the same representative utilities.

If all representative utilities exist and are unique, they are given by a function defined on the set of all utility vectors. In addition, continuity of the social-evaluation ordering ensures that the representative-utility function is continuous. It follows that the representative-utility function is a social-evaluation function that represents the social-evaluation ordering. All social-evaluation functions must be increasing transformations of the representative utility function.

When there are two people in the population, inequality is an unambiguous characteristic of a utility vector: if total utility is fixed, one vector is more equal than another if and only if the utility level of the worst-off person is larger in the first than in the second. That convenient property is not shared by vectors for populations of three or more people, however. Early in the twentieth century, Lorenz (1905) proposed a quasi-ordering of distributions with the same total. To rank distributions, the Lorenz curve is constructed by calculating the total utility that is experienced by the worst-off person, the worst-off two people, the worst-off three people, and so on, and the result is plotted. The Lorenz quasi-ordering declares one distribution to be at least as equal as another if and only if the Lorenz curve for the first is nowhere below the Lorenz curve for the second. Thus, one distribution is unambiguously as equal as another if and only if the Lorenz curve for the first coincides with the curve for the second, and it is unambiguously more equal if and only if the Lorenz curve for the first is nowhere below and somewhere above the curve for the other.

Lorenz curves for distributions of 100 units of utility among a population of four people are illustrated in Figure 4.4. a is $(10, 20, 30, 40)$; b is $(15, 30, 20, 35)$; and c is $(15, 45, 20, 20)$. In distribution a, the worst-off person has 10, the worst-off two have 30, the worst-off three have 60, and the worst-off four have 100. The Lorenz curve is constructed by joining these points to each other and to the bottom-left corner of the rectangle with straight lines. The Lorenz curve for a is the labeled solid line in both the upper and lower panels of the figure. The Lorenz curves for distributions b and c are the dashed lines in the upper and lower panels, respectively.

The upper panel of the figure makes it clear that distribution b is unambiguously more equal than distribution a. Distributions c and a, whose Lorenz curves appear in the lower panel, are not ranked by the Lorenz criterion: it is

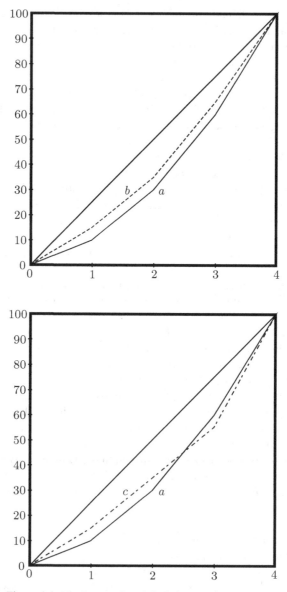

Figure 4.4. The Lorenz Quasi-Ordering.

not the case that c is unambiguously at least as equal as a and it is not the case that a is unambiguously at least as equal as c.

The Lorenz quasi-ordering is identical to a quasi-ordering proposed by Pigou (1912) and Dalton (1920) that is generated by the principle of transfers. It declares any two distributions that are permutations of each other, and therefore have the same Lorenz curve, to be equally unequal and, if utility is transferred from a better-off to a worse-off person without reversing their positions in the distribution, the resulting distribution is seen as unambiguously more equal.

Identity of the two quasi-orderings can be illustrated as follows.[3] Starting with distribution a, transfer 5 units from person 4 to person 1 to produce the unambiguously more equal distribution (15, 20, 30, 35). Because this distribution and b are permutations of each other, they have the same Lorenz curve and are equally unequal by both criteria. As a consequence, b is unambiguously more equal than a according to both. Now consider distributions c and a. To create the distribution (15, 20, 20, 45), which is as equal as c, by transfers from a, it is necessary to make a transfer to person 1 from someone who is better off *and* to make a transfer to person 4 from someone who is worse off. Consequently, distributions c and a are not ranked by either quasi-ordering.

Anonymous social-evaluation orderings that are weakly or strictly consistent with the Lorenz quasi-ordering are called weakly inequality averse or strictly inequality averse. If one utility vector is unambiguously as equal as another with the same total, they must be permutations of each other and they are ranked as equally good by both weakly and strictly inequality-averse orderings. In addition, if one utility vector is unambiguously more equal than another with the same total, a weakly inequality-averse ordering ranks it as no worse and a strictly inequality-averse ordering ranks it as better. The utilitarian social-evaluation ordering is, therefore, weakly inequality averse but not strictly so. Social-evaluation functions that represent weakly or strictly inequality-averse orderings are also called weakly and strictly inequality averse.

4.2 ANONYMOUS SOCIAL-EVALUATION ORDERINGS

We now turn to the most commonly used anonymous social-evaluation orderings. Each of these corresponds to a welfarist fixed-population principle (social-evaluation functional): the ranking of any pair of alternatives is the same as the ranking of the associated utility vectors according to the social-evaluation ordering.

Each of the social-evaluation orderings considered in this section other than maximin satisfies strong Pareto and, apart from the leximin ordering, all are continuous. The maximin ordering satisfies weak Pareto and Pareto weak preference.

Strictly inequality-averse social-evaluation orderings give priority to worse-off individuals.[4] Suppose a single person is to be chosen to receive a one-unit increase in his or her utility level. According to any strictly inequality-averse ordering, the best choice is the worst-off person, the second-best choice is the second-worst-off person, and so on (if two people have the same utility level, either can be chosen).

---

[3] See Hardy, Littlewood, and Pólya (1934) for a proof.

[4] See Parfit (1997).

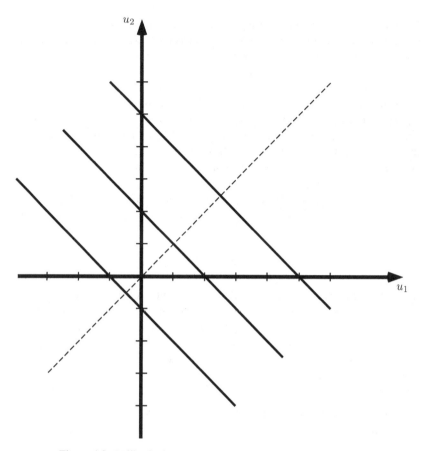

Figure 4.5. Utilitarianism.

The utilitarian social-evaluation ordering ranks utility vectors on the basis of total or average utility. That is, utility vector u is at least as good as utility vector v if and only if total or average utility is at least as great in u. Because population is fixed, average and total utilities are increasing transformations of each other and both average utility and total utility are social-evaluation functions for the utilitarian ordering. Any other increasing transformation of average or total utility is also a social-evaluation function for utilitarianism.

Utilitarian iso-value sets in the two-person case are drawn in Figure 4.5 and several two-person vectors appear in Table 4.1. Utility vector a is $(100, 60)$ and vectors b, c, d, and e exhibit complete equality. For any social-evaluation ordering, representative utilities for b, c, d, and e are (by definition) 80, 70, 65, and 60, respectively. Any ordering that satisfies minimal increasingness therefore ranks b better than c better than d better than e.

Because total (average) utility is the same in a and b, the utilitarian ordering ranks them as equally good. Consequently, representative utility for a is 80,

Table 4.1. *Two-Person Utility Vectors*

Utility Vector	Person 1's Utility	Person 2's Utility
a	100	60
b	80	80
c	70	70
d	65	65
e	60	60

average utility. It is easy to show that, for any number of people and any utility vector, representative utility for the utilitarian ordering is average utility.

There are two general types of strictly inequality-averse social-evaluation orderings. The first is level based and the second is position based. Level-based inequality aversion is represented by a subclass of the generalized utilitarian class. Those orderings rank utility vectors on the basis of sums (or averages) of transformed utilities.[5] Two possible transformations appear in Figure 4.6. In both cases, we have normalized the transformations so that the transformed value of zero is zero. This can be done without loss of generality.

Suppose a utility level is to increase by one unit. Then, if the transforming function is strictly concave, as in the upper panel of Figure 4.6, the change in the transformed value of utility decreases as the starting level of utility increases. Thus, strict priority is given to worse-off individuals. Broome (2004b) argued that generalized utilitarian orderings with strictly concave transformations provide the best fit with Parfit's (1997) prioritarianism (see also Fleurbaey 2004).

An example of a transformation like the one in the upper panel is $1 - \exp(-\tau)$, where τ is the utility level and exp is the exponential function. In that case, the sum of transformed utilities is (approximately) the same in a and in the vector $(61, 61)$. Consequently, representative utility is 61 according to that ordering. It ranks b as best, followed by c, then d, then a, and then e.

A different transformation is employed in the lower panel of Figure 4.6. Transformed utility is equal to the utility level itself if utility is nonnegative and equal to twice the utility level if utility is negative. Thus, priority is given to people whose lives are not worth living. The resulting generalized utilitarian social-evaluation ordering is weakly inequality averse but not strictly so. It does exhibit some instances of strict inequality aversion, however. If vectors u and v have the same average or total and the number of people with negative utilities is smaller in u, u is better. According to any generalized utilitarian social-evaluation ordering, transformed representative utility is equal to the average of transformed utilities.

The second possibility for inequality-aversion focuses on positions in the distribution of utilities. The best known of these is the maximin ordering, which

---

[5] The transformation must be continuous and increasing.

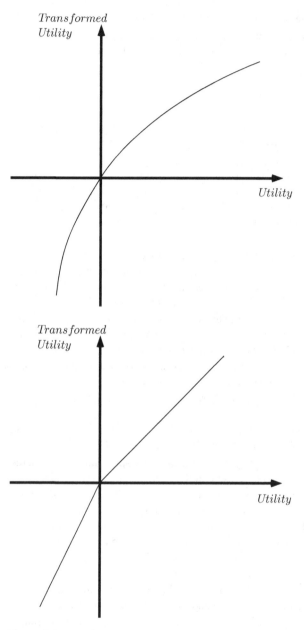

Figure 4.6. Transformations.

ranks utility vectors by comparing the smallest utilities. Therefore, it gives priority to the worst-off person. In the example of Table 4.1, a and e are equally good according to maximin and, as a consequence, a's representative utility is 60, minimum utility. The maximin ordering exhibits weak but not strict inequality aversion: reductions in inequality among individuals whose utility levels exceed the minimum are ranked as equally good, not better. The maximin ordering does not satisfy strong Pareto but it satisfies weak Pareto and continuity and, thus, Pareto weak preference and minimal increasingness.

A social-evaluation ordering that is closely related to the maximin ordering is the leximin ordering. It coincides with maximin when the minimum utility level in one vector exceeds the minimum in another but, when minimum utilities are equal, it ranks one as better if the second smallest utility level is bigger. If the two smallest utilities are the same as well, it compares the third smallest, and so on. Consequently, it ranks two utility vectors as equally good if and only if one is a permutation of the other. Leximin is not continuous and representative utilities do not exist for utility vectors that are not on the ray of equality. It is strictly inequality averse and satisfies strong Pareto and, thus, all other Pareto conditions and minimal increasingness.

In the example of Table 4.1, both leximin and maximin rank b, c, d, and e in that order but they disagree about the ranking of a and e: maximin finds them equally good but leximin ranks a as better.

Although maximin and leximin are not generalized utilitarian orderings, they can be approximated by strictly inequality-averse generalized utilitarian orderings. One example is the Kolm-Pollak class of generalized utilitarian orderings. Each of them is associated with a particular value of a positive parameter and, as that parameter becomes large, maximin and leximin are approximated.

Maximin and leximin are not the only position-based social-evaluation orderings. The generalized Gini orderings (Mehran 1976, Weymark 1981) use a weighted sum of ranked utilities to order utility vectors. Weights are positive and, if weights for higher utility levels are no greater than those for lower utility levels, these orderings are weakly inequality averse. If, in addition, the weights are all different, inequality aversion is strict. The generalized Gini orderings are continuous and satisfy strong Pareto.

The best-known generalized Gini ordering is the Gini ordering itself (Blackorby and Donaldson 1978). It is closely related to the Gini inequality index and it ranks utility vectors with weights that are proportional to the first n positive odd numbers. The largest utility receives a weight of 1, the second largest a weight of 3, and so on. Iso-value sets for a society of two people are illustrated in Figure 4.7.

In the example of Table 4.1, sums of weighted utilities for a through e are 280, 320, 280, 260, and 240. Consequently, a and c are equally good and representative utility for a is 70. It follows that the Gini social-evaluation ordering ranks b as best, followed by the equally good a and c, then by d and by e.

There are two subclasses of generalized Gini orderings known as the single-parameter Ginis or S-Ginis and their illfare-ranked counterparts (Donaldson

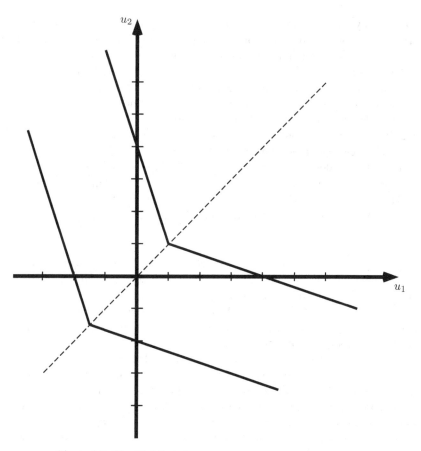

Figure 4.7. The Gini Ordering.

and Weymark 1980). The members of each subclass are associated with particular values of a single parameter. The utilitarian ordering is associated with a parameter value of one in both subclasses and both maximin and leximin can be approximated in each.

It is possible for a social-evaluation ordering to combine level-based and position-based considerations. One of these is the Gini ordering applied to transformed utilities.

Table 4.2 provides a summary of the basic properties of the social-evaluation orderings discussed in this section. All the orderings satisfy minimal increasingness and Pareto weak preference.

The social-evaluation orderings discussed above have different information requirements. In a multiagent setting, the measurability assumptions introduced in Chapter 2 no longer are sufficient to describe an informational environment – in addition, the extent to which utilities can be compared interpersonally must be specified. In particular, we consider information requirements where utility

Table 4.2. *Properties of Fixed-Population Principles*

	Continuity	Pareto		Inequality Aversion	
		Weak	Strong	Weak	Strict
Utilitarianism	•	•	•	•	
Gen. Utilitarianism (concave transformation)	•	•	•	•	
Gen. Utilitarianism (strictly concave transformation)	•	•	•	•	•
Gini	•	•	•	•	•
Gen. Gini (distinct weights)	•	•	•	•	•
Maximin	•	•		•	
Leximin		•	•	•	•

differences or utility levels (or both) can be compared interpersonally. This is the case, for example, if the informational environment is described by cardinal unit comparability: the application of any vector of transformations such that each utility function is multiplied by a common positive scaling factor and a constant (which may be different for different individuals) is added to each individual utility leads to an informationally equivalent utility profile. In this informational environment, utility differences but not utility levels can be compared interpersonally. Ordinal full comparability allows for the comparability of utility levels but not of utility differences. In that case, each utility function can be transformed with a common increasing transformation to arrive at an informationally equivalent profile. Interpersonal comparability of both utility levels and utility differences is guaranteed by cardinal full comparability, in which case each utility function can be multiplied by a common positive scaling factor and a common constant can be added.

The utilitarian ordering is consistent with cardinal measurability and unit comparability; this means that interpersonal comparisons of utility differences are meaningful but comparisons of levels are not needed. An example is provided by $a = (100, 60)$ and $b = (80, 80)$ in Table 4.1. If we move from b to a, person 1 gains 20 units and person 2 loses 20 units. We can transform utilities by multiplying each one by the same positive number and adding or subtracting a number that can be different for different people. If the multiplying number is 2, the gain to person 1 and the loss to person 2 become 40 and 40 and, as before, a and b are equally good. In addition, if we were to add 100 to person 1's utility and subtract 50 from person 2's utility, utility levels for a would be 300 and 70 and utility levels for b would be 260 and 110, so a and b still would be ranked as equally good.

The generalized utilitarian orderings have information requirements that depend on the utility transformation used. If the one shown in the lower panel of Figure 4.6 is used, utilities can be ratio-scale measurable and interpersonally fully comparable. The maximin and leximin orderings do not require cardinal measurability of utilities. For them, ordinal measurability and full interpersonal comparability, which together allow levels of utility to be compared, are sufficient. All the generalized Gini orderings are consistent with cardinal measurability and full interpersonal comparability.

4.3 INEQUALITY INDEXES AND AVERAGE-UTILITY–INEQUALITY TRADE-OFFS

One objection to the unitary approach of social-evaluation orderings is based on the observation that they appear to claim that representative utility is all that matters. It has been argued that both average (or total) utility and utility inequality matter for social evaluation. To make this position precise, inequality should be measured by an index. An inequality index is equal to zero for all vectors of equal utilities and is positive for all other vectors. In addition, an index must be consistent with the Lorenz quasi-ordering and the principle of transfers: an unambiguous increase in inequality (reduction in equality) must be associated with a higher value of the index.

Given an inequality index, alternatives can be ranked by computing both average utility and utility inequality for the associated utility vectors and ranking the average-utility–inequality (AUI) pairs with a goodness relation that is reflexive and transitive. A pair that has an average utility that is no smaller than another and an inequality level that is no greater than another should be ranked as no worse. If, in addition, the average is greater or inequality is smaller, it should be ranked as better. This does not provide a complete ranking of AUI pairs, however. There are comparisons in which both average utility and inequality are bigger or smaller.

Suppose, therefore, there is a goodness relation for AUI pairs that is a quasi-ordering. It follows that there is a social-evaluation quasi-ordering of utility vectors that can be used to rank some pairs of utility vectors. Such a principle is welfarist in the sense that utilities are all the information that is needed to make social judgments (see Chapter 7 for discussions of incomplete rankings). If the quasi-ordering of AUI pairs is complete, we refer to it as an AUI ordering, and it can be used to generate a principle for social evaluation (a social-evaluation functional). The social-evaluation ordering of utility vectors is generated by the AUI ordering, and alternatives can be ranked by either ordering.

An AUI ordering is illustrated in Figure 4.8. We suppose the index of inequality is bounded by zero (complete equality) and one, and we have drawn two iso-value sets. Because inequality is bad, AUI pairs in iso-value set I are better than those in iso-value set II.

There is a difficulty with this approach (Parfit 1997). Suppose inequality is measured by the Gini index. For two people, it can be calculated by computing the weighted average of the higher and lower utilities with weights of $1/4$ and $3/4$, respectively, dividing this number by average utility and subtracting the resulting number from one. Thus, for the utility vector (100, 20), the weighted

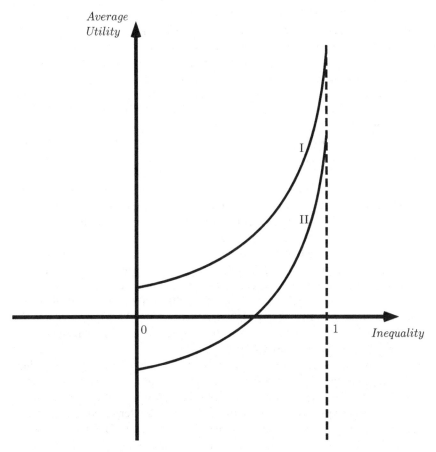

Figure 4.8. An AUI Ordering.

average is 40, average utility is 60, and the Gini index is $1 - 2/3 = 1/3$. The value of the Gini index is equal to zero for the utility vector (10, 10). Suppose AUI pairs are ranked with the product of average utility and one minus the value of the inequality index to the sixth power. This principle satisfies all the above requirements but the associated social-evaluation ordering satisfies neither weak Pareto nor Pareto weak preference. To see this, we note that the product is $60 \times (2/3)^6 = 5.27$ for (100, 20) and 10 for (10, 10). Thus, this principle ranks (10, 10) as better than (100, 20) even though each person is better off in the latter vector.

One response to this difficulty is to restrict attention to AUI orderings whose associated social-evaluation orderings satisfy at least one of the Pareto requirements. Alternatively, one might reject the Pareto axioms and defend the resulting principle. Our intuitions favor the former course, primarily because we find the axiom minimal individual goodness attractive. Theorem 3.1 shows that any welfarist social-evaluation functional that satisfies it must satisfy Pareto weak preference, which does not allow (10, 10) to be ranked as better than (100, 20). We suggest, therefore, that departures from weak Pareto can be reasonably defended only if Pareto weak preference is satisfied.

The above discussion shows that an AUI-ordering approach can be used to generate social-evaluation orderings. The direction can be reversed, however: inequality indexes and AUI orderings can be derived from social-evaluation orderings as long as representative utility functions exist. These indexes are called ethical indexes.

The Atkinson-Kolm-Sen (AKS) index was introduced by Kolm (1969), independently proposed by Atkinson (1970), and investigated by Sen (1973). It is derived from any strictly inequality-averse social-evaluation ordering and it measures inequality by computing the difference between average utility and representative utility and dividing by the absolute value of average utility.[6] For all utility vectors other than those that are equal, representative utility is less than average utility; this ensures that the index is positive for all such vectors. In addition, because the social-evaluation ordering is strictly inequality averse, the AKS inequality index ranks all unambiguous increases in inequality as more unequal.

Suppose, as an example, the Gini social-evaluation ordering for a population of two people is used. Then the vectors (100, 20) and (40, 40) are equally good, and representative utility for (100, 20) is therefore 40. Consequently, the AKS index for (100, 20) is equal to $1 - 40/60 = 1/3$, which is the value of the Gini index for (100, 20) as computed previously.

The procedure can be reversed. Representative utility is equal to the product of average utility and one minus the AKS index if average utility is positive and the product of average utility and one plus the AKS index if average utility is negative. Consequently, representative utility can be interpreted as inequality-adjusted average utility. Because the representative-utility function is a social-evaluation function, the social-evaluation ordering is completely determined by the AKS index. In addition, any inequality index, if interpreted as an AKS index, determines a social-evaluation ordering. This can be done in the example discussed previously. The Gini inequality index for (100, 20) is 1/3 so, interpreting the Gini index as an AKS index, representative utility is $60 \times 2/3 = 40$. Similarly, the Gini index for (10, 10) is 0 and representative utility is therefore 10. Because 40 is greater than 10, (100, 20) is better than (10, 10), which is consistent with both strong and weak Pareto. If an AKS index corresponds to a social-evaluation ordering that satisfies strong Pareto (weak Pareto; minimal increasingness and Pareto weak preference), the AKS procedure can be used to produce an AUI ordering that satisfies strong Pareto (weak Pareto; minimal increasingness and Pareto weak preference).

Kolm (1969) proposed a second ethical inequality index. For any strictly inequality-averse social-evaluation ordering, it is the difference between

---

[6] The AKS index is not defined when average utility is zero. Dividing by the absolute value is not needed in income-inequality analysis because attention typically is restricted to income vectors with positive averages.

average utility and representative utility. Using the Gini social-evaluation ordering for a population of two, representative utility for (100, 20) is 40 and the Kolm index is $60 - 40 = 20$. Like the AKS index, the Kolm index can be used to recover the representative-utility function and, therefore, the social-evaluation ordering: representative utility is equal to average utility less the value of the index. If a Kolm index corresponds to a social-evaluation ordering that satisfies strong Pareto (weak Pareto; minimal increasingness and Pareto weak preference), the Kolm procedure can be reversed to produce an AUI ordering that satisfies strong Pareto (weak Pareto; minimal increasingness and Pareto weak preference).

Some inequality indexes are relative indexes, depending on individual shares of total utility alone. Such indexes rank a distribution and all its positive multiples as equally unequal. It is well known that the AKS index is relative if and only if the social-evaluation ordering possesses a property called homotheticity: multiplying each component of two utility vectors by any positive number preserves their ranking.[7]

Other inequality indexes are absolute indexes, depending on utility differences only. Those indexes rank a distribution and all distributions that can be obtained by adding the same constant to each component as equally unequal. The Kolm index is an absolute index if and only if the social-evaluation ordering is translatable: adding the same amount to each of the components of any two utility vectors leaves their ranking unchanged.

Suppose an AUI ordering is used to rank utility vectors and the corresponding AKS and Kolm indexes are derived. Both of these indexes agree with the AUI ordering's ranking of utility vectors with the same total or average utility, but the indexes may disagree about the inequality rankings of utility vectors with different totals or averages.

AKS and Kolm indexes are not the only possibilities. Bossert and Pfingsten (1990), Kolm (1976a, 1976b), and Pfingsten (1986) have investigated other families. They can be used to produce intermediate indexes that lie between relative and absolute indexes. Ethical social index numbers other than inequality indexes include poverty indexes and indexes of deprivation, which are discussed by Chakravarty (1990).

4.4 OTHER AXIOMS

Suppose a social change affects only a subset of the population such as the citizens of India or the present generation. To evaluate such a change, it is necessary to compare the complete utility vectors before and after the change, because the utility levels of the unaffected individuals may matter. An example is provided in Table 4.3. The utilities of persons 1 and 2 are identical in a and c and in b and d. In moving from a to b or from c to d, person 3 is unaffected.

---

[7] For discussions, see Blackorby, Bossert, and Donaldson (1999e) and Chakravarty (1990).

Table 4.3. *Unaffected Individuals*

Utility Vector	Person 1's Utility	Person 2's Utility	Person 3's Utility
a	100	−10	−50
b	80	−5	−50
c	100	−10	20
d	80	−5	20

According to the utilitarian ordering, a is better than b and c is better than d; the utility level of person 3 makes no difference. In addition, any generalized utilitarian ordering makes comparisons that are independent of the utilities of the unaffected. Suppose, as an example, that transformed utility is the utility level for nonnegative utilities and five times the utility level for negative utilities. Total transformed utilities are -200 for a, -195 for b, 70 for c, and 75 for d. As a consequence, b is better than a and d is better than c.

Suppose, by contrast, that the Gini social-evaluation ordering is used to rank the two pairs. Weights are equal to 1, 3, and 5 on the highest, middle, and lowest utilities, respectively, and sums of weighted utilities are $100 - 30 - 250 = -180$ for a, $80 - 15 - 250 = -185$ for b, $100 - 50 + 60 = 110$ for c, and $80 - 25 + 60 = 115$ for d. Consequently, the Gini social-evaluation ordering ranks a as better than b and d as better than c: the utility level of the unaffected person makes a difference.

If maximin is used to rank the two pairs in Table 4.3, a and b are ranked as equally good but d is ranked as better than c. If, however, leximin is used, b is better than a and d is better than c. The utility level of person 3 makes a difference when maximin is used but not when leximin is used.

Same-people independence is an axiom that requires rankings of utility vectors to be independent of the utility levels of unaffected individuals. It ensures that well-defined social-evaluation orderings exist for population subgroups. If a change affects only the members of the subgroup, the social evaluation of the change is independent of utility levels outside the group. The example of Table 4.3 shows that the Gini and maximin social-evaluation orderings do not satisfy same-people independence.

For populations of at least three people, an anonymous social-evaluation ordering satisfies strong Pareto, continuity, and same-people independence if and only if it is a generalized utilitarian ordering. Consequently, none of the strictly inequality-averse generalized Gini orderings (including the Gini) satisfies same-people independence.

In our view, same-people independence is a compelling axiom. In addition to its ethical appeal, it has the effect of reducing the information needed to make social evaluations. Because information about the utilities of those who are long dead or of those who will be alive in the distant future is often difficult or impossible to obtain, principles that satisfy the axiom have a practical advantage.

If weak inequality-aversion is added to the above axioms, all the ethically acceptable social-evaluation orderings are generalized utilitarian with concave

Table 4.4. *Transplant Example*

	Without Transplant	With Transplant
Person 1's Utility	50	110
Person 2's Utility	80	150

transformations. The utilitarian ordering is one of these, and we may ask whether it has any significant advantages over the other generalized utilitarian orderings.

Suppose several people are candidates for a liver transplant and only one of them can receive it. Without the transplant, death will soon follow. Lifetime utilities are given in Table 4.4.

Person 2 is younger than person 1 and the additional years of life (in good health) will be slightly greater for her. Because the benefit to person 2 (70) would be greater than the benefit to person 1 (60), a case can be made that it would be better if she were to receive the transplant and this is what utilitarianism recommends. But person 1 has a lower starting point than person 2 does, and we might well ask whether that is a reason to select him. Because any strictly inequality-averse social-evaluation ordering that satisfies continuity and weak Pareto would favor him as long as the difference between benefits is small enough, it might be argued that it would be better to select him.

The difference between these intuitions can be captured by the axiom incremental equity. If a single person is to receive a benefit and the benefit is the same no matter who receives it, the axiom asserts that the identity of the person selected does not matter: it sees all possible outcomes as equally good. This axiom is very powerful. A social ordering satisfies minimal increasingness and incremental equity if and only if it is the utilitarian ordering. Thus, the axiom provides a thought experiment that enables us to distinguish between the strict inequality aversion of generalized utilitarian orderings with strictly concave transformations and the absence of inequality aversion of utilitarianism.

4.5 CONSISTENT FIXED-POPULATION SOCIAL EVALUATION

Suppose we consider all populations of a particular size and use the same social-evaluation ordering for each. This does not mean the orderings can be used to rank alternatives in which different individuals are alive (ever live). Given this approach, we consider a sequence of social-evaluation orderings, one for each population size, and require the members of a sequence to satisfy various consistency requirements.[8]

---

[8] Our use of the term consistency differs from that employed in the literature on resource allocation. We use consistency to refer to a class of conditions that impose restrictions on comparisons performed by different members of the sequence, whereas the consistency principle for resource-allocation mechanisms as surveyed by Thomson (1990) is more specific. It requires a resource-allocation mechanism to be insensitive to the departure of an agent in the sense that the mechanism

Table 4.5. *Replication Invariance*

Utility Vector	Person 1	Person 2	Person 3	Person 4
u	10	40		
v	50	5		
u'	10	40	10	40
v'	50	5	50	5

A basic consistency condition is called replication invariance, and it was first proposed by Dalton (1920) in the context of income-inequality measurement. Suppose $u = (u_1, \ldots, u_n)$ is a utility vector for a population of size n. For any positive integer k, the utility vector u' for population size kn is a k-fold replication of u if and only if each component of u is replicated k times in u' (given anonymity, the order does not matter). An example is given in Table 4.5. Utility vectors u and v contain two components and utility vectors u' and v' contain four components. Because the utilities in u and v are replicated in u' and v', u' and v' are 2-fold replications of u and v.

A sequence of social-evaluation orderings is replication invariant if and only if, for any two utility vectors of population size n, the social-evaluation ordering for population size kn ranks the k-fold replications in the same way the social-evaluation ordering for population size n ranks the original vectors. In the example, this means that, if u is ranked as better than v, u' must be ranked as better than v'.

Suppose the sequence of social-evaluation orderings consists of the Gini orderings. Then, in the example of Table 4.5, u is better than v because $40 + 30 = 70$ and $50 + 15 = 65$, and u' is better than v' because $40 + 120 + 50 + 70 = 280$ and $50 + 150 + 25 + 35 = 260$. It is straightforward to verify that the Gini sequence satisfies replication invariance.

Consider, however, a sequence of generalized Gini orderings, each of which assigns the weight 1 to the smallest utility level, $1/2$ to the second smallest, $1/4$ to the next smallest, and, in general, $1/2^{i-1}$ to the ith smallest. In the example, that sequence declares u and v to be equally good because $10 + 20 = 30$ and $5 + 25 = 30$. Replication invariance requires u' and v' to be ranked as equally good as well but, because $10 + 5 + 10 + 5 = 30$ and $5 + 2.5 + 12.5 + 6.75 = 26.75$, u' is ranked as better than v' and replication invariance is not satisfied.

Another example is provided by a sequence of generalized utilitarian orderings, which use the same transformation for all population sizes (the utilitarian sequence is one of these). Suppose u' and v' are k-fold replications of u and v. Then, if the sum of transformed utilities in u is greater (equal to; less than) the sum of transformed utilities in v, the same is true for u' and v': the sum for both is k times the sum for the originals.

prescribes the same allocation for the remaining agents before and after the departure of this agent with her or his allocation.

Replication invariance can be used to make a selection from the set of all possible sequences of orderings. Consider all the sequences of generalized utilitarian orderings, allowing for the possibility that the transformations may be different for different population sizes. A generalized utilitarian sequence is replication invariant if and only if the transformations for different population sizes are positive multiples of each other.[9] Because the multiple makes no difference to the orderings, this means any replication-invariant sequence can be written with the same transformation for all population sizes.

The generalized-Gini sequences were investigated by Donaldson and Weymark (1980), who provided a characterization of all the generalized Gini sequences that satisfy replication invariance. Two subsequences were also considered. Each of these uses a single sequence of weights. The weights in the first sequence are nondecreasing with the first weight assigned to the highest utility, the next to the second highest, and so on. The weights in the second sequence are nonincreasing, with the first assigned to the lowest utility, the second to the second lowest, and so on. If two or more utilities are equal, they may be ranked in either order. The two subsequences have the utilitarian sequence in common.

All the members of the two subsequences that satisfy replication invariance are characterized by a positive parameter. Because of this, they are called the (illfare-ranked) single-parameter Ginis or S-Ginis. There are two cases. In the first, a parameter value of 1 produces the utilitarian sequence, a value of 2 produces the Gini sequence, and, as the parameter becomes large, the maximin and leximin sequences are approximated. And, as long as the parameter is greater than 1, each ordering in the sequence is strictly inequality averse. In the second case, a parameter value of 1 produces the utilitarian sequence, and, as the parameter approaches zero, maximin and leximin are approximated. In both cases, the single-parameter coefficient for the utility of the ith individual in the ranking is given by the difference $i^\delta - (i-1)^\delta$ where δ is the single parameter. In the first (welfare-ranked) case, the utilities are ordered from highest to lowest, and δ must be greater than or equal to one; in the second (the illfare-ranked case), utilities are ranked from lowest to highest, and δ is between zero and one (one included, zero excluded).

If minimal increasingness is satisfied, replication invariance is equivalent to conditions on representative-utility functions (provided they exist) and on AKS and Kolm inequality indexes. Any utility vector and a vector of its representative utilities are equally good by definition. Consequently, replication invariance implies that a k-fold replication of u and a k-fold replication of the vector of its representative utilities are equally good. It follows that the representative utility for a k-fold replication of u is equal to the representative utility for u. Because average utility is replication invariant, the sequences of AKS and Kolm inequality indexes also must be replication invariant. It is straightforward to show that replication invariance of either sequence of inequality indexes

[9] This assumes that the transformations are all normalized so that they are zero when utility is zero.

implies replication invariance of representative utilities, which, in turn, implies replication invariance of the sequence of social-evaluation orderings.

Replication invariance is a weak condition that can be satisfied by some of the generalized Gini sequences. The population substitution principle is a stronger condition. Suppose that, in any utility vector, each of a population subgroup's utilities is replaced with a representative utility, which is calculated from the social-evaluation ordering appropriate to the subgroup's size. The vector for the subgroup and the vector of representative utilities are ranked as equally good by the subgroup social-evaluation ordering, and the population substitution principle requires the two utility vectors to be ranked as equally good by the social-evaluation ordering for the whole population.

Any sequence that satisfies the population substitution principle necessarily satisfies replication invariance. Consider vectors u and v for population size n and let ξ and ζ be their representative utilities. By definition, u and an n-vector of ξs are equally good and v and an n-vector of ζs are equally good. Now consider k-fold replications u' and v' of u and v. In u', replace each occurrence of the vector u with an n-vector of ξs; in v', replace each occurrence of v with an n-vector of ζs. The population substitution principle implies that each of these two vectors and its antecedent are equally good. By definition, their representative utilities are ξ and ζ and, because utility vectors can be ranked by their representative utilities, u' and v' are ranked in the same way as u and v, and replication invariance is satisfied.

The population substitution principle implies replication invariance but the converse is not true. A consequence of the population substitution principle is that each social-evaluation ordering in the sequence satisfies same-people independence. It follows that, if each ordering is assumed to satisfy continuity and strong Pareto and the population substitution principle is satisfied, each same-number ordering must be generalized utilitarian. Because replication invariance is implied by the population substitution principle, the same transformation can be used for each population size. The same result follows if each ordering satisfies continuity, strong Pareto, and same-people independence and the sequence satisfies replication invariance.

Part B

We begin the second part of this chapter by introducing and discussing some basic axioms for fixed-population social evaluation in Section 4.6. Classes of social-evaluation orderings such as those corresponding to generalized utilitarianism and the generalized Ginis are presented in Section 4.7, and ethical indexes of inequality are discussed in Section 4.8. In addition to axiom statements and proofs for claims discussed in Part A, we also consider the effect of limitations of information concerning measurability and interpersonal comparability of utilities in Section 4.9. These restrictions are used to select a subset of all possible social-evaluation orderings that satisfy our other axioms.

Section 4.10 presents several characterization results for generalized utilitarianism and utilitarianism, and Section 4.11 considers sequences of social-evaluation orderings.

4.6 BASIC PROPERTIES OF FIXED-POPULATION PRINCIPLES

To introduce some fundamental axioms for fixed-population social evaluation, we restrict attention to alternatives with a fixed, finite, and nonempty population $\bar{N} \subset \mathcal{Z}_{++}$ and, therefore, to the subset $X^{\bar{N}} = \{x \in X \mid \mathbf{N}(x) = \bar{N}\}$ of X. As in Chapter 3, we choose, without loss of generality, $\bar{N} = \{1, \ldots, n\}$, where $n = |\bar{N}|$. Given welfarism, all social-evaluation principles for that population can be formulated in terms of social-evaluation ordering R^n defined on the set of possible utility vectors $\mathcal{R}^n$.

All the social-evaluation principles considered in this chapter except for the strongly dictatorial orderings satisfy same-people anonymity. It ensures that the ordering R^n treats individuals impartially, paying no attention to their identities. Thus, any permutation of a given utility vector must be as good as the utility vector itself. This is a strengthening of Arrow's (1951, 1963) condition that prevents the existence of a dictator.

Same-People Anonymity. For all $u \in \mathcal{R}^n$ and for all bijections $\rho^n : \{1, \ldots, n\} \to \{1, \ldots, n\}$,

$$u I^n \big(u_{\rho^n(1)}, \ldots, u_{\rho^n(n)} \big).$$

Pareto axioms require social-evaluation orderings to respond positively to increases in well-being. Because Pareto indifference is satisfied by all welfarist principles (it is implied by reflexivity of the ordering R^n), we do not need to consider it explicitly in this chapter and, therefore, restrict attention to axioms that require social betterness or, at least, equal goodness to result from versions of unanimity among the individuals.

The weak-Pareto principle requires an increase in everyone's utility to be regarded as a social improvement.

Weak Pareto. For all $u, v \in \mathcal{R}^n$, if $u \gg v$, then $u P^n v$.

The strong-Pareto requirement extends weak Pareto to cases in which no one's utility level falls and at least one increases.

Strong Pareto. For all $u, v \in \mathcal{R}^n$, if $u > v$, then $u P^n v$.

A possible objection to either of the above Pareto requirements is that, even if each person's well-being increases, inequality of well-being also may increase and the increase in inequality may count against the increases in well-being.

Pareto weak preference requires that, if each person is no worse off in one utility vector than in another, the first must be ranked as no worse than the second. Therefore, it permits an increase in inequality to weigh against the gains in well-being but only to the extent of allowing the change to be ranked as equally good. Because Pareto weak preference is a consequence of minimal individual goodness, we believe acceptable social-evaluation orderings should satisfy it.

Pareto Weak Preference. For all $u, v \in \mathcal{R}^n$, if $u > v$, then $u R^n v$.

As is straightforward to verify, any social-evaluation ordering that satisfies strong Pareto satisfies both weak Pareto and Pareto weak preference.

Minimal increasingness is a very weak form of the requirement that unanimity be respected. It applies only to utility vectors in which all utilities are equal and demands increases in the common level to be ranked as better. Because it is implied by weak (and, therefore, strong) Pareto, it is needed only if neither of those two axioms is used.

Minimal Increasingness. For all $a, b \in \mathcal{R}$, if $a > b$, then $a\mathbf{1}_n P^n b\mathbf{1}_n$.

Continuity is a condition of a different nature. It is a regularity condition ensuring that "small" changes in individual utilities do not lead to "large" changes in the social ranking. This can be expressed by requiring the sets of utility vectors that are at least (at most) as good as a given vector u to be closed in $\mathcal{R}^n$ for any choice of u. An equivalent formulation requires that the sets of utility vectors that are better (worse) than u are open in $\mathcal{R}^n$. As a consequence, if utility vector v is better than utility vector u and u, in turn, is better than utility vector w, then any continuous path from v to w must contain at least one utility vector that is as good as u.

Continuity. For all $u \in \mathcal{R}^n$, the sets $\{v \in \mathcal{R}^n \mid v R^n u\}$ and $\{v \in \mathcal{R}^n \mid u R^n v\}$ are closed in $\mathcal{R}^n$.

A continuous social-evaluation ordering that satisfies weak Pareto also satisfies Pareto weak preference. By way of contradiction, suppose R^n satisfied weak Pareto and continuity but violates Pareto weak preference. Then there exist $u, v \in \mathcal{R}^n$ such that $u > v$ and $v P^n u$. Because R^n is continuous, the worse-than set corresponding to v is open and, therefore, there exists a neighborhood of u such that $v P^n w$ for all w in this neighborhood. Because this neighborhood contains points w such that $w \gg u$ and thus $w \gg v$, this contradicts weak Pareto.

To motivate some equity conditions, we introduce some concepts from the theory of inequality measurement. Although much of the literature on economic inequality focuses on income inequality, most of the definitions translate readily into our framework where utility vectors rather than income distributions are to be compared. The Lorenz (1905) quasi-ordering provides a partial ranking of utility vectors with a common total or average utility. Its definition uses illfare-ranked permutations of utility vectors: for $u \in \mathcal{R}^n$, $(u_{[1]}, \ldots, u_{[n]})$ is a permutation of u such that $u_{[i]} \leq u_{[i+1]}$ for all $i \in \{1, \ldots, n-1\}$. For $u, v \in \mathcal{R}^n$ with $\sum_{i=1}^{n} u_i = \sum_{i=1}^{n} v_i$, u is unambiguously at least as equal as v if and only if

$$\sum_{i=1}^{k} u_{[i]} \geq \sum_{i=1}^{k} v_{[i]} \qquad (4.1)$$

for all $k \in \{1, \ldots, n-1\}$. (4.1) means the sum of the utilities of the k worst-off people is no smaller in u than in v. It follows that u is unambiguously more equal than v if and only if one of the inequalities in (4.1) is strict.

The Lorenz quasi-ordering is equivalent to the quasi-ordering produced by the principle of transfers (Hardy, Littlewood, and Pólya 1934). The Pigou-Dalton (Pigou 1912, Dalton 1920) transfer principle requires that if utility is transferred from a better-off individual to a worse-off person without reversing their relative ranks, the resulting distribution is more equal. The quasi-ordering based on this principle declares vector u to be unambiguously at least as equal as vector v if and only if u is a permutation of v or u can be obtained from v by a finite sequence of Pigou-Dalton transfers.

If u is unambiguously at least as equal as v according to the Lorenz quasi-ordering, there exists an $n \times n$ bistochastic matrix B such that $u = Bv$. A bistochastic matrix has nonnegative elements and rows and columns that sum to one. If u is unambiguously more equal than v, then Bv is not a permutation of v. Each bistochastic matrix can be written as a convex combination of the permutation matrices. See Marshall and Olkin (1979) for an extensive discussion of bistochastic matrices and their properties.

A social-evaluation ordering is inequality averse if it agrees, weakly or strictly, with the Lorenz quasi-ordering on each subset of $\mathcal{R}^n$ with constant total utility.

Weak Inequality Aversion. For all $u \in \mathcal{R}^n$ and for all $n \times n$ bistochastic matrices B, $Bu R^n u$.

Strict Inequality Aversion. For all $u \in \mathcal{R}^n$ and for all $n \times n$ bistochastic matrices B, $Bu R^n u$ and, if Bu is not a permutation of u, $Bu P^n u$.

Because anonymity of R^n is implied by the definition of weak inequality aversion, only anonymous social-evaluation orderings can be inequality averse. If a social-evaluation function represents the ordering R^n, it must be symmetric, and it is said to be weakly inequality averse or S-concave if R^n is weakly inequality averse and strictly inequality averse or strictly S-concave if R^n is strictly inequality averse. For a detailed discussion of S-concavity (Schur-concavity), see Marshall and Olkin (1979).

Finally, we introduce an equity axiom that prevents the social ordering from exhibiting a strong version of preference for inequality. Suppose the only difference between two utility vectors u and v is that individual j is better off in both vectors than individual i, j's utility is lower in u than in v and i is better off in u than in v. Minimal equity requires that there is at least one instance of such a configuration where u is at least as good as v. Note that, unlike the inequality-aversion axioms introduced earlier, the scope of this axiom is not limited to situations in which total utility is the same in u and in v.

Minimal Equity. There exist $u, v \in \mathcal{R}^n$ and $i, j \in \{1, \ldots, n\}$ such that $u_k = v_k$ for all $k \in \{1, \ldots, n\} \setminus \{i, j\}$, $v_j > u_j > u_i > v_i$, and $u R^n v$.

See d'Aspremont (1985), d'Aspremont and Gevers (1977), Deschamps and Gevers (1978), and Hammond (1976) for this and related equity conditions.

Continuity, Pareto weak preference, and minimal increasingness together ensure the existence of a particular continuous representation of the social-evaluation ordering R^n. This representation is analogous to the equally distributed equivalent income that is familiar from the literature on income inequality measurement; see, for example, Atkinson (1970); Blackorby, Bossert, and Donaldson (1999e, 2002b); Dalton (1920); Kolm (1969); and Sen (1973). It can be used to construct ethical indexes of inequality of well-being. For any $u \in \mathcal{R}^n$, representative utility is the level of utility ξ that, if assigned to each individual, produces a vector that is as good as u. Thus, $\xi \mathbf{1}_n I^n u$. If the representative utility exists for every utility vector and is unique, it can be written as function Ξ^n. Ξ^n is a representation of R^n with an intuitive interpretation. It associates each utility vector with a utility value that, if experienced by everyone, leads to a vector that is equally good. Geometrically, for each utility vector u, we find the vector on the ray of equality that is equally good (the existence and uniqueness of this vector is ensured by our axioms; see the proof of the following theorem) and assign the value of its (equal) components as u's value according to the representation. The representation result and some important properties of the representative utility function are summarized in the following theorem.

Theorem 4.1. *If R^n satisfies continuity, Pareto weak preference, and minimal increasingness, then there exists a continuous function $\Xi^n \colon \mathcal{R}^n \to \mathcal{R}$, increasing along the ray of equality, such that:*

    (i) $\Xi^n(u) \in [\min\{u_1, \ldots, u_n\}, \max\{u_1, \ldots, u_n\}]$ for all $u \in \mathcal{R}^n$;
    (ii) $\Xi^n(u)\mathbf{1}_n I^n u$ for all $u \in \mathcal{R}^n$;
    (iii) $\Xi^n(\xi\mathbf{1}_n) = \xi$ for all $\xi \in \mathcal{R}$;
    (iv) $u R^n v \Leftrightarrow \Xi^n(u) \geq \Xi^n(v)$ for all $u, v \in \mathcal{R}^n$.

Proof. First, note that, for any $u \in \mathcal{R}^n$, we have $a\mathbf{1}_n R^n u$ for all $a \geq \max\{u_1, \ldots, u_n\}$ and $u R^n b\mathbf{1}_n$ for all $b \leq \min\{u_1, \ldots, u_n\}$. This follows from reflexivity (if $u = a\mathbf{1}_n$ or $u = b\mathbf{1}_n$) and from Pareto weak preference (if $a\mathbf{1}_n > u$ or $u > b\mathbf{1}_n$). Because R^n is continuous, there exists $\xi \in [\min \{u_1, \ldots, u_n\}, \max\{u_1, \ldots, u_n\}]$ such that $\xi\mathbf{1}_n I^n u$. By minimal increasingness, ξ is unique. Define the function Ξ^n so that

$$\Xi^n(u) = \xi \Leftrightarrow u I^n \xi\mathbf{1}_n,$$

and (i), (ii), and (iii) are satisfied.

To demonstrate continuity of Ξ^n, for any $u \in \mathcal{R}^n$, let $\xi = \Xi^n(u)$ and consider a sequence $(v_j)_{j \in \mathcal{Z}_{++}}$ such that $\lim_{j \to \infty} v_j = u$. Let $\zeta_j = \Xi^n(v_j)$ for all $j \in \mathcal{Z}_{++}$. Because continuity of R^n implies that the iso-value set for v_j approaches the iso-value set for u as j approaches infinity, $\lim_{j \to \infty} \zeta_j = \xi$ and Ξ^n is continuous.

For any $u, v \in \mathcal{R}^n$, let $\xi = \Xi^n(u)$ and $\zeta = \Xi^n(v)$. By the definition of Ξ^n and minimal increasingness,

$$u R^n v \Leftrightarrow \xi\mathbf{1}_n R^n \zeta\mathbf{1}_n \Leftrightarrow \xi \geq \zeta,$$

and (iv) is established. That Ξ^n is increasing on the ray of equality follows immediately from minimal increasingness and (iv). ∎

The function Ξ^n is the representative-utility function corresponding to R^n and, by part (iv) of Theorem 4.1, it is a representation of R^n. Consequently, all social-evaluation functions that represent R^n are increasing transformations of Ξ^n.

In the statement of Theorem 4.1, Pareto weak preference and minimal increasingness can be replaced by weak or strong Pareto. The same proof works and the representative-utility function has stronger properties than increasingness on the ray of equality. In particular, weak Pareto implies that Ξ^n is weakly increasing and strong Pareto implies that Ξ^n is increasing and that $\Xi^n(u)$ is in the open interval $(\min\{u_1, \ldots, u_n\}, \max\{u_1, \ldots, u_n\})$ for all $u \in \mathcal{R}^n$ that are not equal distributions. See also Wold (1943a, 1943b).

4.7 FIXED-POPULATION SOCIAL-EVALUATION ORDERINGS

In this section, we present some examples of welfarist social-evaluation orderings and their representative-utility functions.

The social-evaluation orderings that play the most prominent role in this book belong to the class of generalized utilitarian orderings. Those orderings make social comparisons using the sum of transformed utilities. A social-evaluation ordering R^n is generalized utilitarian if and only if there exists a continuous and increasing function $g^n: \mathcal{R} \to \mathcal{R}$ with $g^n(0) = 0$ such that, for all $u, v \in \mathcal{R}^n$,

$$u R^n v \Leftrightarrow \sum_{i=1}^{n} g^n(u_i) \geq \sum_{i=1}^{n} g^n(v_i).$$

$g^n(u_i)$ is the transformed value of u_i. The normalization $g^n(0) = 0$ is used for mathematical convenience and involves no loss of generality. If transformation $\bar{g}^n$ does not satisfy it, it can be replaced with transformation g^n, where $g^n(u) = \bar{g}^n(u) - \bar{g}^n(0)$, without affecting the social-evaluation ordering. All generalized utilitarian social-evaluation orderings satisfy continuity, same-people anonymity, and strong (and thus weak) Pareto. If the transformation applied to individual utilities is concave, the resulting ordering is weakly inequality averse, and, if the transformation is strictly concave, the ordering is strictly inequality averse (Berge 1963). If g^n is concave, minimal equity is satisfied as well. The representative-utility function for generalized utilitarianism is given by

$$\Xi^n(u) = (g^n)^{-1} \left(\frac{1}{n} \sum_{i=1}^{n} g^n(u_i) \right)$$

for all $u \in \mathcal{R}^n$.

Utilitarianism is a special case of generalized utilitarianism in which the continuous and increasing transformation g^n is the identity mapping. Thus, the utilitarian social-evaluation ordering uses the sum of the individual utilities to make social comparisons. According to utilitarianism, for all $u, v \in \mathcal{R}^n$,

$$u R^n v \Leftrightarrow \sum_{i=1}^{n} u_i \geq \sum_{i=1}^{n} v_i.$$

The representative-utility function for utilitarianism is average utility.

The class of social-evaluation orderings whose members respect all strict rankings of utility vectors according to utilitarianism is the class of weakly utilitarian orderings (Deschamps and Gevers 1978). R^n is weakly utilitarian if and only if, for all $u, v \in \mathcal{R}^n$,

$$\sum_{i=1}^{n} u_i > \sum_{i=1}^{n} v_i \Rightarrow u P^n v.$$

The class of weakly utilitarian orderings is of interest because some sets of axioms imply that the social betterness relation must respect the utilitarian betterness relation, but equal goodness according to utilitarianism does not imply equal goodness according to any social ordering satisfying the axioms; see Deschamps and Gevers (1978) for an example.

Utilitarianism is often criticized because it pays no attention to utility inequality. If the transformation is strictly concave, the corresponding generalized utilitarian principle does not suffer from this defect because it satisfies strict inequality aversion. We now turn to some important special cases of generalized utilitarianism.

A prominent example of a subclass of generalized utilitarian orderings is the class of symmetric global means of order r. R^n is a symmetric global mean of order r if and only if there exist $\beta, r \in \mathcal{R}_{++}$ such that, for all $u, v \in \mathcal{R}^n$,

$$
u R^n v \Leftrightarrow \sum_{\substack{i \in \{1,\ldots,n\}: \\ u_i \geq 0}} (u_i)^r - \beta \left(\sum_{\substack{i \in \{1,\ldots,n\}: \\ u_i < 0}} (-u_i)^r \right)
$$
$$
\geq \sum_{\substack{i \in \{1,\ldots,n\}: \\ v_i \geq 0}} (v_i)^r - \beta \left(\sum_{\substack{i \in \{1,\ldots,n\}: \\ v_i < 0}} (-v_i)^r \right). \tag{4.2}
$$

In this case, the transformation g^n is such that $g^n(\tau) = \tau^r$ for all $\tau \geq 0$ and $g^n(\tau) = -\beta(-\tau)^r$ for all $\tau < 0$. The special cases of (4.2) with $r = 1$ and $\beta \geq 1$ are of particular interest. They represent the only cases that exhibit weak inequality aversion on the entire utility space $\mathcal{R}^n$ (Blackorby and Donaldson 1982). If $\beta > 1$, the resulting orderings are modifications of utilitarianism such that negative utilities get a higher weight than positive utilities (see the lower panel of Figure 4.6).

On restricted utility domains, additional means of order r are available. For any $\kappa \in \mathcal{R}$, the set $\mathcal{R}^n_{\kappa++} = \{u \in \mathcal{R}^n \mid u \gg \kappa \mathbf{1}_n\}$ is the set of utility vectors whose components are greater than κ. R^n is a κ-translated mean of order r if and only if there exists $r \in \mathcal{R}$ such that, for all $u, v \in \mathcal{R}^n_{\kappa++}$,

$$
u R^n v \Leftrightarrow \left(\sum_{i=1}^n (u_i - \kappa)^r \right)^{1/r} \geq \left(\sum_{i=1}^n (v_i - \kappa)^r \right)^{1/r}
$$

if $r \neq 0$, and

$$
u R^n v \Leftrightarrow \sum_{i=1}^n \ln(u_i - \kappa) \geq \sum_{i=1}^n \ln(v_i - \kappa)
$$

if $r = 0$. Representative utilities are given by

$$
\Xi^n(u) = \begin{cases} \left(\frac{1}{n} \sum_{i=1}^n (u_i - \kappa)^r \right)^{1/r} + \kappa & \text{if } r \neq 0, \\ \prod_{i=1}^n (u_i - \kappa)^{1/n} + \kappa & \text{if } r = 0 \end{cases} \tag{4.3}
$$

for all $u \in \mathcal{R}^n_{\kappa++}$. A κ-translated mean of order r is weakly inequality averse if and only if $r \leq 1$ and it is strictly inequality averse if and only if $r < 1$.

To use a κ-translated mean of order r, the domain must be such that all utility levels are greater than κ. Because of this, κ must be a numerically significant and interpersonally fully comparable utility level. We have normalized neutrality to zero, so cardinal measurability and one additional norm are sufficient for numerical full comparability. Because we cannot reasonably expect all lifetime-utility levels to be positive, κ must be negative.

The class of Kolm-Pollak orderings (Kolm 1969, Pollak 1971) is another example of a subclass of generalized utilitarian orderings. R^n is a Kolm-Pollak ordering if and only if R^n is utilitarian or there exists $\gamma \in \mathcal{R}_{++}$ such that, for all $u, v \in \mathcal{R}^n$,

$$u R^n v \Leftrightarrow -\sum_{i=1}^{n} \exp(-\gamma u_i) \geq -\sum_{i=1}^{n} \exp(-\gamma v_i).$$

Utilitarianism is the limiting case when γ approaches zero. Therefore, the utilitarian social-evaluation ordering can be defined as the Kolm-Pollak ordering with a parameter value of $\gamma = 0$. As γ approaches infinity, the maximin ordering (defined below) is approximated. The representative-utility functions for the Kolm-Pollak orderings are given by

$$\Xi^n(u) = -\frac{1}{\gamma} \ln \left(\frac{1}{n} \sum_{i=1}^{n} \exp(-\gamma u_i) \right)$$

for all $u \in \mathcal{R}^n$.

Within the class of weakly inequality-averse orderings satisfying the weak Pareto principle, the utilitarian social-evaluation ordering is the only one that pays no attention to utility inequality. At the opposite extreme within that class are the maximin and leximin orderings: both exhibit complete inequality aversion. Neither ordering is generalized utilitarian but both can be approximated arbitrarily closely by a generalized utilitarian ordering.[10] For $u \in \mathcal{R}^n$, let $(u_{(1)}, \ldots, u_{(n)})$ be a permutation of u such that $u_{(i)} \geq u_{(i+1)}$ for all $i \in \{1, \ldots, n-1\}$. The maximin ordering is defined as follows. For all $u, v \in \mathcal{R}^n$,

$$u R^n v \Leftrightarrow u_{(n)} \geq v_{(n)}.$$

Leximin is a modified version of maximin in which utility vector u is better than utility vector v if the worst-off individual in u is better off than the worst-off individual in v. If those individuals are equally well off, the utilities of the next-worse-off individuals are used to determine the social ranking, and the procedure continues until either there is a strict ranking or the two utility vectors are permutations of each other, in which case they are declared equally good. Thus, the better-than relation corresponding to leximin respects the better-than relation of maximin. If the utilities of the worst-off individuals are the same in two utility vectors, however, the two differ. Whereas maximin declares the two vectors to be equally good in this case, leximin continues by comparing the next-to-worst-off individuals and so on. The leximin ordering is given by

$$u R^n v \Leftrightarrow u \text{ is a permutation of } v \text{ or there exists } j \in \{1, \ldots, n\}$$
$$\text{such that } u_{(i)} = v_{(i)} \text{ for all } i > j \text{ and } u_{(j)} > v_{(j)}$$

for all $u, v \in \mathcal{R}^n$. Maximin is continuous and satisfies Pareto weak preference as well as weak Pareto but not strong Pareto. Leximin is not continuous and

---

[10] See Donaldson and Roemer (1987) for a characterization of maximin in economic environments.

satisfies strong Pareto. Maximin is weakly inequality averse but not strictly so and leximin is strictly inequality averse. Both orderings satisfy minimal equity.

The extremely equality-averse counterpart of leximin is the leximax ordering. It begins by comparing the utilities of the best-off individuals and, in case of equality, moves on to the second-best-off individuals, and so on. Thus, the order in which the utilities are considered is reversed compared with leximin. R^n is the leximax ordering if and only if, for all $u, v \in \mathcal{R}^n$,

$$u R^n v \Leftrightarrow u \text{ is a permutation of } v \text{ or there exists } j \in \{1, \dots, n\}$$
$$\text{such that } u_{(i)} = v_{(i)} \text{ for all } i < j \text{ and } u_{(j)} > v_{(j)}.$$

Leximax is not continuous, satisfies strong Pareto, and does not satisfy minimal equity. Neither leximin nor leximax is generalized utilitarian because these orderings are not representable and, thus, a function g^n as in the definition of generalized utilitarianism does not exist.

The generalized Gini social-evaluation orderings (Mehran 1976, Weymark 1981) use weighted sums of utilities to rank alternatives.[11] The weights depend on the rank orders of the individuals rather than their identities and, thus, the generalized Ginis are anonymous. Recall that $(u_{(1)}, \dots, u_{(n)})$ denotes a rank-ordered permutation of $u \in \mathcal{R}^n$ such that $u_{(i)} \geq u_{(i+1)}$ for all $i \in \{1, \dots, n-1\}$. R^n is a generalized Gini social-evaluation ordering if and only if there exist $a_1^n, \dots, a_n^n \in \mathcal{R}_{++}^n$ such that, for all $u, v \in \mathcal{R}^n$,

$$u R^n v \Leftrightarrow \sum_{i=1}^n a_i^n u_{(i)} \geq \sum_{i=1}^n a_i^n v_{(i)}.$$

All the generalized-Gini orderings are continuous and satisfy strong Pareto. A generalized-Gini ordering is weakly inequality averse if and only if $a_i^n \leq a_{i+1}^n$ for all $i \in \{1, \dots, n-1\}$ and strictly inequality averse if and only if $a_i^n < a_{i+1}^n$ for all $i \in \{1, \dots, n-1\}$. Thus, a weakly inequality-averse generalized Gini cannot assign a higher weight to a higher utility and a strictly inequality-averse generalized Gini assigns a higher weight to lower utilities. The restrictions of the iso-value sets to rank-ordered subspaces of $\mathcal{R}^n$ are hyperplanes.

Two subclasses of the generalized-Gini social-evaluation orderings (Donaldson and Weymark 1980) provide single-parameter control of the degree of inequality aversion. A social-evaluation ordering R^n is a single-parameter Gini (S-Gini) ordering if and only if there exists a real number $\delta \geq 1$ such that, for all $u, v \in \mathcal{R}^n$,

$$u R^n v \Leftrightarrow \sum_{i=1}^n \left[i^\delta - (i-1)^\delta \right] u_{(i)} \geq \sum_{i=1}^n \left[i^\delta - (i-1)^\delta \right] v_{(i)}.$$

For $\delta = 1$, we obtain utilitarianism and, as δ approaches infinity, maximin and leximin are approximated. The case $\delta = 2$ yields the Gini social-evaluation ordering, which corresponds to the Gini index of inequality (Blackorby and

---

[11] These orderings are also investigated by Bossert (1990a) and in Donaldson and Weymark (1980).

Donaldson 1978). In that case, weights are proportional to the first n positive odd numbers and, for all $u, v \in \mathcal{R}^n$,

$$u R^n v \Leftrightarrow \sum_{i=1}^n [2i - 1] u_{(i)} \geq \sum_{i=1}^n [2i - 1] v_{(i)}.$$

All single-parameter Ginis satisfy continuity, strong Pareto, weak inequality aversion, and minimal equity. Inequality aversion is strict if $\delta > 1$. Representative utilities are given by

$$\Xi^n(u) = \frac{1}{n^\delta} \left[\sum_{i=1}^n \left[i^\delta - (i - 1)^\delta \right] u_{(i)} \right] \tag{4.4}$$

for all $u \in \mathcal{R}^n$.

The illfare-ranked single-parameter Gini orderings rank alternatives using a weighted sum of illfare-ranked utilities. Letting $(u_{[1]}, \ldots, u_{[n]})$ denote an illfare-ranked permutation of $u \in \mathcal{R}^n$ – that is, $u_{[i]} \leq u_{[i+1]}$ for all $i \in \{1, \ldots, n - 1\}$, R^n is an illfare-ranked single-parameter Gini ordering if and only if there exists $\delta \in (0, 1]$ such that, for all $u, v \in \mathcal{R}^n$,

$$u R^n v \Leftrightarrow \sum_{i=1}^n \left[i^\delta - (i - 1)^\delta \right] u_{[i]} \geq \sum_{i=1}^n \left[i^\delta - (i - 1)^\delta \right] v_{[i]}.$$

The utilitarian ordering is given by $\delta = 1$ and, as δ approaches zero, maximin and leximin are approximated. The class of illfare-ranked single-parameter Ginis does not coincide with the class of single-parameter Ginis. For example, the Gini is a single-parameter Gini (it is obtained for $\delta = 2$) but it is not an illfare-ranked single-parameter Gini. All illfare-ranked single-parameter Ginis satisfy continuity, strong Pareto, weak inequality aversion, and minimal equity. Strict inequality aversion is satisfied for all $\delta \in (0, 1)$.

The only member of the class of generalized-Gini orderings that also belongs to the generalized utilitarian class is utilitarianism, which is obtained when $a_i^n = a_j^n$ for all $i, j \in \{1, \ldots, n\}$. None of the other generalized Ginis, including the single-parameter Ginis with $\delta \neq 1$, has the additive structure of generalized utilitarianism. However, all generalized Ginis possess a weaker additivity property: they are additive in rank-ordered subspaces of $\mathcal{R}^n$.

Finally, we introduce the strongly dictatorial social-evaluation orderings. These orderings pay attention to the utility of a single individual only. That is, R^n is strongly dictatorial if and only if there exists an individual $k \in \{1, \ldots, n\}$ such that, for all $u, v \in \mathcal{R}^n$,

$$u R^n v \Leftrightarrow u_k \geq v_k.$$

The strongly dictatorial social-evaluation orderings satisfy continuity, weak Pareto, and minimal equity. Strong Pareto and same-number anonymity are violated.

4.8 ETHICAL INDEXES OF INEQUALITY OF WELL-BEING

If representative-utility functions exist, strictly inequality-averse social-evaluation orderings can be used to construct ethical indexes of inequality. An inequality index is a function $Q^n: \mathcal{R}^n \rightarrow \mathcal{R}_+$, which is equal to zero for all utility vectors on the ray of equality and, in addition, on each hyperplane of constant total utility, it must be consistent with the Lorenz quasi-ordering. These two properties imply that the inequality measure has a positive value for all utility vectors that are not equal distributions. Thus, $Q^n(Bu) \leq Q^n(u)$ for all $u \in \mathcal{R}^n$ and for all $n \times n$ bistochastic matrices B with a strict inequality whenever Bu is not a permutation of u. This property is called strict S-convexity; see Marshall and Olkin (1979).

Most, but not all, indexes of income inequality are relative: they are invariant with respect to equal proportional changes in all incomes – that is, they are homogeneous of degree zero. This invariance property is sometimes replaced by translation invariance (invariance with respect to equal absolute changes in all incomes), and the resulting indexes are called absolute. A generalization of the notion of a relative index, which also approximates absolute invariance as a limiting case requires invariance with respect to a convex combination of relative and absolute changes. The same distinction applies to indexes of utility inequality, and we discuss ethical inequality indexes motivated by all these invariance conditions.

The best known ethical inequality index is the AKS index (Atkinson 1970, Kolm 1969, Sen 1973). It is defined only for utility vectors such that total or average utility is not equal to zero. Writing average utility for utility vector $u \in \mathcal{R}^n$ as $\mu^n(u) = (1/n)\sum_{i=1}^{n} u_i$, the AKS index that corresponds to the strictly inequality-averse ordering R^n is given by

$$Q^n_{AKS}(u) = \frac{\mu^n(u) - \Xi^n(u)}{|\mu^n(u)|}. \tag{4.5}$$

It is equal to the percentage shortfall of representative utility from average utility. Because R^n is strictly inequality averse, Q^n_{AKS} is strictly S-convex. Moreover, representative utility is equal to average utility when utilities are equally distributed and the index has a value of zero at equality. Thus, the AKS index satisfies the appropriate properties for an inequality index. That the index is positive for all unequal distributions is an immediate consequence of strict S-convexity and the zero-at-equality property: for any unequal distribution, representative utility is less than average utility, because R^n is strictly inequality averse and the positivity of the inequality index follows immediately from the definition of Q^n_{AKS}. The absolute value in the denominator is necessary to produce a positive value for unequal utility vectors with negative means.

Conversely, if an inequality index is interpreted as an AKS index, the corresponding representative-utility function and social-evaluation ordering can be found. Using (4.5), representative utility is given by

$$\Xi^n(u) = \begin{cases} \mu^n(u)\big[1 - Q^n_{AKS}(u)\big] & \text{if } \mu^n(u) > 0, \\ \mu^n(u)\big[1 + Q^n_{AKS}(u)\big] & \text{if } \mu^n(u) < 0. \end{cases} \tag{4.6}$$

Without further assumptions, an AKS index need not be a relative index. Because the motivation underlying the index is based on a relative notion – the percentage shortfall of representative utility from average utility – it is of interest to identify the circumstances under which the index belongs to the class of relative inequality measures. A social-evaluation ordering is homothetic if and only if the ranking of any two vectors is the same as the ranking of the two vectors that are obtained by multiplying both of them by the same positive number.

Homotheticity. For all $u, v \in \mathcal{R}^n$ and for all $\lambda \in \mathcal{R}_{++}$,

$$u R^n v \Leftrightarrow \lambda u R^n \lambda v.$$

If R^n is homothetic, writing $\xi = \Xi^n(u)$, it follows that $u I^n \xi \mathbf{1}_n$ and $\lambda u I^n \lambda \xi \mathbf{1}_n$, which implies $\Xi^n(\lambda u) = \lambda \Xi^n(u)$, and the representative-utility function is homogeneous of degree one. The AKS index is a relative index, depending on individual shares of total utility only, if and only if it is homogeneous of degree zero. In that case, because μ^n is homogeneous of degree one, Ξ^n also must be homogeneous of degree one. Consequently, an AKS index is a relative index if and only if R^n is homothetic. Although relative indexes are commonly used in the measurement of income inequality, the property is not of obvious interest in the measurement of inequality of well-being. Moreover, even in the case of income inequality, alternative invariance properties can be considered appropriate; see, for example, Kolm (1976a, 1976b).

As an example of an ethical inequality index, consider the well-known Gini index. Because the Gini social-evaluation ordering is homothetic, the corresponding AKS index is relative. The Gini representative utility is

$$\Xi^n(u) = \frac{1}{n^2} \sum_{i=1}^{n} (2i - 1) u_{(i)}$$

and the Gini relative index (the standard Gini coefficient) is given by

$$Q^n(u) = \frac{n^2 \mu^n(u) - \sum_{i=1}^{n}(2i - 1)u_{(i)}}{n^2 |\mu^n(u)|}.$$

If (4.4) is used in conjunction with (4.5), the S-Gini family of inequality indexes results. Because the S-Gini orderings are homothetic, all these indexes are relative.

A second index of utility inequality is the Kolm index (Kolm 1969). It measures inequality as the shortfall of representative utility from average utility and, thus, is based on an absolute notion. The Kolm index, which corresponds to the strictly inequality-averse social-evaluation ordering R^n is given by

$$Q_K^n(u) = \mu^n(u) - \Xi^n(u) \tag{4.7}$$

for all $u \in \mathcal{R}^n$. As is the case for the AKS index, the Kolm index satisfies all the requisite properties for an inequality index.

If an inequality index is interpreted as a Kolm index, (4.7) can be used to find the corresponding representative-utility function and the social-evaluation ordering. Solving, representative utility is given by

$$\Xi^n(u) = \mu^n(u) - Q_K^n(u) \tag{4.8}$$

for all $u \in \mathcal{R}^n$.

The main difference between the AKS index and the Kolm index is that the former is based on a relative notion of the shortfall of representative utility from average utility, whereas the latter uses the absolute shortfall. For that reason, the Kolm index is associated with an absolute rather than a relative concept of inequality. Absolute ethical indexes are linked to social-evaluation orderings with a translatability property. This link is analogous to that between relative indexes and homotheticity. A social-evaluation ordering is translatable if and only if any two vectors are ranked in the same way as the two vectors that are obtained by adding the same positive constant to all components of both.

Translatability. For all $u, v \in \mathcal{R}^n$ and for all $\delta \in \mathcal{R}_{++}$,

$$u R^n v \Leftrightarrow (u + \delta \mathbf{1}_n) R^n (v + \delta \mathbf{1}_n).$$

If R^n is translatable, the representative-utility function is unit translatable, satisfying the equality $\Xi^n(u + \delta \mathbf{1}_n) = \Xi^n(u) + \delta$. The Kolm index is an absolute index, depending on utility differences only, if and only if it is translation invariant, with $Q_K^n(u + \delta \mathbf{1}_n) = Q_K^n(u)$ for all $u \subset \mathcal{R}^n$ and for all $\delta \subset \mathcal{R}_{++}$. Because μ^n is unit translatable, Q_K^n is an absolute index if and only if R^n is translatable. Again, it is not obvious that indexes of utility inequality should be absolute; relative indexes, among others, constitute a possible alternative.

Because the S-Gini social-evaluation orderings are translatable, the corresponding Kolm indexes are absolute. They are given by

$$Q^n(u) = \mu^n(u) - \frac{1}{n^\delta} \sum_{i=1}^n \left[i^\delta - (i-1)^\delta \right] u_{(i)}$$

for all $u \in \mathcal{R}^n$. All the generalized Gini orderings are both homothetic and translatable. This property, together with others imposed on sequences of social-evaluation orderings, can be used to characterize the (illfare-ranked) S-Ginis; see Section 4.11.

There is another general ethical inequality index – namely, the Bossert and Pfingsten (1990) index.[12] It is best suited to the creation of intermediate indexes, which can be thought of as occupying the space between relative and absolute indexes. The Bossert-Pfingsten (BP) index for parameter value $\kappa \in \mathcal{R}_-$ is defined for all $u \in \mathcal{R}^n$ such that $\mu^n(u) \neq \kappa$ and is given by

$$Q_\kappa^n(u) = (1 - \kappa)\frac{\mu^n(u) - \Xi^n(u)}{|\mu^n(u) - \kappa|} \tag{4.9}$$

for all $u \in \mathcal{R}^n$. The BP index for $\kappa = 0$ is the AKS index and the Kolm index is the limit of the BP index as κ approaches minus infinity.

If an inequality index is interpreted as a BP index, the corresponding representative-utility function and social-evaluation ordering can be found. Using (4.9), representative utility is given by

$$\Xi^n(u) = \begin{cases} \dfrac{\mu^n(u)[1 - \kappa] - Q_{BP}^n(\mu^n(u) - \kappa)}{1 - \kappa} & \text{if } \mu^n(u) > \kappa, \\[2mm] \dfrac{\mu^n(u)[1 - \kappa] + Q_{BP}^n(\mu^n(u) - \kappa)}{1 - \kappa} & \text{if } \mu^n(u) < \kappa. \end{cases} \tag{4.10}$$

An inequality index is κ-intermediate for $\kappa \in \mathcal{R}_-$ if and only if

$$Q^n\big(\lambda(u - \kappa\mathbf{1}_n) + \kappa\mathbf{1}_n\big) = Q^n(u)$$

for all $u \in \mathcal{R}^n$ and for all $\lambda \in \mathcal{R}_{++}$. Intermediate indexes are constant along rays through $\kappa\mathbf{1}_n$. Thus, geometrically, the point $\kappa\mathbf{1}_n$ acts as a reference point and, as is the case for relative and absolute indexes, iso-inequality sets are invariant along rays passing through the reference point $\kappa\mathbf{1}_n$ and the relative and absolute indexes are obtained as limiting cases for $\kappa = 0$ and as κ approaches $-\infty$. Thus, intermediate inequality can be thought of as a natural compromise between the relative and absolute views.

A social-evaluation ordering R^n is κ-translated homothetic if and only if, for all $u, v \in \mathcal{R}^n$ and for all $\lambda \in \mathcal{R}_{++}$,

$$uR^nv \Leftrightarrow \big[\lambda(u - \kappa\mathbf{1}_n) + \kappa\mathbf{1}_n\big]R^n\big[\lambda(v - \kappa\mathbf{1}_n) + \kappa\mathbf{1}_n\big]. \tag{4.11}$$

This property is a natural generalization of homotheticity and translatability, which are obtained for $\kappa = 0$ and in the limit as κ approaches minus infinity.

Ξ^n is κ-translated homogeneous of degree one if and only if, for all $u \in \mathcal{R}^n$ and for all $\lambda \in \mathcal{R}_{++}$,

$$\Xi^n(\lambda(u - \kappa\mathbf{1}_n) + \kappa\mathbf{1}_n) = \lambda(\Xi^n(u) - \kappa) + \kappa. \tag{4.12}$$

This condition on Ξ^n is equivalent to κ-translated homotheticity of R^n. We provide a formal proof of this observation. Note again the analogy to the

---

[12] Kolm (1976a, 1976b) proposed a similar index that he calls centrist.

equivalence of homotheticity (translatability) of R^n and homogeneity of degree one (unit translatability) of Ξ^n.

Theorem 4.2. R^n *is κ-translated homothetic if and only if Ξ^n is κ-translated homogenous of degree one.*

Proof. First, suppose R^n is κ-translated homothetic. For $u \in \mathcal{R}^n$, let $\xi = \Xi^n(u)$. Because $u I^n \xi \mathbf{1}_n$,

$$\big[\lambda(u - \kappa \mathbf{1}_n) + \kappa \mathbf{1}_n\big] I^n \big[\lambda(\xi \mathbf{1}_n - \kappa \mathbf{1}_n) + \kappa \mathbf{1}_n\big] = \big[\lambda(\xi - \kappa) + \kappa\big]\mathbf{1}_n,$$

which implies (4.12).

Now suppose Ξ^n is κ-translated homogeneous of degree one. Then, for all $u, v \in \mathcal{R}^n$ and for all $\lambda \in \mathcal{R}_{++}$,

$$\big[\lambda(u - \kappa \mathbf{1}_n) + \kappa \mathbf{1}_n\big] R^n \big[\lambda(v - \kappa \mathbf{1}_n) + \kappa \mathbf{1}_n\big]$$
$$\Leftrightarrow \Xi^n\big(\lambda(u - \kappa \mathbf{1}_n) + \kappa \mathbf{1}_n\big) \geq \Xi^n\big(\lambda(v - \kappa \mathbf{1}_n) + \kappa \mathbf{1}_n\big)$$
$$\Leftrightarrow \lambda\big[\Xi^n(u) - \kappa\big] + \kappa \geq \lambda\big[\Xi^n(v) - \kappa\big] + \kappa$$
$$\Leftrightarrow \Xi^n(u) \geq \Xi^n(v)$$
$$\Leftrightarrow u R^n v$$

and (4.11) is satisfied. ∎

Next, we show that a BP index is κ-intermediate if and only if the social-evaluation R^n is κ-translated homothetic.

Theorem 4.3. Q^n_{BP} *is a κ-intermediate inequality index if and only if R^n is κ-translated homothetic.*

Proof. First, suppose Q^n_{BP} is a κ-intermediate inequality index. Then, for all $u \in \mathcal{R}^n$ and for all $\lambda \in \mathcal{R}_{++}$, $Q^n_{BP}(\lambda(u - \kappa \mathbf{1}_n) + \kappa \mathbf{1}_n) = Q^n_{BP}(u)$. Because μ^n is κ-translated homogeneous of degree one,

$$(1 - \kappa)\frac{\lambda(\mu^n(u) - \kappa) + \kappa - \Xi^n\big(\lambda(u - \kappa \mathbf{1}_n) + \kappa \mathbf{1}_n\big)}{|\lambda(\mu^n(u) - \kappa)|}$$
$$= (1 - \kappa)\frac{(\mu^n(u) - \kappa) - (\Xi^n(u) - \kappa)}{|\mu^n(u) - \kappa|},$$

which implies

$$\Xi^n\big(\lambda(u - \kappa \mathbf{1}_n) + \kappa \mathbf{1}_n\big) = \lambda\big[\Xi^n(u) - \kappa\big] + \kappa.$$

Consequently, Ξ^n is κ-translated homogeneous of degree one and, by Theorem 4.2, R^n is κ-translated homothetic.

Now suppose R^n is κ-translated homothetic. By Theorem 4.2, Ξ^n is κ-translated homogeneous of degree one. It follows that

$$
\begin{aligned}
Q^n_{BP}&\left(\lambda(u - \kappa\mathbf{1}_n) + \kappa\mathbf{1}_n\right)\\
&= (1 - \kappa)\frac{\mu^n\left(\lambda(u - \kappa\mathbf{1}_n) + \kappa\mathbf{1}_n\right) - \Xi^n\left(\lambda(u - \kappa\mathbf{1}_n) + \kappa\mathbf{1}_n\right)}{|\mu^n\left(\lambda(u - \kappa\mathbf{1}_n) + \kappa\mathbf{1}_n\right) - \kappa|}\\
&= (1 - \kappa)\frac{\lambda\left[\mu^n(u) - \kappa\right] + \kappa - \lambda\left[\Xi^n(u) - \kappa\right] - \kappa}{|\lambda\left[\mu^n(u) - \kappa\right] + \kappa - \kappa|}\\
&= (1 - \kappa)\frac{\mu^n(u) - \Xi^n(u)}{|\mu^n(u) - \kappa|} = Q^n_{BP}(u)
\end{aligned}
$$

for all $u \in \mathcal{R}^n$ and for all $\lambda \in \mathcal{R}_{++}$. Consequently, Q^n_{BP} is κ-intermediate. ∎

All the generalized-Gini orderings are κ-translated homothetic. Because of that, representative-utility functions for the S-Gini orderings [given by (4.4)] can be used in conjunction with (4.9) to produce the S-Gini family of intermediate indexes. In addition, if κ is a negative number such that all utilities are above it, the representative-utility functions for the κ-translated means of order r [given by (4.3)] with $r < 1$ can be used to produce the corresponding intermediate indexes. In contrast to the S-Gini family, that family embodies level-based inequality aversion.

If an index of inequality is known, it can be interpreted as an AKS, Kolm, or BP index and used to derive the corresponding social-evaluation ordering using (4.6) (AKS), (4.8) (Kolm), or (4.10) (BP). Blackorby and Donaldson (1978) used (4.6) with the Gini index to derive the Gini social-evaluation ordering. (4.6), (4.8), and (4.10) all imply that representative utility is equal to average utility adjusted for inequality.

An alternative approach proceeds as follows (Blackorby and Donaldson 1984b, Ebert 1987). Suppose that, instead of starting with a social-evaluation ordering, we begin with an AUI quasi-ordering $\mathring{R}^n$. This quasi-ordering is interpreted as an explicit formulation of the trade-offs between average utility and utility inequality in social evaluation. Once an index of inequality Q^n is specified, the AUI quasi-ordering can be used to generate a social-evaluation quasi-ordering by defining, for all $u, v \in \mathcal{R}^n$,

$$
uR^nv \Leftrightarrow \left(\mu^n(u), Q^n(u)\right)\mathring{R}^n\left(\mu^n(v), Q^n(v)\right). \tag{4.13}
$$

(4.13) allows us to define social-evaluation criteria with an aggregation property: the social goodness depends on average utility and inequality only. We require $\mathring{R}^n$ to rank increases in average utility as better and increases in inequality as worse but that is not sufficient to ensure that weak Pareto or Pareto weak preference is satisfied (see the example in Part A). If the AUI quasi-ordering is complete, R^n, as defined in (4.13), is an ordering and the principle is welfarist.

Suppose an AUI ordering is used to find a social-evaluation ordering R^n and all representative-utility functions exist. Then AKS, Kolm, and BP indexes of inequality can be derived, and we may ask how the indexes are related. It is clear from (4.13) that on any hyperplane of constant total utility, the three indexes order utility vectors in the same way. In general, they may differ in the way they compare utility vectors with different means.

Suppose Q^n is an absolute index and $\overset{\circ}{R}{}^n$ is complete. In that case, we say that R^n satisfies the absolute-inequality aggregation property.[13] Relative indexes are included in a generalization of intermediate indexes that is discussed briefly after the following analysis of absolute indexes.

Absolute-Inequality Aggregation Property. There exists an absolute inequality index $Q^n : \mathcal{R}^n \to \mathcal{R}$ and an ordering $\overset{\circ}{R}{}^n$ on $Q^n = \{(\mu, q) \mid \exists u \in \mathcal{R}^n$ such that $\mu^n(u) = \mu$ and $Q^n(u) = q\}$ such that, for all $u, v \in \mathcal{R}^n$,

$$u R^n v \Leftrightarrow \left(\mu^n(u), Q^n(u)\right) \overset{\circ}{R}{}^n \left(\mu^n(v), Q^n(v)\right).$$

If R^n satisfies the absolute-inequality aggregation property, representative utility can be written as a function $\overset{\circ}{\Xi}{}^n : Q^n \to \mathcal{R}$ of average utility and the inequality index, with

$$\Xi^n(u) = \overset{\circ}{\Xi}{}^n \left(\mu^n(u), Q^n(u)\right)$$

for all $u \in \mathcal{R}^n$. Ξ^n must be increasing on all lines of translation because Q^n is constant on each of them. The absolute-inequality aggregation property does not guarantee that Ξ^n is unit translatable, however, which implies that the corresponding Kolm index may not be absolute. But there is a way to derive indexes that are ordinally equivalent to Q^n from the social-evaluation ordering.

The translation function corresponding to Ξ^n is $T^n : \mathcal{R}^{n+1} \to \mathcal{R}$ and it is defined by

$$T^n(\xi, u) = \max\{t \mid \Xi^n(u - t\mathbf{1}_n) \geq \xi\}.$$

The value of the function is the amount (possibly negative) by which each element of the vector u must be decreased to reach the iso-value set on which representative utility is equal to ξ. For all ξ, T^n is unit translatable in u. That is,

$$\begin{aligned}
T^n(\xi, u + \delta\mathbf{1}_n) &= \max\{t \mid \Xi^n(u - (t - \delta)\mathbf{1}_n) \geq \xi\} \\
&= \max\{(t - \delta) \mid \Xi^n(u - (t - \delta)\mathbf{1}_n) \geq \xi\} + \delta \\
&= T^n(\xi, u) + \delta
\end{aligned}$$

for all $u \in \mathcal{R}^n$ and for all $\delta \in \mathcal{R}_{++}$. T^n is decreasing in its first argument. By definition,

$$T^n(\xi, u) = 0 \Leftrightarrow \Xi^n(u) = \xi,$$

so Ξ^n can be recovered from T^n.

---

[13] See Blackorby and Donaldson (1984b) and Ebert (1987). Both consider only relative indexes on a restricted domain.

The representative-utility function that corresponds to $T^n(\xi, \cdot)$ is $\bar{T}^n(\xi, u) = T^n(\xi, u) - T^n(\xi, 0 1_n)$. For a given value of ξ, the Blackorby-Donaldson (BD) index (Blackorby and Donaldson 1980) is the Kolm index that corresponds to $T^n(\xi, \cdot)$ and is given by

$$Q^n_{BD}(\xi, u) = \mu^n(u) - \bar{T}^n(\xi, u).$$

It is an absolute index and may be different for different values of ξ. If R^n is translatable, $T^n(\xi, u) = \Xi^n(u) - \xi$ and, in that case, $\bar{T}^n(\xi, u) = \Xi^n(u)$, so Q^n_{BD} is the Kolm index.

If R^n satisfies the absolute-inequality aggregation property, all the BD indexes are ordinally equivalent to each other and to the index Q^n. In the theorem statement that follows, $\overset{o}{=}$ means "is ordinally equivalent to."

Theorem 4.4. *Suppose that Ξ^n exists and is increasing on translation lines. R^n satisfies the absolute-inequality aggregation property if and only if, for all $\xi, \zeta \in \mathcal{R}$,*

$$Q^n_{BD}(\xi, \cdot) \overset{o}{=} Q^n_{BD}(\zeta, \cdot). \tag{4.14}$$

Proof. If R^n satisfies the absolute-inequality aggregation property, the translation function T^n exists. The absolute-inequality aggregation property implies that there exists a function $\overset{o}{\Xi}{}^n$, increasing in its first argument, such that

$$\Xi^n(u) = \overset{o}{\Xi}{}^n\big(\mu^n(u), Q^n(u)\big)$$

for all $u \in \mathcal{R}^n$. Because Q^n is translation invariant, Ξ^n is increasing on translation lines. Consequently,

$$T^n(\xi, u) = \max\left\{t \mid \overset{o}{\Xi}{}^n(\mu^n(u - t1_n), Q^n(u - t1_n)) \geq \xi\right\}$$
$$= \max\left\{t \mid \overset{o}{\Xi}{}^n(\mu^n(u) - t, Q^n(u)) \geq \xi\right\}.$$

Because $\overset{o}{\Xi}{}^n$ is increasing in its first argument, there exists a function $H^n \colon \mathcal{H}^n \to \mathcal{R}$, where $\mathcal{H}^n = \{(\xi, q) \mid \exists u \in \mathcal{R}^n \text{ such that } \Xi^n(u) = \xi \text{ and } Q^n(u) = q\}$, such that, for all $u \in \mathcal{R}^n$,

$$T^n(\xi, u) = \mu^n(u) - H^n\big(\xi, Q^n(u)\big)$$

where H^n is increasing in its first argument. Hence,

$$\bar{T}^n(\xi, u) = \mu^n(u) + \big[H^n(\xi, 0) - H^n\big(\xi, Q^n(u)\big)\big],$$

and the BD index is given by

$$Q^n_{BD}(\xi, u) = H^n\big(\xi, Q^n(u)\big) - H^n(\xi, 0)$$

and (4.14) follows.

If Ξ^n is increasing along translation lines, the index Q_{BD}^n is well-defined. (4.14) implies that there exists a function $K^n \colon \mathcal{H}^n \to \mathcal{R}$, increasing in its second argument, such that

$$Q_{BD}^n(\xi, u) = K^n\big(\xi, Q^n(u)\big)$$

where Q^n is one of the BD indexes. For all $u \in \mathcal{R}^n$,

$$\bar{T}^n(\xi, u) = \mu^n(u) - K^n\big(\xi, Q^n(u)\big)$$

and, because $\bar{T}^n(\xi, u) = T^n(\xi, u) - T^n(\xi, 01_n)$,

$$T^n(\xi, u) = \mu^n(u) - K^n\big(\xi, Q^n(u)\big) + T^n(\xi, 01_n).$$

Because $T^n(\xi, u) = 0$ if and only if $\xi = \Xi^n(u)$,

$$\Xi^n(u) = \overset{\circ}{\Xi}{}^n\big(\mu^n(u), Q^n(u)\big)$$

for all $u \in \mathcal{R}^n$. ∎

Theorem 4.4 shows that it is possible to test any social-evaluation ordering for the absolute-inequality aggregation property. All that is needed is to compute the BD indexes and to find out whether all of them are ordinally equivalent. If they are, then the property is satisfied and, in that case, any of the BD indexes can be used to construct an AUI ordering.

An equivalence similar to the one sketched above can be found for AUI orderings and κ-intermediate indexes but the domain on which the indexes are defined must be restricted to $\mathcal{R}_{\kappa++}^n$. Because the BP index with $\kappa = 0$ is the AKS index, that case is also covered. See Blackorby and Donaldson (1984b); for a general discussion of ordinal indexes, see Ebert (1987). For a comprehensive discussion of ethical social index numbers, see Chakravarty (1990).

4.9 INFORMATION REQUIREMENTS

Information-invariance conditions, which restrict the available information regarding the measurability and interpersonal comparability of individual utilities, can be used to provide selection criteria for social-evaluation orderings. The most common way to represent informational environments is to define the set of invariance transformations ϕ that can be applied to utility vectors. Information invariance with respect to the information assumption represented by the set of admissible transformations then requires that the ranking of any two utility vectors u and v is the same as the ranking of the transformed vectors $\phi(u)$ and $\phi(v)$.[14] It is also possible to define the information-invariance

---

[14] This approach was developed in contributions such as that of d'Aspremont and Gevers (1977), Roberts (1980a, 1980b), and Sen (1974). See Basu (1983); Bossert (1991, 2000); Bossert and Stehling (1992, 1994); Falmagne (1981), Fishburn, Marcus-Roberts, and Roberts (1988); Fishburn and Roberts (1989); and Krantz, Luce, Suppes, and Tversky (1971) for discussions of information-invariance assumptions in terms of meaningful statements and their relations to uniqueness properties of measurement scales.

requirements for social-evaluation functionals but, given our welfarist focus, we employ the equivalent formulations for social-evaluation orderings. See also the discussion of the measurability of individual utilities in Chapter 2, which is conducted without a welfarism assumption and without reference to interpersonal comparability.

An invariance transformation is a vector $\phi = (\phi_1, \ldots, \phi_n)$ of functions $\phi_i \colon \mathcal{R} \to \mathcal{R}$ for all $i \in \{1, \ldots, n\}$ whose application to a utility vector $u \in \mathcal{R}^n$ results in the utility vector $\phi(u) = (\phi_1(u_1), \ldots, \phi_n(u_n)) \in \mathcal{R}^n$. Let Φ^A denote the set of invariance transformations that are admissible given an information assumption A. Information invariance with respect to Φ^A is defined as follows.

Information Invariance with Respect to Φ^A. For all $u, v \in \mathcal{R}^n$ and for all $\phi \in \Phi^A$, $u R^n v \Leftrightarrow \phi(u) R^n \phi(v)$.

The following collection of information assumptions includes those that are commonly used in the literature on fixed-population social evaluation.[15]

If the only information that can be used is ordinal utility information without interpersonal comparability, we obtain the informational environment corresponding to ordinal noncomparability.

Ordinal Noncomparability. $\phi \in \Phi^{ONC}$ if and only if ϕ_i is increasing for all $i \in \{1, \ldots, n\}$.

If $\phi^A = \phi^{ONC}$ we say that utilities are ordinally measurable and interpersonally noncomparable. Ordinal noncomparability allows us to compare utility levels intrapersonally. This is the case because statements such as $u_i \geq v_i$ are preserved by any increasing transformation ϕ_i applied to both sides of the inequality. In contrast, interpersonal comparisons of utility levels are ruled out because the statement $u_i \geq u_j$ is not necessarily preserved if an increasing transformation ϕ_i is applied to i's utility values and another transformation ϕ_j is applied to j's utilities. For example, if $u_i = 1$, $v_j = 0$ and the increasing functions ϕ_i, ϕ_j are such that $\phi_i(u_i) = u_i$ for all $u_i \in \mathcal{R}$ and $\phi_j(u_j) = u_j + 2$ for all $u_j \in \mathcal{R}$, it follows that $u_i = 1 > 0 = u_j$ and $\phi_i(u_i) = 1 < 2 = \phi_j(u_j)$ so that the interpersonal comparison is not meaningful: it is not preserved for all vectors of admissible transformations. Strong dictatorships are compatible with the information environment defined by ϕ^{ONC} but none of the other examples presented earlier is.

If utility levels are comparable both intrapersonally and interpersonally but no further information is available, we obtain ordinal full comparability.

---

[15] See Blackorby and Donaldson (1982); Blackorby, Donaldson, and Weymark (1984); Bossert and Weymark (2004); d'Aspremont and Gevers (1977, 2002); DeMeyer and Plott (1971); Dixit (1980); Gevers (1979); Roberts (1980b); and Sen (1970a, 1974, 1977a, 1986), among others, for detailed treatments.

Ordinal Full Comparability. $\phi \in \Phi^{OFC}$ if and only if there exists an increasing function $\phi_0: \mathcal{R} \to \mathcal{R}$ such that $\phi_i = \phi_0$ for all $i \in \{1, \ldots, n\}$.

With ordinal full comparability, the interpersonal comparison of utility levels is meaningful because, for all $u_i, u_j \in \mathcal{R}$ and for all increasing functions ϕ_0, it follows that $u_i \geq u_j$ if and only if $\phi_0(u_i) \geq \phi_0(u_j)$ and, thus, all interpersonal level comparisons are preserved by all admissible vectors of transformations. Strong dictatorships, maximin, leximin, and leximax satisfy information invariance with respect to ordinal full comparability.

If utilities are cardinally measurable, individual utilities are unique up to increasing affine transformations, thereby allowing for intrapersonal comparisons of utility differences. If no requirements regarding the interpersonal comparison of utilities are imposed, we obtain the information assumption cardinal noncomparability.

Cardinal Noncomparability. $\phi \in \Phi^{CNC}$ if and only if there exist $a_1, \ldots, a_n \in \mathcal{R}_{++}$ and $b_1, \ldots, b_n \in \mathcal{R}$ such that $\phi_i(\tau) = a_i \tau + b_i$ for all $\tau \in \mathcal{R}$ and for all $i \in \{1, \ldots, n\}$.

If formulated for social-evaluation functionals, information invariance with respect to ordinal noncomparability is stronger than information invariance with respect to cardinal noncomparability. However, in the presence of unlimited domain and binary independence of irrelevant alternatives, the two information-invariance properties are equivalent; see Sen (1970a). Thus, for a social-evaluation ordering defined on $\mathcal{R}^n$ (the existence of which implies that the underlying social-evaluation functional satisfies binary independence of irrelevant alternatives – see the welfarism theorem presented in Chapter 3), we obtain the following equivalence result; see Blackorby, Donaldson, and Weymark (1984) for a geometric illustration.

Theorem 4.5. *R^n satisfies information invariance with respect to cardinal noncomparability if and only if R^n satisfies information invariance with respect to ordinal noncomparability.*

Proof. Clearly, information invariance with respect to ordinal noncomparability implies information invariance with respect to cardinal noncomparability. To prove the converse implication, suppose R^n satisfies information invariance with respect to cardinal noncomparability. Let $\phi \in \Phi^{ONC}$ – that is, the functions $\phi_1, \ldots, \phi_n$ are increasing. We need to show that, for all $u, v \in \mathcal{R}^n$, uR^nv if and only if $\phi(u)R^n\phi(v)$. Let $i \in \{1, \ldots, n\}$. If $u_i = v_i$, let $a_i = 1$ and $b_i = \phi_i(u_i) - u_i$. If $u_i \neq v_i$, let

$$a_i = \frac{\phi_i(v_i) - \phi_i(u_i)}{v_i - u_i} \tag{4.15}$$

and

$$b_i = \frac{v_i\phi_i(u_i) - u_i\phi_i(v_i)}{v_i - u_i}.$$

Note that a_i as defined in (4.15) is positive because ϕ_i is increasing. In either case, it follows that $\phi_i(u_i) = a_i u_i + b_i$ and $\phi_i(v_i) = a_i v_i + b_i$. By information invariance with respect to cardinal noncomparability, $u R^n v$ if and only if $\phi(u) R^n \phi(v)$. ∎

If individual utilities are cardinally measurable and some interpersonal comparisons of utility are considered meaningful, the increasing affine transformations in the definition of cardinal noncomparability must be restricted across individuals. An example is cardinal unit comparability. In that information environment, admissible transformations are increasing affine functions and, in addition, the scaling factor is the same for all individuals. This information assumption allows for interpersonal comparisons of utility differences but utility levels cannot be compared interpersonally because the intercepts of the affine transformations may differ across individuals.

Cardinal Unit Comparability. $\phi \in \Phi^{CUC}$ if and only if there exist $a \in \mathcal{R}_{++}$ and $b_1, \ldots, b_n \in \mathcal{R}$ such that $\phi_i(\tau) = a\tau + b_i$ for all $\tau \in \mathcal{R}$ and for all $i \in \{1, \ldots, n\}$.

Because $u_i - v_i \geq u_j - v_j$ if and only if $a u_i + b_i - (a v_i + b_i) \geq a u_j + b_j - (a v_j + b_j)$ for all $a \in \mathcal{R}_{++}$ and for all $b_i, b_j, u_i, v_i, u_j, v_j \in \mathcal{R}$, utility differences can be compared interpersonally. Suppose now that $u_i = 1$, $v_j = 0$, $a = 1$, $b_i = 0$, and $b_j = 2$. Then $u_i = 1 > 0 = v_j$ and $a u_i + b_i = 1 < 2 = a v_j + b_j$, which implies that utility levels cannot be compared interpersonally. Strong dictatorships and utilitarianism satisfy information invariance with respect to cardinal unit comparability.

If utilities are cardinally measurable and fully interpersonally comparable, both utility levels and utility differences can be compared interpersonally. In this case, the only admissible transformations are increasing affine transformations, which are identical across individuals.

Cardinal Full Comparability. $\phi \in \Phi^{CFC}$ if and only if there exist $a \in \mathcal{R}_{++}$ and $b \in \mathcal{R}$ such that $\phi_i(\tau) = a\tau + b$ for all $\tau \in \mathcal{R}$ and for all $i \in \{1, \ldots, n\}$.

That interpersonal comparisons of utility differences and of utility levels are meaningful follows immediately from the equivalences $u_i \geq u_j$ if and only if $a u_i + b \geq a u_j + b$ and $u_i - v_i \geq u_j - v_j$ if and only if $a u_i + b - (a v_i + b) \geq a u_j + b - (a v_j + b)$ for all $a \in \mathcal{R}_{++}$ and for all $b, u_i, v_i, u_j, v_j \in \mathcal{R}$. Strong dictatorships, maximin, leximin, leximax, utilitarianism, and the generalized Ginis satisfy information invariance with respect to cardinal full comparability.

An information environment that provides more information than cardinal unit comparability is one in which the unit of measurement is numerically significant. In this case, utilities are said to be translation-scale measurable. Utility differences are interpersonally comparable and, in addition, their numerical values are meaningful. Because the functions ϕ_i may be different for each person, utility levels are not interpersonally comparable.

Translation-Scale Noncomparability. $\phi \in \Phi^{TNC}$ if and only if there exist $b_1, \ldots, b_n \in \mathcal{R}$ such that $\phi_i(\tau) = \tau + b_i$ for all $\tau \in \mathcal{R}$ and for all $i \in \{1, \ldots, n\}$.

Utility differences are meaningful because $u_i - v_i = u_i + b_i - (v_i + b_i)$ for all $b_i, u_i, v_i \in \mathcal{R}$. That utility levels cannot be compared interpersonally follows using the same example as that used in cardinal unit comparability. Among the social-evaluation orderings introduced earlier, strong dictatorships and utilitarianism are the only ones that satisfy information invariance with respect to translation-scale noncomparability.

If, in the definition of translation-scale noncomparability, the constants b_i are required to be the same across individuals, we obtain translation-scale full comparability: in addition to having a numerically significant unit of measurement for utilities, utility levels can be compared interpersonally.

Translation-Scale Full Comparability. $\phi \in \Phi^{TFC}$ if and only if there exists $b \in \mathcal{R}$ such that $\phi_i(\tau) = \tau + b$ for all $\tau \in \mathcal{R}$ and for all $i \in \{1, \ldots, n\}$.

Interpersonal comparisons of utility levels are possible in this environment because $u_i \geq u_j$ if and only if $u_i + b \geq u_j + b$ for all $b, u_i, u_j \in \mathcal{R}$. Strong dictatorships, utilitarianism, maximin, leximin, leximax, the Kolm-Pollak orderings, and the generalized Ginis all satisfy information invariance with respect to translation-scale full comparability.

If, instead of a translation scale (with or without full interpersonal comparability), a ratio scale is used to measure utility, the following information assumptions are obtained.

Ratio-Scale Noncomparability. $\phi \in \Phi^{RNC}$ if and only if there exist $a_1, \ldots, a_n \in \mathcal{R}_{++}$ such that $\phi_i(\tau) = a_i \tau$ for all $\tau \in \mathcal{R}$ and for all $i \in \{1, \ldots, n\}$.

If utilities are ratio-scale noncomparable, the zero level of utility is meaningful both intrapersonally and interpersonally. Utility ratios are meaningful because $u_i/v_i = a_i u_i/(a_i v_i)$ for all $a_i \in \mathcal{R}_{++}$ and for all $u_i, v_i \in \mathcal{R}$ with $v_i \neq 0$. Of our examples, only strong dictatorships satisfy information invariance with respect to ratio-scale noncomparability.

Ratio-Scale Full Comparability. $\phi \in \Phi^{RFC}$ if and only if there exists $a \in \mathcal{R}_{++}$ such that $\phi_i(\tau) = a\tau$ for all $\tau \in \mathcal{R}$ and for all $i \in \{1, \ldots, n\}$.

Comparisons of utility levels and ratios are meaningful both intrapersonally and interpersonally: $u_i \geq u_j$ if and only if $au_i \geq au_j$ and, provided that $u_j \neq 0$ and $u_\ell \neq 0$, $u_i/u_j \geq u_k/u_\ell$ if and only if $au_i/au_j \geq au_k/au_\ell$. Strong dictatorships, utilitarianism, maximin, leximin, leximax, the symmetric global means of order

r, and the generalized Ginis satisfy information invariance with respect to ratio-scale full comparability.

If all the information in a utility vector is considered meaningful, we say that utilities are numerically measurable and fully interpersonally comparable. In this case, the only admissible transformation is the identity mapping.

Numerical Full Comparability. $\phi \in \Phi^{NFC}$ if and only if $\phi_i(\tau) = \tau$ for all $\tau \in \mathcal{R}$ and for all $i \in \{1, \ldots, n\}$.

In general, increases in available information reduce the restrictions on social-evaluation orderings. For example, information invariance with respect to translation-scale measurability is a weaker restriction than information invariance with respect to cardinal unit comparability, and invariance with respect to numerical full comparability imposes no restriction at all.

If neutrality is normalized to zero, then cardinal unit comparability is equivalent to ratio-scale full comparability for all profiles that respect the normalization. Further, if there are two norms that are interpersonally comparable, then cardinal noncomparability is equivalent to numerical full comparability. It follows that cardinal measurability and two norms are sufficient to apply any social-evaluation ordering.

4.10 CHARACTERIZATIONS OF FIXED-POPULATION PRINCIPLES

In this section, we present a summary of some results that characterize several classes of fixed-population social-evaluation orderings. We begin with a variant of Arrow's (1951, 1963) theorem stated for social-evaluation orderings. It shows that information invariance with respect to ordinal or cardinal noncomparability is too strong an assumption because, if combined with continuity and weak Pareto, it characterizes strong dictatorships. Thus, an informational environment that permits at least some form of interpersonal comparability of well-being is needed to obtain reasonable principles for social evaluation.

Theorem 4.6. *R^n satisfies continuity, weak Pareto, and information invariance with respect to ordinal (cardinal) noncomparability if and only if R^n is strongly dictatorial.*

The ordinal version of Theorem 4.6 is a variant of Arrow's (1951, 1963) theorem – see also Blau (1957). The cardinal version is an analogue of Sen's (1970a) strengthening of Arrow's theorem.

Arrow's nondictatorship axiom is a condition on social-evaluation functionals. It prevents the existence of an individual whose strict preferences are always replicated in the social ordering. Because the domain of an Arrovian social-welfare function consists of profiles of individual goodness orderings, the corresponding social-evaluation functionals must satisfy ordinal noncomparability. Translated into our framework, the best-known version of his theorem states that there is no social-evaluation functional that satisfies information invariance with respect to ordinal noncomparability, unlimited domain, binary independence of irrelevant alternatives, weak Pareto, and nondictatorship (Sen 1970a). Blackorby, Donaldson, and Weymark (1984) provide a geometric proof of Arrow's theorem for $n = 2$, and a generalization to an arbitrary finite number of individuals is given by Blackorby, Donaldson, and Weymark (1990).

If, in the conditions of Theorem 4.6, continuity is dropped and weak Pareto is replaced with strong Pareto, a serial dictatorship results. In that case, there is an ordered list of individuals. To rank any two alternatives, the orderings of the people on the list are consulted in sequence and the first strict preference is replicated in the social ordering. If all individuals find the alternatives equally good, the social ordering agrees.[16]

A distinguishing feature of generalized utilitarian social-evaluation orderings is that they possess an additive structure. This property is closely related to several independence conditions that limit the influence of the well-being of unconcerned individuals on the social ordering, and these conditions, together with some of our earlier axioms, can be used to provide characterizations of generalized utilitarianism.

Suppose a social change affects only the utilities of the members of a population subgroup. Same-people independence requires the social assessment of the change to be independent of the utility levels of people outside the subgroup.

Same-People Independence. For all M such that $\emptyset \neq M \subset \{1, \ldots, n\}$ and for all $u, v, \bar{u}, \bar{v} \in \mathcal{R}^n$, if $[u_i = v_i$ and $\bar{u}_i = \bar{v}_i]$ for all $i \in M$ and $[u_j = \bar{u}_j$ and $v_j = \bar{v}_j]$ for all $j \in \{1, \ldots, n\} \setminus M$, then

$$u R^n v \Leftrightarrow \bar{u} R^n \bar{v}.$$

In this definition, the individuals in M are unconcerned – they are equally well off in u and v and in $\bar{u}$ and $\bar{v}$. Same-people independence requires the ranking of u and v to depend on the utilities of the concerned individuals – those not in M – only. If expressed in terms of a representation, this axiom is referred to as complete strict separability (Blackorby, Primont, and Russell 1978). The corresponding separability axiom for social-evaluation functionals is given by d'Aspremont and Gevers (1977), where it is called separability with respect to unconcerned individuals. D'Aspremont and Gevers' separability axiom is called "elimination of (the influence of) indifferent individuals" by Maskin (1978) and by Roberts (1980b).

In the case of two individuals, this axiom is implied by strong Pareto. Therefore, it typically is applied to societies with at least three individuals. In that

---

[16] See Blackorby, Donaldson, and Weymark (1990) for a proof.

case, we obtain the following characterization of generalized utilitarianism. Note that no information-invariance condition is needed.

Theorem 4.7. *Suppose $n \geq 3$. R^n satisfies continuity, same-people anonymity, strong Pareto, and same-people independence if and only if R^n is generalized utilitarian.*

Proof. That generalized utilitarianism satisfies the required axioms is straightforward to verify. Conversely, let $n \geq 3$ and suppose R^n satisfies continuity, same-people anonymity, strong Pareto, and same-people independence. Applying Debreu's (1959, pp. 56–59) representation theorem or Theorem 4.1, there exists a continuous function $f: \mathcal{R}^n \to \mathcal{R}$ such that, for all $u, v \in \mathcal{R}^n$,

$$u R^n v \Leftrightarrow f(u) \geq f(v).$$

By strong Pareto, f is increasing in all arguments, and same-people anonymity implies that f is symmetric. In addition, same-people independence implies that $\{1, \ldots, n\} \setminus M$ is separable from its (nonempty) complement M for any choice of M such that $\emptyset \neq M \subset \{1, \ldots, n\}$. Gorman's (1968) theorem on overlapping separable sets of variables (Aczél 1966, p. 312; Blackorby, Primont, and Russell 1978, p. 127) implies that f is additively separable. Therefore, there exist continuous and increasing functions $H: \mathcal{R} \to \mathcal{R}$ and $g_i^n: \mathcal{R} \to \mathcal{R}$ for all $i \in \{1, \ldots, n\}$ such that

$$f(u) = H\left(\sum_{i=1}^{n} g_i^n(u_i) \right)$$

for all $u \in \mathcal{R}^n$. Because f is symmetric, each g_i^n can be chosen to be independent of i, and we define $g^n = g_i^n$ for all $i \in \{1, \ldots, n\}$. Therefore, because f is a representation of R^n,

$$u R^n v \Leftrightarrow H\left(\sum_{i=1}^{n} g^n(u_i) \right) \geq H\left(\sum_{i=1}^{n} g^n(v_i) \right)$$

$$\Leftrightarrow \sum_{i=1}^{n} g^n(u_i) \geq \sum_{i=1}^{n} g^n(v_i)$$

for all $u, v \in \mathcal{R}^n$. Without loss of generality, g^n can be chosen so that $g^n(0) = 0$. ∎

See also Debreu (1960) and Fleming (1952) for variants of this theorem. Due to the presence of same-people anonymity, same-people independence could be weakened by suitably restricting the possible sets of unconcerned individuals. We could, for example, designate a single group that lived in the past with no less than two and no more than $n - 1$ members as the unconcerned. We have, however, chosen the stronger axiom to avoid unnecessary notational complexity.

The ethical appeal of generalized utilitarianism rests, in part, on its separability properties. Utilitarianism is but one possibility within that class of social-evaluation orderings, and it is appropriate to ask whether it should have special status. The arguments for utilitarianism that we present in the following theorems use, for the most part, information-invariance conditions.

In an informational environment that allows for cardinal unit comparability at least, the utilitarian social-evaluation ordering can be employed. This is not the case for generalized utilitarianism – many generalized utilitarian orderings do not satisfy information invariance with respect to cardinal, translation-scale or ratio-scale full comparability. The application of generalized utilitarianism is restricted to informational environments that allow (at least) for the comparability properties described by the set of admissible transformations in the following theorem.

Theorem 4.8. *Suppose $n \geq 2$ and Φ contains n-tuples of continuous and increasing functions only. Generalized utilitarianism with a continuous and increasing function g^n satisfies information invariance with respect to Φ if and only if, for each $\phi \in \Phi$, there exist $a \in \mathcal{R}_{++}$ and $b_1, \ldots, b_n \in \mathcal{R}$ such that*

$$\phi_i(\tau) = (g^n)^{-1}\left(ag^n(\tau) + b_i\right) \tag{4.16}$$

for all $\tau \in \mathcal{R}$ and for all $i \in \{1, \ldots, n\}$.

Proof. That generalized utilitarianism satisfies information invariance with respect to Φ if (4.16) is satisfied can be verified by substitution.

Now suppose generalized utilitarianism, generated by a function g^n, satisfies information invariance with respect to Φ and Φ contains continuous and increasing transformations only. Information invariance requires that an admissible transformation $\phi = (\phi_1, \ldots, \phi_n) \in \Phi$ must satisfy the condition

$$\sum_{i=1}^{n} g^n\left(\phi_i(u_i)\right) \geq \sum_{i=1}^{n} g^n\left(\phi_i(v_i)\right) \Leftrightarrow \sum_{i=1}^{n} g^n(u_i) \geq \sum_{i=1}^{n} g^n(v_i)$$

for all $u, v \in \mathcal{R}^n$. This condition is equivalent to the functional equation

$$\sum_{i=1}^{n} g^n\left((\phi_i(u_i)\right) = H\left(\sum_{i=1}^{n} g^n(u_i)\right) \tag{4.17}$$

for all $u \in \mathcal{R}^n$, where H is increasing. Letting $z_i = g^n(u_i)$ and $G_i = g^n \circ \phi_i \circ (g^n)^{-1}$ for all $i \in \{1, \ldots, n\}$, (4.17) can be rewritten as

$$\sum_{i=1}^{n} G_i(z_i) = H\left(\sum_{i=1}^{n} z_i\right),$$

a Pexider equation, and it follows that there exist $a \in \mathcal{R}_{++}$ and $b_i \in \mathcal{R}$ such that $G_i(\zeta) = a\zeta + b_i$ for all $\zeta \in g^n(\mathcal{R})$ and for all $i \in \{1, \ldots, n\}$.[17] Therefore, $g^n(\phi_i((g^n)^{-1}(\zeta))) = a\zeta + b_i$ and, letting $\tau = (g^n)^{-1}(z_i)$, we obtain $\phi_i(\tau) = (g^n)^{-1}(ag^n(\tau) + b_i)$ for all $i \in \{1, \ldots, n\}$.   ∎

The above theorem states, in effect, that the information environment must support cardinal unit comparability of the transformed utilities $(g^n(u_1), \ldots, g^n(u_n))$ because (4.16) is equivalent to $g^n(\phi_i(\tau)) = ag^n(\tau) + b_i$. If, for example, $g^n(\tau) = 1 - \exp(-\tau)$, neither cardinal unit comparability nor cardinal full comparability of utilities provides sufficient information. Without norms, it is difficult to justify such an information environment unless the function g^n is affine, in which case we are back to utilitarianism. Therefore, the informational difficulties involved in applying generalized utilitarian principles other than utilitarianism suggest that the utilitarian social-evaluation functional has an important advantage over the other members of that class unless two interpersonally comparable utility norms are employed.

Next, we provide a characterization of utilitarianism using, in addition to weak Pareto, an axiom that we call incremental equity (Blackorby, Bossert, and Donaldson 2002b). We use the notation $\mathbf{1}_n^j$ for the vector $w \in \mathcal{R}^n$ such that $w_j = 1$ and $w_i = 0$ for all $i \in \{1, \ldots, n\} \setminus \{j\}$.

Incremental Equity. For all $u \in \mathcal{R}^n$, for all $\delta \in \mathcal{R}$, and for all $j, k \in \{1, \ldots, n\}$,

$$\left(u + \delta\mathbf{1}_n^j\right) I^n \left(u + \delta\mathbf{1}_n^k\right). \tag{4.18}$$

Incremental equity is an impartiality property with respect to utility increases or decreases. If a single individual's utility level changes by the amount δ, it does not matter whose utility changes. Incremental equity and minimal increasingness together characterize utilitarianism. This result is a strengthening of one by Blackorby, Bossert, and Donaldson (2002b).

Theorem 4.9. *R^n satisfies minimal increasingness and incremental equity if and only if R^n is utilitarian.*

Proof. That the utilitarian social-evaluation ordering satisfies minimal increasingness and incremental equity is easily checked.

Conversely, suppose that R^n satisfies the two axioms. If $n = 1$, minimal increasingness alone implies the result. Now let $n \geq 2$. (4.18) implies that

$$u I^n \left(u - \delta\mathbf{1}_n^j + \delta\mathbf{1}_n^k\right) \tag{4.19}$$

---

[17] See Aczél (1966, Chapter 3) for a detailed discussion of Pexider equations and their solutions. Because the functions ϕ_i and g^n (and thus the inverse of g^n) are continuous, the domains of H and of the G_i are nondegenerate intervals, which ensures that the requisite functional equations results apply.

for all $u \in \mathcal{R}^n$, for all $\delta \in \mathcal{R}$, and for all $j, k \in \{1, \ldots, n\}$. (4.19) implies

$$
u I^n \left(\frac{1}{n} \sum_{i=1}^n u_i, u_2, \ldots, u_n + u_1 - \frac{1}{n} \sum_{i=1}^n u_i \right)
$$

$$
I^n \left(\frac{1}{n} \sum_{i=1}^n u_i, \frac{1}{n} \sum_{i=1}^n u_i, \ldots, u_n + u_1 + u_2 - \frac{2}{n} \sum_{i=1}^n u_i \right) \tag{4.20}
$$

$$
\vdots
$$

$$
I^n \left(\frac{1}{n} \sum_{i=1}^n u_i, \ldots, \sum_{i=1}^n u_i - \frac{n-1}{n} \sum_{i=1}^n u_i \right) = \left(\frac{1}{n} \sum_{i=1}^n u_i \right) \mathbf{1}_n
$$

for all $u \in \mathcal{R}^n$. Together with minimal increasingness, this implies

$$
u R^n v \Leftrightarrow \sum_{i=1}^n u_i \geq \sum_{i=1}^n v_i
$$

for all $u, v \in \mathcal{R}^n$. ∎

Equation (4.19) in the above proof shows that incremental equity requires that transfers of utility from one individual to another do not affect social goodness. Consequently, all utility distributions where total utility is constant must be regarded as equally good, and utilitarianism results from minimal increasingness.

Incremental equity is related to same-people anonymity and to information invariance with respect to translation-scale noncomparability. First, (4.20) shows that incremental equity implies same-people anonymity, and Theorem 4.9 itself shows that minimal increasingness and incremental equity together imply information invariance with respect to translation-scale noncomparability. Furthermore, as demonstrated in the following theorem, which is also due to Blackorby, Bossert, and Donaldson (2002b), same-people anonymity and information invariance with respect to translation-scale noncomparability together imply incremental equity.

Theorem 4.10. *If R^n satisfies same-people anonymity and information invariance with respect to translation-scale noncomparability, then R^n satisfies incremental equity.*

Proof. Suppose R^n satisfies same-people anonymity and information invariance with respect to translation-scale noncomparability. The latter axiom implies

$$
\left(u + \delta \mathbf{1}_n^j \right) R^n \left(u + \delta \mathbf{1}_n^k \right) \Leftrightarrow \delta \mathbf{1}_n^j R^n \delta \mathbf{1}_n^k \tag{4.21}
$$

for all $u \in \mathcal{R}^n$, for all $\delta \in \mathcal{R}$ and for all $j, k \in \{1, \ldots, n\}$. By same-people anonymity, $\delta \mathbf{1}_n^j I^n \delta \mathbf{1}_n^k$ and, thus, (4.21) implies

$$
\left(u + \delta \mathbf{1}_n^j \right) I^n \left(u + \delta \mathbf{1}_n^k \right),
$$

which establishes that incremental equity is satisfied. ∎

By combining Theorems 4.9 and 4.10, we can provide an alternative proof of a known characterization of utilitarianism. The result is a strengthening of a theorem due to d'Aspremont and Gevers (1977). They use the stronger axioms weak Pareto and information invariance with respect to cardinal unit comparability instead of minimal increasingness and information invariance with respect to translation-scale noncomparability. See also Blackwell and Girshick (1954), Milnor (1954), and Roberts (1980b). A detailed proof can be found in Bossert and Weymark (2004).

Theorem 4.11. R^n *satisfies same-people anonymity, minimal increasingness, and information invariance with respect to translation-scale noncomparability if and only if R^n is utilitarian.*

Proof. That the utilitarian social-evaluation ordering satisfies the required axioms is easily verified. Conversely, suppose R^n satisfies same-people anonymity, minimal increasingness, and information invariance with respect to translation-scale measurability. By Theorem 4.10, R^n satisfies incremental equity. By Theorem 4.9, R^n is utilitarian. ∎

An alternative characterization of utilitarianism can be obtained for the case $n \geq 3$ by employing continuity, same-people anonymity, strong Pareto, same-people independence, and information invariance with respect to cardinal full comparability. This theorem is due to Maskin (1978); see also Deschamps and Gevers (1978).

Theorem 4.12. *Suppose $n \geq 3$. R^n satisfies continuity, same-people anonymity, strong Pareto, same-people independence, and information invariance with respect to cardinal full comparability if and only if R^n is utilitarian.*

Proof. That utilitarianism satisfies the required axioms is easy to verify. Now suppose a social-evaluation ordering R^n satisfies continuity, same-people anonymity, strong Pareto, same-people independence, and information invariance with respect to cardinal full comparability. By Theorem 4.7, R^n is generalized utilitarian. Because any increasing linear transformation of g^n leads to the same ordering of utility vectors, we can assume that $g^n(1) = 1$. It remains to be shown that, given this normalization, g^n must be the identity mapping.

Information invariance with respect to cardinal full comparability requires

$$\sum_{i=1}^{n} g^n(au_i + b) \geq \sum_{i=1}^{n} g^n(av_i + b) \Leftrightarrow \sum_{i=1}^{n} g^n(u_i) \geq \sum_{i=1}^{n} g^n(v_i)$$

for all $u, v \in \mathcal{R}^n$, for all $a \in \mathcal{R}_{++}$ and for all $b \in \mathcal{R}$. This is equivalent to the functional equation

$$\sum_{i=1}^{n} g^n(au_i + b) = H_{a,b}\left(\sum_{i=1}^{n} g^n(u_i) \right) \tag{4.22}$$

for all $u \in \mathcal{R}^n$, for all $a \in \mathcal{R}_{++}$ and for all $b \in \mathcal{R}$, where $H_{a,b}$ is increasing. Letting $z_i = g^n(u_i)$ and $G_{a,b}(z_i) = g^n(a(g^n)^{-1}(z_i) + b)$, (4.22) can be rewritten as

$$\sum_{i=1}^{n} G_{a,b}(z_i) = H_{a,b}\left(\sum_{i=1}^{n} z_i \right).$$

Continuity of g^n ensures that $G_{a,b}$ and $H_{a,b}$ are continuous. Consequently, all solutions to this Pexider equation are such that $G_{a,b}(z_i) = A(a, b)z_i + B(a, b)$. Substituting back using the definition of $G_{a,b}$, we obtain the equation

$$g^n(a\tau + b) = A(a, b)g^n(\tau) + B(a, b) \qquad (4.23)$$

for all $a \in \mathcal{R}_{++}$ and for all $b, \tau \in \mathcal{R}$, where we use τ instead of u_i for simplicity. Setting $\tau = 0$ and using the normalization $g^n(0) = 0$, we obtain $B(a, b) = g^n(b)$, and choosing $\tau = 1$ in (4.23) yields, together with the normalization $g^n(1) = 1$, $A(a, b) = g^n(a + b) - g^n(b)$. Therefore, (4.23) is equivalent to

$$g^n(a\tau + b) = \left[g^n(a + b) - g^n(b) \right] g^n(\tau) + g^n(b) \qquad (4.24)$$

for all $a \in \mathcal{R}_{++}$ and for all $b, \tau \in \mathcal{R}$. Setting $b = 0$, we obtain

$$g^n(a\tau) = g^n(a)g^n(\tau) \qquad (4.25)$$

for all $a \in \mathcal{R}_{++}$ and for all $\tau \in \mathcal{R}$. Analogously, choosing $a = 1$ in (4.24) yields

$$g^n(\tau + b) = \left[g^n(1 + b) - g^n(b) \right] g^n(\tau) + g^n(b) \qquad (4.26)$$

for all $b, \tau \in \mathcal{R}$. Equation (4.26) is a special case of Equation 3.1.3(3) of Aczél (1966, p. 150)[18] and, together with the increasingness of g^n, it follows that either there exists $c \in \mathcal{R}_{++}$ such that

$$g^n(\tau) = \frac{\exp(c\tau) - 1}{\exp(c) - 1} \qquad (4.27)$$

for all $\tau \in \mathcal{R}$, or $g^n(\tau) = \tau$ for all $\tau \in \mathcal{R}$. Because (4.27) is incompatible with (4.25), this completes the proof. ∎

Continuity plays a crucial role in Theorem 4.12. Deschamps and Gevers (1978) examined the consequences of dropping this axiom. They showed that, if R^n satisfies same-people anonymity, strong Pareto, same-people independence, and information invariance with respect to cardinal full comparability, then R^n must be weakly utilitarian, leximin, or leximax. It is remarkable that these axioms narrow down the possible social-evaluation orderings to that extent. When minimal equity is added, only weakly utilitarian principles and leximin are left because leximax violates minimal equity. Therefore, we obtain the following theorem, which is due to Deschamps and Gevers (1978); see their paper for a proof.

---

[18] To see this, set $f(x) = k(x) = g^n(\tau)$ and $h(y) = g^n(1 + b) - g^n(b)$ in Aczél [1966, Equation 3.1.3(3)].

Theorem 4.13. *Suppose $n \geq 3$. If R^n satisfies same-people anonymity, strong Pareto, minimal equity, same-people independence, and information invariance with respect to cardinal full comparability, then R^n is leximin or weakly utilitarian.*

The above theorem is not a characterization result because its statement is an implication and not an equivalence. The reason is that not all weakly utilitarian orderings satisfy all the required axioms. They may, for example, violate anonymity on hyperplanes of constant total utility.

Next, we present some characterizations of subclasses of generalized utilitarianism that include the utilitarian ordering. We begin with a characterization of the symmetric global means of order r, due to Blackorby and Donaldson (1982). This result is obtained by replacing information invariance with respect to cardinal full comparability in Theorem 4.12 with information invariance with respect to ratio-scale full comparability. A proof can be found elsewhere (Blackorby and Donaldson 1982). If the utility domain were restricted to $\mathcal{R}^n_{++}$, additional orderings would satisfy the axioms.

Theorem 4.14. *Suppose $n \geq 3$. R^n satisfies continuity, same-people anonymity, strong Pareto, same-people independence, and information invariance with respect to ratio-scale full comparability if and only if R^n is a symmetric global mean of order r.*

Analogously, using translation-scale full comparability instead of ratio-scale full comparability, the Kolm-Pollak orderings can be characterized. Again, see Blackorby and Donaldson (1982) for a proof.

Theorem 4.15. *Suppose $n \geq 3$. R^n satisfies continuity, same-people anonymity, strong Pareto, same-people independence, and information invariance with respect to translation-scale full comparability if and only if R^n is a Kolm-Pollak ordering.*

We conclude this section by stating two characterizations of the leximin ordering. The first is based on an information assumption – namely, information invariance with respect to ordinal full comparability. This result is due to d'Aspremont and Gevers (1977); see also d'Aspremont (1985).

Theorem 4.16. *R^n satisfies same-people anonymity, strong Pareto, minimal equity, same-people independence, and information invariance with respect to ordinal full comparability if and only if R^n is leximin.*

A second characterization of leximin employs a strengthening of minimal equity – namely, Hammond equity (Hammond 1976). It uses neither same-people independence nor information invariance with respect to ordinal full comparability. Hammond equity extends minimal equity to all pairs of utility vectors and, furthermore, replaces the at-least-as-good-as requirement with betterness.

Hammond Equity. For all $u, v \in \mathcal{R}^n$ and for all $i, j \in \{1, \ldots, n\}$, if $u_k = v_k$ for all $k \in \{1, \ldots, n\} \setminus \{i, j\}$ and $v_j > u_j > u_i > v_i$, then $u P^n v$.

The following characterization is due to Hammond (1976). See also Bossert and Weymark (2004) for a proof.

Theorem 4.17. R^n *satisfies same-people anonymity, strong Pareto, and Hammond equity if and only if R^n is leximin.*

4.11 CONSISTENT SEQUENCES OF FIXED-POPULATION ORDERINGS

Suppose the same social-evaluation ordering is used for all populations of the same size. Then we may consider a sequence of fixed-population orderings $(R^n)_{n \in \mathcal{Z}_{++}}$, which consists of one social-evaluation ordering for each possible population size. For simplicity, we say that a sequence of social-evaluation orderings satisfies a fixed-population axiom if and only if each member of the sequence has the property.

Consistency conditions may be imposed on sequences of fixed-population orderings in a variety of different ways.[19] We conclude this chapter with a discussion of these conditions and illustrate their use in identifying ethically attractive sequences of principles.

A basic consistency condition was suggested by Dalton (1920). It requires replications of any two n-vectors to be ranked in the same way that the original vectors are.

Replication Invariance. For all $n, k \in \mathcal{Z}_{++}$ and for all $u, v \in \mathcal{R}^n$,

$$u R^n v \Leftrightarrow (\underbrace{u, \ldots, u}_{k \text{ times}}) R^{nk} (\underbrace{v, \ldots, v}_{k \text{ times}}).$$

Replication invariance is satisfied if and only if the sequence of corresponding representative-utility functions also satisfies a replication-invariance property (see, for example, Lemma 1 of Bossert 1990c).

Theorem 4.18. *Suppose that the representative-utility function Ξ^n exists for all $n \in \mathcal{Z}_{++}$. The sequence $(R^n)_{n \in \mathcal{Z}_{++}}$ satisfies replication invariance if and only if, for all $n, k \in \mathcal{Z}_{++}$ and for all $u \in \mathcal{R}^n$,*

$$\Xi^{nk}(\underbrace{u, \ldots, u}_{k \text{ times}}) = \Xi^n(u). \tag{4.28}$$

---

[19] As mentioned in Part A, we use the term consistency to refer to an entire class of conditions that impose restrictions on comparisons performed by different members of a sequence of social-evaluation orderings, as opposed to the more narrow meaning that is attached to this term in the literature on resource-allocation mechanisms; see, for instance, Thomson (1990).

Proof. Suppose the sequence $(R^n)_{n \in \mathcal{Z}_{++}}$ satisfies replication invariance. By definition, for all $n \in \mathcal{Z}_{++}$ and for all $u \in \mathcal{R}^n$, $uI^n\xi\mathbf{1}_n$ where $\xi = \Xi^n(u)$. Replication invariance implies that

$$\underbrace{(u, \ldots, u)}_{k \text{ times}} I^{nk}\xi\mathbf{1}_{nk}$$

and (4.28) follows.

If (4.28) is satisfied, then, for all $n, k \in \mathcal{Z}_{++}$ and for all $u, v \in \mathcal{R}^n$,

$$u R^n v \Leftrightarrow \Xi^n(u) \geq \Xi^n(v)$$
$$\Leftrightarrow \Xi^{nk}(\underbrace{u, \ldots, u}_{k \text{ times}}) \geq \Xi^{nk}(\underbrace{v, \ldots, v}_{k \text{ times}}) \Leftrightarrow (\underbrace{u, \ldots, u}_{k \text{ times}}) R^{nk} (\underbrace{v, \ldots, v}_{k \text{ times}})$$

and the sequence $(R^n)_{n \in \mathcal{Z}_{++}}$ is replication invariant. ∎

If each member of a sequence of orderings is a generalized utilitarian ordering, replication invariance is satisfied if and only if the transformations can be chosen to be the same for all population sizes.

Theorem 4.19. *A sequence of generalized utilitarian fixed-population orderings* $(R^n)_{n \in \mathcal{Z}_{++}}$ *satisfies replication invariance if and only if there exists a continuous and increasing function* $g: \mathcal{R} \to \mathcal{R}$ *with* $g(0) = 0$ *such that, for all* $n \in \mathcal{Z}_{++}$ *and for all* $u, v \in \mathcal{R}^n$,

$$u R^n v \Leftrightarrow \sum_{i=1}^{n} g(u_i) \geq \sum_{i=1}^{n} g(v_i). \tag{4.29}$$

Proof. Suppose that R^n is generalized utilitarian for all $n \in \mathcal{Z}_{++}$ and $(R^n)_{n \in \mathcal{Z}_{++}}$ satisfies replication invariance. This implies, for all $n, k \in \mathcal{Z}_{++}$ and for all $u \in \mathcal{R}^n$,

$$(g^n)^{-1}\left(\frac{1}{n}\sum_{i=1}^{n} g^n(u_i)\right) = (g^{nk})^{-1}\left(\frac{1}{nk}\sum_{i=1}^{n} kg^{nk}(u_i)\right)$$
$$= (g^{nk})^{-1}\left(\frac{1}{n}\sum_{i=1}^{n} g^{nk}(u_i)\right). \tag{4.30}$$

Define $z_i = g^n(u_i)$, $\psi_i^{n,k}(z_i) = g^{nk}((g^n)^{-1}(z_i)) = g^{nk}(u_i)$ and let $G^{n,k}$ be such that $G^{n,k}(t) = ng^{nk}((g^n)^{-1}(t/n))$ for all $t \in \mathcal{R}$. Then (4.30) becomes

$$G^{n,k}\left(\sum_{i=1}^{n} z_i\right) = \sum_{i=1}^{n} \psi_i^{n,k}(z_i),$$

a Pexider equation whose solution is

$$\psi_i^{n,k}(t) = a(n, k)t + b_i(n, k)$$

for all $t \in \mathcal{R}$ with constants $a(n, k) \in \mathcal{R}_{++}$ and $b_i(n, k) \in \mathcal{R}$ for all $i \in \{1, \ldots, n\}$. This implies

$$g^{nk}\big((g^n)^{-1}(t)\big) = a(n, k)t + b_i(n, k). \tag{4.31}$$

Defining $\tau = (g^n)^{-1}(t)$, (4.31) becomes

$$g^{nk}(\tau) = a(n, k)g^n(\tau) + b_i(n, k). \tag{4.32}$$

Because $g^n(0) = g^{nk}(0) = 0$, $b_i(n, k) = 0$ for all $i \in \{1, \ldots, n\}$.

Now consider any $n, m \in \mathcal{Z}_{++}$. By (4.32) with $b_i(n, k) = 0$, $g^{nm}(\tau) = a(n, m)g^n(\tau)$ and $g^{nm}(\tau) = a(m, n)g^m(\tau)$ for all $\tau \in \mathcal{R}$. Consequently, $g_n(\tau) = [a(m, n)/a(n, m)]g_m(\tau)$ for all $\tau \in \mathcal{R}$. Let $g = g^1$. It follows that, for all $n \in \mathcal{Z}_{++}$, $g^n(\tau) = [a(1, n)/a(n, 1)]g(\tau) = \tilde{a}(n)g(\tau)$ for all $\tau \in \mathcal{R}$. Because R^n is unaffected if g^n is replaced by any positive scalar multiple, we may choose $g^n = g$ for all $n \in \mathcal{Z}_{++}$ and (4.29) results.

Conversely, if each member of the sequence $(R^n)_{n \in \mathcal{Z}_{++}}$ is generalized utilitarian with $g^n = g$ for some continuous and increasing function g, replication invariance is immediate. ∎

The population substitution principle (Blackorby and Donaldson 1984a) is a consistency condition that is stronger than replication invariance. It applies to population subgroups. If, in any utility vector, the utilities of a subgroup are replaced by the subgroup's representative utility, calculated as if the subgroup were the whole population, the axiom requires the resulting vector and the original to be ranked as equally good.

Population Substitution Principle. For all $n \in \mathcal{Z}_{++}$, for all M such that $\emptyset \neq M \subset \{1, \ldots, n\}$ and for all $u, v \in \mathcal{R}^n$ such that $v_i = \Xi^{|M|}((u_i)_{i \in M})$ for all $i \in M$ and $v_i = u_i$ for all $i \in \{1, \ldots, n\} \setminus M$, $u I^n v$.

The following theorem establishes the implication mentioned above. If a sequence of social-evaluation orderings satisfies the population substitution principle, it must be replication invariant.

Theorem 4.20. *If the sequence $(R^n)_{n \in \mathcal{Z}_{++}}$ satisfies the population substitution principle, then $(R^n)_{n \in \mathcal{Z}_{++}}$ satisfies replication invariance.*

Proof. For all $n, k \in \mathcal{Z}_{++}$ and for all $u \in \mathcal{R}^n$, the population substitution principle implies

$$\underbrace{(u, \ldots, u)}_{k \text{ times}} I^{nk} \Big(\underbrace{\Xi^n(u)\mathbf{1}_n, \ldots, \Xi^n(u)\mathbf{1}_n}_{k \text{ times}} \Big) = \Xi^n(u)\mathbf{1}_{nk}.$$

Consequently,

$$\Xi^{nk}(\underbrace{u, \ldots, u}_{k \text{ times}}) = \Xi^n(u)$$

and, by Theorem 4.18, replication invariance is satisfied. ∎

The population substitution principle implies that for all $n \geq 3$, the representation Ξ^n of R^n must be additively separable and, therefore, it provides an alternative way of characterizing generalized utilitarianism in the presence of continuity, same-people anonymity, and strong Pareto.

Theorem 4.21. *The sequence* $(R^n)_{n \in \mathcal{Z}_{++}}$ *satisfies continuity, same-people anonymity, strong Pareto, and the population substitution principle if and only there exists a continuous and increasing function* $g \colon \mathcal{R} \to \mathcal{R}$ *with* $g(0) = 0$ *such that, for all* $n \in \mathcal{Z}_{++}$, R^n *is a generalized utilitarian social-evaluation ordering with*

$$u R^n v \Leftrightarrow \sum_{i=1}^{n} g(u_i) \geq \sum_{i=1}^{n} g(v_i) \tag{4.33}$$

for all $u, v \in \mathcal{R}^n$.

Proof. It is straightforward to show that if each member of the sequence $(R^n)_{n \in \mathcal{Z}_{++}}$ is a generalized utilitarian ordering satisfying (4.33) for some increasing and continuous function $g \colon \mathcal{R} \to \mathcal{R}$ with $g(0) = 0$, then continuity, same-people anonymity, strong Pareto, and the population substitution principle are satisfied.

Now suppose $(R^n)_{n \in \mathcal{Z}_{++}}$ satisfies continuity, same-people anonymity, strong Pareto, and the population substitution principle. Then, for any $n \geq 3$ and any M such that $\emptyset \neq M \subset \{1, \ldots, n\}$, the population substitution principle implies that M is strictly separable from its complement in Ξ^n. Gorman's (1968) theorem on overlapping separable sets of variables implies that Ξ^n is additively separable. Therefore, there exist continuous and increasing functions $H^n \colon \mathcal{R} \to \mathcal{R}$ and $g_i^n \colon \mathcal{R} \to \mathcal{R}$ for all $i \in \{1, \ldots, n\}$ such that

$$\Xi^n(u) = H^n \left(\sum_{i=1}^{n} g_i^n(u_i) \right)$$

for all $u \in \mathcal{R}^n$. By same-people anonymity, each g_i^n can be chosen to be independent of i, and we let $g^n = g_i^n$ for all $i \in \{1, \ldots, n\}$. Therefore, because Ξ^n is a representation of R^n,

$$u R^n v \Leftrightarrow \sum_{i=1}^{n} g^n(u_i) \geq \sum_{i=1}^{n} g^n(v_i)$$

for all $u, v \in \mathcal{R}^n$. Without loss of generality, g^n can be chosen so that $g^n(0) = 0$.

Because the population substitution principle implies replication invariance (Theorem 4.18), we may choose $g = g^n$ for all $n \geq 3$. For $n = 1$, strong Pareto implies that (4.33) is satisfied. For $n = 2$, let $u \in \mathcal{R}^2$ and choose any $\tau \in \mathcal{R}$. Then the population substitution principle implies

$$(u, \tau) I^3 \left(\Xi^2(u), \Xi^2(u), \tau \right)$$

and (4.33) implies that

$$g(u_1) + g(u_2) + g(\tau) = 2g\big(\Xi^2(u)\big) + g(\tau)$$

and, hence,

$$\Xi^2(u) = g^{-1}\left(\frac{1}{2}\sum_{i=1}^{2} g(u_i)\right)$$

which implies (4.33) for all $u, v \in \mathcal{R}^2$. ∎

The proof of Theorem 4.21 implies that same-people independence and replication invariance can replace the population substitution principle in the theorem statement.

Theorem 4.22. *The sequence* $(R^n)_{n \in \mathcal{Z}_{++}}$ *satisfies continuity, same-people anonymity, strong Pareto, same-people independence, and replication invariance if and only there exists a continuous and increasing function* $g : \mathcal{R} \to \mathcal{R}$ *with* $g(0) = 0$ *such that, for all* $n \in \mathcal{Z}_{++}$, R^n *is a generalized utilitarian social-evaluation ordering with*

$$u R^n v \Leftrightarrow \sum_{i=1}^{n} g(u_i) \geq \sum_{i=1}^{n} g(v_i)$$

for all $u, v \in \mathcal{R}^n$.

Along with some other axioms, replication invariance can be used to characterize the (illfare-ranked) single-parameter Gini sequences of social-evaluation orderings. These axiomatizations are obtained by combining characterizations of the single-series Ginis and their illfare-ranked counterparts due to Bossert (1990a) with a result of Donaldson and Weymark (1980) establishing that the only (illfare-ranked) single-series Ginis satisfying replication invariance are the (illfare-ranked) S-Ginis. We conclude this chapter with these characterization results.

The single-series Gini sequences use weights that are independent of population size. That is, for all $n \in \mathcal{Z}_{++}$ and for all $u, v \in \mathcal{R}^n$,

$$u R^n v \Leftrightarrow \sum_{i=1}^{n} a_i u_{(i)} \geq \sum_{i=1}^{n} a_i v_{(i)}$$

where $(a_i)_{i \in \mathcal{Z}_{++}}$ is a sequence of positive weights with $a_i \leq a_{i+1}$ for all $i \in \mathcal{Z}_{++}$. Single-series Gini sequences possess the following recursivity property, which is a weakening of the population substitution principle. It requires the conclusion of the population substitution principle to hold only in situations in which the subgroup whose utilities are replaced by the representative utility of their subgroup consists of all but the worst-off individual.

Recursivity. For all $n \in \mathcal{Z}_{++}$ and for all $u \in \mathcal{R}^{n+1}$,

$$u I^{n+1} \left(\Xi^n(u_{(1)}, \ldots, u_{(n)}) \mathbf{1} n, u_{(n+1)} \right).$$

Together with minimal increasingness, weak inequality-aversion, homothetic-ity and translatability, recursivity can be used to characterize the single-series Ginis (Bossert 1990a). Combining this result with Donaldson and Weymark's (1980) observation that the S-Ginis are the only single-series Ginis satisfying replication invariance, we obtain the following characterization.[20]

Theorem 4.23. *Suppose that the representative-utility function Ξ^n exists for all $n \in \mathcal{Z}_{++}$. The sequence $(R^n)_{n \in \mathcal{Z}_{++}}$ satisfies minimal increasingness, weak inequality-aversion, homotheticity, translatability, recursivity, and replication invariance if and only if $(R^n)_{n \in \mathcal{Z}_{++}}$ is a single-parameter Gini sequence.*

The illfare-ranked single-series Gini sequence is given by

$$u R^n v \Leftrightarrow \sum_{i=1}^n a_i u_{[i]} \geq \sum_{i=1}^n a_i v_{[i]}$$

for all $n \in \mathcal{Z}_{++}$ and for all $u \in \mathcal{R}^n$, where $(a_i)_{i \in \mathcal{Z}_{++}}$ is a sequence of positive weights with $a_i \geq a_{i+1}$ for all $i \in \mathcal{Z}_{++}$.

Analogously to the single-series Ginis, the illfare-ranked single-series Ginis satisfy a weakening of the population substitution principle that applies to the subgroup of all but the best-off individuals.

Illfare-Ranked Recursivity. For all $n \in \mathcal{Z}_{++}$ and for all $u \in \mathcal{R}^{n+1}$,

$$u I^{n+1} \left(\Xi^n(u_{[1]}, \ldots, u_{[n]}) \mathbf{1} n, u_{[n+1]} \right).$$

If recursivity is replaced with its illfare-ranked counterpart in the statement of Theorem 4.23, we obtain a characterization of the illfare-ranked S-Ginis. See, again, Bossert (1990a) and Donaldson and Weymark (1980) for details.

Theorem 4.24. *Suppose the representative-utility function Ξ^n exists for all $n \in \mathcal{Z}_{++}$. The sequence $(R^n)_{n \in \mathcal{Z}_{++}}$ satisfies minimal increasingness, weak inequality-aversion, homotheticity, translatability, illfare-ranked recursivity, and replication invariance if and only if $(R^n)_{n \in \mathcal{Z}_{++}}$ is an illfare-ranked single-parameter Gini sequence.*

---

[20] Minimal increasingness is not required in Bossert's (1990a) result. This is the case because he considers a different domain.

CHAPTER 5

Population Principles

Part A

In this chapter, we introduce population principles and explore their properties. Because the principles that we consider are both welfarist and anonymous, each one can be defined by a single anonymous ordering of utility vectors (see Chapter 3). We follow standard practice and normalize utilities so that a utility level of zero represents neutrality.

Most population principles have value functions that represent their social-evaluation orderings. If a value function exists, utility vector u is at least as good as utility vector v if and only if the value associated with u is no less than the value associated with v.

Our investigation uses same-number extensions of fixed-population axioms such as Pareto weak preference and continuity and additional axioms that apply to population principles alone. We prove, in Chapter 6, that there is no population principle that satisfies all our axioms. It is possible, however, to find ethically attractive population principles that satisfy some of them.

We present and examine the critical-level generalized utilitarian class, the restricted critical-level generalized utilitarian class, the number-sensitive critical-level generalized utilitarian class, the restricted number-sensitive critical-level generalized utilitarian class, the number-dampened generalized utilitarian class (Ng 1986), and the restricted number-dampened generalized utilitarian class (Hurka 2000). All these principles rank alternatives with the same population size using generalized utilitarianism. In addition, each class contains a subclass whose members rank same-number alternatives with utilitarianism. In addition to the above classes of principles, we consider variable-population extensions of maximin and leximin as well as classes of principles that have been suggested by Carlson (1998) and Sider (1991).

Because the presentation is more straightforward, we consider only the utilitarian subclasses of the generalized utilitarian principles in Part A. The whole of these classes as well as the variable-population extensions of maximin and leximin are discussed in Part B.

All the principles are well-defined if individual well-being is numerically measurable and fully interpersonally comparable. If, however, individual utilities are cardinally measurable and two utility levels – such as neutrality and a utility level that represents an excellent life above neutrality – are given particular values such as zero and one hundred, numerical measurability and full interpersonal comparability results (see Chapter 2). Not all the principles require such complete information, and we therefore consider the information requirements of the various classes separately.

5.1 AXIOMS, VALUE FUNCTIONS, AND CRITICAL LEVELS

Fixed-population axioms are needed to examine anonymous population principles and, in each case, we say that such an axiom is satisfied if and only if its same-number analogue is satisfied for each same-number subprinciple. The basic axioms that we employ are continuity, weak Pareto, strong Pareto, Pareto weak preference, and minimal increasingness. In addition, we call a principle inequality averse if and only if each same-number subprinciple is inequality averse.

If a principle satisfies continuity, Pareto weak preference and minimal increasingness (or continuity and weak Pareto), unique representative utilities exist for all utility vectors. In that case, the social-evaluation ordering for a population principle can be completely described by an ordering of population-size–representative-utility pairs. If a value function exists, it follows that it can be written in terms of population size and representative utility. When that is done, we call the resulting function a reduced-form value function.

Continuity, Pareto weak preference and minimal increasingness are not sufficient to ensure the existence of a (reduced-form) value function, however. For that, a stronger axiom is needed. Called extended continuity, it requires the continuity property to apply across dimensions and ensures that small changes in utilities do not lead to large changes in the social ranking. If a principle has a value function, its reduced form must be increasing in representative utility.

Carter (1999) and, implicitly, Parfit (1984) have suggested that value functions for principles whose same-number subprinciples are utilitarian should be expressible in terms of average utility and total utility. Because population size is equal to total utility divided by average utility, any such principle can be described in terms of population size and average utility (which is representative utility for same-number-utilitarian principles). Carter suggests, however, that principles should respond positively to increases in both. Any continuous principle with this property necessarily ranks as better some additions of people whose utility levels are below neutrality. Consequently, if value functions are written in terms of average and total utility, they should not be increasing in both. For simplicity of presentation, we work with the representative-utility–population-size representation.

Some of our axioms refer to critical levels, which are defined as follows. For any alternative, consider another with one additional person alive and suppose

Table 5.1. *Handicapped Child Example*

	Parent	First Child	Second Child	Euclid
x	60	50		u_E
y	60	0	60	u_E

that each member of the common population has the same level of well-being in both. A critical level for the utility vector that corresponds to the first alternative is a level of utility for the added person that makes the two alternatives equally good. Although critical levels are defined by using a hypothetical comparison in which the common population is unaffected, any two alternatives with different population sizes can be ranked by using critical levels and the same-number subprinciple for the larger population size as long as critical levels exist for all utility vectors.

We use three axioms that deal with the existence of critical levels: existence of critical levels requires their existence for all utility vectors, intermediate existence of critical levels requires the existence of at least one vector with a critical level for each population size, and weak existence of critical levels requires the existence of at least one utility vector with a critical level.

The axioms that follow are not the only ones that have been suggested but they are, in our view, the most important.

5.1.1 Independence

Suppose a single parent has a handicapped child whose lifetime utility would be zero (neutrality) without the expenditure of additional resources. Two alternatives are available. In the first, which we call x, resources are devoted to improving the child's well-being, resulting in utilities of 50 for the child and 60 for the parent. In the second, which we call y, no additional resources are used to raise the level of well-being of the disabled child, but a second child is born and the same resources are devoted to it, resulting in lifetime utility levels of 60 for the second child and the parent and zero for the first child. The parent and his or her children are not the only people who ever live, however. There is one other – Euclid – who is long dead and has the same utility level (u_E) in both alternatives.[1] See Table 5.1 for a summary.

The parent wants to know which alternative is better. Parfit (1976, 1982) considered this example and he assumed that utility levels other than those of family members and potential members are irrelevant. That assumption is satisfied if principles such as classical utilitarianism, whose value function is the sum of utilities, are used to rank the alternatives. The classical-utilitarian ranking of x and y is independent of Euclid's utility level and even of his existence. But it ranks y as better than x and this contradicts the moral intuition of many.

---

[1] This example, without Euclid, is due to Parfit (1976, 1982).

If, however, average utilitarianism, whose value function is average utility, is used to rank the alternatives, the ranking of x and y is not independent of Euclid's level of well-being. If his utility level is 40, average utility is 50 in x and 40 in y and, if his utility level is -100, average utility is $10/3$ in x and 5 in y: average utilitarianism declares x to be better if Euclid's life was good and y to be better if it was not. In addition, if Euclid's existence is disregarded, average utility is 55 in x and 40 in y so x is ranked as better in that case.

Independence axioms require the ranking of alternatives to be independent of the utility levels and, in one case, the existence of people whose well-being or existence is regarded as morally irrelevant. The weakest of these is same-number independence. It requires the ranking of any two alternatives with the same population size to be independent of the utilities of individuals who have the same utility levels in both. It is equivalent to satisfaction of same-people independence (Chapter 4) for every fixed population. Same-number independence is satisfied by all principles whose same-number subprinciples are generalized utilitarian.

Utility independence requires the ranking of any two alternatives to be independent of the utility levels of individuals who have the same utilities in both. It implies same-number independence, but it applies to comparisons in which population sizes are different as well as to those in which they are the same. In the example of Table 5.1, utility independence requires the ranking of x and y to be independent of Euclid's utility level but not necessarily of his existence.

Existence independence requires the ranking of any two alternatives to be independent of the existence of individuals who ever live and have the same utility levels in both. It implies the other two and is, therefore, the strongest of our independence axioms.[2] It allows population principles to be applied to affected individuals only.

Which independence axiom is appropriate for population ethics? To answer the question, we consider an example. Suppose that, in the near future, a small group of humans leaves Earth on a spaceship and, after travelling through space for several generations, establishes a colony on a planet that belongs to a distant star. The colonists lose contact with Earth and, in all possible alternatives, the two groups have nothing to do with each other from then on. No decision made by the members of either group affects the other in any way.

Now suppose the colonists are considering an important social decision and want to know which of the associated alternatives is best. If the population principle satisfies existence independence, the other group can be disregarded: the ranking of the feasible alternatives is independent of its existence and, therefore, of both the number and utility levels of its members. In this case, the population principle can be applied to the colonists alone.

If, however, the population principle satisfies utility independence but not existence independence, the ranking of the feasible alternatives may depend on

---

[2] In intertemporal settings, we call a related axiom "independence of the utilities of the dead" (see Blackorby, Bossert, and Donaldson 1995b, 1996b, 1997a). Hammond (1988) and McMahan (1981) have suggested similar axioms.

Table 5.2. *Carlson's Example*

	Period 1		Period 2	
	Pop. Size	Utility Level	Pop. Size	Utility Level
x	0	–	5 billion	60
y	0	–	10 billion	30
z	10 billion	60	5 billion	60
w	10 billion	60	10 billion	30

the number of people in the other group even though the number is unaffected by the decisions under consideration. And, if the population principle satisfies same-number independence only, the ranking of the feasible alternatives may depend on the utility levels or number of people in the other group, as is the case for average utilitarianism.

We find existence independence ethically attractive because of examples such as the ones discussed previously. In the presence of anonymity, existence independence cannot be reserved for particular groups. If it applies to groups such as the long dead, it must apply to all groups. A case for utility independence alone could be made, however; it would focus on the total number of people who ever live. In that case, the numbers of the long dead, of unaffected independent groups, or of unaffected people in the far future could count in social rankings. Consider a two-period example of Carlson (1998), which is illustrated in Table 5.2. In the first period, either no one lives or 10 billion well-off people live and each has a utility level of 60. In the second period, there are also two possibilities: in the first, 5 billion live with a utility level of 60; in the second, 10 billion live with a utility level of 30. Let x and y be alternatives with no one alive in period one and the two options for period two, respectively, and let z and w be alternatives with the second possibility in period one and the two options for period two. If existence independence is satisfied, the ranking of x and y must be the same as the ranking of z and w. But Carlson claims that it is not unreasonable to rank y above x and z above w. If so, existence independence must be rejected. But it does not follow that utility independence must be rejected as well. The weaker axiom allows Carlson's ranking because the period-one population size is different in the two cases. Utility independence does require the rankings to be independent of the utilities of period-one people, however.

Existence independence is attractive for practical reasons as well. Information about the number and utility levels of the long dead or of future people whose existence and well-being are unaffected by decisions taken in the present is very difficult to obtain.

5.1.2 The Negative Expansion Principle

Suppose someone whose utility level is below neutrality is added to a utility-unaffected population. Because that person's life is not worth living, it is reasonable to require all such additions to be ranked as bad and we call the resulting axiom the negative expansion principle.[3] If all critical levels exist, the negative expansion principle implies that all critical levels are nonnegative. This follows from the definition of a critical level: if a critical level is negative the addition of a person whose utility is equal to the critical level would be as good as the original. In addition, if strong Pareto is satisfied, the requirement that critical levels be nonnegative implies the negative expansion principle. To see this, suppose a ceteris-paribus addition of a person with a negative utility level is ranked as no worse. Then the critical level must be less than or equal to the utility level of the added person and the critical level is negative.[4]

5.1.3   The Repugnant Conclusion

A population principle implies the repugnant conclusion (Parfit 1976, 1982, 1984) if and only if any alternative in which each member of the population has a positive utility level, no matter how high, is ranked as worse than some alternative in which a larger population has a utility level that is above neutrality but arbitrarily close to it.[5] Such principles may recommend the creation of a large population in which each person is poverty-stricken. As Heyd (1992, p. 57) remarked, "What is the good in a world swarming with people having lives barely worth living, even if *overall* the aggregation of the 'utility' of its members supersedes that of any alternative, smaller world?" On the other hand, Tännsjö (2002) argued that we should accept the repugnant conclusion.

Classical utilitarianism leads to the repugnant conclusion and this is a significant shortcoming. In addition, any principle whose same-number subprinciples are generalized utilitarian and has critical levels that are nonpositive implies the repugnant conclusion. Those principles are not alone, however. We say that a principle is minimally inequality averse if and only if every utility vector is ranked as no better than one in which each person receives its average utility level. Any principle that satisfies minimal increasingness is minimally inequality averse, and has critical levels that are all nonpositive implies the repugnant conclusion.[6] This result is illustrated by a principle proposed by Sider (1991), which he calls geometrism. It uses a positive constant between zero and one, which we write as κ and ranks alternatives with a weighted sum

---

[3] Arrhenius (2000a) calls this axiom the negative mere addition principle.

[4] Parfit's mere addition principle requires the ceteris-paribus addition of a person whose lifetime-utility level is above neutrality to be ranked as no worse and Sikora's (1978) Pareto-plus axiom requires it to be ranked as an improvement. If critical levels exist, Sikora's axiom requires them to be nonpositive.

[5] See also Cowen (1996).

[6] See, in addition to the proof in Part B: Arrhenius (2000a); Blackorby, Bossert, Donaldson, and Fleurbaey (1998); Blackorby and Donaldson (1991); Carlson (1998); McMahan (1981); and Parfit (1976, 1982, 1984).

of utilities: the jth-highest nonnegative utility level receives a weight of κ^{j-1} and the lth-lowest negative utility receives a weight of κ^{l-1}. Critical levels are all zero and the repugnant conclusion is avoided but, because weights on higher positive utilities exceed weights on lower ones, the principle prefers inequality of positive utilities over equality (Arrhenius and Bykvist 1995). If, therefore, the repugnant conclusion is to be avoided and equality aversion is ruled out, some critical levels must be positive. As an example, average utilitarianism is a minimally inequality-averse principle, which has some positive critical levels and does not imply the repugnant conclusion.

We, therefore, adopt an axiom that we call avoidance of the repugnant conclusion. Its most obvious effect is to rule out classical utilitarianism.

5.1.4 Priority for Lives Worth Living

The axiom priority for lives worth living requires all alternatives in which each person is above neutrality to be ranked as better than all those in which each person is below it.

A weaker axiom, suggested by Arrhenius (2000a, 2000b), requires population principles to avoid the "strong sadistic conclusion" that obtains if and only if every alternative in which each person is below neutrality is ranked as better than some alternative in which each person is above neutrality.[7] Any principle that satisfies priority for lives worth living necessarily avoids the strong sadistic conclusion. We have chosen to work with the priority axiom because we believe it best captures the intuition that lies behind this and several related axioms.

Arrhenius (2000a) also suggested that principles should avoid the "sadistic conclusion" that obtains if and only if, when adding people to a utility-unaffected population, the addition of people with negative utility levels can be ranked as better than the addition of a possibly different number of people with positive utility levels. Any principle whose same-number subprinciples are utilitarian and ranks no one-person alternative above all those with larger populations cannot avoid both the sadistic and repugnant conclusions. The condition on one-person alternatives is implied by the existence of critical levels. Consequently, all these principles that avoid the repugnant conclusion necessarily imply the sadistic conclusion. This occurs because avoidance of the sadistic conclusion requires the addition of any number of people at a positive but arbitrarily small utility level to be ranked as no worse than the addition of a single person at an arbitrarily small negative utility level.[8]

---

[7] We do not consider the requirement that principles avoid the "reverse repugnant conclusion," which is implied by all principles that imply the strong sadistic conclusion. It is difficult to see why it is repugnant and, for that reason, we have omitted it. See Blackorby, Bossert, Donaldson, and Fleurbaey (1998); Carlson (1998); and Mulgan (2002).

[8] Arrhenius (2000a, 2000b) provides a more general impossibility theorem using avoidance of the sadistic conclusion as one axiom among others. See also Ng (1989).

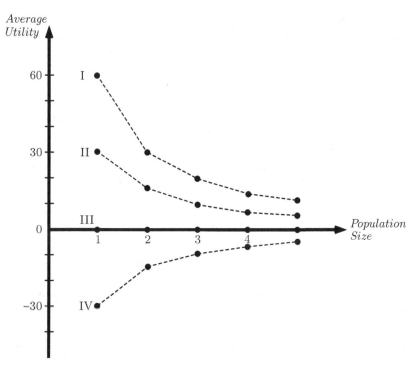

Figure 5.1. Classical Utilitarianism.

5.2 WELFARIST POPULATION PRINCIPLES

We now turn to population principles. Almost all the classes of principles discussed in this part of the chapter have same-number subprinciples that are utilitarian. The larger classes whose same-number principles are generalized utilitarian are presented in Part B.

All welfarist principles can be extended to cover the null alternative, the one in which no one ever lives. This can be accomplished by positioning the null alternative anywhere in the social ranking.

5.2.1 Classical Utilitarianism

The value function for classical utilitarianism (CU) is the sum of utilities and its reduced form is written as the product of population size and average utility. As a consequence, if average utility is constant, increases in population size are good if average utility is positive and bad if average utility is negative.[9]

CU is illustrated in Figure 5.1. The dotted lines join points of equal value and we refer to the resulting curves as iso-value curves. Points on iso-value curve I

---

[9] The sum-of-utilities value function for CU depends on the normalization of neutrality to zero. It is possible to normalize neutrality to any number but, in that case, the definition of the principle must be changed. If neutrality is normalized to η, the value function for classical utilitarianism is $\sum_{i=1}^{n}(u_i - \eta)$.

are better than points on II, which are better than points on III, which are better than points on IV. The four curves join average-utility–population-size pairs, which are as good as utility vectors in which one person has a utility level of 60, 30, 0, and −30, respectively.

Because the addition of an individual with a utility level of zero to a utility-unaffected population does not change total utility, critical levels exist for all utility vectors and are equal to zero. CU satisfies existence (and, therefore, utility and same-number) independence, the negative expansion principle and priority for lives worth living. As is well known, however, it leads to the repugnant conclusion. The repugnant conclusion is implied because the iso-value curve for any average-utility–population-size pair with positive average utility approaches the population-size axis as population size increases. This is true, in particular, of iso-value curves I and II in Figure 5.1. As a consequence, for any utility vector in which each person experiences the same positive utility level, it is possible to find a larger population size so that an arbitrarily small average-utility level paired with that population size is better.

5.2.2   Critical-Level Utilitarianism

Critical-level utilitarianism (CLU) is a class of population principles, one for each value of a *fixed* level of utility, which is the critical level for every utility vector.[10] If the critical level is zero, CU results. The CLU value function can be computed by subtracting the critical level from average utility and multiplying by population size or by subtracting the critical level from the utility level of each person and adding the resulting numbers.

CLU with a critical level of 30 is illustrated in Figure 5.2. The four iso-value curves are constructed in the same way as the iso-value curves of Figure 5.1. If average utility is constant, increases in population size are good if average utility is above the critical level and bad if average utility is below the critical level. Any alternative with average utility above the critical level is ranked as better than any alternative with average utility below it.

Iso-value curves for average-utility–population-size pairs with average utility above the critical level do not drop below iso-value curve II. All CLU principles with positive critical levels avoid the repugnant conclusion.

If avoidance of the repugnant conclusion is regarded as desirable, a CLU principle with a positive critical level should be chosen. Any such principle violates priority for lives worth living, however. This can be seen in Figure 5.2 by looking at iso-value curve IV, which crosses the population-size axis from below and stays above it. Any alternative in which one person is alive with a utility level of −30 is ranked as better than any alternative in which each of four people has a utility level of 10. A similar comparison can be found for any

---

[10] Fixed critical levels were proposed by Parfit (1976, 1982, 1984) and the critical-level generalized utilitarian class is characterized by Blackorby, Bossert, and Donaldson (1995b, 1998) and Blackorby and Donaldson (1984a).

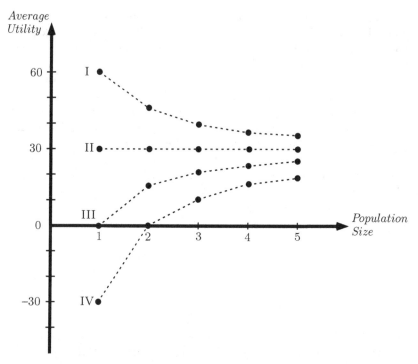

Figure 5.2. Critical-Level Utilitarianism.

alternative in which population size is arbitrary and each person's utility level is negative.

In the example of Table 5.1, the one-child alternative x is better than the two-child alternative y if and only if the critical level is greater than 10. This is a reflection of a general consequence of a positive critical level: the principle is more conservative than CU about population expansion. In addition, it is easy to check that the ranking of the two alternatives is independent of the existence of Euclid and, therefore, of his utility level. If CLU with a critical level of 20 is applied to the family alone, values are 70 for x and 60 for y.

CLU satisfies existence independence and, therefore, utility and same-number independence.

5.2.3   Restricted Critical-Level Utilitarianism

Critical-level utilitarian principles with positive critical levels can be modified so that all members of the resulting class avoid the repugnant conclusion and satisfy priority for lives worth living. The positive critical level for a CLU principle becomes the critical-level parameter for the corresponding principle. The value function is given by the CLU value function if average utility is greater than the critical-level parameter. If average utility is positive and no greater than the parameter, it can be found by subtracting one from average utility divided

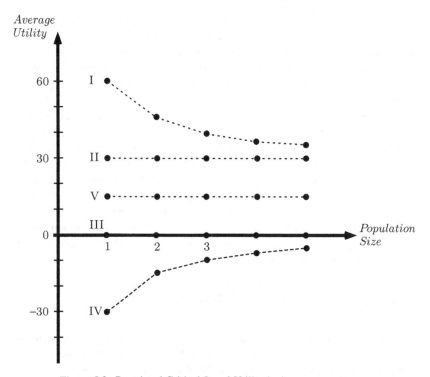

Figure 5.3. Restricted Critical-Level Utilitarianism.

by the parameter and, if average utility is nonpositive, by subtracting one from total utility. The value function is illustrated for a parameter value of 30 in Figure 5.3 (iso-value curves I to IV are defined as before and iso-value curve V is added). We call the resulting class restricted critical-level utilitarianism (RCLU). It ranks alternatives whose average utilities are greater than 30 using CLU (iso-value curve I), alternatives whose average utilities are positive and no greater than 30 using average utilitarianism (iso-value curves II and V), and alternatives whose average utilities are nonpositive with CU (iso-value curves III and IV). In addition, alternatives in the first group are ranked as better than those in the second, which, in turn, are ranked as better than those in the third.

Suppose average utility is constant. If it is above the critical-level parameter, population increases are good; if it is nonnegative and no greater than the parameter, population increases are neither good nor bad; and if it is negative, population increases are bad.

Critical levels are equal to the critical-level parameter for utility vectors whose average utility is above it, average utility for alternatives whose average utility is positive and no greater than the parameter, and zero for alternatives whose average utility is nonpositive. Consequently, all critical levels are nonnegative and the negative expansion principle is satisfied.

Because the iso-value curves for average-utility–population-size pairs with average utility above the parameter (such as iso-value curve I) do not approach the population-size axis, the repugnant conclusion is avoided. In addition, because the iso-value curves for average-utility–population-size pairs with negative average utilities such as IV do not cross the population-size axis, priority for lives worth living is satisfied.

These principles satisfy neither utility nor existence independence. Consider, again, the example of the disabled child summarized in Table 5.1 and suppose RCLU with the critical-level parameter equal to 20 is used to rank x and y. If Euclid's utility level is 100, average utility is 70 in x and 55 in y, which are both greater than 20. Consequently, values are 150 for x and 140 for y, and the alternative with one child is better. Now suppose Euclid's utility level is -140. Then average utilities are -10 for x and -5 for y and values are -31 for x and -21 for y and the two-child alternative is better. It follows that utility independence is violated and, because existence independence implies utility independence, it is also not satisfied.

5.2.4   Number-Sensitive Critical-Level Utilitarianism

The number-sensitive critical-level utilitarian (NCLU) class of principles allows critical levels to depend on population size but not on utility levels and includes CLU as a special case. We write the critical level for population size n as c_n. If the null alternative is included, its critical level is c_0 and, if not, c_0 can be chosen arbitrarily (it makes no difference to the rankings). The NCLU value function for a utility vector of dimension n can be found by subtracting the average of $c_0, \ldots, c_{n-1}$ from average utility and multiplying by population size. Equivalently, it can be found by adding the first utility level less c_0, the second less c_1, and so on.

NCLU is illustrated in Figure 5.4. In it, critical levels are 0 for population size one and 30 for population sizes greater than one. If average utility is constant, population increases are bad for average-utility–population-size pairs that lie below iso-value curve III (and have negative average utility) but, for pairs that are above curve III, the goodness or badness of population-size increases depends on how large the population is. In the figure, NCLU coincides with CU for population sizes one and two and, as population size becomes large, it approximates CLU with a critical level of 30.

If the negative expansion principle is satisfied, critical levels must all be nonnegative. If, in addition, critical levels are nondecreasing, the repugnant conclusion is avoided if and only if there is at least one positive critical level. Nondecreasingness of critical levels ensures, in that case, that all the critical levels for higher population sizes are positive. See Chapter 6 for further discussion of NCLU and the repugnant conclusion.

If critical levels are not all the same, utility independence is satisfied but existence independence is not. To see that, consider the disabled-child example summarized in Table 5.1 and suppose critical levels are equal to 0 for population

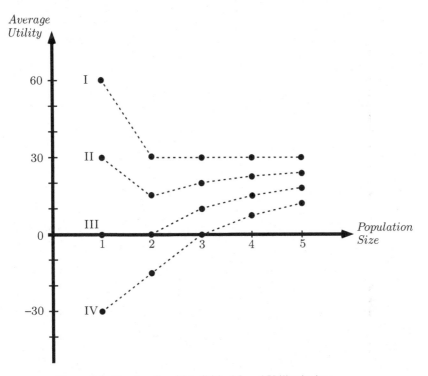

Figure 5.4. Number-Sensitive Critical-Level Utilitarianism.

sizes one to three and 90 for population sizes above three. Without loss of generality, c_0 may be chosen to be zero. Values are $110 + u_E$ for x and $120 + u_E$ for y and y is better than x for all values of u_E. Suppose, now, we discover that Euclid had an identical twin brother whose lifetime-utility level was also equal to u_E. In that case, values are $110 + 2u_E$ for x and $30 + 2u_E$ for y, so x is better. Although the ranking of the two alternatives is independent of the utilities of the Euclids, it is not independent of their number.

All members of the NCLU class that avoid the repugnant conclusion fail to satisfy priority for lives worth living. This can be seen in Figure 5.4 by noting that iso-value curve IV crosses the population-size axis. We show, in the following subsection, that it is possible to modify these principles so they avoid the repugnant conclusion and satisfy priority for lives worth living but, in that case, neither existence nor utility independence is satisfied.

5.2.5 Restricted Number-Sensitive Critical-Level Utilitarianism

The restricted number-sensitive critical-level utilitarian (RNCLU) class of principles is a modification of NCLU with nonnegative, nondecreasing critical levels and at least one positive critical level. It uses the critical levels for NCLU as parameters and we write $\bar{c}_n$ as the average of $c_0, \dots, c_{n-1}$ where c_0 is

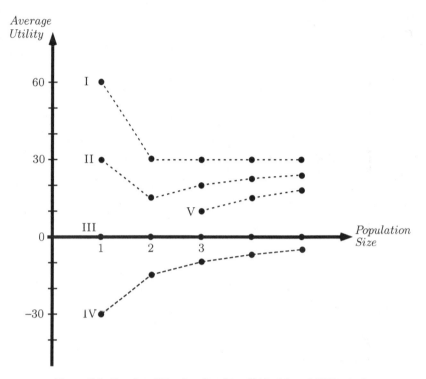

Figure 5.5. Restricted Number-Sensitive Critical-Level Utilitarianism.

nonnegative. The value function is equal to the value of the corresponding NCLU value function if average utility is greater than $\bar{c}_n$. If average utility is positive and no greater than $\bar{c}_n$, it can be found by subtracting one from average utility divided by $\bar{c}_n$ and, if average utility is nonpositive, by subtracting one from total utility. RNCLU with $c_0 = c_1 = c_2 = 0$ and $c_n = 30$ for all population sizes greater than two is illustrated in Figure 5.5. Note that there are no average-utility – population-size pairs on iso-value curve V for population sizes one and two. This occurs when some of the critical-level parameters are zero and some are positive, and does not occur when all are positive. All average-utility – population-size pairs with average utility greater than $\bar{c}_n$ are better than all pairs whose average utility is positive and no greater than $\bar{c}_n$ and these are, in turn, better than all pairs in which average utility is nonpositive. RNCLU ranks alternatives with average utilities above $\bar{c}_n$ with the corresponding NCLU principle and alternatives with nonpositive average utilities with CU.

The critical level for a utility vector of dimension n is c_n if average utility is greater than $\bar{c}_n$, positive and no greater than $\bar{c}_n$ if average utility is positive and no greater than $\bar{c}_n$, and zero if average utility is nonpositive. Consequently, all the RNCLU principles satisfy the negative expansion principle.

Because the critical-level parameters are, by assumption, nondecreasing and at least one is positive, the repugnant conclusion is avoided by all RNCLU principles.

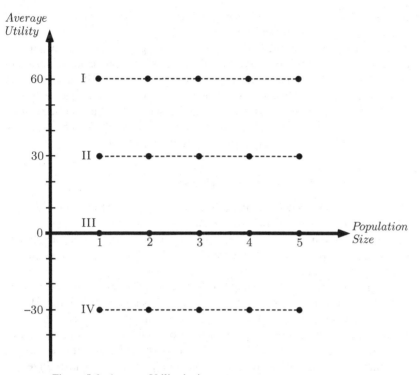

Figure 5.6. Average Utilitarianism.

All the RNCLU principles satisfy priority for lives worth living because all alternatives with positive average utility are ranked as better than all those with negative average utility. An illustration is provided by iso-value curve IV in Figure 5.5: it does not cross the population-size axis.

Restricted number-sensitive principles satisfy neither existence nor utility independence. An example is provided by the one discussed in connection with the RCLU class because those principles also belong to the RNCLU class.

5.2.6   Average Utilitarianism

Average utilitarianism (AU) ranks alternatives with a value function that is equal to average utility. It is illustrated in Figure 5.6. The flat iso-value curves indicate that, if average utility is constant, the principle is indifferent to changes in population size. As a consequence, the principle makes some stark trade-offs: an alternative with a population of any size in which each person is equally well off is ranked as worse than an alternative in which a single person experiences a trivially higher utility level.

Because the addition of a person whose utility level is equal to the average utility of an unaffected population does not change average utility, the critical level for any utility vector is average utility. Consequently, critical levels for alternatives with negative average utilities are negative and the negative expansion principle is not satisfied.

Iso-value curves for alternatives in which average utility is positive do not approach the population-size axis, and this means the repugnant conclusion is avoided. In addition, all alternatives with positive average utility are ranked as better than all those with negative average utility and, as a consequence, priority for lives worth living is satisfied. The discussion of average utilitarianism following the disabled-child example summarized in Table 5.1 demonstrates that AU satisfies neither utility nor existence independence.

5.2.7   Number-Dampened Utilitarianism

The number-dampened utilitarian (NDU) class (Ng 1986) has both CU and AU as members. Its value function is equal to average utility multiplied by a positive-valued function of population size. If the function is equal to population size or any positive multiple, the principle is CU and, if the function is equal to any positive constant, AU results.

It is possible for an NDU principle to approximate CU for "small" population sizes and AU for "large" ones, a property originally suggested by Hurka (1983). Such a case is illustrated in Figure 5.7. For that principle, the function takes on the values 1, 2, 2.6, and 3 for population sizes one, two, three, and four or more, respectively. For population sizes one and two, the value function coincides with that of CU and alternatives with population sizes greater than three are ranked by AU.

Critical levels for NDU are equal to a multiple of average utility and the multiple can depend on population size. In the example of Figure 5.7, the ratios of critical levels to average utilities are 0, 0.31, 0.47, and 1 for population sizes one, two, three, and four or more.

A subclass specializes NDU in a way that is parallel to the way that constant critical levels specialize NCLU. In that subclass, the ratio of critical levels to average utilities is a positive constant between zero and one. A second subclass also uses a positive constant k less than one and makes the function that multiplies average utility equal to the sum $1 + k + \cdots + k^{n-1}$ (Arrhenius 2000a, 2000b). Because critical levels for the NDU principles are equal to a multiple of average utility, they have some negative critical levels unless the ratio is equal to zero. In that case, however, the principle is CU: all other members of the class have some negative critical levels and, therefore, fail to satisfy the negative expansion principle.

Some members of the NDU class, such as CU, imply the repugnant conclusion and others, such as AU, do not. The repugnant conclusion is avoided if and only if the multiplying function does not increase without limit as population size increases. All NDU principles for which the ratio of critical levels to average utilities is a positive constant between zero and one lead to the repugnant conclusion. If the ratio is nonconstant, the requirement that it be nondecreasing is consistent with Hurka's suggestion and Carlson's intuition (discussed in

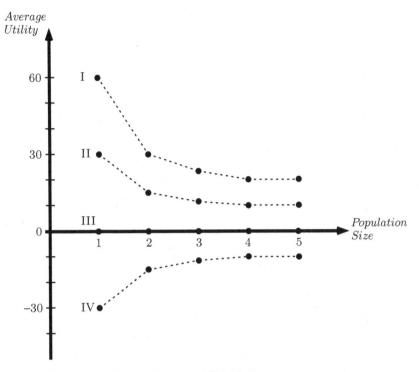

Figure 5.7. Number-Dampened Utilitarianism.

Subsection 5.1.1). To avoid the repugnant conclusion, any NDU principle for which the ratio of critical levels to average utilities is nondecreasing and between zero and one must approximate average utilitarianism as population size becomes large. That is true when the multiplying function is $1 + k + \cdots + k^{n-1}$. In addition, the sum itself approaches $1/(1 - k)$ as population size becomes large and the repugnant conclusion is avoided.

Because every NDU principle ranks all alternatives with positive average utilities as better than all alternatives with negative average utilities, all the NDU principles satisfy priority for lives worth living. Every member of the NDU class satisfies same-number independence but none of them other than CU satisfies either utility or existence independence.

5.2.8   Restricted Number-Dampened Utilitarianism

Suggested by Hurka (2000), the restricted number-dampened utilitarian (RNDU) class of principles provides a partial solution to one of the most important defects of the number-dampened class – namely, that all those principles other than CU do not satisfy the negative expansion principle.

The value function for a restricted principle coincides with the NDU value function when average utility is positive and with the CU value function when

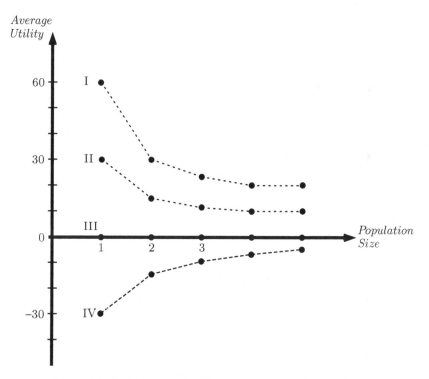

Figure 5.8. Restricted Number-Dampened Utilitarianism.

average utility is nonpositive. The restricted version of the example of Figure 5.7 is illustrated in Figure 5.8. Above the population-size axis, the iso-value curves are the same for both principles. But below the population-size axis, iso-value curves for the restricted principle approach the population-size axis for large population sizes, reflecting the fact that the value function coincides with the CU value function for negative average utilities.

Because of this, critical levels for alternatives with nonpositive average utilities are zero and, hence, nonnegative. Critical levels for alternatives with positive average utilities are not necessarily nonnegative, however. Suppose the function that multiplies average utility takes on the values one and four for population sizes one and two and consider an alternative in which a single person has a utility level of four. Then the critical level is -2. For any NDU principle, the ratios of critical levels to average utilities are nonnegative if and only if the ratio of the multiplying function to population size does not increase as population size increases. This condition, applied to RNDU principles, is necessary and sufficient for nonnegative critical levels and, therefore, for the negative expansion principle.

Several special cases of RNDU have, however, nonnegative critical levels for all utility vectors. The first of these is restricted AU (RAU). Its value function is equal to average utility when average utility is positive and is equal to total utility when average utility is nonpositive. Its critical levels are equal to average utility for utility vectors with positive average utility and are equal to zero for utility vectors whose average utility is nonpositive. The restricted version of NDU for which the ratio of critical levels to average utilities is a constant between zero and one also has nonnegative critical levels: they are equal to the constant multiplied by average utility when average utility is positive and are equal to zero when average utility is nonpositive. And when the multiplying function is $1 + k + \cdots + k^{n-1}$, critical levels for the restricted principle are positive for all alternatives with positive average utility and zero otherwise.

The repugnant conclusion refers to alternatives with positive average utilities only. Because value functions for the RNDU principles coincide with the value functions for their unrestricted counterparts when average utility is positive, the conditions for avoidance of the repugnant conclusion are the same for the restricted and unrestricted classes.

It is difficult to justify the use of a multiplying function such as $1 + k + \cdots + k^{n-1}$ in an RNDU principle because the choice of the constant k has no obvious ethical interpretation. In addition, because the ratio of the critical level to average utility is positive for all population sizes and rises with population size, CU is not approximated at small population sizes unless k is "very close" to one. In Part B, we suggest a two-parameter principle that coincides with CU for all population sizes that are no less than some fixed population size $\bar{n}$ and then moves toward AU as population size increases. Without further investigation, the choice of the parameter values is arbitrary.

As is the case for the NDU principles, all members of the RNDU class rank all alternatives with positive average utilities as better than all those with negative average utilities. Consequently, they all satisfy priority for lives worth living. Of all the RNDU principles, only CU satisfies utility and existence independence. This follows from the discussion of independence and the NDU principles.

5.2.9 Population Principles and the Axioms: A Summary

Table 5.3 summarizes the analysis of this section. The first part of the table lists classes of principles that can be regarded as generalizations of CU and the second lists classes that can be thought of as generalizations of AU. The first group consists of all the unrestricted and restricted critical-level principles and the second consists of all the unrestricted and restricted number-dampened principles. In the second group, we have included RAU, which is a member of the restricted number-dampened class and three cases of number-dampened principles and their restricted counterparts. The first group of number-dampened principles consists of the whole of the NDU class, the second selects members of the class in which the ratios of critical levels to average utilities are equal to a constant between zero and one, and the third selects NDU principles for which the ratios of critical levels to average utilities are positive, are nondecreasing, and approach one as population size becomes large. The last group approximates AU as population size increases. There is no anonymous

Table 5.3. *Properties of Population Principles*

	Utility Independence	Existence Independence	Negative Expansion	Avoidance of the Repugnant Conclusion	Priority for Lives Worth Living
CU[1]	•	•	•		•
CLU[2]	•	•	•	•	•
RCLU[3]			•	•	
NCLU[4]	•		•	•	
RNCLU[5]			•	•	•
AU[6]				•	•
RAU[7]			•	•	•
NDU[8]					•
RNDU[9]				•	•
NDU[10]					•
RNDU[11]			•	•	•
NDU[12]					•
RNDU[13]			•	•	•

1. Classical utilitarianism.
2. Critical-level utilitarianism: positive critical level.
3. Restricted critical-level utilitarianism: positive critical-level parameter.
4. Number-sensitive critical-level utilitarianism: nonnegative, nondecreasing critical levels; some positive.
5. Restricted number-sensitive critical-level utilitarianism: restricted version of 4.
6. Average utilitarianism.
7. Restricted average utilitarianism.
8. Number-dampened utilitarianism: general case.
9. Restricted number-dampened utilitarianism: general case.
10. Number-dampened utilitarianism: ratio of critical level to average utility is a positive constant less than one.
11. Restricted number-dampened utilitarianism: restricted version of 10.
12. Number-dampened utilitarianism: ratio of critical level to average utility is positive, nondecreasing, and approaches one as population size increases.
13. Restricted number-dampened utilitarianism: restricted version of 12.

population principle that satisfies continuity, strong Pareto, intermediate existence of critical levels, utility independence, avoidance of the repugnant conclusion, and priority for lives worth living. It is also true that there is no population principle that satisfies continuity, strong Pareto, weak existence of critical levels, existence independence, avoidance of the repugnant conclusion, and priority for lives worth living (proofs are presented in Chapter 6). In comparing principles, therefore, we should bear in mind that no principle can be completely satisfactory.

We regard satisfaction of the negative expansion principle as an essential property of population principles and use it to eliminate some of the subclasses in the table. None of the classes in the first group is eliminated but all of the unrestricted principles in the second are. For the same reason, the general case of RNDU principles is eliminated. As a consequence, we focus on RAU and the second and third restricted number-dampened classes.

Many investigators, among them Heyd (1992) and Parfit (1976, 1982, 1984), make a strong case for avoidance of the repugnant conclusion. If we accept that view, we may eliminate CU and all but the last of the restricted versions of NDU. The principles that remain fall into two categories: those that satisfy utility or existence independence but violate priority for lives worth living; and those that satisfy neither utility nor existence independence but satisfy priority for lives worth living. We consider the two groups in turn.

The NCLU class, which includes CLU, is the only one that can satisfy utility independence and all axioms other than priority for lives worth living. Of the members of this class that do not imply the repugnant conclusion, the most attractive are those whose critical levels do not decrease as population size increases.[11] In that case, avoidance of the repugnant conclusion requires critical levels to be positive after some population size is reached. If there is more than one critical level, however, existence independence is not satisfied: that axiom requires constant critical levels. Therefore, if existence independence is thought to be desirable, members of the critical-level class with positive critical levels are the only satisfactory principles.

The principles in the second group avoid the repugnant conclusion, satisfy priority for lives worth living, but necessarily violate both utility and existence independence. Subclasses in Table 5.3 that have the requisite characteristics are RCLU, RNCLU, RAU, and RNDU such that the ratios of critical levels to average utilities are positive, are nondecreasing, and approach one as numbers increase. Of these, RAU retains the stark trade-offs of AU for alternatives with positive average utilities.

The last of these subclasses has its own problems, however. All members of this subclass other than RAU must have ratios of critical levels to average utilities that are different for some population sizes. As a consequence, some moral significance must be attached to certain absolute numbers. If the

---

[11] Nondecreasing critical levels are consistent with Carlson's intuition, which is discussed in Subsection 5.1.1.

principle approximates CU at small population sizes and AU at large ones, some numerical meaning for "small" and "large" must be found so that the "speed" of the transition between the two limiting cases can be chosen. It is, however, very difficult to see how this can be done without reference to the carrying capacity of the universe. If that occurs, then value becomes confounded with constraints. The same consideration applies to the NCLU principles.

An axiom, proposed by Zoli (2002), that deals with this problem is called extended replication invariance. It requires replications of any two utility vectors to be ranked in the same way as the originals. Thus, it is stronger than replication invariance (Chapter 4). The axiom suggests that relative, rather than absolute, population size matters. The only NCLU principles that satisfy it are the CLU principles.

Both the restricted and unrestricted critical-level principles require the choice of a single parameter that must be positive if the repugnant conclusion is to be avoided. In both cases, that parameter places a floor on the trade-off between average utility and population size: alternatives with average utility above the parameter are better than all others. Feldman (1995, 1997) defended CLU with the critical level set equal to "some modest level of happiness that people deserve merely in virtue of being people" and added that, if a person has a positive utility level that is below the critical level, "it does not make the world better" and "may make the world worse" (Feldman 1997, p. 194).[12] These comments are consistent with both the unrestricted and the restricted critical-level principles. Feldman allows for different levels of desert for different people and they can be based on nonwelfare characteristics such as industriousness. Even with multiple critical levels, however, the resulting principles rank same-population alternatives with utilitarianism: the critical levels play no role. In addition, such principles prefer the ceteris-paribus addition of a person with a low critical level to the addition of a person with a high critical level provided they are expected to have the same lifetime-utility level. Consequently, it may be better to regard the critical level as an ethical parameter that is independent of desert.

We do not have to choose principles whose same-number subprinciples are utilitarian. All the utilitarian principles discussed above are members of larger classes whose same-number subprinciples are generalized utilitarian. The axioms we employ do not rule out giving priority to the interests of low-utility individuals and the resulting inequality aversion that generalized utilitarian principles can represent. Carlson's (1998) combined principle is unsatisfactory because it is not continuous and satisfies neither weak nor strong Pareto, but it is possible to find an acceptable principle that accords with his intuitions. His principle gives priority to the well-being of individuals who are below neutrality. This can be accomplished with generalized utilitarian same-number subprinciples by using a transformation like the one illustrated in the lower panel of Figure 4.6. Although Carlson rejects existence independence, the example

---

[12] See also Arrhenius (2000b, 2003).

he discusses is consistent with utility independence. If utility independence is accepted, then number-sensitive critical-level generalized utilitarian principles satisfy his requirements. To be consistent with his intuition, critical levels would have to be nondecreasing and nonconstant. If utility independence is rejected, a restricted number-sensitive generalized utilitarian principle or a restricted number-dampened generalized utilitarian principle with a suitable choice of the multiplying function would be appropriate.

5.3   EXAMPLES AND APPLICATIONS

In this section, we use examples in addition to the disabled-child example to compare CLU with a positive critical level, RCLU with a positive critical-level parameter, NCLU, RNCLU, and RNDU such that the ratio of critical levels to average utility is positive. In all cases, critical levels exist and are nonnegative for all utility vectors with positive average utility and positive for some. We do not consider the generalized versions of these principles when the qualitative results are similar.

Some population problems require more complex considerations than the examples considered here, and two of them are discussed in Chapter 11. In the first, a developing country receives foreign aid, which can be used for consumption or resource-using population control (prevention of births). CLU is used to find the best combination of these activities. In the second, the use of animals in research and food production is examined. The human population is assumed to be fixed, but animal population sizes depend on animal use. CLU is extended to give the animals moral standing and best (first-best) and second-best policies are investigated.

5.3.1   Giving Weight to Unfragmented Lives

If a population principle's same-number subprinciples are utilitarian, a positive critical level has the effect of giving weight to unfragmented lives. Suppose that, in alternative x, person 1 has a lifetime-utility level of 100 and, in alternative y, persons 1 and 2 live instead with utility levels of 50 each (see Table 5.4). If no one else is affected (the utility vectors of all others are given by u° in both alternatives in the table), CU declares the two equally good but any principle with a positive critical level for the original utility vector (of all those that ever live) ranks the first alternative as better: weight is given to the fact that a single

Table 5.4. *Fragmented Life Example*

	Person 1	Person 2	Other People
x	100		u°
y	50	50	u°

person experiences a utility of 100. CLU and NCLU with positive critical levels have this property. If the critical level associated with x is zero, NCLU ranks x and y as equally good.

If average utility in x is positive, RCLU, RNCLU with a positive critical level for the utility vector in x, and RNDU rank x as better than y. If, however, average utility in x is nonpositive, all these principles rank x and y as equally good. Note that this can occur when the utility levels of persons 1 and 2 are positive. If the property of giving more weight to less fragmented lives is regarded as important, therefore, CLU and NCLU have an obvious advantage over the restricted principles. It is worth noting that the effect does not depend on the utility levels of the contemporaries of persons 1 and 2 alone but, rather, on the utilities of all those who ever live.

It is interesting to observe the behavior of the unrestricted number-dampened principles when average utility in x is negative. In that case, the critical level is negative and y is ranked as better than x: the principle favors fragmentation of lives.

If a principle has same-number subprinciples that are inequality-averse generalized utilitarian, weight may not be given to unfragmented lives even if critical levels are positive. In that case, classical generalized utilitarianism ranks alternative y as better. A positive critical level for the utility vector in x is not always sufficient to make x better, however. If, for example, $g(\tau) = 1 - \exp(-\tau/10)$ and the critical level is c, x is better than y if c is less than 43.1 and y is better than x if c is greater than 43.1. This result may be interpreted as an argument against inequality aversion.

5.3.2   Abortion

Suppose a pregnant woman is considering an abortion and wants to know whether it would result in a better state of affairs. She is unaffected, in utility terms, by the decision, as are all other people. If the abortion does not take place, the embryo will become a person with a lifetime-utility level of u_e, which may be above or below neutrality. The embryo is not yet sentient and does not have experiences.

Standard arguments about the ethics of abortion claim that it matters whether the embryo has moral standing as a person. But, for CU, that distinction is irrelevant. The abortion has good consequences if and only if u_e is negative (below neutrality).

Now suppose the critical level for the original utility vector (without the embryo) is positive. In that case, it matters whether the embryo has moral standing as a person. Suppose it is regarded as a person. Then the decision to abort does not affect population size and abortion is equivalent to euthanasia. The abortion has good consequences if u_e is negative. Suppose, however, the embryo does *not* have moral standing as a person. In that case, the decision to abort affects population size. Although this does not matter to the CU ranking, it does matter when the critical level is positive. In that case, the abortion has good consequences when u_e is less than the critical level. It follows that, for positive critical levels, if the embryo has moral standing, abortion is permissible in fewer cases than when it does not.[13] This judgment is made by all CLU and NCLU principles with positive critical levels.

The restricted principles make more complex judgments. If the embryo has moral standing, all of them agree that abortion is equivalent to euthanasia and that it has good consequences only when u_e is negative. If the embryo does not have moral standing, the judgment depends on the critical level which, in turn, depends on the average utility of all those who ever live. If that average utility is nonpositive, the restricted principles rank the alternatives in the same way CU does.

5.3.3   Wrongful Births

If the critical level of lifetime utility is positive, principles distinguish between killing someone and preventing his or her existence. Once an individual has been born, he or she is alive in all feasible states, and all positive utility levels have value. Reducing his or her lifetime utility in any way, including killing, is socially and morally undesirable, other things equal. Suppose that, in alternative x, a person is killed and this reduces his or her lifetime well-being by τ units (others are unaffected). In alternative y, the existence of a person who would have a lifetime utility level of τ is prevented. As long as the critical level is positive and the same-number subprinciples are generalized utilitarian, x is ranked as worse than y.[14] Thus preventing someone's death is more important than bringing about new lives when the consequences for total utility are the same. CLU principles with positive critical levels (including the number-sensitive CLU principles) make this judgment in all cases but the restricted principles make it only when the average utility of all those who ever live is positive; if it is negative, they rank the two alternatives as equally good.

If CLU with a positive critical level is used to rank alternatives, it would be better if some, but not necessarily all, individuals with lifetime-utility levels that are positive but below the critical level had not be born. However, preventing the existence of all people whose lifetime utilities are below the critical level is not appropriate in general. If everyone's standard of living in an equal, over-populated world were below the critical level and the prevention of births were costless, it would have been better if *some,* but not all, people had not been born – it does not matter which ones as long as the utilities of the remaining people are above the critical level. If, however, someone's lifetime utility is *necessarily* below the critical level because of a serious incurable chronic illness, say, it

---

[13] Glannon (1997) provided a discussion of the relationship between human life and status as a person. See also Bermúdez (1996) for a discussion of the question of the moral standing of embryos and fœtuses and the significance of birth. Singer (1994) discussed the ethics of preventing and preserving human and nonhuman life.

[14] McMahan (1996) argued that impersonal theories must rank x and y as equally good, but he assumed that critical levels are zero.

Table 5.5. *Asteroid Example*

	Population Size	Average Utility
x	10 billion	50
y	20 billion	40

would have been better if his or her existence had been prevented. A similar observation applies to the restricted principles as long as the average utility of all those who ever live is positive.

5.3.4   Future Generations

Suppose that, in the year 2100, astronomers discover an asteroid on a collision course with Earth that will obliterate life on the planet if nothing is done (alternative x). If, however, resources are committed to a costly international program, the asteroid can be diverted and the planet saved (alternative y).

The example is illustrated in Table 5.5. If the asteroid is not diverted, 10 billion people live with an average utility of 50. If the asteroid is diverted, the number of people who ever live is doubled and their average utility is 40; average well-being is lower because of the resources used to divert the asteroid. Average utilitarianism declares x to be better and classical utilitarianism ranks y as better.

Critical-level utilitarianism ranks x as better if the critical level is greater than 30 and y as better if the critical level is less than 30. A similar observation applies to number-sensitive CLU. Suppose the critical levels are 5 for population sizes 1 to 9,999,999,999, 15 for population sizes 10 billion to 14,999,999,999, and 35 for all larger populations. In that case, writing billion as b, the NCLU value of x is $10b(50 - 5) = 450b$ and the value of y is $10b(50 - 5) + 5b(40 - 15) + 5b(40 - 35) = 600b$. Consequently, y is better. Restricted CLU and restricted NCLU make the same judgments as their unrestricted counterparts.

Suppose, now, that restricted number-dampened utilitarianism is used. If the function of population size that multiplies average utility is $1 + k + \ldots + k^{n-1}$ where k is a constant between 0 and 1, k must be *very* close to 1 to avoid having x ranked as better. If k is 0.999999 or less, x is better. To make a judgment that is not equivalent to that of AU, k must be much closer to one. If, for example, k is the billionth root of 0.9, values are 20.5 for x and 26.1 for y and, in that case, y is better.

5.4   INFORMATION REQUIREMENTS

Population principles have information requirements that differ from those of the fixed-population counterparts of their same-number subprinciples. For example, fixed-population utilitarianism is well-defined if utilities are cardinally measurable and unit comparable. By contrast, same-number utilitarianism requires full interpersonal comparability. The reason is that same-number utilitarianism ranks as equally good any two alternatives whose associated utility vectors are permutations of each other. Consequently, equality of utilities must be preserved across admissible transformations. This argument can be applied to any anonymous principle: all of them require full interpersonal comparability.

Cardinal full comparability is not compatible with classical utilitarianism. Because the sum of utilities is a value function for that principle, the zero level of utility must represent neutrality. Consequently, classical utilitarianism requires that utilities satisfy ratio-scale full comparability: the principle is invariant to scaling all utilities by a common positive multiple.

Critical-level utilitarianism requires the critical level of utility as a norm but does not need the normalization of neutrality to zero. If utilities are cardinally measurable and fully comparable and the critical level is a norm, CLU is well-defined. If, instead, utilities are cardinally measurable and there are two norms, numerical full comparability results, and any principle can be applied. However, adding a single norm to cardinal measurability and full interpersonal comparability does not allow us to apply number-sensitive CLU with more than one critical-level parameter or any of the restricted critical-level principles with nonzero critical-level parameters.

Because neutrality plays no role in average utilitarianism, this principle does not need the normalization of neutrality to zero. Therefore, AU is consistent with cardinal full comparability. Restricted average utilitarianism does need the zero normalization, however, and it follows that cardinal full comparability does not provide a suitable informational base – a weaker invariance condition such as that with respect to ratio-scale full comparability is required to apply that principle. The same observation applies to (restricted) number-dampened utilitarian principles other than (restricted) AU.

If a principle has same-number subprinciples that are generalized utilitarian, the situation is more complex. The information-invariance assumptions compatible with generalized utilitarianism depend on the transformation g used to define a principle. For that reason, this approach to the information problem is arbitrary, and we suggest that cardinal measurability and two interpersonally comparable norms be used instead to produce numerical full comparability.

Part B

As established in the previous chapter, the representative-utility function associated with a fixed-population social-evaluation ordering is a convenient representation that exists under fairly weak conditions. In a variable-population setting, however, knowledge of the representative utilities of two utility vectors of different dimension is not sufficient to rank them. We begin Part B with a representation theorem, which shows that, given several assumptions, there is an ordering of population-size–representative-utility pairs, which can be used, along with the representative-utility functions, to establish the social-evaluation ordering. Moreover, we show that, if extended continuity is satisfied, a value function exists. We then turn to formal statements of some important axioms and prove two theorems concerning their compatibility. Definitions and discussions of some important population principles follow (see also Part A). In addition to some generalized utilitarian principles, we examine the extended maximin and critical-level leximin principles.

5.5 BASIC AXIOMS AND REPRESENTATIONS

A fundamental result in population ethics states that if the representative-utility functions exist, knowledge of representative utilities and population sizes is sufficient to establish the social-evaluation ordering R on the set of all utility vectors $\Omega = \cup_{n \in \mathcal{Z}_{++}} \mathcal{R}^n$. If R satisfies an extended-continuity axiom, this observation can be extended to a representation theorem. It establishes the existence of a reduced-form value function that depends on representative utility and population size. To present these results, we begin by formulating continuity, the various versions of the Pareto principles, and minimal increasingness for the anonymous variable-population ordering R. As in Chapter 3, because these axioms merely require the same-number analogue of the requisite fixed-population axiom to be satisfied for all population sizes, we use the same names for the variable-population versions. The interpretation of these properties is analogous to that of their fixed-population counterparts.

Continuity. For all $n \in \mathcal{Z}_{++}$ and for all $u \in \mathcal{R}^n$, the sets $\{v \in \mathcal{R}^n \mid vRu\}$ and $\{v \in \mathcal{R}^n \mid uRv\}$ are closed in $\mathcal{R}^n$.

Weak Pareto. For all $n \in \mathcal{Z}_{++}$ and for all $u, v \in \mathcal{R}^n$, if $u \gg v$, then uPv.

Strong Pareto. For all $n \in \mathcal{Z}_{++}$ and for all $u, v \in \mathcal{R}^n$, if $u > v$, then uPv.

Pareto Weak Preference. For all $n \in \mathcal{Z}_{++}$ and for all $u, v \in \mathcal{R}^n$, if $u > v$, then uRv.

Minimal Increasingness. For all $n \in \mathcal{Z}_{++}$, and for all $a, b \in \mathcal{R}$, if $a > b$, then $a\mathbf{1}_n P b\mathbf{1}_n$.

For each $n \in \mathcal{Z}_{++}$, continuity, Pareto weak preference, and minimal increasingness guarantee the existence of the representative-utility function $\Xi^n \colon \mathcal{R}^n \to \mathcal{R}$ with the properties established in Theorem 4.1. Furthermore, because R is anonymous, each Ξ^n is symmetric.

In contrast to the fixed-population case, knowledge of the representative utilities $\Xi^n(u)$ and $\Xi^m(v)$ for two utility vectors $u \in \mathcal{R}^n$ and $v \in \mathcal{R}^m$ is not sufficient to rank u and v if $n \neq m$. For variable-population comparisons, the only information that is required in addition to representative utility is population

size. This is the essence of a result due to Blackorby and Donaldson (1984a).
Note that no assumptions other than the fixed-population axioms continuity,
Pareto weak preference, and minimal increasingness are required.

Theorem 5.1. *If R satisfies continuity, Pareto weak preference, and minimal
increasingness, then there exists an ordering* **R** *on* $\mathcal{Z}_{++} \times \mathcal{R}$ *such that, for all
$n \in \mathcal{Z}_{++}$ and for all $\xi, \zeta \in \mathcal{R}$,*

$$(n, \xi)\mathbf{R}(n, \zeta) \Leftrightarrow \xi \geq \zeta \tag{5.1}$$

and, for all $n, m \in \mathcal{Z}_{++}$, for all $u \in \mathcal{R}^n$, and for all $v \in \mathcal{R}^m$,

$$u R v \Leftrightarrow \left(n, \Xi^n(u)\right)\mathbf{R}\left(m, \Xi^m(v)\right). \tag{5.2}$$

Proof. The existence of the representative-utility function Ξ^n for all $n \in \mathcal{Z}_{++}$
follows from Theorem 4.1. Now define the relation **R** on $\mathcal{Z}_{++} \times \mathcal{R}$ by letting,
for all $(n, \xi), (m, \zeta) \in \mathcal{Z}_{++} \times \mathcal{R}$,

$$(n, \xi)\mathbf{R}(m, \zeta) \Leftrightarrow \xi \mathbf{1}_n R \zeta \mathbf{1}_m. \tag{5.3}$$

Clearly, **R** is an ordering. Because $\Xi^n(\gamma \mathbf{1}_n) = \gamma$ for all $n \in \mathcal{Z}_{++}$ and for all
$\gamma \in \mathcal{R}$, it follows that $u I \Xi^n(u)\mathbf{1}_n$ for all $n \in \mathcal{Z}_{++}$ and for all $u \in \mathcal{R}^n$. Together
with (5.3) and the transitivity of R, (5.2) follows. (5.1) is a consequence of the
fact that each Ξ^n is a representation of the restriction of R to $\mathcal{R}^n$. ∎

We call **R** a reduced-form social-evaluation ordering and use **P** and **I** to denote
its asymmetric and symmetric factors.

Theorem 5.1 reduces the information necessary to establish a variable-
population principle, but it is not a representation result: some of the reduced-
form orderings characterized in the theorem orderings do not have representations. For example, the lexicographic ordering defined by

$$(n, \xi)\mathbf{R}(m, \zeta) \Leftrightarrow \xi > \zeta \text{ or } \left[\xi = \zeta \text{ and } n \geq m\right]$$

for all $(n, \xi), (m, \zeta) \in \mathcal{Z}_{++} \times \mathcal{R}$, is not representable. This can be verified
by using an argument analogous to that employed by Debreu (1959). It is
important that the continuous variable ξ has lexicographic priority over the
discrete variable n in this example. The lexicographic ordering obtained by
reversing priorities, given by

$$(n, \xi)\mathbf{R}(m, \zeta) \Leftrightarrow n > m \text{ or } \left[n = m \text{ and } \xi \geq \zeta\right] \tag{5.4}$$

for all $(n, \xi), (m, \zeta) \in \mathcal{Z}_{++} \times \mathcal{R}$, does have a representation: the function
$W: \mathcal{Z}_{++} \times \mathcal{R} \to \mathcal{R}$ defined by

$$W(n, \xi) = \begin{cases} n - 1 + \frac{1}{2}\exp(\xi) & \text{if } \xi \leq 0, \\ n - \frac{1}{2}\exp(-\xi) & \text{if } \xi > 0 \end{cases}$$

for all $(n, \xi) \in \mathcal{Z}_{++} \times \mathcal{R}$ represents the ordering defined in (5.4) because $W(n, \mathcal{R}) = (n - 1, n)$ for all $n \in \mathcal{Z}_{++}$ and W is increasing in its second argument.

The existence of a representation of **R** (and, thus, of a representation of R) can be guaranteed by strengthening continuity to the following variable-population version; see the extended-continuity axiom introduced in Chapter 2.

Extended Continuity. For all $n, m \in \mathcal{Z}_{++}$ and for all $u \in \mathcal{R}^n$, the sets $\{v \in \mathcal{R}^m \mid vRu\}$ and $\{v \in \mathcal{R}^m \mid uRv\}$ are closed in $\mathcal{R}^m$.

Unlike continuity, extended continuity imposes restrictions across dimensions. Consider utility vector u of dimension n. For any population size m (not necessarily equal to n), the set of all utility vectors of dimension m that are at least as good as (at most as good as) u must be a closed set. It follows that small changes in utilities cannot lead to large changes in the social ranking of utility vectors: for any utility vector $v \in \mathcal{R}^m$ that is better (worse) than $u \in \mathcal{R}^n$, there exists a neighborhood of v in $\mathcal{R}^m$ such that all vectors in this neighborhood are better (worse) than u as well.

If extended continuity obtains, a representation, continuous and increasing in its second argument, exists. Proofs of the following representation theorem are given by Blackorby, Bossert, and Donaldson (2001a, 2001b) and Broome (2003).

Theorem 5.2. *If R satisfies extended continuity, Pareto weak preference, and minimal increasingness, then there exist a value function $V: \Omega \to \mathcal{R}$ and a reduced-form value function $W: \mathcal{Z}_{++} \times \mathcal{R} \to \mathcal{R}$, such that, for all $n, m \in \mathcal{Z}_{++}$, for all $u \in \mathcal{R}^n$, and for all $v \in \mathcal{R}^m$,*

$$uRv \Leftrightarrow V(u) = W\big(n, \Xi^n(u)\big) \geq W\big(m, \Xi^m(v)\big) = V(v),$$

where the restriction of V to $\mathcal{R}^n$ is continuous for all $n \in \mathcal{Z}_{++}$ and W is continuous and increasing in its second argument.

The statement of the above theorem could be modified. Pareto weak preference and minimal increasingness are not required to obtain a representation of R. However, without those axioms, the representative-utility functions would no longer be well-defined and would have to be replaced with less structured fixed-population aggregators.

Theorem 5.2 can be extended if the null alternative – the alternative in which no one is alive – is added to X. In that case, the domain of the value function V becomes $\Omega \cup \{u_\emptyset\}$ and the domain of the reduced-form value function W becomes $(\mathcal{Z}_{++} \times \mathcal{R}) \cup \{(0, u_\emptyset)\}$, where $u_\emptyset$ is assigned to the null alternative in place of a utility vector. The null alternative can be positioned anywhere in the social ranking.

5.6 POPULATION AXIOMS

We now introduce some axioms that are genuine variable-population axioms in the sense that they go beyond extending fixed-population axioms to all possible populations – they involve comparisons of utility vectors of different dimensions.

We begin with some variable-population extensions of the separability property same-people independence. First, we formulate same-number independence as a property of R, which requires the fixed-population property to be satisfied for all populations. When reformulated for anonymous orderings, same-people independence becomes same-number independence.

Same-Number Independence. For all $n, m \in \mathcal{Z}_{++}$, for all $u, v \in \mathcal{R}^n$, and for all $w, s \in \mathcal{R}^m$,

$$(u, w)R(v, w) \Leftrightarrow (u, s)R(v, s).$$

A natural generalization of the axiom requires that the ranking of any two utility vectors should not depend on the utilities of those who are unconcerned even if the number of concerned individuals is not the same in the two vectors, provided that the number of unconcerned and their utilities are the same in the two utility vectors. Let $\Omega_\emptyset = \Omega \cup \{u_\emptyset\}$. In the statement of the utility-independence axiom that follows, inclusion of the utility vector corresponding to the null alternative is not in conflict with the assumption that population size is positive for all alternatives. We use $u_\emptyset$ merely to allow for the possibility that nobody is added to a nonempty population but total population is nonempty in all alternatives involved. Thus, all utility vectors to be ranked are in Ω.

Utility Independence. For all $u, v \in \Omega_\emptyset$, for all $r \in \mathcal{Z}_{++}$, and for all $w, s \in \mathcal{R}^r$,

$$(u, w)R(v, w) \Leftrightarrow (u, s)R(v, s).$$

Utility independence extends same-number independence to situations in which the number of concerned individuals may differ in the alternatives to be compared. The number of the unconcerned is the same in both alternatives. A natural generalization of the axiom requires that the ranking of any two utility vectors should be independent not only of the utilities of those who are unconcerned but also of whether they exist. This axiom, whose motivation appears to be as plausible as that of utility independence in a variable-population setting, is a strengthening of utility independence and we call it existence independence.

Existence Independence. For all $u, v, w \in \Omega$,

$$(u, w)R(v, w) \Leftrightarrow uRv.$$

That existence independence indeed implies utility independence can be seen as follows. Suppose R satisfies existence independence, and let $u, v \in \Omega_\emptyset$,

$r \in \mathcal{Z}_{++}$, and $w, s \in \mathcal{R}^r$. Applying existence independence twice, we obtain

$$(u, w)R(v, w) \Leftrightarrow (u, w, s)R(v, w, s) \Leftrightarrow (u, s)R(v, s)$$

and utility independence is satisfied.

Next, we consider axioms that impose restrictions on the response of R to specific additions to a given population. A critical level associated with utility vector $u \in \Omega$ is a level of utility $c \in \mathcal{R}$ such that (u, c) is as good as u. Thus, a critical level for a utility vector u is a utility level such that the ceteris-paribus addition of an individual at this critical level to an existing population leads to an alternative that is as good as the original. Clearly, without further assumptions, critical levels may depend on the original utility vector. Moreover, critical levels need not exist and if they do, they need not be unique. However, if R satisfies strong Pareto and a critical level exists for $u \in \Omega$, then it must be unique – that is, no other utility level is a critical level for u. If a unique critical level exists for every utility vector in Ω, we can describe the critical levels by means of a critical-level function $C: \Omega \to \mathcal{R}$. Critical levels can also be defined for alternatives rather than utility vectors. Given that we restrict attention to welfarist orderings, we use the formulation in terms of utilities.

Several versions of existence requirements for critical levels are employed. The first requires critical levels to exist for all utility vectors.

Existence of Critical Levels. For all $u \in \Omega$, there exists $c \in \mathcal{R}$ such that $(u, c)Iu$.

A weaker axiom requires, for each possible population size n, the existence of at least one utility vector $u \in \mathcal{R}^n$ that possesses a critical level.

Intermediate Existence of Critical Levels. For all $n \in \mathcal{Z}_{++}$, there exist $u \in \mathcal{R}^n$ and $c \in \mathcal{R}$ such that $(u, c)Iu$.

A further weakening is obtained if we merely require the existence of one utility vector in Ω with a critical level.

Weak Existence of Critical Levels. There exist $u \in \Omega$ and $c \in \mathcal{R}$ such that $(u, c)Iu$.

In all the axioms requiring the existence of (some) critical levels, no restriction is imposed on the critical levels for different utility vectors – in particular, critical levels can be different for different utility vectors.

Weak existence of critical levels does not imply intermediate existence of critical levels, and intermediate existence of critical levels does not imply existence of critical levels. However, as shown later, these implications are true if additional axioms are imposed.

If the null alternative is included, its utility vector $u_\emptyset$ has critical level $c_\emptyset$ and if a (reduced-form) value function exists, then $V(u_\emptyset) = W(0, u_\emptyset) = W(1, c_\emptyset) = V((c_\emptyset))$.

The previous axioms only impose the existence of critical levels in various forms, but their properties are not specified. We now turn to more specific consequences of population expansions.

A desirable property of a population principle is that the addition of a person to a utility-unaffected population should be ranked as bad if the utility level of the added person is negative.

Negative Expansion Principle. For all $u \in \Omega$ and for all $d \in \mathcal{R}_{--}$, $u P(u, d)$.

The negative expansion principle is closely related to a condition on critical levels that we call nonnegative critical levels. It requires that, if a critical level exists, it must not be below zero, the level of utility representing neutrality.

Nonnegative Critical Levels. For all $u \in \Omega$ and for all $c \in \mathcal{R}$, if $(u, c)Iu$, then $c \geq 0$.

The negative expansion principle implies nonnegative critical levels. To see that this is the case, suppose the negative expansion principle is satisfied and that $(u, c)Iu$ for some $u \in \Omega$ and $c \in \mathcal{R}$. If $c \in \mathcal{R}_{--}$, the negative expansion principle implies $u P(u, c)$, contradicting our hypothesis. Thus, we must have $c \geq 0$.

Without further axioms, nonnegative critical levels does not imply the negative expansion principle. For example, the ordering R that declares $u \in \Omega$ at least as good as $v \in \Omega$ if and only if the number of individuals in u is greater than or equal to the number of people in v satisfies nonnegative critical levels because critical levels do not exist and violates the negative expansion principle.

However, if all critical levels exist and strong Pareto is satisfied, the two axioms are equivalent. To see that the negative expansion principle is implied by strong Pareto, existence of critical levels and nonnegative critical levels, suppose $u \in \Omega$ and $d \in \mathcal{R}_{---}$. By existence of critical levels, there exists $c \in \mathcal{R}$ such that $(u, c)Iu$. By nonnegative critical levels, $c \geq 0$ and thus $c > d$. Strong Pareto implies $(u, c)P(u, d)$ and, by transitivity, we obtain $u P(u, d)$.

A stronger property than nonnegative critical levels, which is more difficult to defend, requires all critical levels to be equal to the utility level representing neutrality.

Zero Critical Levels. For all $u \in \Omega$ and for all $c \in \mathcal{R}$, if $(u, c)Iu$, then $c = 0$.

An interpretation of zero critical levels is that of a variable-population extension of Pareto indifference. We do not find this axiom very compelling and we therefore do not endorse it. While, by definition of neutrality, it is true that a person who leads a neutral life considers this life to be as good as a life without any experiences, this is not the scenario of the axiom statement. Note that, of the two alternatives to be ranked, the individual in question exists in one but not in the other and, therefore, an appeal to a Pareto-like conclusion is not suitable. To defend the axiom on Paretian grounds, it has to be argued that the person considers both alternatives equally good. We do not think it makes sense to think of an individual who does not exist as being able to express such assessments and, therefore, our view is that zero critical levels is not a compelling axiom. Moreover, together with some rather uncontroversial axioms, it leads to the repugnant conclusion (to be defined shortly), which is an important reason why we suggest rejecting it.

A population principle implies the repugnant conclusion (Parfit 1976, 1982, 1984) if and only if, for any population size $n \in \mathcal{Z}_{++}$, any positive utility level ξ, and any utility level $\varepsilon \in (0, \xi)$, there exists a population size $m > n$ such that an m-person alternative in which every individual experiences utility level ε is ranked as better than an n-person society in which every individual's utility level is ξ. Note that the repugnant conclusion requires the existence of a population size m with the previously mentioned properties for *any* choice of n, ξ, and ε. The axiom that requires the repugnant conclusion to be avoided is defined as follows.

Avoidance of the Repugnant Conclusion. There exist $n \in \mathcal{Z}_{++}$, $\xi \in \mathcal{R}_{++}$, and $\varepsilon \in (0, \xi)$ such that, for all $m > n$, $\xi \mathbf{1}_n R \varepsilon \mathbf{1}_m$.

There is a conflict between zero critical levels and avoidance of the repugnant conclusion, provided minimal increasingness and a minimal inequality-aversion property are satisfied. Minimal inequality aversion requires that an equal distribution is at least as good as any utility vector with the same total utility.

Minimal Inequality Aversion. For all $n \in \mathcal{Z}_{++}$ and for all $u \in \mathcal{R}^n$, $[(1/n) \sum_{i=1}^{n} u_i] \mathbf{1}_n R u$.

Clearly, minimal inequality aversion is implied by weak inequality aversion.

We now obtain the following impossibility result, variants of which can be found elsewhere (Blackorby, Bossert, Donaldson, and Fleurbaey 1998; Blackorby and Donaldson 1991; Carlson 1998; McMahan 1981; Parfit 1976, 1982, 1984).[15]

Theorem 5.3. *There exists no population principle R that satisfies minimal increasingness, zero critical levels, avoidance of the repugnant conclusion, and minimal inequality aversion.*

Proof. We show that every population principle R that satisfies minimal increasingness, zero critical levels, and minimal inequality aversion implies the

---

[15] Blackorby, Bossert, Donaldson, and Fleurbaey (1998) proved a stronger result. First, they showed that minimal inequality aversion can be replaced with a condition that, in the presence of minimal increasingness, is weaker. Second, zero critical levels can be replaced with a weaker condition requiring that the addition of an individual with zero utility to a utility-unaffected population leads to an alternative that is at least as good as the original one.

repugnant conclusion. Let $n \in \mathcal{Z}_{++}$, $\xi \in \mathcal{R}_{++}$, and $\varepsilon \in (0, \xi)$, and suppose $m \in \mathcal{Z}_{++}$ is such that $m > 2n\xi/\varepsilon$. By minimal increasingness,

$$\varepsilon \mathbf{1}_m P \frac{2n\xi}{m} \mathbf{1}_m. \tag{5.5}$$

By minimal inequality aversion,

$$\frac{2n\xi}{m} \mathbf{1}_m R(2\xi \mathbf{1}_n, 0 \mathbf{1}_{m-n}). \tag{5.6}$$

By zero critical levels,

$$(2\xi \mathbf{1}_n, 0 \mathbf{1}_{m-n}) I 2\xi \mathbf{1}_n. \tag{5.7}$$

Using minimal increasingness again, we obtain

$$2\xi \mathbf{1}_n P \xi \mathbf{1}_n. \tag{5.8}$$

Now we can employ transitivity and combine (5.5), (5.6), (5.7), and (5.8) to obtain the repugnant conclusion. ∎

Theorem 5.3 remains true if zero critical levels is replaced with the requirement that all critical levels be nonpositive. In addition, if a principle has nonpositive critical levels and same-number subprinciples that are generalized utilitarian, it leads to the repugnant conclusion. This result does not require an inequality-aversion axiom.

A population principle implies the sadistic conclusion (Arrhenius 2000a) if and only if, when adding people to a utility-unaffected population, it can be better to add people with negative utilities rather than a possibly different number of people with positive utilities. To formulate the axiom avoidance of the sadistic conclusion, we define $\Omega_{++} = \cup_{n \in \mathcal{Z}_{++}} \mathcal{R}_{++}^n$ and $\Omega_{--} = \cup_{n \in \mathcal{Z}_{++}} \mathcal{R}_{--}^n$.

Avoidance of the Sadistic Conclusion. For all $u \in \Omega$, for all $v \in \Omega_{++}$, and for all $w \in \Omega_{--}$, $(u, v)R(u, w)$.

If the same-number subprinciples of R are utilitarian, there is a conflict between avoidance of the repugnant conclusion and avoidance of the sadistic conclusion, provided a weak regularity condition is satisfied. This regularity condition requires that, for any utility level ξ, there exists a society that is at least as good as the one-person society where the only individual alive has a utility of ξ. We call this property minimal one-person trade-off.

Minimal One-Person Trade-Off. For all $\xi \in \mathcal{R}$, there exists $u \in \Omega \setminus \mathcal{R}^1$ such that $u R \xi \mathbf{1}_1$.

Minimal one-person trade-off is implied by existence of critical levels. We obtain the following impossibility result.

Theorem 5.4. *There exists no population principle R that has utilitarian same-number subprinciples and satisfies avoidance of the repugnant conclusion, avoidance of the sadistic conclusion, and minimal one-person trade-off.*

Proof. Suppose, by way of contradiction, that R has utilitarian same-number subprinciples and satisfies avoidance of the repugnant conclusion, avoidance of the sadistic conclusion, and minimal one-person trade-off. For any $n \in \mathcal{Z}_{++} \setminus \{1\}$, $\xi \in \mathcal{R}_{++}$, $\varepsilon \in (0, \xi)$, and $\delta \in (0, \varepsilon)$, let $\zeta = (n\xi + \delta)/(n - 1)$. By same-number utilitarianism,

$$(\zeta \mathbf{1}_{n-1}, -\delta) I \xi \mathbf{1}_n. \tag{5.9}$$

By avoidance of the sadistic conclusion,

$$(\zeta \mathbf{1}_{n-1}, \delta \mathbf{1}_m) R (\zeta \mathbf{1}_{n-1}, -\delta) \tag{5.10}$$

for all $m \in \mathcal{Z}_{++}$. Because $\delta < \varepsilon$, there exists $\bar{m} \in \mathcal{Z}_{++} \setminus \{1\}$ such that

$$\frac{(n - 1)\zeta + \bar{m}\delta}{n - 1 + \bar{m}} < \varepsilon.$$

By same-number utilitarianism,

$$\varepsilon \mathbf{1}_{n-1+\bar{m}} P (\zeta \mathbf{1}_{n-1}, \delta \mathbf{1}_{\bar{m}}). \tag{5.11}$$

(5.11), (5.10), (5.9) and the transitivity of R imply

$$\varepsilon \mathbf{1}_{n-1+\bar{m}} P \xi \mathbf{1}_n. \tag{5.12}$$

Now let $n = 1$. By minimal one-person trade-off, there exist $\hat{n} \in \mathcal{Z}_{++} \setminus \{1\}$ and $\hat{u} \in \mathcal{R}^{\hat{n}}$ such that

$$\hat{u} R \xi \mathbf{1}_1. \tag{5.13}$$

Choose $\omega \in \mathcal{R}_{++}$ such that $\omega \geq \xi$ and $\omega > \hat{u}_i$ for all $i \in \{1, \ldots, \hat{n}\}$. By same-number utilitarianism,

$$\omega \mathbf{1}_{\hat{n}} P \hat{u}. \tag{5.14}$$

By the argument used to obtain (5.12), there exists $\hat{m} \in \mathcal{Z}_{++}$ such that

$$\varepsilon \mathbf{1}_{\hat{n}-1+\hat{m}} P \omega \mathbf{1}_{\hat{n}}. \tag{5.15}$$

(5.15), (5.14), (5.13), and the transitivity of R imply $\varepsilon \mathbf{1}_{\hat{n}-1+\hat{m}} P \xi \mathbf{1}_1$. This, in turn, together with (5.12), implies the repugnant conclusion, a contradiction. ∎

We consider the repugnant conclusion to be more objectionable than the sadistic conclusion and, therefore, our recommendation to deal with this impossibility is to accept the sadistic conclusion.

Arrhenius (2000a) also suggested an axiom that he called the strong sadistic conclusion. A principle implies the strong sadistic conclusion if and only if, for any population size $n \in \mathcal{Z}_{++}$ and any negative utility level ξ, there exist a population size m and a positive utility level ε such that an alternative in which n people experience utility level ξ is better than an alternative in which m people have utility ε. The intuition behind an axiom requiring the avoidance of this conclusion is also captured in a condition introduced by Carlson (1998). The following axiom summarizes the essential features of these suggestions. It requires every alternative in which all levels of well-being are above neutrality to be ranked as better than every alternative in which everyone's well-being is below neutrality.

Priority for Lives Worth Living. For all $u \in \Omega_{++}$ and for all $v \in \Omega_{--}$, $u P v$.

Priority for lives worth living implies avoidance of Arrhenius's (2000a) strong sadistic conclusion.

Some principles require absolute, rather than relative, population sizes to be significant. An axiom that rules this out is extended replication invariance (Zoli 2002). It is stronger than replication invariance because it applies to all pairs of utility vectors rather than to those of the same dimension, and we state it to conclude our summary of important axioms for population principles.

Extended Replication Invariance. For all $u, v \in \Omega$ and for all $k \in \mathcal{Z}_{++}$,

$$u R v \Leftrightarrow \underbrace{(u, \ldots, u)}_{k \text{ times}} R \underbrace{(v, \ldots, v)}_{k \text{ times}}.$$

5.7 CRITICAL-LEVEL PRINCIPLES

Most of the principles considered in this book are variable-population extensions of generalized utilitarianism. It is important to keep in mind that lifetime utilities are normalized so that a utility level of zero represents a neutral life. With different normalizations, our definitions would have to be adjusted accordingly.[16]

In this section, we introduce the critical-level generalized utilitarian principles, the number-sensitive critical-level generalized utilitarian principles, their restricted counterparts, and a variable-population extension of leximin called critical-level leximin. All those principles except critical-level leximin satisfy continuity, strong Pareto, and existence of critical levels. Critical-level leximin satisfies strong Pareto and existence of critical levels but not continuity. Throughout, the transformation $g: \mathcal{R} \to \mathcal{R}$ is assumed to be continuous and increasing with $g(0) = 0$.

We begin with classical (or total) generalized utilitarianism (CGU), which ranks alternatives on the basis of their total transformed utility. That is, for all $n, m \in \mathcal{Z}_{++}$, for all $u \in \mathcal{R}^n$, and for all $v \in \mathcal{R}^m$,

$$u R v \Leftrightarrow \sum_{i=1}^{n} g(u_i) \geq \sum_{i=1}^{m} g(v_i).$$

---

[16] See Dasgupta (1993, 1994), for example, who normalized neutrality to a negative number.

The reduced-form value function for classical generalized utilitarianism is

$$W(n, \xi) = ng(\xi)$$

for all $(n, \xi) \in \mathcal{Z}_{++} \times \mathcal{R}$. ξ is given by the representative-utility function Ξ^n for generalized utilitarianism as defined in Chapter 4 – that is, $\Xi^n(u) = g^{-1}[(1/n) \sum_{i=1}^{n} g(u_i)]$ for all $u \in \mathcal{R}^n$. Critical levels are zero for all $u \in \Omega$ and the negative expansion principle is satisfied. That priority for lives worth living is satisfied is evident. However, the repugnant conclusion is implied. To see this, note that, for any $n \in \mathcal{Z}_{++}$, $\xi \in \mathcal{R}_{++}$, and $\varepsilon \in (0, \xi)$, we can choose $m > n\xi/\varepsilon > n$ so that $\varepsilon \mathbf{1}_m P \xi \mathbf{1}_n$ and the repugnant conclusion follows.

Critical-level generalized utilitarianism (CLGU) is a class of principles that contains CGU as a special case. The critical level is a constant $\alpha \in \mathcal{R}$, not necessarily equal to zero. That is, for all $n, m \in \mathcal{Z}_{++}$, for all $u \in \mathcal{R}^n$, and for all $v \in \mathcal{R}^m$,

$$u R v \Leftrightarrow \sum_{i=1}^{n} \left[g(u_i) - g(\alpha) \right] \geq \sum_{i=1}^{m} \left[g(v_i) - g(\alpha) \right].$$

The reduced-form value functions for the critical-level generalized utilitarian principles can be written as

$$W(n, \xi) = n \left[g(\xi) - g(\alpha) \right]$$

for all $(n, \xi) \in \mathcal{Z}_{++} \times \mathcal{R}$. Different principles are obtained for different values of α. According to critical-level generalized utilitarianism, the critical level is equal to α for all $u \in \Omega$. For $\alpha = 0$, classical generalized utilitarianism obtains. Principles with negative values of α violate the negative expansion principle. If α is positive (the range of parameter values we recommend), critical-level generalized utilitarianism satisfies the negative expansion principle and avoidance of the repugnant conclusion. The repugnant conclusion is avoided because a population size $m > n$ with the property of the repugnant conclusion does not exist if $\xi > \alpha$ and $\varepsilon < \alpha$. Priority for lives worth living is violated if $\alpha > 0$. For example, if $\alpha = 20$ and g is the identity mapping, the utility vector $u = (10, 10, 10, 10)$ is worse than $v = (-10)$.

An example of a subclass of CLGU orderings consists of the critical-level κ-translated means of order r. They have three parameters, and we have to distinguish two cases regarding the sign of one of them. For $\kappa \in \mathcal{R}_+$, the transformation g in critical-level generalized utilitarianism is given by

$$g(\tau) = \begin{cases} (\tau - \kappa)^r + \beta \kappa^r & \text{if } \tau \geq \kappa, \\ -\beta(\kappa - \tau)^r + \beta \kappa^r & \text{if } \tau < \kappa \end{cases} \tag{5.16}$$

for all $\tau \in \mathcal{R}$, where $\beta, r \in \mathcal{R}_{++}$ and $\kappa \in \mathcal{R}_+$ are parameters. For $\kappa = 0$, the critical-level means of order r are obtained. If $\kappa \in \mathcal{R}_{--}$, we obtain

$$g(\tau) = \begin{cases} (\tau - \kappa)^r - (-\kappa)^r & \text{if } \tau \geq \kappa, \\ -\beta(\kappa - \tau)^r - (-\kappa)^r & \text{if } \tau < \kappa \end{cases}$$

for all $\tau \in \mathcal{R}$, where $\beta, r \in \mathcal{R}_{++}$ and $\kappa \in \mathcal{R}_{--}$ are parameters. A critical-level zero-translated mean of order r is called a critical-level mean of order r.

The restricted critical-level generalized utilitarian (RCLGU) class of principles is a generalization of restricted critical-level utilitarianism, which is obtained if g is affine. For these principles, α is the critical-level parameter, which is assumed to be positive; it is not the critical level for all utility vectors. The major interest of this class of principles is that its members satisfy avoidance of the repugnant conclusion and priority for lives worth living. R is represented by the value function $V \colon \Omega \to \mathcal{R}$, where

$$V(u) = \begin{cases} \sum_{i=1}^{n} \left[g(u_i) - g(\alpha) \right] & \text{if } \sum_{i=1}^{n} g(u_i) > n g(\alpha), \\ \sum_{i=1}^{n} g(u_i) / \left[n g(\alpha) \right] - 1 & \text{if } 0 < \sum_{i=1}^{n} g(u_i) \leq n g(\alpha), \\ \sum_{i=1}^{n} g(u_i) - 1 & \text{if } \sum_{i=1}^{n} g(u_i) \leq 0 \end{cases}$$

for all $n \in \mathcal{Z}_{++}$ and for all $u \in \mathcal{R}^n$. $V(u)$ is equal to a representation of CLGU when average transformed utility is greater than $g(\alpha)$, equal to the percentage shortfall of average transformed utility from $g(\alpha)$ less one when average transformed utility is positive and less than or equal to $g(\alpha)$, and equal to total transformed utility less one when average transformed utility is nonpositive. Consequently, all utility vectors whose average transformed utilities are above $g(\alpha)$ are better than all whose average transformed utilities are positive and no greater than it, and these utility vectors in turn are better than all whose average transformed utilities are nonpositive. Critical levels are equal to α for all utility vectors in the first set. In the second set, the critical level c must satisfy

$$V(u, c) = \frac{\sum_{i=1}^{n} g(u_i)}{n g(\alpha)} - 1. \tag{5.17}$$

It can be verified that the second case applies to (u, c) as well and, therefore, (5.17) becomes

$$\frac{\sum_{i=1}^{n} g(u_i) + g(c)}{(n+1) g(\alpha)} - 1 = \frac{\sum_{i=1}^{n} g(u_i)}{n g(\alpha)} - 1$$

and, solving for c,

$$c = g^{-1} \left(\frac{1}{n} \sum_{i=1}^{n} g(u_i) \right).$$

Therefore, the transformed critical level is equal to average transformed utility for the utility vectors in the second set. For the third set, critical levels are equal to zero.

Clearly, these principles satisfy the negative expansion principle. Avoidance of the repugnant conclusion is satisfied because utility vectors in the first set are better than all others, and priority for lives worth living is satisfied because utility vectors in the first two sets are better than all those in the third.

A generalization of CLGU allows critical levels to depend on population size but not on individual utilities. This class of number-sensitive critical-level generalized utilitarian (NCLGU) social-evaluation orderings is defined by

$$u R v \Leftrightarrow \sum_{i=1}^{n} g(u_i) - A_g(n) \geq \sum_{i=1}^{m} g(v_i) - A_g(m)$$

for all $n, m \in \mathcal{Z}_{++}$, for all $u \in \mathcal{R}^n$, and for all $v \in \mathcal{R}^m$, where $A_g: \mathcal{Z}_{++} \to \mathcal{R}$ is an arbitrary function. The special case of CLGU is obtained for the function defined by $A_g(n) = n\alpha$ for all $n \in \mathcal{Z}_{++}$ with a constant $\alpha \in \mathcal{R}$. For $n \in \mathcal{Z}_{++}$ and $u \in \mathcal{R}^n$, the critical level for u is given by $C(u) = c_n = g^{-1}(A_g(n + 1) - A_g(n))$. Thus, an alternative way of defining number-sensitive critical-level generalized utilitarianism is

$$u R v \Leftrightarrow \sum_{i=1}^{n} \left[g(u_i) - g(c_{i-1}) \right] \geq \sum_{i=1}^{m} \left[g(v_i) - g(c_{i-1}) \right]$$

for all $n, m \in \mathcal{Z}_{++}$, for all $u \in \mathcal{R}^n$, and for all $v \in \mathcal{R}^m$, where c_0 is arbitrary. Thus, we have $A_g(n) = \sum_{i=1}^{n} g(c_{i-1})$. The NCLGU orderings satisfy the negative expansion principle if and only if A_g is nondecreasing, and avoidance of the repugnant conclusion if and only if the inferior limit of $A_g(n)/n$ is positive. Priority for lives worth living is violated if avoidance of the repugnant conclusion is satisfied. For these results, see Chapter 6.

As is the case for CLGU, the restricted number-sensitive critical-level generalized utilitarian (RNCLGU) class can be defined. In the following definition, we assume that $c_0 \geq 0$, the c_n are nondecreasing, and at least one c_n is positive. R is represented by the value function V, where

$$V(u) = \begin{cases} \sum_{i=1}^{n} \left[g(u_i) - g(c_{i-1}) \right] & \text{if } \sum_{i=1}^{n} g(u_i) > \sum_{i=1}^{n} g(c_{i-1}), \\ \sum_{i=1}^{n} g(u_i) / \sum_{i=1}^{n} g(c_{i-1}) - 1 & \text{if } 0 < \sum_{i=1}^{n} g(u_i) \leq \sum_{i=1}^{n} g(c_{i-1}), \\ \sum_{i=1}^{n} g(u_i) - 1 & \text{if } \sum_{i=1}^{n} g(u_i) \leq 0 \end{cases}$$

$$(5.18)$$

for all $n \in \mathcal{Z}_{++}$ and for all $u \in \mathcal{R}^n$. It is possible to have $\sum_{i=1}^{n} g(c_{i-1}) = 0$ for some n and, in that case, the middle branch of (5.18) does not apply. Given our assumptions regarding the values of the c_n, these principles satisfy the negative expansion principle, avoidance of the repugnant conclusion, and priority for lives worth living; this can be shown analogously to the corresponding properties of restricted critical-level generalized utilitarianism. Again, the primary interest of these principles is that they satisfy both avoidance of the repugnant conclusion and priority for lives worth living.

If the function g is affine, the special cases obtained for the principles defined above are classical utilitarian (CU), critical-level utilitarian (CLU), restricted critical-level utilitarian (RCLU), number-sensitive critical-level utilitarian (NCLU), and restricted number-sensitive critical-level utilitarian

(RNCLU). CU is defined by

$$uRv \Leftrightarrow \sum_{i=1}^{n} u_i \geq \sum_{i=1}^{m} v_i$$

for all $n, m \in \mathcal{Z}_{++}$, for all $u \in \mathcal{R}^n$, and for all $v \in \mathcal{R}^m$. CLU is given by

$$uRv \Leftrightarrow \sum_{i=1}^{n}[u_i - \alpha] \geq \sum_{i=1}^{m}[v_i - \alpha]$$

for all $n, m \in \mathcal{Z}_{++}$, for all $u \in \mathcal{R}^n$, and for all $v \in \mathcal{R}^m$, where $\alpha \in \mathcal{R}$. RCLU is represented by the value function V, where

$$V(u) = \begin{cases} \sum_{i=1}^{n}[u_i - \alpha] & \text{if } \sum_{i=1}^{n} u_i > n\alpha, \\ \sum_{i=1}^{n} u_i/[n\alpha] - 1 & \text{if } 0 < \sum_{i=1}^{n} u_i \leq n\alpha, \\ \sum_{i=1}^{n} u_i - 1 & \text{if } \sum_{i=1}^{n} u_i \leq 0 \end{cases}$$

for all $n \in \mathcal{Z}_{++}$ and for all $u \in \mathcal{R}^n$, and α is positive. NCLU is defined by

$$uRv \Leftrightarrow \sum_{i=1}^{n}[u_i - c_{i-1}] \geq \sum_{i=1}^{m}[v_i - c_{i-1}]$$

for all $n, m \in \mathcal{Z}_{++}$, for all $u \in \mathcal{R}^n$, and for all $v \in \mathcal{R}^m$, where $c_n \in \mathcal{R}$ for all $n \in \mathcal{Z}_+$. Finally, RNCLU is represented by the value function V, where

$$V(u) = \begin{cases} \sum_{i=1}^{n}[u_i - c_{i-1}] & \text{if } \sum_{i=1}^{n} u_i > \sum_{i=1}^{n} c_{i-1}, \\ \sum_{i=1}^{n} u_i/\sum_{i=1}^{n} c_{i-1} - 1 & \text{if } 0 < \sum_{i=1}^{n} u_i \leq \sum_{i=1}^{n} c_{i-1}, \\ \sum_{i=1}^{n} u_i - 1 & \text{if } \sum_{i=1}^{n} u_i \leq 0 \end{cases}$$

for all $n \in \mathcal{Z}_{++}$ and for all $u \in \mathcal{R}^n$, $c_0 \geq 0$, the c_n are nondecreasing, and at least one c_n is positive.

We conclude this section with a class of critical-level principles whose same-number subprinciples are not generalized utilitarian – the critical-level leximin principles. Letting R_{lex}^n denote the leximin ordering on $\mathcal{R}^n$ for $n \in \mathcal{Z}_{++}$, R is a critical-level leximin ordering if and only if there exists $\alpha \in \mathcal{R}$ such that, for all $n, m \in \mathcal{Z}_{++}$, for all $u \in \mathcal{R}^n$, and for all $v \in \mathcal{R}^m$,

$$uRv \Leftrightarrow \begin{bmatrix} n = m \text{ and } u R_{\text{lex}}^n v \end{bmatrix} \text{ or } \\ \begin{bmatrix} n > m \text{ and } u R_{\text{lex}}^n (v, \alpha \mathbf{1}_{n-m}) \end{bmatrix} \text{ or } \\ \begin{bmatrix} n < m \text{ and } (u, \alpha \mathbf{1}_{m-n}) R_{\text{lex}}^n v \end{bmatrix}.$$

The critical level is α for all $u \in \Omega$. As is the case for critical-level generalized utilitarianism, critical-level leximin satisfies the negative expansion principle and avoidance of the repugnant conclusion if the critical level α is positive. Priority for lives worth living is violated for positive values of α.

The axiom extended replication invariance can be used to distinguish the critical-level generalized utilitarian principles from all other number-sensitive critical-level generalized utilitarian principles. We conclude this section with a formal statement and proof of this observation.

Theorem 5.5. *A number-sensitive critical-level generalized utilitarian principle R satisfies extended replication invariance if and only if it is critical-level generalized utilitarian.*

Proof. It is straightforward to show that R satisfies extended replication invariance if it is critical-level generalized utilitarian.

Let R be number-sensitive critical-level generalized utilitarian and suppose it satisfies extended replication invariance. Without loss of generality, let $c_0 = c_1 = \beta \in \mathcal{R}$. Then, for all $n, m, k \in \mathcal{Z}_{++}$, for all $u \in \mathcal{R}^n$, and for all $v \in \mathcal{R}^m$,

$$\sum_{i=1}^{n} g(u_i) - \sum_{i=1}^{n} g(c_{i-1}) \geq \sum_{i=1}^{m} g(v_i) - \sum_{i-1}^{m} g(c_{i-1})$$

$$\Leftrightarrow k \sum_{i=1}^{n} g(u_i) - \sum_{i=1}^{kn} g(c_{i-1}) \geq k \sum_{i=1}^{m} g(v_i) - \sum_{i=1}^{km} g(c_{i-1}).$$

This implies

$$\sum_{i=1}^{n} g(u_i) - \sum_{i=1}^{m} g(v_i) = \sum_{i=1}^{n} g(c_{i-1}) - \sum_{i=1}^{m} g(c_{i-1})$$

$$\Leftrightarrow \sum_{i=1}^{n} g(u_i) - \sum_{i=1}^{m} g(v_i) = \frac{1}{k} \sum_{i=1}^{kn} g(c_{i-1}) - \frac{1}{k} \sum_{i=1}^{km} g(c_{i-1}).$$

Set $m = 1$ to get

$$\sum_{i=1}^{n} g(c_{i-1}) - g(\beta) = \frac{1}{k} \sum_{i=1}^{kn} g(c_{i-1}) - \frac{1}{k} \sum_{i=1}^{k} g(c_{i-1})$$

which implies

$$\sum_{i=1}^{kn} g(c_{i-1}) = k \sum_{i=1}^{n} g(c_{i-1}) + \sum_{i=1}^{k} g(c_{i-1}) - kg(\beta). \tag{5.19}$$

Interchange k and n to obtain

$$\sum_{i=1}^{kn} g(c_{i-1}) = n \sum_{i=1}^{k} g(c_{i-1}) + \sum_{i=1}^{n} g(c_{i-1}) - ng(\beta). \tag{5.20}$$

(5.19) and (5.20) together imply

$$k \sum_{i=1}^{n} g(c_{i-1}) + \sum_{i=1}^{k} g(c_{i-1}) - kg(\beta)$$

$$= n \sum_{i=1}^{k} g(c_{i-1}) + \sum_{i=1}^{n} g(c_{i-1}) - ng(\beta).$$

Rewriting,

$$\sum_{i=1}^{n} g(c_{i-1})(k-1) = \sum_{i=1}^{k} g(c_{i-1})(n-1) - g(\beta)(n-k).$$

Now suppose that $n > 2$ and let $k = n - 1$. Then

$$\sum_{i=1}^{n} g(c_{i-1})(n-2) = \sum_{i=1}^{n-1} g(c_{i-1})(n-1) - g(\beta)$$

or

$$\frac{1}{n} \sum_{i=1}^{n} g(c_{i-1}) = \frac{(n-1)^2 \left[\frac{1}{n-1} \sum_{i=1}^{n-1} g(c_{i-1}) \right] - g(\beta)}{n(n-2)}. \tag{5.21}$$

If $\sum_{i=1}^{n-1} g(c_{i-1})/(n-1) = g(\beta)$, (5.21) implies $\sum_{i=1}^{n} g(c_{i-1})/n = g(\beta)$. Because $c_0 = c_1 = \beta$, $\sum_{i=1}^{n} g(c_{i-1})/n = g(\beta)$ for $n \in \{1, 2\}$. Consequently, $\sum_{i=1}^{n} g(c_{i-1})/n = g(\beta)$ for all $n \in \mathcal{Z}_{++}$ and R is critical-level generalized utilitarian. ∎

5.8 OTHER POPULATION PRINCIPLES

We now define some additional population principles that have been discussed in the literature. Some of them have critical levels that depend on the utilities of the existing population. All except extended maximin satisfy continuity, strong Pareto, and existence of critical levels. Extended maximin satisfies continuity, existence of critical levels, and weak (but not strong) Pareto. Again, the transformation $g: \mathcal{R} \to \mathcal{R}$ is assumed to be continuous and increasing with $g(0) = 0$.

Average generalized utilitarianism (AGU) employs average transformed utilities to rank utility vectors. The corresponding social-evaluation ordering is defined by

$$u R v \Leftrightarrow \frac{1}{n} \sum_{i=1}^{n} g(u_i) \geq \frac{1}{m} \sum_{i=1}^{m} g(v_i)$$

for all $n, m \in \mathcal{Z}_{++}$, for all $u \in \mathcal{R}^n$, and for all $v \in \mathcal{R}^m$. For $n \in \mathcal{Z}_{++}$ and $u \in \mathcal{R}^n$, the critical level c for u has to satisfy

$$\frac{1}{n+1} \sum_{i=1}^{n} g(u_i) + \frac{1}{n+1} g(c) = \frac{1}{n} \sum_{i=1}^{n} g(u_i),$$

which implies

$$c = g^{-1}\left(\frac{1}{n}\sum_{i=1}^{n} g(u_i)\right).$$

Consequently, the transformed critical level is equal to average transformed utility, which is equal to transformed representative utility. AGU violates the negative expansion principle because all alternatives with negative average transformed utility have negative critical levels. It satisfies avoidance of the repugnant conclusion because average transformed utility in a society where everyone has utility ξ is greater than average transformed utility if everyone has utility $\varepsilon < \xi$. The same reasoning implies that priority for lives worth living is satisfied.

Number-dampened generalized utilitarianism (NDGU) is defined by

$$u R v \Leftrightarrow \frac{f(n)}{n}\sum_{i=1}^{n} g(u_i) \geq \frac{f(m)}{m}\sum_{i=1}^{m} g(v_i) \tag{5.22}$$

for all $n, m \in \mathcal{Z}_{++}$, for all $u \in \mathcal{R}^n$, and for all $v \in \mathcal{R}^m$, where $f: \mathcal{Z}_{++} \to \mathcal{R}_{++}$ is a positive-valued function. The critical level c for $n \in \mathcal{Z}_{++}$ and $u \in \mathcal{R}^n$ is

$$c = g^{-1}\left(h(n)\sum_{i=1}^{n} g(u_i)\right) \tag{5.23}$$

where $h: \mathcal{Z}_{++} \to \mathcal{R}$ is given by

$$h(n) = \frac{(n+1)f(n) - nf(n+1)}{nf(n+1)} \tag{5.24}$$

for all $n \in \mathcal{Z}_{++}$. The transformed critical level is average transformed utility multiplied by a function of population size. We consider only principles such that the argument of g^{-1} in (5.23) is in the image of g for all $n \in \mathcal{Z}_{++}$ and for all $u \in \mathcal{R}^n$ to ensure that the principles satisfy the existence of critical levels. Thus, the term NDGU refers to those principles defined by (5.22) such that the argument of g^{-1} in (5.23) is in the image of g for all $n \in \mathcal{Z}_{++}$ and for all $u \in \mathcal{R}^n$. Note that the expression in (5.23) is in the image of g in the case in which g is unbounded.

AGU and CGU are obtained as the special cases of NDGU where f is constant and where f is increasing linear, respectively. All NDGU principles satisfy priority for lives worth living and all except classical generalized utilitarianism violate the negative expansion principle. NDGU principles satisfy avoidance of the repugnant conclusion if and only if f is bounded.

Restricted number-dampened generalized utilitarianism (RNDGU) employs the value function V, where

$$V(u) = \begin{cases} f(n)\sum_{i=1}^{n} g(u_i)/n & \text{if } \sum_{i=1}^{n} g(u_i) > 0, \\ \\ \sum_{i=1}^{n} g(u_i) & \text{if } \sum_{i=1}^{n} g(u_i) \leq 0 \end{cases}$$

for all $n \in \mathcal{Z}_{++}$ and for all $u \in \mathcal{R}^n$. The value function coincides with that of NDGU for positive average transformed utilities and with that of classical generalized utilitarianism for nonpositive average transformed utilities. Critical levels are given by the critical levels for NDGU for utility vectors with positive average transformed utilities and are equal to zero for all others. All the RNDGU principles satisfy priority for lives worth living but not all satisfy the negative expansion principle and avoidance of the repugnant conclusion (Blackorby, Bossert, and Donaldson 2002c). Restricted average generalized utilitarianism is the special case of RNDGU that corresponds to AGU.

For affine functions g, we again obtain principles that reduce to utilitarianism in same-number comparisons. Average utilitarianism (AU) is defined by

$$u R v \Leftrightarrow \frac{1}{n} \sum_{i=1}^{n} u_i \geq \frac{1}{m} \sum_{i=1}^{m} v_i$$

for all $n, m \in \mathcal{Z}_{++}$, for all $u \in \mathcal{R}^n$, and for all $v \in \mathcal{R}^m$. Number-dampened utilitarianism (NDU) (Ng 1986) is defined by

$$u R v \Leftrightarrow \frac{f(n)}{n} \sum_{i=1}^{n} u_i \geq \frac{f(m)}{m} \sum_{i=1}^{m} v_i$$

for all $n, m \in \mathcal{Z}_{++}$, for all $u \in \mathcal{R}^n$, and for all $v \in \mathcal{R}^m$ where, as before, $f: \mathcal{Z}_{++} \to \mathcal{R}_{++}$ is a positive-valued function. Restricted number-dampened utilitarianism (RNDU) (Hurka 2000) is represented by the value function V, where

$$V(u) = \begin{cases} f(n) \sum_{i=1}^{n} u_i / n & \text{if } \sum_{i=1}^{n} u_i > 0, \\ \\ \sum_{i=1}^{n} u_i & \text{if } \sum_{i=1}^{n} u_i \leq 0 \end{cases}$$

for all $n \in \mathcal{Z}_{++}$, and for all $u \in \mathcal{R}^n$.

It is possible to generate a subclass of the NDU principles by assuming that $h(n)$ in (5.24) is independent of n and equal to $\gamma \in (0, 1)$. In that case, we obtain

$$f(n) = \begin{cases} 1 & \text{if } n = 1, \\ \left(\frac{2}{1+\gamma}\right) \cdots \left(\frac{n}{n-1+\gamma}\right) & \text{if } n \geq 2 \end{cases}$$

for all $n \in \mathcal{Z}_{++}$.

A second special case of (restricted) NDU, discussed by Arrhenius (2000a), is obtained by setting

$$f(n) = \sum_{i=1}^{n} k^{i-1} \tag{5.25}$$

for all $n \in \mathcal{Z}_{++}$, where $k \in (0, 1)$ is a parameter. Because $0 < k < 1$ by assumption, f is bounded and, thus, the resulting population principle avoids the repugnant conclusion. As is the case for all number-dampened (generalized) utilitarian principles, priority for lives worth living is satisfied. However, the unrestricted principles violate the negative expansion principle. To see this, note that, for example, the critical level for $u = (-1)$ is $(k-1)/(k+1) < 0$.

Another special case generalizes the one above and makes NDU equivalent to CU for all population sizes that are no less than $\bar{n} \in \mathcal{Z}_{++}$. In that case,

$$
f(n) = \begin{cases} n & \text{if } n \leq \bar{n}, \\ \bar{n} + \sum_{i=1}^{n-\bar{n}} k^{i-1} & \text{if } n > \bar{n}. \end{cases}
$$

Sider (1991) proposed a rank-ordered variant of a principle that uses powers of a number between zero and one as weights. This principle uses higher weights for lower utilities below neutrality but lower weights for lower utilities at or above neutrality. To define Sider's (1991) principle, we use the following notation. For $u \in \Omega$, let n_u^+ be the number of nonnegative components of u, and let n_u^{--} be the number of negative components of u. Arrange the nonnegative components of u in descending order to obtain the vector $u^{(+)} = \left(u_{(1)}^{(+)}, \ldots, u_{(n_u^+)}^{(+)} \right)$, and arrange the negative components in ascending order to obtain the vector $u^{[--]} = \left(u_{[1]}^{[--]}, \ldots, u_{[n_u^{--}]}^{[--]} \right)$. Thus, $u^{(+)}$ is welfare-ranked and $u^{[--]}$ is illfare-ranked. Finally, let $\kappa \in (0, 1)$ be a parameter. According to Sider's (1991) principle,

$$
u R v \Leftrightarrow \sum_{i=1}^{n_u^+} \kappa^{i-1} u_{(i)}^{(+)} + \sum_{i=1}^{n_u^{--}} \kappa^{i-1} u_{[i]}^{[--]} \geq \sum_{i=1}^{n_v^+} \kappa^{i-1} v_{(i)}^{(+)} + \sum_{i=1}^{n_v^{--}} \kappa^{i-1} v_{[i]}^{[--]}
$$

for all $u, v \in \Omega$. This principle satisfies strong Pareto, zero critical levels, avoidance of the repugnant conclusion, and priority for lives worth living. However, it fails to satisfy minimal inequality aversion because it gives higher priority to higher utilities for nonnegative levels of well-being. For example, if $u = (0, 2)$ and $v = (1, 1)$, we obtain $u P v$ for any value of the parameter $\kappa \in (0, 1)$, contradicting minimal inequality aversion.

Carlson (1998) proposed a criterion that combines the above-mentioned special case of number-dampened utilitarianism (Arrhenius 2000a) with Sider's (1991) principle. In particular, his suggestion is to use a value function that, for any $u \in \Omega$, applies number-dampened utilitarianism with (5.25) to the subvector $u^+ = \left(u_1^+, \ldots, u_{n_u^+}^+ \right)$ of u (consisting of all nonnegative components of u) and Sider's principle to $u^{[--]}$. Thus, we obtain the ordering

$$
u R v \Leftrightarrow \frac{\sum_{i=1}^{n_u^+} \kappa^{i-1}}{n_u^+} \sum_{i=1}^{n_u^+} u_i^+
$$

$$
+ \sum_{i=1}^{n_u^{--}} \kappa^{i-1} u_{[i]}^{[--]} \geq \frac{\sum_{i=1}^{n_v^+} \kappa^{i-1}}{n_v^+} \sum_{i=1}^{n_v^+} v_i^+ + \sum_{i=1}^{n_v^{--}} \kappa^{i-1} v_{[i]}^{[--]}
$$

for all $u, v \in \Omega$ where, again, $\kappa \in (0, 1)$ is a parameter. This principle avoids the repugnant conclusion and satisfies priority for lives worth living [see Carlson (1998) for a discussion].

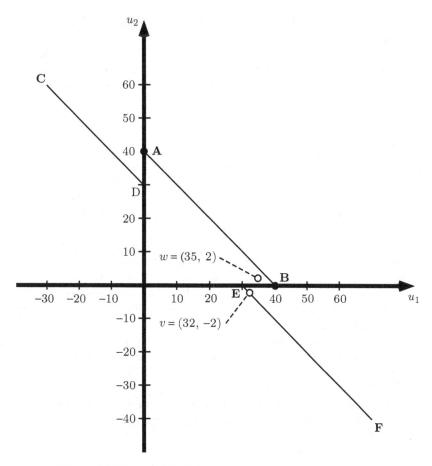

Figure 5.9. Carlson's Principle.

However, as Carlson (1998) noted, the principle fails to satisfy continuity. Consider the restriction of R to $\mathcal{R}^2$ and let $\kappa = 1/2$. At $v = (32, -2)$, value is 30 and the set of utility vectors in $\mathcal{R}^2$ that are as good as v is shown in Figure 5.9. It consists of AB, including A and B, CD, not including D, and EF, not including E. This set is not connected, and the at-least-as-good-as set for v is

$$\{u \in \mathcal{R}_+^2 \mid 3(u_1 + u_2)/4 \geq 30\} \cup \{u \in \{\mathcal{R}_+ \times \mathcal{R}_{--}\}$$
$$\cup \{\mathcal{R}_{--} \times \mathcal{R}_+\} \mid u_1 + u_2 \geq 30\},$$

which is not closed.

In addition, as Carlson also noted, the principle fails to satisfy both weak Pareto and Pareto weak preference. To see this, let $\kappa = 1/2$, $v = (32, -2)$ and $w = (35, 2)$. Because $w \gg v$, both weak Pareto and Pareto weak preference require wRv. But the value function is equal to 27.75 at w and equal to 30 at

v, and Carlson's principle ranks v as better than w. In Figure 5.9, note that w lies below AB and v is on EF.

Finally, we introduce a variable-population extension of maximin. As before, for $n \in \mathcal{Z}_{++}$ and $u \in \mathcal{R}^n$, we use $(u_{(1)}, \ldots, u_{(n)})$ to denote a permutation of u such that $u_{(i)} \geq u_{(i+1)}$ for all $i \in \{1, \ldots, n-1\}$. Extended maximin is defined by

$$u R v \Leftrightarrow u_{(n)} \geq v_{(m)}$$

for all $n, m \in \mathcal{Z}_{++}$, for all $u \in \mathcal{R}^n$, and for all $v \in \mathcal{R}^m$. This principle is extremely inequality averse: only the utilities of the worst-off individuals matter in comparing two utility vectors. According to extended maximin, $u_{(n)}$ is a critical level for all $n \in \mathcal{Z}_{++}$ and for all $u \in \mathcal{R}^n$. Critical levels for extended maximin are not unique (note that extended maximin does not satisfy strong Pareto): any $c \in \mathcal{R}$ with $c \geq u_{(n)}$ is a critical level for $u \in \mathcal{R}^n$.

Extended maximin fails to satisfy the negative expansion principle because the smallest component of a utility vector may be negative. Avoidance of the repugnant conclusion is satisfied. To see this, note that the smallest components of $\xi \mathbf{1}_n$ and $\varepsilon \mathbf{1}_m$ are ξ and ε so $\xi \mathbf{1}_n$ is better than $\varepsilon \mathbf{1}_m$ whenever $\xi > \varepsilon$, thereby avoiding the repugnant conclusion. That priority for lives worth living is satisfied is immediate.

We conclude this section with an impossibility result. There is no population principle with constant critical levels whose same-number subprinciples are maximin.

Theorem 5.6. *There exists no social-evaluation ordering R that has same-number maximin subprinciples such that there exists $\alpha \in \mathcal{R}$ with $(u, \alpha)I u$ for all $u \in \Omega$.*

Proof. If $(u, \alpha)I u$ for all $u \in \Omega$, then $\alpha \mathbf{1}_1 I(\alpha, \alpha)$ and $(\alpha + 1)\mathbf{1}_1 I(\alpha + 1, \alpha)$. By same-number maximin, it follows that

$$\alpha \mathbf{1}_1 I(\alpha, \alpha) I(\alpha + 1, \alpha) I(\alpha + 1)\mathbf{1}_1,$$

which implies $(\alpha + 1)\mathbf{1}_1 I \alpha \mathbf{1}_1$. Again using same-number maximin, we obtain $(\alpha + 1)\mathbf{1}_1 P \alpha \mathbf{1}_1$, and a contradiction is established.   ∎

5.9   INFORMATION INVARIANCE

In a variable-population setting, individual invariance transformations must be identical if anonymity is satisfied. This is the case because the identities of the individuals alive cannot matter in anonymous social evaluation. Therefore, the components of a vector of invariance transformations cannot be assigned to specific individuals. It follows that an invariance transformation can be described by a single function $\phi_0 \colon \mathcal{R} \to \mathcal{R}$. The application of ϕ_0 to utility vector $u \in \mathcal{R}^n$ results in the transformed vector $(\phi_0(u_1), \ldots, \phi_0(u_n))$. We use Φ_0^A to denote the set of invariance transformations that are admissible given an information assumption A. As usual, we consider only information assumptions A such that the relation is-informationally-equivalent-to generated by Φ_0^A is an equivalence relation. Information invariance with respect to Φ_0^A is defined as follows.

Information Invariance with Respect to Φ_0^A. For all $n, m \in \mathcal{Z}_{++}$, for all $u \in \mathcal{R}^n$, for all $v \in \mathcal{R}^m$, and for all $\phi_0 \in \Phi_0^A$,

$$u R v \Leftrightarrow \big(\phi_0(u_1), \ldots, \phi_0(u_n)\big) R \big(\phi_0(v_1), \ldots, \phi_0(v_m)\big).$$

The following is a list of information assumptions that will be used in the remainder of this book. They are analogous to the corresponding fixed-population properties introduced in Chapter 4 and, therefore, we do not repeat the discussions of their features and interpretations. Assumptions such as cardinal unit comparability do not appear because the ϕ_i cannot be person specific. Information assumptions with person-specific transformations can be imposed on the nonanonymous ordering $\overset{*}{R}$ (see Chapter 3), however.

Ordinal Full Comparability. $\phi_0 \in \Phi_0^{OFC}$ if and only if ϕ_0 is increasing.

Cardinal Full Comparability. $\phi_0 \in \Phi_0^{CFC}$ if and only if there exist $a \in \mathcal{R}_{++}$ and $b \in \mathcal{R}$ such that $\phi_0(\tau) = a\tau + b$ for all $\tau \in \mathcal{R}$.

Ratio-Scale Full Comparability. $\phi_0 \in \Phi_0^{RSF}$ if and only if there exists $a \in \mathcal{R}_{++}$ such that $\phi_0(\tau) = a\tau$ for all $\tau \in \mathcal{R}$.

Numerical Full Comparability. $\phi_0 \in \Phi_0^{NFC}$ if and only if $\phi_0(\tau) = \tau$ for all $\tau \in \mathcal{R}$.

In addition, we introduce the following class of reference ratio-scale full-comparability assumptions. This class is a generalization of ratio-scale full comparability that is obtained by allowing for arbitrary values $u^0 \in \mathcal{R}$ as reference values of utility. Ratio-scale full comparability is obtained as the special case where $u^0 = 0$.

Reference Ratio-Scale Full Comparability $[u^0]$. $\phi_0 \in \Phi_0^{RRSF[u^0]}$ if and only if there exists $a \in \mathcal{R}_{++}$ such that $\phi_0(\tau) = u^0 + a(\tau - u^0)$ for all $\tau \in \mathcal{R}$.

Reference ratio-scale full comparability is a translated version of ratio-scale full comparability. This is analogous to the translated-homotheticity condition introduced in Chapter 4.

Because of the restrictive nature of the invariance transformations that are available in a variable-population setting if anonymity is satisfied, it may be more natural to use norms as in Chapter 2. Norms provide a way of restricting the set of possible utility profiles to those respecting the normalization represented by the norm, thereby permitting interpersonal comparisons of utility at the norm level. For instance, if we use zero as the utility level associated with a neutral life, we consider only utility profiles respecting this normalization. Thus, the standard welfarist framework with an unrestricted domain is inadequate to define norms. We propose using norms to restrict the domain of a variable-population social-evaluation functional.[17]

For $U \in \mathcal{U}$ and $i \in \mathcal{Z}_{++}$, let $\eta_i(U_i)$ denote the level of utility individual i assigns to a neutral life, given the utility function $U_i \colon X_i \to \mathcal{R}$.[18] Suppose, in addition, that a second norm identifies a life above neutrality at some satisfactory or excellent level (not necessarily a critical level). Given these norms, we may represent the value of a neutral life by a utility level of 0 and the value of an excellent life by a utility level of 100. Letting $\mu_i(U_i)$ denote the utility level representing an excellent life according to i's utility function U_i, the restricted domain that respects both normalizations is given by

$$\mathcal{D}_{\eta\mu} = \{\Upsilon \in \mathcal{U} \times \mathcal{K} \mid \eta_i(U_i) = 0 \text{ and } \mu_i(U_i) = 100 \text{ for all } i \in \mathcal{Z}_{++}\}.$$

Thus, the profiles in $\mathcal{D}_{\eta\mu}$ are such that everyone's utility associated with neutrality and everyone's utility associated with an excellent life are the same, so interpersonal comparisons at those two utility levels are possible. All arguments in the welfarism theorems presented in Chapter 3 remain true if the unlimited domain is replaced with $\mathcal{D}_{\eta\mu}$.

These normalizations allow us to start with cardinal noncomparability on the full domain and yet obtain possibility results by restricting attention to the profiles respecting our normalizations. For $U \in \mathcal{U}$ and an invariance transformation ϕ, we use $\phi \circ U$ to denote the vector of composite functions $(\phi_i \circ U_i)_{i \in \mathcal{Z}_{++}}$. In terms of a variable-population social-evaluation functional F, information invariance and the assumptions used in the remainder of this section are defined as follows.

Information Invariance with Respect to Φ^A. For all $\Upsilon = (U, K) \in \mathcal{D}$ and for all $\phi \in \Phi^A$ such that $(\phi \circ U, K) \in \mathcal{D}$, $F(U, K) = F(\phi \circ U, K)$.

Cardinal Noncomparability. $\phi \in \Phi^{CNC}$ if and only if there exist $a_i \in \mathcal{R}_{++}$ and $b_i \in \mathcal{R}$ for all $i \in \mathcal{Z}_{++}$ such that $\phi_i(\tau) = a_i\tau + b_i$ for all $\tau \in \mathcal{R}$ and for all $i \in \mathcal{Z}_{++}$.

Numerical Full Comparability. $\phi \in \Phi^{NFC}$ if and only if $\phi_i(\tau) = \tau$ for all $\tau \in \mathcal{R}$ and for all $i \in \mathcal{Z}_{++}$.

The following result establishes that two interpersonally comparable norms can be used to generate an environment that allows for numerical full comparability of utilities even if utilities are merely cardinally measurable and interpersonally

---

[17] See Tungodden (1998) for a discussion of a single norm in combination with ordinally measurable utilities.

[18] Recall that X_i is the set of alternatives in which individual i is alive and, therefore, her or his lifetime utility $U_i(x)$ is well-defined for all $x \in X_i$.

noncomparable on the entire domain. Information invariance with respect to cardinal noncomparability implies that individual utilities are unique up to independent increasing affine transformations. Adding our two norms uniquely determines the parameters of these transformations everywhere on the restricted domain where the normalizations are respected: the scaling factors a_i must be equal to one and the additive constants b_i must be equal to zero for all individuals $i \in \mathcal{Z}_{++}$. Therefore, only the identity mapping is permitted on the restricted domain and numerical full comparability obtains.

Theorem 5.7. *Let $F: \mathcal{D} \to \mathcal{O}$ be a variable-population social-evaluation functional such that $\mathcal{D}_{\eta\mu} \subseteq \mathcal{D}$. If F satisfies information invariance with respect to cardinal noncomparability, then the restriction of F to $\mathcal{D}_{\eta\mu}$ satisfies information invariance with respect to numerical full comparability.*

Proof. Suppose F satisfies information invariance with respect to cardinal noncomparability. Let $\Upsilon = (U, K) \in \mathcal{D}_{\eta\mu}$. By definition, $\eta_i(U_i) = 0$ and $\mu_i(U_i) = 100$, and it follows that $\phi_i(0) = 0$ and $\phi_i(100) = 100$ for all $i \in \mathcal{Z}_{++}$. Consequently, $a_i = 1$ and $b_i = 0$ for all $i \in \mathcal{Z}_{++}$. ∎

In the above theorem, only cardinal noncomparability is required on the full domain of F – full interpersonal comparability on the restricted domain is provided by the two norms. Thus, the theorem shows that, if utilities are cardinally measurable and two norms are employed, utilities on the resulting restricted domain are numerically measurable and fully interpersonally comparable. Therefore, the norms generate sufficient additional information to apply any social-evaluation functional. Similar results involving a single norm can be found elsewhere (Blackorby, Bossert, and Donaldson 1999b).

CHAPTER 6

Characterizations and Possibilities

Part A

A characterization establishes an equivalence between a set of axioms and a class of population principles. Thus, each member of the class satisfies all the axioms and, in addition, no principle outside the class satisfies all of them. Impossibility theorems reveal inconsistencies among axioms and remind us that axioms should not be considered in isolation. In this chapter, we present characterizations of most of the population principles discussed in Chapter 5 together with a pair of closely related impossibility theorems. Many of the axioms used here are introduced in Chapters 4 and 5. We say that a population principle or social-evaluation ordering satisfies a fixed-population axiom if and only each same-number subprinciple or same-number social-evaluation ordering satisfies it.

Consider the number-sensitive critical-level generalized utilitarian (NCLGU) class, for example. As mentioned in Chapter 5, each member of the class satisfies continuity, strong Pareto, same-number independence, and utility independence. In addition, all critical levels exist, are independent of utility levels, and may depend on population size. Although these properties can be used as axioms to characterize the NCLGU class, some are redundant: same-number independence is implied by utility independence, and intermediate existence of critical levels and utility independence together imply that all critical levels exist and are independent of utilities. It follows that a smaller set of axioms – continuity, strong Pareto, intermediate existence of critical levels, and utility independence – characterizes the NCLGU class. In addition, the axioms are independent: there are non-NCLGU principles that satisfy the axioms in every proper subset.

A short list of axioms characterizes the same-number generalized utilitarian class of principles, each member of which has same-number subprinciples that are generalized utilitarian with the same transformation for each population size. The class is characterized by continuity, strong Pareto, and the population substitution principle or by continuity, strong Pareto, same-number independence, and replication invariance. A subclass is the same-number utilitarian class, each of whose members has same-number subprinciples that are utilitarian. That class is characterized by minimal increasingness and incremental equity.

6.1 CRITICAL-LEVEL PRINCIPLES

The class of number-sensitive critical-level generalized-utilitarian (NCLGU) principles is characterized by five axioms: continuity, strong Pareto, intermediate existence of critical levels, and utility independence. Any population principle that is not in this class therefore must fail to satisfy one of the axioms. Average utilitarianism, for example, violates utility independence; see the discussion of the disabled-child example following Table 5.1. In addition, any axiom that is not implied by the five must be violated by *some* member of the NCLGU class. As demonstrated in Chapter 5, existence independence is violated by all NCLGU principles with at least two distinct critical levels.

An important subclass of the NCLGU class is the critical-level generalized utilitarian class. It is characterized by continuity, strong Pareto, weak existence of critical levels, and existence independence. Note that existence independence, which is stronger than utility independence, permits a weaker condition on the existence of critical levels: the axiom requires the existence of only one critical level.

It is easy to see why critical levels must be the same for all utility vectors in the presence of existence independence. Let u be a utility vector of any dimension whose critical level exists and is equal to c. Then consider any other utility vector v of any dimension (which may or may not be the same as the dimension of u). By definition of a critical level, the vectors u and (u, c) are equally good. By existence independence, (u, v) and (u, v, c) are equally good and, using existence independence again, v and (v, c) are equally good. Consequently, a critical level for v exists and is equal to c. Strong Pareto implies that critical levels are unique. If critical levels are constant, the criterion for ranking an addition to a utility-unaffected population is independent of the number and utility levels of the existing population. This property of the critical-level principles, which is implied by existence independence, is ethically attractive in its own right and is weaker than existence independence.

To characterize the number-sensitive critical-level utilitarian (NCLU) and critical-level utilitarian (CLU) classes, axioms that focus on the same-number utilitarian class are needed. That can be accomplished by using minimal increasingness and incremental equity and the requirement that critical levels be utility independent or constant.

Critical-level leximin can be characterized by using the Hammond-equity axiom (Chapter 4). Strong Pareto, weak existence of critical levels, existence independence, and Hammond equity together characterize critical-level leximin.

6.2 AVERAGE UTILITARIANISM AND ITS GENERALIZATIONS

Knowledge of representative utilities is not sufficient, in general, to rank utility vectors of different dimensions. There are, however, some replication-invariant principles with that property and we call them representative-utility principles. Each member of that class has a value function that is equal to representative utility or any increasing transformation. The average generalized utilitarian class consists of all representative-utility principles that are same-number generalized utilitarian and average utilitarianism is the representative-utility principle that is same-number utilitarian. These are not the only members of the class, however. Population principles whose value functions are equal to any S-Gini representative utility with $\delta \neq 1$ and the extended maximin principle, whose value function is equal to minimum utility, are representative-utility principles that are not same-number generalized utilitarian.

Our characterization of the representative-utility class depends on a strengthening of replication invariance to replication equivalence, which requires any vector of utilities u and a k-fold replication of itself to be ranked as equally good. Thus, utility vectors u, (u, u), (u, u, u) and so on are equally good. This axiom, continuity, Pareto weak preference, and minimal increasingness together characterize the representative-utility principles.

Average utilitarianism (AU) is characterized by continuity, strong Pareto, same-number independence, existence of critical levels, replication invariance, and information invariance with respect to cardinal full comparability. Extended maximin is characterized by continuity, Pareto weak preference, minimal increasingness, minimal inequality-aversion, and minimum critical levels. The last axiom requires minimum utility to be a critical level for any utility vector.

It is easy to criticize the representative-utility principles. Consider any alternative in which each of at least two people has the same utility level and a second alternative in which only one person ever lives and has a trivially higher utility level. All the representative-utility principles rank the second alternative as better than the first, no matter how small the difference between the two utility levels is.

6.3 CHARACTERIZATIONS THAT USE PROPERTIES OF CRITICAL-LEVEL FUNCTIONS

All principles that satisfy strong Pareto and have critical levels for all utility vectors have an important property that can be used in characterization theorems: same-number subprinciples (or representative-utility functions) and critical-level functions are sufficient to rank all pairs of utility vectors. Suppose, for example, we want to rank $(9, 4, 3, 8)$ and $(9, 9)$ and know that the same-number subprinciples are utilitarian and that critical levels are equal to one-third of average utility (which is representative utility). The critical level for $(9, 9)$ is 3, so $(9, 9)$ and $(9, 9, 3)$ are equally good. Because the critical level for $(9, 9, 3)$ is $7/3$, $(9, 9, 3)$ and $(9, 9, 3, 7/3)$ are equally good and, by transitivity, $(9, 9, 3, 7/3)$ and $(9, 9)$ are equally good. Consequently, the ranking of $(9, 4, 3, 8)$ and $(9, 9)$ is the same as the ranking of $(9, 4, 3, 8)$ and $(9, 9, 3, 7/3)$. Because total (or average) utility is greater in $(9, 4, 3, 8)$ than in $(9, 9, 3, 7/3)$, $(9, 4, 3, 8)$ is better than $(9, 9)$.

To characterize number-dampened generalized utilitarianism (NDGU), an axiom that we call number-dampened critical levels is employed. It states that, if a principle is same-number generalized utilitarian, the transformed critical level for any utility vector u must be equal to a multiple of average transformed utility in u. The multiple can depend on population size and must be greater than $-n$ where n is the dimension of u. This axiom, continuity, strong Pareto, and the population substitution principle together characterize the NDGU principles. Same-number independence and replication invariance may be used instead of the population substitution principle. Number-dampened utilitarianism (NDU) is characterized by minimal increasingness, incremental equity, and number-dampened critical levels.

To characterize the restricted number-dampened generalized utilitarian (RNDGU) principles, we again use an axiom that imposes structure on critical-level functions. Restricted number-dampened critical levels applies only to same-number generalized utilitarian principles and it requires transformed critical levels to be a nonnegative utility-independent multiple of average transformed utility when average transformed utility is positive and zero otherwise. If this axiom replaces number-dampened critical levels in the characterizations of the unrestricted principles, RNDGU and RNDU are characterized.

A similar approach permits characterizations of the restricted critical-level principles. In that case, the axiom restricted existence-independent critical levels is used. It applies to same-number generalized utilitarian principles only and requires the critical level to be equal to a positive constant α if representative utility exceeds α, representative utility itself if representative utility is positive and no greater than α, and zero otherwise. Continuity, strong Pareto, the population substitution principle, and restricted existence-independent critical levels together characterize restricted critical-level generalized utilitarianism (RCLGU). In addition, minimal increasingness, incremental equity, and restricted existence-independent critical levels characterize restricted critical-level utilitarianism (RCLU).

Although we do not do it, it is possible to use an axiom that structures critical levels to characterize the restricted number-sensitive generalized utilitarian and restricted number-sensitive utilitarian classes.

6.4 IMPOSSIBILITIES

The critical-level generalized utilitarian (CLGU) subclass with positive critical levels is characterized by continuity, strong Pareto, weak existence of critical levels, existence independence, and avoidance of the repugnant conclusion. It might be thought desirable to add priority for lives worth living to the set of axioms. There is no principle that satisfies the axioms on the augmented list, however. As a consequence, choices must be made. In the case at hand, dropping the priority axiom is one possibility. That choice leaves us with the CLGU class. Eliminating existence independence is another possibility, but that alternative is not without its difficulties. There is no principle that satisfies continuity, strong Pareto, intermediate existence of critical levels, utility independence, avoidance of the repugnant conclusion, and priority for lives worth living. Consequently, if priority for lives worth living is regarded as an essential property of population principles and attention is restricted to the same-number generalized utilitarian class, both existence and utility independence must be abandoned. This may be a significant price to pay: in the spaceship example of Chapter 5, neither the utility levels of the colonists nor their number can be disregarded by the home population.

What is the class of principles characterized by continuity, strong Pareto, existence of critical levels, same-number independence, replication invariance, avoidance of the repugnant conclusion, and priority for lives worth living? This is an open question, but we know that the class is a large subclass of the same-number generalized utilitarian class and that it includes the restricted NCLGU principles that avoid the repugnant conclusion.

Part B

We now present the characterization and impossibility theorems discussed in Part A. First, in Section 6.5, we characterize the same-number generalized utilitarian class and its utilitarian counterpart. In Section 6.6, we characterize number-sensitive critical-level generalized utilitarianism (NCLGU) using the utility-independence axiom. Strengthening utility independence to existence independence allows us to characterize critical-level generalized utilitarianism (CLGU) and critical-level leximin in Section 6.7.

Section 6.8 focuses on average utilitarianism and Section 6.9 is concerned with the more general class of representative-utility principles whose reduced-form value functions are independent of population size.

Number-dampened generalized utilitarianism (NDGU) is discussed in Section 6.10. Section 6.11 presents characterizations of the restricted number-dampened generalized utilitarian (RNDGU) class and the restricted critical-level generalized utilitarian (RCLGU) class.

Several characterizations that use information-invariance properties conclude the chapter in Section 6.12.

6.5   SAME-NUMBER GENERALIZED UTILITARIANISM

The same-number generalized utilitarian class of principles consists of all those whose same-number subprinciples are generalized utilitarian with the same transformation for each population size. Thus, R is same-number generalized utilitarian if and only if there exists a continuous and increasing function $g: \mathcal{R} \to \mathcal{R}$ with $g(0) = 0$ such that, for all $n \in \mathcal{Z}_{++}$ and for all $u, v \in \mathcal{R}^n$,

$$u R v \Leftrightarrow \sum_{i=1}^{n} g(u_i) \geq \sum_{i=1}^{n} g(v_i).$$

The same-number utilitarian class, which is a subclass of the same-number generalized utilitarian class, consists of all principles whose same-number sub-principles are utilitarian.

The appeal of same-number generalized utilitarianism is based on a notion of coherence across population sizes. Because the same transformation is employed for all dimensions, features of the principle such as the degree of inequality aversion as expressed by the curvature of g are preserved when moving from one population size to another. No coherence property for variable-population comparisons is implied, however.

The same-number generalized utilitarian class can be characterized in several ways, and we present two of them. One of the characterizations uses the population substitution principle. The following theorem is a consequence of Theorem 4.21 and the proof is omitted.

Theorem 6.1. *R satisfies continuity, strong Pareto, and the population substitution principle if and only if R is same-number generalized utilitarian.*

A second characterization uses same-number independence, the weakest of the independence axioms. Because it applies to same-number subprinciples separately, a requirement that links utility vectors of different dimensions is needed in addition. We say that a population principle satisfies replication invariance if and only if the sequence of same-number subprinciples satisfies replication invariance. In conjunction with continuity and strong Pareto, these two axioms characterize the same-number generalized utilitarian class. The following theorem is a direct consequence of Theorem 4.22 and, again, we omit its proof.

Theorem 6.2. *R satisfies continuity, strong Pareto, same-number independence, and replication invariance if and only if R is same-number generalized utilitarian.*

The incremental-equity axiom can be employed to characterize the same-number utilitarian class whose members all have utilitarian same-number subprinciples. *R* satisfies incremental equity if and only if each same-number subprinciple does. The proof of this characterization result is omitted because it follows immediately from Theorem 4.9.

Theorem 6.3. *R satisfies minimal increasingness and incremental equity if and only if R is same-number utilitarian.*

We conclude this section with an observation regarding the critical-level function C for same-number generalized utilitarian principles that satisfy existence of critical levels. Suppose R is such a principle. By existence of critical levels, the critical-level function C is well-defined. For all $n \in \mathcal{Z}_{++}$ and for all $u \in \mathcal{R}^n$, if $c = C(u)$, then $uI(u, c)$ by definition. Because all members of the same-number generalized-utilitarian class satisfy the population substitution principle, it follows that $(\Xi^n(u)\mathbf{1}_n, c)I(u, c)$ and, because $uI\Xi^n(u)\mathbf{1}_n$ by definition, $\Xi^n(u)\mathbf{1}_n I(\Xi^n(u)\mathbf{1}_n, c)$. Consequently, c is also the critical level for $\Xi^n(u)\mathbf{1}_n$. Therefore, the critical-level function can be written in terms of population size and representative utility, with

$$C(u) = C\left(\Xi^n(u)\mathbf{1}_n\right) = \mathbf{C}\left(n, \Xi^n(u)\right).$$

6.6 NUMBER-SENSITIVE CRITICAL LEVELS

Combined with the axioms continuity and strong Pareto, utility independence and intermediate existence of critical levels can be used to provide a characterization of NCLGU. As a preliminary result, we show that utility independence and intermediate existence of critical levels together imply existence of critical levels and that, in the presence of strong Pareto, critical levels are unique and may depend on the size of the existing population but not on the utilities of its members.

Theorem 6.4. *(i) If R satisfies intermediate existence of critical levels and utility independence, then R satisfies existence of critical levels.*

(ii) If R satisfies strong Pareto, intermediate existence of critical levels and utility independence, then the critical-level function C is well-defined and, for all $n \in \mathcal{Z}_{++}$ and for all $u, v \in \mathcal{R}^n$, $C(u) = C(v)$.

Proof. (i) Let $n \in \mathcal{Z}_{++}$. By intermediate existence of critical levels, there exist $\bar{u} \in \mathcal{R}^n$ and $c \in \mathcal{R}$ such that

$$(\bar{u}, c)I\bar{u}. \tag{6.1}$$

Let $r = n$, $u = (c)$, $v = u_\emptyset$, $w = \bar{u}$ and $s \in \mathcal{R}^n$ in the definition of utility independence (see Section 5.6). By (6.1) and utility independence, $(s, c)Is$ and, because $s \in \mathcal{R}^n$ was chosen arbitrarily, c must be a critical level for any n-dimensional utility vector. Because this argument applies for any value of $n \in \mathcal{Z}_{++}$, this proves that R satisfies existence of critical levels.

Part (ii) follows immediately from the above argument and the observation that critical levels are unique if R satisfies strong Pareto. ∎

Theorem 6.4 is employed in the proof of the following characterization result.

Theorem 6.5. *R satisfies continuity, strong Pareto, intermediate existence of critical levels, and utility independence if and only if R is NCLGU.*

Proof. That all NCLGU principles satisfy the axioms of the theorem statement is straightforward to verify.

Now suppose R satisfies continuity, strong Pareto, intermediate existence of critical levels, and utility independence. Because utility independence implies same-number independence and R is anonymous, Theorem 4.7 implies that, for all $n \geq 3$, there exists a continuous and increasing function $g^n : \mathcal{R} \to \mathcal{R}$ with $g^n(0) = 0$ such that, for all $u, v \in \mathcal{R}^n$,

$$uRv \Leftrightarrow \sum_{i=1}^{n} g^n(u_i) \geq \sum_{i=1}^{n} g^n(v_i). \tag{6.2}$$

Next, we prove that, for all $n \geq 3$, the functions g^n and g^{n+1} can be chosen to be the same. Let $u, v \in \mathcal{R}^n$. By Theorem 6.4, there exists a critical level $c_n \in \mathcal{R}$ for all utility vectors in $\mathcal{R}^n$ and, consequently,

$$uRv \Leftrightarrow (u, c_n)R(v, c_n). \tag{6.3}$$

By (6.2),

$$uRv \Leftrightarrow \sum_{i=1}^{n} g^n(u_i) \geq \sum_{i=1}^{n} g^n(v_i) \tag{6.4}$$

and

$$(u, c_n)R(v, c_n) \Leftrightarrow \sum_{i=1}^{n} g^{n+1}(u_i) + g^{n+1}(c_n) \geq \sum_{i=1}^{n} g^{n+1}(v_i) + g^{n+1}(c_n)$$

$$\Leftrightarrow \sum_{i=1}^{n} g^{n+1}(u_i) \geq \sum_{i=1}^{n} g^{n+1}(v_i). \tag{6.5}$$

Therefore, using (6.3), (6.4) and (6.5),

$$\sum_{i=1}^{n} g^n(u_i) \geq \sum_{i=1}^{n} g^n(v_i) \Leftrightarrow \sum_{i=1}^{n} g^{n+1}(u_i) \geq \sum_{i=1}^{n} g^{n+1}(v_i),$$

which means that the same function can be used for g^n and for g^{n+1}. Because this is true for all $n \geq 3$, it follows that the functions g^n can be chosen independently of n, and we write $g = g^n$ for all $n \geq 3$. Together with (6.2), it follows that, for all $n \geq 3$ and for all $u, v \in \mathcal{R}^n$,

$$uRv \Leftrightarrow \sum_{i=1}^{n} g(u_i) \geq \sum_{i=1}^{n} g(v_i). \tag{6.6}$$

Next, we prove that (6.6) must be true for $n \in \{1, 2\}$ as well. Let $u, v \in \mathcal{R}^1$. By strong Pareto and the increasingness of g,

$$uRv \Leftrightarrow u_1 \geq v_1 \Leftrightarrow g(u_1) \geq g(v_1). \tag{6.7}$$

If $u, v \in \mathcal{R}^2$, utility independence and (6.6) together imply

$$uRv \Leftrightarrow (u, c_2)R(v, c_2) \Leftrightarrow \sum_{i=1}^{2} g(u_i) + g(c_2) \geq \sum_{i=1}^{2} g(v_i) + g(c_2)$$

$$\Leftrightarrow \sum_{i=1}^{2} g(u_i) \geq \sum_{i=1}^{2} g(v_i). \tag{6.8}$$

(6.6), (6.7), and (6.8) imply that all fixed-population comparisons are carried out according to generalized utilitarianism with the same transformation for all population sizes.

To complete the proof, let $n, m \in \mathcal{Z}_{++}$ with $n \neq m$, $u \in \mathcal{R}^n$, and $v \in \mathcal{R}^m$. Suppose $n > m$. By definition of the critical levels and letting $c_0 \in \mathcal{R}$ be arbitrary,

$$uRv \Leftrightarrow uR(v, c_m, \ldots, c_{n-1})$$

$$\Leftrightarrow \sum_{i=1}^{n} g(u_i) \geq \sum_{i=1}^{m} g(v_i) + \sum_{i=m+1}^{n} g(c_{i-1})$$

$$\Leftrightarrow \sum_{i=1}^{n} g(u_i) - \sum_{i=1}^{n} g(c_{i-1}) \geq \sum_{i=1}^{m} g(v_i) - \sum_{i=1}^{m} g(c_{i-1})$$

and, defining $A_g(n) = \sum_{i=1}^{n} g(c_{i-1})$ for all $n \in \mathcal{Z}_{++}$, it follows that R is number-sensitive generalized utilitarian. A similar argument applies to the case $n < m$. ∎

If avoidance of the repugnant conclusion is added to the requirements of Theorem 6.5, the values of the function A_g must obey some restrictions as n becomes large. Because avoidance of the repugnant conclusion is an important axiom, it is of interest to provide a precise formulation of these restrictions.

Suppose $(a_n)_{n \in \mathcal{Z}_{++}}$ is a sequence in $\mathcal{R}$. A point $t \in \mathcal{R}$ is a point of accumulation of $(a_n)_{n \in \mathcal{Z}_{++}}$ if and only if, for all $\varepsilon \in \mathcal{R}_{++}$ and for all $n \in \mathcal{Z}_{++}$, there exists $m \geq n$ such that $a_m \in (t - \varepsilon, t + \varepsilon)$. Thus, a point of accumulation of a sequence is a point such that any neighborhood of this point contains infinitely many elements of the sequence. Note that a number $s \in \mathcal{R}$ may appear more than once as an element of a sequence. This implies that the set of real numbers s such that there exists an index m with $a_m = s \in (t - \varepsilon, t + \varepsilon)$ need not be infinite – the set that has to be infinite is the set of all m such that a_m is in the requisite interval. For example, the sequence defined by $a_n = 1$ if n is odd and $a_n = -1$ if n is even has two points of accumulation – namely, 1 and -1. Clearly, if $t \in \mathcal{R}$ is a point of accumulation of $(a_n)_{n \in \mathcal{Z}_{++}}$, the sequence has a subsequence that converges to t.

The inferior limit of the sequence $(a_n)_{n \in \mathcal{Z}_{++}}$, denoted by $\liminf a_n$, is equal to $+\infty$ if the sequence has no point of accumulation and diverges to $+\infty$, equal to the smallest point of accumulation of $(a_n)_{n \in \mathcal{Z}_{++}}$ if the sequence is bounded below and has at least one point of accumulation, and equal to $-\infty$ otherwise. We can now characterize all number-sensitive critical-level generalized utilitarian principles that avoid the repugnant conclusion.

Theorem 6.6. *R satisfies continuity, strong Pareto, intermediate existence of critical levels, utility independence, and avoidance of the repugnant conclusion if and only if R is NCLGU and $\lim\inf A_g(n)/n > 0$.*

Proof. By Theorem 6.5, number-sensitive critical-level generalized utilitarianism is the only class of principles satisfying the first four axioms of the theorem statement. The proof is completed by establishing that the repugnant conclusion is implied if and only if $\lim\inf A_g(n)/n \le 0$.

Suppose the repugnant conclusion is satisfied. If the sequence $(A_g(n)/n)_{n \in \mathcal{Z}_{++}}$ is not bounded below, then $\lim\inf A_g(n)/n = -\infty \le 0$. If this sequence is bounded below, consider $\varepsilon \in \mathcal{R}_{++}$ and $n \in \mathcal{Z}_{++}$. Choose $\xi > \varepsilon$ so that $g(\xi) > A_g(n)/n$. Note that the existence of a ξ with this property is guaranteed by the definition of A_g. The repugnant conclusion implies that there exists $m > n$ such that

$$m\big[g(\varepsilon) - A_g(m)/m\big] > n\big[g(\xi) - A_g(n)/n\big] > 0$$

which implies

$$A_g(m)/m < g(\varepsilon).$$

Now fix $\varepsilon \in \mathcal{R}_{++}$ and, beginning with $m_1 = 1$, construct a subsequence $(A_g(m_j)/m_j)_{j \in \mathcal{Z}_{++}}$ of $(A_g(n)/n)_{n \in \mathcal{Z}_{++}}$ by finding $m_{j+1} > m_j$ such that $A_g(m_{j+1})/m_{j+1} < g(\varepsilon)$ for all $j \in \mathcal{Z}_{++}$. Because $(A_g(n)/n)_{n \in \mathcal{Z}_{++}}$ is bounded below, this sequence contains a subsequence which converges to $\overset{*}{a}_\varepsilon$ with $\overset{*}{a}_\varepsilon \le g(\varepsilon)$. Because $g(0) = 0$ and ε can be arbitrarily close to zero, $\lim\inf A_g(n)/n \le 0$.

Conversely, if $\lim\inf A_g(n)/n \le 0$, there exists a subsequence $(A_g(m_j)/m_j)_{j \in \mathcal{Z}_{++}}$ of $(A_g(n)/n)_{n \in \mathcal{Z}_{++}}$ which converges to this nonpositive inferior limit if it is finite and diverges to $-\infty$ if it is not. Let $n \in \mathcal{Z}_{++}$, $\zeta \in \mathcal{R}_{++}$, and $\varepsilon \in (0, \xi)$. It follows that the sequence $m_j(g(\varepsilon) - A_g(m_j)/m_j)_{j \in \mathcal{Z}_{++}}$ diverges to $+\infty$. This implies that we can find $m > n$ such that

$$m\big[g(\varepsilon) - A_g(m)/m\big] > n\big[g(\xi) - A_g(n)/n\big]$$

and the repugnant conclusion is satisfied. ∎

Because a finite inferior limit of a sequence is a point of accumulation and, thus, the sequence has a subsequence converging to the inferior limit, Theorem 6.6 implies that NCLGU avoids the repugnant conclusion if and only if there exists no subsequence of $(A_g(n)/n)_{n \in \mathcal{Z}_{++}}$ that converges to a non-positive number or diverges to minus infinity.

As an immediate consequence of Theorem 6.6, we obtain the following result. If critical levels are assumed to be non-decreasing in population size, a

NCLGU principle avoids the repugnant conclusion if and only if it has at least one positive critical level.

Theorem 6.7. *Suppose that R is an NCLGU principle with nondecreasing critical levels. R avoids the repugnant conclusion if and only if it has at least one positive critical level.*

Given the axioms characterizing NCLGU, avoidance of the repugnant conclusion and priority for lives worth living are incompatible. Thus, no population principle can satisfy all those requirements, and trade-offs between axioms have to be made to avoid impossibilities. We conclude this section with a statement and proof of this result.

Theorem 6.8. *There exists no social-evaluation ordering R that satisfies continuity, strong Pareto, intermediate existence of critical levels, utility independence, avoidance of the repugnant conclusion, and priority for lives worth living.*

Proof. Suppose, by way of contradiction, that R satisfies continuity, strong Pareto, intermediate existence of critical levels, utility independence, avoidance of the repugnant conclusion, and priority for lives worth living. By Theorem 6.5, R must be an NCLGU principle. If A_g is constant, we obtain classical generalized utilitarianism and, therefore, a contradiction to avoidance of the repugnant conclusion. If A_g is not constant, there exist $n, m \in \mathcal{Z}_{++}$ such that $A_g(n) - A_g(m) > 0$. Let $\xi \in \mathcal{R}_{++}$ and $\varepsilon \in \mathcal{R}_{--}$ be such that $ng(\xi) - mg(\varepsilon) < A_g(n) - A_g(m)$. The existence of ξ and ε with this property is guaranteed by the assumption $g(0) = 0$ and the continuity of g. Letting $u = \xi \mathbf{1}_n \in \Omega_{++}$ and $v = \varepsilon \mathbf{1}_m \in \Omega_{--}$, it follows that

$$\sum_{i=1}^{n} g(u_i) - A_g(n) = ng(\xi) - A_g(n) < mg(\varepsilon) - A_g(m)$$

$$= \sum_{i=1}^{m} g(v_i) - A_g(m),$$

contradicting priority for lives worth living.   ∎

6.7   CONSTANT CRITICAL LEVELS

Existence independence is a strengthening of utility independence that requires the social ranking to be independent not only of the utilities of the unconcerned but also of their existence. In conjunction with continuity, strong Pareto, and weak existence of critical levels, it can be used to characterize critical-level generalized utilitarianism (CLGU). If continuity is replaced with Hammond equity in this list of axioms, critical-level leximin is obtained. These two axiomatizations are the main results of this section. Because existence independence has strong intuitive appeal, the two characterizations provide a solid argument for these principles. Among critical-level generalized utilitarianism and critical-level leximin, we favor the former class because it satisfies continuity, which we consider an essential property. However, both results are of a fundamental nature in population ethics.

In the presence of existence independence, weak existence of critical levels and existence of critical levels are equivalent and, if strong Pareto is added, the critical-level function C is well-defined and constant. Thus, we obtain the following result, which is analogous to Theorem 6.4. It will play an important role in proving the characterization theorems of this section.

Theorem 6.9. (i) If R satisfies weak existence of critical levels and existence independence, then R satisfies existence of critical levels.

(ii) If R satisfies strong Pareto, weak existence of critical levels and existence independence, then the critical-level function C is well-defined and there exists $c \in \mathcal{R}$ such that $C(u) = c$ for all $u \in \Omega$.

Proof. (i) By weak existence of critical levels, there exist $\bar{u} \in \Omega$ and $c \in \mathcal{R}$ such that

$$(\bar{u}, c)I\bar{u}. \tag{6.9}$$

Let $u \in \Omega$ be arbitrary. Applying existence independence twice, we obtain

$$(u, c)Ru \Leftrightarrow (u, \bar{u}, c)R(u, \bar{u}) \Leftrightarrow (\bar{u}, c)R\bar{u}$$

which, together with (6.9), implies $(u, c)Iu$. Therefore, c is a critical level for all $u \in \Omega$.

As in the proof of Theorem 6.4, part (ii) is immediate. ∎

We can now use Theorems 6.5 and 6.9 to obtain a characterization of CLGU.

Theorem 6.10. R satisfies continuity, strong Pareto, weak existence of critical levels, and existence independence if and only if R is CLGU.

Proof. That the CLGU principles satisfy the axioms of the theorem statement is straightforward to verify.

Now suppose R satisfies continuity, strong Pareto, weak existence of critical levels, and existence independence. By part (i) of Theorem 6.9, R satisfies existence of critical levels and thus intermediate existence of critical levels. In addition, existence independence implies utility independence. Therefore, we can apply Theorem 6.5 and conclude that R is NCLGU. Part (ii) of Theorem 6.9 implies that the critical-level function is well-defined and constant and, setting the constant critical level equal to α, CLGU results. ∎

The axioms of Theorem 6.10 do not restrict the value of the critical-level parameter α. If additional requirements are imposed, some critical-level principles are excluded. For example, if R is required to satisfy the negative expansion principle, α must be nonnegative. Furthermore, given Theorem 6.10, the following result is immediate.

Theorem 6.11. *R satisfies continuity, strong Pareto, weak existence of critical levels, existence independence, and avoidance of the repugnant conclusion if and only if R is CLGU with $\alpha > 0$.*

Note that, if $\alpha > 0$, priority for lives worth living is not satisfied. For $\alpha = 0$, priority for lives worth living is satisfied but the repugnant conclusion is implied. The following theorem is an immediate consequence of Theorems 6.10 and 6.11. It differs from Theorem 6.8 in two ways: a stronger independence axiom is employed and the existence of only one critical level is required.

Theorem 6.12. *There exists no social-evaluation ordering R that satisfies continuity, strong Pareto, weak existence of critical levels, existence independence, avoidance of the repugnant conclusion, and priority for lives worth living.*

As a consequence of this impossibility theorem, choices must be made among the axioms listed in the theorem statement. Dropping the priority axiom is one possibility and it leaves us with the critical-level generalized utilitarian class with positive critical levels. This choice is the one we consider most suitable. There are other options, however. Eliminating existence independence is a possibility, but that alternative is has its own difficulties. There is no principle that satisfies continuity, strong Pareto, intermediate existence of critical levels, utility independence, avoidance of the repugnant conclusion, and priority for lives worth living. Therefore, if priority for lives worth living is regarded as an essential property of population principles and attention is restricted to the same-number generalized utilitarian class, both existence independence and utility independence must be dropped.

We now employ Hammond equity to characterize critical-level leximin. This axiom replaces continuity in the list of requirements of Theorem 6.10.

Hammond Equity. For all $n \in \mathcal{Z}_{++}$, for all $u, v \in \mathcal{R}^n$ and for all $i, j \in \{1, \ldots, n\}$, if $u_k = v_k$ for all $k \in \{1, \ldots, n\} \setminus \{i, j\}$ and $v_j > u_j > u_i > v_i$, then uPv.

We obtain the following characterization (see Blackorby, Bossert, and Donaldson 1996b for an intertemporal version of this result).

Theorem 6.13. *R satisfies strong Pareto, weak existence of critical levels, existence independence, and Hammond equity if and only if R is critical-level leximin.*

Proof. That the critical-level leximin principles satisfy the axioms of the theorem statement is straightforward to verify.

Now suppose R satisfies strong Pareto, weak existence of critical levels, existence independence, and Hammond equity. Let $n, m \in \mathcal{Z}_{++}$, $u \in \mathcal{R}^n$, and $v \in \mathcal{R}^m$. Because R is anonymous, the case $n = m$ is covered by Theorem 4.17. If $n \neq m$, suppose, without loss of generality, that $n > m$; the case $n < m$ is analogous. Theorem 6.9 implies that there exists $\alpha \in \mathcal{R}$ such that $C(u) = \alpha$ for all $u \in \Omega$. Therefore,

$$vI(v, \alpha)I \ldots I(v, \alpha\mathbf{1}_{n-m})$$

and we obtain

$$uRv \Leftrightarrow uR(v, \alpha\mathbf{1}_{n-m}). \tag{6.10}$$

Because u and $(v, \alpha\mathbf{1}_{n-m})$ both have dimension n, Theorem 4.17 implies

$$uRv \Leftrightarrow uR_{\text{lex}}^n(v, \dot{\alpha}\mathbf{1}_{n-m}),$$

which completes the proof. ∎

6.8 AVERAGE UTILITARIANISM

The characterization of average utilitarianism (AU) presented in this section uses same-number independence, replication invariance, and information invariance with respect to cardinal full comparability in addition to some standard axioms. Without replication invariance, average utilitarianism is implied for $n \geq 3$ only.[1]

Theorem 6.14. *R satisfies continuity, strong Pareto, same-number independence, existence of critical levels, replication invariance, and information invariance with respect to cardinal full comparability if and only if R is AU.*

Proof. That AU satisfies the required axioms is straightforward to verify. Now suppose R satisfies continuity, strong Pareto, same-number independence, existence of critical levels, replication invariance, and information invariance with respect to cardinal full comparability. By Theorem 4.12, same-number comparisons involving at least three individuals must be made according to utilitarianism. Replication invariance extends this result to $n = 2$ and the case $n = 1$ is implied by strong Pareto. Therefore, all same-number comparisons are utilitarian.

Strong Pareto and existence of critical levels together imply that the critical-level function is well-defined and that $(u, C(u))Iu$ for all $u \in \Omega$. Information invariance with respect to cardinal full comparability requires, for all $n \in \mathcal{Z}_{++}$,

---

[1] This restricted characterization result is due to Blackorby, Bossert, and Donaldson (1999b). There is an omission in the statement of the relevant result (Theorem 5): the restriction to population sizes greater than 2 is not stated explicitly. The proof does not apply to smaller population sizes because Maskin's (1978) theorem (see our Theorem 4.12) is valid for the case $n \geq 3$ only.

for all $u \in \mathcal{R}^n$, for all $a \in \mathcal{R}_{++}$, and for all $b \in \mathcal{R}$,

$$\left(au_1 + b, \ldots, au_n + b, aC(u) + b\right) I \left(au_1 + b, \ldots, au_n + b\right).$$

By definition of a critical level, we obtain

$$\left(au_1 + b, \ldots, au_n + b, C(au_1 + b, \ldots, au_n + b)\right) I$$
$$\left(au_1 + b, \ldots, au_n + b\right).$$

Because R is transitive, we obtain

$$\left(au_1 + b, \ldots, au_n + b, C(au_1 + b, \ldots, au_n + b)\right) I$$
$$\left(au_1 + b, \ldots, au_n + b, aC(u) + b\right)$$

and strong Pareto implies

$$C(au_1 + b, \ldots, au_n + b) = aC(u) + b. \tag{6.11}$$

Aczél (1966, pp. 234–236) characterized all restrictions of C to a fixed $\mathcal{R}^n$ satisfying (6.11). For our purposes, it is sufficient to show that (6.11) implies that

$$C(\gamma \mathbf{1}_n) = \gamma \tag{6.12}$$

for all $n \in \mathcal{Z}_{++}$ and for all $\gamma \in \mathcal{R}$.

To prove (6.12), consider first the case $\gamma = 0$. Setting $b = 0$ and $u = \gamma \mathbf{1}_n$, (6.11) implies that $C(0 \mathbf{1}_n) = aC(0 \mathbf{1}_n)$ for all $a \in \mathcal{R}_{++}$, so that

$$C(0 \mathbf{1}_n) = 0. \tag{6.13}$$

Now consider the case $\gamma > 0$ and $\gamma \neq 1$. Let $a = 1/\gamma$, $b = \gamma - 1$, and $u = \gamma \mathbf{1}_n$. By (6.11),

$$C(\gamma \mathbf{1}_n) = \frac{1}{\gamma} C(\gamma \mathbf{1}_n) + \gamma - 1,$$

and (6.12) results.

If $\gamma = 1$, let $a = b = 1$ and $u = 0 \mathbf{1}_n$. Substitution into (6.11) together with (6.13) produces (6.12).

Finally, suppose $\gamma < 0$. Let $a = -1/\gamma$, $b = 1 - \gamma$, and $u = \gamma \mathbf{1}_n$. By (6.11),

$$C(-\gamma \mathbf{1}_n) = -\frac{1}{\gamma} C(\gamma \mathbf{1}_n) + 1 - \gamma.$$

Because $-\gamma > 0$, the result for $\gamma > 0$ implies $C(-\gamma \mathbf{1}_n) = -\gamma$. Thus,

$$-\frac{1}{\gamma} C(\gamma \mathbf{1}_n) = C(-\gamma \mathbf{1}_n) - 1 + \gamma = -1$$

and we obtain (6.12).

Now let $n \in \mathcal{Z}_{++}$ and $u \in \mathcal{R}^n$. Because same-number comparisons must be made according to utilitarianism, it follows that

$$u I \left(\frac{1}{n} \sum_{i=1}^{n} u_i \right) \mathbf{1}_n$$

and

$$(u, C(u)) I \left(\left(\frac{1}{n} \sum_{i=1}^{n} u_i \right) \mathbf{1}_n, C(u) \right).$$

Therefore,

$$\left(\left(\frac{1}{n} \sum_{i=1}^{n} u_i \right) \mathbf{1}_n \right) I u I (u, C(u)) I \left(\left(\frac{1}{n} \sum_{i=1}^{n} u_i \right) \mathbf{1}_n, C(u) \right),$$

which implies that $C\left(((1/n) \sum_{i=1}^{n} u_i) \mathbf{1}_n \right) = C(u)$. From (6.12),

$$C(u) = \frac{1}{n} \sum_{i=1}^{n} u_i. \tag{6.14}$$

Therefore, the critical level is given by average utility for all $u \in \Omega$.

Now consider $u \in \mathcal{R}^n$ and $v \in \mathcal{R}^m$ and, without loss of generality, suppose $n > m$. By repeated application of (6.14), it follows that

$$v I \left(v, \frac{1}{m} \sum_{i=1}^{m} v_i \right) I \ldots I \left(v, \left(\frac{1}{m} \sum_{i=1}^{m} v_i \right) \mathbf{1}_{n-m} \right)$$

and, therefore,

$$u R v \Leftrightarrow u R \left(v, \left(\frac{1}{m} \sum_{i=1}^{m} v_i \right) \mathbf{1}_{n-m} \right). \tag{6.15}$$

Because u and $(v, ((1/m) \sum_{i=1}^{m} v_i) \mathbf{1}_{n-m})$ have the same population size n and same-number comparisons must be made according to utilitarianism, it follows that

$$u R \left(v, \left(\frac{1}{m} \sum_{i=1}^{m} v_i \right) \mathbf{1}_{n-m} \right) \Leftrightarrow \sum_{i=1}^{n} u_i \geq \sum_{i=1}^{m} v_i + \frac{n-m}{m} \sum_{i=1}^{m} v_i,$$

which is equivalent to

$$u R \left(v, \left(\frac{1}{m} \sum_{i=1}^{m} v_i \right) \mathbf{1}_{n-m} \right) \Leftrightarrow \frac{1}{n} \sum_{i=1}^{n} u_i \geq \frac{1}{m} \sum_{i=1}^{m} v_i.$$

By (6.15), we obtain AU.   ∎

The reason why the above theorem requires replication invariance is that same-number independence has no power if there are fewer than three individuals. For example, define the value function V by

$$
V(u) = \begin{cases} \frac{1}{n} \sum_{i=1}^{n} u_i & \text{if } n \in \mathcal{Z}_{++} \setminus \{2\} \text{ and } u \in \mathcal{R}^n, \\ \frac{5}{12} u_{(1)} + \frac{7}{12} u_{(2)} & \text{if } u \in \mathcal{R}^2. \end{cases}
$$

The ordering represented by this value function satisfies all the required axioms except replication invariance.

A comparison of Theorems 4.12 and 6.14 illustrates the additional force of information-invariance requirements in a variable-population setting. Together with the additional axiom existence of critical levels, the variable-population version of information invariance with respect to cardinal full comparability implies that critical levels are given by average utility and, thus, a specific variable-population extension of the same-number utilitarian principles characterized in Theorem 4.12 results. Because critical levels are important ethical parameters of population principles, however, it is unsatisfactory to have them determined by an information assumption.

6.9   REPRESENTATIVE-UTILITY PRINCIPLES

As illustrated in Chapter 5, knowledge of representative utilities is, in general, not sufficient to rank utility vectors of different dimension. However, only representative utility is required to define the average generalized utilitarian principles. This is the case because their reduced-form value functions do not depend on population size. In this section, we discuss a more general class of principles whose members have reduced-form value functions that depend on representative utility only. Although the average generalized utilitarian principles are members, the class is larger because the same-number subprinciples need not be generalized utilitarian.

The representative-utility principles can be criticized on the grounds that they recommend driving the population toward zero in the presence of resource constraints. Consider an example with two alternatives. In the first, each of at least two people has the same utility level; in the second, only one person ever lives and has a higher utility level. All the representative-utility principles rank the second alternative as better than the first, no matter how small the difference between the two utility levels.

We now prove a general characterization result concerning these principles to illustrate some of the ethical principles on which they are based. In addition, we discuss the special case of extended maximin.

We begin by introducing a replication-equivalence condition that ensures that no information other than the sequence of representative-utility functions is needed to establish R. This property requires that a utility vector and any replication of it are equally good.

Replication Equivalence. For all $u \in \Omega$ and for all $k \in \mathcal{Z}_{++}$,

$$\underbrace{(u, \ldots, u)}_{k \text{ times}} I u.$$

Replication equivalence implies replication invariance. To see this, let $n, k \in \mathcal{Z}_{++}$ and $u, v \in \mathcal{R}^n$. By replication equivalence,

$$\underbrace{(u, \ldots, u)}_{k \text{ times}} I u$$

and

$$\underbrace{(v, \ldots, v)}_{k \text{ times}} I v.$$

Therefore,

$$\underbrace{(u, \ldots, u)}_{k \text{ times}} R \underbrace{(v, \ldots, v)}_{k \text{ times}} \Leftrightarrow u R v$$

and replication invariance is satisfied. The reverse implication is not true: it is easy to find examples of population principles that satisfy replication invariance but violate replication equivalence.

The ordering R is a representative-utility principle if and only if there exists a sequence of continuous, weakly increasing, and symmetric representative-utility functions $\Xi^n : \mathcal{R}^n \to \mathcal{R}$ for all $n \in \mathcal{Z}_{++}$ such that

$$u R v \Leftrightarrow \Xi^n(u) \geq \Xi^m(v) \tag{6.16}$$

for all $n, m \in \mathcal{Z}_{++}$, for all $u \in \mathcal{R}^n$, and for all $v \in \mathcal{R}^m$, and

$$\Xi^{kn} \underbrace{(u, \ldots, u)}_{k \text{ times}} = \Xi^n(u) \tag{6.17}$$

for all $n, k \in \mathcal{Z}_{++}$, and for all $u \in \mathcal{R}^n$.

Together with the axioms guaranteeing the existence of the representative utility functions Ξ^n, replication equivalence can be used to characterize the class of representative-utility principles.

Theorem 6.15. *R satisfies continuity, Pareto weak preference, minimal increasingness, and replication equivalence if and only if R is a representative-utility principle.*

Proof. Clearly, the representative-utility principles satisfy continuity, Pareto weak preference, and minimal increasingness, given the continuity and weak increasingness of Ξ^n for all $n \in \mathcal{Z}_{++}$. Replication equivalence follows from (6.16) and (6.17).

Now suppose R satisfies continuity, Pareto weak preference, minimal increasingness, and replication equivalence. The existence of a sequence of continuous, weakly increasing, and symmetric representative-utility functions follows from Theorem 4.1 and the anonymity of R.

By Theorem 5.1, there exists an ordering $\mathbf{R}$ on $\mathcal{Z}_{++} \times \mathcal{R}$ such that, for all $n \in \mathcal{Z}_{++}$ and for all $\xi, \zeta \in \mathcal{R}$,

$$(n, \xi)\mathbf{R}(n, \zeta) \Leftrightarrow \xi \geq \zeta \tag{6.18}$$

and, for all $n, m \in \mathcal{Z}_{++}$, for all $u \in \mathcal{R}^n$, and for all $v \in \mathcal{R}^m$,

$$u\,Rv \Leftrightarrow \big(n, \Xi^n(u)\big)\mathbf{R}\big(m, \Xi^m(v)\big). \tag{6.19}$$

Replication equivalence requires

$$\big(kn, \Xi^{kn}(\underbrace{u, \ldots, u})\big)\mathbf{I}\big(n, \Xi^n(u)\big)$$
$$\qquad\qquad\;\; {}_{k \text{ times}}$$

for all $n, k \in \mathcal{Z}_{++}$ and for all $u \in \mathcal{R}^n$. In particular, we can choose $n = 1$ and $u = (\xi)$ to obtain

$$\big(k, \Xi^k(\xi\mathbf{1}_k)\big)\mathbf{I}\big(1, \Xi^1(\xi)\big)$$

for all $k \in \mathcal{Z}_{++}$ and for all $\xi \in \mathcal{R}$. Because $\Xi^n(\xi\mathbf{1}_n) = \xi$ for all $n \in \mathcal{Z}_{++}$, we obtain

$$(k, \xi)\mathbf{I}(1, \xi) \tag{6.20}$$

for all $k \in \mathcal{Z}_{++}$ and for all $\xi \in \mathcal{R}$. Using (6.18), (6.19), (6.20), and transitivity, we obtain

$$u\,Rv \Leftrightarrow \big(n, \Xi^n(u)\big)\mathbf{R}\big(m, \Xi^m(v)\big) \Leftrightarrow \big(1, \Xi^n(u)\big)\mathbf{R}\big(1, \Xi^m(v)\big)$$
$$\Leftrightarrow \Xi^n(u) \geq \Xi^m(v)$$

for all $n, m \in \mathcal{Z}_{++}$, for all $u \in \mathcal{R}^n$, and for all $v \in \mathcal{R}^m$, which implies (6.16). Given (6.16), (6.17) follows immediately from replication equivalence. ∎

The average generalized utilitarian (AGU) class is a subclass of the representative-utility principles, and it can be characterized by adding same-number independence to the list of axioms in Theorem 6.15. The representative-utility class includes many other principles, such as those whose value functions are the representative-utility functions for the S-Gini same-number principles.

As another example of a representative-utility principle, we provide a characterization of extended maximin. In addition to the axioms guaranteeing the existence of the representative-utility functions and the axiom minimal inequality aversion, we employ a requirement that imposes a specific critical level for all $u \in \Omega$. The critical-level axiom requires minimal utility to be a critical level for every utility vector. Thus, the axiom strengthens existence of critical levels. Strong Pareto is not satisfied by extended maximin and, as a consequence, critical levels need not be unique. We call the axiom minimum critical levels.

Minimum Critical Levels. For all $n \in \mathcal{Z}_{++}$ and for all $u \in \mathcal{R}^n$, $(u, u_{(n)})Iu$.

Extended maximin is an interesting case of a population principle in that specifying critical levels is sufficient to recover the ordering R itself. This is not true in general, even if critical levels are unique for each $u \in \Omega$. For example, average utility is a critical-level function not only for average utilitarianism but also for orderings such as the one defined by

$$uRv \Leftrightarrow \gamma \frac{1}{n} \sum_{i=1}^{n} u_i + (1 - \gamma)u_{(n)} \geq \gamma \frac{1}{m} \sum_{i=1}^{m} v_i + (1 - \gamma)v_{(m)}$$

for all $n, m \in \mathcal{Z}_{++}$, for all $u \in \mathcal{R}^n$, and for all $v \in \mathcal{R}^m$, where $\gamma \in (0, 1)$. The function $C : \Omega \to \mathcal{R}$ such that $C(u)$ is equal to average utility for all $u \in \Omega$ is a critical-level function for R because adding an individual at average utility changes neither average nor minimum utility. Therefore, average utility is a critical-level function for orderings that are represented by convex combinations of average utility and minimum utility.

The following theorem characterizes extended maximin.

Theorem 6.16. *R satisfies continuity, Pareto weak preference, minimal increasingness, minimal inequality aversion, and minimum critical levels if and only if R is extended maximin.*

Proof. That extended maximin satisfies the required axioms is easy to see. Now suppose R satisfies continuity, Pareto weak preference, minimal increasingness, minimal inequality aversion, and minimum critical levels. By Theorem 5.1, there exists an ordering $\mathbf{R}$ on $\mathcal{Z}_{++} \times \mathcal{R}$ such that, for all $n \in \mathcal{Z}_{++}$ and for all $\xi, \zeta \in \mathcal{R}$,

$$(n, \xi)\mathbf{R}(n, \zeta) \Leftrightarrow \xi \geq \zeta$$

and, for all $n, m \in \mathcal{Z}_{++}$, for all $u \in \mathcal{R}^n$, and for all $v \in \mathcal{R}^m$,

$$uRv \Leftrightarrow \left(n, \Xi^n(u)\right)\mathbf{R}\left(m, \Xi^m(v)\right).$$

Therefore, minimum critical levels requires

$$\left(n + 1, \Xi^{n+1}(u, u_{(n)})\right)\mathbf{I}\left(n, \Xi^n(u)\right)$$

for all $n \in \mathcal{Z}_{++}$ and for all $u \in \mathcal{R}^n$. This implies, for all $n \in \mathcal{Z}_{++}$ and for all $\xi \in \mathcal{R}$,

$$\left(n + 1, \Xi^{n+1}(\xi \mathbf{1}_{n+1})\right)\mathbf{I}\left(n, \Xi^n(\xi \mathbf{1}_n)\right)$$

and, because $\Xi^n(\xi \mathbf{1}_n) = \Xi^{n+1}(\xi \mathbf{1}_{n+1}) = \xi$,

$$(n + 1, \xi)\mathbf{I}(n, \xi). \tag{6.21}$$

Repeated application of (6.21) and transitivity implies

$$(n, \xi)\mathbf{I}(1, \xi)$$

and, as in the proof of Theorem 6.15, it follows that

$$u R v \Leftrightarrow \left(n, \Xi^n(u)\right) \mathbf{R}\left(m, \Xi^m(v)\right) \Leftrightarrow \left(1, \Xi^n(u)\right) \mathbf{R}\left(1, \Xi^m(v)\right)$$

$$\Leftrightarrow \Xi^n(u) \geq \Xi^m(v) \tag{6.22}$$

for all $n, m \in \mathcal{Z}_{++}$, for all $u \in \mathcal{R}^n$, and for all $v \in \mathcal{R}^m$. Repeated application of minimum critical levels yields

$$\Xi^{n+m}(u, u_{(n)}\mathbf{1}_m) = \Xi^n(u) \tag{6.23}$$

for all $n, m \in \mathcal{Z}_{++}$ and for all $u \in \mathcal{R}^n$. Minimal inequality aversion implies that representative utility is less than or equal to average utility and, thus,

$$\Xi^{n+m}(u, u_{(n)}\mathbf{1}_m) \leq \frac{1}{n+m} \sum_{i=1}^{n} u_i + \frac{m}{n+m} u_{(n)}. \tag{6.24}$$

Using (6.23), (6.24) implies

$$u_{(n)} \leq \Xi^n(u) \leq \frac{1}{n+m} \sum_{i=1}^{n} u_i + \frac{m}{n+m} u_{(n)},$$

where the first inequality follows from the observation that representative utility is no less than minimum utility. Taking limits as m approaches infinity, we obtain

$$u_{(n)} \leq \Xi^n(u) \leq u_{(n)}$$

and, thus, $\Xi^n(u) = u_{(n)}$ for all $n \in \mathcal{Z}_{++}$ and for all $u \in \mathcal{R}^n$. By (6.22), this implies that R is extended maximin. ∎

6.10   NUMBER-DAMPENED GENERALIZED UTILITARIANISM

We now consider number-dampened generalized utilitarianism together with restrictions that are imposed by additional axioms.

The theorems in this section and the next make use of a general property of any principle that has a well-defined critical-level function: knowledge of the same-number subprinciples and the critical-level function is sufficient to rank any two utility vectors. To see this, let $n > m$, $u \in \mathcal{R}^n$ and $v \in \mathcal{R}^m$. Then define the vector $v' \in \mathcal{R}^n$ so that $v'_i = v_i$ for all $i \in \{1, \ldots, m\}$ and $v'_i = C(v'_1, \ldots, v'_{i-1})$ for all $i \in \{m+1, \ldots, n\}$. By the definition of critical levels, $v' I v$. Consequently, the ranking of u and v is the same as the ranking of u and v'. It follows that the ranking of u and v is determined by the same-number subprinciple for population size n.

To characterize number-dampened generalized utilitarianism, we employ a critical-level condition stating that, provided R is same-number generalized utilitarian, each transformed critical level is equal to the product of average transformed utility and a function of population size.

Number-Dampened Critical Levels. If R is same-number generalized utilitarian, then there exists a function $h: \mathcal{Z}_{++} \to \mathcal{R}$ with $h(n) > -n$ for all $n \in \mathcal{Z}_{++}$ such that, for all $n \in \mathcal{Z}_{++}$ and for all $u \in \mathcal{R}^n$,

$$C(u) = g^{-1}\left(\frac{h(n)}{n}\sum_{i=1}^{n} g(u_i)\right). \tag{6.25}$$

As is the case for minimum critical levels, number-dampened critical levels strengthens existence of critical levels by specifying some properties of critical levels, in addition to assuming their existence.

We use number-dampened critical levels in conjunction with continuity, strong Pareto, and the population substitution principle to characterize number-dampened generalized utilitarianism. Alternatively, same-number independence and replication invariance could be employed instead of the population substitution principle.

Theorem 6.17. *R satisfies continuity, strong Pareto, the population substitution principle, and number-dampened critical levels if and only if R is NDGU.*

Proof. That continuity, strong Pareto, and the population substitution principle are satisfied by NDGU is straightforward to verify.

To prove that number-dampened critical levels is satisfied, we define the function $h: \mathcal{Z}_{++} \to \mathcal{R}$ by

$$h(n) = \frac{(n+1)f(n) - nf(n+1)}{f(n+1)}$$

for all $n \in \mathcal{Z}_{++}$, which implies, using the critical levels for number-dampened generalized utilitarianism derived in Chapter 5, that (6.25) is satisfied. It remains to be shown that $h(n) > -n$ for all $n \in \mathcal{Z}_{++}$. Because $f(n) > 0$ for all $n \in \mathcal{Z}_{++}$,

$$(n+1)f(n) > 0 \Rightarrow (n+1)f(n) - nf(n+1) > -nf(n+1)$$
$$\Rightarrow \frac{(n+1)f(n) - nf(n+1)}{f(n+1)} > -n$$
$$\Rightarrow h(n) > -n.$$

Conversely, suppose R satisfies the required axioms. By Theorem 6.1, R must be same-number generalized utilitarian. By number-dampened critical levels, there exists a function h such that (6.25) is satisfied. Let $f(1) = 1$ and

$$f(n) = \prod_{j=1}^{n} \frac{j}{j-1+h(j-1)}$$

for all $n \in \mathcal{Z}_{++}\backslash\{1\}$. Because $h(n) > -n$ for all $n \in \mathcal{Z}_{++}$, $f(n) > 0$ for all $n \in \mathcal{Z}_{++}$. As is straightforward to verify, the NDGU ordering defined by f has critical levels given by (6.25). Because the ordering R is determined by its same-number subprinciples (which are determined by the function g) and by the critical-level function (see the demonstration at the beginning of this section), this completes the proof.   ■

As argued earlier, the negative expansion principle is an important property of a population principle. Without it, adding individuals whose lifetime utilities are below neutrality to an otherwise unaffected population is considered desirable in some circumstances. All number-dampened generalized utilitarian (NDGU) principles other than classical generalized utilitarianism (CGU) fail to satisfy this fundamental axiom. This is a serious shortcoming of this class of principles.

Theorem 6.18. *Let R be an NDGU principle. R satisfies the negative expansion principle if and only if R is CGU.*

Proof. Suppose R is NDGU. Clearly, the special case of CGU satisfies the negative expansion principle because all critical levels are zero and, thus, nonnegative. Conversely, suppose R is an NDGU principle that satisfies the negative expansion principle. Therefore, critical levels must be nonnegative, and it follows that

$$\frac{h(n)}{n} \sum_{i=1}^{n} g(u_i) \geq 0$$

for all $n \in \mathcal{Z}_{++}$ and for all $u \in \mathcal{R}^n$. Because, for any $n \in \mathcal{Z}_{++}, u, v \in \mathcal{R}^n$ may be chosen so that $\sum_{i=1}^{n} g(u_i)$ is positive and $\sum_{i=1}^{n} g(v_i)$ is negative, this implies that $h(n) = 0$ for all $n \in \mathcal{Z}_{++}$. By definition of h, this requires

$$(n + 1)f(n) - nf(n + 1) = 0$$

or, equivalently,

$$\frac{f(n)}{n} = \frac{f(n + 1)}{n + 1}$$

which implies that $f(n) = an$ for all $n \in \mathcal{Z}_{++}$, where $a \in \mathcal{R}_{++}$ is a constant. The resulting ordering is CGU.   ■

Now we examine number-dampened generalized utilitarianism with respect to its capability of avoiding the repugnant conclusion. Our next result provides a necessary and sufficient condition: the repugnant conclusion is implied if and only if the function f is unbounded.

Theorem 6.19. *Let R be an NDGU principle. R satisfies avoidance of the repugnant conclusion if and only the function f is bounded.*

Proof. Suppose R is NDGU. Clearly, it is sufficient to prove that the unboundedness of f implies and is implied by the repugnant conclusion.

Suppose first that f is unbounded. Let $n \in \mathcal{Z}_{++}$, $\xi \in \mathcal{R}_{++}$, and $\varepsilon \in (0, \xi)$. Because f is unbounded, there exists $m > n$ such that $f(m) > f(n)g(\xi)/g(\varepsilon)$, which implies the repugnant conclusion.

Now suppose the repugnant conclusion is satisfied. Then, for all $n \in \mathcal{Z}_{++}$, for all $\xi \in \mathcal{R}_{++}$, and for all $\varepsilon \in (0, \xi)$, there exists $m > n$ such that $f(m) > f(n)g(\xi)/g(\varepsilon)$. For fixed n and ξ, the right side increases without limit as ε approaches zero because $g(0) = 0$ and g is continuous. Therefore, f is unbounded. ∎

An important subclass of NDGU consists of the principles for which the function h is a positive constant with $h(n) = \gamma \in (0, 1)$ for all $n \in \mathcal{Z}_{++}$.[2] The function f that corresponds to such an h is given by

$$f(n) = \begin{cases} 1 & \text{if } n = 1, \\ \left(\frac{2}{1+\gamma}\right) \cdots \left(\frac{n}{n-1+\gamma}\right) & \text{if } n \geq 2. \end{cases}$$

The following theorem shows that all members of this subclass of NDGU imply the repugnant conclusion. In the proof, we use Abel's theorem (see, for example, Brand 1955, p. 52), which states that if $(a_n)_{n \in \mathcal{Z}_{++}}$ is a positive and decreasing sequence and $\sum_{i=1}^n a_i$ converges, then $\lim_{n \to \infty} na_n = 0$.

Theorem 6.20. *If R is NDGU with $h(n) = \gamma$ for all $n \in \mathcal{Z}_{++}$ where $\gamma \in (0, 1)$, then R implies the repugnant conclusion.*

Proof. Suppose that f is bounded. Because f is increasing in n, it is bounded if and only if it converges and, because $i/(i - 1 + \gamma) > 1$ for all $i \geq 2$, the limit is at least one. Because $f(1) = 1$ and, for $n \geq 2$,

$$f(n) = \prod_{i=1}^{n-1} \frac{i+1}{i+\gamma},$$

the product

$$\prod_{i=1}^n \frac{i+1}{i+\gamma}$$

converges to the same limit. Therefore, the logarithm

$$\sum_{i=1}^n \ln\left(\frac{i+1}{i+\gamma}\right)$$

converges as well. The individual terms $\ln((i + 1)/(i + \gamma))$ are positive and decreasing in i because $\gamma < 1$. By Abel's theorem,

$$\lim_{n \to \infty} n \ln\left(\frac{n+1}{n+\gamma}\right) = 0$$

---

[2] For further details on the properties of this subclass, see Blackorby and Donaldson (1984a).

and, therefore,

$$\lim_{n \to \infty} \ln \left(\frac{n+1}{n+\gamma} \right)^n = 0.$$

Because $\ln \big((n+1)/(n+\gamma) \big)$ converges to zero,

$$\lim_{n \to \infty} \ln \left(\frac{n+1}{n+\gamma} \right)^n + \lim_{n \to \infty} \ln \left(\frac{n+1}{n+\gamma} \right) = \lim_{n \to \infty} \ln \left(\frac{n+1}{n+\gamma} \right)^{n+1} = 0,$$

which implies

$$\lim_{n \to \infty} \left(\frac{n+1}{n+\gamma} \right)^{n+1} = 1.$$

Inverting both sides,

$$\lim_{n \to \infty} \left(\frac{n+\gamma}{n+1} \right)^{n+1} = \lim_{n \to \infty} \left(1 + \frac{\gamma-1}{n+1} \right)^{n+1} = 1.$$

But

$$\lim_{n \to \infty} \left(1 + \frac{\gamma-1}{n+1} \right)^{n+1} = \exp(\gamma - 1),$$

which is less than one for all $\gamma \in (0, 1)$ and a contradiction is obtained. Consequently, f is not bounded and, by Theorem 6.19, R implies the repugnant conclusion. ∎

A related result states that if the repugnant conclusion is to be avoided for nondecreasing functions h such that $h(n) \in (0, 1]$ for all $n \in \mathcal{Z}_{++}$, it follows that $h(n)$ must approach 1 as n becomes large. To see why this is the case, note first that $h(n)$ must have a limit as n approaches infinity because h is nondecreasing and bounded, and this limit must be in the interval $(0, 1]$ as well. A straightforward modification of the proof of Theorem 6.20 shows that, if the limit is less than 1, then the repugnant conclusion is implied. Consequently, to avoid the repugnant conclusion, the limit must be equal to 1 and the principle must approximate average generalized utilitarianism as n becomes large.

We conclude this section with an observation concerning the relationship between specific properties of the functions f and h. In particular, the function h assumes nonnegative values only if and only if $f(n)/n$ is nonincreasing. To see why this is the case, note that, according to the definition of h,

$$h(n) \geq 0 \Leftrightarrow \frac{(n+1)f(n) - nf(n+1)}{f(n+1)} \geq 0$$
$$\Leftrightarrow (n+1)f(n) \geq nf(n+1)$$
$$\Leftrightarrow \frac{f(n)}{n} \geq \frac{f(n+1)}{n+1}$$

for all $n \in \mathcal{Z}_{++}$.

6.11 RESTRICTED PRINCIPLES

The characterization of number-dampened generalized utilitarianism in Theorem 6.17 uses an axiom that specifies the functional form of the critical-level function. A characterization of the restricted number-dampened principles can be obtained by using a modification of number-dampened critical levels.

Restricted Number-Dampened Critical Levels. If R is same-number generalized utilitarian, then there exists a function $h: \mathcal{Z}_{++} \to \mathcal{R}_+$ such that, for all $n \in \mathcal{Z}_{++}$ and for all $u \in \mathcal{R}^n$,

$$
C(u) = \begin{cases} g^{-1}\left(\frac{h(n)}{n} \sum_{i=1}^{n} g(u_i) \right) & \text{if } \sum_{i=1}^{n} g(u_i) > 0, \\ 0 & \text{if } \sum_{i=1}^{n} g(u_i) \le 0. \end{cases}
$$

Note that, in the axiom statement, $h(n)$ must be nonnegative. It follows that, if R is same-number generalized utilitarian and satisfies restricted number-dampened critical levels, the negative expansion principle is satisfied. Restricted number-dampened generalized utilitarianism (RNDGU) is characterized in the following theorem. Because the proof is almost identical to the proof of Theorem 6.17, it is omitted.

Theorem 6.21. *R satisfies continuity, strong Pareto, the population substitution principle, and restricted number-dampened critical levels if and only if R is RNDGU.*

An axiom that is similar to restricted number-dampened critical levels can be used in a characterization of restricted critical-level generalized utilitarianism.

Restricted Existence-Independent Critical Levels. If R is same-number generalized utilitarian, then there exists $\alpha \in \mathcal{R}_{++}$ such that

$$
C(u) = \begin{cases} \alpha & \text{if } \sum_{i=1}^{n} g(u_i) > ng(\alpha), \\ g^{-1}\left(\frac{1}{n} \sum_{i=1}^{n} g(u_i) \right) & \text{if } 0 < \sum_{i=1}^{n} g(u_i) \le ng(\alpha), \\ 0 & \text{if } \sum_{i=1}^{n} g(u_i) \le 0. \end{cases}
$$

The axiom name indicates that, in certain cases, a kind of existence independence is satisfied. If we know that the representative utility of those who ever live exceeds α or is nonpositive, then the critical level is independent of their number and their utility levels. If representative utility is positive and no greater than α, the critical level is equal to representative utility. A characterization of restricted critical-level generalized utilitarianism (RCLGU) is easily obtained by using this axiom.

Theorem 6.22. *R satisfies continuity, strong Pareto, the population substitution principle, and restricted existence-independent critical levels if and only if R is RCLGU.*

It is also possible to obtain a characterization of restricted number-sensitive critical-level utilitarianism by means of an appropriate critical-level axiom. Because that axiom and the resulting theorem are similar to restricted existence-independent critical levels and Theorem 6.22, they are omitted.

6.12 INFORMATION-INVARIANCE CONDITIONS

We conclude this chapter by illustrating how information-invariance conditions can be used to obtain characterizations of specific critical-level principles. However, as mentioned in Chapter 5, the possibilities for such characterizations are limited because, in the absence of norms, variable-population information-invariance assumptions are very demanding.

First, we show that many variable-population information-invariance assumptions are incompatible with number-sensitive critical-level generalized utilitarianism. In particular, if there is a population size such that the critical level is the same for all utility vectors of that size, all admissible transformations according to an information-invariance assumption A must map the critical level into itself.

Theorem 6.23. *Suppose R satisfies strong Pareto, existence of critical levels, and information invariance with respect to Φ^A. If there exist $n \in \mathcal{Z}_{++}$ and $c \in \mathcal{R}$ such that $C(u) = c$ for all $u \in \mathcal{R}^n$, then $\phi_i(c) = c$ for all $\phi \in \Phi^A$ and for all $i \in \mathcal{Z}_{++}$.*

Proof. Let $n \in \mathcal{Z}_{++}$ and suppose $C(u) = c$ for all $u \in \mathcal{R}^n$. By definition, $u I(u, c)$ for all $u \in \mathcal{R}^n$. The anonymity of R implies that $\Phi^A \subseteq \Phi^{OFC}$. Hence, for all $\phi \in \Phi^A$, there exists an increasing function $\phi_0: \mathcal{R} \to \mathcal{R}$ such that $\phi_i = \phi_0$ for all $i \in \mathcal{Z}_{++}$. Therefore, information invariance with respect to Φ^A implies, for all $\phi \in \Phi^A$,

$$\big(\phi_0(u_1), \ldots, \phi_0(u_n)\big) I \big(\phi_0(u_1), \ldots, \phi_0(u_n), \phi_0(c)\big)$$

and, using the definition of a critical level again,

$$\big(\phi_0(u_1), \ldots, \phi_0(u_n)\big) I \big(\phi_0(u_1), \ldots, \phi_0(u_n), c\big).$$

Transitivity of R implies

$$\big(\phi_0(u_1), \ldots, \phi_0(u_n), \phi_0(c)\big) I \big(\phi_0(u_1), \ldots, \phi_0(u_n), c\big).$$

By strong Pareto, $\phi_0(c) = c$ and thus $\phi_i(c) = c$ for all $i \in \mathcal{Z}_{++}$. ∎

Clearly, existence of critical levels could be weakened by requiring the existence of critical levels for a single population size only without changing the conclusion of Theorem 6.23.

Theorem 6.23 implies that any information assumption allowing for invariance transformations that do not leave the critical level unchanged is incompatible with NCLGU. Therefore, information assumptions such as cardinal full comparability are ruled out because, according to it, the transformed value of the critical level c is given by $ac + b$, which can be different from c. Among the information assumptions listed in Chapter 5, only information invariance with respect to reference ratio-scale full comparability $[c]$ and with respect to numerical full comparability are compatible with a constant critical level c.

We now turn to characterizations of special classes of CLGU principles. If information invariance with respect to ratio-scale full comparability is added to the axioms continuity, strong Pareto, weak existence of critical levels, and existence independence, we obtain a characterization of the classical means of order r. See Blackorby and Donaldson (1982) for a characterization of the same-number restrictions of these principles. The proof of the following theorem is an adaptation of an argument used in the proof of Theorem 7 by Bossert (1997). A classical mean of order r is a critical-level zero-translated mean of order r with a critical level of zero; see Chapter 5.

Theorem 6.24. *R satisfies continuity, strong Pareto, weak existence of critical levels, existence independence, and information invariance with respect to ratio-scale full comparability if and only if R is a classical mean of order r.*

Proof. That the classical means of order r satisfy the required axioms is straightforward to verify. Now suppose R satisfies the axioms. Together with the anonymity of R, Theorem 1 and Corollary 1.1 of Blackorby and Donaldson (1982) imply that there exist $\beta, r \in \mathcal{R}_{++}$ such that, for all $n \geq 3$ and for all $u, v \in \mathcal{R}^n$,

$$uRv \Leftrightarrow \sum_{\substack{i \in \{1,\dots,n\}: \\ u_i \geq 0}} u_i^r - \beta \sum_{\substack{i \in \{1,\dots,n\}: \\ u_i < 0}} (-u_i)^r$$

$$\geq \sum_{\substack{i \in \{1,\dots,n\}: \\ v_i \geq 0}} v_i^r - \beta \sum_{\substack{i \in \{1,\dots,n\}: \\ v_i < 0}} (-v_i)^r. \tag{6.26}$$

By Theorem 6.9, there exists $c \in \mathcal{R}$ such that $(u, c)Iu$ for all $u \in \Omega$, and an argument analogous to the one employed in the proof of Theorem 6.5 implies that (6.26) is true for $n \in \{1, 2\}$ as well. Suppose first that $c > 0$. Adding m individuals with utility c to $u \in \mathcal{R}^n$ and n individuals with utility c to $v \in \mathcal{R}^m$, we can apply (6.26) and simplify to obtain

$$uRv \Leftrightarrow \sum_{\substack{i \in \{1,\dots,n\}: \\ u_i \geq 0}} u_i^r - \beta \sum_{\substack{i \in \{1,\dots,n\}: \\ u_i < 0}} (-u_i)^r - nc^r$$

$$\geq \sum_{\substack{i \in \{1,\dots,m\}: \\ v_i \geq 0}} v_i^r - \beta \sum_{\substack{i \in \{1,\dots,m\}: \\ v_i < 0}} (-v_i)^r - mc^r \tag{6.27}$$

for all $n, m \in \mathcal{Z}_{++}$, for all $u \in \mathcal{R}^n$, and for all $v \in \mathcal{R}^m$. By definition of the critical level c, we must have $c\mathbf{1}_2 I c\mathbf{1}_1$, and information invariance with respect to ratio-scale full comparability implies, in particular, that $2^{1/r}c\mathbf{1}_2 I 2^{1/r}c\mathbf{1}_1$. But according to (6.27), $2^{1/r}c\mathbf{1}_2 P 2^{1/r}c\mathbf{1}_1$, a contradiction. The assumption $c < 0$ leads to an analogous contradiction, and it follows that c must be equal to zero. Substituting $c = 0$ in (6.27) implies that R is a classical mean of order r. ■

Theorem 6.24 illustrates why the choice of zero in the invariance assumption with respect to ratio-scale full comparability is arbitrary: there is no reason why classical generalized utilitarianism should result without any reference to the notion of a neutral life. A generalization of the theorem is obtained by replacing this information assumption with information invariance with respect to reference ratio-scale full comparability $[\alpha]$, which leads to a characterization of the class of critical-level α-translated means of order r, where α is the critical level for all $u \in \Omega$. Note that the translation parameter κ must be equal to the critical-level parameter α in this result. This is the case because the definition of information invariance with respect to reference ratio-scale full comparability $[\alpha]$ is contingent on α.

Theorem 6.25. *R satisfies continuity, strong Pareto, weak existence of critical levels, existence independence, and information invariance with respect to reference ratio-scale full comparability $[\alpha]$ if and only if R is a critical-level α-translated mean of order r with critical level α.*

The proof of Theorem 6.25 can be obtained from the proof of Theorem 6.24 by noting that information invariance with respect to reference ratio-scale full comparability $[\alpha]$ differs from information invariance with respect to ratio-scale full comparability in that the property of the admissible transformations $\phi_0(0) = 0$ is replaced with $\phi_0(\alpha) = \alpha$. With that modification, the remaining steps are the same in both proofs.

CHAPTER 7

Uncertainty and Incommensurabilities

Part A

In this chapter, we investigate several variations on our basic model. First, we incorporate uncertainty and extend our characterizations of the critical-level utilitarian (CLU) and number-sensitive critical-level utilitarian (NCLU) classes of population principles. The resulting classes are called ex-ante CLU and ex-ante NCLU.

Our theorems are variants and extensions of Harsanyi's (1955, 1977) well-known social-aggregation theorem. Additional axioms are used to extend fixed-population principles to the variable-population environment. Although Harsanyi used a single-profile setting, we investigate the multiprofile case but note that the single-profile approach could be extended to the variable-population model as well.

Second, we examine incommensurabilities in social rankings by employing social-decision functionals, which associate a quasi-ordering (rather than an ordering) on the set of alternatives with each utility profile. Several new axioms are used to characterize the critical-band generalized utilitarian class of principles. The band is an interval and, according to those principles, one alternative is at least as good as another if and only if it is at least as good according to critical-level generalized utilitarianism for all critical levels in the band.

7.1 UNCERTAINTY

The principles presented and discussed in Chapters 3 to 6 can be used to rank actions or combinations of institutional arrangements (including legal and educational ones), customs, and moral rules, taking account of the constraints of history and human nature. If each of these leads with certainty to a particular social alternative, they can be ranked with any welfarist principle. This approach does not make a strong distinction between ends and means: actions are embedded in the associated alternatives.

There are different ways to make use of the resulting rankings. One is to take a maximizing approach and recommend to governments and individuals

Table 7.1. *An Uncertain Alternative*

States	1	2	3
Probabilities	1/4	1/8	5/8
Alternatives	x	y	z

alike that they choose the best feasible action, a position taken by act utilitarians such as Sidgwick (1907, 1966). Other utilitarians realize that it may be impossible or impractical for individuals to engage in complicated assessments of consequences and, instead, follow general rules that are "constantly evolving, but on the whole stable, such that their use in moral education, including self-education, and their consequent acceptance by society at large, will lead to the nearest possible approximation to archangelic thinking" (Hare 1982, p. 33), a position sometimes called rule utilitarianism. Furthermore, the best actions may require an individual, state, or generation to make very great sacrifices. Because concern for others is bounded, it may be important to choose rules that limit the sacrifices of agents or declare some actions to be supererogatory: beyond the call of duty.[1] Mill (1861, 1979b), a utilitarian who took such considerations seriously, did not advocate maximization in all circumstances (see, for example, Barry 1989, Chapter 12, Brown 1972).

If consequences are uncertain, the problem is more difficult. One way of solving it is to consider the various possibilities and to attach probabilities to them. Such a possibility is illustrated in Table 7.1. The table has three possible outcomes, x, y, z, and probabilities are 1/4, 1/8, and 5/8. We refer to such combinations as uncertain alternatives or U-alternatives. Possibilities are indexed in the top row of the table and we refer to them as states (after the term states of nature in decision theory).

The number of states may be different in different alternatives, but some of this complexity can be reduced if the maximal number of states is finite, which we assume. In that case, each U-alternative can be converted into one with that number of states by adding states whose associated probabilities are zero. Thus, we can assume that the number of states is the same for all U-alternatives.

Table 7.2 illustrates a four-state version of the U-alternative of Table 7.1. In the table, state 4 has a probability of zero and the associated alternative is z. The alternative chosen has, of course, no significance: any alternative will do.

If a U-alternative represents a certain outcome, it can be represented in different ways when the number of states is greater than one. The two U-alternatives in Table 7.3 illustrate the case in which alternative x is certain and the number of states is four. In the U-alternative on the left side of

---

[1] See also Heyd (1982) and Blackorby, Bossert, and Donaldson (2000) for a discussion of limited altruism.

Table 7.2. *Another Description*

States	1	2	3	4
Probabilities	1/4	1/8	5/8	0
Alternatives	x	y	z	z

the table, x occurs with probability one in state one; probabilities for the other states are zero. On the right side, probabilities are arbitrary, provided they are nonnegative and add to one. In both cases, x occurs with probability one and the two U-alternatives are equivalent.

In any U-alternative, the individuals who ever live may differ from state to state, a possibility that is illustrated in Table 7.4. In that U-alternative, only individuals 2, 42, 56, and 87 live in at least one state and each person has actual or ex-post utility levels defined only in states in which he or she is alive. Of the four individuals, only person 56 is alive in all states.

An ex-ante utility level can be defined for each individual who is alive in all states. It represents an assessment of the U-alternative before the uncertainty is resolved. If a person's ex-ante utility level is greater in one such U-alternative than in another, then it is better for him or her. We assume individual ex-ante utilities are consistent with ex-post utilities so that the ex-ante value of a U-alternative in which the same alternative occurs in every state is the same as the actual utility level. As a consequence, if ex-ante values are specified for all U-alternatives in which the individual is alive in all states, ex-post utilities can be derived. On the set of those U-alternatives, the ex-ante utilities define an ex-ante utility function. We assume that the probabilities employed in these assessments are the same for all individuals. Because probabilities are used normatively, they may be thought to be based on the best information available.

The expected-utility hypothesis (von Neumann and Morgenstern 1944, 1947) and the Bernoulli hypothesis (Arrow 1972, Broome 1991) provide particular structures for individual ex-ante utility functions. The Bernoulli hypothesis makes individual ex-ante utilities equal to the expected value of ex-post utilities. Thus, in the example of Table 7.4, an ex-ante utility is defined for person 56 only and is given by $(1/4)20 + (1/8)64 + (1/2)64 + (1/8)40$, which is equal to 50. Ex-ante utilities for the other three people are not defined.

Table 7.3. *A Certain Outcome*

States	1	2	3	4	1	2	3	4
Probabilities	1	0	0	0	p_1	p_2	p_3	p_4
Alternatives	x	y	z	w	x	x	x	x

Table 7.4. *Different Populations in Different States*

States	1	2	3	4
Probabilities	1/4	1/8	1/2	1/8
Alternatives	x	y	z	w
Utility of Person 2	−15		50	
Utility of Person 42		80	60	
Utility of Person 56	20	64	64	40
Utility of Person 87		42		

The expected-utility hypothesis requires the ex-ante utility function to be ordinally equivalent to the expected value of a von Neumann–Morgenstern (vNM) function, which, in turn, is ordinally equivalent to the ex-post utility function. Suppose that, in the example of Table 7.4, the vNM value u_{M56} for person 56 for ex-post utility level u_{56} is equal to $1 - \exp(-u_{56}/1{,}000)$. Then vNM values for person 56 are 0.0198, 0.0620, 0.0620, and 0.0392 for x, y, z, and w, respectively, and the expected value is 0.0486. To satisfy our consistency requirement that links ex-ante and ex-post utilities, ex-ante utility must be equal to a transformed value of the expected vNM value where the transformation is the inverse of the one that links ex-post utilities and vNM values. In the example, the inverse transformation is $-1{,}000 \ln(1 - u_{M56})$, so ex-ante utility is $-1000 \ln(0.9514) = 49.82$.

The expected-utility hypothesis allows individual ex-ante utility functions to express an attitude toward utility uncertainty. In the above example, the ex-ante utility function is averse to utility uncertainty: a U-alternative in which the expected value of the ex-post utilities is realized with certainty is ranked as better than the original U-alternative. In the example, the expected value of the ex-post utilities is 50 and, if received with certainty, the ex-ante utility is also 50, which is greater than 49.82.

The Bernoulli hypothesis requires uncertainty neutrality: a U-alternative in which the expected value of the ex-post utilities is realized with certainty is as good as the original U-alternative. In the example, if the Bernoulli hypothesis holds, the ex-ante values of the U-alternative and of an alternative in which an ex-post utility of 50 (the expected value of the ex-post utilities) is realized with certainty are the same.

Two special subsets of the set of U-alternatives are considered in this chapter. The first is a set of lotteries. In it, the alternatives that are realized in the various states are fixed, but probabilities are allowed to take on any possible values. The second is a set of prospects. In that set, probabilities are fixed and the probability associated with each state is positive. The alternatives realized in the various states are unconstrained.

Harsanyi's (1955, 1977) social-aggregation theorem investigates the possibilities for consistency of individual utilities and social preferences in a fixed-population lottery framework. There is a single profile of ex-ante (and ex-post) utility functions and all possible lotteries are considered. Individual ex-ante utility functions are assumed to satisfy the Bernoulli hypothesis, and social preferences are required to satisfy the expected-utility hypothesis. In addition, social preferences over lotteries satisfy ex-ante Pareto indifference, which requires society to rank any two lotteries as equally good whenever they are equally valuable for each individual. Given this, there must be a vector of individual weights such that lotteries are ranked with the weighted sum of ex-ante utilities. The theorem has been investigated extensively and many refinements have been made (see the citations in Part B).

7.2 SOCIAL AGGREGATION: THE FIXED-POPULATION CASE

We first investigate the possibilities for social aggregation in a prospect environment with two or more states, a fixed vector of positive probabilities, and a set of alternatives with at least three members. The positivity requirement for probabilities involves no loss of generality as long as there are at least two states with positive probabilities; states with zero probabilities can be dropped. There are multiple profiles of ex-ante utility functions and, implicitly, a single profile of nonwelfare information. However, it is possible to extend the results of this chapter to the case of multiple nonwelfare information profiles by using the results of Chapter 3.

An ex-ante social-evaluation functional for prospects is defined, and it is assumed to satisfy the following axioms:

(i) individual Bernoulli domain, which requires the domain to consist of all possible ex-ante profiles satisfying the Bernoulli hypothesis;

(ii) the social expected-utility hypothesis, which requires social orderings of prospects to satisfy the expected-utility hypothesis;

(iii) ex-ante Pareto indifference, which requires any two prospects to be equally good if each person's ex-ante assessment is the same in both;

(iv) ex-ante binary independence of irrelevant alternatives, which requires the social ordering of any two prospects to depend on their ex-ante utilities only;

(v) ex-ante minimal increasingness, which applies to pairs of prospects in which ex-ante utilities are the same for all individuals and requires increases in the common level to be ranked as social improvements; and

(vi) ex-ante same-people anonymity, which requires any two prospects to be ranked as equally good if their associated ex-ante utility vectors are permutations of each other.

These axioms are satisfied if and only if the ex-ante social-evaluation functional is ex-ante utilitarian; that is, prospects are ranked with the sum (or average) of ex-ante utilities. In addition, because of the link between ex-post and ex-ante utilities established by the Bernoulli hypothesis, ex-post assessments must be utilitarian as well.

This result depends critically on the assumption that individual ex-ante utilities satisfy the Bernoulli hypothesis. If individual Bernoulli domain is replaced with the axiom individual expected-utility domain, which requires the domain to consist of all profiles that satisfy the expected-utility hypothesis, an impossibility results. The reason is that the expected-utility domain is larger and, thus, the scope of the other axioms is expanded.

The theorems for prospects can be extended to the set of all U-alternatives. To do this, the ex-ante social-evaluation functional is required to rank all U-alternatives and the axioms are extended to the larger environment.

7.3   SOCIAL AGGREGATION: THE VARIABLE-POPULATION CASE

To extend our fixed-population results to the set of all prospects, we assume that the set of possible people is indexed by the positive integers, as in Chapter 3. In addition, we assume that the number of alternatives for each population is greater than the number of states. Ex-ante utilities are defined only for prospects in which the individual is alive in all states. Specification of the ex-ante utility functions is sufficient to determine ex-post utility functions. We define complete prospects to be those prospects in which all individuals who are alive in at least one state are alive in all.

The axioms used in our fixed-population utilitarianism theorem are easily extended to the variable-population environment. The extended versions of the axioms that characterize fixed-population ex-ante utilitarianism imply that complete prospects in which the same number of people live must be ranked with ex-ante utilitarianism. Thus, the principle is same-number ex-ante utilitarian on the set of complete prospects.

In the fixed-population case, our axioms imply that the utilitarian ordering must be used for ex-post social evaluation as well. Without additional axioms, that result obtains only for same-number comparisons of complete prospects in the variable-population environment. Rankings of all other prospects have not been characterized. To do that, we employ axioms that extend the ex-post same-number orderings to cover variable-population comparisons. They assert that ex-post critical levels exist and that they are respected by the overall orderings of prospects.

The extended critical-level population principle requires the existence of a fixed nonnegative critical level c with a property that is best illustrated with an example. Consider prospects $\mathbf{x}$ and $\bar{\mathbf{x}}$, which are outlined in Table 7.5. There are two states. In prospect $\mathbf{x}$, person 1 is alive in both states with ex-post utility levels 10 and 20, but person 2 is alive in state 1 only with a utility level of 12. Consequently, an ex-ante utility level is not defined for person 2. Prospect $\bar{\mathbf{x}}$ is complete, persons 1 and 2 live in both states, person 1's utilities are 10 and 20, and person 2's utilities are 12 and c. The extended critical-level population

Table 7.5. *Extended Critical-Level Population Principle*

	Prospect **x**		Prospect **x̄**	
	State 1	State 2	State 1	State 2
Person 1	10	20	10	20
Person 2	12		12	c

principle asserts that the ranking of **x** and any prospect **y** is the same as the ranking of **x̄** and **y**. The requirement that c is nonnegative ensures that an uncertainty version of the negative expansion principle is satisfied.

If the extended critical-level population principle is added to the other axioms, ex-ante CLU with a nonnegative critical level is characterized. It requires prospects to be ranked with the expected value of the CLU value function with a fixed nonnegative critical level equal to c in the axiom statement.

It may be thought that the extended critical-level population principle is overly strong. An alternate axiom is much weaker. Critical-level consistency asserts that there is an ex-post critical-level function that can be used instead of a fixed critical level. Critical levels can depend on the utilities of those alive in a state as well as their number. As in the case of the extended critical-level population principle, the critical levels are required to be nonnegative.

An important implication of the axiom is illustrated in Table 7.6. As in the previous example, there are two states. In prospects **x** and **y**, the population is $\{1, \ldots, n\}$ and, in prospects **x̄** and **ȳ**, person $n + 1$ is added. u_i^j is the utility level of person i in state j and $EU_i = p_1 u_i^1 + p_2 u_i^2$ is the expected utility of person i. Because each person has the same expected utility in prospects **x** and **y**, they are equally good by ex-ante Pareto indifference.

Table 7.6. *Critical-Level Consistency*

	Prospect **x**		Prospect **y**	
	State 1	State 2	State 1	State 2
Person 1	u_1^1	u_1^2	EU_1	EU_1
⋮	⋮	⋮	⋮	⋮
Person n	u_n^1	u_n^2	EU_n	EU_n

	Prospect **x̄**		Prospect **ȳ**	
	State 1	State 2	State 1	State 2
Person 1	u_1^1	u_1^2	EU_1	EU_1
⋮	⋮	⋮	⋮	⋮
Person n	u_n^1	u_n^2	EU_n	EU_n
Person n + 1	$C(u_1^1, \ldots, u_n^1)$	$C(u_1^2, \ldots, u_n^2)$	$C(EU_1, \ldots, EU_n)$	$C(EU_1, \ldots, EU_n)$

Table 7.7. *Asteroid Example with Uncertainty*

	Population Size	Average Utility
x	10 billion	50
y	20 billion	40
z	10 billion	35

In prospects $\bar{x}$ and $\bar{y}$, the utilities of persons $1, \dots, n$ are the same as in prospects x and y. In $\bar{x}$ and $\bar{y}$, the added person has utility levels given by the critical-level function whose existence is guaranteed by critical-level consistency. Repeated application of that axiom implies that prospects $\bar{x}$ and $\bar{y}$ are equally good. Because the social-evaluation functional is same-number ex-ante utilitarian, it must be true that expected utilities for person $n + 1$ are the same in prospects $\bar{x}$ and $\bar{y}$. Thus, the critical level for the vector $(EU_1, \dots, EU_n)$ must be equal to the expected value of the critical levels for $(u_1^1, \dots, u_n^1)$ and $(u_1^2, \dots, u_n^2)$, or

$$C\left(EU_1, \dots, EU_n\right) = p_1 C\left(u_1^1, \dots, u_n^1\right) + p_2 C\left(u_1^2, \dots, u_n^2\right).$$

Not all critical-level functions satisfy this equation. Our axioms imply that C can depend on population size but not on utility levels. Thus, the orderings of ex-post utility vectors must be NCLU. The implication is that prospects are ranked with the expected value of a number-sensitive critical-level value function with nonnegative critical levels. We call the class of such principles ex-ante NCLU.

These results may be extended to the set of all U-alternatives. Two classes of principles correspond to modified versions of the extended critical-level population principle and critical-level consistency. In the first case, U-alternatives are ranked with the expected value of a CLU value function with a nonnegative critical level and, in the second, U-alternatives are ranked with the expected value of an NCLU value function with nonnegative critical levels.

An extension of the asteroid example of Chapter 5 illustrates the application of these classes of social-evaluation functionals. In the example, astronomers discover, in the year 2100, that an asteroid is on a collision course with Earth and will obliterate life on the planet if nothing is done (alternative x). If, however, resources are committed to a costly international program, the asteroid might be diverted and the planet saved. The probability of success (alternative y) is $1/2$. If the program fails, alternative z is realized. Population sizes and average utilities are given in Table 7.7.

If nothing is done (x), 10 billion people live with an average utility level of 50. If the asteroid is diverted (y), the number of people who ever live is doubled and their average utility is 40: average well-being is lower because of the resources used to divert the asteroid. If the attempt to divert the asteroid

Table 7.8. *Critical-Level Consistency and Ex-Post Critical Levels*

| | Prospects $\mathbf{x}$, $\bar{\mathbf{x}}$ | | Prospects $\mathbf{y}$, $\bar{\mathbf{y}}$ | |
	State 1	State 2	State 1	State 2
Person 1	0	60	30 (EU_1)	30 (EU_1)
Person 2	−20	80	30 (EU_2)	30 (EU_2)
Person 3 (CLU)	α	α	α	α
Person 3 (AU)	−10	70	30	30
Person 3 (RAU)	0	70	30	30

fails (z), 10 billion people live with an average utility of 35; average utility is still lower because of the sacrifice of the initial population.

According to ex-ante CLU with critical level α, taking action is better than doing nothing if and only if

$$\frac{1}{2}\big[20(40 - \alpha)\big] + \frac{1}{2}\big[10(35 - \alpha)\big] > 10(50 - \alpha),$$

which obtains if and only if $\alpha < 15$. Alternatively, suppose critical levels are equal to zero below 15 billion and $\bar{c} > 0$ otherwise. In that case, according to ex-ante NCLU, taking action is better than doing nothing if and only if

$$\frac{1}{2}\big[15(40) + 5(40 - \bar{c})\big] + \frac{1}{2}\big[10(35)\big] > 10(50),$$

which obtains if and only if $\bar{c} < 30$.

The nonnegativity requirement for critical levels in critical-level consistency is of crucial importance to the theorem that characterizes ex-ante NCLU. Without it, additional possibilities become available and they include all principles that rank prospects with the expectation of the value functions for the number-dampened utilitarian class. This is illustrated in Table 7.8 with an example based on the example in Table 7.6. There are two states and probabilities are $1/2$ and $1/2$. In prospects $\mathbf{x}$ and $\mathbf{y}$, persons 1 and 2 are alive. Because, in prospect $\mathbf{y}$, each person's utility in both states is equal to expected utility in $\mathbf{x}$, the two prospects are equally good. In prospects $\bar{\mathbf{x}}$ and $\bar{\mathbf{y}}$, person 3 is added without affecting the others. The table presents three cases: (i) ex-post critical levels are equal to α, (ii) ex-post critical levels are equal to average utility, and (iii) ex-post critical levels are equal to average utility when it is nonnegative and zero otherwise. The first case corresponds to CLU, the second to average utilitarianism (AU), and the third to restricted average utilitarianism (RAU), which is a restricted number-dampened principle.

In each case, critical-level consistency requires person 3's expected utility to be the same in $\bar{\mathbf{x}}$ and $\bar{\mathbf{y}}$. Because expected utility is the average of actual utilities when probabilities are equal, that is clearly true in the first two cases, but it is not true in the third. Although all the number-dampened utilitarian critical-level functions satisfy this part of critical-level consistency, all of them have some negative values unless critical levels are all zero (which is the classical-utilitarian case) and, as a result, all but classical utilitarianism are ruled out. The restricted principles other than classical utilitarianism (which is the restricted version of itself) have critical-level functions whose values are always nonnegative, but they do not satisfy the consistency property. That can be seen easily in the table. The RAU critical level in state 1 is zero because average utility in **x** for persons 1 and 2 is negative. Because expected utilities are positive, the consistency property does not hold.

The only principles that satisfy critical-level consistency belong to the ex-ante NCLU class with nonnegative critical levels. It contains the ex-ante CLU class and, therefore, ex-ante classical utilitarianism. All other principles, including the restricted principles other than classical utilitarianism, are ruled out by critical-level consistency and, as a consequence, a strong case against them is made.

7.4 SOCIAL-AGGREGATION THEOREMS AND THE CASE FOR UTILITARIANISM

The fixed-population versions of the social-aggregation theorem have been widely interpreted as making a case for utilitarianism. It is important to realize, however, that the results of the theorem and its variable-population extensions depend critically on the assumption that individual utility functions satisfy the Bernoulli hypothesis.[2]

The Bernoulli hypothesis requires each person's ex-ante utility function to express a particular attitude toward utility uncertainty called uncertainty neutrality: any prospect is as good as one in which the expected value of ex-post utilities is achieved with certainty. It is tempting, therefore, to ask whether the theorem can be modified to cover other attitudes toward utility uncertainty. If all such attitudes are admitted into the domain of the ex-ante social-evaluation functional, an impossibility results, but that is not the case if individual ex-ante utility functions are required to express a single attitude that is different from uncertainty neutrality. If that is done (see the example in Part B), the social attitude toward utility uncertainty and inequality must be the same as the individual attitude toward uncertainty. Thus, ex-ante social preferences are generalized utilitarian in ex-ante utilities and ex-post social preferences are generalized utilitarian with a specific transformation.[3] There are, of course, many attitudes toward uncertainty and each depends on the transformation employed.

Analogously, variants of the variable-population social-aggregation theorems are obtained by requiring individual ex-ante utility functions to express a single attitude toward utility uncertainty. This move characterizes ex-ante number-sensitive critical-level generalized utilitarianism using the same transformation that determines the ex-ante attitude toward utility uncertainty. The

---

[2] See Broome (1991) for a case in favor of the Bernoulli hypothesis.

[3] For discussions, see Blackorby, Donaldson, and Weymark (2004); Roemer (2004); and Weymark (1991, 1995).

ex-ante versions of all other principles are ruled out. Again, some way must be found to select the transformation that determines the attitude toward utility uncertainty and utility inequality.

The most important lesson of the various social-aggregation theorems is that everyone who thinks seriously about population principles must deal with the questions they raise. If the expected-utility hypothesis provides a normative standard of rationality in the face of uncertainty and critical-level consistency is an appropriate axiom in the variable-population case, then all the ex-ante restricted principles must be rejected.

7.5 INCOMMENSURABILITIES

A possible intuition regarding the ranking of pairs of alternatives with different population sizes is that neither can be better than the other. This intuition and others like it cannot be sensibly expressed by social-evaluation functionals. Because rankings of alternatives are orderings, it is necessary to rank such alternatives as equally good. In that case, however, all alternatives must be equally good. The reason is that any two alternatives must be as good as a third alternative with a different population size and, because equal goodness is transitive, all same-number alternatives also must be equally good. To accommodate such intuitions, we therefore must allow alternatives to be unranked. In that case, we say that they are incommensurable.

Two interpretations of incommensurabilities are possible. The first is that the alternatives cannot be ranked because of incompleteness of information or uncertainty about the choice of an appropriate principle, and the other is that, even with complete information, social rankings of some alternatives are meaningless. Our investigation is consistent with both.

A social-decision functional associates a quasi-ordering on the set of alternatives (a reflexive and transitive at-least-as-good-as relation) with every information profile. Because orderings are also quasi-orderings, social-evaluation functionals are social-decision functionals. Two alternatives are not ranked (incommensurable) if and only if neither is at least as good as the other. As an example, let the set of alternatives be $\{x, y, z\}$ and suppose each alternative is at least as good as itself, x is at least as good as y, x is at least as good as z, y is at least as good as x, y is not at least as good as z, z is not at least as good as x, and z is not at least as good as y. Then x and y are equally good, x is better than z, and y and z are not ranked.

The welfarism theorems of Chapter 3 are easily extended to the case of social-decision functionals and they imply that there is a single quasi-ordering of utility vectors such that, for all profiles and all pairs of alternatives x and y, x is at least as good as y if and only if the utility vector that corresponds to x is ranked as at least as good as the utility vector that corresponds to y by the single quasi-ordering. Thus, x and y are unranked if and only if the corresponding utility vectors are unranked.

Broome (1991, 1992a, 1992b, 1992c) has criticized CLU because of its fixed critical level. According to CLU, any alternative with an average utility

Table 7.9. *Critical-Band Utilitarianism*

	x	y	z
Person 1	50	20	80
Person 2	70	80	
Person 3		40	

level above the critical level is inferior to another alternative with a suitably large population and an average level above the critical level but arbitrarily close to it. Therefore, Broome argued, we should reject CLU for low critical levels. On the other hand, if the critical level is high, CLU tells us to prevent the existence of people whose lifetime utilities would be just below it when the existing population's levels of well-being are unaffected. Because of this, Broome rejects CLU.

In this chapter, we assume that the social quasi-ordering ranks utility vectors of the same dimension (same population size) completely. Consider any utility vector and its comparison with one in which a single person is added without affecting the utilities of the existing people. If there is a critical level for the original vector and strong Pareto holds, then all such expansions are ranked. To allow for incommensurabilities, we assume there are at least two utility levels for the added person such that the two vectors are not ranked and the set of such values, which we call the critical set, is bounded above and below. Given strong Pareto, the result is that the critical set must be an interval, which is consistent with a suggestion of Parfit (1976, 1982, 1984). The interval might be all utility values from 0 to 30, for example, and may include one or both end points. A second axiom asserts that further expansions, if unranked against the preceding utility vector, are also unranked against the original vector. And a third axiom, called the critical-set population principle, requires the critical set to be the same for all utility vectors.[4]

If continuity, strong Pareto, and the population substitution principle are added to the above axioms, the class of critical-band generalized utilitarian (CBGU) population principles is characterized.[5] Each member of the class is associated with an interval (the band) of critical levels and a transformation that is applied to all utilities. One alternative is at least as good as another if and only if it is at least as good according to critical-level generalized utilitarianism for all critical levels in the band. Critical-band utilitarianism (CBU) results if the transformation is the identity mapping. If two alternatives have different population sizes, they cannot be equally good according to CBGU. This occurs because equal goodness requires equality of the CLGU values at more than one value of the critical level, which is impossible.

An example may clarify the application of the principle. In Table 7.9, there are three alternatives and, in each, some or all of three individuals are alive, and

---

[4] Broome (2004a) performs a similar exercise using supervaluation theory.

[5] The critical-band name was suggested by John Broome.

utility levels are given by the numbers in the appropriate boxes. Suppose CBU is used to rank the alternatives with the band equal to all utility levels from 0 to 25, including the end points. Using CLU with critical level α, the CLU values for x, y, and z are $120 - 2\alpha$, $140 - 3\alpha$, and $80 - \alpha$. Because $120 - 2\alpha \geq 140 - 3\alpha$ for all $\alpha \geq 20$ and $120 - 2\alpha \leq 140 - 3\alpha$ for all $\alpha \leq 20$, x and y are not ranked. And, because $120 - 2\alpha \geq 80 - \alpha$ for all $\alpha \leq 40$, x is better than z. Similarly, it is easy to confirm that y is better than z.

One interesting possibility arises if a utility vector is expanded (original utilities unchanged) by adding more than one person. If all the added utilities are inside the band, the expanded vector and the original are not ranked by assumption. But suppose some or all of the added utilities are outside the band. If the principle is same-number utilitarian, then the expanded vector and another in which each added person receives the average utility of the added people in the original expansion are equally good. Thus, the first expanded vector and the original vector are unranked if the average utility of the added people is in the band and ranked otherwise.

CBGU avoids the repugnant conclusion if and only if the upper value in the band is positive. In addition, the negative expansion principle is satisfied if and only if the lower value is nonnegative. Broome's criticism of the critical-level principles is also avoided: the upper value provides a floor on the trade-off between average transformed utility (average utility in the CBU case) and population size, but prevention of expansions with utilities just below that floor is not recommended (such expansions are unranked against the original alternative).

A further possibility for incommensurabilities arises if individual utility functions are not completely determined. An individual might have several candidate utility functions and either there is no way to know which one is correct or the only meaningful information is that which all the functions have in common. In either case, we can rank alternatives by ranking one alternative as at least as good as another if and only if it is at least as good according to the population principle when each of the candidate utility profiles is used. The result is a quasi-ordering of the alternatives.

It is possible to combine the approaches of this chapter in several ways. First, U-alternatives can be ranked with ex-ante CBU, which ranks one U-alternative as at least as good as another if and only if it is at least as good according to ex-ante CLU for each critical level in the band. Second, the probability approach can be extended to the choice of critical levels or candidate utility functions, thus producing complete rankings of alternatives or U-alternatives. Third, probability assignments can be rejected completely, ranking alternatives ex ante if and only if they are ranked in the same way ex post in every state.

Part B

We begin Part B of this chapter with a description of a formal model that generalizes social-evaluation functionals so that they incorporate uncertainty. In each of them, probabilities are assigned to the various possibilities, and social and individual probabilities are assumed to coincide. Although our results are extended to the set of all uncertain alternatives, our main focus is on prospects: uncertain alternatives for which probabilities are fixed and outcomes are allowed to vary. We introduce a multiprofile welfarist model in Section 7.6, which is consistent with the multiprofile approach employed throughout the book. In the context of this model, we first provide a prospect formulation of Harsanyi's (1955) characterization of ex-ante utilitarianism in a fixed-population frame-work and, in addition, prove an impossibility theorem. These results are presented in Section 7.7. Section 7.8 extends the characterization result to variable-population comparisons. A difficulty that arises in this setting is that in-dividuals may be alive in some states of the world but not in others. Two axioms, one weaker than the other, are employed to deal with the issue. Extensions to uncertain alternatives, in which both probabilities and outcomes may vary, are discussed in Section 7.9. Incommensurabilities are investigated in Section 7.10. We make use of social-decision functionals, which associate a quasi-ordering on the set of alternatives with each information profile. The critical-band gen-eralized utilitarian (CBGU) and critical-band utilitarian (CBU) classes are characterized.

7.6 UNCERTAIN ALTERNATIVES, LOTTERIES AND PROSPECTS

We now incorporate uncertainty into our basic model. One way of doing so is to assume that there are a fixed number of states and to specify a probability and an alternative that materializes for each of them. We let $M = \{1, \ldots, m\}$ be a set of $m \geq 2$ states, where m is finite. An uncertain alternative (U-alternative) consists of a probability vector $p = (p_1, \ldots, p_m) \in \mathbf{P} = \{p \in \mathcal{R}_+^m \mid \sum_{j=1}^m p_j = 1\}$ and a vector of alternatives $\mathbf{x} \in \mathbf{X}$, where $\mathbf{X}$ is the m-fold Cartesian product of the set of all alternatives X. Thus, a U-alternative is a pair $(p, \mathbf{x})$. $\mathbf{x}_j$ is the outcome in state j, and it occurs with probability p_j. The social probability distribution and all individual probability distributions coincide and may be thought of as based on the best information available.

Two special cases of U-alternatives are of special interest. They are lotter-ies and prospects. Lotteries are U-alternatives where $\mathbf{x} \in \mathbf{X}$ is fixed. Because the state-specific outcomes are fixed, they may be described by their proba-bility vectors alone. In contrast, prospects are U-alternatives for some fixed probability vector $p \in \mathbf{P}$ with positive probabilities only. Because the proba-bility vector is fixed, prospects may be described by vectors of state-specific outcomes.

We use the notation introduced in the certainty environment: for all $n \in \mathcal{Z}_{++}$, $X^n \subseteq X$ denotes the set of all alternatives in which the set of individuals alive is given by $\{1, \ldots, n\}$ (because we assume anonymity throughout, this covers any fixed-population case – the identities of the n individuals do not matter). For all $i \in \mathcal{Z}_{++}$, X_i is the set of all alternatives x in which individual i is one of the individuals alive in x. Thus, we use the X_i when formulating assumptions regarding individuals, X^n when investigating uncertainty in models where the population is fixed and given by the set of individuals $\{1, \ldots, n\}$, and X when dealing with variable-population social evaluation.

Harsanyi (1955, 1977) employed several assumptions on individual and social orderings of lotteries. These requirements are analogous to those we use in our model and, for that reason, we do not discuss the Harsanyi lottery axioms in detail. He showed that there must exist a vector of individual weights $\gamma \in \mathcal{R}^n$ such that lottery p is socially at least as good as lottery q if and only if the weighted sum of individual expected utilities in p is greater than or equal to the weighted sum of individual expected utilities in q. In this approach, individual utility functions are assumed to represent actual well-being and, in addition, are used as individual von-Neumann–Morgenstern (vNM) functions (von Neumann and Morgenstern 1944, 1947). Thus, the Bernoulli hypothesis is satisfied (see Part A and Section 7.7). The model operates with a fixed profile of utility functions – only the probabilities vary.

The result described above is called Harsanyi's social-aggregation theorem.[6] Because Harsanyi's single-profile approach has been extensively studied, we present a variant of Harsanyi's theorem and a variable-population extension based on a multiprofile model.[7]

7.7 THE SOCIAL-AGGREGATION THEOREM FOR PROSPECTS

For all $n \in \mathcal{Z}_{++}$, we assume that X^n contains at least three alternatives. Because probabilities are assumed to be fixed, any state with a probability of zero may be dropped and, as long as there are at least two states with positive probabilities, the positivity requirement on p involves no loss of generality. In the fixed-population case, a prospect is a vector $\mathbf{x} \in \mathbf{X}^n$ where $\mathbf{X}^n = (X^n)^m$ is the set of all fixed-population prospects.[8] For all $j \in \{1, \ldots, m\}$, $\mathbf{x}_j \in X^n$ is the alternative that materializes in state j. For $x \in X^n$, the prospect $x\mathbf{1}_m = (x, \ldots, x) \subset \mathbf{X}^n$ is that in which the alternative x occurs with certainty (that is, x materializes

---

[6] Border (1981) presented an elegant proof, which is reproduced in expanded form by Weymark (1994). For further discussions and variations of Harsanyi's fundamental theorem, see Blackorby, Bossert, and Donaldson (1998); Blackorby, Donaldson, and Weymark (1999, 2004); Broome (1990, 1991); Coulhon and Mongin (1989); De Meyer and Mongin (1995); Domotor (1979); Fishburn (1984); Hammond (1981, 1983); Mongin (1994, 1995, 1998); Mongin and d'Aspremont (1998); Weymark (1993, 1994, 1995); and Zhou (1997a). Weymark (1994), as well as some others of these papers, investigated conditions under which the weights γ are unique and positive or nonnegative.

[7] Multiprofile models of social choice under uncertainty are discussed, for example, by Blackorby, Donaldson, and Weymark (1999, 2004); Hammond (1981, 1983); Mongin (1994); and Mongin and d'Aspremont (1998).

[8] $(X^n)^m$ is the m-fold Cartesian product of X^n. Because the number of states m is fixed, the notation $\mathbf{X}^n$ is unambiguous even though m does not appear explicitly.

in all possible states). An ex-ante ordering is an ordering defined on the set of prospects $\mathbf{X}^n$ and the set of all ex-ante orderings on $\mathbf{X}^n$ is denoted by $\mathcal{O}_E^n$.

Individual i's ex-ante utility function is $U_{Ei}^n \colon \mathbf{X}^n \to \mathcal{R}$, that is, $U_{Ei}^n(\mathbf{x})$ is the value of the prospect $\mathbf{x} \in \mathbf{X}^n$ to individual $i \in \{1, \dots, n\}$.[9] A profile of ex-ante utility functions is an n-tuple $U_E^n = (U_{E1}^n, \dots, U_{En}^n)$, and the set of all possible ex-ante profiles is $\mathcal{U}_E^n$. For $\mathbf{x} \in \mathbf{X}^n$, $U_E^n(\mathbf{x}) = (U_{E1}^n(\mathbf{x}), \dots, U_{En}^n(\mathbf{x}))$.

For $i \in \{1, \dots, n\}$, an individual vNM function is a mapping $U_{Mi}^n \colon X^n \to \mathcal{R}$. A vNM profile is an n-tuple $U_M^n = (U_{M1}^n, \dots, U_{Mn}^n) \in \mathcal{U}^n$ (where $\mathcal{U}^n$ is the set of all possible profiles). $U_i^n \colon X^n \to \mathcal{R}$ is i's actual or ex-post utility function. Throughout, we assume that ex-ante and ex-post utilities satisfy the fundamental consistency requirement that their assessments of certain outcomes are identical: if an alternative materializes in every possible state, ex-ante utility coincides with ex-post utility. That is, for all $i \in \{1, \dots, n\}$ and for all $x \in X^n$,

$$U_{Ei}^n(x\mathbf{1}_m) = U_i^n(x). \tag{7.1}$$

(7.1) implies that the ex-ante utility function U_{Ei}^n determines the ex-post utility function U_i^n, although the converse is not true.

An ex-ante social-evaluation functional is a mapping $F_E^n \colon \mathcal{D}_E^n \to \mathcal{O}_E^n$ with $\emptyset \neq \mathcal{D}_E^n \subseteq \mathcal{U}_E^n$. F_E^n assigns a social ordering on $\mathbf{X}^n$ to each profile of ex-ante utility functions in its domain $\mathcal{D}_E^n$. We use the notation $R_{U_E^n}^n = F_E^n(U_E^n)$ for all $U_E^n \in \mathcal{D}_E^n$, and $P_{U_E^n}^n$ and $I_{U_E^n}^n$ are the asymmetric and symmetric factors of $R_{U_E^n}^n$.

The individual expected-utility hypothesis requires that the ex-ante ranking of any two prospects $\mathbf{x}$ and $\mathbf{y}$ for individual i is determined by the expected values of i's vNM function obtained for $\mathbf{x}$ and $\mathbf{y}$ for all $i \in \{1, \dots, n\}$. In one of our results, we require the ex-ante social-evaluation functional to produce a social ordering for each utility profile that is composed of individual ex-ante utilities satisfying the hypothesis. Thus, the expected-utility hypothesis is formulated as a domain assumption. The expected-utility domain $\mathcal{D}_M^n \subseteq \mathcal{U}_E^n$ is defined as follows. For all $U_E^n \in \mathcal{U}_E^n$, $U_E^n \in \mathcal{D}_M^n$ if and only if there exists a profile $U_M^n \in \mathcal{U}^n$ of vNM functions such that, for all $i \in \{1, \dots, n\}$ and for all $\mathbf{x}, \mathbf{y} \in \mathbf{X}^n$,

$$U_{Ei}^n(\mathbf{x}) \geq U_{Ei}^n(\mathbf{y}) \Leftrightarrow \sum_{j=1}^m p_j U_{Mi}^n(\mathbf{x}_j) \geq \sum_{j=1}^m p_j U_{Mi}^n(\mathbf{y}_j). \tag{7.2}$$

Clearly, (7.2) is satisfied if and only if there exists an increasing function $\varphi_i \colon \mathcal{R} \to \mathcal{R}$ such that, for all $\mathbf{x} \in \mathbf{X}^n$,

$$U_{Ei}^n(\mathbf{x}) = \varphi_i \left(\sum_{j=1}^m p_j U_{Mi}^n(\mathbf{x}_j) \right). \tag{7.3}$$

In this case, (7.1) implies $U_i^n(x) = \varphi_i(U_{Mi}^n(x))$ for all $x \in X^n$. We obtain the following domain assumption.

---

[9] The superscript n is used only because the domain of definition is restricted to $\mathbf{X}^n$.

Individual Expected-Utility Domain. $\mathcal{D}_E^n = \mathcal{D}_M^n$.

The Bernoulli hypothesis imposes a more stringent restriction on individual ex-ante utilities than the expected-utility hypothesis: it requires the function φ_i in (7.3) to be affine. Because i's actual or ex-post utility $U_i^n(x)$ of alternative $x \in X^n$ is given by the ex-ante value of the prospect that yields x with certainty, the Bernoulli hypothesis requires

$$U_i^n(x) = U_{Ei}^n(x\mathbf{1}_m) = a_i U_{Mi}^n(x) + b_i$$

where $a_i \in \mathcal{R}_{++}$ and $b_i \in \mathcal{R}$ are the parameters of the affine function φ_i. Thus, the Bernoulli hypothesis implies that the actual utility function U_i^n is an increasing affine transformation of the vNM function U_{Mi}^n and, therefore, is a particular vNM function itself. (7.3) can therefore be written as

$$U_{Ei}^n(\mathbf{x}) = a_i \sum_{j=1}^m p_j U_{Mi}^n(\mathbf{x}_j) + b_i = \sum_{j=1}^m p_j U_i^n(\mathbf{x}_j). \tag{7.4}$$

(7.4) shows that if the Bernoulli hypothesis is satisfied, the individual utility functions U_i^n play two roles: they are indicators of actual well-being and, in addition, they are vNM functions. Thus, the value of a prospect $\mathbf{x} \in X^n$ to $i \in \{1, \ldots, n\}$ according to U_{Ei}^n is the expected utility of $\mathbf{x}$ given the probabilities p and the actual utility function U_i^n.

As is the case for the individual expected-utility hypothesis, the individual Bernoulli hypothesis is expressed as a domain restriction. The Bernoulli domain $\mathcal{D}_B^n \subseteq \mathcal{U}_E^n$ is defined as follows. For all $U_E^n \in \mathcal{U}_E^n$, $U_E^n \in \mathcal{D}_B^n$ if and only if there exists a profile $U^n \in \mathcal{U}^n$ such that, for all $i \in \{1, \ldots, n\}$ and for all $\mathbf{x} \in X^n$,

$$U_{Ei}^n(\mathbf{x}) = \sum_{j=1}^m p_j U_i^n(\mathbf{x}_j). \tag{7.5}$$

The axiom individual Bernoulli domain can now be formulated by specifying the domain of the ex-ante social-evaluation functional F_E^n.

Individual Bernoulli domain. $\mathcal{D}_E^n = \mathcal{D}_B^n$.

It is interesting to note that, in our multiprofile setting, individual Bernoulli domain is a less demanding requirement than individual expected-utility domain because it requires the social-evaluation functional to produce a social ordering on a smaller domain. In contrast, the individual Bernoulli hypothesis is the stronger assumption in the single-profile case because each axiom merely requires the single profile to belong to the appropriate domain.

Social orderings are assumed to satisfy the expected-utility hypothesis. This requires the existence of a social vNM function such that the social ranking of two prospects is obtained by comparing their social expected vNM values.

Social Expected-Utility Hypothesis. There exists a function $U_0^n: X^n \times \mathcal{D}_E^n \to \mathcal{R}$ such that, for all $\mathbf{x}, \mathbf{y} \in X^n$ and for all $U_E^n \in \mathcal{D}_E^n$,

$$\mathbf{x} R_{U_E^n}^n \mathbf{y} \Leftrightarrow \sum_{j=1}^m p_j U_0^n (\mathbf{x}_j, U_E^n) \geq \sum_{j=1}^m p_j U_0^n (\mathbf{y}_j, U_E^n).$$

The social vNM function U_0^n is allowed be profile dependent. In our multiprofile setting, if this function were not allowed to depend on U_E^n, an imposed social ranking would result. In Harsanyi's lottery framework, there is only a single profile of ex-ante utility functions and the second argument is not needed.

We first prove a version of the welfarism theorem for ex-ante utilities. The first part is a straightforward reformulation of the standard welfarism theorem: on the Bernoulli domain, ex-ante versions of Pareto indifference and binary independence together are equivalent to the existence of an ex-ante social-evaluation ordering R_E^n on $\mathcal{R}^n$ such that, for any ex-ante profile in the domain of F_E^n and for any two prospects $\mathbf{x}$ and $\mathbf{y}$, the ranking of $\mathbf{x}$ and $\mathbf{y}$ according to $R_{U_E^n}^n$ is determined by the ranking of the associated ex-ante utility vectors according to R_E^n. The second part shows that comparisons of prospects in which an alternative occurs with certainty must be performed according to the ex-ante social-evaluation ordering R_E^n as well.

The ex-ante versions of the welfarism axioms are defined as follows.

Ex-Ante Pareto Indifference. For all $\mathbf{x}, \mathbf{y} \in X^n$ and for all $U_E^n \in \mathcal{D}_E^n$, if $U_E^n(\mathbf{x}) = U_E^n(\mathbf{y})$, then $\mathbf{x} I_{U_E^n}^n \mathbf{y}$.

Ex-Ante Binary Independence of Irrelevant Alternatives. For all $\mathbf{x}, \mathbf{y} \in X^n$ and for all $U_E^n, \bar{U}_E^n \in \mathcal{D}_E^n$, if $U_E^n(\mathbf{x}) = \bar{U}_E^n(\mathbf{x})$ and $U_E^n(\mathbf{y}) = \bar{U}_E^n(\mathbf{y})$, then

$$\mathbf{x} R_{U_E^n}^n \mathbf{y} \Leftrightarrow \mathbf{x} R_{\bar{U}_E^n}^n \mathbf{y}.$$

We obtain the following result (see also Blackorby, Donaldson, and Weymark 2004; Mongin 1994; Mongin and d'Aspremont 1998).

Theorem 7.1. *If F_E^n satisfies individual Bernoulli domain, ex-ante Pareto indifference, and ex-ante binary independence of irrelevant alternatives, then there exists a social-evaluation ordering R_E^n on $\mathcal{R}^n$ such that, for all $\mathbf{x}, \mathbf{y} \in X^n$ and for all $U_E^n \in \mathcal{D}_E^n$,*

$$\mathbf{x} R_{U_E^n}^n \mathbf{y} \Leftrightarrow U_E^n(\mathbf{x}) R_E^n U_E^n(\mathbf{y}) \tag{7.6}$$

and, for all $x, y \in X^n$ and for all $U^n \in \mathcal{U}^n$,

$$x \mathbf{1}_m R_{U_E^n}^n y \mathbf{1}_m \Leftrightarrow U^n(x) R_E^n U^n(y) \tag{7.7}$$

where U_E^n is the ex-ante profile corresponding to U^n according to (7.5).

Proof. Suppose F_E^n satisfies the individual Bernoulli hypothesis, ex-ante Pareto indifference and ex-ante binary independence of irrelevant alternatives. The proof of the existence of an ordering R_E^n such that (7.6) is satisfied is analogous to that of the welfarism theorem under certainty presented in Chapter 3.

It remains to be shown that (7.7) is satisfied for the same ordering R_E^n. Let $x, y \in X^n$ and $U^n \in \mathcal{U}^n$. Setting $\mathbf{x} = x\mathbf{1}_m$ and $\mathbf{y} = y\mathbf{1}_m$ in (7.6), the individual Bernoulli hypothesis implies (7.7). ∎

Next, we show that any ex-ante social-evaluation functional satisfying the axioms of Theorem 7.1 and the social expected-utility hypothesis must possess a property that is equivalent to the requirement that R_E^n satisfy information invariance with respect to translation-scale noncomparability.[10]

Theorem 7.2. *If F_E^n satisfies individual Bernoulli domain, the social expected-utility hypothesis, ex-ante Pareto indifference, and ex-ante binary independence of irrelevant alternatives, then, for all $u, v, b \in \mathcal{R}^n$,*

$$u R_E^n v \Leftrightarrow (u + b) R_E^n (v + b) \tag{7.8}$$

where R_E^n is the ex-ante social-evaluation ordering corresponding to F_E^n.

Proof. Let $u, v, b \in \mathcal{R}^n$. By individual Bernoulli domain, $\mathcal{D}_E^n = \mathcal{D}_B^n$. The social expected-utility hypothesis implies that there exists a function $U_0^n \colon X^n \times \mathcal{D}_B^n \to \mathcal{R}$ such that, for all $\mathbf{x}, \mathbf{y} \in X^n$ and for all $U_E^n \in \mathcal{D}_B^n$,

$$\mathbf{x} R_{U_E^n}^n \mathbf{y} \Leftrightarrow \sum_{j=1}^m p_j U_0^n(\mathbf{x}_j, U_E^n) \geq \sum_{j=1}^m p_j U_0^n(\mathbf{y}_j, U_E^n).$$

Combined with (7.6), this yields

$$U_E^n(\mathbf{x}) R_E^n U_E^n(\mathbf{y}) \Leftrightarrow \sum_{j=1}^m p_j U_0^n(\mathbf{x}_j, U_E^n) \geq \sum_{j=1}^m p_j U_0^n(\mathbf{y}_j, U_E^n) \tag{7.9}$$

for all $\mathbf{x}, \mathbf{y} \in X^n$ and for all $U_E^n \in \mathcal{D}_B^n$.

Because X^n contains at least three alternatives, we can choose $x, y, z \in X^n$ and $U^n \in \mathcal{U}^n$ so that

$$U^n(x) = \frac{1}{p_1} u - \frac{\sum_{j=2}^m p_j}{p_1} v + b,$$

$$U^n(y) = v + b,$$

---

[10] A weaker version of this theorem that requires X^n to contain at least four alternatives is proven by Blackorby, Bossert, and Donaldson (2002b). The more general result is taken from Blackorby, Bossert, and Donaldson (2003b). See Mongin (1994) and Mongin and d'Aspremont (1998) for a similar theorem.

and

$$U^n(z) = v - \frac{p_1}{\sum_{j=2}^m p_j}b.$$

Let $\mathbf{x}, \mathbf{y}, \mathbf{z}, \mathbf{w} \in \mathbf{X}^n$ be such that $\mathbf{x}_1 = \mathbf{z}_1 = x$, $\mathbf{y}_1 = \mathbf{w}_1 = y$, $\mathbf{x}_j = \mathbf{y}_j = z$ for all $j \in \{2, \ldots, m\}$ and $\mathbf{z}_j = \mathbf{w}_j = y$ for all $j \in \{2, \ldots, m\}$. By individual Bernoulli domain, the profile $U_E^n \in \mathcal{D}_B^n$ that corresponds to U^n satisfies

$$U_E^n(\mathbf{x}) = \sum_{j=1}^m p_j U^n(\mathbf{x}_j) = u,$$

$$U_E^n(\mathbf{y}) = \sum_{j=1}^m p_j U^n(\mathbf{y}_j) = v,$$

$$U_E^n(\mathbf{z}) = \sum_{j=1}^m p_j U^n(\mathbf{z}_j) = u + b,$$

and

$$U_E^n(\mathbf{w}) = \sum_{j=1}^m p_j U^n(\mathbf{w}_j) = v + b.$$

Substituting into (7.9), we obtain

$$u R_E^n v \Leftrightarrow p_1 U_0^n(x, U_E^n) + \sum_{j=2}^m p_j U_0^n(z, U_E^n) \geq p_1 U_0^n(y, U_E^n)$$

$$+ \sum_{j=2}^m p_j U_0^n(z, U_E^n) \Leftrightarrow p_1 U_0^n(x, U_E^n) \geq p_1 U_0^n(y, U_E^n)$$

$$(7.10)$$

and, using (7.9) with $\mathbf{x} = \mathbf{z}$ and $\mathbf{y} = \mathbf{w}$,

$$(u + b) R_E^n(v + b) \Leftrightarrow p_1 U_0^n(x, U_E^n) + \sum_{j=2}^m p_j U_0^n(y, U_E^n)$$

$$\geq p_1 U_0^n(y, U_E^n) + \sum_{j=2}^m p_j U_0^n(y, U_E^n)$$

$$\Leftrightarrow p_1 U_0^n(x, U_E^n) \geq p_1 U_0^n(y, U_E^n). \quad (7.11)$$

Combining (7.10) and (7.11), (7.8) follows. ∎

The property of R_E^n established in Theorem 7.2 is identical to information invariance with respect to translation-scale noncomparability defined for the ex-ante ordering. Therefore, we can apply the result of Theorem 4.11 to characterize utilitarianism in the present framework. To do so, we introduce ex-ante versions of minimal increasingness and same-people anonymity.

Ex-Ante Minimal Increasingness. For all $a, b \in \mathcal{R}$, for all $\mathbf{x}, \mathbf{y} \in \mathbf{X}^n$, and for all $U_E^n \in \mathcal{D}_E^n$, if $U_E^n(\mathbf{x}) = a\mathbf{1}_n \gg b\mathbf{1}_n = U_E^n(\mathbf{y})$, then $\mathbf{x}P_{U_E^n}^n\mathbf{y}$.

Ex-Ante Same-People Anonymity. For all $\mathbf{x}, \mathbf{y} \in \mathbf{X}^n$ and for all $U_E^n \in \mathcal{D}_E^n$, if there exists a bijection $\rho^n: \{1, \ldots, n\} \rightarrow \{1, \ldots, n\}$ such that $U_{Ei}^n(\mathbf{x}) = U_{E\rho^n(i)}^n(\mathbf{y})$ for all $i \in \{1, \ldots, n\}$, then $\mathbf{x}I_{U_E^n}^n\mathbf{y}$.

The social-evaluation functional characterized in the following theorem is an ex-ante version of utilitarianism. We call the corresponding principle ex-ante utilitarianism and it is defined as follows. For all $\mathbf{x}, \mathbf{y} \in \mathbf{X}^n$ and for all $U_E^n \in \mathcal{D}_E^n$,

$$\mathbf{x}R_{U_E^n}^n\mathbf{y} \Leftrightarrow \sum_{i=1}^n U_{Ei}^n(\mathbf{x}) \geq \sum_{i=1}^n U_{Ei}^n(\mathbf{y})$$

$$\Leftrightarrow \sum_{j=1}^m p_j \sum_{i=1}^n U_i^n(\mathbf{x}_j) \geq \sum_{j=1}^m p_j \sum_{i=1}^n U_i^n(\mathbf{y}_j)$$

where U^n is the profile corresponding to U_E^n according to (7.5). The following theorem is a generalization of a result with a more restrictive domain assumption due to Mongin (1994).

Theorem 7.3. *Suppose F_E^n satisfies individual Bernoulli domain. F_E^n satisfies the social expected-utility hypothesis, ex-ante Pareto indifference, ex-ante binary independence of irrelevant alternatives, ex-ante minimal increasingness, and ex-ante same-people anonymity if and only if F_E^n is ex-ante utilitarian.*

Proof. The "only-if" part follows from combining Theorems 4.11 and 7.2. To prove the "if" part, we show that ex-ante utilitarianism satisfies the social expected-utility hypothesis; all other axioms are easily verified. We define the function U_0^n as follows. For all $x \in X^n$ and for all $U_E^n \in \mathcal{D}_B^n$,

$$U_0^n(x, U_E^n) = \sum_{i=1}^n U_{Ei}^n(x\mathbf{1}_m).$$

Substituting, the social expected-utility hypothesis is satisfied.   ∎

If the ex-post utilities in any two prospects differ in a single state only, the prospects can be ranked with the sum of ex-ante utilities or with the sum of ex-post utilities in that state. Thus, there is a utilitarian ex-post social-evaluation functional that applies to each state. Consequently, the social-evaluation functional is both ex-ante and ex-post welfarist. Ex-post welfarism is implied; it need not be assumed.

The characterization result of Theorem 7.3 requires the social-evaluation functional to produce a social ordering only for profiles of ex-ante utilities satisfying the Bernoulli hypothesis.[11] An immediate issue raised by this

---

[11] See Broome (1991) for arguments in favor of the individual Bernoulli hypothesis.

observation is how the result is affected by requiring individual expected-utility domain instead. In contrast to the single-profile setting, the individual expected-utility domain is a stronger requirement because the social-evaluation functional has to produce a social ordering on a larger domain and, thus, the scope of the other axioms is widened. As a consequence, we obtain an impossibility result.

Theorem 7.4. *There exists no ex-ante social-evaluation functional F_E^n that satisfies individual expected-utility domain, the social expected-utility hypothesis, ex-ante Pareto indifference, ex-ante binary independence of irrelevant alternatives, ex-ante minimal increasingness, and ex-ante same-people anonymity.*

Proof. Suppose F_E^n satisfies the axioms in the theorem statement. Clearly, $\mathcal{D}_B^n \subseteq \mathcal{D}_M^n$. Theorem 7.3 implies that, for all $\mathbf{x}, \mathbf{y} \in \mathbf{X}^n$ and for all $U_E^n \in \mathcal{D}_B^n$,

$$\mathbf{x} R_{U_E^n}^n \mathbf{y} \Leftrightarrow U_E^n(\mathbf{x}) R_E^n U_E^n(\mathbf{y})$$

or, equivalently,

$$\mathbf{x} R_{U_E^n}^n \mathbf{y} \Leftrightarrow \left(\sum_{j=1}^m p_j U_{M1}^n(\mathbf{x}_j), \ldots, \sum_{j=1}^m p_j U_{Mn}^n(\mathbf{x}_j) \right)$$
$$R_E^n \left(\sum_{j=1}^m p_j U_{M1}^n(\mathbf{y}_j), \ldots, \sum_{j=1}^m p_j U_{Mn}^n(\mathbf{y}_j) \right)$$

for some $U_M^n \in \mathcal{U}^n$, where R_E^n satisfies

$$u R_E^n v \Leftrightarrow \sum_{i=1}^n u_i \geq \sum_{i=1}^n v_i \tag{7.12}$$

for all $u, v \in \mathcal{R}^n$.

Let $\varphi : \mathcal{R} \to \mathcal{R}$ be an increasing, surjective and non-affine function, and define the subset $\mathcal{D}_\varphi^n$ of $\mathcal{D}_M^n$ as follows. For all $U_E^n \in \mathcal{D}_M^n$, $U_E^n \in \mathcal{D}_\varphi^n$ if and only if there exists a profile $U_M^n \in \mathcal{U}^n$ such that, for all $i \in \{1, \ldots, n\}$ and for all $\mathbf{x} \in \mathbf{X}^n$,

$$U_{Ei}^n(\mathbf{x}) = \varphi \left(\sum_{j=1}^m p_j U_{Mi}^n(\mathbf{x}_j) \right). \tag{7.13}$$

Now define the ordering R_φ^n on $\mathcal{R}^n$ by

$$u R_\varphi^n v \Leftrightarrow \left(\varphi(u_1), \ldots, \varphi(u_n) \right) R_E^n \left(\varphi(v_1), \ldots, \varphi(v_n) \right) \tag{7.14}$$

for all $u, v \in \mathcal{R}^n$. Because φ is a bijection, its inverse φ^{-1} exists and (7.14) is equivalent to

$$u R_E^n v \Leftrightarrow \left(\varphi^{-1}(u_1), \ldots, \varphi^{-1}(u_n) \right) R_\varphi^n \left(\varphi^{-1}(v_1), \ldots, \varphi^{-1}(v_n) \right) \tag{7.15}$$

for all $u, v \in \mathcal{R}^n$. Let $U_E^n \in \mathcal{D}_\varphi^n$. By definition, there exists a vNM profile $U_M^n \in \mathcal{U}^n$ such that (7.13) is satisfied for all $\mathbf{x} \in \mathbf{X}^n$. Therefore, for any two prospects

$\mathbf{x}, \mathbf{y} \in \mathbf{X}^n$, it follows that

$$U_E^n(\mathbf{x}) R_E^n U_E^n(\mathbf{y}) \Leftrightarrow \left(\varphi \left(\sum_{j=1}^m p_j U_{M1}^n(\mathbf{x}_j) \right), \ldots, \varphi \left(\sum_{j=1}^m p_j U_{Mn}^n(\mathbf{x}_j) \right) \right)$$

$$R_E^n \left(\varphi \left(\sum_{j=1}^m p_j U_{M1}^n(\mathbf{y}_j) \right), \ldots, \varphi \left(\sum_{j=1}^m p_j U_{Mn}^n(\mathbf{y}_j) \right) \right)$$

and, by (7.14),

$$U_E^n(\mathbf{x}) R_E^n U_E^n(\mathbf{y}) \Leftrightarrow \left(\sum_{j=1}^m p_j U_{M1}^n(\mathbf{x}_j), \ldots, \sum_{j=1}^m p_j U_{Mn}^n(\mathbf{x}_j) \right)$$

$$R_\varphi^n \left(\sum_{j=1}^m p_j U_{M1}^n(\mathbf{y}_j), \ldots, \sum_{j=1}^m p_j U_{Mn}^n(\mathbf{y}_j) \right).$$

Letting $\bar{U}_{Ei}^n(\mathbf{x}) = \sum_{j=1}^m p_j U_{Mi}^n(\mathbf{x}_j)$ for all $\mathbf{x} \in \mathbf{X}^n$ and for all $i \in \{1, \ldots, n\}$, this implies

$$\bar{U}_E^n(\mathbf{x}) R_\varphi^n \bar{U}_E^n(\mathbf{y}) \Leftrightarrow \left(\sum_{j=1}^m p_j U_{M1}^n(\mathbf{x}_j), \ldots, \sum_{j=1}^m p_j U_{Mn}^n(\mathbf{x}_j) \right)$$

$$R_\varphi^n \left(\sum_{j=1}^m p_j U_{M1}^n(\mathbf{y}_j), \ldots, \sum_{j=1}^m p_j U_{Mn}^n(\mathbf{y}_j) \right).$$

Because, by definition, $\bar{U}_E^n \in \mathcal{D}_B^n$, it follows that

$$\bar{U}_E^n(\mathbf{x}) R_\varphi^n \bar{U}_E^n(\mathbf{y}) \Leftrightarrow \mathbf{x} R_{\bar{U}_E^n}^n \mathbf{y}.$$

Applying Theorem 7.3, we obtain

$$u R_\varphi^n v \Leftrightarrow \sum_{i=1}^n u_i \geq \sum_{i=1}^n v_i$$

for all $u, v \in \mathcal{R}^n$. Together with (7.12) and (7.15), it follows that

$$\sum_{i=1}^n u_i \geq \sum_{i=1}^n v_i \Leftrightarrow \sum_{i=1}^n \varphi^{-1}(u_i) \geq \sum_{i=1}^n \varphi^{-1}(v_i) \tag{7.16}$$

for all $u, v \in \mathcal{R}^n$. (7.16) is equivalent to the existence of an increasing function $H: \mathcal{R} \rightarrow \mathcal{R}$ such that

$$\sum_{i=1}^n \varphi^{-1}(u_i) = H \left(\sum_{i=1}^n u_i \right) \tag{7.17}$$

for all $u, v \in \mathcal{R}^n$. (7.17) is a Pexider equation and, as in the proof of Theorem 4.8, it follows that φ^{-1} must be affine (see Aczél 1966, Chapter 3, for Pexider equations and their solutions). This implies that φ is affine as well, a contradiction. ∎

The proof of Theorem 7.4 shows that, when the increasing transformations $\varphi_1, \ldots, \varphi_n$ are identical and non-affine, prospects must be ranked according to their sums of expected utilities. This means, however, that R_E^n must depend on φ, contradicting the welfarism axioms. A variant of Theorem 7.4 is obtained if anonymity is replaced by continuity.[12]

In a single-profile setting, the impossibility is avoided because, with a single ex-ante profile, the individual expected-utility hypothesis is a weaker axiom than the individual Bernoulli hypothesis and ex-ante social-evaluation functionals other than ex-ante utilitarianism become available. Blackorby, Donaldson, and Weymark (2004) prove that, in the single-profile case, R_E^n must be generalized utilitarian if the individual expected-utility hypothesis is satisfied and utilitarian if the individual Bernoulli hypothesis is satisfied. We believe, however, that the multiprofile framework employed here represents a suitable way of formulating social-choice problems under uncertainty and that Theorems 7.3 and 7.4 provide a convincing argument in favor of utilitarianism.

One possible relaxation of the axioms in Harsanyi's result (and our Theorem 7.3) is to drop the social expected-utility hypothesis, a move that has been suggested by Diamond (1967) and by Sen (1976, 1977b, 1986). They argued that ex-ante social-evaluation functionals that satisfy the social expected-utility hypothesis cannot take account of the fairness of procedures by which outcomes are generated (see also Weymark 1991).

An interesting alternative, however, is to relax the ex-ante welfarism axioms. The form of ex-ante welfarism of Theorem 7.1 is not applied to actual well-being, and this suggests that ex-post welfarism may be more appropriate and ethically easier to defend than ex-ante welfarism. Given our axioms, ex-ante welfarism implies ex-post welfarism but the converse implication is not true. A second way to relax the assumptions of Theorem 7.3, therefore, is provided by requiring ex-post welfarism only.

Suppose, for example, that when the ex-post profile is U^n, such a principle produces an ex-post ordering, which ranks prospect $\mathbf{x}$ as at least as good as prospect $\mathbf{y}$ if and only if

$$\sum_{j=1}^m p_j \frac{1}{n^2} \sum_{i=1}^n (2i - 1) U_{(i)}^n(\mathbf{x}_j) \geq \sum_{j=1}^m p_j \frac{1}{n^2} \sum_{i=1}^n (2i - 1) U_{(i)}^n(\mathbf{y}_j)$$

where, for all $x \in X^n$, $(U_{(1)}^n(x), \ldots, U_{(n)}^n(x))$ is a permutation of $(U_1^n(x), \ldots, U_n^n(x))$ such that $U_{(i)}^n(x) \geq U_{(i+1)}^n(x)$ for all $i \in \{1, \ldots, n - 1\}$. In this case, alternatives are ranked, ex post, with a social-evaluation functional that expresses aversion to utility inequality. This principle is not consistent with ex-ante Pareto indifference if individual ex-ante utilities satisfy the Bernoulli hypothesis. Thus, prospect $\mathbf{x}$ may be regarded as better than prospect $\mathbf{y}$ although $\mathbf{x}$ and $\mathbf{y}$ are equally good for each person. With such a principle, therefore, social rationality trumps individual rationality.

[12] See also Blackorby, Donaldson, and Weymark (1999, 2004); Roemer (1996); Sen (1976); and Weymark (1991).

A generalization of Theorem 7.3 requires individual ex-ante utility functions to express a single attitude toward utility uncertainty. In that case, the vNM function for each person is an increasing transformation $\varphi: \mathcal{R} \to \mathcal{R}$ of actual utility and the ex-ante utility function for person i is given by

$$U_{Ei}^n(\mathbf{x}) = \varphi^{-1}\Big(\sum_{j=1}^m p_j U_{Mi}^n(\mathbf{x}_j) \Big) = \varphi^{-1}\Big(\sum_{j=1}^m p_j \varphi\big(U_i^n(\mathbf{x}_j)\big) \Big), \quad (7.18)$$

where the transformation φ^{-1} is a consequence of (7.1). If φ is (strictly) concave, individuals are (strictly) uncertainty averse.

If, instead of the Bernoulli domain, the single-attitude domain given by (7.18) is employed, a theorem that is similar to Theorem 7.3 can be proved. It requires social preferences to satisfy

$$\mathbf{x} R_{U_E^n}^n \mathbf{y} \Leftrightarrow \sum_{i=1}^n \varphi\big(U_{Ei}^n(\mathbf{x})\big) \geq \sum_{i=1}^n \varphi\big(U_{Ei}^n(\mathbf{y})\big)$$

$$\Leftrightarrow \sum_{j=1}^m p_j \sum_{i=1}^n \varphi\big(U_i^n(\mathbf{x}_j)\big) \geq \sum_{j=1}^m p_j \sum_{i=1}^n \varphi\big(U_i^n(\mathbf{y}_j)\big) \quad (7.19)$$

$$\Leftrightarrow \sum_{i=1}^n \sum_{j=1}^m p_j U_{Mi}^n(\mathbf{x}_j) \geq \sum_{i=1}^n \sum_{j=1}^m p_j U_{Mi}^n(\mathbf{y}_j).$$

The result is that the individual attitude toward utility uncertainty and the social attitude toward uncertainty and utility inequality must match.[13] The last line of (7.19) indicates that knowledge of the vNM functions is sufficient to establish the ordering. The appropriate vNM functions are uniquely determined in each profile and, because of (7.18), must satisfy

$$U_i^n(x) = u \Leftrightarrow U_{Mi}^n(x) = \varphi(u)$$

for all $i \in \{1, \dots, n\}$ and for all $x \in X^n$. This requires a particular vNM function to be selected. In each case, the ex-post principles are generalized utilitarian.

The single-attitude domain is not without its difficulties. To use it, some way must be found to choose the transformation φ. If it is chosen to reflect a social attitude toward ex-post inequality, then individual ex-ante utilities must express the same attitude toward utility uncertainty.

7.8 EX-ANTE POPULATION PRINCIPLES FOR PROSPECTS

We now extend the fixed-population model to cover situations in which the population may vary within and among prospects. Suppose, again, that there are $m \geq 2$ states with fixed positive probabilities. For all nonempty and finite $N \subseteq \mathcal{Z}_{++}$, $\mathbf{X}^N$ is the set of alternatives in which the individuals in N are alive in

---

[13] See Blackorby, Donaldson, and Weymark (2004) and Weymark (1991).

all states. That is,

$$\mathbf{X}^N = \left\{ \mathbf{x} \in \mathbf{X} \mid \mathbf{N}(\mathbf{x}_j) = N \text{ for all } j \in \{1, \ldots, m\} \right\}.$$

We assume that $|\mathbf{X}^N| \geq m + 1$ for all possible populations N.[14] The set of all ex-ante orderings on the set of prospects $\mathbf{X}$ is denoted by $\mathcal{O}_E$.

We define $\mathbf{N}_E(\mathbf{x}) = \bigcup_{j=1}^{m} \mathbf{N}(\mathbf{x}_j)$ and $\mathbf{n}_E(\mathbf{x}) = |\mathbf{N}_E(\mathbf{x})|$ for all $\mathbf{x} \in \mathbf{X}$, that is, $\mathbf{N}_E(\mathbf{x})$ is the set of individuals alive in at least one state of prospect $\mathbf{x}$ and $\mathbf{n}_E(\mathbf{x})$ is their number. Furthermore, let

$$\mathbf{X}_\theta = \left\{ \mathbf{x} \in \mathbf{X} \mid \mathbf{N}(\mathbf{x}_j) = \mathbf{N}(\mathbf{x}_k) \text{ for all } j, k \in \{1, \ldots, m\} \right\}.$$

The set $\mathbf{X}_\theta$ is the set of complete prospects. In them, everyone who is alive in at least one state is alive in all states. For $\mathbf{x} \in \mathbf{X}$, we let $\mathbf{N}_\theta(\mathbf{x}) = \{ i \in \mathcal{Z}_{++} \mid i \in \mathbf{N}(\mathbf{x}_j) \text{ for all } j \in \{1, \ldots, m\}\}$.

For $i \in \mathcal{Z}_{++}$, let

$$\mathbf{X}_i = \left\{ \mathbf{x} \in \mathbf{X} \mid i \in \mathbf{N}(\mathbf{x}_j) \text{ for all } j \in \{1, \ldots, m\} \right\}.$$

The set $\mathbf{X}_i$ contains all prospects such that $i \in \mathcal{Z}_{++}$ is alive in all states. Individual i's ex-ante utility function is $U_{Ei} \colon \mathbf{X}_i \to \mathcal{R}$, that is, $U_{Ei}(\mathbf{x})$ is the value of the prospect $\mathbf{x} \in \mathbf{X}_i$ to individual $i \in \mathcal{Z}_{++}$. A profile of ex-ante utility functions is an infinite-dimensional vector $U_E = (U_{Ei})_{i \in \mathcal{Z}_{++}}$, and the set of all possible ex-ante profiles is $\mathcal{U}_E$. For $\mathbf{x} \in \mathbf{X}$ such that $\mathbf{N}_\theta(\mathbf{x})$ is nonempty, we let $U_E(\mathbf{x}) = (U_{Ei}(\mathbf{x}))_{i \in \mathbf{N}_\theta(\mathbf{x})}$. Note that U_{Ei} is defined on the domain $\mathbf{X}_i$, that is, on the set of prospects in which i is alive in all states. Thus, we do not assign ex-ante utility values to prospects in which an individual is not alive in all states. As is the case in a certainty framework, there is no reasonable interpretation of individual utility values for situations in which the individual does not exist. Again, we assume that ex-ante utility and ex-post utility coincide in the presence of certainty. That is, for all $i \in \mathcal{Z}_{++}$ and for all $x \in X_i$,

$$U_{Ei}(x \mathbf{1}_m) = U_i(x).$$

As in the fixed-population case, ex-post utility functions are determined by ex-ante utility functions even though the ex-ante functions are not defined for all prospects.

An ex-ante social-evaluation functional is a mapping $F_E \colon \mathcal{D}_E \to \mathcal{O}_E$ with $\emptyset \neq \mathcal{D}_E \subseteq \mathcal{U}_E$. F_E assigns a social ordering on $\mathbf{X}$ to each admissible profile of ex-ante utility functions. We let $R_{U_E} = F_E(U_E)$ for all $U_E \in \mathcal{D}_E$, and we use P_{U_E} and I_{U_E} to denote the asymmetric and symmetric factors of R_{U_E}.

The formulation of the Bernoulli hypothesis is easily adapted to our variable-population setting. The extended Bernoulli domain $\mathcal{D}_B \subseteq \mathcal{U}_E$ is defined as follows. For all $U_E \in \mathcal{U}_E$, $U_E \in \mathcal{D}_B$ if and only if there exists a profile

---

[14] This assumption is necessary for the application of the extended critical-level population principle and critical-level consistency.

$U \in \mathcal{U}$ such that, for all nonempty and finite $N \subseteq \mathcal{Z}_{++}$, for all $i \in N$, and for all $\mathbf{x} \in \mathbf{X}^N$,

$$U_{Ei}(\mathbf{x}) = \sum_{j=1}^{m} p_j U_i(\mathbf{x}_j). \tag{7.20}$$

Individual Bernoulli domain is extended to the following domain restriction.

Extended Individual Bernoulli Domain. $\mathcal{D}_E = \mathcal{D}_B$.

The only change that is required in order to adapt the social expected-utility hypothesis to the variable-population setting is to require the existence of a social vNM function that can be used to rank the prospects in $\mathbf{X}^N$ for all nonempty and finite $N \subseteq \mathcal{Z}_{++}$.

Extended Social Expected-Utility Hypothesis. For all nonempty and finite $N \subseteq \mathcal{Z}_{++}$, there exists a function $U_0^N : X^N \times \mathcal{D}_E \to \mathcal{R}$ such that, for all $\mathbf{x}, \mathbf{y} \in \mathbf{X}^N$ and for all $U_E \in \mathcal{D}_E$,

$$\mathbf{x} R_{U_E} \mathbf{y} \Leftrightarrow \sum_{j=1}^{m} p_j U_0^N(\mathbf{x}_j, U_E) \geq \sum_{j=1}^{m} p_j U_0^N(\mathbf{y}_j, U_E).$$

The variable-population versions of the welfarism axioms are defined as follows.

Ex-Ante Pareto Indifference. For all nonempty and finite $N \subseteq \mathcal{Z}_{++}$, for all $\mathbf{x}, \mathbf{y} \in \mathbf{X}^N$, and for all $U_E \in \mathcal{D}_E$, if $U_E(\mathbf{x}) = U_E(\mathbf{y})$, then $\mathbf{x} I_{U_E} \mathbf{y}$.

Ex-Ante Binary Independence of Irrelevant Alternatives. For all nonempty and finite $N \subseteq \mathcal{Z}_{++}$, for all $\mathbf{x}, \mathbf{y} \in \mathbf{X}^N$, and for all $U_E, \bar{U}_E \in \mathcal{D}_E$, if $U_E(\mathbf{x}) = \bar{U}_E(\mathbf{x})$ and $U_F(\mathbf{y}) = \bar{U}_F(\mathbf{y})$, then

$$\mathbf{x} R_{U_E} \mathbf{y} \Leftrightarrow \mathbf{x} R_{\bar{U}_E} \mathbf{y}.$$

Ex-ante minimal increasingness translates into the variable-population framework analogously.

Ex-Ante Minimal Increasingness. For all nonempty and finite $N \subseteq \mathcal{Z}_{++}$, for all $a, b \in \mathcal{R}$, for all $\mathbf{x}, \mathbf{y} \in \mathbf{X}^N$, and for all $U_E \in \mathcal{D}_E$, if $U_E(\mathbf{x}) = a\mathbf{1}_n \gg b\mathbf{1}_n = U_E(\mathbf{y})$, then $\mathbf{x} P_{U_E} \mathbf{y}$.

Following our standard convention, we use the same names for the last three axioms as for their fixed-population counterparts because they require the corresponding fixed-population axiom to be satisfied for every population. Finally, we define a variable-population version of ex-ante anonymity. This axiom is the uncertainty analogue of extended welfare anonymity introduced in Chapter 3.

Extended Ex-Ante Anonymity. For all $\mathbf{x}, \mathbf{y} \in \mathbf{X}_\theta$ and for all $U_E \in \mathcal{D}_E$, if there exists a bijection $\rho: \mathbf{N}_\theta(\mathbf{x}) \to \mathbf{N}_\theta(\mathbf{y})$ such that $U_{Ei}(\mathbf{x}) = U_{E\rho(i)}(\mathbf{y})$ for all $i \in \mathbf{N}_\theta(\mathbf{x})$, then $\mathbf{x} I_{U_E} \mathbf{y}$.

If an ex-ante social-evaluation functional F_E satisfies extended individual Bernoulli domain, ex-ante Pareto indifference, ex-ante binary independence of irrelevant alternatives, and extended ex-ante anonymity, then complete prospects are ranked by a single anonymous ordering of vectors of ex-ante utilities. The result follows from the variable-population version of the welfarism theorem without uncertainty and is omitted.

Theorem 7.5. *If F_E satisfies extended individual Bernoulli domain, ex-ante Pareto indifference, ex-ante binary independence of irrelevant alternatives, and extended ex-ante anonymity, then there exists an anonymous ordering R_E on Ω such that, for all $\mathbf{x}, \mathbf{y} \in \mathbf{X}_\theta$ and for all $U_E \in \mathcal{D}_E$,*

$$\mathbf{x} R_{U_E} \mathbf{y} \Leftrightarrow U_E(\mathbf{x}) R_E U_E(\mathbf{y}).$$

Theorems 7.3 and 7.5 together imply that the same-number subprinciples of R_E must be utilitarian. We call any principle with this property a same-number utilitarian principle.

.Theorem 7.6. *If F_E satisfies extended individual Bernoulli domain, the extended social expected-utility hypothesis, ex-ante Pareto indifference, ex-ante binary independence of irrelevant alternatives, ex-ante minimal increasingness and extended ex-ante anonymity, then, for all non-empty and finite $N \subseteq \mathcal{Z}_{++}$, for all $\mathbf{x}, \mathbf{y} \in \mathbf{X}^N$, and for all $U_E \in \mathcal{D}_E$,*

$$\mathbf{x} R_{U_E} \mathbf{y} \Leftrightarrow \sum_{i \in N} U_{Ei}(\mathbf{x}) \geq \sum_{i \in N} U_{Ei}(\mathbf{y})$$

$$\Leftrightarrow \sum_{i \in N} \sum_{j=1}^{m} p_j U_i(\mathbf{x}_j) \geq \sum_{i \in N} \sum_{j=1}^{m} p_j U_i(\mathbf{y}_j)$$

$$\Leftrightarrow \sum_{j=1}^{m} p_j \sum_{i \in N} U_i(\mathbf{x}_j) \geq \sum_{j=1}^{m} p_j \sum_{i \in N} U_i(\mathbf{y}_j)$$

where $U \in \mathcal{U}$ is the profile corresponding to U_E according to (7.20).

The fixed-population characterization of Theorem 7.3 can now be extended to a variable-population setting by employing, in addition to the variable-population versions of the axioms introduced above, the extended critical-level population principle. This axiom is the uncertainty analogue of Blackorby and Donaldson's (1984a) critical-level population principle. It requires the existence of a critical level $c \in \mathcal{R}_+$ with the following property. Consider two prospects $\mathbf{x}, \mathbf{y} \in \mathbf{X}$ and a profile $U_E \in \mathcal{D}_E$, and suppose there is a person $k \in \mathcal{Z}_{++}$ who is not alive in state j for some $j \in \{1, \ldots, m\}$; that is, $k \notin \mathbf{N}(\mathbf{x}_j)$. Now consider a prospect $\bar{\mathbf{x}} \in \mathbf{X}$ and a profile $\bar{U}_E \in \mathcal{D}_E$ such that individual k is alive in state j in $\bar{\mathbf{x}}$ with utility level $\bar{U}_k(\bar{\mathbf{x}}_j) = c$, other things the same. The extended critical-level population principle requires that the ranking of $\mathbf{x}$ and $\mathbf{y}$ according to R_{U_E} is the same as the ranking of $\bar{\mathbf{x}}$ and $\mathbf{y}$ according to $R_{\bar{U}_E}$. Note that the axiom applies to the extended Bernoulli domain only – the individual ex-post utility functions U_i rather than the ex-ante utility functions U_{Ei} are referred to. We require the critical level to be nonnegative to ensure that the uncertainty analogue of the negative expansion principle is satisfied. We could impose the axiom separately but, because its formulation is more complex in the present setting, we incorporate it into the critical-level axiom to simplify our exposition.

Extended Critical-Level Population Principle. If $\mathcal{D}_E = \mathcal{D}_B$, then there exists $c \in \mathcal{R}_+$ such that, for all $\mathbf{x}, \mathbf{y}, \bar{\mathbf{x}} \in \mathbf{X}$, for all $U_E, \bar{U}_E \in \mathcal{D}_E$, for all $j \in \{1, \ldots, m\}$, and for all $k \in \mathcal{Z}_{++} \setminus \mathbf{N}(\mathbf{x}_j)$, if

$$\bar{U}(\mathbf{y}_\ell) = U(\mathbf{y}_\ell)$$

for all $\ell \in \{1, \ldots, m\}$,

$$\mathbf{N}(\bar{\mathbf{x}}_\ell) = \mathbf{N}(\mathbf{x}_\ell)$$

for all $\ell \in \{1, \ldots, m\} \setminus \{j\}$,

$$\bar{U}_i(\bar{\mathbf{x}}_\ell) = U_i(\mathbf{x}_\ell)$$

for all $\ell \in \{1, \ldots, m\}$ and for all $i \in \mathbf{N}(\mathbf{x}_\ell)$,

$$\mathbf{N}(\bar{\mathbf{x}}_j) = \mathbf{N}(\mathbf{x}_j) \cup \{k\},$$

and

$$\bar{U}_k(\bar{\mathbf{x}}_j) = c,$$

then

$$\mathbf{x} R_{U_E} \mathbf{y} \Leftrightarrow \bar{\mathbf{x}} R_{\bar{U}_E} \mathbf{y}.$$

A variable-population extension of ex-ante utilitarianism is given by ex-ante critical-level utilitarianism, which is defined as follows. There exists $\alpha \in \mathcal{R}$ such that, for all $\mathbf{x}, \mathbf{y} \in \mathbf{X}$ and for all $U_E \in \mathcal{D}_E$,

$$\mathbf{x} R_{U_E} \mathbf{y} \Leftrightarrow \sum_{j=1}^{m} p_j \sum_{i \in \mathbf{N}(\mathbf{x}_j)} [U_i(\mathbf{x}_j) - \alpha] \geq \sum_{j=1}^{m} p_j \sum_{i \in \mathbf{N}(\mathbf{y}_j)} [U_i(\mathbf{y}_j) - \alpha]$$

$$(7.21)$$

where U is the profile corresponding to U_E according to (7.20). We obtain the following characterization of ex-ante critical-level utilitarianism with a nonnegative critical level α.

Theorem 7.7. *Suppose F_E satisfies extended individual Bernoulli domain. F_E satisfies the extended social expected-utility hypothesis, ex-ante Pareto indifference, ex-ante binary independence of irrelevant alternatives, ex-ante minimal increasingness, extended ex-ante anonymity, and the extended critical-level population principle if and only if F_E is ex-ante critical-level utilitarian with $\alpha \geq 0$.*

Proof. That ex-ante critical-level utilitarianism with a nonnegative critical level satisfies the required axioms is straightforward to verify. Now suppose F_E satisfies the axioms. By Theorem 7.3, for all nonempty and finite $N \subseteq \mathcal{Z}_{++}$, for all $\mathbf{x}, \mathbf{y} \in \mathbf{X}^N$, and for all $U_E \in \mathcal{D}_B$,

$$\mathbf{x} R_{U_E} \mathbf{y} \Leftrightarrow \sum_{j=1}^{m} p_j \sum_{i \in N} U_i(\mathbf{x}_j) \geq \sum_{j=1}^{m} p_j \sum_{i \in N} U_i(\mathbf{y}_j) \tag{7.22}$$

where $U \in \mathcal{U}$ is the profile corresponding to U_E according to (7.20). By the extended critical-level population principle, there exists $c \in \mathcal{R}_+$ with the properties described in the axiom. Let $\alpha = c$ and consider two prospects $\mathbf{x}, \mathbf{y} \in \mathbf{X}$. Let $\bar{\mathbf{x}}, \bar{\mathbf{y}} \in \mathbf{X}$ and $\bar{U}_E \in \mathcal{D}_B$ be such that

$$\mathbf{N}(\bar{\mathbf{x}}_j) = \mathbf{N}_E(\mathbf{x}) \text{ and } \mathbf{N}(\bar{\mathbf{y}}_j) = \mathbf{N}_E(\mathbf{y})$$

for all $j \in \{1, \ldots, m\}$,

$$\bar{U}_i(\bar{\mathbf{x}}_j) = U_i(\mathbf{x}_j) \text{ and } \bar{U}_k(\bar{\mathbf{y}}_j) = U_k(\mathbf{y}_j)$$

for all $j \in \{1, \ldots, m\}$, for all $i \in \mathbf{N}(\mathbf{x}_j)$, and for all $k \in \mathbf{N}(\mathbf{y}_j)$,

$$\bar{U}_i(\bar{\mathbf{x}}_j) = \alpha \text{ and } \bar{U}_k(\bar{\mathbf{y}}_j) = \alpha$$

for all $j \in \{1, \ldots, m\}$, for all $i \in \mathbf{N}_E(\mathbf{x}) \setminus \mathbf{N}(\mathbf{x}_j)$, and for all $k \in \mathbf{N}_E(\mathbf{y}) \setminus \mathbf{N}(\mathbf{y}_j)$. By repeated application of the extended critical-level population principle,

$$\mathbf{x} R_{U_E} \mathbf{y} \Leftrightarrow \bar{\mathbf{x}} R_{\bar{U}_E} \bar{\mathbf{y}}. \tag{7.23}$$

Suppose that $\mathbf{n}_E(\bar{\mathbf{x}}) = \mathbf{n}_E(\bar{\mathbf{y}})$. By extended ex-ante anonymity, we can, without loss of generality, assume that $\mathbf{N}_E(\bar{\mathbf{x}}) = \mathbf{N}_E(\bar{\mathbf{y}})$, and we denote this common set of individuals by N_E. By (7.22), it follows that

$$\bar{\mathbf{x}} R_{\bar{U}_E} \bar{\mathbf{y}} \Leftrightarrow \sum_{j=1}^{m} p_j \left[\sum_{i \in \mathbf{N}(\mathbf{x}_j)} U_i(\mathbf{x}_j) + \sum_{i \in N_E \setminus \mathbf{N}(\mathbf{x}_j)} \alpha \right]$$

$$\geq \sum_{j=1}^{m} p_j \left[\sum_{i \in \mathbf{N}(\mathbf{y}_j)} U_i(\mathbf{y}_j) + \sum_{i \in N_E \setminus \mathbf{N}(\mathbf{y}_j)} \alpha \right].$$

This inequality is equivalent to

$$\sum_{j=1}^{m} p_j \left[\sum_{i \in N(\mathbf{x}_j)} U_i(\mathbf{x}_j) + \sum_{i \in N_E} \alpha - \sum_{i \in N(\mathbf{x}_j)} \alpha \right]$$

$$\geq \sum_{j=1}^{m} p_j \left[\sum_{i \in N(\mathbf{y}_j)} U_i(\mathbf{y}_j) + \sum_{i \in N_E} \alpha - \sum_{i \in N(\mathbf{y}_j)} \alpha \right].$$

Simplifying, we obtain

$$\sum_{j=1}^{m} p_j \left[\sum_{i \in N(\mathbf{x}_j)} U_i(\mathbf{x}_j) - \sum_{i \in N(\mathbf{x}_j)} \alpha \right]$$

$$\geq \sum_{j=1}^{m} p_j \left[\sum_{i \in N(\mathbf{y}_j)} U_i(\mathbf{y}_j) - \sum_{i \in N(\mathbf{y}_j)} \alpha \right]$$

and, therefore,

$$\bar{\mathbf{x}} R_{\bar{U}_E} \bar{\mathbf{y}} \Leftrightarrow \sum_{j=1}^{m} p_j \sum_{i \in N(\mathbf{x}_j)} [U_i(\mathbf{x}_j) - \alpha] \geq \sum_{j=1}^{m} p_j \sum_{i \in N(\mathbf{y}_j)} [U_i(\mathbf{y}_j) - \alpha].$$

Together with (7.23), this implies (7.21).

Now suppose $\mathbf{n}_E(\bar{\mathbf{x}}) \neq \mathbf{n}_E(\bar{\mathbf{y}})$. Without loss of generality, suppose $\mathbf{n}_E(\bar{\mathbf{x}}) < \mathbf{n}_E(\bar{\mathbf{y}})$ and, by extended ex-ante anonymity, we can assume that $\mathbf{N}_E(\bar{\mathbf{x}}) \subset \mathbf{N}_E(\bar{\mathbf{y}}) = \mathbf{N}_E(\mathbf{y})$. Let $\hat{\mathbf{x}} \in \mathbf{X}$ and $\hat{U}_E \in \mathcal{D}_B$ be such that

$$\hat{U}(\bar{\mathbf{y}}_j) = \bar{U}(\bar{\mathbf{y}}_j)$$

for all $j \in \{1, \ldots, m\}$,

$$\mathbf{N}(\hat{\mathbf{x}}_j) = \mathbf{N}_E(\mathbf{y})$$

for all $j \in \{1, \ldots, m\}$,

$$\hat{U}_i(\hat{\mathbf{x}}_j) = \bar{U}_i(\bar{\mathbf{x}}_j)$$

for all $j \in \{1, \ldots, m\}$ and for all $i \in \mathbf{N}_E(\bar{\mathbf{x}})$, and

$$\hat{U}_i(\hat{\mathbf{x}}_j) = \alpha$$

for all $j \in \{1, \ldots, m\}$ and for all $i \in \mathbf{N}_E(\mathbf{y}) \setminus \mathbf{N}_E(\bar{\mathbf{x}})$. Again applying the extended critical-level population principle repeatedly, we obtain

$$\bar{\mathbf{x}} R_{\bar{U}_E} \bar{\mathbf{y}} \Leftrightarrow \hat{\mathbf{x}} R_{\hat{U}_E} \bar{\mathbf{y}}. \tag{7.24}$$

By (7.22), it follows that

$$\hat{\mathbf{x}}R_{\hat{U}_E}\bar{\mathbf{y}} \Leftrightarrow \sum_{j=1}^{m} p_j \left[\sum_{i\in N(\mathbf{x}_j)} U_i(\mathbf{x}_j) + \sum_{i\in N_E(\mathbf{x})\backslash N(\mathbf{x}_j)} \alpha + \sum_{i\in N_E(\mathbf{y})\backslash N_E(\mathbf{x})} \alpha \right]$$

$$\geq \sum_{j=1}^{m} p_j \left[\sum_{i\in N(\mathbf{y}_j)} U_i(\mathbf{y}_j) + \sum_{i\in N_E(\mathbf{y})\backslash N(\mathbf{y}_j)} \alpha \right].$$

Rewriting, the inequality becomes

$$\sum_{j=1}^{m} p_j \left[\sum_{i\in N(\mathbf{x}_j)} U_i(\mathbf{x}_j) - \sum_{i\in N(\mathbf{x}_j)} \alpha + \sum_{i\in N_E(\mathbf{y})} \alpha \right]$$

$$\geq \sum_{j=1}^{m} p_j \left[\sum_{i\in N(\mathbf{y}_j)} U_i(\mathbf{y}_j) - \sum_{i\in N(\mathbf{y}_j)} \alpha + \sum_{i\in N_E(\mathbf{y})} \alpha \right]$$

which is equivalent to

$$\sum_{j=1}^{m} p_j \left[\sum_{i\in N(\mathbf{x}_j)} U_i(\mathbf{x}_j) - \sum_{i\in N(\mathbf{x}_j)} \alpha \right]$$

$$\geq \sum_{j=1}^{m} p_j \left[\sum_{i\in N(\mathbf{y}_j)} U_i(\mathbf{y}_j) - \sum_{i\in N(\mathbf{y}_j)} \alpha \right].$$

Therefore, we obtain

$$\hat{\mathbf{x}}R_{\hat{U}_E}\bar{\mathbf{y}} \Leftrightarrow \sum_{j=1}^{m} p_j \sum_{i\in N(\mathbf{x}_j)} [U_i(\mathbf{x}_j) - \alpha] \geq \sum_{j=1}^{m} p_j \sum_{i\in N(\mathbf{y}_j)} [U_i(\mathbf{y}_j) - \alpha]$$

and, together with (7.23) and (7.24), this implies (7.21).   ∎

A natural question that arises is what additional principles become available if the critical levels in the extended critical-level population principle are allowed to differ across utility vectors. The resulting axiom is a weakening of the extended critical-level population principle.

Critical-Level Consistency. If $\mathcal{D}_E = \mathcal{D}_B$, then there exists a function $C: \Omega \to \mathcal{R}_+$ such that, for all $\mathbf{x}, \mathbf{y}, \bar{\mathbf{x}} \in \mathbf{X}$, for all $U_E, \bar{U}_E \in \mathcal{D}_E$, for all $j \in \{1, \ldots, m\}$, and for all $k \in \mathcal{Z}_{++} \backslash N(\mathbf{x}_j)$, if

$$\bar{U}(\mathbf{y}_\ell) = U(\mathbf{y}_\ell)$$

for all $\ell \in \{1, \ldots, m\}$,

$$N(\bar{\mathbf{x}}_\ell) = N(\mathbf{x}_\ell)$$

for all $\ell \in \{1, \ldots, m\} \setminus \{j\}$,

$$\bar{U}_i(\bar{\mathbf{x}}_\ell) = U_i(\mathbf{x}_\ell)$$

for all $\ell \in \{1, \ldots, m\}$ and for all $i \in \mathbf{N}(\mathbf{x}_\ell)$,

$$\mathbf{N}(\bar{\mathbf{x}}_j) = \mathbf{N}(\mathbf{x}_j) \cup \{k\},$$

and

$$\bar{U}_k(\bar{\mathbf{x}}_j) = C\Big[U(\mathbf{x}_j)\Big],$$

then

$$\mathbf{x}R_{U_E}\mathbf{y} \Leftrightarrow \bar{\mathbf{x}}R_{\bar{U}_E}\mathbf{y}.$$

In the axiom statement, the (ex-post) critical level used in the expansion is given by a function that can depend on the utilities of those alive and their number in the state in question. Again, because the range of the critical-level function C is assumed to be $\mathcal{R}_+$, an uncertainty version of the negative expansion principle is incorporated into the axiom.

Replacing the extended critical-level population principle with the above axiom yields a characterization of a subclass of an ex-ante version of the number-sensitive critical-level utilitarian orderings. This is a quite remarkable result. Critical-level consistency is very weak because it allows critical levels to depend on the utility vector of the state in which an individual is added. In conjunction with some other axioms, however, it implies that critical levels may depend on the number of individuals in that state but not on their utilities. To make the formal proof of this observation (which is part of the proof of the next characterization theorem) more transparent, we provide an illustration (see also Table 7.6 of Part A for a simplified version of the example with two states only).

Suppose that, in prospects $\mathbf{x}$ and $\mathbf{y}$, there are n individuals $\{1, \ldots, n\}$ and, in prospects $\bar{\mathbf{x}}$ and $\bar{\mathbf{y}}$, an additional individual $n + 1$ is alive. In prospect $\mathbf{x}$, the utility of person $i \in \{1, \ldots, n\}$ in state $j \in \{1, \ldots, m\}$ is u_i^j. In prospect $\mathbf{y}$, each individual $i \in \{1, \ldots, n\}$ experiences her or his expected utility of $\mathbf{x}$, $\sum_{j=1}^m p_j u_i^j$, in each of the m states. In prospects $\bar{\mathbf{x}}$ and $\bar{\mathbf{y}}$, the utilities of individuals $1, \ldots, n$ are the same as in prospects $\mathbf{x}$ and $\mathbf{y}$. The added individual $n + 1$ has the utility levels $C(u_1^j, \ldots, u_n^j)$ in state $j \in \{1, \ldots, m\}$ in prospect $\bar{\mathbf{x}}$. In prospect $\bar{\mathbf{y}}$, the utility of individual $n + 1$ is $C(\sum_{j=1}^m p_j u_1^j, \ldots, \sum_{j=1}^m p_j u_n^j)$ in all m states. The existence of the critical-level function C is guaranteed by critical-level consistency.

Because each person has the same expected utility in prospects $\mathbf{x}$ and $\mathbf{y}$, they are equally good by ex-ante Pareto indifference. Moreover, repeated application of critical-level consistency implies that prospects $\bar{\mathbf{x}}$ and $\bar{\mathbf{y}}$ are equally good. Because the social-evaluation functional is same-number ex-ante utilitarian, expected utilities for person $n + 1$ are the same in prospects $\bar{\mathbf{x}}$ and $\bar{\mathbf{y}}$. Thus, the critical level for the vector $(EU_1, \ldots, EU_n)$ of expected utilities, must be equal to the expected value of the critical levels for the $(u_1^j, \ldots, u_n^j)$. That is,

$$C\left(\sum_{j=1}^{m} p_j u_1^j, \ldots, \sum_{j=1}^{m} p_j u_n^j\right) = \sum_{j=1}^{m} p_j C(u_1^j, \ldots, u_n^j).$$

Not all critical-level functions satisfy this equation. As shown in the proof below, the solutions to this equation must be such that C can depend on population size but not on utility levels. Thus, the orderings of ex-post utility vectors must be number-sensitive critical-level utilitarian. It follows that prospects are ranked with the expected value of a number-sensitive critical-level value function with nonnegative critical levels. We call the class of such principles ex-ante number-sensitive critical-level utilitarianism.

F_E is ex-ante number-sensitive critical-level utilitarian if and only if there exists a function $A: \mathcal{Z}_{++} \to \mathcal{R}$ such that, for all $\mathbf{x}, \mathbf{y} \in \mathbf{X}$ and for all $U_E \in \mathcal{D}_E$,

$$\mathbf{x} R_{U_E} \mathbf{y} \Leftrightarrow \sum_{j=1}^{m} p_j \left[\sum_{i \in \mathbf{N}(\mathbf{x}_j)} U_i(\mathbf{x}_j) - A\big(\mathbf{n}(\mathbf{x}_j)\big) \right]$$

$$\geq \sum_{j=1}^{m} p_j \left[\sum_{i \in \mathbf{N}(\mathbf{y}_j)} U_i(\mathbf{y}_j) - A\big(\mathbf{n}(\mathbf{y}_j)\big) \right]$$

where U is the profile corresponding to U_E according to (7.20). The function A can be written as

$$A(n) = \sum_{k=1}^{n} c_{k-1}$$

for all $n \in \mathcal{Z}_{++}$, where $c_0 \in \mathcal{R}$ is arbitrary and $c_k \in \mathcal{R}_+$ is the ex-post critical level for population size $k \in \{1, \ldots, n - 1\}$. Note that the ex-post critical levels can depend on population size but not on utilities. All critical levels are nonnegative if and only if A is nondecreasing. We obtain the following characterization.

Theorem 7.8. *Suppose F_E satisfies extended individual Bernoulli domain. F_E satisfies the extended social expected-utility hypothesis, ex-ante Pareto indifference, ex-ante binary independence of irrelevant alternatives, ex-ante minimal increasingness, extended ex-ante anonymity, and critical-level consistency if and only if F_E is ex-ante number-sensitive critical-level utilitarian with a nondecreasing function A.*

Proof. That the ex-ante number-sensitive critical-level utilitarian ex-ante social-evaluation functionals with a nondecreasing function A satisfy the required axioms is straightforward to verify. Now suppose F_E satisfies the axioms. By critical-level consistency, there exists a function $C: \Omega \to \mathcal{R}_+$ with the requisite properties. Let $n \in \mathcal{Z}_{++}$ be arbitrary and consider four prospects $\mathbf{x}, \mathbf{y}, \bar{\mathbf{x}}, \bar{\mathbf{y}} \in X_\theta$ and two profiles $U_E, \bar{U}_E \in \mathcal{D}_B$ such that

$$\mathbf{N}_\theta(\mathbf{x}) = \mathbf{N}_\theta(\mathbf{y}) = \{1, \ldots, n\},$$

$$U_i(\mathbf{y}_j) = \sum_{k=1}^m p_k U_i(\mathbf{x}_k)$$

for all $i \in \{1, \ldots, n\}$ and for all $j \in \{1, \ldots, m\}$,

$$\mathbf{N}_\theta(\bar{\mathbf{x}}) = \mathbf{N}_\theta(\bar{\mathbf{y}}) = \{1, \ldots, n+1\},$$

$$\bar{U}_i(\bar{\mathbf{x}}_j) = U_i(\mathbf{x}_j) \text{ and } \bar{U}_i(\bar{\mathbf{y}}_j) = U_i(\mathbf{y}_j)$$

for all $i \in \{1, \ldots, n\}$ and for all $j \in \{1, \ldots, m\}$, and

$$\bar{U}_{n+1}(\bar{\mathbf{x}}_j) = C\left(U(\mathbf{x}_j)\right) \text{ and } \bar{U}_{n+1}(\bar{\mathbf{y}}_j) = C\left(U(\mathbf{y}_j)\right)$$

for all $j \in \{1, \ldots, m\}$, where $U, \bar{U} \in \mathcal{U}$ are the profiles of actual utilities corresponding to U_E and $\bar{U}_E$. Using Theorem 7.6, it follows that $\mathbf{x} I_{U_E} \mathbf{y}$. By repeated application of critical-level consistency, this implies $\bar{\mathbf{x}} I_{\bar{U}_E} \bar{\mathbf{y}}$. Again using Theorem 7.6, it follows that

$$\sum_{j=1}^m p_j C\left(U(\mathbf{x}_j)\right) = C\left(\sum_{j=1}^m p_j U(\mathbf{x}_j)\right).$$

Because, for any m vectors $u^1, \ldots, u^m \in \mathcal{R}^n$, a profile $U \in \mathcal{U}$ with the above properties can be chosen so that $U(\mathbf{x}_j) = u^j$ for all $j \in \{1, \ldots, m\}$, the function C must satisfy

$$\sum_{j=1}^m p_j C(u^j) = C\left(\sum_{j=1}^m p_j u^j\right) \tag{7.25}$$

for all $u^1, \ldots, u^m \in \mathcal{R}^n$. By Theorem 7.6 and critical-level consistency,

$$C(u^j) = C\left(\frac{1}{n} \sum_{i=1}^n u_i^j \mathbf{1}_n\right) \tag{7.26}$$

and

$$C\left(\sum_{j=1}^m p_j u^j\right) = C\left(\left[\sum_{j=1}^m p_j \frac{1}{n} \sum_{i=1}^n u_i^j\right] \mathbf{1}_n\right) \tag{7.27}$$

for all $j \in \{1, \ldots, m\}$ and for all $u^j \in \mathcal{R}^n$. Fix $n \in \mathcal{Z}_{++}$ and define $\bar{C}^n(\tau) = C(\tau \mathbf{1}_n)$ for all $\tau \in \mathcal{R}$. Letting $t_j = (1/n) \sum_{i=1}^n u_i^j$ for all $j \in \{1, \ldots, m\}$, (7.25), (7.26), and (7.27) together imply

$$\sum_{j=1}^m p_j \bar{C}^n(t_j) = \bar{C}^n\left(\sum_{j=1}^m p_j t_j\right) \tag{7.28}$$

for all $t \in \mathcal{R}^m$. Letting $z_j = p_j t_j$ for all $t \in \mathcal{R}^m$ and for all $j \in \{1, \ldots, m\}$, (7.28) becomes

$$\sum_{j=1}^m p_j \bar{C}^n(z_j/p_j) = \bar{C}^n \left(\sum_{j=1}^m z_j \right)$$

for all $z \in \mathcal{R}^m$. Defining $\hat{C}_j^n(z_j) = p_j \bar{C}^n(z_j/p_j)$ for all $z \in \mathcal{R}^m$ and for all $j \in \{1, \ldots, m\}$, we obtain

$$\sum_{j=1}^m \hat{C}_j^n(z_j) = \bar{C}^n \left(\sum_{j=1}^m z_j \right) \tag{7.29}$$

for all $z \in \mathcal{R}^m$. This is a Pexider equation, which has the solutions

$$\hat{C}_j^n(\tau) = d_n \tau + \bar{c}_j^n \tag{7.30}$$

and

$$\bar{C}^n(\tau) = d_n \tau + \sum_{j=1}^m \bar{c}_j^n \tag{7.31}$$

for all $\tau \in \mathcal{R}$ and for all $j \in \{1, \ldots, m\}$, where $d_n \in \mathcal{R}$ and $\bar{c}_j^n \in \mathcal{R}$ for all $j \in \{1, \ldots, m\}$. To establish that there are no further solutions, we show that the $\hat{C}_j^n$ (and, thus, $\bar{C}^n$) must be bounded below on a nondegenerate interval (see Aczél 1966, pp. 34, 142). Let $j \in \{1, \ldots, m\}$ and consider an arbitrary $z \in \mathcal{R}^m$. Given z, let $\bar{z} \in \mathcal{R}^m$ be such that $\bar{z}_k = z_k$ for all $k \in \{1, \ldots, m\} \setminus \{j\}$ and $\bar{z}_j = z_0$ where $z_0 \in \mathcal{R}$ is fixed. Applying Theorem 7.6 and critical-level consistency, it follows that

$$\sum_{k=1}^m z_k + \sum_{k=1}^m \hat{C}_k^n(z_k) \geq \sum_{k=1}^m \bar{z}_k + \sum_{k=1}^m \hat{C}_k^n(\bar{z}_k) \Leftrightarrow \sum_{k=1}^m z_k \geq \sum_{k=1}^m \bar{z}_k.$$
$$\tag{7.32}$$

Substituting the definition of $\bar{z}$ and rearranging, (7.32) implies that

$$\hat{C}_j^n(z_j) \geq \hat{C}_j^n(z_0) + z_0 - z_j$$

for all $z_j \geq z_0$. This implies that $\hat{C}_j^n$ is bounded below on any interval $[a, b]$ with $z_0 < a < b$ and, therefore, the only solutions of (7.29) are given by (7.30) and (7.31). Using (7.26), (7.28), and the definition of $\bar{C}^n$, substituting back yields

$$C(u^j) = C \left(\frac{1}{n} \sum_{i=1}^n u_i^j \mathbf{1}_n \right) = \bar{C}^n \left(\frac{1}{n} \sum_{i=1}^n u_i^j \right) = \frac{d_n}{n} \sum_{i=1}^n u_i^j + c_n$$

for all $j \in \{1, \ldots, m\}$ and for all $u^j \in \mathcal{R}^n$, where $c_n = \sum_{j=1}^n \bar{c}_j^n$. By critical-level consistency, critical levels must be nonnegative and, because average utility can be arbitrarily high or arbitrarily low for any given value of n, it follows that d_n must be equal to zero for all $n \in \mathcal{Z}_{++}$. Thus, there exists a sequence $(c_n)_{n \in \mathcal{Z}_{++}}$ such that the critical-level function C is given by $C(u) = c_n$ for all

$n \in \mathcal{Z}_{++}$ and for all $u \in \mathcal{R}^n$. Because the range of C is $\mathcal{R}_+$, it follows that $c_n \geq 0$ for all $n \in \mathcal{Z}_{++}$. Letting $c_0 \in \mathcal{R}$ be arbitrary, setting $A(n) = \sum_{i=1}^{n} c_{i-1}$ for all $n \in \mathcal{Z}_{++}$ and using the definition of critical levels as in the proof of Theorem 7.7, it follows that F_E is number-sensitive critical-level utilitarian. Because the c_n are nonnegative for all $n \in \mathcal{Z}_{++}$, A is nondecreasing. ∎

7.9 UNCERTAIN ALTERNATIVES

The theorems of Sections 7.7 and 7.8 can be extended so that all uncertain alternatives and not only prospects are ranked. $(p, \mathbf{x}) \in \mathbf{P} \times \mathbf{X}$ is a U-alternative in which $\mathbf{x}_j$ is realized with probability p_j for all $j \in \{1, \ldots, m\}$. Because probabilities are allowed to be zero, the case in which the number of states is U-alternative dependent is implicitly covered.

We first turn to the fixed-population case and, as in Section 7.7, let the population be $\{1, \ldots, n\}$. Individual ex-ante utility functions can depend on the probability vector p. $U_{UEi}^n : \mathbf{P} \times \mathbf{X}^n \to \mathcal{R}$ is the individual ex-ante utility function for person i and $\mathcal{U}_{UE}^n$ is the set of all profiles of such functions. If the individual Bernoulli hypothesis is satisfied,

$$U_{UEi}^n(p, \mathbf{x}) = \sum_{j=1}^{m} p_j U_i^n(\mathbf{x}_j)$$

where U_i^n is person i's ex-post utility function. $\mathcal{D}_{UB}^n$ is the set of all profiles of ex-ante utility functions that satisfy the Bernoulli hypothesis.

An ex-ante social-evaluation functional is a mapping $F_{UE}^n : \mathcal{D}_{UE}^n \to \mathcal{O}_{UE}^n$ where $\mathcal{D}_{UE}^n \subseteq \mathbf{P} \times \mathcal{U}_{UE}^n$ is the nonempty domain and $\mathcal{O}_{UE}^n$ is the set of all orderings on $\mathbf{P} \times \mathbf{X}^n$. We write $R_{U_{UE}^n}^n = F_{U_{UE}^n}^n(U_{UE}^n)$ and use $P_{U_{UE}^n}^n$ and $I_{U_{UE}^n}^n$ to denote the asymmetric and symmetric factors of $R_{U_{UE}^n}^n$.

The fixed-population axioms are straightforward generalizations of the fixed-population axioms of Section 7.7.

Uncertainty Individual Bernoulli Domain. $\mathcal{D}_{UE}^n = \mathbf{P} \times \mathcal{D}_{UB}^n$.

Uncertainty Social Expected-Utility Hypothesis. There exists a function $U_{U0}^n : \mathbf{P} \times \mathbf{X}^n \times \mathcal{D}_{UE}^n \to \mathcal{R}$ such that, for all $(p, \mathbf{x}), (q, \mathbf{y}) \in \mathbf{P} \times \mathbf{X}^n$ and for all $U_{UE}^n \in \mathcal{D}_{UE}^n$,

$$(p, \mathbf{x}) R_{U_{UE}^n}^n (q, \mathbf{y}) \Leftrightarrow \sum_{j=1}^{m} p_j U_{U0}^n(\mathbf{x}_j, U_{UE}^n) \geq \sum_{j=1}^{m} q_j U_{U0}^n(\mathbf{y}_j, U_{UE}^n).$$

Uncertainty Ex-Ante Pareto Indifference. For all $(p, \mathbf{x}), (q, \mathbf{y}) \in \mathbf{P} \times \mathbf{X}^n$ and for all $U_{UE}^n \in \mathcal{D}_{UE}^n$, if $U_{UE}^n(p, \mathbf{x}) = U_{UE}^n(q, \mathbf{y})$, then $(p, \mathbf{x}) I_{U_{UE}^n}^n (q, \mathbf{y})$.

Uncertainty Ex-Ante Binary Independence of Irrelevant Alternatives. For all $(p, \mathbf{x}), (q, \mathbf{y}) \in \mathbf{P} \times \mathbf{X}^n$ and for all $U_{UE}^n, \bar{U}_{UE}^n \in \mathcal{D}_{UE}^n$, if $U_{UE}^n(p, \mathbf{x}) = \bar{U}_{UE}^n(p, \mathbf{x})$ and $U_{UE}^n(q, \mathbf{y}) = \bar{U}_{UE}^n(q, \mathbf{y})$, then

$$(p, \mathbf{x})R_{U_{UE}^n}^n(q, \mathbf{y}) \Leftrightarrow (p, \mathbf{x})R_{\bar{U}_{UE}^n}^n(q, \mathbf{y}).$$

Uncertainty Ex-Ante Minimal Increasingness. For all $a, b \in \mathcal{R}$, for all $(p, \mathbf{x}), (q, \mathbf{y}) \in \mathbf{P} \times \mathbf{X}^n$, and for all $U_{UE}^n \in \mathcal{D}_{UE}^n$, if $U_{UE}^n(p, \mathbf{x}) = a\mathbf{1}_n \gg b\mathbf{1}_n = U_{UE}^n(q, \mathbf{y})$, then $(p, \mathbf{x})P_{U_{UE}^n}^n(q, \mathbf{y})$.

Uncertainty Ex-Ante Same-People Anonymity. For all $(p, \mathbf{x}), (q, \mathbf{y}) \in \mathbf{P} \times \mathbf{X}^n$ and for all $U_{UE}^n \in \mathcal{D}_{UE}^n$, if there exists a bijection $\rho^n: \{1, \ldots, n\} \to \{1, \ldots, n\}$ such that $U_{UEi}^n(p, \mathbf{x}) = U_{UE\rho^n(i)}^n(q, \mathbf{y})$ for all $i \in \{1, \ldots, n\}$, then $(p, \mathbf{x})I_{U_{UE}^n}^n(q, \mathbf{y})$.

The following theorem generalizes Theorem 7.1.

Theorem 7.9. *If F_{UE}^n satisfies uncertainty individual Bernoulli domain, uncertainty ex-ante Pareto indifference, and uncertainty ex-ante binary independence of irrelevant alternatives, then there exists a social-evaluation ordering R_{UE}^n on $\mathcal{R}^n$ such that, for all $(p, \mathbf{x}), (q, \mathbf{y}) \in \mathbf{P} \times \mathbf{X}^n$ and for all $U_{UE}^n \in \mathcal{D}_{UE}^n$,*

$$(p, \mathbf{x})R_{U_{UE}^n}^n(q, \mathbf{y}) \Leftrightarrow U_{UE}^n(p, \mathbf{x})R_{UE}^n U_{UE}^n(q, \mathbf{y}). \qquad (7.33)$$

The social-evaluation functional F_{UE}^n is ex-ante utilitarian if and only if, for all $(p, \mathbf{x}), (q, \mathbf{y}) \in \mathbf{P} \times \mathbf{X}^n$ and for all $U_{UE}^n \in \mathcal{D}_{UE}^n$,

$$(p, \mathbf{x})R_{U_{UE}^n}^n(q, \mathbf{y}) \Leftrightarrow \sum_{i=1}^n U_{UEi}^n(p, \mathbf{x}) \geq \sum_{i=1}^n U_{UEi}^n(q, \mathbf{y})$$

$$\Leftrightarrow \sum_{i=1}^n \sum_{j=1}^m p_j U_i^n(\mathbf{x}_j) \geq \sum_{i=1}^n \sum_{j=1}^m q_j U_i^n(\mathbf{y}_j)$$

$$\Leftrightarrow \sum_{j=1}^m p_j \sum_{i=1}^n U_i^n(\mathbf{x}_j) \geq \sum_{j=1}^m q_j \sum_{i=1}^n U_i^n(\mathbf{y}_j).$$

The following theorem is a consequence of Theorems 7.3 and 7.9.

Theorem 7.10. *Suppose F_{UE}^n satisfies uncertainty individual Bernoulli domain. F_{UE}^n satisfies the uncertainty social expected-utility hypothesis, uncertainty ex-ante Pareto indifference, uncertainty ex-ante binary independence of irrelevant alternatives, uncertainty ex-ante minimal increasingness, and uncertainty ex-ante same-people anonymity if and only if F_{UE}^n is ex-ante utilitarian.*

Proof. If F_{UE}^n is ex-ante utilitarian, it is straightforward to show that all the axioms are satisfied. Now suppose that F_{UE}^n satisfies the axioms of the theorem statement. By Theorem 7.9, there exists an ordering R_{UE}^n on $\mathcal{R}^n$ such that (7.33) is satisfied. Because R_{UE}^n is independent of probabilities, it can be found by examining the restriction of $R_{U_{UE}^n}$ to $\{\bar{p}\} \times \mathbf{X}^n$ where $\bar{p} \in \mathbf{P} \cap \mathcal{R}_{++}^m$. Theorem 7.3 implies that, for all $u, v \in \mathcal{R}^n$,

$$u R_{UE}^n v \Leftrightarrow \sum_{i=1}^n u_i \geq \sum_{i=1}^n v_i$$

and, as a consequence, F_{UE}^n is ex-ante utilitarian. ∎

Although notational complexities have persuaded us not to include a formal demonstration, the results of Theorems 7.7 and 7.8 can be extended to cover all U-alternatives. To do so, the axioms presented in Section 7.8 must be extended to the variable-population environment of U-alternatives. In addition, it is a simple matter to rewrite the extended critical-level population principle and critical-level consistency in a similar way. The domain of the resulting social-evaluation functional is $\mathcal{D}_{UE}$.

Using the argument in the proof of Theorem 7.10, it is immediate that all complete U-alternatives (in which each person is alive in all states or in none) with the same number of people must be ranked with ex-ante utilitarianism. Given the modified basic axioms and the modified extended critical-level population principle, the uncertainty ex-ante critical-level utilitarian principles with a nonnegative critical level are characterized. That is, there exists $\alpha \geq 0$ such that, for all $(p, \mathbf{x}), (q, \mathbf{y}) \in \mathbf{P} \times \mathbf{X}$ and for all $U_{UE} \in \mathcal{D}_{UE}$,

$$(p, \mathbf{x}) R_{U_{UE}}(q, \mathbf{y}) \Leftrightarrow \sum_{j=1}^m p_j \sum_{i \in \mathbf{N}(\mathbf{x}_j)} \left[U_i(\mathbf{x}_j) - \alpha \right]$$

$$\geq \sum_{j=1}^m q_j \sum_{i \in \mathbf{N}(\mathbf{y}_j)} \left[U_i(\mathbf{y}_j) - \alpha \right]. \tag{7.34}$$

If the modified version of critical-level consistency is used instead, the argument in the proof of Theorem 7.8 establishes that ex-post critical levels are utility independent but may depend on the number of people alive. We therefore obtain a characterization of uncertainty ex-ante number-sensitive critical-level utilitarianism with a nondecreasing function A. That is, there exists a non-decreasing function $A: \mathcal{Z}_{++} \to \mathcal{R}$ such that, for all $(p, \mathbf{x}), (q, \mathbf{y}) \in \mathbf{P} \times \mathbf{X}$ and for all $U_{UE} \in \mathcal{D}_{UE}$,

$$(p, \mathbf{x}) R_{U_{UE}}(q, \mathbf{y}) \Leftrightarrow \sum_{j=1}^m p_j \left[\sum_{i \in \mathbf{N}(\mathbf{x}_j)} U_i(\mathbf{x}_j) - A\left(\mathbf{n}(\mathbf{x}_j)\right) \right]$$

$$\geq \sum_{j=1}^m q_j \left[\sum_{i \in \mathbf{N}(\mathbf{y}_j)} U_i(\mathbf{y}_j) - A\left(\mathbf{n}(\mathbf{y}_j)\right) \right]. \tag{7.35}$$

As in Section 7.8, the function A can be written as

$$A(n) = \sum_{k=1}^{n} c_{k-1}$$

for all $n \in \mathcal{Z}_{++}$, where $c_0 \in \mathcal{R}$ is arbitrary and $c_k \in \mathcal{R}_+$ is the ex-post critical level for population size $k \in \{1, \ldots, n-1\}$.

If, instead of the Bernoulli domain, an expected-utility domain, which consists of all profiles with a single attitude toward utility uncertainty expressed by the transformation φ as in (7.18), is chosen instead, principles that are extensions of (7.34) and (7.35) result (see the discussion at the end of Section 7.7). Their associated ex-post principles are critical-level generalized utilitarian and number-sensitive critical-level generalized utilitarian.

7.10 QUASI-ORDERINGS AND POPULATION PRINCIPLES

In employing a critical-level generalized utilitarian principle, the choice of the parameter α is of crucial importance. There are compelling reasons to choose a positive critical level (see the discussions in the previous two chapters) but the exact choice can be very difficult: if α is small, the repugnant conclusion is approximated and if α is large, the principle may recommend against bringing people into existence whose lives are well worth living.

In this section, we allow for incommensurabilities by relaxing the assumption that the population principle ranks all pairs of alternatives. A social-decision functional is employed which produces a quasi-ordering (rather than an ordering) of the alternatives for every utility profile. Thus, given any profile and any two alternatives $x, y \in X$, x is at least as good as y, y is at least as good as x, or neither is true, in which case we say that x and y are not ranked.

If the welfarism axioms (unlimited domain, Pareto indifference, and binary independence of irrelevant alternatives) are imposed, the principle is welfarist in the sense that the ranking of any two alternatives is given by the ranking of the corresponding utility vectors by a single quasi-ordering.[15] Thus, if the profile is $U \in \mathcal{U}$,

$$x R_U y \Leftrightarrow U(x) R U(y)$$

for all $x, y \in X$, where R is a social quasi-ordering (reflexive and transitive but not necessarily complete).

We investigate social quasi-orderings that employ a critical set rather than a single critical level. These rankings are incomplete variants of critical-level generalized utilitarianism. If a single individual is added to a utility unaffected

---

[15] The welfarism theorems of Chapter 3 are easily extended to social-decision functionals.

population, the new alternative and the original are not ranked if the lifetime utility of the added person is in the set.[16]

For a utility vector $u \in \Omega$, let $\mathbf{Q}(u)$ denote the set of all utility levels $c \in \mathcal{R}$ such that the vector obtained by augmenting u by one individual with utility c and the original vector u are not ranked by the social quasi-ordering R. That is, for all $u \in \Omega$,

$$\mathbf{Q}(u) = \{c \in \mathcal{R} \mid \text{not } (u, c)Ru \text{ and not } uR(u, c)\}.$$

We call $\mathbf{Q}(u)$ a critical set for u, and we assume that this set has at least two elements and is bounded for all utility vectors. The assumption that the critical set contains at least two elements ensures that any utility vector and at least two of its augmentations are not ranked.

Regularity of Critical Sets. For all $u \in \Omega$, $\mathbf{Q}(u)$ has at least two elements and is bounded.

Together with the strong Pareto principle, regularity of critical sets has remarkably strong consequences. We summarize them in the following theorem.

Theorem 7.11. *Suppose R is a quasi-ordering on Ω. If R satisfies strong Pareto and regularity of critical sets, then, for all $u \in \Omega$:*

(i) *there exists no $c \in \mathcal{R}$ such that $(u, c)Iu$;*
(ii) *$\mathbf{Q}(u)$ is a non-degenerate and bounded interval;*
(iii) *$(u, d)Pu$ for all $d \in \mathcal{R}$ such that $d > c$ for all $c \in \mathbf{Q}(u)$;*
(iv) *$uP(u, d)$ for all $d \in \mathcal{R}$ such that $d < c$ for all $c \in \mathbf{Q}(u)$.*

Proof. To prove part (i), suppose, by way of contradiction, that there exists $u \in \Omega$ and $c \in \mathcal{R}$ such that $(u, c)Iu$. By strong Pareto and transitivity, $(u, d)Pu$ for all $d > c$ and $uP(u, d)$ for all $d < c$. But this implies $\mathbf{Q}(u) = \emptyset$, contradicting regularity of critical sets.

To establish (ii), let $u \subset \Omega$ and suppose $c, d, e \in \mathcal{R}$ are such that $c \prec d \prec e$ and $c, e \in \mathbf{Q}(u)$. If $(u, d)Pu$, strong Pareto and transitivity together imply $(u, e)Pu$, contradicting the hypothesis $e \in \mathbf{Q}(u)$. If $uP(u, d)$, strong Pareto and transitivity together imply $uP(u, c)$, contradicting $c \in \mathbf{Q}(u)$. By part (i), $(u, d)Iu$ is ruled out, and it follows that $d \in \mathbf{Q}(u)$. Thus, $\mathbf{Q}(u)$ must be an interval. That $\mathbf{Q}(u)$ is nondegenerate and bounded follows immediately from regularity of critical sets.

We conclude by proving (iii); the proof of (iv) is analogous. Let $u \in \Omega$, and suppose $d > c$ for all $c \in \mathbf{Q}(u)$. This implies $d \notin \mathbf{Q}(u)$ and, by part (i), we must have $(u, d)Pu$ or $uP(u, d)$. If $uP(u, d)$ is true, strong Pareto, regularity

---

[16] Parfit (1976, 1982, 1984) suggested that the set in which ceteris-paribus additions to a population are not ranked should be an interval. Theorem 7.11 shows that this is a consequence of a regularity axiom and strong Pareto.

of critical sets, and transitivity together imply $uP(u, c)$ for some $c \in \mathbf{Q}(u)$, a contradiction. Therefore, we obtain $(u, d)Pu$.   ∎

We introduce two further critical-set axioms that are used in the main result of this section. The noncomparable factor of a quasi-ordering is not necessarily transitive. In our critical-sets framework, however, it is natural to assume that if a succession of individuals is added and each augmentation is such that the utility of the added person is in the requisite critical set, the resulting vector and the original are non-comparable. The axiom that formalizes this intuition is the critical-set extension principle.

Critical-Set Extension Principle. For all $u \in \Omega$, for all $K \in \mathcal{Z}_{++}$, and for all $d_1, \ldots, d_K \in \mathcal{R}$, if $d_0 = u_\emptyset$ and $d_k \in \mathbf{Q}(u, d_0, \ldots, d_{k-1})$ for all $k \in \{1, \ldots, K\}$, then not $(u, d_1, \ldots, d_K)Ru$ and not $uR(u, d_1, \ldots, d_K)$.

Analogously to the critical-level population principle which requires the existence of a constant critical level, the critical-set population principle requires the critical set to be independent of the utility vector u.

Critical-Set Population Principle. There exists $Q \subseteq \mathcal{R}$ such that, for all $u \in \Omega$, $\mathbf{Q}(u) = Q$.

R is a critical-band generalized utilitarian social-evaluation quasi-ordering if and only if there exist a nondegenerate and bounded interval $Q \subseteq \mathcal{R}$ and a continuous and increasing function $g: \mathcal{R} \to \mathcal{R}$ with $g(0) = 0$ such that, for all $n, m \in \mathcal{Z}_{++}$, for all $u \in \mathcal{R}^n$, and for all $v \in \mathcal{R}^m$,

$$uRv \Leftrightarrow \sum_{i=1}^{n}[g(u_i) - g(c)] \geq \sum_{i=1}^{m}[g(v_i) - g(c)] \text{ for all } c \in Q.$$

The following theorem, which is the main result of this section, characterizes the critical-band generalized utilitarian class.

Theorem 7.12. *Suppose R is a quasi-ordering and the restriction of R to $\mathcal{R}^n$ is an ordering for all $n \in \mathcal{Z}_{++}$. R satisfies continuity, strong Pareto, the population substitution principle, regularity of critical sets, the critical-set extension principle, and the critical-set population principle if and only if R is critical-band generalized utilitarian.*

Proof. That the principles defined in the theorem statement satisfy the required axioms is easy to verify. Now suppose R satisfies the axioms. By Theorem 4.21, R must be same-number generalized utilitarian. As is straightforward to verify, R is critical-band generalized utilitarian if and only if there exist a nondegenerate and bounded interval $Q \subseteq \mathcal{R}$ and a continuous and increasing function $g: \mathcal{R} \to \mathcal{R}$ with $g(0) = 0$ such that, for all $n, m \in \mathcal{Z}_{++}$, for all $u \in \mathcal{R}^n$, and for all $v \in \mathcal{R}^m$,

$$uRv \Leftrightarrow \left[n = m \text{ and } \sum_{i=1}^n g(u_i) \geq \sum_{i=1}^m g(v_i) \right] \text{ or}$$

$$\left[n \neq m \text{ and } \sum_{i=1}^n \left[g(u_i) - g(c) \right] \right.$$

$$\left. > \sum_{i=1}^m \left[g(v_i) - g(c) \right] \text{ for all } c \in Q \right].$$

Let $n, m \in \mathcal{Z}_{++}, u \in \mathcal{R}^n$, and $v \in \mathcal{R}^m$. If $n = m$, the result follows immediately from Theorem 4.21.

Now consider the case $n \neq m$. Without loss of generality, suppose $n > m$. It is sufficient to show that: (i) if

$$\sum_{i=1}^n \left[g(u_i) - g(c) \right] > \sum_{i=1}^m \left[g(v_i) - g(c) \right] \tag{7.36}$$

for all $c \in Q$, then uPv; and (ii) if there exist $c, d \in Q$ such that

$$\sum_{i=1}^n \left[g(u_i) - g(c) \right] \geq \sum_{i=1}^m \left[g(v_i) - g(c) \right] \quad \text{and}$$

$$\sum_{i=1}^n \left[g(u_i) - g(d) \right] \leq \sum_{i=1}^m \left[g(v_i) - g(d) \right], \tag{7.37}$$

then not uRv and not vRu.

To prove (i), suppose that (7.36) is satisfied for all $c \in Q$. This is equivalent to

$$\sum_{i=1}^n g(u_i) > \sum_{i=1}^m g(v_i) + (n - m)g(c)$$

for all $c \in Q$. Because g is continuous and increasing and Q is bounded, there exists $d \in \mathcal{R}$ such that $d > c$ for all $c \in Q$ and

$$\sum_{i=1}^n g(u_i) > \sum_{i=1}^m g(v_i) + (n - m)g(d).$$

Because u and $(v, d\mathbf{1}_{n-m})$ are both of dimension n, we obtain $uP(v, d\mathbf{1}_{n-m})$. Part (iii) of Theorem 7.11 and the transitivity of R together imply $(v, d\mathbf{1}_{n-m})Pv$ and, again employing transitivity, it follows that uPv.

Finally, we establish (ii). Suppose there exist $c, d \in Q$ such that (7.37) is true. Because g is continuous and Q is an interval, it follows that there exists $e \in Q$ such that

$$\sum_{i=1}^n \left[g(u_i) - g(e) \right] = \sum_{i=1}^m \left[g(v_i) - g(e) \right].$$

This is equivalent to

$$\sum_{i=1}^{n} g(u_i) = \sum_{i=1}^{m} g(v_i) + (n - m)g(e)$$

and, because same-number comparisons are made according to generalized utilitarianism with the transformation g, we obtain

$$u I(v, e\mathbf{1}_{n-m}). \tag{7.38}$$

Because $e \in Q$, the critical-set extension principle implies

$$\text{not } (v, e\mathbf{1}_{n-m})Rv \tag{7.39}$$

and

$$\text{not } vR(v, e\mathbf{1}_{n-m}). \tag{7.40}$$

If $u Rv$, transitivity and (7.38) imply $vR(v, e\mathbf{1}_{n-m})$, a contradiction to (7.40). Analogously, if $v R u$, transitivity and (7.38) imply $(v, e\mathbf{1}_{n-m})Rv$, contradicting (7.39). This establishes (ii) and completes the proof of the theorem. ∎

An important special case of the critical-band generalized utilitarian quasi-orderings is obtained if g is affine. In this case, there exists a nondegenerate and bounded interval $Q \subseteq \mathcal{R}$ such that, for all $n, m \in \mathcal{Z}_{++}$, for all $u \in \mathcal{R}^n$, and for all $v \in \mathcal{R}^m$,

$$u Rv \Leftrightarrow \sum_{i=1}^{n} [u_i - c] \ge \sum_{i=1}^{m} [v_i - c] \text{ for all } c \in Q.$$

We call this class of quasi-orderings the critical-band utilitarian class. It can be characterized by adding the critical-set axioms to the axioms characterizing same-number utilitarianism in Theorem 4.9.

Theorem 7.13. *Suppose R is a quasi-ordering and the restriction of R to $\mathcal{R}^n$ is an ordering for all $n \in \mathcal{Z}_{++}$. R satisfies minimal increasingness, incremental equity, regularity of critical sets, the critical-set extension principle, and the critical-set population principle if and only if R is critical-band utilitarian.*

Proof. That critical-band utilitarianism satisfies the required axioms is straightforward to verify. Now suppose R satisfies the axioms. By Theorem 4.9, R is same-number utilitarian. Therefore, R satisfies strong Pareto and, thus, Theorem 7.11 applies. The rest of the proof is analogous to the proof of Theorem 7.12 with Theorem 4.21 replaced by Theorem 4.9. ∎

CHAPTER 8

Independence of the Existence of the Dead

Part A

In this and the following chapter, we use an explicit intertemporal structure for variable-population social evaluation. Nonwelfare information includes the birth dates and lifetimes of those alive in each alternative and all other nonwelfare information is assumed to be fixed. We examine the consequences of weakening Pareto indifference and strong Pareto so that birth dates or lifetimes (or both) may matter. In addition, we impose a natural independence condition, called independence of the existence of the dead, that requires the ranking of any two alternatives to be independent of the existence of individuals whose lives are over and who had the same lifetime utilities, birth dates, and lifetimes in both alternatives.[1]

8.1 AN INTERTEMPORAL ENVIRONMENT

To investigate population principles in an intertemporal setting, we employ a period analysis with arbitrary period length. There are multiple information profiles that provide, for each possible person, lifetime utility, birth date, and length of life in each alternative in which the person is alive. Other nonwelfare information, which is assumed to be fixed, can be disregarded, as in the case of a single nonwelfare-information profile. We assume that no person can live more than a fixed number of periods. The maximal lifetime is finite but can be arbitrarily large.

Information about a possible alternative is displayed in Table 8.1. In it, individuals 2, 21, 1,024, and 1,729 are alive in periods 4 to 9, 1 to 6, 7 only, and 3 to 5, and their lifetime utilities are 70, 25, 0, and 22. In the problems investigated in this chapter, it is not necessary to assign individual utility values to the periods themselves; all that is needed is lifetime utility.

A social-evaluation functional associates an ordering of the alternatives with every information profile. We employ the axioms extended unlimited domain,

---

[1] In previous work, we called this axiom independence of the utilities of the dead.

Table 8.1. *Intertemporal Information*

	1	2	3	4	5	6	7	8	9	10	...	Lifetime Utility
Person 2				•	•	•	•	•	•			70
Person 21	•	•	•	•	•	•						25
Person 1024							•					0
Person 1729			•	•	•							22

extended binary independence, and extended anonymity, which are defined in Chapter 3. Extended unlimited domain allows birth dates and lifetimes to be different in different alternatives. When this axiom is combined with Pareto indifference and extended binary independence, welfarism results (Theorem 3.11) and, as a consequence, dates of birth and lengths of life cannot affect social orderings. To investigate such influences, therefore, it is necessary to consider weaker axioms.

If, in any two alternatives, the same individuals are alive and have the same utility levels, birth dates, and lengths of life, conditional Pareto indifference requires them to be ranked as equally good. This axiom rules out orderings based solely on the names of the alternatives or on the fixed nonwelfare information. If a social-evaluation functional satisfies extended unlimited domain, conditional Pareto indifference, extended binary independence of irrelevant alternatives, and extended anonymity, there is a single anonymous ordering of compound vectors of individual utilities, birth dates, and lifetimes that, together with the information in a profile, can be used to rank the alternatives. We call this ordering R_{SL}. Because nonwelfare information can influence the social ordering, such principles may not be welfarist.

8.2 INDEPENDENCE OF THE EXISTENCE OF THE DEAD

In Chapter 5, we used the axiom existence independence to characterize critical-level generalized utilitarianism and offered, as a justification, the idea that the existence of people who are long dead should not influence the ranking of feasible alternatives (which necessarily have a common past). Within the framework employed in this chapter, we are able to formulate the corresponding property explicitly.

Suppose that two alternatives are to be ranked. In each, the individuals whose lives are over by period t, which can be any period, are the dead, from the point of view of that period. If, in both alternatives, the same individuals are dead and each of them has the same lifetime-utility level, birth date, and length of life, then independence of the existence of the dead requires the ranking of the alternatives to be unchanged if the existence of the dead is disregarded. This condition is weak but, in the presence of other axioms, it has significant implications.

To prove our theorems, we formulate intertemporal versions of continuity, weak existence of critical levels, and the (conditional) strong-Pareto axioms that are appropriate to the intertemporal environment. Each axiom is a property required of the ordering R_{SL}, which ranks compound vectors of utility levels, birth dates, and lengths of life. Intertemporal continuity is a natural extension of continuity, and intertemporal weak existence of critical levels requires the existence of at least one critical level for some birth date and lifetime of the added individual. Intertemporal strong Pareto requires (i) two vectors to be ranked as equally good if all utilities are the same in both, and (ii) one vector to be ranked as better than another if no utility level is lower in it and at least one is higher; conditional strong Pareto restricts the strong-Pareto axiom to apply only to vectors in which birth dates and lengths of life are the same; birth-date conditional strong Pareto applies only to vectors in which birth dates are the same; and lifetime conditional strong Pareto applies to vectors in which lengths of life are the same.

Some of our results use individual intertemporal equivalence axioms. Individual intertemporal equivalence and its conditional, birth-date conditional and lifetime conditional counterparts assert that, by suitably changing an individual's lifetime utility, his or her birth date can be changed to any prespecified period without changing the social ranking. These axioms imply that there are nondegenerate trade-offs between birth dates or lifetimes and utilities. They also rule out principles such as one whose value function is the discounted sum of the average utilities of those born in each period (for all periods in which at least one person is born).

The ordering R_{SL} is a birth-date- and lifetime-dependent critical-level generalized utilitarian ordering if and only if it is represented by a value function that is equal to the sum of the differences between conditionally transformed individual utility and a conditionally transformed fixed critical level, where the summation is done over all individuals alive. The transformation, which we call a conditional transformation, is increasing and continuous in individual utility and is conditional on birth date and length of life. R_{SL} is a birth-date-dependent critical-level generalized utilitarian ordering if and only if the conditional transformation is independent of lengths of life, a lifetime-dependent critical-level generalized utilitarian ordering if and only if the conditional transformation is independent of birth dates, and an intertemporal critical-level generalized utilitarian ordering if and only if the conditional transformation is independent of birth dates and lengths of life. Except for the last class of principles, an additional richness property regarding the image of the requisite principle is required in each of their definitions.

We show that R_{SL} satisfies: (i) intertemporal continuity, conditional strong Pareto, intertemporal weak existence of critical levels, individual intertemporal equivalence, and independence of the existence of the dead if and only if it is birth-date- and lifetime-dependent critical-level generalized utilitarian; (ii) intertemporal continuity, birth-date-conditional strong Pareto, intertemporal weak existence of critical levels, birth-date-conditional individual intertemporal equivalence, and independence of the existence of the dead if and only if it is birth-date-dependent critical-level generalized utilitarian; (iii) intertemporal continuity, lifetime-conditional strong Pareto, intertemporal weak existence of critical levels, lifetime-conditional individual intertemporal equivalence, and independence of the existence of the dead if and only if it is lifetime-dependent critical-level generalized utilitarian; and (iv) intertemporal continuity, intertemporal strong Pareto, intertemporal weak existence of critical levels, and independence of the existence of the dead if and only if it is intertemporal critical-level generalized utilitarian.

Result (iv) does not use an individual intertemporal equivalence axiom because that axiom is implied by intertemporal strong Pareto. In that case, neither birth dates nor lengths of life can matter in social evaluation and it follows that critical levels, if they exist, also must be independent of the birth date and lifetime of the added person. In addition, it is easy to see that existence independence is implied. Consequently, R_{SL} must be intertemporal critical-level generalized utilitarian.

Should we allow population principles to be sensitive to birth dates or lengths of life? Suppose R_{SL} is birth-date- and lifetime-dependent critical-level generalized utilitarian. Sensitivity to birth date requires the conditional transformation to be sensitive to it and, in that case, there exist a utility level, a lifetime, and two different birth dates such that the transformed value of the utility level is different, given the lifetime at the two values for birth date. Now consider an alternative in which a person is alive with the particular utility level and lifetime. We wish to assess the desirability of moving from one of the two birth dates to the other, all else equal. Because the conditional transformation is sensitive to birth date at that utility level and lifetime, one birth date will be ranked as better than the other. Because the transformation is continuous in utility, betterness is preserved for some small decrease in utility. Thus, the principle approves of changes in birth dates even when, in terms of well-being, no one gains and someone loses. A similar argument applies to sensitivity to lifetimes. This suggests that we should reject the conditional Pareto axioms and, instead, opt in favor of intertemporal strong Pareto. If this is done, intertemporal critical-level generalized utilitarianism results.

In spite of these difficulties, special forms of birth-date-dependent principles are employed frequently in economic models. In particular, principles that employ geometric discounting are widely used and, for that reason, we investigate them in some detail.

8.3 STATIONARITY AND DISCOUNTING

Many studies in economics and other social sciences employ criteria based on geometrically discounted utilities to guide policy recommendations. This discounting of utility should be distinguished from the discounting of consumption, a common practice in cost-benefit analysis.

In models that employ geometric discounting, a discount factor between zero and one is used, and each person's lifetime utility is multiplied by the discount factor raised to a power equal to the individual's birth date less one. Because the discount factor may be equal to one or greater than one, the cases of no discounting (all generations receive equal weights) and of "upcounting" (later generations receive higher weights) are included. For simplicity, we use the term discounting for all possible values of the discount factor.

If the population is fixed, the discounted utilities are added. A more general principle uses transformed utilities, where the transformation is independent of birth date and length of life. The class of geometric birth-date-dependent critical-level generalized utilitarian principles employs the sum of the discounted differences between transformed utility and a transformed fixed critical level. Because the transformation can be the identity map, it includes the subclass of geometric birth-date-dependent critical-level utilitarian principles.

Some members of the birth-date-dependent critical-level generalized utilitarian class of population principles employ geometric discounting but many others do not. If an axiom are added to the list that characterizes this class, geometric discounting can be characterized.

Suppose the birth date of every person who is alive in each of two alternatives is moved forward in time by a given number of periods. Stationarity requires their ranking to be unchanged. If it is added to the axioms that characterize the birth-date-dependent critical-level generalized utilitarian orderings, orderings that discount geometrically result. Thus geometric birth-date-dependent critical-level generalized utilitarianism is characterized by intertemporal continuity, birth-date-conditional strong Pareto, intertemporal weak existence of critical levels, birth-date-conditional individual intertemporal equivalence, independence of the existence of the dead, and stationarity. These principles use value functions that are equal to the sum of the discounted values of the differences between unconditionally transformed utilities and an unconditionally transformed fixed critical level.

An ethically attractive property of the principles in the geometric birth-date-dependent critical-level generalized utilitarian class is that critical levels are constant and, therefore, independent of the birth date of the added person. The repugnant conclusion is avoided if and only if the constant critical level is positive.

Although geometric discounting has some properties that can be used in its defense, it has some ethically unattractive features as well. At any time, people are alive who have different birth dates. If geometric discounting is employed, the transformed utilities of the old receive higher weights than those of the young. In addition, these principles favor earlier births, other things equal. And, because of the continuity property, earlier births are favored even at the expense of small decreases in lifetime well-being.[2]

---

[2] This is, of course, a special case of the criticism directed toward all principles that are sensitive to birth date that was discussed in the previous section.

An argument sometimes made in favor of discounting with a discount factor below one is that, if there is an infinite number of periods and no discounting is employed, the resulting value function may not be well-defined because it may fail to yield a finite number for some alternatives. Because the lifetime of the universe is known to be finite, this argument is based on an impossibility. But there is a related argument that is more attractive. It is possible that very large sacrifices by those currently alive may be justified by larger gains to people who will exist in the distant future, and discounting therefore might be thought to be appropriate. This argument rests on the claim that discounting necessarily increases the well-being of the present generation. That claim is, however, not true.

Consider two alternatives x and y in which three people live and are born in periods 1, 2, and 3. In x, utility levels are 28, 4, and 44; in y, utility levels are 24, 24, and 24. If intertemporal critical-level utilitarianism with a critical level of zero is used to evaluate the alternatives, x is better than y and the utility level of person 1, who represents the present generation, is 28. Now suppose geometric birth-date-dependent critical-level utilitarianism with a critical level of zero and a discount factor of $1/2$ is used instead. In that case, values for x and y are $28 + 2 + 11 = 41$ and $24 + 12 + 6 = 42$, so y is better and person 1's utility is 24. Discounting has made the present generation worse off.

Our view of the matter is that, for the purpose of social evaluation, the well-being of future generations should not be discounted. If the present generation finds that maximization requires it to sacrifice most of its consumption for the benefit of others, then such an action, while morally permissible, would be supererogatory: desirable but beyond the call of duty. The same problem arises in a single period. If rich people behave in a way that maximizes a world value function, they may be required to make great sacrifices for the sake of large populations of poor people. We do not and should not attempt to solve the problem by giving the disadvantaged a smaller weight in the world value function. Instead, a sufficiently high level of well-being for the present generation can be guaranteed by imposing a floor on their utility as an additional constraint in an intertemporal choice problem. This seems to be a far more natural way of dealing with the supererogation issue than by transforming an ethically appropriate value function into one that fails to treat generations or contemporaries impartially. See Blackorby, Bossert, and Donaldson (2000) for a detailed discussion, including some counterintuitive comparative-statics results if (geometric or more general) discounting is employed. In addition, see Cowen (1992) and Cowen and Parfit (1992), who present a Paretian argument against discounting.[3]

8.4   FIXED BIRTH DATES

A possible objection to our model is the claim that any individual's birth date is fixed and, thus, that our domain that allows us to assign any birth date to an

---

[3] See also Broome (1992c, pp. 92–108) for further discussions of discounting.

individual is too large. Although it is true that a person cannot be born at a completely arbitrary time, because of the fact that the duration of pregnancy is not
fixed, his or her birth date may vary over several months.[4] Given intertemporal
strong Pareto, this possibility is sufficient to rule out discounting.

Our response to the above objection is subject to another criticism – namely,
that any change in birth date, even if it is only a matter of a single period,
does not allow us to treat the individual born in period t as the same individual
as a person born in period $t + 1$ instead, all else (including lifetime utilities)
the same. This position corresponds to the view that every person's birth date
is a characteristic of that person and cannot be changed without changing the
person. There is an alternative to the approach that we have taken that can
accommodate this criticism. If the domain of the social-evaluation functional
is restricted so that each individual has a fixed birth date, intertemporal strong
Pareto and anonymity can be replaced with a single axiom that extends the
Pareto condition so that it applies anonymously to alternatives with the same
population size. If two alternatives have the same population size and the list
of utilities in the first is a permutation of the list of utilities in the second,
anonymous intertemporal strong Pareto implies that the two alternatives are
ranked as equally good.[5] This possibility is sufficient to rule out discounting.
Similar combined axioms correspond to the other Pareto axioms. We think the
combined axioms have strong ethical appeal and, as a consequence, can serve
as a convincing defense against the objection.

Part B

In an intertemporal environment, we now formalize a special case of the model
employed in Chapter 3. This variation of our model is important because most
variable-population problems are intertemporal in nature; population growth
occurs over time. Instead of abstract nonwelfare information, we focus on birth
dates and lifetimes of those alive to capture intertemporal features of social
evaluation. All other nonwelfare information is assumed to be fixed and therefore can be ignored. It is possible, however, to accommodate multiple profiles
of all nonwelfare information. To investigate population principles in an intertemporal setting, we employ a period analysis with arbitrary period length.
Time is treated as a sequence of periods of finite duration. An information profile provides, for each person, lifetime utility, birth date, and length of life in
each alternative in which the person is alive. We assume that no one can live
more than a fixed number of periods. The maximal lifetime is finite but can be
arbitrarily large.

---

[4] Similarly, although it is unlikely, the date of conception may vary because spermatozoa may
survive for some time.

[5] See also Suppes's (1966) grading principle.

8.5 INTERTEMPORAL SOCIAL EVALUATION

Recall, from Chapter 3, that a variable-population lifetime-utility profile has a countably infinite number of components, one for each potential person. We write it as $U = (U_i)_{i \in Z_{++}}$ where $U_i : X_i \to \mathcal{R}$ for all $i \in Z_{++}$. The set of all possible utility profiles is $\mathcal{U}$. A profile of nonwelfare-information functions is given by $K = (S, L) = ((S_i)_{i \in Z_{++}}, (L_i)_{i \in Z_{++}})$ where $S_i : X_i \to Z_+$ and $L_i : X_i \to \{1, \ldots, \bar{L}\}$ assign the period of birth less one and the length of life of individual $i \in Z_{++}$ to each alternative in which i is alive. No individual can live more than $\bar{L} \in Z_{++}$ periods. The set of all possible period-before-birth-date profiles is S and the set of all possible lifetime profiles is $\mathcal{L}$.

A social-evaluation functional is a mapping $F : \mathcal{D} \to \mathcal{O}$ where $\emptyset \neq \mathcal{D} \subseteq \mathcal{U} \times S \times \mathcal{L}$ and $\mathcal{O}$ is the set of all orderings on X. We write $\Upsilon = (U, S, L)$ and $R_\Upsilon = F(\Upsilon)$ for all $\Upsilon \in \mathcal{D}$. The asymmetric and symmetric factors of R_Υ are P_Υ and I_Υ. Extended unlimited domain is defined in Chapter 3, and it requires that the domain $\mathcal{D}$ is equal to $\mathcal{U} \times S \times \mathcal{L}$.

We assume that, for each possible population, there are at least three alternatives with that population. For $x \in X$, we let $\Pi(x)$ be the vector of identities of those alive in x (see Chapter 3). Utilities, periods before birth, and lifetimes of those alive in x are

$$\mathbf{U}(x) = \big(\mathbf{U}_1(x), \ldots, \mathbf{U}_{\mathbf{n}(x)}(x)\big) = \big(U_{\Pi_1(x)}(x), \ldots, U_{\Pi_{\mathbf{n}(x)}(x)}(x)\big) \in \mathcal{R}^{\mathbf{n}(x)},$$

$$\mathbf{S}(x) = \big(\mathbf{S}_1(x), \ldots, \mathbf{S}_{\mathbf{n}(x)}(x)\big) = \big(S_{\Pi_1(x)}(x), \ldots, S_{\Pi_{\mathbf{n}(x)}(x)}(x)\big) \in Z_+^{\mathbf{n}(x)},$$

and

$$\mathbf{L}(x) = \big(\mathbf{L}_1(x), \ldots, \mathbf{L}_{\mathbf{n}(x)}(x)\big) = \big(L_{\Pi_1(x)}(x), \ldots, L_{\Pi_{\mathbf{n}(x)}(x)}(x)\big)$$
$$\in \{1, \ldots, \bar{L}\}^{\mathbf{n}(x)}.$$

The set of possible combinations of utility vectors, vectors of periods before birth, and lifetime vectors is $\Gamma = \bigcup_{n \in Z_{++}} \mathcal{R}^n \times Z_+^n \times \{1, \ldots, \bar{L}\}^n$. $(u_\emptyset, s_\emptyset, \ell_\emptyset)$ is the compound vector corresponding to the null alternative. For $n \in Z_{++}$, $i \in \{1, \ldots, n\}$, and $u \in \mathcal{R}^n$, we define

$$u_{-i} = \begin{cases} (u_1, \ldots, u_{i-1}, u_{i+1}, \ldots, u_n) & \text{if } n \in Z_{++} \setminus \{1\}, \\ u_\emptyset & \text{if } n = 1. \end{cases}$$

s_{-i} and ℓ_{-i} are defined analogously.

In the context of the intertemporal model considered in this chapter, we explore the implications of weakening the Pareto axioms. First, consider Pareto indifference. If, in addition to lifetime utilities, we allow birth dates and lengths of life to matter in social evaluation, we obtain the following axiom.

Conditional Pareto Indifference. For all $x, y \in X$ such that $\mathbf{N}(x) = \mathbf{N}(y)$ and for all $\Upsilon \in \mathcal{D}$, if $U_i(x) = U_i(y)$, $S_i(x) = S_i(y)$, and $L_i(x) = L_i(y)$ for all $i \in \mathbf{N}(x)$, then $x I_\Upsilon y$.

We assume that the social-evaluation functional satisfies extended binary independence of irrelevant alternatives and extended anonymity as defined in Chapter 3. The following theorem specifies the information that can be used in social evaluation if conditional Pareto indifference is added. Because its proof is analogous to the proofs of the welfarism theorems of Chapter 3, it is omitted. Let $n \in \mathcal{Z}_{++}$. An ordering R_{SL}^n on $\mathcal{R}^n \times \mathcal{Z}_+^n \times \{1, \dots, \bar{L}\}^n$ is anonymous if and only if, for all $(u, s, \ell) \in \mathcal{R}^n \times \mathcal{Z}_+^n \times \{1, \dots, \bar{L}\}^n$ and for all bijections $\rho^n \colon \{1, \dots, n\} \to \{1, \dots, n\}$,

$$\left((u_{\rho^n(1)}, \dots, u_{\rho^n(n)}), (s_{\rho^n(1)}, \dots, s_{\rho^n(n)}), (\ell_{\rho^n(1)}, \dots, \ell_{\rho^n(n)})\right) I_{SL}^n (u, s, \ell).$$

An ordering R_{SL} on Γ is anonymous if and only if, for all $n \in \mathcal{Z}_{++}$, the restriction of R_{SL} to $\mathcal{R}^n \times \mathcal{Z}_+^n \times \{1, \dots, \bar{L}\}^n$ is anonymous.

Theorem 8.1. *Suppose F satisfies extended unlimited domain. F satisfies conditional Pareto indifference, extended binary independence of irrelevant alternatives, and extended anonymity if and only if there exists an anonymous social-evaluation ordering R_{SL} on Γ such that, for all $x, y \in X$ and for all $\Upsilon \in \mathcal{D}$,*

$$x R_\Upsilon y \Leftrightarrow (\mathbf{U}(x), \mathbf{S}(x), \mathbf{L}(x)) R_{SL} (\mathbf{U}(y), \mathbf{S}(y), \mathbf{L}(y)).$$

8.6 INTERTEMPORAL AXIOMS

Given Theorem 8.1, we can formulate intertemporal axioms in terms of the ordering R_{SL}. In addition to our basic axioms, we introduce conditional versions of the strong Pareto principle and three variants of a new axiom, which ensures that the birth date of an individual can be changed to a specific birth date (common for all individuals) without changing the social ranking, provided the individual's lifetime utility is suitably adjusted. We begin with intertemporal versions of continuity and strong Pareto.

Continuity can be adapted to the intertemporal model in a straightforward manner. We require the social ranking to be continuous in lifetime utilities for any possible fixed population size and for any fixed pair of birth-date vectors and lifetime vectors.

Intertemporal Continuity. For all $n \in \mathcal{Z}_{++}$ and for all $(u, s, \ell) \in \mathcal{R}^n \times \mathcal{Z}_+^n \times \{1, \dots, \bar{L}\}^n$, the sets $\{v \in \mathcal{R}^n \mid (v, s, \ell) R_{SL}(u, s, \ell)\}$ and $\{v \in \mathcal{R}^n \mid (u, s, \ell) R_{SL}(v, s, \ell)\}$ are closed in $\mathcal{R}^n$.

The intertemporal version of the strong Pareto principle has two parts, each of which applies to fixed-population comparisons only. First, if each individual has the same lifetime utilities in two alternatives, they are ranked as equally good by the social ranking. Second, if everyone's utility is greater than or equal in one alternative than in another with at least one strict inequality, the former is better than the latter.

Intertemporal Strong Pareto. For all $n \in \mathcal{Z}_{++}$ and for all $(u, s, \ell), (v, r, k) \in \mathcal{R}^n \times \mathcal{Z}_+^n \times \{1, \ldots, \bar{L}\}^n$,

   (i) if $u = v$, then $(u, s, \ell) I_{SL}(v, r, k)$;
   (ii) if $u > v$, then $(u, s, \ell) P_{SL}(v, r, k)$.

Whereas intertemporal strong Pareto rules out the influence of nonutility information, the following conditional versions of the axiom permit some nonwelfare information to matter. The axioms apply the principle conditionally on birth dates and lifetimes, on birth dates only, and on lifetimes only, respectively.

Conditional Strong Pareto. For all $n \in \mathcal{Z}_{++}$ and for all $(u, s, \ell), (v, r, k) \in \mathcal{R}^n \times \mathcal{Z}_+^n \times \{1, \ldots, \bar{L}\}^n$,

   (i) if $s = r$, $\ell = k$, and $u = v$, then $(u, s, \ell) I_{SL}(v, r, k)$;
   (ii) if $s = r$, $\ell = k$, and $u > v$, then $(u, s, \ell) P_{SL}(v, r, k)$.

Birth-Date Conditional Strong Pareto. For all $n \in \mathcal{Z}_{++}$ and for all (u, s, ℓ), $(v, r, k) \in \mathcal{R}^n \times \mathcal{Z}_+^n \times \{1, \ldots, \bar{L}\}^n$,

   (i) if $s = r$ and $u = v$, then $(u, s, \ell) I_{SL}(v, r, k)$;
   (ii) if $s = r$ and $u > v$, then $(u, s, \ell) P_{SL}(v, r, k)$.

Lifetime Conditional Strong Pareto. For all $n \in \mathcal{Z}_{++}$ and for all (u, s, ℓ), $(v, r, k) \in \mathcal{R}^n \times \mathcal{Z}_+^n \times \{1, \ldots, \bar{L}\}^n$,

   (i) if $\ell = k$ and $u = v$, then $(u, s, \ell) I_{SL}(v, r, k)$;
   (ii) if $\ell = k$ and $u > v$, then $(u, s, \ell) P_{SL}(v, r, k)$.

Part (i) of conditional strong Pareto is redundant because R_{SL} is an ordering and, therefore, reflexive. We have included it to use the same structure as in the other strong Pareto axioms.

An intertemporal version of weak existence of critical levels requires the existence of at least one critical level for some birth date and lifetime of the added individual.

Intertemporal Weak Existence of Critical Levels. There exist $(u, s, \ell) \in \Gamma$ and $(c, \sigma, \lambda) \in \mathcal{R} \times \mathcal{Z}_+ \times \{1, \ldots, \bar{L}\}$ such that $((u, c), (s, \sigma), (\ell, \lambda)) I_{SL}(u, s, \ell)$.

Finally, we introduce an axiom we call individual intertemporal equivalence and two conditional versions of it. Individual intertemporal equivalence and its conditional counterparts ensure that, by suitably changing an individual's lifetime utility, the birth date of the person can be moved to a prespecified period without changing the social ranking. These conditions imply that nondegenerate trade-offs between birth dates or lifetimes and utilities are possible.

Individual Intertemporal Equivalence. There exists $\lambda_0 \in \{1, \ldots, \bar{L}\}$ such that, for all $(d, \sigma, \lambda) \in \mathcal{R} \times \mathcal{Z}_+ \times \{1, \ldots, \bar{L}\}$ and for all $\sigma_0 \in \mathcal{Z}_+$, there exists $\hat{d} \in \mathcal{R}$ such that, for all $n \in \mathcal{Z}_{++}$, for all $(u, s, \ell) \in \mathcal{R}^n \times \mathcal{Z}_+^n \times \{1, \ldots, \bar{L}\}^n$, and for all $i \in \{1, \ldots, n\}$,

$$\big((u_{-i}, \hat{d}), (s_{-i}, \sigma_0), (\ell_{-i}, \lambda_0)\big) \, I_{SL}\big((u_{-i}, d), (s_{-i}, \sigma), (\ell_{-i}, \lambda)\big).$$

Birth-Date Conditional Individual Intertemporal Equivalence. There exists $\lambda_0 \in \{1, \ldots, \bar{L}\}$ such that, for all $(d, \sigma) \in \mathcal{R} \times \mathcal{Z}_+$ and for all $\sigma_0 \in \mathcal{Z}_+$, there exists $\hat{d} \in \mathcal{R}$ such that, for all $n \in \mathcal{Z}_{++}$, for all $(u, s) \in \mathcal{R}^n \times \mathcal{Z}_+^n$, and for all $i \in \{1, \ldots, n\}$,

$$\big((u_{-i}, \hat{d}), (s_{-i}, \sigma_0), \lambda_0 \mathbf{1}_n\big) \, I_{SL}\big((u_{-i}, d), (s_{-i}, \sigma), \lambda_0 \mathbf{1}_n\big).$$

Lifetime Conditional Individual Intertemporal Equivalence. There exist $\sigma_0 \in \mathcal{Z}_+$ and $\lambda_0 \in \{1, \ldots, \bar{L}\}$ such that, for all $(d, \lambda) \in \mathcal{R} \times \{1, \ldots, \bar{L}\}$, there exists $\hat{d} \in \mathcal{R}$ such that, for all $n \in \mathcal{Z}_{++}$, for all $(u, \ell) \in \mathcal{R}^n \times \{1, \ldots, \bar{L}\}^n$, and for all $i \in \{1, \ldots, n\}$,

$$\big[(u_{-i}, \hat{d}), \sigma_0 \mathbf{1}_n, (\ell_{-i}, \lambda_0)\big] \, I_{SL}\big[(u_{-i}, d), \sigma_0 \mathbf{1}_n, (\ell_{-i}, \lambda)\big].$$

8.7 INTERTEMPORAL INDEPENDENCE

When policy decisions are made in period t, all feasible alternatives have a common history but the lifetime utilities of some members of society may not be fixed. If person i is alive in period $t - 1$, there may be alternatives in which i's life extends to period t and possibly beyond, whereas, in other alternatives, i dies at the end of period $t - 1$. This suggests that history must matter to some extent if lifetime utilities are to be taken into consideration. On the other hand, the same arguments that can be made in favor of the existence-independence axiom in an atemporal model apply in this intertemporal framework. If, at any time, an individual's life is over in two alternatives and he or she had the same lifetime utility, birth date, and lifetime in both, a plausible requirement is that the ranking of the two alternatives does not depend on whether that individual existed. In the present setting, this leads to an independence condition whose scope is limited: it applies only if the sets of those whose lives are over are identical in two alternatives and, moreover, everyone in this set had the same lifetime utility, the same birth date, and the same length of life in both.

Independence of the Existence of the Dead. For all $n, m, q \in \mathcal{Z}_{++}$, for all $(u, s, \ell) \in \mathcal{R}^n \times \mathcal{Z}_+^n \times \{1, \ldots, \bar{L}\}^n$, for all $(v, r, k) \in \mathcal{R}^m \times \mathcal{Z}_+^m \times \{1, \ldots, \bar{L}\}^m$, for all $(\bar{u}, \bar{s}, \bar{\ell}) \in \mathcal{R}^q \times \mathcal{Z}_+^q \times \{1, \ldots, \bar{L}\}^q$, and for all $t \in \mathcal{Z}_{++}$, if

$\bar{s}_i + \bar{\ell}_i < t$ for all $i \in \{1, \ldots, q\}$, $s_i + 1 \geq t$ for all $i \in \{1, \ldots, n\}$ and $r_i + 1 \geq t$ for all $i \in \{1, \ldots, m\}$, then

$$\big((u, \bar{u}), (s, \bar{s}), (\ell, \bar{\ell})\big) R_{SL}\big((v, \bar{u}), (r, \bar{s}), (k, \bar{\ell})\big) \Leftrightarrow (u, s, \ell) R_{SL}(v, r, k).$$

Independence of the existence of the dead is a weak separability condition because it applies to individuals whose lives are over before period t only and not to all unconcerned individuals. Thus, if all generations overlap, it does not impose any restrictions. However, when combined with intertemporal strong Pareto or one of the conditional versions thereof, the axiom becomes more powerful.

The main result of this chapter provides characterizations of critical-level generalized utilitarianism and related principles in our intertemporal setting. In each of the definitions of the first three classes of principles, a condition regarding the possibility of equalizing the values of the requisite transformation for different birth dates or lifetimes is imposed. This condition is required to ensure that the relevant individual intertemporal equivalence property is satisfied.

R_{SL} is a birth-date- and lifetime-dependent critical-level generalized utilitarian principle if and only if there exist a function $h: \mathcal{R} \times \mathcal{Z}_+ \times \{1, \ldots, \bar{L}\} \to \mathcal{R}$, continuous and increasing in its first argument, $\lambda_0 \in \{1, \ldots, \bar{L}\}$, and $\alpha \in \mathcal{R}$ such that $h(0, 0, \lambda_0) = 0$, $h(\mathcal{R}, \sigma_0, \lambda_0) \cap h(\mathcal{R}, \sigma, \lambda) \neq \emptyset$ for all $\sigma_0, \sigma \in \mathcal{Z}_+$, and for all $\lambda \in \{1, \ldots, \bar{L}\}$, and for all $n, m \in \mathcal{Z}_{++}$, for all $(u, s, \ell) \in \mathcal{R}^n \times \mathcal{Z}_+^n \times \{1, \ldots, \bar{L}\}^n$, and for all $(v, r, k) \in \mathcal{R}^m \times \mathcal{Z}_+^m \times \{1, \ldots, \bar{L}\}^m$,

$$(u, s, \ell) R_{SL}(v, r, k) \Leftrightarrow \sum_{i=1}^{n} [h(u_i, s_i, \ell_i) - h(\alpha, 0, \lambda_0)]$$

$$\geq \sum_{i=1}^{m} [h(v_i, r_i, k_i) - h(\alpha, 0, \lambda_0)].$$

Analogously, R_{SL} is a birth-date-dependent critical-level generalized utilitarian principle if and only if there exist a function $f: \mathcal{R} \times \mathcal{Z}_+ \to \mathcal{R}$, continuous and increasing in its first argument, and $\alpha \in \mathcal{R}$ such that $f(0, 0) = 0$, $f(\mathcal{R}, \sigma_0) \cap f(\mathcal{R}, \sigma) \neq \emptyset$ for all $\sigma_0, \sigma \in \mathcal{Z}_+$ and for all $n, m \in \mathcal{Z}_{++}$, for all $(u, s, \ell) \in \mathcal{R}^n \times \mathcal{Z}_+^n \times \{1, \ldots, \bar{L}\}^n$, and for all $(v, r, k) \in \mathcal{R}^m \times \mathcal{Z}_+^m \times \{1, \ldots, \bar{L}\}^m$,

$$(u, s, \ell) R_{SL}(v, r, k) \Leftrightarrow \sum_{i=1}^{n} [f(u_i, s_i) - f(\alpha, 0)]$$

$$\geq \sum_{i=1}^{m} [f(v_i, r_i) - f(\alpha, 0)].$$

R_{SL} is a lifetime-dependent critical-level generalized utilitarian principle if and only if there exist a function $e: \mathcal{R} \times \{1, \ldots, \bar{L}\} \to \mathcal{R}$, continuous and increasing in its first argument, $\lambda_0 \in \{1, \ldots, \bar{L}\}$, and $\alpha \in \mathcal{R}$ such that $e(0, \lambda_0) = 0$, $e(\mathcal{R}, \lambda_0) \cap e(\mathcal{R}, \lambda) \neq \emptyset$ for all $\lambda \in \{1, \ldots, \bar{L}\}$, and for all $n, m \in \mathcal{Z}_{++}$, for all $(u, s, \ell) \in \mathcal{R}^n \times \mathcal{Z}_+^n \times \{1, \dots, \bar{L}\}^n$, and for all $(v, r, k) \in \mathcal{R}^m \times \mathcal{Z}_+^m \times \{1, \dots, \bar{L}\}^m$,

$$(u, s, \ell) R_{SL}(v, r, k) \Leftrightarrow \sum_{i=1}^{n} [e(u_i, \ell_i) - e(\alpha, \lambda_0)]$$

$$\geq \sum_{i=1}^{m} [e(v_i, k_i) - e(\alpha, \lambda_0)].$$

Finally, R_{SL} is an intertemporal critical-level generalized utilitarian principle if and only if there exist a continuous and increasing function $g: \mathcal{R} \to \mathcal{R}$ and $\alpha \in \mathcal{R}$ such that $g(0) = 0$ and for all $n, m \in \mathcal{Z}_{++}$, for all $(u, s, \ell) \in \mathcal{R}^n \times \mathcal{Z}_+^n \times \{1, \dots, \bar{L}\}^n$, and for all $(v, r, k) \in \mathcal{R}^m \times \mathcal{Z}_+^m \times \{1, \dots, \bar{L}\}^m$,

$$(u, s, \ell) R_{SL}(v, r, k) \Leftrightarrow \sum_{i=1}^{n} [g(u_i) - g(\alpha)] \geq \sum_{i=1}^{m} [g(v_i) - g(\alpha)].$$

We now provide characterizations of these intertemporal principles by combining independence of the existence of the dead with the various intertemporal versions of strong Pareto.

Theorem 8.2.
  (i) R_{SL} satisfies intertemporal continuity, conditional strong Pareto, intertemporal weak existence of critical levels, individual intertemporal equivalence, and independence of the existence of the dead if and only if R_{SL} is birth-date- and lifetime-dependent critical-level generalized utilitarian.
  (ii) R_{SL} satisfies intertemporal continuity, birth-date conditional strong Pareto, intertemporal weak existence of critical levels, birth-date conditional individual intertemporal equivalence, and independence of the existence of the dead if and only if R_{SL} is birth-date-dependent critical-level generalized utilitarian.
  (iii) R_{SL} satisfies intertemporal continuity, lifetime conditional strong Pareto, intertemporal weak existence of critical levels, lifetime conditional individual intertemporal equivalence, and independence of the existence of the dead if and only if R_{SL} is lifetime-dependent critical-level generalized utilitarian.
  (iv) R_{SL} satisfies intertemporal continuity, intertemporal strong Pareto, intertemporal weak existence of critical levels, and independence of the existence of the dead if and only if R_{SL} is intertemporal critical-level generalized utilitarian.

Proof. First, we consider Part (i). That the birth-date- and lifetime-dependent critical-level generalized utilitarian principles satisfy the axioms is straightforward to verify. Note that the nonemptiness of $h(\mathcal{R}, \sigma_0, \lambda_0) \cap h(\mathcal{R}, \sigma, \lambda)$ for all $\sigma_0, \sigma \in \mathcal{Z}_+$ and for all $\lambda \in \{1, \dots, \bar{L}\}$ in the definition of the principles guarantees that individual intertemporal equivalence is satisfied.

Now suppose R_{SL} is an anonymous ordering satisfying the required axioms. The proof that R_{SL} is birth-date- and lifetime-dependent critical-level generalized utilitarian proceeds as follows. We define an ordering R on Ω (that is, an ordering of utility vectors) as the restriction of R_{SL} that is obtained by fixing all birth dates and lengths of life. We then show that R satisfies the axioms of Theorem 6.10 and, thus, must be critical-level generalized utilitarian. Finally, we show that all comparisons according to R_{SL} can be carried out by applying R to utilities that depend on birth dates and lifetimes, resulting in birth-date- and lifetime-dependent critical-level generalized utilitarianism.

Let λ_0 be as in the definition of individual intertemporal equivalence. Define the ordering R on Ω by letting, for all $n, m \in \mathcal{Z}_{++}$, for all $u \in \mathcal{R}^n$, and for all $v \in \mathcal{R}^m$,

$$u R v \Leftrightarrow (u, 01_n, \lambda_0 1_n) R_{SL} (v, 01_m, \lambda_0 1_m).$$

Clearly, R is an anonymous ordering satisfying continuity and strong Pareto.

Next, we show that R satisfies weak existence of critical levels. By intertemporal weak existence of critical levels, there exist $n \in \mathcal{Z}_{++}, (u, s, \ell) \in \mathcal{R}^n \times \mathcal{Z}_+^n \times \{1, \dots, \bar{L}\}^n$ and $(c, \sigma, \lambda) \in \mathcal{R} \times \mathcal{Z}_+ \times \{1, \dots, \bar{L}\}$ such that

$$((u, c), (s, \sigma), (\ell, \lambda)) I_{SL}(u, s, \ell).$$

By repeated application of individual intertemporal equivalence, there exist $\lambda_0 \in \{1, \dots, \bar{L}\}, \bar{u} \in \mathcal{R}^n$, and $\bar{c} \in \mathcal{R}$ such that

$$(\bar{u}, 01_n, \lambda_0 1_n) I_{SL}(u, s, \ell)$$

and

$$((\bar{u}, \bar{c}), 01_{n+1}, \lambda_0 1_{n+1}) I_{SL} ((u, c), (s, \sigma), (\ell, \lambda)).$$

Note that $\bar{u}_i$ may depend on (u_i, s_i, ℓ_i) for all $i \in \{1, \dots, n\}$ and $\bar{c}$ may depend on (c, σ, λ). By transitivity, we obtain

$$((\bar{u}, \bar{c}), 01_{n+1}, \lambda_0 1_{n+1}) I_{SL}(\bar{u}, 01_n, \lambda_0 1_n)$$

which, by definition of R, is equivalent to

$$(\bar{u}, \bar{c}) I \bar{u}.$$

Thus, $\bar{c}$ is a critical level for $\bar{u}$ and weak existence of critical levels is satisfied.

The last remaining property of R to be established is existence independence. Let $n, m, q \in \mathcal{Z}_{++}, u \in \mathcal{R}^n, v \in \mathcal{R}^m$, and $w \in \mathcal{R}^q$. By repeated application of individual intertemporal equivalence, there exist $\lambda_0 \in \{1, \dots, \bar{L}\}, \hat{u} \in \mathcal{R}^n$ and $\hat{v} \in \mathcal{R}^m$ such that

$$\left((\hat{u}, w), (\bar{L}1_n, 01_q), \lambda_0 1_{n+q}\right) I_{SL}\left((u, w), 01_{n+q}, \lambda_0 1_{n+q}\right)$$

and

$$\left((\hat{v}, w), (\bar{L}\mathbf{1}_m, 0\mathbf{1}_q), \lambda_0\mathbf{1}_{m+q}\right) I_{SL}\left((v, w), 0\mathbf{1}_{m+q}, \lambda_0\mathbf{1}_{m+q}\right).$$

Thus,

$$\begin{aligned}
\left((u, w), 0\mathbf{1}_{n+q}, \lambda_0\mathbf{1}_{n+q}\right) & R_{SL}\left((v, w), 0\mathbf{1}_{m+q}, \lambda_0\mathbf{1}_{m+q}\right) \\
& \Leftrightarrow \left((\hat{u}, w), (\bar{L}\mathbf{1}_n, 0\mathbf{1}_q), \lambda_0\mathbf{1}_{n+q}\right) R_{SL} \left((\hat{v}, w), (\bar{L}\mathbf{1}_m, 0\mathbf{1}_q), \lambda_0\mathbf{1}_{m+q}\right).
\end{aligned}$$
$$(8.1)$$

By independence of the existence of the dead,

$$\begin{aligned}
\left((\hat{u}, w), (\bar{L}\mathbf{1}_n, 0\mathbf{1}_q), \lambda_0\mathbf{1}_{n+q}\right) & R_{SL} \left((\hat{v}, w), (\bar{L}\mathbf{1}_m, 0\mathbf{1}_q), \lambda_0\mathbf{1}_{m+q}\right) \\
& \Leftrightarrow \left(\hat{u}, \bar{L}\mathbf{1}_n, \lambda_0\mathbf{1}_n\right) R_{SL} \left(\hat{v}, \bar{L}\mathbf{1}_m, \lambda_0\mathbf{1}_m\right).
\end{aligned}$$
$$(8.2)$$

Because

$$\left(\hat{u}, \bar{L}\mathbf{1}_n, \lambda_0\mathbf{1}_n\right) I_{SL}(u, 0\mathbf{1}_n, \lambda_0\mathbf{1}_n)$$

and

$$\left(\hat{v}, \bar{L}\mathbf{1}_m, \lambda_0\mathbf{1}_m\right) I_{SL}(v, 0\mathbf{1}_m, \lambda_0\mathbf{1}_m)$$

by individual intertemporal equivalence, it follows that

$$\begin{aligned}
\left(\hat{u}, \bar{L}\mathbf{1}_n, \lambda_0\mathbf{1}_n\right) & R_{SL} \left(\hat{v}, \bar{L}\mathbf{1}_m, \lambda_0\mathbf{1}_m\right) \\
& \Leftrightarrow (u, 0\mathbf{1}_n, \lambda_0\mathbf{1}_n) R_{SL}(v, 0\mathbf{1}_m, \lambda_0\mathbf{1}_m).
\end{aligned}$$
$$(8.3)$$

Combining (8.1), (8.2), and (8.3), we obtain

$$\begin{aligned}
\left((u, w), 0\mathbf{1}_{n+q}, \lambda_0\mathbf{1}_{n+q}\right] & R_{SL}\left[(v, w), 0\mathbf{1}_{m+q}, \lambda_0\mathbf{1}_{m+q}\right) \\
& \Leftrightarrow (u, 0\mathbf{1}_n, \lambda_0\mathbf{1}_n) R_{SL}(v, 0\mathbf{1}_m, \lambda_0\mathbf{1}_m),
\end{aligned}$$

which, by definition, is equivalent to

$$(u, w)R(v, w) \Leftrightarrow u R v$$

and existence independence is satisfied.

By Theorem 6.10, R is critical-level generalized utilitarian and, thus, there exist a continuous and increasing function $g: \mathcal{R} \to \mathcal{R}$ with $g(0) = 0$ and a critical level $\alpha \in \mathcal{R}$ such that

$$u R v \Leftrightarrow \sum_{i=1}^{n} \left[g(u_i) - g(\alpha)\right] \geq \sum_{i=1}^{m} \left[g(v_i) - g(\alpha)\right]$$

for all $n, m \in \mathcal{Z}_{++}$, for all $u \in \mathcal{R}^n$, and for all $v \in \mathcal{R}^m$.

Let $\lambda_0 \in \{1, \dots, \bar{L}\}$ be as in the definition of individual intertemporal equivalence and define the function $\bar{h}: \mathcal{R} \times \mathcal{Z}_+ \times \{1, \dots, \bar{L}\} \to \mathcal{R}$ by

$$\bar{h}(d, \sigma, \lambda) = \gamma \Leftrightarrow (d, \sigma, \lambda) I_{SL}(\gamma, 0, \lambda_0)$$

for all $(d, \sigma, \lambda) \in \mathcal{R} \times \mathcal{Z}_+ \times \{1, \dots, \bar{L}\}$ and for all $\gamma \in \mathcal{R}$. This function is well-defined because of individual intertemporal equivalence.

Now let $n, m \in \mathcal{Z}_{++}$, $(u, s, \ell) \in \mathcal{R}^n \times \mathcal{Z}_+^n \times \{1, \dots, \bar{L}\}^n$, and $(v, r, k) \in \mathcal{R}^m \times \mathcal{Z}_+^m \times \{1, \dots, \bar{L}\}^m$. By repeated application of individual intertemporal equivalence,

$$\left(\left(\bar{h}(u_i, s_i, \ell_i) \right)_{i=1}^n, 0\mathbf{1}_n, \lambda_0 \mathbf{1}_n \right) I_{SL}(u, s, l)$$

and

$$\left(\left(\bar{h}(v_i, r_i, k_i) \right)_{i=1}^m, 0\mathbf{1}_m, \lambda_0 \mathbf{1}_m \right) I_{SL}(v, r, k).$$

Therefore,

$$(u, s, \ell) R_{SL}(v, r, k)$$
$$\Leftrightarrow \left(\left(\bar{h}(u_i, s_i, \ell_i) \right)_{i=1}^n, 0\mathbf{1}_n, \lambda_0 \mathbf{1}_n \right) R_{SL} \left(\left(\bar{h}(v_i, r_i, k_i) \right)_{i=1}^m, 0\mathbf{1}_m, \lambda_0 \mathbf{1}_m \right)$$
$$\Leftrightarrow \left(\bar{h}(u_i, s_i, \ell_i) \right)_{i=1}^n R \left(\bar{h}(v_i, r_i, k_i) \right)_{i=1}^m$$
$$\Leftrightarrow \sum_{i=1}^n \left[g \left(\bar{h}(u_i, s_i, \ell_i) \right) - g(\alpha) \right] \geq \sum_{i=1}^m \left[g \left(\bar{h}(v_i, r_i, k_i) \right) - g(\alpha) \right].$$

Noting that $\bar{h}(\alpha, 0, \lambda_0) = \alpha$ by definition and letting $h = g \circ \bar{h}$, it follows that

$$(u, s, \ell) R_{SL}(v, r, k) \Leftrightarrow \sum_{i=1}^n \left[h(u_i, s_i, \ell_i) - h(\alpha, 0, \lambda_0) \right]$$
$$\geq \sum_{i=1}^m \left[h(v_i, r_i, k_i) - h(\alpha, 0, \lambda_0) \right].$$

That h satisfies $h(0, 0, \lambda_0) = 0$ and $h(\mathcal{R}, \sigma_0, \lambda_0) \cap h(\mathcal{R}, \sigma, \lambda) \neq \emptyset$ for all $\sigma_0, \sigma \in \mathcal{Z}_+$ and for all $\lambda \in \{1, \dots, \bar{L}\}$ follows from the definitions of $\bar{h}$ and h.

The proofs of Parts (ii) through (iv) of the theorem are analogous. Because R_{SL} is independent of lifetimes in Part (ii) and independent of birth dates in Part (iii), the corresponding weakenings of individual intertemporal equivalence are sufficient for the characterization results. In Part (iv), the axiom can be dispensed with altogether because, by intertemporal strong Pareto, the ordering cannot depend on either birth dates or lifetimes. ∎

8.8 GEOMETRIC DISCOUNTING

We now turn to an important subclass of the birth-date-dependent critical-level generalized utilitarian principles. A common procedure for allowing birth dates to matter is to employ geometric discounting. In that case, a fixed discount factor $\delta \in \mathcal{R}_{++}$ is chosen and the difference between person i's transformed utility and the transformed critical level is multiplied by δ^{s_i}. Thus, we define a class of birth-date-dependent principles as follows. The ordering R_{SL} is geometric birth-date-dependent critical-level generalized utilitarian if and only if there exist a continuous and increasing function $g: \mathcal{R} \to \mathcal{R}$, $\alpha \in \mathcal{R}$, and $\delta \in \mathcal{R}_{++}$ such that $g(0) = 0$ and, for all $n, m \in \mathcal{Z}_{++}$, for all $(u, s, \ell) \in \mathcal{R}^n \times \mathcal{Z}_+^n \times \{1, \dots, \bar{L}\}^n$, and for all $(v, r, k) \in \mathcal{R}^m \times \mathcal{Z}_+^m \times \{1, \ldots, \bar{L}\}^m$,

$$(u, s, \ell) R_{SL}(v, r, k) \Leftrightarrow \sum_{i=1}^{n} \delta^{s_i} [g(u_i) - g(\alpha)]$$

$$\geq \sum_{i=1}^{m} \delta^{r_i} [g(v_i) - g(\alpha)].$$

We do not endorse these principles because we believe that intertemporal strong Pareto is a compelling axiom and, thus, only utility information should matter. However, because of the important status geometric discounting enjoys in intertemporal economic models, we provide a characterization of these principles to illustrate their properties and the ethical judgments underlying their use.

A characterization can be obtained by adding an axiom to the set of properties employed in Part (ii) of Theorem 8.2. Stationarity requires that the ranking of any two elements of Γ is unchanged if, ceteris paribus, the birth date of everyone alive is moved into the future by any number of periods in both. This is one of the most commonly used restrictions on multiperiod social-evaluation principles.

Stationarity. For all $n, m \in \mathcal{Z}_{++}$, for all $(u, s, \ell) \in \mathcal{R}^n \times \mathcal{Z}_+^n \times \{1, \ldots, \bar{L}\}^n$, for all $(v, r, k) \in \mathcal{R}^m \times \mathcal{Z}_+^m \times \{1, \ldots, \bar{L}\}^m$, and for all $\tau \in \mathcal{Z}_{++}$,

$$(u, s + \tau \mathbf{1}_n, \ell) R_{SL}(v, r + \tau \mathbf{1}_m, k) \Leftrightarrow (u, s, \ell) R_{SL}(v, r, k).$$

We now obtain a characterization of geometric birth-date-dependent critical-level generalized utilitarianism.

Theorem 8.3. *R_{SL} satisfies intertemporal continuity, birth-date conditional strong Pareto, intertemporal weak existence of critical levels, birth-date conditional individual intertemporal equivalence, independence of the existence of the dead, and stationarity if and only if R_{SL} is geometric birth-date-dependent critical-level generalized utilitarian.*

Proof. That geometric birth-date-dependent critical-level generalized utilitarianism satisfies the axioms of the theorem statement is straightforward to verify.

Conversely, suppose R_{SL} satisfies the required axioms. By Theorem 8.2, R_{SL} is birth-date-dependent critical-level generalized utilitarian. Let f and α be as in the definition of birth-date-dependent critical-level generalized utilitarianism and define the function $g: \mathcal{R} \to \mathcal{R}$ by $g(d) = f(d, 0)$ for all $d \in \mathcal{R}$. It is sufficient to show that there exists $\delta \in \mathcal{R}_{++}$ such that

$$f(d, \sigma) = \delta^\sigma [g(d) - g(\alpha)] + g(\alpha)$$

for all $(d, \sigma) \in \mathcal{R} \times \mathcal{Z}_+$.

Stationarity implies that, for all $(u, \ell), (v, k) \in \mathcal{R}^2 \times \{1, \ldots, \bar{L}\}^2$ and for all $\sigma, \tau \in \mathcal{Z}_{++}$,

$$(u, (\sigma + \tau)\mathbf{1}_2, \ell) R_{SL}(v, (\sigma + \tau)\mathbf{1}_2, k) \Leftrightarrow (u, \sigma \mathbf{1}_2, \ell) R_{SL}(v, \sigma \mathbf{1}_2, k).$$

Applying birth-date-dependent critical-level generalized utilitarianism, this is equivalent to

$$f(u_1, \sigma + \tau) + f(u_2, \sigma + \tau) \geq f(v_1, \sigma + \tau) + f(v_2, \sigma + \tau)$$
$$\Leftrightarrow f(u_1, \sigma) + f(u_2, \sigma) \geq f(v_1, \sigma) + f(v_2, \sigma).$$

Thus, for each $\tau \in \mathcal{Z}_+$, there exists an increasing function $\varphi_\tau : \mathcal{R} \to \mathcal{R}$ such that

$$f(u_1, \sigma + \tau) + f(u_2, \sigma + \tau) = \varphi_\tau(f(u_1, \sigma) + f(u_2, \sigma))$$

for all $u \in \mathcal{R}^2$ and for all $\sigma, \tau \in \mathcal{Z}_+$. For each $\sigma \in \mathcal{Z}_+$, define the function $\bar{g}_\sigma : f(\mathcal{R}, \sigma) \to \mathcal{R}$ by

$$\bar{g}_\sigma(\gamma) = d \Leftrightarrow f(d, \sigma) = \gamma$$

for all $\gamma \in f(\mathcal{R}, \sigma)$ and for all $d \in \mathcal{R}$ – that is, $\bar{g}_\sigma$ is the inverse of f with respect to its first argument for the fixed value σ of its second argument. Now let $x = f(u_1, \sigma)$, $y = f(u_2, \sigma)$, and $\bar{f}(z, \sigma + \tau) = f(\bar{g}_\sigma(z), \sigma + \tau)$ to obtain the functional equation

$$\bar{f}(x, \sigma + \tau) + \bar{f}(y, \sigma + \tau) = \varphi_\tau(x + y).$$

This is a Pexider equation in the variables x and y, the solution of which satisfies

$$\bar{f}(z, \sigma + \tau) = a(\tau)z + b(\tau).$$

a and b do not depend on σ because φ_τ does not. Substituting back into the definition of $\bar{f}$, we obtain

$$f(d, \sigma + \tau) = a(\tau)f(d, \sigma) + b(\tau) \tag{8.4}$$

for all $d \in \mathcal{R}$ and for all $\sigma, \tau \in \mathcal{Z}_+$. Setting $\sigma = 0$, it follows that

$$f(d, \tau) = a(\tau)f(d, 0) + b(\tau) = a(\tau)g(d) + b(\tau) \tag{8.5}$$

for all $d \in \mathcal{R}$ and for all $\tau \in \mathcal{Z}_+$. Therefore,

$$f(d, \sigma + \tau) = a(\sigma + \tau)g(d) + b(\sigma + \tau) \tag{8.6}$$

for all $d \in \mathcal{R}$ and for all $\sigma, \tau \in \mathcal{Z}_+$. Setting $\tau = 0$ in (8.5), we obtain

$$f(d, 0) = a(0)g(d) + b(0)$$

for all $d \in \mathcal{R}$. Because $f(d, 0) = g(d)$ for all $d \in \mathcal{R}$ and $g(0) = 0$, this implies that $a(0) = 1$ and $b(0) = 0$. Substituting (8.5) into (8.4), we obtain, for all $d \in \mathcal{R}$ and for all $\sigma, \tau \in \mathcal{Z}_+$,

$$f(d, \sigma + \tau) = a(\tau)[a(\sigma)g(d) + b(\sigma)] + b(\tau). \tag{8.7}$$

Combining (8.6) and (8.7), it follows that

$$a(\sigma + \tau)g(d) + b(\sigma + \tau) = a(\tau)[a(\sigma)g(d) + b(\sigma)] + b(\tau)$$

or, equivalently,

$$[a(\sigma + \tau) - a(\tau)a(\sigma)]g(d) = a(\tau)b(\sigma) + b(\tau) - b(\sigma + \tau).$$

Because g is increasing and the right side of this equation is independent of d, it must be the case that both sides are identically zero, which requires

$$a(\sigma + \tau) = a(\tau)a(\sigma) \tag{8.8}$$

for all $\sigma, \tau \in \mathcal{Z}_+$. Defining $\delta = a(1)$, repeated application of (8.8) implies, for all $\sigma \in \mathcal{Z}_+$, $a(\sigma + 1) = \delta^{\sigma+1}$. By (8.5),

$$f(d, \sigma) = a(\sigma)g(d) + b(\sigma) = \delta^{\sigma} g(d) + b(\sigma) \tag{8.9}$$

for all $d \in \mathcal{R}$ and for all $\sigma \in \mathcal{Z}_+$. Because R_{SL} is birth-date-dependent critical-level generalized utilitarian, stationarity implies $f(\alpha, \sigma) = f(\alpha, 0) = g(\alpha)$. It follows that

$$f(\alpha, 0) = g(\alpha) = \delta^{\sigma} g(\alpha) + b(\sigma) = f(\alpha, \sigma)$$

and, therefore,

$$b(\sigma) = g(\alpha) - \delta^{\sigma} g(\alpha)$$

for all $\sigma \in \mathcal{Z}_+$. Substituting into (8.9) yields

$$f(d, \sigma) = \delta^{\sigma} [g(d) - g(\alpha)] + g(\alpha).$$

By birth-date conditional strong Pareto, δ must be positive. ∎

CHAPTER 9

Temporal Consistency

Part A

In this chapter, we consider an intertemporal model in which individual well-being in each period when a person is alive is measured by a utility function. This allows us to formulate consistency conditions across periods. The first of these requires the ranking of any two alternatives whose per-period utilities differ in a single period only to be independent of utilities in other periods. Thus, social evaluations can be made on a per-period basis. The second, which is weaker, requires the ranking of two alternatives with a common past to be independent of past utilities but permits utilities in the present and future to influence it. When combined with some standard axioms, both consistency properties have undesirable consequences, the most important of which is that the repugnant conclusion is implied. Counterintuitive recommendations about killing are avoided, but at a significant cost. We conclude that both temporal-consistency axioms should be abandoned in favor of axioms such as independence of the existence of the dead, which allows history to matter by taking account of the possibility that individual lives may be over in some alternatives but continue into the present in others.

9.1 WELL-BEING IN EACH PERIOD

As in Chapter 8, we employ a multiperiod model with arbitrary period length. If a person ever lives, he or she is alive in a collection of contiguous periods and the maximum lifetime (in periods) is fixed at a finite number greater than one. An information profile provides, for each alternative and each potential person, a utility level for each period in which the person is alive (see Chapter 2 for a discussion) together with periods before birth, lengths of life, and other fixed nonwelfare information. Information for a possible alternative is provided in Table 9.1. In it, individuals 2, 21, 1,024, and 1,729 are alive in periods 4 to 9, 1 to 6, 7 only, and 3 to 5 with per-period utilities given by the entries in the table. Neutrality in a period is represented by a per-period utility of zero.

Table 9.1. *Per-Period Utilities*

	1	2	3	4	5	6	7	8	9	10	...
Person 2				30	20	0	15	15	−10		
Person 21	−10	15	−10	15	10	5					
Person 1024							0				
Person 1729			32	−10	0						

A temporal social-evaluation functional associates an ordering of the alternatives with each information profile. If the functional satisfies temporal analogues of the axioms extended unlimited domain, Pareto indifference (which allows us to disregard birth dates and lengths of life), binary independence of irrelevant alternatives, and extended anonymity, then there is a single ordering of arrays of per-period utility information (called matrices in Part B), such as the one in Table 9.1, augmented with blank entries for all those people who never live. The ordering can be used, together with utility information in a profile, to rank alternatives. This is the temporal analogue of the standard welfarism theorem (see Chapter 3).

For each individual, lifetime utility is a function of utility levels for periods when the person is alive (see Chapter 2). These aggregator functions are assumed to possess several fundamental properties. The axiom individual welfarism requires, for each possible length of life, lifetime utility to be a continuous and increasing function of per-period utilities. Furthermore, if a person lives for a single period only, lifetime utility is equal to the utility level in that period. Thus, in the alternative represented in Table 9.1, individual 1,024's lifetime utility is zero. Finally, the addition of a single period at neutrality, utility levels in other periods unchanged, leaves lifetime utility unchanged. Although we consider multiple profiles of per-period utility functions, we assume there is a single profile of aggregator functions. Together with the per-period utility functions, these functions produce standard lifetime-utility functions, which are defined on the set of alternatives.

9.2 TEMPORAL CONSISTENCY

Full temporal consistency guarantees that per-period social evaluations can be performed in a meaningful way. Consider any period t and two alternatives such that the per-period utility information is the same in all periods other than t. The axiom full temporal consistency requires their ranking to be independent of the (common) per-period utilities in the other periods. As a consequence, a well-defined per-period ranking that is consistent with the overall ordering exists for each period. We formulate the full-temporal-consistency axiom as a property of the welfarist ranking of arrays of per-period utilities. This is simpler than defining it for the underlying temporal social-evaluation functional and involves no loss of generality in the presence of the welfarism axioms.

Table 9.2. *Full Temporal Consistency*

	Alternative x				Alternative y			
	1	2	3	4	1	2	3	4
Person 2		20	20			20	20	
Person 5		12				12	8	

Full temporal consistency is a very demanding requirement. In particular, together with some standard axioms, it implies that both the overall social ranking and the implied per-period orderings satisfy the repugnant conclusion. To illustrate, consider the alternatives x and y described in Table 9.2.

In x and y, individuals 2 and 5 are the only people who ever live. Person 2 is alive in periods two and three in both alternatives, and person 5 is alive in period two only in x and in periods two and three in y. Utility information differs in period three only and principles for per-period social evaluation may be applied to the utility levels in that period alone. For example, from the viewpoint of period three, average utilitarianism and critical-level utilitarianism with a critical level of 10 both rank x as better but classical utilitarianism ranks y as better. By individual welfarism and Pareto indifference, however, x is as good, from a timeless point of view, as an alternative in which person 2's utilities are unchanged but person 5 lives in periods two and three with utility levels of 12 and 0. Therefore, the period-three critical level is zero. It follows that full temporal consistency and the multiperiod formulation of strong Pareto require y to be ranked as better than x. The argument can be generalized to show that, from the point of view of any single period after period one, critical levels must be zero. In Part B, we demonstrate that critical levels for period one also must be zero.

If a critical level for a per-period ordering is positive, counterintuitive recommendations about killing can occur. In the example, average utilitarianism and critical-level utilitarianism with a critical level of 10 rank x as better. Thus, it would be better if person 5 were to die, painlessly and unexpectedly, at the end of period two even though, in alternative y, his or her life is worth living in period three. Individual welfarism prevents this and it follows that critical levels must be zero.

Full temporal consistency and our other axioms imply further restrictions. The functions that aggregate per-period utilities into lifetime utility must be the same for each individual and must exhibit an additively separable structure where the same transformation is used in each period. In addition, the implied per-period orderings must be classical generalized utilitarian using the same transformation as the one used in the aggregator functions. Thus, the transformation represents an attitude toward inequality of per-period utilities over each individual's lifetime and it also represents the social attitude toward inequality of utilities in each period. This result, together with the requirement that all critical levels be zero, implies that all principles that satisfy full temporal consistency and our other axioms imply the repugnant conclusion.

This suggests that full temporal consistency is much too strong and that we should look for less demanding axioms. One such possibility is forward-looking consistency. At any time, it permits alternatives to be ranked by looking at information from that time forward only, without consideration of past information, provided that the alternatives have a common past.

Forward-looking consistency provides no relief from the strictures of full temporal consistency, however. Together with our other axioms, it has the same implications for the individual aggregator functions, for the timeless social ranking, and for the implied per-period orderings. Thus, again, any principle that satisfies the axioms leads to the repugnant conclusion.

Full temporal consistency and forward-looking consistency have been investigated with weaker Pareto axioms that permit discounting (Blackorby, Bossert, and Donaldson 1997a). Although this enlarges the set of possible population principles considerably, the discounting (or upcounting) of future utilities does not provide an escape from the ethically unattractive consequences of the temporal consistency conditions in the no-discounting environment. Similar restrictions on the individual aggregator functions result and all principles that satisfy the axioms imply the repugnant conclusion.

We conclude from these results that both full temporal consistency and forward-looking consistency are requirements that are much too strong and suggest that less demanding axioms, such as independence of the existence of the dead, be employed instead. That axiom permits history to matter by taking account of the possibility that some people who were born in the past have lives that may extend into the present or future.

Part B

We now consider a model in which, in addition to lifetime utilities, birth dates, and lifetimes, per-period utilities (utilities experienced in each period of the lifetime of an individual) may matter. Thus, for each individual who is alive, we record, in addition to lifetime utility, a utility number for each period of his or her life. This allows us to impose independence conditions across periods. For example, we can now require the social ranking of two alternatives to be independent of past per-period utilities if, from the viewpoint of a given time period, the two alternatives have a common past. We investigate the consequences of axioms of that nature in the remaining sections of this chapter.

9.3 TEMPORAL SOCIAL EVALUATION

To define a suitable framework for temporal social evaluation, it is convenient to use the following convention regarding individual per-period utilities. Consider an individual $i \in \mathcal{Z}_{++}$ and a time period $t \in \mathcal{Z}_{++}$. If, in an alternative in X, i is alive in period t, i's per-period utility in t is a real number; if i is not alive in t, this situation is described by assigning the per-period null alternative $w_\emptyset$ to i and t. Thus, we can define a family of per-period utility functions $W_i^t: X \to \mathcal{R} \cup \{w_\emptyset\}$, where $W_i^t(x) \in \mathcal{R}$ if individual i is alive in period t in $x \in X$ and $W_i^t(x) = w_\emptyset$ otherwise. Neutrality in a period is represented by a per-period utility level of zero. We assume that: (i) for all $x \in X$, the set of individuals $i \in \mathcal{Z}_{++}$ such that there exists a period $t \in \mathcal{Z}_{++}$ with $W_i^t(x) \neq w_\emptyset$ is nonempty and finite; and (ii) for all $x \in X$ and for all $i \in \mathcal{Z}_{++}$, the set of periods $t \in \mathcal{Z}_{++}$ such that $W_i^t(x) \neq w_\emptyset$ is composed of at most $\bar{L} \geq 2$ contiguous periods. A per-period utility profile is $W = (W_i^t)_{i, t \in \mathcal{Z}_{++}}$. The set of all possible per-period utility profiles is $\mathcal{W}$. We let $W(x) = (W_i^t(x))_{i, t \in \mathcal{Z}_{++}}$ for all $x \in X$.

Clearly, once $W(x)$ is known for some $x \in X$, we can identify the set of individuals alive in x and, for each of them, his or her birth date and lifetime. This is accomplished by defining

$$\mathbf{N}(x) = \{i \in \mathcal{Z}_{++} \mid \exists t \in \mathcal{Z}_{++} \text{ such that } W_i^t(x) \in \mathcal{R}\}$$

and, for all $i \in \mathbf{N}(x)$,

$$S_i(x) = \min\{t \in \mathcal{Z}_{++} \mid W_i^t(x) \in \mathcal{R}\} - 1$$

and

$$L_i(x) = \max\{t \in \mathcal{Z}_{++} \mid W_i^t(x) \in \mathcal{R}\} - S_i(x).$$

$\mathbf{N}(x)$ as well as $S_i(x)$ and $L_i(x)$ for all $i \in \mathbf{N}(x)$ are well-defined because of restrictions (i) and (ii) introduced above. Other nonwelfare information is assumed to be fixed. Because it plays no role in our theorems, we do not include it in our notation.

For an alternative $x \in X$, we can think of $W(x)$ as an infinite-dimensional matrix satisfying the following restrictions. Let $\mathbf{W}$ be the set of all matrices $\mathbf{w}$ with typical entry $w_i^t \in \mathcal{R} \cup \{w_\emptyset\}$ such that: (i) the set of $i \in \mathcal{Z}_{++}$ such that there exists $t \in \mathcal{Z}_{++}$ with $w_i^t \neq w_\emptyset$ is nonempty and finite; and (ii) for all $i \in \mathcal{Z}_{++}$, the set of periods $t \in \mathcal{Z}_{++}$ such that $w_i^t \neq w_\emptyset$ is composed of at most $\bar{L}$ contiguous periods. It follows that $W(x) \in \mathbf{W}$ for all $x \in X$. For $\mathbf{w} \in \mathbf{W}$ and for $t \in \mathcal{Z}_{++}$, we define

$$\Theta_t(\mathbf{w}) = \{i \in \mathcal{Z}_{++} \mid w_i^t \in \mathcal{R}\}$$

and

$$\Theta(\mathbf{w}) = \{i \in \mathcal{Z}_{++} \mid \exists t \in \mathcal{Z}_{++} \text{ such that } i \in \Theta_t(\mathbf{w})\}.$$

That is, $\Theta_t(\mathbf{w})$ is the set of all individuals who are alive in period t in $\mathbf{w}$ and $\Theta(\mathbf{w})$ is the set of all individuals who ever live in $\mathbf{w}$.

For $i \in \Theta(\mathbf{w})$, we let $\sigma_i(\mathbf{w})$ be the period before i is born and we use $\lambda_i(\mathbf{w})$ to denote the lifetime of individual i. Let $\mathbf{W}_{\bar{L}n}$ be the subset of $\mathbf{W}$ that contains all matrices $\mathbf{w}$ such that $\Theta_t(\mathbf{w}) = \{1, \ldots, n\}$ for all $t \in \{1, \ldots, \bar{L}\}$ and $\Theta_t(\mathbf{w}) = \emptyset$ for all $t > \bar{L}$. $\mathbf{W}_{\bar{L}n}$ is the set of all matrices where the n individuals $1, \ldots, n$ ever live and they all are born in period 1 and live for $\bar{L}$ periods. For a given individual $i \in \mathcal{Z}_{++}$, we define w_i to be the vector of all real components w_i^t of $\mathbf{w}$. Analogously, for a given period $t \in \mathcal{Z}_{++}$, w^t is the vector of all real components w_i^t of $\mathbf{w}$. Finally, for $\mathbf{w} \in \mathbf{W}_{\bar{L}n}$, $w \in \mathcal{R}^{\bar{L}n}$ consists of all real entries in $\mathbf{w}$.

A temporal social-evaluation functional is a mapping $G \colon \mathcal{E} \to \mathcal{O}$ where $\emptyset \neq \mathcal{E} \subseteq \mathcal{W}$ and, as before, $\mathcal{O}$ is the set of all orderings on X. We write $R_W = G(W)$ for all $W \in \mathcal{E}$. The asymmetric and symmetric factors of R_W are P_W and I_W. As in Chapter 8, we assume that, for each possible population, there are at least three alternatives with that population.

We obtain the following temporal versions of an unlimited-domain assumption, a Pareto-indifference condition, an independence-of-irrelevant-alternatives axiom, and extended anonymity.

Temporal Extended Unlimited Domain. $\mathcal{E} = \mathcal{W}$.

Temporal Pareto Indifference. For all x, $y \in X$ and for all $W \in \mathcal{E}$, if $W(x) = W(y)$, then $x I_W y$.

Temporal Extended Binary Independence of Irrelevant Alternatives. For all x, $y \in X$ and for all W, $\bar{W} \in \mathcal{E}$, if $W(x) = \bar{W}(x)$ and $W(y) = \bar{W}(y)$, then

$$x R_W y \Leftrightarrow x R_{\bar{W}} y.$$

Temporal Extended Anonymity. For all x, $y \in X$ and for all $W \in \mathcal{E}$, if there exists a bijection $\rho \colon \mathcal{Z}_{++} \to \mathcal{Z}_{++}$ such that $W_i^t(x) = W_{\rho(i)}^t(y)$ for all $i, t \in \mathcal{Z}_{++}$, then $x I_W y$.

An ordering $\mathbf{R}_T$ on $\mathbf{W}$ is anonymous if and only if, for all $\mathbf{w}$, $\mathbf{v} \in \mathbf{W}$ and for all bijections $\rho \colon \mathcal{Z}_{++} \to \mathcal{Z}_{++}$, if $w_i^t = v_{\rho(i)}^t$ for all $i, t \in \mathcal{Z}_{++}$, then $\mathbf{w} I_T \mathbf{v}$.

As in Chapters 3 and 8, we can now identify the information required to rank the alternatives for each profile given the above axioms. We obtain the following theorem which is analogous to Theorem 3.14.

Theorem 9.1. *Suppose G satisfies temporal extended unlimited domain. G satisfies temporal Pareto indifference, temporal extended binary independence of irrelevant alternatives, and temporal extended anonymity if and only if there exists an anonymous temporal social-evaluation ordering $\mathbf{R}_T$ on $\mathbf{W}$ such that, for all x, $y \in X$ and for all $W \in \mathcal{E}$,*

$$x R_W y \Leftrightarrow W(x) \mathbf{R}_T W(y).$$

We now impose some restrictions on the ordering $\mathbf{R}_T$. First, we introduce an axiom that requires individual lifetime utilities to be functions of the per-period utilities. In addition, we normalize utilities so that the lifetime utility of an agent who is alive in a single period only is equal to the single per-period utility. Moreover, the addition of a period of life at neutrality leaves lifetime utility unchanged. We call this axiom individual welfarism; see Chapter 2 for a suitably formulated continuity condition guaranteeing the existence of a representation of an ordering of individual per-period utility vectors.

Individual Welfarism. For all $i \in \mathcal{Z}_{++}$, there exists a function $U_i^W : \bigcup_{\ell_i=1}^{\bar{L}} \mathcal{R}^{\ell_i} \to \mathcal{R}$, whose restrictions to $\mathcal{R}^{\ell_i}$ are continuous and increasing for all $\ell_i \in \{1, \ldots, \bar{L}\}$, such that:

(i) $U_i^W(w_i) = w_i$ for all $w_i \in \mathcal{R}$;
(ii) $U_i^W(w_i, 0) = U_i^W(w_i)$ for all $w_i \in \bigcup_{\ell_i=1}^{\bar{L}-1} \mathcal{R}^{\ell_i}$.

The following continuity axiom is a multiperiod version adapted to the ordering $\mathbf{R}_T$. We require the axiom to hold only for each fixed population size $n \in \mathcal{Z}_{++}$ where each of the n individuals is born in period one and has a lifetime of $\bar{L}$.

Multiperiod Continuity. For all $n \in \mathcal{Z}_{++}$ and for all $\mathbf{w} \in \mathbf{W}_{\bar{L}n}$, the sets $\{v \in \mathcal{R}^{\bar{L}n} \mid v\mathbf{R}_T\mathbf{w}\}$ and $\{v \in \mathcal{R}^{\bar{L}n} \mid \mathbf{w}\mathbf{R}_Tv\}$ are closed in $\mathcal{R}^{\bar{L}n}$.

As usual, the strong Pareto principle applies to situations of unanimity regarding individual lifetime utilities. The indifference part of the axiom is now required explicitly because the temporal Pareto-indifference axiom introduced earlier applies to per-period utilities rather than lifetime utilities.

Multiperiod Strong Pareto. For all $n \in \mathcal{Z}_{++}$ and for all $\mathbf{w}, \mathbf{v} \in \mathbf{W}$ such that $\Theta(\mathbf{w}) = \{1, \ldots, n\}$,

(i) if $U_i^W(w_i) = U_i^W(v_i)$ for all $i \in \Theta(\mathbf{w})$, then $\mathbf{w}\mathbf{I}_T\mathbf{v}$;
(ii) if $U_i^W(w_i) \geq U_i^W(v_i)$ for all $i \in \Theta(\mathbf{w})$ with at least one strict inequality, then $\mathbf{w}\mathbf{P}_T\mathbf{v}$.

An anonymity condition with respect to lifetime utilities follows from the anonymity of $\mathbf{R}_T$, individual welfarism and multiperiod strong Pareto.

Multiperiod Anonymity. For all $\mathbf{w}, \mathbf{v} \in \mathbf{W}_{\bar{L}n}$, if there exists a bijection $\rho : \Theta(\mathbf{w}) \to \Theta(\mathbf{v})$ such that $U_i^W(w_i) = U_{\rho(i)}^W(v_{\rho(i)})$ for all $i \in \Theta(\mathbf{w})$, then $\mathbf{w}\mathbf{I}_T\mathbf{v}$.

9.4   FULL TEMPORAL CONSISTENCY

The first consistency condition we impose in this temporal model is full temporal consistency. Consider any time period t. The axiom requires that, if any two elements of $\mathbf{W}$ differ in column $t \in \mathcal{Z}_{++}$ only, their ranking according to $\mathbf{R}_T$ does not depend on the entries in periods other than t. This means that $\mathbf{R}_T$ induces a per-period ordering for each period and, using this per-period ordering, social evaluations can be made in each period t based on the per-period utilities experienced in t only.

Full Temporal Consistency. For all $\mathbf{w}, \mathbf{v}, \bar{\mathbf{w}}, \bar{\mathbf{v}} \in \mathbf{W}$ and for all $t \in \mathcal{Z}_{++}$, if $w_i^t = \bar{w}_i^t$ and $v_i^t = \bar{v}_i^t$ for all $i \in \mathcal{Z}_{++}$, and $w_i^\tau = v_i^\tau$ and $\bar{w}_i^\tau = \bar{v}_i^\tau$ for all $i \in \mathcal{Z}_{++}$ and for all $\tau \in \mathcal{Z}_{++} \setminus \{t\}$, then

$$\mathbf{w}\mathbf{R}_T\mathbf{v} \Leftrightarrow \bar{\mathbf{w}}\mathbf{R}_T\bar{\mathbf{v}}.$$

Full temporal consistency is a powerful axiom. The following theorem identifies the principles that satisfy full temporal consistency and some basic properties. All these principles have zero critical levels and, thus, lead to the repugnant conclusion. Moreover, the functions U_i^W must be identical for all $i \in \mathcal{Z}_{++}$. Clearly, different people may have different attitudes toward the intertemporal substitution of individual well-being and, therefore, this equality cannot be expected to be satisfied in general. Whenever the individual functions U_i^W differ, the axioms are incompatible and, as a consequence, we conclude that full temporal consistency is much too demanding.

Theorem 9.2. *Suppose individual welfarism is satisfied.* $\mathbf{R}_T$ *satisfies multi-period continuity, multiperiod strong Pareto, and full temporal consistency if and only if there exists a continuous and increasing function* $g: \mathcal{R} \to \mathcal{R}$ *with* $g(0) = 0$ *such that:*

(i) *for all* $i \in \mathcal{Z}_{++}$, *for all* $s_i \in \mathcal{Z}_+$, *for all* $\ell_i \in \{1, \ldots, \bar{L}\}$, *and for all* $w_i \in \mathcal{R}^{\ell_i}$,

$$U_i^W(w_i) = g^{-1}\left(\sum_{t=s_i+1}^{s_i+\ell_i} g(w_i^t)\right);$$

(ii) *for all* $\mathbf{w}, \mathbf{v} \in \mathbf{W}$,

$$\mathbf{w}\mathbf{R}_T\mathbf{v} \Leftrightarrow \sum_{i\in\Theta(\mathbf{w})} g\left(U_i^W(w_i)\right) \geq \sum_{i\in\Theta(\mathbf{v})} g\left(U_i^W(v_i)\right)$$

$$\Leftrightarrow \sum_{i\in\Theta(\mathbf{w})} \sum_{t=\sigma_i(\mathbf{w})+1}^{\sigma_i(\mathbf{w})+\lambda_i(\mathbf{w})} g(w_i^t) \geq \sum_{i\in\Theta(\mathbf{v})} \sum_{t=\sigma_i(\mathbf{v})+1}^{\sigma_i(\mathbf{v})+\lambda_i(\mathbf{v})} g(v_i^t).$$

Proof. Clearly, the principles defined in the theorem statement satisfy the axioms.

Now let $n \geq 2$. By multiperiod continuity and Debreu's (1959, pp. 56–59) representation theorem, there exists a continuous function $f^n: \mathcal{R}^{\bar{L}n} \to \mathcal{R}$ such that, for all $\mathbf{w}, \mathbf{v} \in \mathbf{W}_{\bar{L}n}$,

$$\mathbf{w}\mathbf{R}_T\mathbf{v} \Leftrightarrow f^n(w) \geq f^n(v). \tag{9.1}$$

Multiperiod strong Pareto implies that f^n is increasing. By full temporal consistency, the vector $w^t \in \mathcal{R}^n$ is separable from its complement in f^n for all $t \in \{1, \ldots, \bar{L}\}$. Thus, using multiperiod continuity and multiperiod strong Pareto, there exist continuous and increasing functions $J^n: \mathcal{R}^{\bar{L}} \to \mathcal{R}$ and $f_1^n, \ldots, f_{\bar{L}}^n: \mathcal{R}^n \to \mathcal{R}$ such that

$$f^n(w) = J^n\left(f_1^n(w^1), \ldots, f_{\bar{L}}^n(w^{\bar{L}})\right)$$

for all $w \in \mathbf{W}_{\bar{L}n}$. Analogously, multiperiod strong Pareto implies that the vector $w_i \in \mathcal{R}^{\bar{L}}$ is separable from its complement in f^n for all $i \in \{1, \ldots, n\}$. This, together with multiperiod continuity and individual welfarism, implies that there exists a continuous and increasing function $G^n: \mathcal{R}^n \to \mathcal{R}$ such that

$$f^n(w) = G^n\left(U_1^W(w_1), \ldots, U_n^W(w_n)\right) \tag{9.2}$$

for all $w \in \mathbf{W}_{\bar{L}n}$. Gorman's (1968) theorem on overlapping separable sets of variables (see also Aczél 1966, p. 312; Blackorby, Primont, and Russell 1978, p. 127) implies that f^n is additively separable and there exist continuous and increasing functions $H^n: \mathcal{R} \to \mathcal{R}$ and $g_{it}^n: \mathcal{R} \to \mathcal{R}$ for all $i \in \{1, \ldots, n\}$ and for all $t \in \{1, \ldots, \bar{L}\}$ such that

$$f^n(w) = H^n\left(\sum_{i=1}^n \sum_{t=1}^{\bar{L}} g_{it}^n(w_i^t)\right) \tag{9.3}$$

for all $w \in \mathbf{W}_{\bar{L}n}$. Without loss of generality, the g_{it}^n can be chosen so that $g_{it}^n(0) = 0$. Furthermore, multiperiod anonymity (which follows from the axioms in the theorem statement) implies that each g_{it}^n can be chosen to be independent of i and we write it as g_t^n.

Let $i \in \{1, \ldots, n\}$ and consider $w \in \mathbf{W}_{\bar{L}n}$ such that $w_j^t = 0$ for all $j \in \{1, \ldots, n\} \setminus \{i\}$ and for all $t \in \{1, \ldots, \bar{L}\}$. Because $g_t^n(0) = 0$ for all $t \in \{1, \ldots, \bar{L}\}$, individual welfarism implies that $U_j^W(w_j) = 0$ for all $j \in \{1, \ldots, n\} \setminus \{i\}$. Substituting into (9.2) and using (9.3) with $g_{it}^n = g_t^n$, it follows that

$$H^n\left(\sum_{t=1}^{\bar{L}} g_t^n(w_i^t)\right) = G^n\left(U_i^W(w_i), 0\mathbf{1}_{n-1}\right)$$

for all $w_i \in \mathcal{R}^{\bar{L}}$. Solving, we obtain the existence of a continuous and increasing function $\Phi_i^n: \mathcal{R} \to \mathcal{R}$ such that

$$U_i^W(w_i) = \Phi_i^n\left(\sum_{t=1}^{\bar{L}} g_t^n(w_i^t)\right) \tag{9.4}$$

for all $w_i \in \mathcal{R}^{\bar{L}}$. Because the left side of (9.4) is independent of n, so is the right side and it follows that we can choose Φ_i^n and the g_t^n to be independent of n. Writing the resulting functions as Φ_i and g_t, (9.4) becomes

$$U_i^W(w_i) = \Phi_i\left(\sum_{t=1}^{\bar{L}} g_t(w_i^t)\right)$$

for all $w_i \in \mathcal{R}^{\bar{L}}$. By definition of U_i^W, it follows that

$$U_i^W(w_i) = \Phi_i \left(\sum_{t=s_i+1}^{s_i+\bar{L}} g_t(w_i^t) \right)$$

for all $s_i \in \mathcal{Z}_+$ and for all $w_i \in \mathcal{R}^{\bar{L}}$. Therefore, g_t can be chosen to be independent of t, and we write it as g. Using $g(0) = 0$ and individual welfarism, it follows that

$$U_i^W(w_i) = g^{-1} \left(\sum_{t=s_i+1}^{s_i+\ell_i} g(w_i^t) \right) \tag{9.5}$$

for all $s_i \in \mathcal{Z}_+$, for all $\ell_i \in \{1, \dots, \bar{L}\}$, and for all $w_i \in \mathcal{R}^{\ell_i}$, establishing Part (i) of the theorem.

Combining (9.1), (9.3), and the observation that $g_{it}^n = g$, it follows that

$$\mathbf{w} \mathbf{R}_T \mathbf{v} \Leftrightarrow \sum_{i=1}^{n} \sum_{t=1}^{\bar{L}} g(w_i^t) \geq \sum_{i=1}^{n} \sum_{t=1}^{\bar{L}} g(v_i^t) \tag{9.6}$$

for all $\mathbf{w}, \mathbf{v} \in \mathbf{W}_{\bar{L}n}$. (9.6) permits us to rank any two matrices in $\mathbf{W}_{\bar{L}n}$ for $n \geq 2$ and, by multiperiod anonymity, any two matrices with the same number of people who all live from period 1 to period $\bar{L}$. This result can be extended to $n = 1$ in a straightforward manner. Let $\mathbf{w}, \mathbf{v} \in \mathbf{W}_{\bar{L}1}$. By multiperiod strong Pareto, (9.5) and the increasingness of g, it follows that

$$\mathbf{w} \mathbf{R}_T \mathbf{v} \Leftrightarrow U_1^W(w_1) \geq U_1^W(v_1)$$

$$\Leftrightarrow g^{-1} \left(\sum_{t=1}^{\bar{L}} g(w_1^t) \right) \geq g^{-1} \left(\sum_{t=1}^{\bar{L}} g(v_1^t) \right)$$

$$\Leftrightarrow \sum_{t=1}^{\bar{L}} g(w_1^t) \geq \sum_{t=1}^{\bar{L}} g(v_1^t)$$

and, thus, (9.6) is true for $n = 1$ as well.

Let $\mathbf{w} \in \mathbf{W}$ and suppose $\Theta(\mathbf{w})$ contains $n \in \mathcal{Z}_{++}$ elements. Consider a matrix $\bar{\mathbf{w}} \in \mathbf{W}$ such that the same n people as in $\mathbf{w}$ are alive and all of them are born in period 1 and have the same lifetimes and per-period utilities as in $\mathbf{w}$. This implies that their lifetime utilities are the same in $\mathbf{w}$ and in $\bar{\mathbf{w}}$ and, by multiperiod strong Pareto, we have $\bar{\mathbf{w}} \mathbf{I}_T \mathbf{w}$. For all individuals $i \in \Theta(\bar{\mathbf{w}}) = \Theta(\mathbf{w})$ whose lifetime is less than $\bar{L}$, replace all entries in columns less than or equal to $\bar{L}$ that are equal to $w_\emptyset$ with zero to obtain the matrix $\mathbf{w}'$. By individual welfarism, $\mathbf{w}' \mathbf{I}_T \bar{\mathbf{w}}$ and transitivity implies $\mathbf{w}' \mathbf{I}_T \mathbf{w}$. By construction, $\mathbf{w}'$ is in $\mathbf{W}_{\bar{L}n}$ and it follows that knowledge of the ranking of all matrices in $\bigcup_{n \in \mathcal{Z}_{++}} \mathbf{W}_{\bar{L}n}$ is sufficient to rank all matrices in $\mathbf{W}$. Within each $\mathbf{W}_{\bar{L}n}$, all comparisons are made according to (9.6). We now determine critical levels to be able to make comparisons across population sizes as well.

Let $n, t \in \mathcal{Z}_{++}$ with $t > 1$ and let $\mathbf{w}, \mathbf{v} \in \mathbf{W}$ be such that $\Theta_t(\mathbf{w}) = \{1, \ldots, n\}$ and $(n + 1) \in \Theta_{t-1}(\mathbf{w})$, and the only difference between $\mathbf{v}$ and $\mathbf{w}$ is that $v_{n+1}^t = 0$ while $w_{n+1}^t = w_\emptyset$. By individual welfarism, the lifetime utility of person $n + 1$ is unchanged when moving from $\mathbf{w}$ to $\mathbf{v}$ and, because no one else is affected by the change, multiperiod strong Pareto implies $\mathbf{v}\mathbf{I}_T\mathbf{w}$. Thus, replacing any $w_\emptyset$ with zero in period t leads to a matrix that is equally good according to $\mathbf{R}_T$.

Now let $n \in \mathcal{Z}_{++}$ and $t = 1$. Let $\mathbf{w}, \mathbf{v} \in \mathbf{W}$ be such that, in $\mathbf{w}$, there are n people alive and everyone is born in period 2 with a lifetime of one and, in $\mathbf{v}$, the same n individuals are alive and are born in period 1 and have a lifetime of one with the same (per-period and lifetime) utility as in $\mathbf{w}$. Multiperiod strong Pareto implies $\mathbf{w}\mathbf{I}_T\mathbf{v}$. Thus, given transitivity, because replacing $w_\emptyset$ with zero in period 2 leads to a matrix that is equally good, the same must be true for replacing $w_\emptyset$ with zero in period 1. It follows that the critical-level result regarding the replacement of $w_\emptyset$ with zero applies to all periods $t \in \mathcal{Z}_{++}$.

Let $\mathbf{w}, \mathbf{v} \in \mathbf{W}$. Suppose there are $n \in \mathcal{Z}_{++}$ people alive in $\mathbf{w}$ and $m \in \mathcal{Z}_{++}$ people are alive in $\mathbf{v}$. Without loss of generality, suppose $n \geq m$, $\Theta(\mathbf{w}) = \{1, \ldots, n\}$, and $\Theta(\mathbf{v}) = \{1, \ldots, m\}$. Let $\mathbf{w}'$, and $\mathbf{v}'$ be such that $\mathbf{w}' \in \mathbf{W}_{\bar{L}n}$, $\mathbf{v}' \in \mathbf{W}_{\bar{L}m}$, $\mathbf{w}'\mathbf{I}_T\mathbf{w}$, and $\mathbf{v}'\mathbf{I}_T\mathbf{v}$. Define $\mathbf{v}'' \in \mathbf{W}_{\bar{L}n}$ by adding $(n - m)$ individuals to $\mathbf{v}'$ who are born in period 1, live for $\bar{L}$ periods, and have a per-period utility of zero in each period. Because zero is a critical level in each period, it follows that $\mathbf{v}'\mathbf{I}_T\mathbf{v}''$ and, by transitivity, $\mathbf{v}\mathbf{I}_T\mathbf{v}''$. Using (9.6), Part (i), and $g(0) = 0$, it follows that

$$\mathbf{w}\mathbf{R}_T\mathbf{v} \Leftrightarrow \mathbf{w}'\mathbf{R}_T\mathbf{v}''$$

$$\Leftrightarrow \sum_{i=1}^{n}\sum_{t=1}^{\bar{L}} g(w_i^t) \geq \sum_{i=1}^{m}\sum_{t=1}^{\bar{L}} g(v_i^t) + (n - m)\bar{L}g(0)$$

$$\Leftrightarrow \sum_{i \in \Theta(\mathbf{w})} g\left(U_i^W(w_i)\right) \geq \sum_{i \in \Theta(\mathbf{v})} g\left(U_i^W(v_i)\right) + (n - m)\bar{L}g(0)$$

$$\Leftrightarrow \sum_{i \in \Theta(\mathbf{w})} g\left(U_i^W(w_i)\right) \geq \sum_{i \in \Theta(\mathbf{v})} g\left(U_i^W(v_i)\right)$$

$$\Leftrightarrow \sum_{i \in \Theta(\mathbf{w})} \sum_{t=\sigma_i(\mathbf{w})+1}^{\sigma_i(\mathbf{w})+\lambda_i(\mathbf{w})} g(w_i^t) \geq \sum_{i \in \Theta(\mathbf{v})} \sum_{t=\sigma_i(\mathbf{v})+1}^{\sigma_i(\mathbf{v})+\lambda_i(\mathbf{v})} g(v_i^t)$$

which establishes Part (ii) of the theorem.   ∎

The principles for per-period social evaluation induced by the orderings of Theorem 9.2 use the sum $\sum_{i \in \Theta_t(\mathbf{w})} g(w_i^t)$ [or zero if $\Theta_t(\mathbf{w}) = \emptyset$] as the criterion for period t rankings. As is the case for $\mathbf{R}_T$, these per-period principles imply the repugnant conclusion. We conclude this section by reemphasizing that the axioms used in the theorem statement (in particular, full temporal consistency) are too demanding. The repugnant conclusion is implied and, moreover, an impossibility results if, as is likely the case, individuals differ with respect to the way they trade off well-being across periods. Thus, more reasonable temporal consistency properties are called for.

9.5 FORWARD-LOOKING CONSISTENCY

Given the result of Theorem 9.2, a natural question is whether more satisfactory multiperiod principles can be obtained if full temporal consistency is replaced by an alternative separability property. A natural candidate is an axiom that requires the present and the future to be separable from the past. Thus, this axiom permits us to define forward-looking orderings, one for each period, that can be employed to perform social evaluations in period t based on present and future utilities only: social evaluations are independent of past utilities if two alternatives to be ranked have a common history.

Forward-Looking Consistency. For all $\mathbf{w}, \mathbf{v}, \bar{\mathbf{w}}, \bar{\mathbf{v}} \in \mathbf{W}$ and for all $t \in \mathcal{Z}_{++}$, if $w_i^\tau = \bar{w}_i^\tau$ and $v_i^\tau = \bar{v}_i^\tau$ for all $i \in \mathcal{Z}_{++}$ and for all $\tau \in \mathcal{Z}_{++}$ with $\tau \geq t$, and $w_i^\tau = v_i^\tau$ and $\bar{w}_i^\tau = \bar{v}_i^\tau$ for all $i \in \mathcal{Z}_{++}$ and for all $\tau \in \mathcal{Z}_{++}$ with $\tau < t$, then

$$\mathbf{w} \mathbf{R}_T \mathbf{v} \Leftrightarrow \bar{\mathbf{w}} \mathbf{R}_T \bar{\mathbf{v}}.$$

Surprisingly, the same negative conclusion as that of Theorem 9.2 obtains when this alternative separability property is employed. If full temporal consistency is replaced with forward-looking consistency in Theorem 9.2, the same class of principles is characterized. Moreover, the functions U_i^W must be the same for all individuals $i \in \mathcal{Z}_{++}$ and the same impossibility as in Theorem 9.2 results if this is not the case. Again, we conclude that the separability axiom is too strong and we should abandon the idea of consistent forward-looking social evaluation based on per-period utilities.

Theorem 9.3. *Suppose individual welfarism is satisfied.* $\mathbf{R}_T$ *satisfies multiperiod continuity, multiperiod strong Pareto, and forward-looking consistency if and only if there exists a continuous and increasing function* $g: \mathcal{R} \to \mathcal{R}$ *with* $g(0) = 0$ *such that:*

(i) *for all* $i \in \mathcal{Z}_{++}$, *for all* $s_i \in \mathcal{Z}_+$, *for all* $\ell_i \in \{1, \dots, \bar{L}\}$, *and for all* $w_i \in \mathcal{R}^{\ell_i}$,

$$U_i^W(w_i) = g^{-1}\left(\sum_{t=s_i+1}^{s_i+\ell_i} g(w_i^t)\right);$$

(ii) *for all* $\mathbf{w}, \mathbf{v} \in \mathbf{W}$,

$$\mathbf{w} \mathbf{R}_T \mathbf{v} \Leftrightarrow \sum_{i \in \Theta(\mathbf{w})} g\left(U_i^W(w_i)\right) \geq \sum_{i \in \Theta(\mathbf{v})} g\left(U_i^W(v_i)\right)$$

$$\Leftrightarrow \sum_{i \in \Theta(\mathbf{w})} \sum_{t=\sigma_i(\mathbf{w})+1}^{\sigma_i(\mathbf{w})+\lambda_i(\mathbf{w})} g(w_i^t) \geq \sum_{i \in \Theta(\mathbf{v})} \sum_{t=\sigma_i(\mathbf{v})+1}^{\sigma_i(\mathbf{v})+\lambda_i(\mathbf{v})} g(v_i^t).$$

Proof. Clearly, the principles defined in the theorem statement satisfy the axioms.

Now let $n \geq 2$. By multiperiod continuity and Debreu's (1959, pp. 56–59) representation theorem, there exists a continuous function $f^n : \mathcal{R}^{\bar{L}n} \to \mathcal{R}$ such that, for all $\mathbf{w}, \mathbf{v} \in \mathbf{W}_{\bar{L}n}$,

$$\mathbf{w} \mathbf{R}_T \mathbf{v} \Leftrightarrow f^n(w) \geq f^n(v).$$

Multiperiod strong Pareto implies that f^n is increasing. By forward-looking consistency, the vector $(w^\tau)_{\tau=t,\ldots,\bar{L}}$ is separable from its complement in f^n for all $t \in \{2, \ldots, \bar{L}\}$. Thus, using multiperiod continuity and multiperiod strong Pareto, there exist continuous and increasing functions $J_t^n : \mathcal{R}^{n(t-1)} \times \mathcal{R} \to \mathcal{R}$ and $F_t^n : \mathcal{R}^{n(\bar{L}-t+1)} \to \mathcal{R}$ such that

$$f^n(w) = J_t^n \left(w^1, \ldots, w^{t-1}, F_t^n(w^t, \ldots, w^{\bar{L}}) \right) \tag{9.7}$$

for all $\mathbf{w} \in \mathbf{W}_{\bar{L}n}$ and for all $t \in \{2, \ldots, \bar{L}\}$. As in the proof of Theorem 9.2, multiperiod strong Pareto implies that the vector $w_i \in \mathcal{R}^{\bar{L}}$ is separable from its complement in f^n for all $i \in \{1, \ldots, n\}$. This, together with multiperiod continuity and individual welfarism, implies that there exists a continuous and increasing function $G^n : \mathcal{R}^n \to \mathcal{R}$ such that

$$f^n(w) = G^n \left(U_1^W(w_1), \ldots, U_n^W(w_n) \right) \tag{9.8}$$

for all $\mathbf{w} \in \mathbf{W}_{\bar{L}n}$. (9.7) and (9.8) generate sufficient overlap so that, again, Gorman's (1968) theorem implies that f^n is additively separable and there exist continuous and increasing functions $H^n : \mathcal{R} \to \mathcal{R}$ and $g_{it}^n : \mathcal{R} \to \mathcal{R}$ for all $i \in \{1, \ldots, n\}$ and for all $t \in \{1, \ldots, \bar{L}\}$ such that

$$f^n(w) = H^n \left(\sum_{i=1}^n \sum_{t=1}^{\bar{L}} g_{it}^n(w_i^t) \right)$$

for all $\mathbf{w} \in \mathbf{W}_{\bar{L}n}$. The rest of the proof proceeds as in the proof of Theorem 9.2. ∎

As an immediate consequence of Theorems 9.2 and 9.3, it follows that full temporal consistency and forward-looking consistency are equivalent in the presence of the remaining axioms in the theorem statements.

The results of this chapter generalize to weaker Pareto principles such as those investigated in Chapter 8; see Blackorby, Bossert, and Donaldson (1997a) for a discussion.

Theorems 9.2 and 9.3 illustrate the difficulties associated with temporal social evaluation based on per-period utilities. The natural candidates for consistency conditions across periods are unacceptably demanding because they lead to the repugnant conclusion. Moreover, they produce impossibility results in the likely case in which individual attitudes toward intertemporal trade-offs of well-being differ. We conclude that per-period utilities cannot be taken into consideration in a satisfactory manner and, therefore, only lifetime utilities should matter. A natural and plausible independence condition in this context is independence of the existence of the dead, which is compatible with attractive principles and permits us to avoid the repugnant conclusion.

CHAPTER 10

Choice Problems and Rationalizability

Part A

Because many policy decisions have population consequences, it is natural to use population principles to guide them. These decision problems are, in most cases, choice problems: one or more options must be selected from a set of feasible alternatives. Examples are decisions involving the allocation of funds to population-control programs or to prenatal care.

The maximizing approach to solving choice problems consists of two steps. First, a social ordering with ethically appropriate properties is identified, a task that is the focus of the previous chapters. Once that is done, choices can be made by selecting the best feasible alternatives (provided that they exist) according to the ordering. The best alternatives in any feasible set are those that are ranked as at least as good as all feasible alternatives. There may be more than one best alternative and, in that case, all the best alternatives are ranked as equally good. For that reason, the actual choice may be any one of them.

Although this is a reasonable way to proceed, it excludes consideration of choice procedures that are not based on social orderings from the outset.[1] In addition, it is natural to ask whether the focus should be on the choices themselves rather than on the social ordering. Requiring that all alternatives can be ranked may be too much to ask of a social decision procedure.

Many of the axioms discussed in the previous chapters are concerned with the trade-offs made by population principles. As an example, principles that imply the repugnant conclusion allow population size to substitute for decreases in individual well-being as long as well-being is above neutrality. It does not follow, however, that such principles recommend the deliberate creation of large, poverty-stricken populations in real-world situations. For that reason, it is important to investigate the properties of choice procedures directly.

A welfarist variable-population choice procedure is rationalizable if and only if it chooses the best feasible alternatives according to a social ordering

---

[1] Thomson (1996a) makes this point in his discussion of Blackorby, Bossert, and Donaldson (1996d).

of the utility vectors associated with the feasible alternatives. In this chapter, we examine the properties of variable-population choice procedures together with requirements for rationalizability. In addition, we investigate several properties of best and undominated choices according to critical-level generalized utilitarian orderings and critical-band generalized utilitarian quasi-orderings.

10.1 RATIONALIZABILITY: THE PURE POPULATION PROBLEM

The simplest choice problem with a population aspect is the pure population problem. In it, a fixed endowment of a single resource is available. Each person who is alive has an identical utility function that depends on that person's consumption. In addition, consumption levels are assumed to be the same for all. A choice consists of a population size and a level of per-capita consumption such that total consumption is no greater than the total amount of the resource. A choice function selects one or more of these for each value of the endowment. The choice of a population size of zero is assumed to be feasible.

A choice function is rationalizable by an ordering of population-size–per-capita-consumption pairs if and only if it selects the best choices, according to the ordering, for every value of the endowment. Note that the same ordering is used for every value. The rationalizing ordering is monotonic if and only if it ranks increases in per-capita consumption as a social improvement, provided that population size is constant. Although the ordering ranks population-size–per-capita-consumption pairs, its existence implies the existence of an ordering of population-size–per-capita-utility pairs that rationalizes choices from the sets of feasible equally distributed utilities. That ordering in turn implies the existence of an ordering of utility vectors in which all utilities are equal.

Only two axioms are needed to ensure that a choice function is rationalizable by a monotonic ordering. The first is efficiency, which requires all of the resource to be consumed and the second is zero consistency, which requires that, if a population size of zero is chosen for some value of the resource endowment, it is also chosen for all smaller values. This rationalizability result applies whether population size is treated as a discrete variable, taking on only integer values, or as a continuous variable.

Our second rationalizability result is valid for the case of a continuous population variable only. In addition to efficiency, it uses three further axioms. Nondegeneracy requires a non-zero population size to be chosen for some value of the endowment, and single-valued choice requires a single population size and per-capita consumption level to be chosen for at least one value. Homogeneity requires the chosen population size to be proportional to the value of the endowment. This is a plausible assumption because, in this simple model, the resource endowment represents the carrying capacity of the universe. Efficiency and these axioms are satisfied if and only if choices of population-size–per-capita-utility pairs can be rationalized by an inequality-sensitive generalized utilitarian ordering with a critical level that is greater than the utility value for zero consumption. Inequality sensitivity requires the transformed utility function to be strictly concave.

An example, which is included in Part B, considers a solution to the pure population problem proposed by Dasgupta (1988). It makes choices by distinguishing between actual and potential people and uses a weighted sum of utilities with a weight of one for actual people and a positive weight that is less than one for potential people. If used to rank utility vectors, this weighted sum does not generate an ordering. For example, suppose that, in alternative x, the population consists of two people with utilities of 10 and 20, and they consider adding another person. In alternative y, the utilities are 10 and 20 for the original population with 4 for the added person and, in alternative z, utilities are 6 and 16 for the original population with 14 for the added person. Suppose the weight for potential people is $1/2$. From the viewpoint of the population in x, y is better than z because the weighted sum for y is $10 + 20 + (1/2)4 = 32$ and for z, the weighted sum is $6 + 16 + (1/2)14 = 29$. But, if y is chosen, then the added person becomes an actual person and z is better than y because the sums are $10 + 20 + 4 = 34$ for y and $6 + 16 + 14 = 36$ for z.

Dasgupta's choice function chooses the smallest population that does not want to add to itself using the above rule. In the example discussed in Part B, the resulting choice function satisfies all four of the above axioms and, as a result, it can be rationalized by an inequality-sensitive critical-level generalized utilitarian ordering, which is, in this case, critical-level utilitarian. As the weight for potential people moves up, the corresponding value for the critical level moves down. In the limit, the weight for potential people is one, the critical level is zero, and the choice function is rationalized by the classical-utilitarian ordering.

10.2   RATIONALIZABILITY: THE GENERAL CASE

Although the pure population problem focuses attention on population issues, actual choice problems combine those issues with others such as population composition and the distribution of well-being. The general choice problem employs a collection of feasible sets of utility vectors and a choice function chooses a subset (which may consist of a single utility vector) of each feasible set.

If a utility vector is chosen in a feasible set, it is said to be at least as good as all others in the feasible set according to the direct revealed-preference relation. As noted by Samuelson (1938, 1948) in the context of consumer-choice theory, a direct revealed preference has to be respected by any rationalizing relation (if one exists). It is easy to see why this is the case: if a utility vector u is directly revealed preferred to a utility vector v, u is chosen when v is feasible. Rationalizability requires that u is a best element in the feasible set according to a rationalizing relation, and it follows that it is at least as good as all elements of the feasible set and, in particular, at least as good as v.

Although necessary, respecting the direct revealed preference relation is not sufficient for rationalizability because a rationalizing relation is required to be transitive. A revealed-preference cycle is a finite sequence of utility vectors such that each is at least as good as the next and the last is better than the first according to the direct revealed-preference relation. The congruence axiom (Richter 1966) states that there can be no revealed-preference cycle. That axiom is necessary and sufficient for rationalizability.

Zero dominance requires chosen utility vectors to consist of nonnegative utility levels only, ensuring that no one is below neutrality. If we assume that the restrictions of the choice function to each population size are rationalizable and that zero dominance is satisfied, then congruence can be weakened to an axiom that we call weak population congruence. It rules out revealed-preference cycles of length four where the elements of the cycle are of alternating dimension. The axiom is a substantial weakening of congruence because it rules out only revealed-preference cycles with a very special structure.

Although this result ensures rationalizability, we know nothing about the rationalizing orderings. However, choice functions that are rationalized by critical-level generalized utilitarian orderings can be characterized with some additional axioms, which we now describe.

The first two axioms are zero dominance and weak population congruence, which are discussed above.

Same-number single-valuedness assumes that at most one utility vector of each population size is chosen. This requirement parallels the single-valuedness assumption in standard models of bargaining and resource allocation. Single-valuedness is satisfied by most bargaining solutions but some exceptions, such as the generalized-Gini bargaining solutions (Blackorby, Bossert, and Donaldson 1994), exist. See Thomson (2004) for a discussion.

Pareto optimality requires that only utility vectors that are not Pareto dominated can be chosen. A utility vector Pareto dominates another utility vector of the same dimension if and only if every component of the first is greater than or equal to the corresponding component of the second with at least one strict inequality. This axiom is the choice-theoretic analogue of the strong Pareto principle. It is also fundamental in Nash's (1950) characterization of his bargaining solution.

Choice continuity requires choices for a sequence of feasible sets to converge to the choices for the limit of the sequence (if it exists). As is the case for the continuity axiom formulated for orderings, the purpose of choice continuity is to rule out "large" changes in choices resulting from "small" changes in the choice problem. In the context of bargaining problems, continuity is discussed, for example, by Jansen and Tijs (1983) and by Salonen (1998).

Choice anonymity parallels its twin formulated for orderings. It ensures that the choice function treats individuals impartially, paying no attention to their identities. If formulated for bargaining solutions, the axiom is stronger than Nash's (1950) symmetry condition, which applies only in situations in which everyone is equal in the description of a problem.

Population consistency requires that, if some people leave with their utilities, the choice of a utility vector for those remaining is unchanged. This is a version of the well-known consistency axiom adapted to our framework. The consistency principle has been applied in many models of bargaining and resource allocation. See Thomson (1990, 1996b) for a general discussion and Blackorby, Bossert, and Donaldson (1996c) and Lensberg (1987) for versions that are particularly relevant for the present setting. Population consistency is a very powerful axiom. It encompasses a separability property because the utility allocation to those remaining does not depend on whether those leaving with their payoffs are present and, therefore, it is analogous to our existence-independence axiom for social orderings. Moreover, the axiom plays a crucial role in establishing the rationalizability of bargaining solutions; see Lensberg (1987) and Thomson and Lensberg (1989) for detailed discussions.

Restricted choice independence limits the influence of utility vectors of other dimensions when deciding on the selection of elements of a given population size. Suppose a utility vector u is the only chosen vector of dimension n for a problem where the feasible sets of utility vectors of all other dimensions contain only negative utilities. Restricted choice independence requires that if an n-dimensional vector is chosen in another choice problem where the set of feasible n-dimensional vectors is unchanged, then this n-dimensional vector should be u. Restricted choice independence has an interesting consequence. In conjunction with other axioms, it guarantees same-number rationalizability.

Finally, the critical-level choice principle is analogous to the critical-level population principle for orderings. It requires the existence of a fixed critical level such that, if a feasible utility vector is augmented by a utility value at the critical level and the augmented vector is feasible, it is chosen if and only if the original vector is.

10.3   RATIONAL CHOICE WITH CRITICAL-BAND GENERALIZED UTILITARIANISM

When social rankings are incomplete, rational choices become somewhat problematic because, in many situations, best utility vectors do not exist. A solution is to choose a member of the set of undominated utility vectors. Undominated choices are feasible and there is no other feasible choice that is better. For example, undominated choices for the strong Pareto quasi-ordering are the Pareto optima. If the social quasi-ordering is complete, undominated choices are best choices.

The critical-band generalized utilitarian quasi-orderings are intersections of critical-level generalized utilitarian orderings: one utility vector is at least as good as another if and only if it is at least as good for all critical levels in the band. Although best elements for the generating orderings are undominated, other utility vectors may be undominated as well. Suppose, for example, that a set of feasible utility vectors consists of (65), $(40, 40)$, and $(35, 35, 35)$ and that the critical-band utilitarian quasi-ordering with the band equal to all critical levels from 0 to 30 including the end points is employed. In that case, the set of undominated alternatives consists of all three utility vectors, but there is no critical level in the band such that (40, 40) is best. See Part B for a discussion of this example.

If it were true that each member of the set of undominated utility vectors were best according to critical-level generalized utilitarianism for some critical level in the band, it would be much simpler to find undominated alternatives. This does occur in some cases. If the set of best population sizes associated with the best alternatives for the critical levels in the band is a set of consecutive integers, then the set of undominated alternatives and the set of best alternatives for critical levels in the band coincide.

This result can be applied to the pure population problem. If the common utility function has a second derivative that is everywhere negative and critical-level generalized utilitarianism with a transformation whose second derivative is everywhere nonpositive is employed, the two sets coincide.

A general comparative-statics result is valid for choices that select best elements according to critical-level generalized utilitarian orderings from an arbitrary nonempty feasible set. If the critical level is raised, then all the best population sizes associated with the higher critical level are no greater than all the best population sizes associated with the lower critical level. This is an important property of the critical-level generalized utilitarian principles and it illustrates the power of a critical level above zero.

Part B

Whether there are population consequences or not, issues related to the design of public policies lead, in most cases, to choice problems: one or more options must be selected from a set of feasible alternatives. Examples for policy-choice problems with possible population consequences are decisions involving the allocation of funds to population-control programs or to prenatal care.

We investigate the maximizing approach to solving choice problems, which consists of two steps. First, a social ordering with ethically appropriate properties is identified, a task that has been analyzed thoroughly in the previous chapters. Once that is done, choices are made by making a selection from the set of best feasible alternatives according to the ordering.

This approach guarantees that choices are made in a consistent manner because they all derive from the same objective. However, by postulating it directly, the maximizing method excludes consideration of choice procedures that are not based on social orderings from the outset. This is noted, for example, by Thomson (1996a). In addition, the question arises whether it may be more natural to make the choices themselves the focus of investigation rather than the social ordering.

As before, we focus on welfarist choice procedures. This means that the choice of alternatives from a feasible set of options can be identified with the choice of utility vectors from a set of feasible utility vectors. In the variable-population case, the set of feasible utility vectors for a given choice problem may contain utility vectors of different dimensions.

A choice function selects a nonempty subset of each feasible set in its domain. Rationalizable choice functions perform this selection in accordance with an ordering on the universal set of objects of choice: the chosen set is the set of best elements in the feasible set with respect to this ordering. The rationalizability of choice functions has been analyzed extensively in the context of consumer theory but more general choice problems are investigated in the literature as well.[2] Furthermore, a growing number of contributions examine issues related to the rationalizability of various group decision procedures (such as bargaining solutions) rather than individual choices.[3] The variable-population aspect that is important in our choice-theoretical approach differs from that appearing in bargaining problems with a variable population that are analyzed, for example, by Blackorby, Bossert, and Donaldson (1996c); Lensberg (1987, 1988); Thomson (1983a, 1983b, 1984, 1985, 1986); and Thomson and Lensberg (1989). In our formulation, population size is to be chosen as well, whereas in the above contributions, a choice has to be made for each possible population, and cross-population restrictions on choices are examined. This difference is essential: although the size and the composition of the population may vary across bargaining problems in the earlier literature, the set of agents is given for each problem and is not a matter of choice.

We begin our analysis of variable-population rational choice in Section 10.4 with a simple problem: the pure population problem. In it, a single resource is to be divided equally among the members of a society, and population size and per-capita consumption are the objects of choice. In this setting, we characterize rationalizability by an arbitrary ordering. In addition, rationalizability by inequality-sensitive critical-level generalized utilitarian principles is characterized. Section 10.5 employs a more general framework where choices from feasible sets of utility vectors (possibly of different dimensions) are analyzed. We identify necessary and sufficient conditions for the rationalizability of a class of general variable-population choice functions. Section 10.6 uses the same basic model as Section 10.5 and provides a characterization of critical-level separable choice functions. Section 10.7 concludes the chapter with a discussion of the relationship between variable-population choices and quasi-orderings.

---

[2] See, for example, Blackorby, Bossert, and Donaldson (1995a); Bossert (1993); Gale (1960); Houthakker (1950); Hurwicz and Richter (1971); Kihlstrom, Mas-Colell, and Sonnenschein (1976); Peters and Wakker (1994); Rose (1958); Samuelson (1938, 1948); and Uzawa (1960, 1971) for studies of rational choice in consumer theory. More general choice problems are considered by Arrow (1959); Baigent and Gaertner (1996); Bossert (2001); Hansson (1968); Richter (1966, 1971); Sen (1971, 1993); and Suzumura (1976), among others.

[3] See, for instance, Blackorby, Bossert, and Donaldson (1994, 1996c); Bossert (1994, 1998); Donaldson and Weymark (1988); Lensberg (1987); Ok and Zhou (1999, 2000); Peters and Wakker (1991); Sanchez (2000); and Zhou (1997b).

10.4 THE PURE POPULATION PROBLEM

Consider an economy with a single resource that is to be distributed equally among the individuals who are alive in a chosen alternative. Each person who is alive has an identical continuous and increasing utility function U defined on the set of possible consumption levels. A choice consists of a population size and a per-capita consumption level. We assume an equal distribution of the resource in order to focus on the population issue.

A pure population problem is defined by the total amount of the resource $\omega \in \mathcal{R}_{++}$ available. The set of population sizes is $\mathcal{N}$, where either $\mathcal{N} = \mathcal{Z}_+$ or $\mathcal{N} = \mathcal{R}_+$. Furthermore, we define $\mathcal{N}_{++} = \mathcal{N} \setminus \{0\}$. Note that this marks our first departure from the assumption that population size is a discrete variable. For some issues in rational-choice theory, we need to go beyond this assumption and allow population size to be a continuous variable. This is the case because integer problems may arise. However, some of our results do not require the assumption that population size is continuous. For those that do, we think of them as approximating the more realistic discrete model.

Our first result does not depend on the choice between a discrete and a continuous model: the theorem is true whether population size is a discrete or a continuous variable. In contrast, as is the case in a variety of economic models, our second theorem requires population size to be a continuous variable. The reason is that we employ a homogeneity property, which cannot be satisfied if the set of possible population sizes is discrete – in that case, the condition can only be approximately satisfied due to integer problems.

Each pure population problem ω induces a set of feasible population-size–per-capita-consumption pairs defined by

$$\mathcal{B}(\omega) = \{(n, x) \mid n \in \mathcal{N}_{++} \text{ and } 0 \leq x \leq \omega/n\} \cup \{(0, 0)\}.$$

The choice of $x = 0$ in the case of a zero population is arbitrary and of no consequence for the results of the paper. Let $\mathcal{P}_+ = \mathcal{N}_{++} \times \mathcal{R}_+$, and let $\mathcal{P} = \mathcal{P}_+ \cup \{(0, 0)\}$. A solution is a choice function defined on $\mathcal{R}_{++}$; that is, a function $\mathcal{C}: \mathcal{R}_{++} \to 2^{\mathcal{P}}$ such that, for all $\omega \in \mathcal{R}_{++}$, $\mathcal{C}(\omega) \subseteq \mathcal{B}(\omega)$.

Throughout this section, we impose an efficiency condition, the intuitive appeal of which is evident. Efficiency requires that the entire amount of the resource available is distributed by a solution.

Efficiency. For all $\omega \in \mathcal{R}_{++}$, for all $n \in \mathcal{N}_{++}$, and for all $x, y \in \mathcal{R}_+$ such that $x > y$, if $(n, x) \in \mathcal{B}(\omega)$, then $(n, y) \notin \mathcal{C}(\omega)$.

A solution $\mathcal{C}$ is rationalizable if and only if there exists an ordering $\succeq$ on $\mathcal{P}$ such that, for all $\omega \in \mathcal{R}_{++}$,

$$\mathcal{C}(\omega) = \{(n, x) \in \mathcal{B}(\omega) \mid (n, x) \succeq (m, y) \text{ for all } (m, y) \in \mathcal{B}(\omega)\}.$$

Thus, $\mathcal{C}$ is rationalizable if and only if there exists an ordering $\succeq$ such that, for each $\omega \in \mathcal{R}_{++}$, the choice function selects the set of best elements in the feasible set $\mathcal{B}(\omega)$ according to $\succeq$. In this case, we say that the social ordering $\succeq$ rationalizes $\mathcal{C}$ or that $\succeq$ is a rationalization of $\mathcal{C}$. The asymmetric and symmetric factors of $\succeq$ are denoted by $\succ$ and $\sim$.

The direct revealed-preference relation R_C corresponding to the choice function $\mathcal{C}$ is defined as follows. For all $(n, x), (m, y) \in \mathcal{P}$, $(n, x)R_C(m, y)$ if and only if there exists $\omega \in \mathcal{R}_{++}$ such that $(n, x) \in \mathcal{C}(\omega)$ and $(m, y) \in \mathcal{B}(\omega)$.

The following axiom imposes a restriction on the choice of a zero population size. Zero consistency requires that if a zero population size is chosen for some amount of the resource, then zero must be the only chosen population size for all lower levels of the resource.

Zero Consistency. If there exists $\bar{\omega} \in \mathcal{R}_{++}$ such that $(0, 0) \in \mathcal{C}(\bar{\omega})$, then $\mathcal{C}(\omega) = \{(0, 0)\}$ for all $\omega < \bar{\omega}$.

The zero-consistency axiom imposes a restriction only on choices that involve a zero population. Therefore, it is considerably weaker than the usual axioms that are required for rational choice. As a consequence of the special structure of pure population problems, this condition is all that is required in addition to efficiency for our first rationalizability result. Moreover, efficiency implies that rationalizing orderings can be chosen such that they possess the following monotonicity property.

Monotonicity. For all $(n, x), (m, y) \in \mathcal{P}$, if $n = m$ and $x > y$, then $(n, x) \succ (m, y)$.

Efficiency and zero consistency together form a set of necessary and sufficient conditions for rationalizability by a monotonic ordering. This observation is stated and proven in the following theorem.

Theorem 10.1. *$\mathcal{C}$ is rationalizable by a monotonic ordering if and only if $\mathcal{C}$ satisfies efficiency and zero consistency.*

Proof. Suppose first that $\succeq$ is a monotonic ordering that rationalizes $\mathcal{C}$. To prove that $\mathcal{C}$ satisfies efficiency, let $\omega \in \mathcal{R}_{++}$, $n \in \mathcal{N}_{++}$, and $x, y \in \mathcal{R}_+$ be such that $x > y$ and $(n, x) \in \mathcal{B}(\omega)$. By way of contradiction, suppose $(n, y) \in \mathcal{C}(\omega)$. Because $\succeq$ rationalizes $\mathcal{C}$, it follows that $(n, y) \succeq (n, x)$, contradicting the monotonicity of $\succeq$.

Now suppose zero consistency is violated. Then there exist $\bar{\omega}$, $\omega \in \mathcal{R}_{++}$ and $(n, x) \in \mathcal{P}_+$ such that $\omega < \bar{\omega}$, $(0, 0) \in \mathcal{C}(\bar{\omega})$ and $(n, x) \in \mathcal{C}(\omega)$. The pair $(0, 0)$ is feasible for any possible amount of the resource and, thus, in particular for the problem ω. Therefore, because $\succeq$ rationalizes $\mathcal{C}$, it follows that $(n, x) \succeq (0, 0)$. Because (n, x) is feasible for the problem ω, it must be feasible for the higher amount of the resource $\bar{\omega}$. Hence, because $(0, 0)$ is chosen for $\bar{\omega}$ and (n, x) is at least as good as $(0, 0)$ according to the rationalizing ordering, it follows that $(n, x) \in \mathcal{C}(\bar{\omega})$. But this contradicts efficiency because $nx \leq \omega < \bar{\omega}$.

Now suppose C is efficient and satisfies zero consistency. To complete the proof, we establish the existence of a monotonic ordering that rationalizes C. Define a relation $\succeq^*$ on P as follows. For all $(n, x), (m, y) \in P, (n, x) \succeq^* (m, y)$ if and only if

$$\left[n \neq m \text{ and } \exists t \in \mathcal{R}_+ \text{ such that } x \geq t \text{ and } (n, t)R_C(m, y) \right]$$
$$\text{or } \left[n = m \text{ and } x \geq y \right].$$

First, we show that $\succeq^*$ is a quasi-ordering. That $\succeq^*$ is reflexive follows immediately. To show that $\succeq^*$ is transitive, suppose $(n, x) \succeq^* (m, y)$ and $(m, y) \succeq^* (r, z)$ for some $(n, x), (m, y), (r, z) \in P$. Suppose $(n, x) \neq (m, y)$ and $(m, y) \neq (r, z)$ (all other cases are trivial). According to the definition of $\succeq^*$, we can distinguish four cases.

(1) $n \neq m$ and there exist $t, s \in \mathcal{R}_+$ such that $x \geq t, (n, t)R_C(m, y), y \geq s$, and $(m, s)R_C(r, z)$. The following five subcases arise according to which of the population sizes in these pairs are equal to zero [note that these are the only possibilities because the case $(n, x) = (m, y)$ or $(m, y) = (r, z)$ is ruled out].

  (i) $n = 0$ and $r = 0$. In this case, $(n, x) = (0, 0) \succeq^* (0, 0) = (r, z)$ follows immediately because $\succeq^*$ is reflexive.

  (ii) $n = 0$ and $m \neq 0$ and $r \neq 0$. It follows that $(n, x) = (0, 0)$ and, because $x \geq t, t = 0$. Therefore, $(0, 0)R_C(m, y)$. Let $\omega, \hat{\omega} \in \mathcal{R}_{++}$ be such that $(0, 0) \in C(\omega), my \leq \omega, (m, s) \in C(\hat{\omega})$, and $rz \leq \hat{\omega}$. By efficiency, $ms = \hat{\omega}$. Furthermore, $\omega \geq my \geq ms$ and, therefore, $\omega \geq \hat{\omega}$. If $\omega = \hat{\omega}$, it follows that $(0, 0) \in C(\hat{\omega})$ and thus $(n, x) = (0, 0)R_C(r, z)$, which implies $(n, x) \succeq^* (r, z)$. The case $\omega > \hat{\omega}$ cannot occur because it contradicts zero consistency.

  (iii) $n \neq 0$ and $m = 0$ and $r \neq 0$. Analogously to (ii), $(m, y) = (m, s) = (0, 0)$ and hence $(0, 0)R_C(r, z)$. Let $\omega, \hat{\omega} \in \mathcal{R}_{++}$ be such that $(n, t) \in C(\omega), (0, 0) \in C(\hat{\omega})$, and $rz \leq \hat{\omega}$. If $\omega < \hat{\omega}$, we obtain a contradiction to zero consistency. Therefore, $\omega \geq \hat{\omega}$, which implies $rz \leq \omega$. Hence, $(r, z) \in B(\omega)$ and it follows that $(n, t)R_C(r, z)$ and thus $(n, x) \succeq^* (r, z)$.

  (iv) $n \neq 0$ and $m \neq 0$ and $r = 0$. It follows that $(r, z) = (0, 0)$. Let $\omega \in \mathcal{R}_{++}$ be such that $(n, t) \in C(\omega)$. Because $(0, 0) \in B(\omega)$, it follows that $(n, t)R_C(0, 0) = (r, z)$ and hence $(n, x) \succeq^* (r, z)$.

  (v) $n \neq 0$ and $m \neq 0$ and $r \neq 0$. Let $\omega, \hat{\omega} \in \mathcal{R}_{++}$ be such that $(n, t) \in C(\omega), my \leq \omega, (m, s) \in C(\hat{\omega})$, and $rz \leq \hat{\omega}$. Efficiency implies $ms = \hat{\omega}$ and we obtain $\omega \geq my \geq ms = \hat{\omega} \geq rz$. Therefore, $(r, z) \in B(\omega)$ and it follows that $(n, t)R_C(r, z)$ and thus $(n, x) \succeq^* (r, z)$.

(2) $n = m$ and $x \geq y$ and $m = r$ and $y \geq z$. In this case, we obtain $n = r$ and $x \geq z$ and thus $(n, x) \succeq^* (r, z)$.

(3) $n \neq m$ and there exists $t \in \mathcal{R}_+$ such that $x \geq t$ and $(n, t)R_C(m, y), m = r$ and $y \geq z$. Because $(m, y) \neq (r, z)$, it follows that $m = r \neq 0$. Let

$\omega \in \mathcal{R}_{++}$ be such that $(n, t) \in \mathcal{C}(\omega)$ and $my \leq \omega$. It follows that $rz = mz \leq my \leq \omega$ and, therefore, $(r, z) \in \mathcal{B}(\omega)$. Hence, $(n, t)R_{\mathcal{C}}(r, z)$ and we obtain $(n, x) \succeq^* (r, z)$.

(4) $n = m$ and $x \geq y$ and $m \neq r$ and there exists $t \in \mathcal{R}_+$ such that $y \geq t$ and $(m, t)R_{\mathcal{C}}(r, z)$. Therefore, $(n, t)R_{\mathcal{C}}(r, z)$. Because $x \geq y \geq t$, this implies $(n, x) \succeq^* (r, z)$.

Next, it is shown that $\succeq^*$ satisfies monotonicity. Suppose $n = m$ and $x > y$. By definition, $(n, x) \succeq^* (n, y)$. $(n, y) \succeq^* (n, x)$ is impossible because $y < x$.

The next step is to show that $\mathcal{C}$ selects the best elements according to $\succeq^*$. Let $\omega \in \mathcal{R}_{++}$ and $(n, x) \in \mathcal{C}(\omega)$. Therefore, $(n, x)R_{\mathcal{C}}(m, y)$ for all $(m, y) \in \mathcal{B}(\omega)$ and hence $(n, x) \succeq^* (m, y)$ for all $(m, y) \in \mathcal{B}(\omega)$. This establishes that

$$\mathcal{C}(\omega) \subseteq \{(n, x) \in \mathcal{B}(\omega) \mid (n, x) \succeq^* (m, y) \text{ for all } (m, y) \in \mathcal{B}(\omega)\}.$$

To establish the reverse set inclusion, suppose $(n, x) \in \mathcal{B}(\omega)$ and $(n, x) \succeq^* (m, y)$ for all $(m, y) \in \mathcal{B}(\omega)$. Let $(r, z) \in \mathcal{C}(\omega)$. If $(r, z) = (n, x)$, we are done. Now suppose $(r, z) \neq (n, x)$. Because this possibility is inconsistent with $n = r = 0$, there are three cases left to consider.

(1) $n = 0$ and $r \neq 0$. Because $n \neq r$, $(n, x) \succeq^* (r, z)$ implies $(0, 0)R_{\mathcal{C}}(r, z)$. Let $\hat{\omega} \in \mathcal{R}_{++}$ be such that $(0, 0) \in \mathcal{C}(\hat{\omega})$ and $rz \leq \hat{\omega}$. Efficiency implies $rz = \omega$ and, therefore, $\omega \leq \hat{\omega}$. If $\omega = \hat{\omega}$, $(n, x) = (0, 0) \in \mathcal{C}(\omega)$ by definition. If $\omega < \hat{\omega}$, $(n, x) = (0, 0) \in \mathcal{C}(\omega)$ by zero consistency.

(2) $n \neq 0$ and $r = 0$. It follows that $(0, 0) \in \mathcal{C}(\omega)$. Because $(n, x) \succeq^* (r, z) = (0, 0)$ and $n \neq 0$, it follows that there exists $t \in \mathcal{R}_+$ such that $x \geq t$ and $(n, t)R_{\mathcal{C}}(0, 0)$. Let $\hat{\omega} \in \mathcal{R}_{++}$ be such that $(n, t) \in \mathcal{C}(\hat{\omega})$. Zero consistency implies $\hat{\omega} \geq \omega$.

(i) If $\hat{\omega} = \omega$, we obtain $(n, t) \in \mathcal{C}(\omega)$, and efficiency implies

$$nt = \omega. \tag{10.1}$$

Furthermore, because $(n, x) \in \mathcal{B}(\omega)$, it follows that $nx \leq \omega$. Together with (10.1) and the observation that $x \geq t$, it follows that $x = t$ and hence $(n, x) \in \mathcal{C}(\omega)$.

(ii) If $\hat{\omega} > \omega$, efficiency can be used to obtain $nx \geq nt = \hat{\omega} > \omega$, contradicting the feasibility of (n, x) for the problem ω.

(3) $n \neq 0$ and $r \neq 0$. There are two subcases.

(i) $n = r$ and $x \geq y$. It follows that $x > y$ because $(n, x) \neq (r, z)$ by assumption. This contradicts efficiency.

(ii) $n \neq r$ and there exists $t \in \mathcal{R}_+$ such that $x \geq t$ and $(n, t)R_{\mathcal{C}}(r, z)$. Let $\hat{\omega} \in \mathcal{R}_{++}$ be such that $(n, t) \in \mathcal{C}(\hat{\omega})$ and $rz \leq \hat{\omega}$. Using efficiency, we obtain $nt = \hat{\omega} \geq rz = \omega \geq nx \geq nt$, which implies $\hat{\omega} = \omega$ and $t = x$. Therefore, $(n, x) \in \mathcal{C}(\omega)$.

We now have established that $\succeq^*$ is a monotonic quasi-ordering such that

$$\mathcal{C}(\omega) = \{(n, x) \in \mathcal{B}(\omega) \mid (n, x) \succeq^* (m, y) \text{ for all } (m, y) \in \mathcal{B}(\omega)\}$$

for all $\omega \in \mathcal{R}_{++}$. Because $\succeq^*$ is not necessarily complete, it remains to be shown that $\succeq^*$ can be extended to a monotonic ordering that rationalizes $\mathcal{C}$. Applying Richter's (1966) proof [which uses Szpilrajn's (1930) extension of an antisymmetric quasi-ordering to an antisymmetric ordering], there exists an ordering extension $\succeq$ of $\succeq^*$ that rationalizes $\mathcal{C}$. To see that $\succeq$ satisfies monotonicity, note that Szpilrajn's extension procedure is applied to the antisymmetric relation induced on the equivalence classes of $\succeq^*$ and, therefore, all strict preferences in $\succeq^*$ that are due to the monotonicity requirement are preserved when extending $\succeq^*$ to $\succeq$. ∎

The standard solutions proposed for pure population problems are rationalized by orderings that rank pairs of population sizes and per-capita utilities rather than per-capita consumption levels. Given efficiency, this makes no difference. Only pairs of the form $(n, \omega/n)$ can be selected, and $\mathcal{C}$ induces a choice function on pairs of the form $(n, U(\omega/n))$. Conversely, because U is increasing and efficiency is satisfied, $\mathcal{C}$ can be recovered uniquely from knowledge of the choice function defined on population-size–per-capita-utility pairs.

Our second result in this section is valid for the continuous case only; that is, we now assume that $\mathcal{N} = \mathcal{R}_+$. We rule out the degenerate solution that always selects only a zero population.

Nondegeneracy. There exist $\hat{\omega} \in \mathcal{R}_{++}$ and $(\hat{n}, \hat{x}) \in \mathcal{P}_+$ such that $(\hat{n}, \hat{x}) \in \mathcal{C}(\hat{\omega})$.

In addition, we require the existence of a pure population problem $\bar{\omega}$ such that $\mathcal{C}(\bar{\omega})$ is a singleton. This condition, together with our other axioms, implies that $\mathcal{C}$ is single-valued: a single population-size–per-capita-utility pair is chosen for each $\omega \in \mathcal{R}_{++}$.

Single-Valued Choice. There exists $\bar{\omega} \in \mathcal{R}_{++}$ such that $|\mathcal{C}(\bar{\omega})| = 1$.

In this continuous framework, an interesting property of a solution is homogeneity: if the amount of the resource ω is multiplied by some positive number λ and $n \in \mathcal{R}_+$ is a chosen population size for ω, then λn is a chosen population size for $\lambda\omega$. This is a plausible requirement because, in a pure population problem, the amount of the resource represents the carrying capacity of the environment.

Homogeneity. For all $\omega, \lambda \in \mathcal{R}_{++}$ and for all $n \in \mathcal{R}_+$, there exists $x \in \mathcal{R}_+$ such that $(n, x) \in \mathcal{C}(\omega)$ if and only if there exists $y \in \mathcal{R}_+$ such that $(\lambda n, y) \in \mathcal{C}(\lambda\omega)$.

Efficiency, nondegeneracy, single-valued choice, and homogeneity can be used to provide a characterization of a subclass of the critical-level generalized utilitarian solutions to pure population problems. Recall that all agents have a common continuous and increasing utility function U. The ordering $\succeq$ is an inequality-sensitive critical-level generalized utilitarian ordering if and only if there exist $\alpha > U(0)$ and a continuous and increasing function $g: \mathcal{R} \to \mathcal{R}$ with $g(0) = 0$ such that $g \circ U$ is strictly concave and, for all $(n, x), (m, y) \in \mathcal{P}$,

$$(n, x) \succeq (m, y) \Leftrightarrow n\big[g(U(x)) - g(\alpha)\big] \geq m\big[g(U(y)) - g(\alpha)\big].$$

The strict concavity of $g \circ U$ and the assumption $\alpha > U(0)$ together guarantee that a unique best element exists in $\mathcal{B}(\omega)$ for all $\omega \in \mathcal{R}_{++}$. We obtain the following characterization result.[4]

Theorem 10.2. *Let* $\mathcal{N} = \mathcal{R}_+$. *$\mathcal{C}$ is rationalizable by an inequality-sensitive critical-level generalized utilitarian ordering if and only if $\mathcal{C}$ satisfies efficiency, nondegeneracy, single-valued choice, and homogeneity.*

Proof. First, suppose $\succeq$ is an inequality-sensitive critical-level generalized utilitarian ordering with critical level $\alpha > U(0)$ that rationalizes $\mathcal{C}$. Clearly, this implies that $\mathcal{C}$ is efficient. Nondegeneracy is obvious and single-valued choice follows from the strict concavity of $g \circ U$. To show that $\mathcal{C}$ is homogeneous, suppose $\omega, \lambda \in \mathcal{R}_{++}$ and $n \in \mathcal{R}_+$. It follows that there exists $x \in \mathcal{R}_+$ such that $(n, x) \in \mathcal{C}(\omega)$ if and only if

$$n\lfloor g(U(x)) - g(\alpha)\rfloor \geq m\big[g(U(y)) - g(\alpha)\big] \tag{10.2}$$

for all $(m, y) \in \mathcal{B}(\omega)$. Because $my \leq \omega$ if and only if $\lambda my \leq \lambda \omega$, $(\lambda m, y) \in \mathcal{B}(\lambda \omega)$ if and only if $(m, y) \in \mathcal{B}(\omega)$. Multiplying both sides of (10.2) by λ, we obtain

$$\lambda n\big[g(U(x)) - g(\alpha)\big] \geq \lambda m\big[g(U(y)) - g(\alpha)\big]$$

for all $(\lambda m, y) \in \mathcal{B}(\lambda \omega)$. Letting $r = \lambda m$, this is equivalent to

$$\lambda n\big[g(U(x)) - g(\alpha)\big] \geq r\big[g(U(y)) - g(\alpha)\big]$$

for all $(r, y) \in \mathcal{B}(\lambda \omega)$, which, in turn, is equivalent to $(\lambda n, x) \in \mathcal{C}(\lambda \omega)$.

Now suppose that $\mathcal{C}$ satisfies efficiency, nondegeneracy, single-valued choice, and homogeneity. By single-valued choice, there exists $\bar{\omega} \in \mathcal{R}_{++}$ such that $\mathcal{C}(\bar{\omega})$ is a singleton $\{(\bar{n}, \bar{x})\}$. If $(\bar{n}, \bar{x}) = (0, 0)$, homogeneity implies $\mathcal{C}(\omega) = \{(0, 0)\}$ for all $\omega \in \mathcal{R}_{++}$ (to see this, set $\lambda = \omega/\bar{\omega}$), contradicting nondegeneracy. Thus, $(\bar{n}, \bar{x}) \in \mathcal{P}_+$. By efficiency, $\bar{x} = \bar{\omega}/\bar{n}$. Using homogeneity and efficiency, it follows that $\mathcal{C}(\omega) = \{(\omega\bar{n}/\bar{\omega}, \bar{\omega}/\bar{n})\}$ for all $\omega \in \mathcal{R}_{++}$.

Let $\phi: \mathcal{R}_+ \to \mathcal{R}$ be a differentiable, increasing, and strictly concave function such that $\phi(0) < 0$, $\phi(\bar{\omega}/\bar{n}) = \bar{\omega}/\bar{n}$, and $\phi'(\bar{\omega}/\bar{n}) = 1$. Clearly, such a function exists. It is immediate that the ordering defined by

$$(n, x) \succeq (m, y) \Leftrightarrow n\phi(x) \geq m\phi(y) \tag{10.3}$$

for all $(n, x), (m, y) \in \mathcal{P}$ rationalizes $\mathcal{C}$.

Finally, we use ϕ to construct a critical level $\alpha > U(0)$ and a function g as in the definition of inequality-sensitive critical-level generalized utilitarianism. Let $\bar{x} = \phi^{-1}(0)$. Because $\phi(0) < 0$ and ϕ is increasing, it follows that $\bar{x} > 0$.

---

[4] Note that zero consistency is not required; it is implied by the other axioms.

Because the utility function U is continuous and increasing, the image of U must be an interval of the form $[a, b)$ with $a \in \mathcal{R}, b \in \mathcal{R} \cup \{\infty\}$ and $a < b$. If $b \in \mathcal{R}$, define the function $\bar{g} \colon \mathcal{R} \to \mathcal{R}$ by

$$\bar{g}(u) = \begin{cases} u + \phi(U^{-1}(a)) - a & \text{if } u \in (-\infty, a); \\ \phi(U^{-1}(u)) & \text{if } u \in [a, b); \\ u + \phi(\lim_{v \to b} U^{-1}(v)) - b & \text{if } u \in [b, \infty); \end{cases}$$

if $b = \infty$, let

$$\bar{g}(u) = \begin{cases} u + \phi[U^{-1}(a)] - a & \text{if } u \in (-\infty, a); \\ \phi(U^{-1}(u)) & \text{if } u \in [a, \infty). \end{cases}$$

Now let $g(u) = \bar{g}(u) - \bar{g}(0)$ for all $u \in \mathcal{R}$. Defining $\alpha = U(\bar{x})$, it follows that $\alpha > U(0)$ because $\bar{x} > 0$ and U is increasing and, because $\phi(\bar{x}) = 0$,

$$\phi(x) = \phi(x) - \phi(\bar{x}) = \bar{g}(U(x)) - \bar{g}(U(\bar{x})) = \bar{g}(U(x)) - \bar{g}(\alpha)$$

for all $x \in \mathcal{R}_+$. Hence,

$$\phi(x) = \bar{g}(U(x)) - \bar{g}(\alpha) = \bar{g}(U(x)) - \bar{g}(0) - \bar{g}(\alpha) + \bar{g}(0)$$
$$= g(U(x)) - g(\alpha) \tag{10.4}$$

for all $x \in \mathcal{R}_+$. The function g is continuous and increasing because U and ϕ are and, furthermore, $g(0) = 0$. $g \circ U$ is strictly concave because ϕ is. Substituting (10.4) into (10.3), it follows that C is rationalized by an inequality-sensitive critical-level generalized utilitarian ordering. ∎

That the axioms employed in Theorem 10.2 are independent is established by the following examples.

For all $\omega \in \mathcal{R}_{++}$, let $C(\omega)$ be the set consisting of the best element in $B(\omega/2)$ according to inequality-sensitive critical-level generalized utilitarianism. This choice function is not efficient but satisfies all other axioms of Theorem 10.2.

If $C(\omega) = \{(0, 0)\}$ for all $\omega \in \mathcal{R}_{++}$, it follows that nondegeneracy is the only condition that is violated.

The choice function defined by $C(\omega) = \{(n, \omega/n) \mid n \in \mathcal{R}_{++}\}$ satisfies all axioms except single-valued choice.

Finally, let $C(\omega) = \{(1, \omega)\}$ for all $\omega \in \mathcal{R}_{++}$. Homogeneity is violated but all other axioms are satisfied.

An interesting choice function for the pure population problem has been suggested by Dasgupta (1988). It chooses the smallest population that does not want to add to itself if a weighted sum of utilities with a weight of one for actual people and a weight of $\beta \in (0, 1)$ for potential people is used as a criterion for the desirability of a population augmentation.

Suppose that the utility function $U \colon \mathcal{R}_+ \to \mathcal{R} \cup \{-\infty\}$ maps into the extended real line and is given by $U(0) = -\infty$ and

$$U(x) = 1 - \frac{1}{x}$$

for all $x \in \mathcal{R}_{++}$. Dasgupta's choice function is given by

$$C(\omega) = \left\{ \left(\frac{\beta\omega}{1 + \beta}, \frac{1 + \beta}{\beta} \right) \right\}$$

for all $\omega \in \mathcal{R}_{++}$. Efficiency, non-degeneracy, single-valued choice and homogeneity are satisfied. Theorem 10.2 implies that there is an inequality-sensitive critical-level generalized utilitarian ordering that rationalizes this choice function.

If the chosen population-size–per-capita-consumption pairs are the best elements according to critical-level utilitarianism with $\alpha \in (0, 1)$, then the choice function is

$$C(\omega) = \left\{ \left(\frac{(1 - \alpha)\omega}{2}, \frac{2}{1 - \alpha} \right) \right\}$$

for all $\omega \in \mathcal{R}_{++}$. Consequently, Dasgupta's choice function with weight β is rationalized by the critical-level utilitarian ordering with critical level α if and only if $\beta/(1 + \beta) = (1 - \alpha)/2$, which requires

$$\alpha - \frac{1 - \beta}{1 + \beta}.$$

As β increases, α decreases. In the limit as β approaches 1, α approaches 0 and the choices are rationalized by the classical-utilitarian ordering.

10.5 VARIABLE-POPULATION RATIONAL CHOICE

Although it is of some interest in assessing the relative merits of different population principles, the pure population problem is highly stylized and it is natural to ask whether the results obtained in that setting can be extended to more general choice problems. In this section, we examine the rationalizability issue in a general variable-population welfarist framework, where the objects to be chosen are feasible utility vectors of variable dimension. Beginning with a choice-theoretic formulation of variable-population problems, we characterize classes of choice functions that are rationalizable by variable-population social orderings. We assume that the information relevant for choice can be summarized by a collection of feasible sets of utility vectors, one set for each possible population size. In addition, to avoid utility levels associated with a very low standard of living, we impose a lower bound on chosen utilities.

The same-number restrictions of our choice functions can be interpreted as bargaining solutions. However, the variable-population aspect that is of particular importance in our model is quite different from that appearing in bargaining problems with a variable population [see, for example, Blackorby, Bossert, and Donaldson (1996c); Lensberg (1987, 1988); Thomson (1983a, 1983b, 1984, 1985, 1986); and Thomson and Lensberg (1989)]. In our formulation, population size is to be chosen in addition to a utility distribution, whereas the variable-population bargaining literature analyzes problems in which a choice has to be made for each possible population. Because of that difference, the interpretation of our results in terms of resource-allocation problems is more natural than a bargaining interpretation. Because of the close formal link to the bargaining literature, we can make use of some results in that area. In particular, the results of Lensberg (1987) play an important role in some of our proofs. For $n \in \mathcal{Z}_{++}$, a set $A \subseteq \mathcal{R}^n$ is comprehensive if and only if, for all $u \in A$ and for all $v \in \mathcal{R}^n$, $v \leq u$ implies $v \in A$. The comprehensive hull of $u \in \mathcal{R}^n$ is defined as $\mathcal{H}(u) = \{v \in \mathcal{R}^n \mid v \leq u\}$. A set $A \subseteq \mathcal{R}^n$ is bounded above if and only if there exist $\beta \in \mathcal{R}^n_{++}$ and $\delta \in \mathcal{R}$ such that $\beta u \leq \delta$ for all $u \in A$.

Let $\bar{n} \in \mathcal{Z}_{++}$ with $\bar{n} \geq 3$, and let $N = \{1, \ldots, \bar{n}\}$. A variable-population choice problem is a feasible set $S = \bigcup_{n \in N} S_n$ where, for all $n \in N$, $S_n \subseteq \mathcal{R}^n$ is nonempty, convex, comprehensive, closed, and bounded above. Furthermore, we assume that there exists $n \in N$ such that $S_n \cap \mathcal{R}^n_+ \neq \emptyset$. The set of all variable-population choice problems is denoted by Σ. For $n \in N$, the subset Σ^n of Σ is defined as follows. For all $S \in \Sigma$, $S \in \Sigma^n$ if and only if $S_m = \mathcal{H}(-\mathbf{1}_m)$ for all $m \in N \setminus \{n\}$. In addition, $\bar{\Sigma}^n \subset \Sigma^n$ consists of all problems $S \in \Sigma^n$ satisfying $S_n \cap \mathcal{R}^n_{++} \neq \emptyset$. To simplify notation, we define $S_+ = \bigcup_{n \in N}(S_n \cap \mathcal{R}^n_+)$.

In the previous definitions, N is the set of feasible population sizes. This set is assumed to be bounded because, if resources are limited, arbitrarily large population sizes are not sustainable. Furthermore, $n \in N$ represents population size and S_n is the set of feasible vectors of lifetime utilities for the individuals labelled $1, \ldots, n$. This formulation could be generalized to allow for different populations with the same size. We use the above formulation for simplicity of exposition.

The purpose of Σ^n is to represent same-number choice problems in the sense that, given the zero-dominance condition introduced below, utility vectors of size n only are chosen for all problems in Σ^n. For that reason, we use a negative vector rather than the origin in the definition of Σ^n. If $\mathcal{H}(0\mathbf{1}_m)$ were used instead of $\mathcal{H}(-\mathbf{1}_m)$ for $m \in N \setminus \{n\}$ in the relevant definition, zero dominance would no longer be sufficient to rule out the choice of $0\mathbf{1}_m$ – that is, the axiom would fail to guarantee that an n-dimensional vector is chosen. The choice of $-\mathbf{1}_m$ in the definition of Σ^n is arbitrary – any negative vector would do. The assumption that there exists at least one population size so that everyone alive experiences a utility level of at least zero rules out degenerate cases in which positive population sizes are never chosen.

We do not require the existence of at least one population size such that the corresponding feasible set of utility vectors contains a vector that strictly dominates the origin. This is another feature that distinguishes our approach from standard axiomatic models of bargaining, where such an assumption is usually made, based on the view that there should be some potential gains for all participants in the bargaining process. In contrast, for the variable-population problems considered here, this is not a natural assumption. Given that one might very well choose a boundary point of $\mathcal{R}^n_+$ for some n, it is inappropriate to exclude feasible sets that contain boundary points but no interior points of $\mathcal{R}_+^n$ from the outset.

Let $\Omega^N = \bigcup_{n \in N} \mathcal{R}^n$ and $\Omega_+^N = \bigcup_{n \in N} \mathcal{R}_+^n$. A variable-population choice function is a mapping $\mathcal{G}: \Sigma \rightarrow 2^{\Omega^N}$ such that $\mathcal{G}(S) \subseteq S$ for all $S \in \Sigma$. Formally, this choice function $\mathcal{G}$ generalizes a bargaining solution. Instead of merely selecting utility vectors for given population sizes, population size itself is chosen.

We impose the following zero-dominance condition throughout.

Zero Dominance. For all $S \in \Sigma$, for all $n \in N$, and for all $u \in S_n$, if $u \in \mathcal{G}(S)$, then $u \in \mathcal{R}_+^n$.

Zero dominance is consistent with the assumption that $\mathcal{G}(S)$ is nonempty for all $S \in \Sigma$ because, by definition, there exists at least one population size n such that $S_n \cap \mathcal{R}_+^n$ is nonempty.

Analogously to the case of the pure population problem, a variable-population choice function $\mathcal{G}$ is rationalizable if and only if there exists an ordering $\succeq$ on Ω^N such that, for all $S \in \Sigma$,

$$\mathcal{G}(S) = \{u \in S \mid u \succeq v \text{ for all } v \in S\}.$$

The direct revealed-preference relation $R_{\mathcal{G}}$ on Ω^N corresponding to the choice function $\mathcal{G}$ is defined as follows. For all $u, v \in \Omega^N$, $u R_{\mathcal{G}} v$ if and only if there exists $S \in \Sigma$ such that $u \in \mathcal{G}(S)$ and $v \in S$.

Richter (1966) showed that the following congruence axiom is necessary and sufficient for the rationalizability of a choice function with an arbitrary domain. Stated in terms of our variable-population choice problems, congruence is defined as follows.

Congruence. For all $S \in \Sigma$, for all $K \in \mathcal{Z}_{++} \setminus \{1\}$, and for all $u^1, \ldots, u^K \in \Omega^N$, if $u^{k-1} R_{\mathcal{G}} u^k$ for all $k \in \{2, \ldots, K\}$, $u^K \in \mathcal{G}(S)$, and $u^1 \in S$, then $u^1 \in \mathcal{G}(S)$.

If there exist $S \in \Sigma$, $K \in \mathcal{Z}_{++} \setminus \{1\}$, and $u^1, \ldots, u^K \in \Omega^N$ such that $u^{k-1} R_{\mathcal{G}} u^k$ for all $k \in \{2, \ldots, K\}$, $u^K \in \mathcal{G}(S)$, and $u^1 \in S \setminus \mathcal{G}(S)$, we say that there exists a revealed-preference cycle of length K. Therefore, an equivalent formulation of congruence is that there exists no revealed-preference cycle of length K for all $K \in \mathcal{Z}_{++} \setminus \{1\}$.

Richter's (1966) result formulated for variable-population choice problems is stated in the following theorem.

Theorem 10.3. *A variable-population choice function $\mathcal{G}$ is rationalizable if and only if $\mathcal{G}$ satisfies congruence.*

Richter's rationalizability result is very general in the sense that it does not require any assumptions regarding the domain of a choice function. In the context of variable-population choice problems as defined above, the question arises whether there may be weaker conditions that, due to the specific structure of the underlying domain, are sufficient for the existence of a rationalizing ordering. Clearly, the rationalizability of same-number restrictions of $\mathcal{G}$ is necessary to obtain full rationality. What is of particular interest is the set of additional restrictions on $\mathcal{G}$ imposed by variable-population considerations. Rationalizability can be obtained by adding an interesting weakening of congruence to same-number rationalizability, provided the variable-population choice function satisfies zero dominance. In particular, revealed-preference cycles involving four utility vectors of alternating population sizes have to be ruled out.

Same-number rationalizability requires that, for each population size $n \in N$, there exists an ordering $\succeq^n$ on $\mathcal{R}^n$ such that, if $\mathcal{G}(S)$ contains any n-dimensional vectors, they must be best elements in S_n according to $\succeq^n$.

Same-Number Rationalizability. There exist orderings $\succeq^n \subseteq \mathcal{R}^n \times \mathcal{R}^n$ for all $n \in N$ such that, for all $S \in \Sigma$ and for all $n \in N$, if $\mathcal{G}(S) \cap S_n \neq \emptyset$, then $\mathcal{G}(S) \cap S_n = \{u \in S_n \mid u \succeq^n v \text{ for all } v \in S_n\}$.

The weakening of congruence mentioned above is defined as follows. Note that only revealed-preference cycles with a very special pattern need to be ruled out; in the presence of zero dominance, the conjunction of this axiom and same-number rationalizability is sufficient to exclude any revealed-preference cycle.

Weak Population Congruence. For all $S \in \Sigma$, for all $n, m \in N$ with $n \neq m$, for all $u^1, u^3 \in \mathcal{R}^n$, and for all $u^2, u^4 \in \mathcal{R}^m$, if $u^{\ell-1} R_\mathcal{G} u^\ell$ for all $\ell \in \{2, 3, 4\}$ and $u^4 \in \mathcal{G}(S)$ and $u^1 \in S$, then $u^1 \in \mathcal{G}(S)$.

Weak population congruence rules out revealed-preference cycles of length four where the elements of the cycle are of alternating dimension. This requirement is substantially weaker than congruence. Note that weak population congruence also rules out cycles of length two involving elements of different dimension because the vectors u^1 and u^3 in the definition of this axiom need not be distinct, and the same is true for u^2 and u^4.

In the presence of zero dominance and same-number rationalizability, weak population congruence is equivalent to a stronger version that rules out revealed-preference cycles involving alternating dimensions of any even size. This axiom is defined as follows.

Strong Population Congruence. For all $S \in \Sigma$, for all $n, m \in N$ with $n \neq m$, for all even $L \geq 4$, for all $u^1, u^3, \ldots, u^{L-1} \in \mathcal{R}^n$, and for all $u^2, u^4, \ldots, u^L \in \mathcal{R}^m$, if $u^{\ell-1} R_\mathcal{G} u^\ell$ for all $\ell \in \{2, \ldots, L\}$ and $u^L \in \mathcal{G}(S)$ and $u^1 \in S$, then $u^1 \in \mathcal{G}(S)$.

If there exist $S \in \Sigma$, $n, m \in N$ with $n \neq m$, an even number $L \geq 4$, $u^1, u^3, \ldots, u^{L-1} \in \mathcal{R}^n$, and $u^2, u^4, \ldots, u^L \in \mathcal{R}^m$ such that $u^{\ell-1} R_{\mathcal{G}} u^\ell$ for all $\ell \in \{2, \ldots, L\}$, $u^L \in \mathcal{G}(S)$, and $u^1 \in S \setminus \mathcal{G}(S)$, we say that there exists an alternating-population revealed-preference cycle of length L. The case $L = 2$ is covered because u^1 and u^3 (u^2 and u^4) can be the same.

The following theorem establishes the equivalence of weak and strong population congruence in the presence of zero dominance and same-number rationalizability.

Theorem 10.4. *Suppose a variable-population choice function $\mathcal{G}$ satisfies zero dominance and same-number rationalizability. $\mathcal{G}$ satisfies weak population congruence if and only if $\mathcal{G}$ satisfies strong population congruence.*

Proof. That strong population congruence implies weak population congruence is obvious. Now suppose $\mathcal{G}$ satisfies zero dominance, same-number rationalizability, and weak population congruence. We proceed by induction on L. By weak population congruence, the conclusion of strong population congruence applies to the case $L = 4$. Now suppose the claim is true for all even $\overline{L} \leq L$ where $L \geq 4$. By way of contradiction, suppose there exists an alternating-population revealed-preference cycle of length $L + 2$. That is, there exist $S \in \Sigma$, $n, m \in N$ with $n \neq m$, $u^1, u^3, \ldots, u^{L+1} \in \mathcal{R}^n$, and $u^2, u^4, \ldots, u^{L+2} \in \mathcal{R}^m$ such that $u^{\ell-1} R_{\mathcal{G}} u^\ell$ for all $\ell \in \{2, \ldots, L+2\}$, $u^{L+2} \in \mathcal{G}(S)$, and $u^1 \in S \setminus \mathcal{G}(S)$. Let $S^3 \in \Sigma$ be such that $u^3 \in \mathcal{G}(S^3)$ and $u^4 \in S^3$. Define $\overline{S} \in \Sigma$ by letting $\overline{S}_n = S^3_n$, $\overline{S}_m = S_m$, and $\overline{S}_r = \mathcal{H}(-\mathbf{1}_r)$ for all $r \in N \setminus \{n, m\}$.

If $u^3 \in \mathcal{G}(\overline{S})$, it follows that $u^1 R_{\mathcal{G}} u^2$, $u^2 R_{\mathcal{G}} u^3$, $u^3 R_{\mathcal{G}} u^{L+2}$, $u^{L+2} \in \mathcal{G}(S)$, and $u^1 \in S \setminus \mathcal{G}(S)$. This implies that there exists an alternating-population revealed-preference cycle of length four, a contradiction.

If $u^3 \notin \mathcal{G}(\overline{S})$, zero dominance and same-number rationalizability imply $u^{L+2} \in \mathcal{G}(\overline{S})$. This, in turn, implies that we have $u^3 R_{\mathcal{G}} u^4, \ldots, u^{L+1} R_{\mathcal{G}} u^{L+2}$, $u^{L+2} \in \mathcal{G}(\overline{S})$, and $u^3 \in \overline{S} \setminus \mathcal{G}(\overline{S})$, which establishes the existence of an alternating-population revealed-preference cycle of length L, again a contradiction. ∎

Theorem 10.4 can be used to prove a general characterization result for rationalizable variable-population choice functions.

Theorem 10.5. *Suppose a variable-population choice function $\mathcal{G}$ satisfies zero dominance. $\mathcal{G}$ is rationalizable if and only if $\mathcal{G}$ satisfies same-number rationalizability and weak population congruence.*

Proof. Clearly, rationalizability implies same-number rationalizability and weak population congruence. Conversely, suppose $\mathcal{G}$ satisfies zero dominance, same-number rationalizability, and weak population congruence. We show by induction on K that $\mathcal{G}$ satisfies congruence which, by Theorem 10.3, is sufficient to complete the proof.

Let $S \in \Sigma$, $n, m \in N$, $u^1 \in \mathcal{R}^n$, and $u^2 \in \mathcal{R}^m$ be such that $u^1 R_{\mathcal{G}} u^2$, $u^2 \in \mathcal{G}(S)$, and $u^1 \in S$. If $n = m$, same-number rationalizability implies $u^1 \in \mathcal{G}(S)$ because the restriction of $R_{\mathcal{G}}$ to $\mathcal{R}^n$ must be a subrelation of $\succeq^n$ [see Richter (1971) and Samuelson (1938)]. If $n \neq m$, $u^1 \in \mathcal{G}(S)$ follows from weak population congruence. Therefore, there exists no revealed-preference cycle of length two.

Now suppose there exists no revealed-preference cycle of length $\overline{K} \leq K$ with $K \geq 2$. By way of contradiction, suppose there exists a revealed-preference cycle of length $K + 1$. That is, there exist $S \in \Sigma$ and $u^1, \ldots, u^{K+1} \in \Omega^N$ such that $u^{k-1} R_{\mathcal{G}} u^k$ for all $k \in \{2, \ldots, K+1\}$, $u^{K+1} \in \mathcal{G}(S)$, and $u^1 \in S \setminus \mathcal{G}(S)$. For all $k \in \{1, \ldots, K\}$, let $S^k \in \Sigma$ be such that $u^k \in \mathcal{G}(S^k)$ and $u^{k+1} \in S^k$. Furthermore, let $S^{K+1} = S$. Clearly, one of the following three cases must occur:

(a) there exist $n \in N$ and $k \in \{1, \ldots, K\}$ such that $u^k, u^{k+1} \in \mathcal{R}^n$;
(b) there exist distinct $n, m, r \in N$ and $k \in \{2, \ldots, K\}$ such that $u^{k-1} \in \mathcal{R}^n$, $u^k \in \mathcal{R}^m$ and $u^{k+1} \in \mathcal{R}^r$;
(c) there exist distinct $n, m \in N$ such that $u^k \in \mathcal{R}^n$ for all odd k and $u^k \in \mathcal{R}^m$ for all even k.

(a) If $u^j \in \mathcal{R}^n$ for all $j \in \{1, \ldots, K+1\}$, we obtain a contradiction to same-number rationalizability. Therefore, n and k can be chosen such that at least one of the following subcases must occur:

(a.i) there exists $m \in N \setminus \{n\}$ such that $u^{k-1} \in \mathcal{R}^m$;
(a.ii) there exists $m \in N \setminus \{n\}$ such that $u^{k+2} \in \mathcal{R}^m$.

(a.i) Let $\overline{S} \in \Sigma$ be such that $\overline{S}_m = S_m^{k-1}$, $\overline{S}_n = S_n^k$, and $\overline{S}_r = \mathcal{H}(-\mathbf{1}_r)$ for all $r \in N \setminus \{n, m\}$.

If $\mathcal{G}(\overline{S}) \cap \overline{S}_m \neq \emptyset$, $u^{k-1} \in \mathcal{G}(\overline{S})$ by same-number rationalizability. Because $u^{k+1} \in \overline{S}$, there exists a revealed-preference cycle of length K, a contradiction.

If $\mathcal{G}(\overline{S}) \cap \overline{S}_m = \emptyset$, zero dominance implies $\mathcal{G}(\overline{S}) \cap \overline{S}_n \neq \emptyset$ and, by same-number rationalizability, $u^k \in \mathcal{G}(\overline{S})$. Because $u^{k-1} \in \overline{S} \setminus \mathcal{G}(\overline{S})$, there exists a revealed-preference cycle of length two, a contradiction.

(a.ii) Let $\overline{S} \in \Sigma$ be such that $\overline{S}_m = S_m^{k+2}$, $\overline{S}_n = S_n^k$, and $\overline{S}_r = \mathcal{H}(-\mathbf{1}_r)$ for all $r \in N \setminus \{n, m\}$.

If $\mathcal{G}(\overline{S}) \cap \overline{S}_n \neq \emptyset$, $u^k \in \mathcal{G}(\overline{S})$ by same-number rationalizability. Because $u^{k+2} \in \overline{S}$, there exists a revealed-preference cycle of length K, a contradiction.

If $\mathcal{G}(\overline{S}) \cap \overline{S}_n = \emptyset$, zero dominance implies $\mathcal{G}(\overline{S}) \cap \overline{S}_m \neq \emptyset$, and by same-number rationalizability, $u^{k+2} \in \mathcal{G}(\overline{S})$. Because $u^{k+1} \in \overline{S} \setminus \mathcal{G}(\overline{S})$, there exists a revealed-preference cycle of length two, a contradiction.

(b) Let $\overline{S} \in \Sigma$ be such that $\overline{S}_n = S_n^{k-1}$, $\overline{S}_m = S_m^k$, $\overline{S}_r = S_r^{k+1}$, and $\overline{S}_t = \mathcal{H}(-\mathbf{1}_t)$ for all $t \in N \setminus \{n, m, r\}$. By zero dominance, $\mathcal{G}(\overline{S}) \cap (\overline{S}_n \cup \overline{S}_m \cup \overline{S}_r) \neq \emptyset$ and, by same-number rationalizability, we must have

$$\mathcal{G}(\overline{S}) \cap \overline{S}_n \neq \emptyset \Rightarrow u^{k-1} \in \mathcal{G}(\overline{S}),$$
$$\mathcal{G}(\overline{S}) \cap \overline{S}_m \neq \emptyset \Rightarrow u^k \in \mathcal{G}(\overline{S}),$$

and

$$\mathcal{G}(\overline{S}) \cap \overline{S}_r \neq \emptyset \Rightarrow u^{k+1} \in \mathcal{G}(\overline{S}).$$

If $u^{k+1} \in \mathcal{G}(\overline{S})$, it follows that $u^k \in \mathcal{G}(\overline{S})$ because there exists no revealed-preference cycle of length two. Analogously, if $u^k \in \mathcal{G}(\overline{S})$, it follows that $u^{k-1} \in \mathcal{G}(\overline{S})$. Therefore, $u^{k-1} \in \mathcal{G}(\overline{S})$ in all possible cases and, because $u^{k+1} \in \overline{S}$, we have $u^{k-1} R_{\mathcal{G}} u^{k+1}$. Therefore, there exists a revealed-preference cycle of length K, a contradiction.[5]

(c) There are two subcases:

(c.i) K is odd;
(c.ii) K is even.

(c.i) In this case, $K + 1$ is even, and we obtain a contradiction to strong population congruence and, by Theorem 10.4, to weak population congruence.

(c.ii) It follows that $u^1, u^{K+1} \in \mathcal{R}^n$. Let $\overline{S} \in \Sigma$ be such that $\overline{S}_n = S_n^{K+1}$, $\overline{S}_m = S_m^2$, and $\overline{S}_r = \mathcal{H}(-\mathbf{1}_r)$ for all $r \in N \setminus \{n, m\}$.

If $\mathcal{G}(\overline{S}) \cap \overline{S}_m \neq \emptyset$, same-number rationalizability implies $u^2 \in \mathcal{G}(\overline{S})$. Because $u^{k+1} \in \mathcal{G}(S^{K+1})$ and $u^1 \in S^{K+1} \setminus \mathcal{G}(S^{K+1})$, same-number rationalizability implies $u^1 \in \overline{S} \setminus \mathcal{G}(\overline{S})$. Therefore, there exists a revealed-preference cycle of length two, a contradiction.

If $\mathcal{G}(\overline{S}) \cap \overline{S}_m = \emptyset$, zero dominance implies $\mathcal{G}(\overline{S}) \cap \overline{S}_n \neq \emptyset$. By same-number rationalizability, $u^{K+1} \in \mathcal{G}(\overline{S})$. Because $u^2 \in \overline{S} \setminus \mathcal{G}(\overline{S})$, we obtain a revealed-preference cycle of length K, a contradiction.   ∎

Weak population congruence cannot be weakened to an axiom that merely rules out alternating-population revealed-preference cycles of length two. This is illustrated in the following example. Let $u^1 = (1, 0)$, $u^2 = (1, 0, 0)$, $u^3 = (0, 1)$, and $u^4 = (0, 1, 0)$. Define the sets $B_2 = \{u^1, u^3\}$, $B_3 = \{u^2, u^4\}$, $C_2 = ([\mathcal{H}(u^1) \cup \mathcal{H}(u^3)] \setminus B_2) \cap \mathcal{R}_+^2$, $C_3 = [(\mathcal{H}(u^2) \cup \mathcal{H}(u^4)] \setminus B_3) \cap \mathcal{R}_+^3$, $A_2 = \mathcal{R}_+^2 \setminus (B_2 \cup C_2)$, and $A_3 = \mathcal{R}_+^3 \setminus (B_3 \cup C_3)$. Clearly, $\{A_2, B_2, C_2\}$ is a partition of $\mathcal{R}_+^2$ and $\{A_3, B_3, C_3\}$ is a partition of $\mathcal{R}_+^3$. Define a relation $\succeq^N$ on Ω^N as follows.

(i) for all $u \in \Omega^N, u \sim u$;
(ii) for all $u \in \Omega_+^N$ and for all $v \in \Omega^N \setminus \Omega_+^N, u \succ v$;
(iii) for all $u, v \in \Omega^N \setminus \Omega_+^N, u \sim v$;
(iv) for all $u \in \mathcal{R}_+^2 \cup \mathcal{R}_+^3$ and for all $v \in \bigcup_{n \in N \setminus \{2,3\}} \mathcal{R}_+^n, u \succ v$;
(v) for all $u \in \mathcal{R}_+^n$ and for all $v \in \mathcal{R}_+^m$ with $n, m \in N \setminus \{2, 3\}, u \succeq v$ if and only if $\sum_{i=1}^n u_i \geq \sum_{i=1}^m v_i$;
(vi) for all $u \in A_2 \cup A_3$ and for all $v \in B_2 \cup C_2 \cup B_3 \cup C_3, u \succ v$;

---

[5] The proof of case (b) is analogous to Sen's (1971) proof of the observation that if the domain of a choice function contains all subsets of cardinality three or less of the universal set under consideration, then the direct revealed-preference relation is an ordering.

(vii) for all $u \in A_2 \cup B_2 \cup A_3 \cup B_3$ and for all $v \in C_2 \cup C_3$, $u \succ v$;

(viii) for all $u \in A_n$ and for all $v \in A_m$ with $n, m \in \{2, 3\}$, $u \succeq v$ if and only if $\sum_{i=1}^{n} u_i \geq \sum_{i=1}^{m} v_i$;

(ix) for all $u \in C_n$ and for all $v \in C_m$ with $n, m \in \{2, 3\}$, $u \succeq v$ if and only if $\sum_{i=1}^{n} u_i \geq \sum_{i=1}^{m} v_i$;

(x) $u^1 \succ u^2, u^1 \succ u^3, u^2 \succ u^3, u^2 \succ u^4, u^3 \succ u^4$, and $u^4 \succ u^1$.

Now let

$$\mathcal{G}(S) = \{u \in S \mid u \succeq v \text{ for all } v \in S\}$$

for all $S \in \Sigma$. It can be checked that $\mathcal{G}$ is well-defined even though $\succeq$ is not an ordering. That $\mathcal{G}$ satisfies zero dominance is easy to verify. To see that same-number rationalizability is satisfied, note that the restriction of $\succeq$ to $\mathcal{R}^n$ is an ordering for all $n \in N$. $\mathcal{G}$ violates weak population congruence because there exists an alternating-population revealed-preference cycle of length four involving the points u^1, u^2, u^3, u^4. Whenever u^1 and u^3 (u^2 and u^4) are both feasible, they are worse than points in A_2 (A_3), which, by convexity, are also feasible. Consequently, neither is chosen in such a situation. Thus, no alternating-population revealed-preference cycle of length two exists, which demonstrates that weak population congruence cannot be weakened in the suggested fashion.

10.6 CRITICAL-LEVEL SEPARABLE CHOICE FUNCTIONS

We now provide a generalization of Lensberg's (1987) characterization of bargaining solutions with an additively separable rationalization. Unlike the axiomatizations of critical-level generalized-utilitarian orderings presented earlier, this is a novel characterization because it is formulated in a general choice-theoretic setting.

Throughout this section, it is assumed that, for all variable-population choice problems S and for all population sizes $n \in N$, the choice function $\mathcal{G}$ selects at most one element from the set S_n of feasible utility vectors of dimension n. This axiom is analogous to the single-valuedness assumption that is usually employed in bargaining models.

Same-Number Single-Valuedness. For all $S \in \Sigma$ and for all $n \in N$, $|\mathcal{G}(S) \cap S_n| \in \{0, 1\}$.

We want to include same-number choice problems as special cases in our model. To formulate the same-number axioms for population size $n \in N$, we use one fixed feasible set for all other population sizes in which all utilities are negative. Same-number single-valuedness allows us to formulate our axioms so that their conclusions apply to single-valued choices only.

The next axiom we introduce is Pareto optimality, suitably adapted to our domain.

Pareto Optimality. For all $S \in \Sigma$, for all $n \in N$, and for all $u \in \mathcal{R}^n$, if $S_m = \mathcal{H}(-\mathbf{1}_m)$ for all $m \in N \setminus \{n\}$ and $\mathcal{G}(S) \cap S_n = \{u\}$, then $u \in \{v \in S_n \mid \nexists\, w \in S_n$ such that $w > v\}$.

As usual, continuity axioms require that "small" changes in the description of a problem lead to only "small" changes in the outcome. For the following definition, convergence is defined in terms of the Hausdorff topology.[6]

Choice Continuity. For all $S \in \Sigma$, for all sequences $(S^k)_{k \in \mathcal{Z}_{++}}$ with $S^k \in \Sigma$ for all $k \in \mathcal{Z}_{++}$, for all $n \in N$, for all sequences $(u^k)_{k \in \mathcal{Z}_{++}}$ with $u^k \in \mathcal{R}^n$ for all $k \in \mathcal{Z}_{++}$, and for all $u \in \mathcal{R}^n$, if $S_m = S_m^k = \mathcal{H}(-\mathbf{1}_m)$ for all $m \in N \setminus \{n\}$ and for all $k \in \mathcal{Z}_{++}$, $\mathcal{G}(S^k) \cap S_n^k = \{u^k\}$ for all $k \in \mathcal{Z}_{++}$, $\mathcal{G}(S) \cap S_n = \{u\}$ and $\lim_{k \to \infty} S_n^k = S_n$, then $\lim_{k \to \infty} u^k = u$.

The choice-theoretic formulation of the anonymity axiom requires that the choice function selects outcomes impartially, paying no attention to the agents' identities. Let $n \in N$, and let $\rho \colon \{1, \ldots, n\} \to \{1, \ldots, n\}$ be a bijection. For $u \in \mathcal{R}^n$ and $A \subseteq \mathcal{R}^n$, let $\rho(u) = (u_{\rho(1)}, \ldots, u_{\rho(n)})$ and $\rho(A) = \{v \in \mathcal{R}^n \mid \exists\, w \in A$ such that $v = \rho(w)\}$.

Choice Anonymity. For all $S, T \in \Sigma$, for all $n \in N$, for all bijections $\rho \colon \{1, \ldots, n\} \to \{1, \ldots, n\}$, and for all $u \in \mathcal{R}^n$, if $S_m = T_m = \mathcal{H}(-\mathbf{1}_m)$ for all $m \in N \setminus \{n\}$, $T_n = \rho(S_n)$ and $\mathcal{G}(S) \cap S_n = \{u\}$, then $\mathcal{G}(T) \cap T_n = \{\rho(u)\}$.

Choice anonymity implies symmetry, which requires that, if S_n is equal to $\rho(S_n)$ for all bijections ρ, then any n-dimensional utility vector that is chosen by the solution must have equal utilities.

The next axiom is a suitably adapted version of Nash's (1950) well-known independence of irrelevant alternatives. To avoid confusion with the binary independence axiom for social-evaluation functionals, we use the term contraction consistency for this condition.

Contraction Consistency. For all $S, T \in \Sigma$, for all $n \in N$, and for all $u \in \mathcal{R}^n$, if $S_m = T_m = \mathcal{H}(-\mathbf{1}_m)$ for all $m \in N \setminus \{n\}$, $T_n \subseteq S_n$ and $\mathcal{G}(S) \cap T_n = \{u\}$, then $\mathcal{G}(T) \cap T_n = \{u\}$.

Zero dominance and contraction consistency together imply that the outcomes selected by a choice function are independent of the points in the feasible set that do not dominate the zero vector (this observation is proven later as a preliminary result for the main theorem in this section). This property is

---

[6] Because our feasible sets are closed but not compact, the Hausdorff "distance" may assume the value infinity. However, this does not create any difficulties here. See Peters (1992, p. 168) for details.

analogous to the axiom independence of nonindividually rational alternatives, which is a well-known property of many bargaining solutions (see, for example, Peters 1992).

Independence of Dominated Alternatives. For all $S, T \in \Sigma$, for all $n \in N$, and for all $u \in \mathcal{R}^n$, if $S_m = T_m = \mathcal{H}(-\mathbf{1}_m)$ for all $m \in N \setminus \{n\}$, $S_n \cap \mathcal{R}^n_+ = T_n \cap \mathcal{R}^n_+ \neq \emptyset$, and $\mathcal{G}(S) \cap S_n = \{u\}$, then $\mathcal{G}(T) \cap T_n = \{u\}$.

The population-consistency principle requires that, if some agents leave with their payoffs, the choice of a utility vector for the remaining agents is unchanged.[7] This axiom has remarkably strong consequences. In addition to encompassing a separability condition, it plays a crucial role in establishing the rationalizability of bargaining solutions; see Lensberg (1987) and Thomson and Lensberg (1989). For $n \in \{2, \ldots, \bar{n}\}$, $u \in \mathcal{R}^n$, and $M \subset \{1, \ldots, n\}$, let $u^M = (u_i)_{i \in M}$. Furthermore, for $S \in \Sigma$, let

$$t^u_M(S_n) = \{v^M \in \mathcal{R}^{|M|} \mid w \in S_n, \text{ where } w_i = u_i \text{ if } i \in \{1, \ldots, n\} \setminus M$$
$$\text{and } w_i = v^M_i \text{ if } i \in M\}.$$

Population consistency can now be defined as follows.

Population Consistency. For all $S, T \in \Sigma$, for all $n \in N$, for all $u \in \mathcal{R}^n$, and for all nonempty $M \subset \{1, \ldots, n\}$, if $S_m = \mathcal{H}(-\mathbf{1}_m)$ for all $m \in N \setminus \{n\}$, $T_m = \mathcal{H}(-\mathbf{1}_m)$ for all $m \in N \setminus \{|M|\}$, $\mathcal{G}(S) \cap S_n = \{u\}$, and $T_{|M|} = t^u_M(S_n)$, then $\mathcal{G}(T) \cap T_{|M|} = \{u^M\}$.

The above axioms are well-known in the context of resource-allocation mechanisms and bargaining solutions. In addition, we use an independence condition that guarantees same-number rationalizability if added to some other axioms.

Restricted Choice Independence. For all $S, T \in \Sigma$, for all $n \in N$, and for all $u \in \mathcal{R}^n$, if $S_m = \mathcal{H}(-\mathbf{1}_m)$ for all $m \in N \setminus \{n\}$, $\mathcal{G}(S) \cap S_n = \{u\}$, $T_n = S_n$ and $\mathcal{G}(T) \cap T_n \neq \emptyset$, then $\mathcal{G}(T) \cap T_n = \{u\}$.

In the presence of same-number single-valuedness, the axioms choice anonymity, contraction consistency, independence of dominated alternatives, population consistency, and restricted choice independence are equivalent to those that are obtained by replacing the equality in their conclusions by the set

---

[7] This axiom is usually referred to as consistency. We use the term population consistency to avoid confusion with other consistency axioms. See Thomson (1990, 1996b) for a general discussion and Blackorby, Bossert, and Donaldson (1996c) and Lensberg (1987) for versions that are analogous to the one employed here.

inclusion $\supseteq$. We have chosen the above versions to use formulations that are analogous to those that are standard in the relevant literature.

Finally, to provide a link between choices involving different population sizes, we impose a choice-theoretic version of the critical-level population principle. It requires that there exists a fixed critical level such that, if a feasible utility vector is augmented by an individual utility at this critical level and the resulting vector is feasible as well, then the augmented vector is chosen if and only if the original vector is chosen.

Critical-Level Choice Principle. There exists $c \in \mathcal{R}$ such that, for all $n \in N \setminus \{\bar{n}\}$, for all $u \in \mathcal{R}^n$, and for all $S \in \Sigma$, if $u \in S$ and $(u, c) \in S$, then $u \in \mathcal{G}(S)$ if and only if $(u, c) \in \mathcal{G}(S)$.

The members of the class of variable-population choice functions characterized in this section are rationalized by critical-level separable orderings. Following the terminology used by Thomson and Lensberg (1989), we refer to these choice functions as critical-level CRS choice functions because they are analogous to the collectively rational bargaining solutions admitting an additively separable representation characterized by Lensberg (1987).

Let $\mathbf{H}$ be the set of continuous, increasing and strictly concave functions $h: \mathcal{R}_+ \to \mathcal{R}$. Consider any continuous, increasing and strictly concave function $h: \mathcal{R}_+ \to \mathcal{R} \cup \{-\infty\}$ such that $h(0) = -\infty$. For all $\beta \in \mathcal{R}^2_{++}$, let

$$\bar{u}^h(\beta) = \arg\max\{h(u_1) + h(u_2) \mid \beta u \leq 1\}.$$

Note that the properties of h ensure that $\bar{u}^h(\beta)$ is well-defined and unique and, furthermore, $\bar{u}^h(\beta) \in \mathcal{R}^2_{++}$ for all $\beta \in \mathcal{R}^2_{++}$. Let $\mathbf{H}_0$ be the set of all continuous, increasing, and strictly concave functions $h: \mathcal{R}_+ \to \mathcal{R} \cup \{-\infty\}$ such that $h(0) = -\infty$ and

$$\lim_{\beta_2 \to \infty} \bar{u}^h(\beta) = (1/\beta_1, 0) \tag{10.5}$$

for all $\beta_1 \in \mathcal{R}_{++}$. For all $n \in N$ and for all $u \in \mathcal{R}^n_+$, let $N_+(u) = \{i \in \{1, \ldots, n\} \mid u_i > 0\}$ and $n_+(u) = |N_+(u)|$.

For $h \in \mathbf{H}$ and $n \in N$, define the ordering $\succeq^n_h$ on $\mathcal{R}^n_+$ by letting, for all $u, v \in \mathcal{R}^n_+$,

$$u \succeq^n_h v \Leftrightarrow \sum_{i=1}^n h(u_i) \geq \sum_{i=1}^n h(v_i).$$

For $h \in \mathbf{H}_0$ and $n \in N$, define the ordering $\succeq^n_h$ on $\mathcal{R}^n_+$ by letting, for all $u, v \in \mathcal{R}^n_+$,

$$u \succeq^n_h v \Leftrightarrow [n_+(u) > n_+(v)] \text{ or}$$

$$\left[n_+(u) = n_+(v) \text{ and } \sum_{i \in N_+(u)} h(u_i) \geq \sum_{i \in N_+(v)} h(v_i) \right].$$

Let $\alpha \in \mathcal{R}_+$ and $h \in \mathbf{H} \cup \mathbf{H}_0$. The ordering $\succeq_{h,\alpha}$ on Ω_+^N is defined as follows. For all $n, m \in N$, for all $u \in \mathcal{R}_+^n$ and for all $v \in \mathcal{R}_+^m$,

$$u \succeq_{h,\alpha} v \Leftrightarrow \begin{cases} u \succeq_h^n v \text{ if } n = m; \\ u \succeq_h^n (v, \alpha\mathbf{1}_{n-m}) \text{ if } n > m; \\ (u, \alpha\mathbf{1}_{m-n}) \succeq_h^n v \text{ if } n < m. \end{cases}$$

$\mathcal{G}$ is a critical-level CRS choice function if and only if there exist $\alpha \in \mathcal{R}_+$ and $h \in \mathbf{H} \cup \mathbf{H}_0$ such that, for all $S \in \Sigma$,

$$\mathcal{G}(S) = \{u \in S_+ \mid u \succeq_{h,\alpha} v \text{ for all } v \in S_+\}.$$

Because of the strict concavity assumption, the class of orderings $\{\succeq_{h,\alpha}\}_{h \in \mathbf{H} \cup \mathbf{H}_0, \alpha \in \mathcal{R}_+}$ does not contain the critical-level utilitarian orderings, which result from choosing h to be affine. These orderings are excluded because the choice functions rationalized by them fail to satisfy same-number single-valuedness.

In the case in which h is an element of $\mathbf{H}$, the definition of $\succeq_{h,\alpha}$ simplifies to

$$u \succeq_{h,\alpha} v \Leftrightarrow \sum_{i=1}^{n} \left[h(u_i) - h(\alpha)\right] \geq \sum_{i=1}^{m} \left[h(v_i) - h(\alpha)\right]$$

for all $n, m \in N$, for all $u \in \mathcal{R}_+^n$, and for all $v \in \mathcal{R}_+^m$.[8]

The restriction (10.5) in the definition of $\mathbf{H}_0$ is needed to ensure that the resulting choice functions are continuous and satisfy Pareto optimality. Note that (10.5) is not satisfied by all continuous, increasing, and strictly concave functions h such that $h(0) = -\infty$; for example, logarithmic functions fail to possess this property. Therefore, Nash-type choice functions are not in the class of functions characterized here. Although the Nash solution and related bargaining solutions are well-behaved on domains that include interior points of $\mathcal{R}_+^n$, they cannot be extended continuously to other problems without violating Pareto optimality. However, $\mathbf{H}_0$ is nonempty. For example, the function $h \colon \mathcal{R}_+ \to \mathcal{R} \cup \{-\infty\}$ defined by

$$h(w) = \begin{cases} -\left[-\ln(w)\right]^q & \text{if } 0 \leq w \leq e^{q-1}; \\ -(1-q)^{1+q} + q(1-q)^{q-1}\ln(w) & \text{if } w > e^{q-1} \end{cases}$$

is an element of $\mathbf{H}_0$ for all parameter values $q \in (0, 1)$.[9]

We now turn to a characterization of the critical-level CRS choice functions. We begin with some preliminary results. The proof of the following theorem is analogous to the proof of Lensberg's (1987) Lemma 1 formulated for bargaining solutions and is omitted.

---

[8] See Blackorby, Bossert, and Donaldson (1998) and Blackorby and Donaldson (1984a).

[9] We thank James Redekop for proving the nonemptiness of $\mathbf{H}_0$ by providing this example.

Theorem 10.6. *If a variable-population choice function $\mathcal{G}$ satisfies same-number single-valuedness, Pareto optimality, choice continuity, and population consistency, then $\mathcal{G}$ satisfies contraction consistency.*

The next result establishes that independence of dominated alternatives is implied by some of our other axioms.

Theorem 10.7. *If a variable-population choice function $\mathcal{G}$ satisfies zero dominance and contraction consistency, then $\mathcal{G}$ satisfies independence of dominated alternatives.*

Proof. Suppose $\mathcal{G}$ satisfies zero dominance and contraction consistency. Let $S, T \in \Sigma$, $n \in N$ and $u \in \mathcal{R}^n$ be such that $S_m = T_m = \mathcal{H}(-\mathbf{1}_m)$ for all $m \in N \setminus \{n\}$, $S_n \cap \mathcal{R}^n_+ = T_n \cap \mathcal{R}^n_+ \neq \emptyset$, and $\mathcal{G}(S) \cap S_n = \{u\}$. Let $W \in \Sigma$ be such that $W_m = \mathcal{H}(-\mathbf{1}_m)$ for all $m \in N \setminus \{n\}$ and $W_n = S_n \cap T_n$. By zero dominance, $\mathcal{G}(S) \cap S_n \cap \mathcal{R}^n_+$ and $\mathcal{G}(T) \cap T_n \cap \mathcal{R}^n_+$ are nonempty and, because $S_n \cap \mathcal{R}^n_+ = T_n \cap \mathcal{R}^n_+$, $W_n \cap \mathcal{R}^n_+ = S_n \cap \mathcal{R}^n_+ = T_n \cap \mathcal{R}^n_+$. Therefore, $\mathcal{G}(S) \cap W_n$ and $\mathcal{G}(T) \cap W_n$ are nonempty, and contraction consistency implies $\mathcal{G}(W) \cap W_n = \mathcal{G}(S) \cap S_n - \{u\}$ and $\mathcal{G}(W) \cap W_n = \mathcal{G}(T) \cap T_n$. Hence, $\mathcal{G}(T) \cap T_n = \mathcal{G}(S) \cap S_n = \{u\}$. ∎

Theorem 10.8 provides an extension of Lensberg's (1987) Theorem 1 to a larger domain. The domain considered by Lensberg (1987) is the standard domain of bargaining solutions with a normalized disagreement point satisfying individual rationality, which is analogous to our zero-dominance condition. A crucial difference between that domain and the one considered here is that Lensberg's is restricted to problems S_n such that $S_n \cap \mathcal{R}^n_{++} \neq \emptyset$ – that is, each same-number problem contains a strictly positive vector.

Lensberg (1987) showed that suitably reformulated versions of Pareto optimality, choice continuity, and population consistency characterize, under an implicit individual-rationality assumption, the class of bargaining solutions that are rationalized by a family of orderings (one for each population size) with a specific additively separable representation. Due to the assumption that there exists a strictly positive vector in each bargaining problem, it is possible that the functions generating this representation have the value $-\infty$ at zero. If this assumption is dropped, the only functions of that type consistent with our axioms are those satisfying (10.5). We add choice anonymity to the list of axioms, which implies that the functions used in the additive representation can be chosen to be the same for all agents. We obtain

Theorem 10.8. *If a variable-population choice function $\mathcal{G}$ satisfies zero dominance, same-number single-valuedness, Pareto optimality, choice continuity, choice anonymity, and population consistency, then there exists a function $h \in \mathbf{H} \cup \mathbf{H}_0$ such that, for all $n \in N$ and for all $S \in \Sigma^n$,*

$$\mathcal{G}(S) = \{u \in S_n \cap \mathcal{R}^n_+ \mid u \succeq^n_h v \text{ for all } v \in S_n \cap \mathcal{R}^n_+\}. \tag{10.6}$$

Proof. By Theorems 10.6 and 10.7, the axioms in the statement of Theorem 10.8 imply that Lensberg's (1987) Theorems 1 and 2 can be invoked to conclude that there exists a continuous, increasing, and strictly concave function $h: \mathcal{R}_+ \to \mathcal{R} \cup \{-\infty\}$ such that, for all $n \in N$ and for all $S \in \bar{\Sigma}^n$, (10.6) is satisfied. Choice anonymity implies that the functions h_i in Lensberg's result can be chosen to be identical for all $i \in N$, and we can therefore write $h = h_i$ for all $i \in N$.

To accommodate problems in $\Sigma^n \setminus \bar{\Sigma}^n$, functions with $h(0) = -\infty$ must satisfy (10.5) to ensure that the resulting choice functions satisfy choice continuity and Pareto optimality. Therefore, only functions in $\mathbf{H} \cup \mathbf{H}_0$ are admissible. To complete the proof, note that, given the properties of h, $\mathcal{G}(S)$ must consist of the (unique) best element in S according to $\succeq_h^n$ for all $S \in \Sigma^n$. ∎

The last preliminary result before stating the characterization theorem of this section shows that same-number rationalizability is implied by some of our other axioms.

Theorem 10.9. *If a variable-population choice function $\mathcal{G}$ satisfies zero dominance, same-number single-valuedness, Pareto optimality, choice continuity, choice anonymity, population consistency, and restricted choice independence, then $\mathcal{G}$ satisfies same-number rationalizability.*

Proof. By Theorem 10.8, there exists a function $h \in \mathbf{H} \cup \mathbf{H}_0$ such that (10.6) is satisfied for all $n \in N$ and for all $S \in \Sigma^n$. Let $n \in N$ and define the ordering $\succeq^n$ on $\mathcal{R}^n$ as follows:

    (i) for all $u, v \in \mathcal{R}_+^n$, $u \succeq^n v$ if and only if $u \succeq_h^n v$;
    (ii) for all $u, v \in \mathcal{R}^n \setminus \mathcal{R}_+^n$, $u \sim^n v$;
    (iii) for all $u \in \mathcal{R}_+^n$ and for all $v \in \mathcal{R}^n \setminus \mathcal{R}_+^n$, $u \succ^n v$.

By Theorem 10.8 and restricted choice independence, it follows that $\mathcal{G}$ satisfies same-number rationalizability with the orderings $\succeq^n$. ∎

The following characterization is the main result of this section.

Theorem 10.10. *A variable-population choice function $\mathcal{G}$ satisfies zero dominance, weak population congruence, same-number single valuedness, Pareto optimality, choice continuity, choice anonymity, population consistency, restricted choice independence, and the critical-level choice principle if and only if $\mathcal{G}$ is a critical-level CRS choice function.*

Proof. That the critical-level CRS choice functions satisfy the required axioms can be verified easily.[10] Now suppose $\mathcal{G}$ satisfies all of the axioms. By weak

---

[10] Note that (10.5) ensures that choice continuity and Pareto optimality are satisfied if $h \in \mathbf{H}_0$.

population congruence, Theorem 10.5 and Theorem 10.9, $\mathcal{G}$ is rationalizable by an ordering $\succeq$ on Ω^N. By zero dominance, only nonnegative utility vectors can be chosen and, therefore, we can restrict attention to vectors in Ω^N_+. The critical-level choice principle implies that there exists a fixed critical level $c \in \mathcal{R}$. Let $\alpha = c$. Consider any $n \in N \setminus \{\bar{n}\}$ and $u \in \mathcal{R}^n_+$, and let $S \in \Sigma$ be such that $S_m = \mathcal{H}(-\mathbf{1}_m)$ for all $m \in N \setminus \{n, n+1\}$, $S_n = \mathcal{H}(u)$, and $S_{n+1} = \mathcal{H}((u, \alpha))$. By zero dominance and Pareto optimality, $u \in \mathcal{G}(S)$ or $(u, \alpha) \in \mathcal{G}(S)$. By the critical-level choice principle, $u \in \mathcal{G}(S)$ and $(u, \alpha) \in \mathcal{G}(S)$. By zero dominance, $\alpha \geq 0$. By definition of a rationalization,

$$u \sim (u, \alpha). \tag{10.7}$$

Let $n, m \in N$, $u \in \mathcal{R}^n_+$ and $v \in \mathcal{R}^m_+$. If $n = m$, Theorems 10.8 and 10.9 imply that there exists a function $h \in \mathbf{H} \cup \mathbf{H}_0$ such that

$$u \succeq v \Leftrightarrow u \succeq^n_h v \Leftrightarrow u \succeq_{h,\alpha} v.$$

If $n > m$, repeated application of (10.7) implies

$$u \succeq v \Leftrightarrow u \succeq (v, \alpha \mathbf{1}_{n-m}) \Leftrightarrow u \succeq^n_h (v, \alpha \mathbf{1}_{n-m}) \Leftrightarrow u \succeq_{h,\alpha} v$$

and, analogously, if $n < m$, we obtain

$$u \succeq v \Leftrightarrow (u, \alpha \mathbf{1}_{m-n}) \succeq v \Leftrightarrow (u, \alpha \mathbf{1}_{m-n}) \succeq^n_h v \Leftrightarrow u \succeq_{h,\alpha} v,$$

which completes the proof. ∎

The axioms used in Theorem 10.10 are independent; see the appendix of Blackorby, Bossert, and Donaldson (2002a) for details.

Critical-level separable orderings are usually defined for all utility vectors, including those with negative components. Instead of using neutrality, the norm in the zero-dominance condition could be set, for example, at a utility level that represents a wretched life or a life that is worse than any person might reasonably experience. Consequently, the ethical judgment that it represents can be made flexible. In addition, it is natural to deal with the problem of utility levels that are "too low" by imposing lower bounds on individual utilities rather than through a modification of the social objective function. This is a position that is analogous to the one advocated by Blackorby, Bossert, and Donaldson (2000) in an examination of the ethical foundations of the common practice of discounting the utilities of the members of future generations. Moreover, imposing a lower bound on individual utilities allows us to respond to a criticism that applies to additively separable orderings with unbounded transformations. These orderings allow sufficiently high utility levels to compensate for arbitrarily low utilities of other individuals. If a condition such as zero dominance is imposed, the objection loses much of its force.

10.7 QUASI-ORDERINGS AND UNDOMINATED CHOICES

If a social ranking is not complete, best elements may not exist in choice problems. However, quasi-orderings can be used to guide choices by finding the set of undominated utility vectors.[11] It is analogous to the set of Pareto optima corresponding to the Pareto quasi-ordering. In this section, we illustrate this methodology by means of the critical-band generalized utilitarian principles.

Suppose $S = \bigcup_{n \in N} S_n$ is a fixed set of feasible utility vectors where, for all $n \in N$, $S_n \subseteq \mathcal{R}^n$ is nonempty. R is the restriction of a critical-band generalized utilitarian quasi-ordering to N if and only if there exist a nondegenerate and bounded interval $Q \subseteq \mathcal{R}$ and a continuous and increasing function $g \colon \mathcal{R} \to \mathcal{R}$ with $g(0) = 0$ such that, for all $n, m \in N$, for all $u \in \mathcal{R}^n$, and for all $v \in \mathcal{R}^m$,

$$u R v \Leftrightarrow \sum_{i=1}^{n} [g(u_i) - g(c)] \geq \sum_{i=1}^{m} [g(v_i) - g(c)] \text{ for all } c \in Q.$$

We fix the transformation g and let $V_c \colon \bigcup_{n \in N} \mathcal{R}^n \to \mathcal{R}$ be the value function for critical-level generalized utilitarianism restricted to N with the critical level $c \in \mathcal{R}$ – that is, $V_c(u) = \sum_{i=1}^{n} [g(u_i) - g(c)]$ for all $n \in N$ and for all $u \in \mathcal{R}^n$.

The set of undominated elements in S consists of all utility vectors for which there exists no utility vector that is better according to critical-band generalized utilitarianism. This set is defined as

$$M^* = \{u \in S \mid \nexists v \in S \text{ such that } V_c(v) > V_c(u) \text{ for all } c \in Q\}.$$

Analogously, the set of undominated population sizes in N is defined as

$$N_M^* = \left\{ n \in N \mid \nexists m \in N \text{ such that} \right.$$

$$\left. \max_{v \in S_m} V_c(v) > \max_{u \in S_n} V_c(u) \text{ for all } c \in Q \right\}.$$

For $c \in \mathcal{R}$, the set of best elements in S is

$$B_c^* = \{u \in S \mid V_c(u) \geq V_c(v) \text{ for all } v \in S\}$$

and we define the set of best elements in S for Q to be

$$B^* = \bigcup_{c \in Q} B_c^*.$$

The set of best population sizes in N for $c \in \mathcal{R}$ is defined as

$$N_{Bc}^* = \left\{ n \in N \mid \max_{u \in S_n} V_c(u) \geq \max_{v \in S_m} V_c(v) \text{ for all } m \in N \right\}$$

and, finally, the set of best population sizes for Q is

$$N_B^* = \bigcup_{c \in Q} N_{Bc}^*.$$

---

[11] Sen (1970a) calls this the set of maximal elements.

If the social ranking is not complete, there are potential difficulties regarding the consistency of sequential choices of undominated alternatives. Consider the following example with three alternatives and two consecutive choice problems.[12] In the first choice problem, the feasible set has two elements: an alternative x and a second choice problem with the feasible set $\{y, z\}$. Suppose a quasi-ordering R on the universal set $\{x, y, z\}$ is such that xPz and all other pairs of distinct alternatives are not ranked. The undominated alternatives are x and y and there is no reason to reject either of the two choices – both lead to undominated alternatives. If the second choice problem is selected rather than x, there is no reason to reject z because it is not dominated in $\{y, z\}$. It is, however, dominated by x, which illustrates the difficulty.

Problems of that nature can be avoided if the set of undominated alternatives is the union of the sets of best alternatives according to the orderings generated by each value of $c \in Q$. This is not always the case, unfortunately. Although the union of the best sets is a subset of the undominated set, the converse set inclusion is not true in general. For example, let $N = \{1, 2, 3\}$ and consider the feasible set of utility vectors $S = \{(65), (40, 40), (35, 35, 35)\}$. Suppose g is the identity mapping and $Q = [0, 30]$. All elements in S are undominated according to critical-band utilitarianism but there exists no $c \in Q$ such that $(40, 40)$ is best: we have $B_c^* = \{(35, 35, 35)\}$ for all $c \in [0, 20)$, $B_{20}^* = \{(65), (35, 35, 35)\}$, and $B_c^* = \{(65)\}$ for all $c \in (20, 30]$.

The following theorem provides a sufficient condition for the set of best elements to coincide with the undominated set. This condition requires that the set of best population sizes N_B^* consist of a set of consecutive elements in N.

Theorem 10.11. *Let R be a critical-band generalized utilitarian quasi-ordering. If there exist $n_L, n_H \in N$ such that $n_L \leq n_H$ and $N_B^* = \{n_L, \ldots, n_H\}$, then $M^* = B^*$.*

Proof. Suppose there exist $n_L, n_H \in N$ such that $n_L \leq n_H$ and $N_B^* = \{n_L, \ldots, n_H\}$. Because $B^* \subseteq M^*$ by definition, it is sufficient to show that, for all $u \in S$, $u \notin B^*$ implies $u \notin M^*$. Let $n \in N$ and $u \in S_n \setminus B^*$. There are two cases:

(a) $n \in N_B^*$;
(b) $n \notin N_B^*$.

(a) If $n \in N_B^*$, it follows that there exists $c_0 \in Q$ such that

$$\max_{v \in S_n} V_{c_0}(v) \geq \max_{w \in S_m} V_{c_0}(w)$$

for all $m \in N$. Because $u \notin B^*$, this implies that $\max_{v \in S_n} V_{c_0}(v) > V_{c_0}(u)$ and, thus, there exists $v \in S_n$ such that $V_{c_0}(v) > V_{c_0}(u)$. Because u and v have the same population size n, it follows that $V_c(v) > V_c(u)$ for all $c \in Q$ and, thus, $u \notin M^*$.

---

[12] See also Hammond (1996).

(b) If $n \notin N_B^*$, our hypothesis implies that $n < n_L$ or $n > n_H$. Without loss of generality, suppose $n < n_L$; the proof in the other case is analogous. Let $c_H = \sup(Q)$.

First, suppose $c_H \notin Q$. There are two subcases:

(b.i) there exists $v \in B^*$ such that $V_{c_H}(v) \geq V_{c_H}(u)$;

(b.ii) $V_{c_H}(u) > V_{c_H}(v)$ for all $v \in B^*$.

(b.i) Let $m \in N$ be such that $v \in S_m$. We obtain

$$\sum_{i=1}^{m} g(v_i) - mg(c_H) \geq \sum_{i=1}^{n} g(u_i) - ng(c_H), \tag{10.8}$$

which is equivalent to

$$\sum_{i=1}^{m} g(v_i) + (n - m)g(c_H) \geq \sum_{i=1}^{n} g(u_i).$$

Because $v \in B^*$, it follows that $m \in N_B^*$ and, because $n < n_L, n < m$. Together with the increasingness of g, this implies

$$\sum_{i=1}^{m} g(v_i) + (n - m)g(c) > \sum_{i=1}^{n} g(u_i) \tag{10.9}$$

for all $c < c_H$ and, thus,

$$\sum_{i=1}^{m} g(v_i) - mg(c) > \sum_{i=1}^{n} g(u_i) - ng(c)$$

for all $c \in Q$. Therefore, $V_c(v) > V_c(u)$ for all $c \in Q$ and, hence, $u \notin M^*$.

(b.ii) Because V_c is continuous in c, it follows that there exists a $c \in Q$ sufficiently close to c_H such that $V_c(u) > V_c(v)$ for all $v \in B^*$. Let $v \in B^*$ be such that v is a best element for c. By definition, it follows that $V_c(v) > V_c(u)$, a contradiction. Thus, this subcase cannot occur.

Finally, suppose $c_H \in Q$. Because $n \notin N_B^*$, there exists $m \in N$ such that

$$\max_{v \in S_m} V_{c_H}(v) > \max_{w \in S_n} V_{c_H}(w).$$

Let $v \in S_m$ be such that $V_{c_H}(v) = \max_{v \in S_m} V_{c_H}(v)$. It follows that (10.8) is satisfied with a strict inequality and (10.9) holds for all $c \leq c_H$ and, therefore, for all $c \in Q$. Again, we obtain $V_c(v) > V_c(u)$ for all $c \in Q$ and $u \notin M^*$ follows. ∎

Blackorby, Bossert, and Donaldson (1996a, Theorem 2) claimed that an alternative sufficient condition is that the set of undominated population sizes N_M^* is a set of consecutive elements in N. However, this claim is not correct. Consider again the critical-band utilitarian example with

$N = \{1, 2, 3\}$, $S = \{(65), (40, 40), (35, 35, 35)\}$, and $Q = [0, 30]$. We have $V_{20}(65) = V_{20}(35, 35, 35) = 45 \geq 40 = V_{20}(40, 40)$, which implies $\{1, 3\} \subseteq N_M^*$. Furthermore, $V_0(40, 40) = 80 \geq 65 = V_0(65)$ and $V_{30}(40, 40) = 20 \geq 15 = V_{30}(35, 35, 35)$ and, therefore, $2 \in N_M^*$. Thus, the set of undominated population sizes is $N_M^* = \{1, 2, 3\}$ but, as established earlier, $M^* \neq B^*$.

An interesting application of Theorem 10.11 is obtained in the context of the pure population problem. The result requires a concave transformation g and, for simplicity of presentation, we assume that g is twice differentiable. Furthermore, we assume that the common utility function U is strongly concave – that is, U is twice differentiable with $U''(x) < 0$ for all $x \in \mathcal{R}_+$. The pure population problem defined by the available amount of the resource $\omega \in \mathcal{R}_{++}$ induces the feasible set

$$S = \bigcup_{n \in N} S_n = \bigcup_{n \in N} \{U(x)\mathbf{1}_n \mid nx \leq \omega\}.$$

To use the same framework throughout this section, we consider only the set N of possible population sizes. However, a zero population could be included without changing the following result.

Theorem 10.12. *Let R be a critical-band generalized utilitarian quasi-ordering. If g is concave and twice differentiable, U is strongly concave, and the feasible set S is induced by a pure population problem, then $M^* = B^*$.*

Proof. Step 1. We first show that, for any $n \in N$, there exists $c \in \mathcal{R}$ such that $n \in N_{Bc}^*$. Let

$$c = g^{-1}\Big(g\big(U(\omega/n)\big) - (\omega/n)g'\big(U(\omega/n)\big)U'(\omega/n)\Big).$$

Because g is concave, it is not bounded below and, therefore, the argument of g^{-1} is in the image of g, so c is well-defined. Define a function $f: \mathcal{R}_{++} \to \mathcal{R}$ by

$$f(t) = t\Big[g\big(U(\omega/t)\big) - g(c)\Big]$$

for all $t \in \mathcal{R}_{++}$. We obtain

$$f'(t) = g\big(U(\omega/t)\big) - g(c) - (\omega/t)g'\big(U(\omega/t)\big)U'(\omega/t)$$

and

$$f''(t) = (\omega^2/t^3)\Big[g''\big(U(\omega/t)\big)\big[U'(\omega/t)\big]^2 + g'\big(U(\omega/t)\big)U''(\omega/t)\Big]$$

for all $t \in \mathcal{R}_{++}$. Because g is concave and U is strongly concave, it follows that $f''(t) < 0$ for all $t \in \mathcal{R}_{++}$. Therefore, the first-order condition $f'(t) = 0$ is sufficient for a maximum of f. This first-order condition is satisfied for $t = n$ and, therefore, $n \in N_{Bc}^*$.

Step 2. Next, we show that, for all $c, d \in \mathcal{R}$, for all $n, m \in N$, for all $u \in B_c^* \cap S_n$, and for all $v \in B_d^* \cap S_m$,

$$c > d \Rightarrow m \geq n.$$

Because $u \in B_c^*$ and $v \in B_d^*$, it follows that

$$\sum_{i=1}^n [g(u_i) - g(c)] \geq \sum_{i=1}^m [g(v_i) - g(c)]$$

and

$$\sum_{i=1}^m [g(v_i) - g(d)] \geq \sum_{i=1}^m [g(u_i) - g(d)].$$

Adding the two inequalities, we obtain

$$(m - n)[g(c) - g(d)] \geq 0. \tag{10.10}$$

If $c > d$, the increasingness of g implies $g(c) > g(d)$ and, by (10.10), we obtain $m \geq n$.

Step 3. Finally, we show that there exist $n_L, n_H \in N$ such that $n_L \leq n_H$ and $N_B^* = \{n_L, \ldots, n_H\}$ which, by Theorem 10.11, completes the proof.

Suppose, by way of contradiction, that there exist $m, n, r \in N$ such that $m < n < r$, $m, r \in N_B^*$, and $n \notin N_B^*$. As shown in Step 1, there exists $c \in \mathcal{R}$ such that $n \in N_{Bc}^*$. Because $n \notin N_B^*$, it follows that $c \notin Q$. The result of Step 2 implies that $c \geq \inf(Q)$ and $c \leq \sup(Q)$. If $\inf(Q) \in Q$, the first inequality must be strict and if $\sup(Q) \in Q$, the second inequality must be strict; this is the case because $c \notin Q$. But Q is an interval, and this contradicts the assumption $c \notin Q$. ∎

Step 2 in the above proof establishes a monotonicity property of chosen population sizes with respect to the critical level. For higher critical levels, the optimal population sizes according to critical-level generalized utilitarianism are less than or equal to those for lower critical levels. This result is not restricted to the pure population problem; the argument in the above proof applies to any choice problem with a solution that selects best elements according to critical-level generalized utilitarianism. We therefore obtain

Theorem 10.13. *Let $S \subseteq \bigcup_{n \in \mathcal{Z}_{++}} \mathcal{R}^n$ be nonempty. If $c, d \in \mathcal{R}$, $n, m \in \mathcal{Z}_{++}$, $u \in \mathcal{R}^n$, and $v \in \mathcal{R}^m$ are such that $u \in B_c^*$, $v \in B_d^*$ and $c > d$, then $n \leq m$.*

CHAPTER 11

Applications

Part A

To illustrate the practical use of the critical-level utilitarian principles discussed in earlier chapters, we examine their use in two economic models. The first analyzes the problem of allocating a foreign-aid budget to different types of expenditures. In it, we assume that aid received by a developing country can be used to fund consumption or population control (prevention of births) and use a two-period model where population size in period two is determined by the amount spent on population control in period one. The second application examines the use of animals in research and food production. We evaluate various policies with a generalization of critical-level utilitarianism that takes account of the interests of nonhuman sentient animals and allows critical levels to differ across species. In both applications, population size is treated as a continuous variable to simplify the analysis.

11.1 FOREIGN AID AND POPULATION POLICY

Population policy is replete with ethical difficulties (Sen 1994, 1995) and policy decisions are complicated by imperfect knowledge of the effectiveness of policy options. Should we rely, for example, on the free choices of potential parents, improved education, or (possibly coercive) family-planning programs? These conundrums are made worse if there is disagreement about the ethical standards that should be used to evaluate possible outcomes. If policies are evaluated using average utilitarianism, for example, the result will be smaller populations than those recommended by classical utilitarianism.

Because developing countries receive economic aid from individual donor countries and international agencies such as the United Nations, population aid has come to be included in aid packages.[1] If developing countries cannot easily avoid using earmarked money for the purposes intended, such aid can be used

---

[1] Multilateral aid is managed by the United Nations Population Fund (United Nations 1995).

to manipulate their behavior. At the same time, developing countries have an interest in controlling their population growth and the aid provided may fill an unmet need.

In this chapter, we consider a single aspect of the ethical dilemma surrounding population aid and assume foreign aid is used in a way that maximizes an ethical value function. A country, a group of countries, or an international agency grants aid to a recipient country, which can be used for consumption or a population-control program. The objective is to decide the optimal combination of the two aspects of the grant, taking account of the relationship between per-capita consumption and population size in the recipient country. The model describes two generations of people, each of which lives for one period without overlap.[2] In the recipient country, a social decision to have fewer children can be taken in the first period, which reduces population size in period two. Such population-control decisions are costly and reduce the resources available for consumption. For mathematical convenience, we assume that the natural population sizes and the amounts of the resource produced are the same in both periods, but the model can easily be generalized to allow for different values in the two periods.

We assume that the developing country has access to a perfect capital market and can borrow and lend at a fixed interest rate. The foreign-aid budget is fixed in present-value terms and production is exogenous and constant. No allowance is made for price or environmental effects as population changes. The model can be generalized to include endogenous production, which depends on population size, or to dispense with perfect capital markets (see Blackorby, Bossert, and Donaldson 1999d).

We employ a critical-level utilitarian population (CLU) principle with a nonnegative critical level to guide population policy. Because classical utilitarianism is a CLU principle with a critical level of zero, that principle is implicitly covered. The results are qualitatively robust to the employment of inequality-averse critical-level generalized utilitarian principles.

In a foreign-aid setting, donor and recipient countries and, perhaps, international agencies as well, may have different views about population ethics. We assume, however, that there is no disagreement and that a particular CLU principle is the ethical position agreed on by all. This avoids some difficult moral issues, but our hope is that the resulting simplification may shed some light on one important aspect of the foreign-aid problem – the effect of resources on optimal population size.

Each person is assumed to have an identical strongly concave utility function (in which marginal utility diminishes as consumption increases). Subsistence consumption, the level that corresponds to neutrality, is assumed to be positive.

Expenditures on population control, which can be made in period one only, affect population size in the second period. The marginal (and average) cost of

---

[2] The model can be generalized to allow overlap.

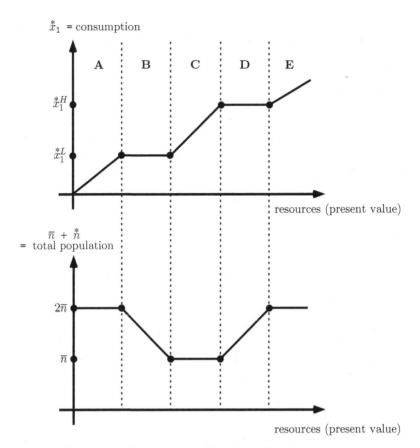

Figure 11.1. Consumption and Population Size.

population reduction is fixed and measured in terms of the resource. The present value of total resources, which includes foreign aid, is equal to the present value of production plus the present value of foreign aid. Without population control, population is $\bar{n}$ in each period.

Choice variables are consumption levels in each period and expenditure on population control, which determines population size in period two. Because utility functions are identical and marginal utility diminishes, consumption should be the same for all in each period. In addition, if the interest rate is zero, consumption should be the same in both periods and, if the interest rate is positive, consumption should be higher in period two. Optimal consumption levels in both periods increase as the present value of resources increases.

Optimal population size also depends on the present value of resources. For the case in which the cost of population control is not so high that it is never used, Figure 11.1 illustrates the relationship between period-one consumption and resources and the relationship between (total) population size and resources. Optimal per-capita consumption in period one is $\overset{*}{x}_1$ and optimal population size

Table 11.1. *Effects of Parameter Changes*

	Region B		Region D	
	Consumption	Population	Consumption	Population
Critical Level	down	down	up	down
Budget	no change	down	no change	up
Cost	up	up	down	?

in period two is $\hat{n}$. There are five regions. In region A, resources are low, there is no population control, and consumption increases as resources increase. In region B, consumption is constant (at $\overset{*}{x}_1^L$), the resource surplus is used for population control, and population size declines as resources increase. In both regions, the utility level of people in generation two is below the critical level, so that their lives contribute negatively to total value. At the same time, the cost of feeding them, in present value terms, is less than the cost of preventing their existence. Thus, allowing a new person to exist in period two raises the consumption levels of people in both generations. Although lives in generation two reduce total value directly, they raise it indirectly, and it is not always optimal to prevent their existence. In region C, no one lives in period two and, as resources rise, consumption in period one rises. In region D, consumption exceeds the critical level and, as resources increase, consumption is constant (at $\overset{*}{x}_1^H$) and population in period two rises. In region E, again there is no population control and consumption rises as resources rise. If endogenous production is included in the model, the flat segments in regions B and D in the upper panel slope upward and consumption rises with resources in those regions.

Suppose, for example, that subsistence consumption corresponds to $100 (current U.S. dollars) per annum. If the consumption level that corresponds to the critical level is $300, regions A and B correspond to consumption levels below $300, regions D and E correspond to consumption levels above $300, and region C makes the transition.

It is interesting to ask how changes in the parameters of the model affect the optimal levels of per-capita consumption and population size in regions B and E (the problem is trivial in the other regions because population size in period two is either zero or $\bar{n}$). Table 11.1 shows the effects of changes in the critical level, the foreign-aid budget, and the cost of population control.

An increase in the critical level decreases population size in both regions, but consumption falls in region B and rises in region D. Increases in the foreign-aid budget increase resources and, as in Figure 11.1, consumption is unaffected in both regions and population falls in region B and rises in region D. An increase in the cost of population control increases consumption when period-two utility is below the critical level (region B) and decreases consumption when period-two utility is above the critical level. In region B, such a change increases population but, in region D, the direction of change cannot be signed.

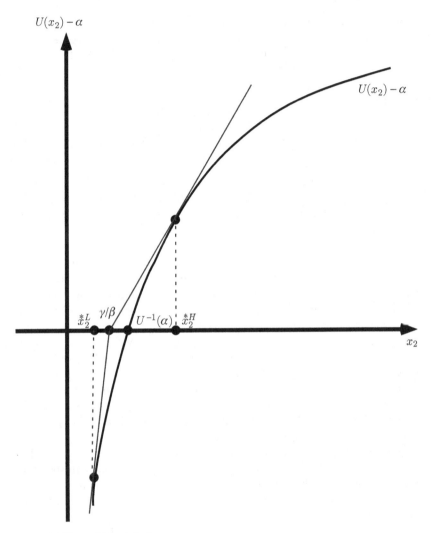

Figure 11.2. Solutions.

The solutions to the optimal levels of per-capita consumption in period two (x_2) can be seen in Figure 11.2. The curve labelled $U(x_2) - \alpha$ is determined by the utility function and the critical level. Optimal consumption levels – $\overset{*}{x}{}_2^L$ in region B and $\overset{*}{x}{}_2^H$ in region D – are determined by tangents to the curve from the point labeled γ/β, which in turn is determined by the cost of population control (γ) and the discount rate. If the critical level increases by a small amount, the curve shifts vertically downward and the points of tangency move in opposite directions: optimal consumption decreases in region B and increases in region D. Because the cost of population control is greater than consumption in region B, a decrease in consumption must be accompanied by a decrease in population size. In region D, cost is less than consumption and population size decreases when consumption increases. If the budget is increased by a small amount, per-capita consumption is constant in regions B and D because nothing changes in Figure 11.2. In region B, cost exceeds consumption, so population size falls and, in region D, cost is less than consumption, so population size rises. If the cost of population control rises, the point labeled γ/β moves to the right, the points of tangency move in opposite directions, $\overset{*}{x}_2^L$ rises, and $\overset{*}{x}_2^H$ falls. In region B, population size cannot fail to rise because that would require a decrease in consumption. Consequently, population size rises. In region D, however, the direction of change in population size cannot be predicted; change in either direction is consistent with a fall in consumption. Thus, the direction of change depends on the specifics of the model.

These results indicate that the choice of population principle matters a great deal. It is important for countries on both sides of foreign-aid transactions to discuss and, if possible, agree on the choice of a critical level. If the ethical approach to population problems is to make any sense at all, there must be a single value function. Therefore, different views about critical levels are not merely matters of preference.

If donor countries believe in higher critical levels than recipient countries do, a plausible possibility given recent international debates, significant disagreements will result. Donor countries may expect ethically responsible recipients to reduce population size as grant levels rise, for example, while recipient countries may want to increase their population sizes. Such disagreements are not perverse or irrational; they can stem from the use of ethical principles that differ in minor ways only.

Although we think our investigation can make a contribution to our understanding of the complex ethical problems surrounding population policy, the simplicity of our models prevents investigation of many important issues. At the same time, it should be clear that progress cannot be made on these issues unless we have defensible population principles.

11.2 MORAL STANDING FOR NONHUMAN ANIMALS

Many policy decisions involving nonhumans have consequences for animal well-being and for the number of animals that ever live. For example, animal exploitation in research and food production has both consequences: animals may suffer pain, discomfort, illness, and isolation and may live short lives; and large numbers of animals are brought into existence.

Much of the writing and thinking about the morality of these activities focuses on the first of these facts. Scientists who use animals in experiments, philosophers, and vegetarians ask whether the suffering can be justified by the gains to humans – better health, longer lives, tastier food, safer cosmetics – that result.

But there is another dimension. If we reduce our consumption of meat, there will be fewer cattle in the world; if we adopt less animal-intensive methods of research, there will be fewer laboratory animals. The number of these animals is significant: in 2002, there were more than 1.3 billion cattle in the world (Foged 2003).

Nonhuman animals that are sentient – capable of having experiences – have interests, and many utilitarian writers have suggested that welfarist calculations should be extended "to the whole sentient creation" (Mill 1861, 1979b, p. 263). Sidgwick (1907, 1966, p. 414) argued, for example, that we should "extend our concern to all the beings capable of pleasure and pain whose feelings are affected by our conduct" and that "it seems arbitrary and unreasonable to exclude . . . any pleasure of any sentient being."

In this chapter, we employ an extension of the CLU class of population principles whose members give animals moral standing. Human and nonhuman levels of well-being are given equal consideration, in accord with Singer's (1975, 1979) arguments, but the qualitative results of the following section and Part B require only that animal interests receive some weight. It is true, of course, that it is difficult to assign utility values to animals, but we are able to provide partial answers to several policy questions nonetheless.

Value functions for multispecies CLU are equal to the sum of the standard CLU value functions for the various species. Because lengths of life and possibilities for good lives vary across species, we allow critical levels to be different for different species. As is the case for humans, critical levels for animals are important ethical parameters because they provide a floor on the trade-off between average well-being and population sizes. A possible choice for animals is the average level of well-being that an individual in the species or a closely related one can expect to face in its natural habitat.[3] This view may face a philosophical difficulty, however. An appealing argument for a positive critical level for humans is that people are sentient beings who are cognizant of their futures and pasts, make plans and pay attention to memories, in addition to experiencing pains and pleasures. Cognition of future and past is present in animals such as gorillas and chimpanzees, but it seems likely that simpler animals, such as mice and rats, have less coherent lives. Indeed, animals with rudimentary brains, such as fish, appear to live in the present only. This suggests that setting the critical level at the "natural" level is appropriate for highly sentient animals, but, for species whose members have less integrated lives, a lower critical level is reasonable, with a level of zero for species whose members exist in the present only.[4]

A significant problem for the application of welfarist principles such as multispecies CLU arises because of the need to make interindividual comparisons of well-being across species. Such comparisons are hard to make between members of our own species, and they have had near taboo status among economists. The qualitative results of our multispecies models follow from the claim that such comparisons are meaningful or possible in principle, but practical judgments demand approximate comparisons at a minimum. The difficulty of

---

[3] This suggestion is consistent with the view of Rolston (1988, Ch. 2).

[4] We thank John Broome and Gary Wedeking for help with this argument.

making them may explain the prevalence of rules of thumb such as "do no harm" or "animals should never be below neutrality."

It is possible to argue that activities such as killing animals for food and experimenting on them have deleterious effects on human character, leading to less respect for life and to harmful behavior. In addition, humans care about animal suffering and may be made worse off by it. In both cases, human well-being is affected and such concerns are, therefore, easily incorporated into welfarist principles. As a consequence, animal losses appear in the value function through their effect on human utilities, and animal well-being has instrumental value. We suggest, however, that this is not a valid substitute for the recognition of the moral standing of all sentient creatures, regardless of human attitudes.

CLU and CLGU principles are not the only ones that can be extended to cover several species. The number-sensitive critical-level principles have similar extensions, with the multispecies value functions equal to sums of the single-species functions with species-specific critical levels that depend on species population size. Restricted versions of critical-level principles can be similarly extended. But number-dampened principles, restricted or not, face several serious difficulties. If, for example, a multispecies value function is equal to the sum, across species, of average utilities, the resulting principle is not consistent with same-number utilitarianism for all species combined and gives the well-being of members of different species weights that are inversely proportional to their numbers. If, on the other hand, the value function is equal to average utility for all species combined, critical levels for one species depend on the well-being of members of other species. Similar observations apply to all extensions of the number-dampened classes other than classical utilitarianism and classical generalized utilitarianism.

Regan (1982, 1983) presented rights-based arguments for vegetarianism and against research on animals. He argued that sentient nonhuman animals have a right to respectful treatment and that this right makes animal exploitation for food or knowledge morally illegitimate. Given such a moral prohibition, the fact that farming and research call forth animal populations that otherwise would not exist is not a problem. If, however, a rights theory were to allow for a trade-off of animal rights against significant benefits to humans, then it could not deal with the population question without an explicit formulation of the trade-off.

This problem is encountered by Lesco's (1988) account of Buddhist ethics toward animals. He argued that the principle of *ahimsa* or no-harm (avoiding unnecessary suffering) leads to vegetarianism and to a prohibition of animal use in cosmetics testing but allows some animal use – in vaccines, for example – because, when there is a trade-off between human and animal suffering, humans take precedence. Multispecies CLU offers an explicit formulation of such ethics.

Not all religious ethical views are as concerned with animal well-being as the Buddhist one, however. In the Biblical creation myth, humans are told to "fill the earth and subdue it, rule over the fish in the sea, the birds of heaven, and every living thing that moves upon the earth" (*New English Bible* 1970, Genesis

1:28). Proper behavior is to be consistent with God's will for animals, but little guidance is offered. Later Christian writers argued that, because animals are part of "the lower order of creation" (Saint Augustine 1961, pp. 147–150), their well-being is less important than that of humans.

11.3 ANIMALS IN RESEARCH AND FOOD PRODUCTION

We now turn to models of animal exploitation in research and farming. Both are highly stylized and attempt to be as simple as possible. In each, the size of the animal population is endogenous and a multispecies CLU principle with nonnegative critical levels is used to find optimal policies.

Our model of animal use in research divides sentient beings into two groups: humans who benefit from research, and guinea pigs who are the subjects of experiments. There is a single human resource, labor, which can be used in grain production or research. The human population is assumed to be constant but research animals are created for the purpose. In addition, the well-being of guinea pigs is affected by the expenditure of resources. For example, it is well-known that guinea pigs are happier when they have cleaner or larger cages. Cleaning requires labor that could be used elsewhere and larger cages are more expensive than small ones.

To keep the problem simple and to avoid obvious measurement difficulties, we assume that the amount of research to be done is fixed. There are, however, substitution possibilities, examples of which are tissue culture and computer-modeling techniques. In the model, the number of guinea pigs used can be reduced by increasing the use of labor in research. We assume that the number of animals always exceeds the level needed for statistical significance; any reduction below that level would be condemned by any moral theory that accords animals moral standing.

Guinea pigs have identical strongly concave utility functions that depend on their treatment in experiments and on grain consumption. We assume that: each animal consumes the same amount and experiences the same pain, suffering, and shortening of life; each guinea pig must consume a minimum amount of grain to be healthy enough to be a good experimental subject; and the utility level that results from consumption of the minimum amount of grain is below the critical level for guinea pigs. Humans have identical strongly concave utility functions that depend on research output (which is fixed) and on grain consumption.

We also assume that, when research is unregulated, researchers are cost minimizers without regard to the well-being of their experimental subjects. We do not suggest that all or even most investigators exhibit this behavior but point out that there are market and social forces (granting institutions) that pull in this direction. Researchers obtain grants on the basis of past performance as measured by their publications. Expenditures on grain that bring the well-being of guinea pigs above the minimum necessary to carry out the experiment reduce the funds available for continued research. This presumably reduces the investigator's research output and hence affects his or her chances of obtaining further funding.

Three possible outcomes are compared: the first describes a competitive equilibrium without regulation; the second describes the social optimum according to the multispecies CLU objective (the first-best); and the third describes the second-best optimum in which the grain consumption of guinea pigs is unregulated (and, therefore at the minimum) but the animal intensity of experiments is chosen socially.

We find that, as long as the utility level of guinea pigs in the first-best solution is not above the (guinea-pig) critical level, the optimal level of animal use in research is lower than the cost-minimizing level and may be equal to zero. In addition, if, as may be expected, the first-best level of grain consumption for guinea pigs exceeds the minimum, the second-best level of animal use is lower than the first-best unless both are zero. This accords well with standard intuitions. If guinea pigs have better lives, the loss of value is smaller and, therefore, increased use becomes permissible. In the same case, a tax on animal use, while reducing the use of animals, does not increase their standard of living; hence, direct controls are necessary. Moreover, an increase in the critical level for guinea pigs reduces the optimal number of animals in both the first-best and second-best cases. These results support the regulation of animal use in experiments and other scientific pursuits by institutions such as animal-care committees. These committees regulate the living conditions of experimental subjects and attempt to lower the animal intensity of the experiments.

Our model does not take account of differences in the condition of animals in different experiments, nor does it deal with the fact that many different species are used in research. In addition, it ignores human inequality. The analysis suggests, however, that animal use can be justified only by the claim that the benefits to humans outweigh the costs to the animals. Thus, to be morally acceptable, experiments that subject animals to a great deal of suffering must result in greater benefits than more benign experiments.

When animals are used for food, their number is affected. If the (competitive) supply of pork (say) is not perfectly inelastic, then individual decisions for vegetarianism reduce the pig population. A second consequence of such decisions is that, as the farm-animal population size falls, resources that can be used for other purposes are released.

We consider a simple model that connects human food consumption, food-animal population size, and the consumption of resources by food animals. In it, the members of a single species of food animal, pigs, consume grain and each pig must consume at least a fixed minimum amount to ensure good health. The utility function for pigs is strongly concave and thus exhibits diminishing marginal utility. Humans consume both grain and pork and have identical strongly concave utility functions. Pork is assumed to be a normal good (quantity consumed increases with total expenditure). The human population size and, hence, the size of the labor force, is fixed.

Three social outcomes are described. The first is an unregulated competitive equilibrium. In it, pigs consume grain at the minimum level. The second is the first-best outcome in which the consumption levels of both humans and pigs are chosen optimally according to multispecies CLU. The pork consumption of humans determines the size of the pig population, so it is also chosen. The third is the second-best outcome in which the grain consumption of pigs is determined by the market (and is therefore at the minimum).

We assume, as in the research model, that the utility level of pigs when they consume the minimum is less that the critical level for pigs. We find that, in the first-best case, pork consumption and, therefore, the size of the pig population, is lower than the market level and may be equal to zero as long as the utility level of pigs is not greater than the critical level. In the second-best case, pork consumption is lower still if the first-best level is positive and zero if it is not. In addition, if the optimal level of consumption in the first-best case exceeds the minimum, the optimal level for pigs cannot be achieved by a tax on pork consumption.

We conclude that there is a case for raising animals for food, but it is possible that the ethical vegetarians are right and that the optimal level of meat consumption is zero. Their case is strengthened by the observation that the taste for meat is not a brute fact but is influenced by acculturation and habituation. Our model indicates as well that if food animals enjoy short but happy lives with humane deaths, the case for complete vegetarianism is weakened and that there is a case for direct regulation of farm-animal welfare through legislation such as Sweden's (Lohr 1988).

Part B

There are numerous applications of population principles, and we discuss two of them in detail. We begin in Section 11.4 with a formal presentation of the foreign-aid problem discussed in Part A together with a derivation and an explanation of the comparative-statics results. Next, we consider our second example – namely, a population model that incorporates the well-being of sentient nonhumans. We define a multispecies generalization of critical-level utilitarianism (CLU) in Section 11.5 and discuss some of its properties. In Sections 11.6 and 11.7, multispecies CLU principles are used to assess the ethics of animal exploitation in research and in food consumption.

11.4 POPULATION POLICY IN A SMALL DEVELOPING COUNTRY

Consider the problem of designing an aid package for a developing country. The donor is a developed country or an international agency. Aid can be given in two forms: consumption aid and population-control aid. There are two periods and there is a single resource that can be used for consumption or devoted to a population-control program. Individuals live for one period. The goal is to find the optimal levels of both types of aid with a CLU objective function. Each person has the same utility function $U: \mathcal{R}_{++} \to \mathcal{R}$, where, for all $x \in \mathcal{R}_{++}$, $U(x)$ is the utility an individual derives from the consumption of x units of the resource. We assume that U is increasing and strongly concave. Furthermore, to ensure that optimal consumption levels are well-defined, we assume that $\lim_{x \to 0} U'(x) = \infty$. The developing country produces $\bar{\omega} \in \mathcal{R}_{++}$ units of the resource in each period. We treat production as exogenous but note that introducing endogenous production would leave most of our conclusions unaffected; see Blackorby, Bossert, and Donaldson (1999d) for a detailed discussion.

In period one, there is a fixed population of size $\bar{n} \in \mathcal{R}_{++}$ in the developing country. The present value of a foreign-aid budget is $D \in \mathcal{R}_{++}$, and aid can be given as consumption aid or as population-control assistance. Spending on population control in period one affects the population size in period two. Without population-control expenditures, the population in period two is $\bar{n}$. We assume that the natural population size and the amount of the resource produced are the same in each period for convenience only. Resources produced and natural population size in period two could be set at $\tilde{\omega} > \bar{\omega}$ and $\tilde{n} > \bar{n}$ without affecting our qualitative results. To reduce the population in period two to $n \in [0, \bar{n})$, the expenditure needed is $\gamma(\bar{n} - n)$ where $\gamma \in \mathcal{R}_+$ is the marginal (and average) cost of population control, expressed in terms of the consumption good.[5] For simplicity, we assume the existence of perfect international capital markets. The absence of such markets does not affect our qualitative results; see again Blackorby, Bossert, and Donaldson (1999d) for details.

Let x_t denote per-capita consumption in the developing country in period $t \in \{1, 2\}$. The present-value price of consumption in period two is $\beta \in \mathcal{R}_{++}$. If the real interest rate is positive, $\beta < 1$ and, if it is zero, $\beta = 1$. The resource constraint is

$$\bar{n} x_1 + n \beta x_2 = (1 + \beta)\bar{\omega} + D - \gamma(\bar{n} - n).$$

Solving for x_2, we obtain

$$x_2 = \frac{(1 + \beta)\bar{\omega} + D - \bar{n}(\gamma + x_1) + \gamma n}{n \beta} \tag{11.1}$$

if $n > 0$ and, trivially, $x_2 = 0$ if $n = 0$. Because population size in the rest of the world and the size of the foreign-aid budget are fixed, only per-capita consumption and population size in the recipient country are to be determined. We solve for the optimal levels according to CLU with a nonnegative critical level α. This yields the social maximization problem

$$\max_{(x_1, n)} \{\bar{n}[U(x_1) - \alpha] + \psi(n, x_1)\} \tag{11.2}$$

where $\psi(0, x_1) = 0$ and

$$\psi(n, x_1) = n \left[U \left(\frac{(1 + \beta)\bar{\omega} + D - \bar{n}(\gamma + x_1) + \gamma n}{n \beta} \right) - \alpha \right]$$

for all $n > 0$ and for all $x_1 \in \mathcal{R}_{++}$. We provide a detailed derivation of the possible solutions to this problem, followed by a discussion of their properties.

[5] Alternative functional forms can be chosen for the cost of population control. We use the above parameterization to facilitate our comparative-statics analysis.

The objective function in (11.2) is not concave but, despite this lack of a suitable global curvature property, the first-order conditions are sufficient for a maximum. To see this, define the function $V: \mathcal{R}_{++} \to \mathcal{R}$ by $V(x) = U(x) - \alpha$ for all $x \in \mathcal{R}_{++}$. Thus,

$$\bar{n}V(x_1) + nV(x_2)$$

is to be maximized subject to

$$\bar{n}x_1 + n\beta x_2 = (1 + \beta)\bar{\omega} + D - \bar{n}\gamma + n\gamma$$

by choice of x_1, x_2, and n. We use a two-stage procedure. First, for fixed n, optimal values $\hat{x}_1(n)$ and $\hat{x}_2(n)$ of x_1 and x_2 are determined. This yields a maximized value of $\bar{n}V(\hat{x}_1(n)) + nV(\hat{x}_2(n))$. In the second stage, n is chosen to maximize that function.

For $n = 0$, the optimal choice of x_1 and x_2 is trivial. Now suppose $n > 0$. Our assumptions on U guarantee the existence of a solution and, because V is concave, the first-order conditions are sufficient for an n-conditional maximum. The first-order conditions are

$$V'(\hat{x}_1(n)) = \hat{\lambda}(n),$$

$$V'(\hat{x}_2(n)) = \beta\hat{\lambda}(n), \tag{11.3}$$

and

$$\bar{n}\hat{x}_1(n) + n\beta\hat{x}_2(n) = (1 + \beta)\bar{\omega} + D - \bar{n}\gamma + n\gamma$$

where $\hat{\lambda}(n)$ is the value of the Lagrange multiplier corresponding to the solution. These conditions are identities in n and, therefore, we can differentiate them to obtain

$$V''(\hat{x}_1(n))\,\hat{x}_1'(n) = \hat{\lambda}'(n), \tag{11.4}$$

$$V''(\hat{x}_2(n))\,\hat{x}_2'(n) = \beta\hat{\lambda}'(n), \tag{11.5}$$

and

$$\bar{n}\hat{x}_1'(n) + n\beta\hat{x}_2'(n) = -[\beta\hat{x}_2(n) - \gamma]. \tag{11.6}$$

Substituting (11.4) and (11.5) into (11.6), we obtain

$$\left[\frac{\bar{n}}{V''(\hat{x}_1(n))} + \frac{n\beta^2}{V''(\hat{x}_2(n))}\right]\hat{\lambda}'(n) = -[\beta\hat{x}_2(n) - \gamma].$$

Now define the function $h: [0, \bar{n}] \to \mathcal{R}$ by

$$h(n) = \bar{n}V(\hat{x}_1(n)) + nV(\hat{x}_2(n))$$

for all $n \in [0, \bar{n}]$. The first derivative of this function is

$$h'(n) = \bar{n}V'(\hat{x}_1(n))\,\hat{x}_1'(n) + nV'(\hat{x}_2(n))\,\hat{x}_2'(n) + V(\hat{x}_2(n))$$
$$= \bar{n}\hat{\lambda}(n)\hat{x}_1'(n) + n\beta\hat{\lambda}(n)\hat{x}_2'(n) + V(\hat{x}_2(n)).$$

Using (11.6), this simplifies to

$$h'(n) = -\hat{\lambda}(n)[\beta\hat{x}_2(n) - \gamma] + V(\hat{x}_2(n)).$$

Differentiating again and using (11.3), we obtain

$$h''(n) = -\hat{\lambda}'(n)[\beta\hat{x}_2(n) - \gamma] - \hat{\lambda}(n)\beta\hat{x}_2'(n) + V'(\hat{x}_2(n))\hat{x}_2'(n)$$

$$= [\beta\hat{x}_2(n) - \gamma]^2 \left[\frac{\bar{n}}{V''(\hat{x}_1(n))} + \frac{n\beta^2}{V''(\hat{x}_2(n))} \right]^{-1}.$$

Because the term in square brackets is negative, $h''(n) \leq 0$ for all $n \in [0, \bar{n}]$. Consequently, h is concave and satisfaction of the first-order conditions is sufficient for a maximum.

We now return to the original maximization problem. For an interior solution $(\overset{*}{x}_1, \overset{*}{n})$ to (11.2), the corresponding optimal second-period consumption level $\overset{*}{x}_2$ is obtained by substituting $\overset{*}{x}_1$ and $\overset{*}{n}$ into (11.1). Using the first-order conditions, $(\overset{*}{x}_1, \overset{*}{x}_2, \overset{*}{n})$ must satisfy

$$\bar{n}[U'(\overset{*}{x}_1) - (1/\beta)U'(\overset{*}{x}_2)] = 0, \tag{11.7}$$

$$U(\overset{*}{x}_2) - \alpha - (\overset{*}{x}_2 - \gamma/\beta)U'(\overset{*}{x}_2) = 0, \tag{11.8}$$

and

$$\bar{n}\overset{*}{x}_1 + \overset{*}{n}(\beta\overset{*}{x}_2 - \gamma) = (1 + \beta)\bar{\omega} + D - \gamma\bar{n}. \tag{11.9}$$

By assumption, $U''(x) < 0$ for all $x \in \mathcal{R}_{++}$ and, therefore, U' is decreasing. From (11.7), it follows that

$$\beta < 1 \Rightarrow \overset{*}{x}_1 < \overset{*}{x}_2,$$

$$\beta = 1 \Rightarrow \overset{*}{x}_1 = \overset{*}{x}_2,$$

and

$$\beta > 1 \Rightarrow \overset{*}{x}_1 > \overset{*}{x}_2.$$

If $\beta = 1$, per-capita consumption is equal in the two periods; if the real interest rate is positive ($\beta < 1$), consumption in period two is higher. Our assumptions imply that an interior solution for $\overset{*}{x}_1$ exists. (11.7) implies

$$\overset{*}{x}_1 = (U')^{-1}(U'(\overset{*}{x}_2)/\beta).$$

The concavity of U implies that a solution $\overset{*}{x}_2$ to (11.8) exists if and only if $U(\gamma/\beta) \leq \alpha$ [see the Appendix of Blackorby, Bossert, and Donaldson (1999d) for details]. Suppose now that this condition is satisfied with a strict inequality. It follows that

$$\frac{U(\overset{*}{x}_2) - \alpha}{\overset{*}{x}_2 - \gamma/\beta} = U'(\overset{*}{x}_2). \tag{11.10}$$

There are two solutions to this equation (see Figure 11.2). These solutions exist for all parameter values but may not satisfy the resource constraint. From (11.10),

$$\text{sign}(\overset{*}{x}_2 - \gamma/\beta) = \text{sign}(\beta\overset{*}{x}_2 - \gamma) = \text{sign}[U(\overset{*}{x}_2) - \alpha].$$

Consequently, one of the solutions to (11.10) is such that $U(\overset{*}{x}_2) > \alpha$ and $(\overset{*}{x}_2 - \gamma/\beta) > 0$, and the other is such that $U(\overset{*}{x}_2) < \alpha$ and $(\overset{*}{x}_2 - \gamma/\beta) < 0$. We label the solutions $\overset{*}{x}_2^H$ and $\overset{*}{x}_2^L$ (for high and low). Because U is increasing, $\overset{*}{x}_2^H > \overset{*}{x}_2^L$. The consumption vectors corresponding to these solutions are $(\overset{*}{x}_1^H, \overset{*}{x}_2^H)$ and $(\overset{*}{x}_1^L, \overset{*}{x}_2^L)$. By (11.1), x_2 is increasing in x_1 and, consequently, $\overset{*}{x}_1^H > \overset{*}{x}_1^L$. The value function is greater at $(\overset{*}{x}_1^H, \overset{*}{x}_2^H)$ than at $(\overset{*}{x}_1^L, \overset{*}{x}_2^L)$ because $\overset{*}{x}_1^H > \overset{*}{x}_1^L$, $U(\overset{*}{x}_2^H) > \alpha$ and $U(\overset{*}{x}_2^L) < \alpha$. Consequently, if $(\overset{*}{x}_1^H, \overset{*}{x}_2^H)$ satisfies the resource constraint, $(\overset{*}{x}_1^L, \overset{*}{x}_2^L)$ will not be chosen. If $\gamma/\beta = U^{-1}(\alpha)$, the two solutions collapse to a single one where $U(\overset{*}{x}_2) = \alpha$.

The solution $(\overset{*}{x}_1^L, \overset{*}{x}_2^L)$ is of special interest. In it, people in generation two are below the critical level, which means their lives contribute negatively to total value. At the same time, the cost of feeding them, $\beta\overset{*}{x}_2^L$ in present-value terms, is less than the cost of preventing their existence, γ. Thus, allowing a new person to exist in period two raises the consumption levels of people in both generations. This solution is characterized by low levels of resources, low consumption levels, and high population-control costs relative to consumption. It may be expected to obtain in very poor developing countries.

These observations permit us to describe all the solutions for population size, including corner solutions (see Figure 11.1). If $\gamma/\beta < U^{-1}(\alpha)$, there are two possible interior solutions to (11.10), $\overset{*}{x}_2^H$ and $\overset{*}{x}_2^L$, both of which satisfy equation (11.9) and result in period-two utilities on both sides of the critical level. If the economy's resources $(1 + \beta)\bar{\omega} + D$ are high enough to sustain consumption levels above $(\overset{*}{x}_1^H, \overset{*}{x}_2^H)$ without any population control, then the largest levels of $(\overset{*}{x}_1, \overset{*}{x}_2)$ with $\overset{*}{n} = \bar{n}$ satisfying (11.7) will obtain (region E). As resources decrease, consumption in both periods will be reduced until $(\overset{*}{x}_1^H, \overset{*}{x}_2^H)$ is reached. At this point, population control begins and, as resources drop further, population is reduced to keep consumption constant at $(\overset{*}{x}_1^H, \overset{*}{x}_2^H)$ (region D). Even smaller resource levels push population in period two to zero. Now the population size cannot be reduced further, so consumption falls (region C). Eventually, consumption reaches $(\overset{*}{x}_1^L, \overset{*}{x}_2^L)$. At this point, the marginal cost of population $\beta\overset{*}{x}_2^L - \gamma$ is negative and, although adding to the population produces negative value, it is worthwhile because it increases consumption. Because of this, further decreases in resources increase population size while maintaining consumption at $(\overset{*}{x}_1^L, \overset{*}{x}_2^L)$ (region B). Eventually, population size in period two reaches its maximum $\bar{n}$ and, as resources approach zero, consumption approaches zero without population-control activity (region A).

The regions can be characterized as follows. The resource constraint must be satisfied, so

$$\bar{n}\overset{*}{x}_1 + \overset{*}{n}(\beta\overset{*}{x}_2 - \gamma) = (1 + \beta)\bar{\omega} + D - \bar{n}\gamma.$$

In region A, $(1 + \beta)\bar{\omega} + D - \bar{n}\gamma$ is not large enough to sustain $(\overset{*L}{x}_1, \overset{*L}{x}_2)$ with a period-two population size of $\bar{n}$, so

$$(1 + \beta)\bar{\omega} + D - \bar{n}\gamma < \bar{n}\overset{*L}{x}_1 + \bar{n}(\beta\overset{*L}{x}_2 - \gamma).$$

Note that $(\beta\overset{*L}{x}_2 - \gamma)$ is negative. In region B, consumption is $(\overset{*L}{x}_1, \overset{*L}{x}_2)$ and, because $0 \leq \overset{*}{n} \leq \bar{n}$,

$$\bar{n}\overset{*L}{x}_1 + \bar{n}(\beta\overset{*L}{x}_2 - \gamma) \leq (1 + \beta)\bar{\omega} + D - \bar{n}\gamma \leq \bar{n}\overset{*L}{x}_1.$$

In region C, $\overset{*}{n} = 0$, and

$$\bar{n}\overset{*L}{x}_1 < (1 + \beta)\bar{\omega} + D - \bar{n}\gamma < \bar{n}\overset{*H}{x}_1.$$

In region D, consumption is $(\overset{*H}{x}_1, \overset{*H}{x}_2)$, so

$$\bar{n}\overset{*H}{x}_1 \leq (1 + \beta)\bar{\omega} + D - \bar{n}\gamma \leq \bar{n}\overset{*H}{x}_1 + \bar{n}(\beta\overset{*H}{x}_2 - \gamma).$$

Note that $(\gamma\overset{*H}{x}_2 - \gamma)$ is positive. In region E, $(1 + \beta)\bar{\omega} + D - \bar{n}\gamma$ is greater than the cost of $(\overset{*H}{x}_1, \overset{*H}{x}_2)$ at $\bar{n}$, and

$$\bar{n}\overset{*H}{x}_1 + \bar{n}(\beta\overset{*H}{x}_2 - \gamma) < (1 + \beta)\bar{\omega} + D - \bar{n}\gamma.$$

These five regions appear if and only if $\gamma/\beta < U^{-1}(\alpha)$. If $\gamma/\beta \geq U^{-1}(\alpha)$, regions B, C, D, and E disappear: population control is so expensive that it is never used.

We conclude this section with a derivation and discussion of some comparative-statics results. In particular, we examine the response of a solution to changes in the cost of population control γ, the foreign-aid budget D, and the critical level α.

For $\overset{*}{x}_2 > 0$, we have the reduced maximization problem

$$\max_{(x_1,n)} \left\{ \bar{n}[U(x_1) - \alpha] \right. $$
$$\left. + n\left[U\left(\frac{(1 + \beta)\bar{\omega} + D - \bar{n}(\gamma + x_1) + \gamma n}{n\beta} \right) - \alpha \right] \right\}$$

which, because $\bar{n}$ and α are fixed, has the same solution as

$$\max_{(x_1,n)} \left\{ \bar{n}U(x_1) + n\left[U\left(\frac{(1 + \beta)\bar{\omega} + D - \bar{n}(\gamma + x_1) + \gamma n}{n\beta} \right) - \alpha \right] \right\}.$$

We obtain the following first-order conditions for an interior solution $(\overset{*}{x}_1, \overset{*}{n})$.

$$\bar{n}[U'(\overset{*}{x}_1) - (1/\beta)U'(\overset{*}{x}_2)] = 0$$

and

$$U(\overset{*}{x}_2) - \alpha - (\overset{*}{x}_2 - \gamma/\beta)U'(\overset{*}{x}_2) = 0.$$

The Hessian matrix of the objective function at a solution is

$$H = \begin{pmatrix} \bar{n}\left[U''(\overset{*}{x}_1) + \frac{\bar{n}}{\overset{*}{n}\beta^2}U''(\overset{*}{x}_2)\right] & \frac{\bar{n}}{\overset{*}{n}\beta}(\overset{*}{x}_2 - \gamma/\beta)U''(\overset{*}{x}_2) \\ \frac{\bar{n}}{\overset{*}{n}\beta}(\overset{*}{x}_2 - \gamma/\beta)U''(\overset{*}{x}_2) & \frac{1}{\overset{*}{n}}(\overset{*}{x}_2 - \gamma/\beta)^2 U''(\overset{*}{x}_2) \end{pmatrix}.$$

Differentiating the first-order conditions with respect to γ, we obtain the system of equations

$$H\begin{pmatrix} \frac{\partial \overset{*}{x}_1}{\partial \gamma} \\ \frac{\partial \overset{*}{n}}{\partial \gamma} \end{pmatrix} = \begin{pmatrix} -\frac{\bar{n}}{\overset{*}{n}\beta^2}(\bar{n} - \overset{*}{n})U''(\overset{*}{x}_2) \\ -\left[\frac{1}{\beta}U'(\overset{*}{x}_2) + \frac{1}{\overset{*}{n}\beta}(\bar{n} - \overset{*}{n})(\overset{*}{x}_2 - \gamma/\beta)U''(\overset{*}{x}_2)\right] \end{pmatrix}.$$

Using Cramer's rule to sign the change in $\overset{*}{x}_1$ with respect to γ, we obtain

$$|H|\frac{\partial \overset{*}{x}_1}{\partial \gamma} = -\frac{\bar{n}}{\overset{*}{n}\beta^2}(\bar{n} - \overset{*}{n})U''(\overset{*}{x}_2)\frac{1}{\overset{*}{n}}(\overset{*}{x}_2 - \gamma/\beta)^2 U''(\overset{*}{x}_2)$$

$$+ \frac{\bar{n}}{\overset{*}{n}\beta}(\overset{*}{x}_2 - \gamma/\beta)U''(\overset{*}{x}_2)$$

$$\times \left[\frac{1}{\beta}U'(\overset{*}{x}_2) + \frac{1}{\overset{*}{n}\beta}(\bar{n} - \overset{*}{n})(\overset{*}{x}_2 - \gamma/\beta)U''(\overset{*}{x}_2)\right]$$

$$= \frac{\bar{n}}{\overset{*}{n}\beta^2}(\overset{*}{x}_2 - \gamma/\beta)U''(\overset{*}{x}_2)U'(\overset{*}{x}_2).$$

Because H is negative definite, $|H| > 0$ and, therefore,

$$\text{sign}\left(\frac{\partial \overset{*}{x}_1}{\partial \gamma}\right) = -\text{sign}(\overset{*}{x}_2 - \gamma/\beta) = -\text{sign}\left[U(\overset{*}{x}_2) - \alpha\right].$$

Using Cramer's rule to sign the change in $\overset{*}{n}$ with respect to γ, we obtain

$$|H|\frac{\partial \overset{*}{n}}{\partial \gamma} = -\bar{n}\left[U''(\overset{*}{x}_1) + \frac{\bar{n}}{\overset{*}{n}\beta^2}U''(\overset{*}{x}_2)\right]$$

$$\times \left[\frac{1}{\beta}U'(\overset{*}{x}_2) + \frac{1}{\overset{*}{n}\beta}(\bar{n} - \overset{*}{n})(\overset{*}{x}_2 - \gamma/\beta)U''(\overset{*}{x}_2)\right]$$

$$+ \frac{\bar{n}}{\overset{*}{n}\beta}(\overset{*}{x}_2 - \gamma/\beta)U''(\overset{*}{x}_2)\frac{\bar{n}}{\overset{*}{n}\beta^2}(\bar{n} - \overset{*}{n})U''(\overset{*}{x}_2)$$

$$= -\frac{\bar{n}}{\beta}U''(\overset{*}{x}_1)U'(\overset{*}{x}_2) - \frac{\bar{n}}{\overset{*}{n}\beta}(\bar{n} - \overset{*}{n})(\overset{*}{x}_2 - \gamma/\beta)U''(\overset{*}{x}_1)U''(\overset{*}{x}_2)$$

$$- \frac{\bar{n}}{\overset{*}{n}\beta^3}U'(\overset{*}{x}_2)U''(\overset{*}{x}_2) - \frac{\bar{n}^2}{\overset{*}{n}^2\beta^3}(\bar{n} - \overset{*}{n})(\overset{*}{x}_2 - \gamma/\beta)[U''(\overset{*}{x}_2)]^2$$

$$+ \frac{\bar{n}^2}{\overset{*}{n}^2\beta^3}(\bar{n} - \overset{*}{n})(\overset{*}{x}_2 - \gamma/\beta)[U''(\overset{*}{x}_2)]^2,$$

which cannot be signed in general. However, if $\overset{*}{x}_2 - \gamma/\beta \leq 0$, then $\partial\overset{*}{n}/\partial\gamma$ is positive.

The comparative-statics result differ dramatically depending on the region where the solution is located. In region B, an increase in the parameter representing population-control cost increases both consumption and population. Thus, when period-two utility is below the critical level, the solution responds to such an increase by substituting consumption for population control because population control has become relatively more expensive. The effects are very different in region D. An increase in the cost of population control decreases consumption and population is unaffected. This sharp contrast suggests that the critical level is of great importance when assessing changes in the cost-parameter value. The response of the solution to such a change depends on the relation between the utility level of consumption and the critical level.

We now turn to the effects of an increase in the foreign-aid budget. Differentiating the first-order conditions with respect to D, we obtain the system of equations

$$H \begin{pmatrix} \frac{\partial \overset{*}{x}_1}{\partial D} \\ \frac{\partial \overset{*}{n}}{\partial D} \end{pmatrix} = \begin{pmatrix} \frac{\bar{n}}{\overset{*}{n}\beta^2} U''(\overset{*}{x}_2) \\ \frac{1}{\overset{*}{n}\beta}(\overset{*}{x}_2 - \gamma/\beta)U''(\overset{*}{x}_2) \end{pmatrix}.$$

Using Cramer's rule, we obtain

$$|H|\frac{\partial \overset{*}{x}_1}{\partial D} = \frac{\bar{n}}{\overset{*}{n}^2\beta^2}(\overset{*}{x}_2 - \gamma/\beta)^2 \left[U''(\overset{*}{x}_2)\right]^2$$
$$- \frac{\bar{n}}{\overset{*}{n}^2\beta^2}(\overset{*}{x}_2 - \gamma/\beta)^2 \left[U''(\overset{*}{x}_2)\right]^2 = 0$$

and

$$|H|\frac{\partial \overset{*}{n}}{\partial D} = \frac{\bar{n}}{\overset{*}{n}\beta}\left[U''(\overset{*}{x}_1) + \frac{\bar{n}}{\overset{*}{n}\beta^2}U''(\overset{*}{x}_2)(\overset{*}{x}_2 - \gamma/\beta)U''(\overset{*}{x}_2)\right]$$
$$- \frac{\bar{n}^2}{\overset{*}{n}^2\beta^3}(\overset{*}{x}_2 - \gamma/\beta)\left[U''(\overset{*}{x}_2)\right]^2$$
$$= \frac{\bar{n}}{\overset{*}{n}\beta}(\overset{*}{x}_2 - \gamma/\beta)U''(\overset{*}{x}_1)U''(\overset{*}{x}_2).$$

Thus,

$$\text{sign}\left(\frac{\partial \overset{*}{n}}{\partial D}\right) = \text{sign}(\overset{*}{x}_2 - \gamma/\beta) = \text{sign}\left[U(\overset{*}{x}_2) - \alpha\right].$$

In regions B and D, consumption is unaffected by an increase in the foreign-aid budget. Population size does change, however, but the effects have opposite signs in the two regions. Population increases in region B but decreases in region D as a consequence of the increase in resources implied by a larger aid budget. Again, care needs to be taken in assessing the consequences of such a parameter change because the population consequences are sensitive with respect to the region where the solution is located.

Finally, differentiating the first-order conditions with respect to α, we obtain the system of equations

$$H \begin{pmatrix} \frac{\partial \overset{*}{x}_1}{\partial \alpha} \\ \frac{\partial \overset{*}{n}}{\partial \alpha} \end{pmatrix} = \begin{pmatrix} 0 \\ 1 \end{pmatrix}.$$

It follows that

$$|H|\frac{\partial \overset{*}{x}_1}{\partial \alpha} = -\frac{\bar{n}}{\overset{*}{n}\beta}(\overset{*}{x}_2 - \gamma/\beta)U''(\overset{*}{x}_2)$$

and

$$\text{sign}\left(\frac{\partial \overset{*}{x}_1}{\partial \alpha}\right) = \text{sign}(\overset{*}{x}_2 - \gamma/\beta) = \text{sign}\left[U(\overset{*}{x}_2) - \alpha\right].$$

Furthermore,

$$|H|\frac{\partial \overset{*}{n}}{\partial \alpha} = \bar{n}\left[U''(\overset{*}{x}_1) + \frac{\bar{n}}{\overset{*}{n}\beta^2}U''(\overset{*}{x}_2)\right] < 0.$$

Comparing the changes in consumption and population caused by an increase in α with those obtained for an increase in the foreign-aid budget D, we note that population size moves in the same direction in both regions (population decreases in region B and in region D), whereas the comparative-statics terms have opposite signs in the case of the response of the optimal level of consumption. In region B, consumption decreases in response to an increase in α, whereas, in region D, consumption increases and we have another instance of the sensitivity of the comparative statics of the model with respect to the location of the solution.

11.5 MULTISPECIES CRITICAL-LEVEL UTILITARIANISM

Suppose there are several sentient species whose well-being is to be taken into consideration in social evaluation. We modify the CLU objective by introducing critical levels that may differ across species. A value function for multispecies CLU is given by the sum of standard CLU value functions, one for each species. However, as mentioned earlier, we allow critical levels to differ across species. Such differences could be justified, for example, because life expectancies and the potential for good lives are different for different species. Moreover, the degree to which the members of a species are capable of living integrated lives may be an important determinant for the choice of its critical level. Cognition of future and past is important for the ability to have coherent lives and, therefore, species whose members have less integrated lives can be assigned lower critical levels, with a level of zero for sentient animals who live in the present only.

However, our model does not require critical levels to be different for different species – equal critical levels are permitted as a special case.

Each of our two applications involves two species: humans and guinea pigs (for research) or humans and pigs (for food). We write the critical levels for the two species as α_H and α_P. Population sizes are n_H and n_P, and the lifetime-utility vectors for the two species are $u^H \in \mathcal{R}^{n_H}$ and $u^P \in \mathcal{R}^{n_P}$. Multispecies CLU is defined as

$$(u_H, u_P)R(v_H, v_P) \Leftrightarrow \sum_{i=1}^{n_H}[u_i^H - \alpha_H] + \sum_{j=1}^{n_P}[u_j^P - \alpha_P]$$

$$\geq \sum_{i=1}^{m_H}[v_i^H - \alpha_H] + \sum_{j=1}^{m_P}[v_j^P - \alpha_P]$$

for all $n_H, n_P, m_H, m_P \in \mathcal{Z}_{++}$, for all $u^H \in \mathcal{R}^{n_H}$, for all $u^P \in \mathcal{R}^{n_P}$, for all $v^H \in \mathcal{R}^{m_H}$, and for all $v^P \in \mathcal{R}^{m_P}$.

Analogously to the single-species case, we obtain a general comparative-statics result regarding the monotonicity of optimal population sizes with respect to changes in the critical levels. This result is analogous to Theorem 10.13 and, because the steps employed in its proof are identical, we do not prove it here. In the statement of the theorem, $B^*_{(c_H, c_P)}$ denotes the set of optimal utility vectors for the critical-level pair (c_H, c_P). We obtain

Theorem 11.1. *Let* $S \subseteq \bigcup_{n \in \mathcal{Z}_{++}} \mathcal{R}^n$ *be nonempty and suppose* $c_H, c_P, d_H,$ $d_P \in \mathcal{R}$, $n_H, n_P, m_H, m_P \in \mathcal{Z}_{++}$, $u^H \in \mathcal{R}^{n_H}$, $u^P \in \mathcal{R}^{n_P}$, $v^H \in \mathcal{R}^{m_H}$, *and* $v^P \in \mathcal{R}^{m_P}$.

(i) *If* $(u^H, u^P) \in B^*_{(c_H, c_P)}$, $(v^H, v^P) \in B^*_{(c_H, d_P)}$ *and* $c_P > d_P$, *then* $n_P \leq m_P$;

(ii) *if* $(u^H, u^P) \in B^*_{(c_H, c_P)}$, $(v^H, v^P) \in B^*_{(d_H, c_P)}$ *and* $c_H > d_H$, *then* $n_H \leq m_H$.

Thus, if the critical level for pigs (humans) increases, the optimal pig (human) population does not increase. Note that the result is very general and does not depend on the specific model under consideration.

11.6 ANIMAL EXPLOITATION: RESEARCH

We model the use of animals in research by identifying two species: humans, who benefit from research, and guinea pigs, who are used in research experiments. The only good in the economy other than research is grain, and it can be consumed by both species. The only factor of production is human labor, which can be employed in the production of grain or in research. Guinea pigs are bred for use as experimental subjects only and, therefore, their population is endogenous. In contrast, we assume the human population to be fixed to focus on the animal-use aspect of the problem.

We consider a simple general-equilibrium model capturing the above assumptions. The predictions of the model under various policy regimes are assessed by employing a multispecies critical-level utilitarian value function. Three scenarios are considered. First, we examine a competitive equilibrium without regulation. Second, the first-best outcome according to the multispecies critical-level utilitarian objective is described. Finally, we analyze a second-best solution in which the grain consumption of guinea pigs is unregulated but the animal intensity of the experimental research is chosen socially.

Suppose, for simplicity, that a fixed amount of research is to be done. The number of guinea pigs used in research can be reduced by increasing the expenditures on other techniques, such as the use of tissue cultures and computer modeling. We summarize alternative research techniques by means of a single variable $L^R \in \mathcal{R}_+$, which we refer to as the amount of labor allocated to research. $n_P \in \mathcal{R}_+$ is the number of guinea pigs, assumed to be a continuous variable for simplicity. Defining $\sigma = n_P/n_H$, the technology constraint can be expressed as

$$L^R = h(\sigma) \tag{11.11}$$

where $h: \mathcal{R}_+ \to \mathcal{R}_+$ is decreasing, continuously differentiable, and strongly convex. The value of h at σ is the amount of human labor required to produce the desired amount of research if the animal population is n_P (recall that both the amount of research to be done and the human population are assumed to be fixed).

The single food source, grain, is produced with human labor as the only input. We assume full employment so the amount of labor devoted to grain production is $n_H - L^R$. For simplicity, suppose a constant-returns-to-scale technology is employed. Thus, the amount of grain produced is $\gamma[n_H - L^R]$ where $\gamma \in \mathcal{R}_{++}$ is a constant. Defining the function $k: \mathcal{R}_+ \to \mathcal{R}_+$ by

$$k(\sigma) = \frac{\gamma}{n_H}[n_H - h(\sigma)]$$

for all $\sigma \in \mathcal{R}_+$ and using (11.11), total grain production can be written as $n_H k(\sigma)$. By definition, k is increasing, continuously differentiable, and strongly concave. We normalize the price of grain to one which, assuming perfect competition, implies that the real wage rate is equal to γ.

Denoting grain consumption by humans and by animals as G_H and G_P, the resource constraint is

$$n_H G_H + n_P G_P = n_H k(\sigma)$$

or, equivalently,

$$G_H = k(\sigma) - \sigma G_P. \tag{11.12}$$

All guinea pigs are assumed to have the same increasing and strongly concave utility function $U_P: \mathcal{R}_+ \to \mathcal{R}$, where $U_P(G_P)$ is the utility of consuming G_P units of grain. The minimum grain consumption of a guinea pig to be healthy enough for experimental use is $\underline{G}_P$. Thus, an additional constraint is given by the inequality

$$G_P \geq \underline{G}_P.$$

We assume that this minimum level of consumption is not sufficient for a utility at or above the critical level, that is, $U_P(\underline{G}_P) < \alpha_P$. Human well-being depends on research and grain consumption but because research output is assumed to be fixed, we can write it as a function of G_H alone – that is, we employ an increasing and strongly concave utility function $U_H: \mathcal{R}_+ \to \mathcal{R}$.

To investigate the normative implications of animal use in research, we now examine the three different scenarios mentioned earlier.

First, we assume scientists are cost minimizers without taking into consideration the well-being of the guinea pigs. Although we do not mean to suggest that most researchers adopt this position, it seems plausible that there are forces (for example, the funding criteria employed by grant-giving institutions) that favor this behavior. Expenditures on the guinea pigs' grain consumption above the minimum divert resources from research use and this presumably lowers research output and, as a consequence, the probability of further funding.

The cost of research is $L^R \gamma + n_P G_P$ and, using (11.11) and the definition of k, this can alternatively be written as $n_H[\gamma - k(\sigma) + \sigma G_P]$. Clearly, cost minimization requires $G_P = \underline{G}_P$ and, thus, it remains to choose σ to minimize

$$n_H[\gamma - k(\sigma) + \sigma \underline{G}_P].$$

The first-order condition for an interior solution is

$$k'(\sigma) = \underline{G}_P.$$

Second, the first-best solution is obtained by choosing σ and G_P to maximize the multispecies CLU value function subject to the constraint $G_P \geq \underline{G}_P$. Substituting our definitions, the objective function is ordinally equivalent to

$$U_H (k(\sigma) - \sigma G_P) + \sigma [U_P(G_P) - \alpha_P].$$

We distinguish three solution types.

1. $\sigma = 0$. In this case, there are no animal experiments. Intuitively, it is associated with high values of α_P, high values of $\underline{G}_P$, and a technology that permits the required research to be done by means of alternative techniques without excessive resource use.
2. $\sigma > 0$ and $G_P = \underline{G}_P$. This solution is the same as that obtained in the second-best case, which is discussed in detail later.
3. $\sigma > 0$ and $G_P > \underline{G}_P$. In this case, the first-order conditions are

$$U_H'(G_H) = U_P'(G_P) \tag{11.13}$$

and

$$U_H'(G_H)\big[k'(\sigma) - G_P\big] + U_P(G_P) - \alpha_P = 0. \tag{11.14}$$

(11.13) requires the marginal utility of grain to be the same for the two species. Solving (11.14), we obtain

$$k'(\sigma) = G_P + [\alpha_P - U_P(G_P)] / U'_H(G_H)$$

and, therefore,

$$k'(\sigma) = G_P \Leftrightarrow U_P(G_P) = \alpha_P.$$

Let σ^c denote the optimal value of σ in the cost-minimizing solution. Analogously, σ^f and G_P^f are the optimal values of σ and G_P in the first-best solution.

If $U_P(G_P^f) < \alpha_P$, let $\bar{\sigma}$ be such that $k'(\bar{\sigma}) = G_P^f$. Because k is concave and $G_P^f > \underline{G}_P$, it follows that $\bar{\sigma} < \sigma^c$. Because $U_P(G_P^f) < \alpha_P$, it follows that $k'(G_P^f) > G_P^f = k'(\bar{\sigma})$. Because k is concave, we obtain $\sigma^f < \bar{\sigma}$. Combining the two relevant inequalities, we obtain $\sigma^f < \sigma^c$. Therefore, animal use is too high in the cost-minimizing solution compared with the first-best optimum. If $U_P(G_P^f) > \alpha_P$, the relative ranking of σ^c and σ^f is ambiguous.

Finally, we consider the second-best solution. In the second-best problem, the multispecies CLU value function is maximized subject to the constraint $G_P = \underline{G}_P$. Substituting, the first-order condition is

$$k'(\sigma) = \underline{G}_P + [\alpha_P - U_P(G_P)] / U'_H(G_H). \tag{11.15}$$

Let σ^s denote the second-best level of σ. By (11.12), $G_H = k(\sigma^s) - \sigma^s \underline{G}_P$. Because $U_P(\underline{G}_P) < \alpha$ by assumption, (11.15) implies $k'(\sigma^s) > \underline{G}_P$ and, because k is concave, it follows that $\sigma^s < \sigma^c$. Thus, cost minimization uses too many guinea pigs compared with the second-best solution as well.

In the case where $G_P^f > \underline{G}_P$ and $U_P(G_P^f) < \alpha$, we can compare the first-best level of σ with that obtained in the second-best problem. Let $G_P \in [\underline{G}_P, G_P^f]$ and consider the problem of maximizing

$$U_H\left(k(\sigma) - \sigma G_P\right) + \sigma\left[U_P(G_P) - \alpha_P\right]$$

by choice of σ. The first-order condition for an interior solution to this problem is

$$U'_H\left(k(\sigma) - \sigma G_P\right)\left[k'(\sigma) - G_P\right] + \left[U_P(G_P) - \alpha_P\right] = 0.$$

The solution to this problem depends on G_P, and we can write it as a function $\overset{*}{\sigma}(G_P)$. Differentiating with respect to G_P and using (11.12), we obtain

$$U''_H(G_H)\left[\left[k'\left(\overset{*}{\sigma}(G_P)\right) - G_P\right]^2 \overset{*}{\sigma}'(G_P) - \overset{*}{\sigma}(G_P)\right]$$
$$+ U'_H(G_H)\left[k''(\overset{*}{\sigma}(G_P))\overset{*}{\sigma}'(G_P) - 1\right] + U'_P(G_P) = 0,$$

which is equivalent to

$$\overset{*}{\sigma}'(G_P)\left[U''_H(G_H)\left[k'\left(\overset{*}{\sigma}(G_P)\right) - G_P\right]^2 + U'_H(G_H)k''\left(\overset{*}{\sigma}(G_P)\right)\right]$$
$$= U'_H(G_H) - U'_P(G_P) + \overset{*}{\sigma}(G_P)U''_H(G_H). \tag{11.16}$$

Because $U_P(\underline{G}_P) < U_P(G_P^f) < \alpha_P$, it follows that $U_H'(G_H) < U_P'(G_P)$ for all $G_P \leq G_P^f$ and, therefore, the right side of (11.16) is negative. The term multiplied by $\overset{*}{\delta}{}'(G_P)$ on the left side of (11.16) is negative and, thus, $\overset{*}{\delta}{}'(G_P) > 0$ for all $G_P \in [G_P, \underline{G}_P^f]$. Thus, $\sigma^f > \sigma^s$.

To summarize our results, we first note that if the utility of guinea pigs in the first-best solution is below their critical level, the optimal level of animal use in experiments is below the level that minimizes cost and may be equal to zero. Moreover, if the level of guinea pig grain consumption in the first-best problem is above the minimum level necessary for research (a plausible assumption), the first-best level of animal use is above that of the second-best level, unless both of these levels are equal to zero. If the critical level for guinea pigs increases, the optimal guinea-pig population decreases both in the first-best case and in the second-best scenario.

11.7 ANIMAL EXPLOITATION: FOOD

To model animal use in food production, we again employ a model with two species: humans and pigs. There are two goods in the economy: grain and pork. Humans consume grain and pork, whereas pigs eat grain only. Pork is assumed to be a normal good. A minimal level of grain consumption is necessary for a pig to be of sufficient health as a food animal. The pig population is endogenous but the human population and, thus, the labor force, is fixed.

Again, we employ multispecies CLU to assess possible outcomes under three alternative scenarios. The first is an unregulated competitive equilibrium. The next is the first-best outcome in which the optimal levels of consumption of both species are chosen according to the multispecies CLU objective. Because the pork consumption of humans determines the pig population, the number of pigs is also determined. Finally, we consider a second-best solution where the grain consumption of pigs is market-determined, which results in choosing the minimal consumption level to make the pigs viable as food animals.

As in the previous section, all pigs have the same increasing and strongly concave utility function $U_P : \mathcal{R}_+ \to \mathcal{R}$ where $U_P(G_P)$ is a pig's utility derived from consuming G_P units of grain. The well-being of each human depends on grain and pork consumption and we represent human well-being by the common increasing and strongly concave utility function $U_H : \mathcal{R}_+^2 \to \mathcal{R}$ where $U_H(G_H, \sigma)$ is the utility of a human consuming G_H units of grain and $\sigma = n_P/n_H$ units of pork. We assume pork is a normal good. n_P denotes the number of pigs (assumed to be a continuous variable for convenience) and n_H is the (fixed) number of humans. Grain production uses one input, human labor, and is constant because human population size n_H is fixed. We denote per-capita grain production by $\bar{G} \in \mathcal{R}_{++}$. The minimal level of grain consumption for a pig to be sufficiently healthy to serve as a food animal is $\underline{G}_P \in \mathcal{R}_{++}$. Thus, the production constraints in the economy are

$$G_P \geq \underline{G}_P$$

and

$$G_H + \sigma G_P \le \bar{G}. \tag{11.17}$$

The price of grain is normalized to one.

The multispecies CLU value function with critical levels α_H for humans and α_P for pigs is

$$n_H [U_H(G_H, \sigma) - \alpha_H] + n_P [U_P(G_P) - \alpha_P],$$

which is ordinally equivalent to

$$U_H(G_H, \sigma) + \sigma [U_P(G_P) - \alpha_P].$$

We now discuss three scenarios in detail: the competitive-market outcome, the first-best solution according to multispecies CLU, and the second-best solution that treats the competitive value of G_P as given.

In a competitive market, cost minimization requires that $G_P = \underline{G}_P$. The long-run (zero-profit) equilibrium price of pork is equal to $\underline{G}_P$ and, in an equilibrium with positive values of G_H and σ, the marginal rate of substitution between pork and grain must be equal to $\underline{G}_P$ as well; that is,

$$\frac{\partial U_H(G_H, \sigma)/\partial \sigma}{\partial U_H(G_H, \sigma)/\partial G_H} = \underline{G}_P.$$

Furthermore, the constraint (11.17) is binding, that is,

$$G_H + \sigma \underline{G}_P = \bar{G}.$$

There are three cases in the first-best optimization problem.

1. $\sigma = 0$. In this case, there are no food animals. It corresponds to high values of α_P, high values of $\underline{G}_P$, and a human utility function that does not put much weight on pork.
2. $\sigma > 0$ and $G_P = \underline{G}_P$. This solution is the same as that obtained in the second-best case and we discuss it below.
3. $\sigma > 0$ and $G_P > \underline{G}_P$. In this case, the first-order conditions are, in addition to the resource constraint (11.17) satisfied with an equality,

$$\frac{\partial U_H(G_H, \sigma)}{\partial G_H} = \lambda,$$

$$\frac{\partial U_H(G_H, \sigma)}{\partial \sigma} + U_P(G_P) - \alpha_P = \lambda G_P,$$

and

$$U_P'(G_P) = \lambda$$

where λ is the Lagrange multiplier associated with the resource constraint. Eliminating the multiplier, we obtain

$$\frac{\partial U_H(G_H, \sigma)}{\partial G_H} = U_P'(G_P) \tag{11.18}$$

and
$$\frac{\partial U_H(G_H, \sigma)/\partial \sigma}{\partial U_H(G_H, \sigma)/\partial G_H} = G_P + \frac{\alpha_P - U_P(G_P)}{\partial U_H(G_H, \sigma)/\partial G_H}. \tag{11.19}$$

The term $\alpha_P - U_P(G_P)$ cannot be signed in general: even though we assume that $U_P(\underline{G}_P) < \alpha_P$, this does not imply that the value of U_P at the first-best level of a pig's grain consumption is below the critical level α_P. If this is the case, however (which we consider a plausible hypothesis), we can compare the resulting pig population to that associated with the competitive solution. Let σ^c and σ^f denote the optimal values of σ in the competitive solution and in the first-best solution. Because G_P is assumed to exceed $\underline{G}_P$ in the first-best outcome, the price of pork to humans is increased compared with the competitive solution. Because pork is a normal good, it follows that $\bar{\sigma}$ – optimal per-capita consumption at the new prices – is below that of the competitive equilibrium. Furthermore, because $U_P(G_P) < \alpha_P$ by assumption, (11.19) implies that $\sigma^f < \bar{\sigma}$. Therefore, we obtain $\sigma^f < \sigma^c$: pork consumption in the competitive outcome is too high compared to the first-best solution.

In the second-best problem, the competitive solution for the grain consumption of the pigs is assumed to be given, and G_H and σ are chosen to maximize the multispecies CLU objective subject to that additional constraint. Assuming that the optimal level of G_H is positive, the first-order conditions imply
$$\frac{\partial U_H(G_H, \sigma)/\partial \sigma}{\partial U_H(G_H, \sigma)/\partial G_H} = \underline{G}_P + \frac{\alpha_P - U_P(\underline{G}_P)}{\partial U_H(G_H, \sigma)/\partial G_H}.$$

Given the assumption $U_P(\underline{G}_P) < \alpha$, this implies
$$\frac{\partial U_H(G_H, \sigma)/\partial \sigma}{\partial U_H(G_H, \sigma)/\partial G_H} > \underline{G}_P.$$

This implies that per-capita pork consumption in the second-best case is lower than in the competitive case.

Some analogies to the research model are worth pointing out. Suppose the pigs' consumption of grain at the minimum level is insufficient to achieve their critical level. In the first-best case, pork consumption (and, thus, the size of the pig population) is lower than in the competitive solution. It may reach zero, provided the pigs' utility level does not exceed their critical level. The second-best case is associated with even lower values of pork consumption than the first-best case, provided that the latter is not already at zero. A zero consumption level in the first-best case implies that the same is true for the second-best scenario as well.

References

Aczél, J., 1966, *Lectures on Functional Equations and Their Applications*, Academic Press, New York.

Aczél, J., 1987, *A Short Course on Functional Equations: Based upon Recent Applications to the Social and Behavioral Sciences*, Reidel, Dordrecht.

Anderson, E., 1999, What is the point of equality?, *Ethics* **109**, 287–337.

Arneson, R., 1989, Equality of opportunity for welfare, *Philosophical Studies* **56**, 77–93.

Arneson, R., 2000a, Luck egalitarianism and prioritarianism, *Ethics* **110**, 339–349.

Arneson, R., 2000b, Perfectionism and politics, *Ethics* **111**, 37–63.

Arrhenius, G., 2000a, An impossibility theorem for welfarist axiologies, *Economics and Philosophy* **16**, 247–266.

Arrhenius, G., 2000b, *Future Generations: A Challenge for Moral Theory*, Ph.D. Dissertation, Department of Philosophy, Uppsala University.

Arrhenius, G., 2003, Feldman's desert-adjusted utilitarianism and population ethics, *Utilitas* **15**, 225–236.

Arrhenius, G. and K. Bykvist, 1995, Future generations and interpersonal compensations, Uppsala Prints and Preprints in Philosophy no. 21, Department of Philosophy, Uppsala University.

Arrow, K., 1951 (2nd ed. 1963), *Social Choice and Individual Values*, Wiley, New York.

Arrow, K., 1959, Rational choice functions and orderings, *Economica* **26**, 121–127.

Arrow, K., 1972, Exposition of the theory of choice under uncertainty, in *Decision and Organization*, C. McGuire and R. Radner, eds., North-Holland, Amsterdam, 19–55.

Atkinson, A., 1970, On the measurement of inequality, *Journal of Economic Theory* **2**, 244–263.

Austen-Smith, D., 1979, Fair rights, *Economics Letters* **4**, 29–32.

Baigent, N. and W. Gaertner, 1996, Never choose the uniquely largest: a characterization, *Economic Theory* **8**, 239–249.

Barry, B., 1989, *Democracy, Power and Justice: Essays in Political Theory*, Clarendon, Oxford.

Basu, K., 1983, Cardinal utility, utilitarianism, and a class of invariance axioms in welfare analysis, *Journal of Mathematical Economics* **12**, 193–206.

Bentham, J., 1973 (originally published in 1789), Principles of morals and legislation, in *The Utilitarians*, Anchor, Garden City, 5–398.

Berge, C., 1963, *Topological Spaces*, Oliver and Boyd, London.

Bermúdez, J., 1996, The moral significance of birth, *Ethics* **106**, 378–403.

Blackorby, C., W. Bossert, and D. Donaldson, 1994, Generalized Ginis and cooperative bargaining solutions, *Econometrica* **62**, 1161–1178.

Blackorby, C., W. Bossert, and D. Donaldson, 1995a, Multi-valued demand and rational choice in the two-commodity case, *Economics Letters* **47**, 5–10.

Blackorby, C., W. Bossert, and D. Donaldson, 1995b, Intertemporal population ethics: critical-level utilitarian principles, *Econometrica* **63**, 1303–1320.

Blackorby, C., W. Bossert, and D. Donaldson, 1996a, Quasi-orderings and population ethics, *Social Choice and Welfare* **13**, 129–150.

Blackorby, C., W. Bossert, and D. Donaldson, 1996b, Leximin population ethics, *Mathematical Social Sciences* **31**, 115–131.

Blackorby, C., W. Bossert, and D. Donaldson, 1996c, Consistency, replication invariance, and generalized Gini bargaining solutions, *Journal of Economic Theory* **69**, 367–386.

Blackorby, C., W. Bossert, and D. Donaldson, 1996d, Intertemporally consistent population ethics: classical utilitarian principles, in *Social Choice Re-Examined*, vol. 2, K. Arrow, A. Sen, and K. Suzumura, eds., Macmillan, London, 137–162.

Blackorby, C., W. Bossert, and D. Donaldson, 1997a, Intertemporally consistent population ethics: birth-date dependent classical principles, *Japanese Economic Review* **48**, 267–292.

Blackorby, C., W. Bossert, and D. Donaldson, 1997b, Critical-level utilitarianism and the population-ethics dilemma, *Economics and Philosophy* **13**, 197–230.

Blackorby, C., W. Bossert, and D. Donaldson, 1997c, Birth-date dependent population ethics: critical-level principles, *Journal of Economic Theory* **77**, 260–284.

Blackorby, C., W. Bossert, and D. Donaldson, 1998, Uncertainty and critical-level population principles, *Journal of Population Economics* **11**, 1–20.

Blackorby, C., W. Bossert, and D. Donaldson, 1999a, Functional equations and population ethics, *Aequationes Mathematicae* **58**, 272–284.

Blackorby, C., W. Bossert, and D. Donaldson, 1999b, Information invariance in variable-population social-choice problems, *International Economic Review* **40**, 403–422.

Blackorby, C., W. Bossert, and D. Donaldson, 1999c, Rationalizable solutions to pure population problems, *Social Choice and Welfare* **16**, 395–407.

Blackorby, C., W. Bossert, and D. Donaldson, 1999d, Foreign aid and population policy: some ethical considerations, *Journal of Development Economics* **59**, 203–232.

Blackorby, C., W. Bossert, and D. Donaldson, 1999e, Income inequality measurement: the normative approach, in *Handbook of Income Inequality Measurement*, J. Silber, ed., Kluwer, Dordrecht, 133–157.

Blackorby, C., W. Bossert, and D. Donaldson, 2000, The value of limited altruism, *Journal of Economic Theory* **95**, 37–70.

Blackorby, C., W. Bossert, and D. Donaldson, 2001a, Population ethics and the existence of value functions, *Journal of Public Economics* **82**, 301–308.

Blackorby, C., W. Bossert, and D. Donaldson, 2001b, A representation theorem for domains with discrete and continuous variables, Discussion Paper 01-22, Department of Economics, University of British Columbia, Vancouver.

Blackorby, C., W. Bossert, and D. Donaldson, 2002a, Rationalizable variable-population choice functions, *Economic Theory* **19**, 355–378.

Blackorby, C., W. Bossert, and D. Donaldson, 2002b, Utilitarianism and the theory of justice, in *Handbook of Social Choice and Welfare*, vol. 1, K. Arrow, A. Sen, and K. Suzumura, eds., Elsevier, Amsterdam, 543–596.

Blackorby, C., W. Bossert, and D. Donaldson, 2002c, Population principles with number-dependent critical levels, *Journal of Public Economic Theory* **4**, 347–368.

Blackorby, C., W. Bossert, and D. Donaldson, 2003a, The axiomatic approach to population ethics, *Politics, Philosophy and Economics* **2**, 342–381.

Blackorby, C., W. Bossert, and D. Donaldson, 2003b, Harsanyi's social aggregation theorem: a multi-profile approach with variable-population extensions, Discussion Paper 03-2003, CIREQ, Université de Montréal.

Blackorby, C., W. Bossert, and D. Donaldson, 2004a, Multi-profile welfarism: a generalization, *Social Choice and Welfare*, forthcoming.

Blackorby, C., W. Bossert, and D. Donaldson, 2004b, Critical-level population principles and the repugnant conclusion, in *The Repugnant Conclusion: Essays on Population Ethics*, J. Ryberg and T. Tännsjö, eds., Kluwer, Dordrecht, forthcoming.

Blackorby, C., W. Bossert, D. Donaldson, and M. Fleurbaey, 1998, Critical levels and the (reverse) repugnant conclusion, *Journal of Economics* **67**, 1–15.

Blackorby, C. and D. Donaldson, 1978, Measures of relative equality and their meaning in terms of social welfare, *Journal of Economic Theory* **18**, 59–80.

Blackorby, C. and D. Donaldson, 1980, A theoretical treatment of indices of absolute inequality, *International Economic Review* **21**, 107–136.

Blackorby, C. and D. Donaldson, 1982, Ratio-scale and translation-scale full interpersonal comparability without domain restrictions: admissible social evaluation functions, *International Economic Review* **23**, 249–268.

Blackorby, C. and D. Donaldson, 1984a, Social criteria for evaluating population change, *Journal of Public Economics* **25**, 13–33.

Blackorby, C. and D. Donaldson, 1984b, Ethically significant ordinal indexes of relative inequality, in *Advances in Econometrics, vol. 3*, R. Basmann and G. Rhodes, eds., JAI Press, Greenwich, 131–147.

Blackorby, C. and D. Donaldson, 1991, Normative population theory: a comment, *Social Choice and Welfare* **8**, 261–267.

Blackorby, C. and D. Donaldson, 1992, Pigs and guinea pigs: a note on the ethics of animal exploitation, *Economic Journal* **102**, 1345–1369.

Blackorby, C. and D. Donaldson, 1993, Adult-equivalence scales and the economic implementation of interpersonal comparisons of well-being, *Social Choice and Welfare* **10**, 335–361.

Blackorby, C., D. Donaldson, and J. Weymark, 1984, Social choice with interpersonal utility comparisons: a diagrammatic introduction, *International Economic Review* **25**, 327–356.

Blackorby, C., D. Donaldson, and J. Weymark, 1990, A welfarist proof of Arrow's theorem, *Recherches Economiques de Louvain* **56**, 259–286.

Blackorby, C., D. Donaldson, and J. Weymark, 1999, Harsanyi's social aggregation theorem for state-contingent alternatives, *Journal of Mathematical Economics* **32**, 365–387.

Blackorby, C., D. Donaldson, and J. Weymark, 2004, Social aggregation and the expected utility hypothesis, in *Justice, Political Liberalism, and Utilitarianism: Themes from Harsanyi and Rawls*, M. Salles and J. Weymark, eds., Cambridge University Press, Cambridge, forthcoming.

Blackorby, C., D. Primont, and R. Russell, 1978, *Duality, Separability, and Functional Structure: Theory and Economic Applications*, North-Holland, Amsterdam.

Blackwell, D. and M. Girshick, 1954, *Theory of Games and Statistical Decisions*, Wiley, New York.

Blau, J., 1957, The existence of social welfare functions, *Econometrica* **25**, 302–313.

Blau, J., 1976, Neutrality, monotonicity, and the right of veto: a comment, *Econometrica* **44**, 603.

Border, K., 1981, Notes on von Neumann–Morgenstern social welfare functions, unpublished manuscript, Division of the Humanities and Social Sciences, California Institute of Technology, Pasadena.

Bordes, G., P. Hammond, and M. Le Breton, 1997, Social welfare functionals on restricted domains and in economic environments, unpublished manuscript, Department of Economics, Stanford University.

Bossert, W., 1990a, An axiomatization of the single-series Ginis, *Journal of Economic Theory* **50**, 82–92.

Bossert, W., 1990b, Maximin welfare orderings with variable population size, *Social Choice and Welfare* **7**, 39–45.

Bossert, W., 1990c, Social evaluation with variable population size: an alternative concept, *Mathematical Social Sciences* **19**, 143–158.

Bossert, W., 1991, On intra- and interpersonal utility comparisons, *Social Choice and Welfare* **8**, 207–219.

Bossert, W., 1993, Continuous choice functions and the strong axiom of revealed preference, *Economic Theory* **3**, 379–385.

Bossert, W., 1994, Rational choice and two-person bargaining solutions, *Journal of Mathematical Economics* **23**, 549–563.

Bossert, W., 1997, Opportunity sets and individual well-being, *Social Choice and Welfare* **14**, 97–112.

Bossert, W., 1998, Welfarism and rationalizability in allocation problems with indivisibilities, *Mathematical Social Sciences* **35**, 133–150.

Bossert, W., 2000, Welfarism and information invariance, *Social Choice and Welfare* **17**, 321–336.

Bossert, W., 2001, Choices, consequences, and rationality, *Synthese* **129**, 343–369.

Bossert, W. and A. Pfingsten, 1990, Intermediate inequality: concepts, indices, and welfare implications, *Mathematical Social Sciences* **19**, 117–134.

Bossert, W. and F. Stehling, 1992, A remark on admissible transformations for interpersonally comparable utilities, *International Economic Review* **33**, 739–744.

Bossert, W. and F. Stehling, 1994, On the uniqueness of cardinally interpreted utility functions, in *Models and Measurement of Welfare and Inequality*, W. Eichhorn, ed., Springer, Berlin, 537–551.

Bossert, W. and J. Weymark, 2004, Utility in social choice, in *Handbook of Utility Theory, vol. 2: Extensions*, S. Barberà, P. Hammond, and C. Seidl, eds., Kluwer, Dordrecht, 1099–1177.

Brand, L., 1955, *Advanced Calculus: An Introduction to Classical Analysis*, Wiley, New York.

Broome, J., 1990, Bolker-Jeffrey expected utility theory and axiomatic utilitarianism, *Review of Economic Studies* **57**, 477–502.

Broome, J., 1991, *Weighing Goods*, Basil Blackwell, Oxford.

Broome, J., 1992a, The value of living, *Recherches Economiques de Louvain* **58**, 125–142.

Broome, J., 1992b, Reply to Blackorby and Donaldson, and Drèze, *Recherches Economiques de Louvain* **58**, 167–171.

Broome, J., 1992c, *Counting the Cost of Global Warming*, White Horse, Cambridge.

Broome, J., 1993, Goodness is reducible to betterness: the evil of death is the value of life, in *The Good and the Economical: Ethical Choices in Economics and Management*, P. Koslowski, ed., Springer, Berlin, 69–83.

Broome, J., 2003, Representing an ordering when the population varies, *Social Choice and Welfare* **20**, 243–246.

Broome, J., 2004a, *Weighing Lives*, Oxford University Press, Oxford.

Broome, J., 2004b, Equality or priority: a useful distinction, in *Fairness and Goodness in Health*, D. Wikler and C. Murray, eds., World Health Organization, Geneva, forthcoming.

Brown, D., 1972, Mill on liberty and morality, *Philosophical Review* **81**, 133–158.

Carlson, E., 1998, Mere addition and the two trilemmas of population ethics, *Economics and Philosophy* **14**, 283–306.

Carter, A., 1999, Moral theory and global population, *Proceedings of the Aristotelian Society* **99**, 289–313.

Chakravarty, S., 1990, *Ethical Social Index Numbers*, Springer, Berlin.

Coulhon, T. and P. Mongin, 1989, Social choice theory in the case of von Neumann–Morgenstern utilities, *Social Choice and Welfare* **6**, 175–187.

Cowen, T., 1992, Consequentialism implies a zero rate of intergenerational discount, in *Justice Between Age Groups and Generations*, P. Laslett and J. Fishkin, eds., Yale University Press, New Haven, 162–168.

Cowen, T., 1996, What do we learn from the repugnant conclusion?, *Ethics* **106**, 754–795.

Cowen, T. and D. Parfit, 1992, Against the social discount rate, in *Justice Between Age Groups and Generations*, P. Laslett and J. Fishkin, eds., Yale University Press, New Haven, 144–161.

Dalton, H., 1920, The measurement of the inequality of incomes, *Economic Journal* **30**, 348–361.

Dasgupta, P., 1988, Lives and well-being, *Social Choice and Welfare* **5**, 103–126.

Dasgupta, P., 1993, *An Inquiry into Well-Being and Destitution*, Clarendon, Oxford.

Dasgupta, P., 1994, Savings and fertility: ethical issues, *Philosophy and Public Affairs* **23**, 99–127.

d'Aspremont, C., 1985, Axioms for social welfare orderings, in *Social Goals and Social Organizations: Essays in Memory of Elisha Pazner*, L. Hurwicz, D. Schmeidler, and H. Sonnenschein, eds., Cambridge University Press, Cambridge, 19–76.

d'Aspremont, C. and L. Gevers, 1977, Equity and the informational basis of collective choice, *Review of Economic Studies* **44**, 199–209.

d'Aspremont, C. and L. Gevers, 2002, Social welfare functionals and interpersonal comparability, in *Handbook of Social Choice and Welfare*, vol. 1, K. Arrow, A. Sen, and K. Suzumura, eds., Elsevier, Amsterdam, 459–541.

Debreu, G., 1959, *Theory of Value: An Axiomatic Analysis of Economic Equilibrium*, Wiley, New York.

Debreu, G., 1960, Topological methods in cardinal utility theory, in *Mathematical Methods in the Social Sciences, 1959; Proceedings*, K. Arrow, S. Karlin, and P. Suppes, eds., Stanford University Press, Stanford, 16–26.

De Meyer, B. and P. Mongin, 1995, A note on affine aggregation, *Economics Letters* **47**, 177–183.

DeMeyer, F. and C. Plott, 1971, A welfare function using 'relative intensity' of preference, *Quarterly Journal of Economics* **85**, 179–186.

Deschamps, R. and L. Gevers, 1978, Leximin and utilitarian rules: a joint characterization, *Journal of Economic Theory* **17**, 143–163.

Diamond, P., 1967, Cardinal welfare, individualistic ethics, and interpersonal comparisons of utility: comment, *Journal of Political Economy* **75**, 765–766.

Dixit, A., 1980, Interpersonal comparisons and social welfare functions, unpublished manuscript, Department of Economics, University of Warwick.

Domotor, Z., 1979, Ordered sum and tensor product of linear utility structures, *Theory and Decision* **11**, 375–399.

Donaldson, D. and J. Roemer, 1987, Social choice in economic environments with dimensional variation, *Social Choice and Welfare* **4**, 253–276.

Donaldson, D. and J. Weymark, 1980, A single-parameter generalization of the Gini indices of inequality, *Journal of Economic Theory* **22**, 67–86.

Donaldson, D. and J. Weymark, 1988, Social choice in economic environments, *Journal of Economic Theory* **46**, 291–308.

Ebert, U., 1987, Size and distribution of incomes as determinants of social welfare, *Journal of Economic Theory* **41**, 23–33.

Eichhorn W., 1978, *Functional Equations in Economics*, Addison-Wesley, Reading.

Falmagne, J.-C., 1981, On a recurrent misuse of a classical functional equation result, *Journal of Mathematical Psychology* **23**, 190–193.

Feldman, F., 1995, Justice, desert, and the repugnant conclusion, *Utilitas* **7**, 189–206. Also published in Feldman, F., 1997, *Utilitarianism, Hedonism, and Desert: Essays in Moral Philosophy*, Cambridge University Press, Cambridge, 193–214.

Feldman, F., 1997, *Utilitarianism, Hedonism, and Desert: Essays in Moral Philosophy*, Cambridge University Press, Cambridge.

Fishburn, P., 1984, On Harsanyi's utilitarian cardinal welfare theorem, *Theory and Decision* **17**, 21–28.

Fishburn, P., H. Marcus-Roberts, and F. Roberts, 1988, Unique finite difference measurement, *SIAM Journal of Discrete Mathematics* **1**, 334–354.

Fishburn, P. and F. Roberts, 1989, Uniqueness in finite measurement, in *Applications of Combinatorics and Graph Theory to the Biological and Social Sciences*, F. Roberts, ed., Springer, New York, 103–137.

Fleming, M., 1952, A cardinal concept of welfare, *Quarterly Journal of Economics* **66**, 366–384.

Fleurbaey, M., 2004, Equality versus priority: how relevant is the distinction?, in *Fairness and Goodness in Health*, D. Wikler and C. Murray, eds., World Health Organization, Geneva, forthcoming.

Fleurbaey, M. and F. Maniquet, 2004, Compensation and responsibility, in *Handbook of Social Choice and Welfare, vol. 2*, K. Arrow, A. Sen, and K. Suzumura, eds., Elsevier, Amsterdam, forthcoming.

Foged, H., 2003, Worldwide trends in number of cattle, horses and sheep, available at http://www.microfeeder.com/news/livestock_trends_uk.htm.

Gaertner, W., 1982, Envy-free rights assignments and self-oriented preferences, *Mathematical Social Sciences* **2**, 199–208.

Gaertner, W., P. Pattanaik, and K. Suzumura, 1992, Individual rights revisited, *Economica* **59**, 161–177.

Gale, D., 1960, A note on revealed preference, *Economica* **27**, 348–354.

Gevers, L., 1979, On interpersonal comparability and social welfare orderings, *Econometrica* **47**, 75–89.

Glannon, W., 1997, Embryos, biotechnology, and future people, unpublished manuscript, Centre for Applied Ethics, University of British Columbia, Vancouver.

Goodin, R., 1991, Utility and the good, in *A Companion to Ethics*, P. Singer, ed., Basil Blackwell, Oxford, 241–248.

Gorman, W., 1968, The structure of utility functions, *Review of Economic Studies* **32**, 369–390.

Griffin, J., 1986, *Well-Being: Its Meaning, Measurement, and Moral Importance*, Clarendon, Oxford.

Griffin, J., 1996, *Value Judgement: Improving Our Ethical Beliefs*, Clarendon, Oxford.

Guha, A., 1972, Neutrality, monotonicity, and the right of veto, *Econometrica* **40**, 821–826.

Hammond, P., 1976, Equity, Arrow's conditions, and Rawls' difference principle, *Econometrica* **44**, 793–804.

Hammond, P., 1979, Equity in two person situations: some consequences, *Econometrica* **47**, 1127–1135.

Hammond, P., 1981, Ex-ante and ex-post welfare optimality under uncertainty, *Economica* **48**, 235–250.

Hammond, P., 1983, Ex-post optimality as a dynamically consistent objective for collective choice under uncertainty, in *Social Choice and Welfare*, P. Pattanaik and M. Salles, eds., North-Holland, Amsterdam, 175–205.

Hammond, P., 1988, Consequentialist demographic norms and parenting rights, *Social Choice and Welfare* **5**, 127–146.

Hammond, P., 1996, Consequentialist decision theory and utilitarian ethics, in *Ethics, Rationality, and Economic Behavior*, F. Farina, F. Hahn, and S. Vannucci, eds., Oxford University Press, Oxford, 92–118.

Hansson, B., 1968, Choice structures and preference relations, *Synthese* **18**, 443–458.

Hardy, G., J. Littlewood, and G. Pólya, 1934, *Inequalities*, Cambridge University Press, Cambridge.

Hare, R., 1982, Ethical theory and utilitarianism, in *Utilitarianism and Beyond*, A. Sen and B. Williams, eds., Cambridge University Press, Cambridge, 23–38.

Harsanyi, J., 1955, Cardinal welfare, individualistic ethics, and interpersonal comparisons of utility, *Journal of Political Economy* **63**, 309–321.

Harsanyi, J., 1977, *Rational Behavior and Bargaining Equilibrium in Games and Social Situations*, Cambridge University Press, Cambridge.

Harsanyi, J., 1982, Morality and the theory of rational behavior, in *Utilitarianism and Beyond*, A. Sen and B. Williams, eds., Cambridge University Press, Cambridge, 39–62.

Heyd, D., 1982, *Supererogation: Its Status in Ethical Theory*, Cambridge University Press, Cambridge.

Heyd, D., 1992, *Genethics: Moral Issues in the Creation of People*, University of California Press, Berkeley.

Houthakker, H., 1950, Revealed preference and the utility function, *Economica* **17**, 159–174.

Hurka, T., 1983, Value and population size, *Ethics* **93**, 496–507.

Hurka, T., 2000, Comment on 'Population principles with number-dependent critical levels,' unpublished manuscript, Department of Philosophy, University of Calgary.

Hurwicz, L. and M. Richter, 1971, Revealed preference without demand continuity assumptions, in *Preferences, Utility, and Demand*, J. Chipman, L. Hurwicz, M. Richter, and H. Sonnenschein, eds., Harcourt Brace Jovanovich, New York, 59–76.

Jansen, M. and S. Tijs, 1983, Continuity of bargaining solutions, *International Journal of Game Theory* **12**, 91–105.

Kelly, J., 1976, The impossibility of a just liberal, *Economica* **43**, 67–75.

Kelsey, D., 1987, The role of information in social welfare judgements, *Oxford Economic Papers* **39**, 301–317.

Kihlstrom, R., A. Mas-Colell, and H. Sonnenschein, 1976, The demand theory of the weak axiom of revealed preference, *Econometrica* **44**, 971–978.

Kolm, S.-C., 1969, The optimal production of social justice, in *Public Economics*, J. Margolis and S. Guitton, eds., Macmillan, London, 145–200.

Kolm, S.-C., 1972, *Justice et Equité*, Editions C.N.R.S., Paris.

Kolm, S.-C., 1976a, Unequal inequalities I, *Journal of Economic Theory* **12**, 416–442.

Kolm, S.-C., 1976b, Unequal inequalities II, *Journal of Economic Theory* **13**, 82–111.

Kolm, S.-C., 1992, *The Impossibility of Utilitarianism*, C.G.P.C., Paris.

Kolm, S.-C., 1996, *Modern Theories of Justice*, MIT Press, Cambridge.

Krantz, D., R. Luce, P. Suppes, and A. Tversky, 1971, *Foundations of Measurement, vol. I: Additive and Polynomial Representations*, Academic Press, New York.

Lensberg, T., 1987, Stability and collective rationality, *Econometrica* **55**, 935–961.

Lensberg, T., 1988, Stability and the Nash solution, *Journal of Economic Theory* **45**, 330–341.

Lesco, P., 1988, To do no harm: a Buddhist view on animal use in research, *Journal of Religion and Health* **27**, 307–312.

Lohr, S., 1988, Livestock liberated by new law in Sweden, *The Globe and Mail*, October 25, A1.

Lorenz, M., 1905, Methods for measuring concentration of wealth, *Journal of the American Statistical Association* **9**, 209–219.

Marshall, A. and I. Olkin, 1979, *Inequalities: Theory of Majorization and Its Applications*, Academic Press, New York.

Maskin, E., 1978, A theorem on utilitarianism, *Review of Economic Studies* **45**, 93–96.

McMahan, J., 1981, Problems of population theory, *Ethics* **92**, 96–127.

McMahan, J., 1996, Wrongful life: paradoxes in the morality of causing people to exist, unpublished manuscript, Department of Philosophy, University of Illinois, Chicago.

Mehran, F., 1976, Linear measures of income inequality, *Econometrica* **44**, 805–809.

Mill, J., 1979a (originally published in 1859), On Liberty, in *Utilitarianism; On Liberty; Essay on Bentham*, J. Mill, Collins, Glasgow, 126–250.

Mill, J., 1979b (originally published in 1861), Utilitarianism, in *Utilitarianism; On Liberty; Essay on Bentham*, J. Mill, Collins, Glasgow, 251–321.

Milnor, J., 1954, Games against nature, in *Decision Processes*, R. Thrall, C. Coombs, and R. Davis, eds., Wiley, New York, 49–59.

Mongin, P., 1994, Harsanyi's aggregation theorem: multi-profile version and unsettled questions, *Social Choice and Welfare* **11**, 331–354.

Mongin, P, 1995, Consistent Bayesian aggregation, *Journal of Economic Theory* **66**, 313–351.

Mongin, P., 1998, The paradox of the Bayesian experts and state-dependent utility theory, *Journal of Mathematical Economics* **29**, 331–361.

Mongin, P. and C. d'Aspremont, 1998, Utility theory in ethics, in *Handbook of Utility Theory, vol. 1: Principles*, S. Barberà, P. Hammond, and C. Seidl, eds., Kluwer, Dordrecht, 371–481.

Mulgan, T., 2002, The reverse repugnant conclusion, *Utilitas* **14**, 360–364.

Nash, J., 1950, The bargaining problem, *Econometrica* **18**, 155–162.

New English Bible, 1970, Oxford University Press, Oxford.

Ng, Y.-K., 1986, Social criteria for evaluating population change: an alternative to the Blackorby-Donaldson criterion, *Journal of Public Economics* **29**, 375–381.

Ng, Y.-K., 1989, What should we do about future generations? Impossibility of Parfit's Theory X, *Economics and Philosophy* **5**, 235–253.

Nussbaum, M., 2000a, *Women and Human Development: The Capabilities Approach*, Cambridge University Press, Cambridge.

Nussbaum, M., 2000b, The central human capabilities, *Ethics* **111**, 6–7.

Ok, E. and L. Zhou, 1999, Revealed group preferences on non-convex choice problems, *Economic Theory* **13**, 671–687.

Ok, E. and L. Zhou, 2000, The Choquet bargaining solutions, *Games and Economic Behavior* **33**, 249–264.

Parfit, D., 1976, On doing the best for our children, in *Ethics and Population*, M. Bayles, ed., Schenkman, Cambridge, 100–102.

Parfit, D., 1982, Future generations, further problems, *Philosophy and Public Affairs* **11**, 113–172.

Parfit, D., 1984, *Reasons and Persons*, Oxford University Press, Oxford.

Parfit, D., 1997, Equality or priority?, *Ratio* **10**, 202–221.

Peters, H., 1992, *Axiomatic Bargaining Game Theory*, Kluwer, Dordrecht.

Peters, H. and P. Wakker, 1991, Independence of irrelevant alternatives and revealed group preferences, *Econometrica* **59**, 1787–1801.

Peters, H. and P. Wakker, 1994, WARP does not imply SARP for more than two commodities, *Journal of Economic Theory* **62**, 152–160.

Pfingsten, A., 1986, Distributionally-neutral tax changes for different inequality concepts, *Journal of Public Economics* **30**, 385–393.

Pigou, A., 1912, *Wealth and Welfare*, Macmillan, London.

Pollak, R., 1971, Additive utility functions and linear Engel curves, *Review of Economic Studies* **38**, 401–414.

Regan, T., 1982, *All That Dwell Therein: Animal Rights and Environmental Ethics*, University of California Press, Berkeley.

Regan, T., 1983, *The Case for Animal Rights*, University of California Press, Berkeley.

Richter, M., 1966, Revealed preference theory, *Econometrica* **34**, 635–645.

Richter, M., 1971, Rational choice, in *Preferences, Utility, and Demand*, J. Chipman, L. Hurwicz, M. Richter, and H. Sonnenschein, eds., Harcourt Brace Jovanovich, New York, 29–58.

Roberts, K., 1980a, Possibility theorems with interpersonally comparable welfare levels, *Review of Economic Studies* **47**, 409–420.

Roberts, K., 1980b, Interpersonal comparability and social choice theory, *Review of Economic Studies* **47**, 421–439.

Roemer, J., 1996, *Theories of Distributive Justice*, Harvard University Press, Cambridge.

Roemer, J., 2004, Harsanyi's impartial observer is *not* a utilitarian, in *Justice, Political Liberalism, and Utilitarianism: Themes from Harsanyi and Rawls*, M. Salles and J. Weymark, eds., Cambridge University Press, Cambridge, forthcoming.

Rolston, H., 1988, *Environmental Ethics: Duties to and Values in the Natural World*, Temple University Press, Philadelphia.

Rose, H., 1958, Consistency of preference: the two-commodity case, *Review of Economic Studies* **25**, 124–125.

Saint Augustine, 1961, *Confessions*, Penguin, London.

Salonen, H., 1998, Egalitarian solutions to *n*-person bargaining games, *Mathematical Social Sciences* **35**, 291–306.

Samuelson, P., 1938, A note on the pure theory of consumer's behavior, *Economica* **5**, 61–71.

Samuelson, P., 1948, Consumption theory in terms of revealed preference, *Economica* **15**, 243–253.

Sanchez, M., 2000, Rationality of bargaining solutions, *Journal of Mathematical Economics* **33**, 389–399.

Sen, A., 1970a, *Collective Choice and Social Welfare*, Holden-Day, San Francisco.

Sen, A., 1970b, The impossibility of a Paretian liberal, *Journal of Political Economy* **78**, 152–157.

Sen, A., 1971, Choice functions and revealed preference, *Review of Economic Studies* **38**, 307–317.

Sen, A., 1973, *On Economic Inequality*, Oxford University Press, Oxford.

Sen, A., 1974, Informational bases of alternative welfare approaches: aggregation and income distribution, *Journal of Public Economics* **3**, 387–403.

Sen, A., 1976, Welfare inequalities and Rawlsian axiomatics, *Theory and Decision* **7**, 243–262.

Sen, A., 1977a, On weights and measures: informational constraints in social welfare analysis, *Econometrica* **45**, 1539–1572.

Sen, A., 1977b, Non-linear social welfare functions: a reply to Professor Harsanyi, in *Foundational Problems in the Special Sciences*, R. Butts and J. Hintikka, eds., Reidel, Dordrecht, 297–302.

Sen, A., 1979, Personal utilities and public judgements: or what's wrong with welfare economics?, *Economic Journal* **89**, 537–558.

Sen, A., 1981, Plural utility, *Proceedings of the Aristotelian Society* **81**, 193–215.

Sen, A., 1985, *Commodities and Capabilities*, Elsevier, Amsterdam.

Sen, A., 1986, Social choice theory, in *Handbook of Mathematical Economics, vol. III*, K. Arrow and M. Intriligator, eds., North-Holland, Amsterdam, 1073–1181.

Sen, A., 1987, *The Standard of Living*, Cambridge University Press, Cambridge.

Sen, A., 1993, Internal consistency of choice, *Econometrica* **61**, 495–521.

Sen, A., 1994, Population: delusion and reality, *New York Review of Books* **41**, 62–71.

Sen, A., 1995, Population policy: authoritarianism versus cooperation, Discussion Paper 63, Development Economics Research Programme, London School of Economics.

Sen, A. and B. Williams, 1982, Introduction, in *Utilitarianism and Beyond*, A. Sen and B. Williams, eds., Cambridge University Press, Cambridge, 1–21.

Sider, T., 1991, Might theory X be a theory of diminishing marginal value?, *Analysis* **51**, 265–271.

Sidgwick, H., 1966 (originally published in 1907), *The Methods of Ethics*, Dover, New York.

Sikora, R., 1978, Is it wrong to prevent the existence of future generations?, in *Obligations to Future Generations*, R. Sikora and B. Barry, eds., Temple University Press, Philadelphia, 112–166.

Singer, P., 1975, *Animal Liberation: A New Ethics For Our Treatment of Animals*, Avon, New York.

Singer, P., 1979, *Practical Ethics*, Cambridge University Press, Cambridge.

Singer, P., 1994, *Rethinking Life and Death*, The Text Publishing Company, Melbourne.

Sumner, L., 1996, *Welfare, Happiness, and Ethics*, Clarendon, Oxford.

Suppes, P., 1966, Some formal models of grading principles, *Synthese* **6**, 284–306.

Suzumura, K., 1976, Rational choice and revealed preference, *Review of Economic Studies* **43**, 149–158.

Suzumura, K., 1982, Equity, efficiency and rights in social choice, *Mathematical Social Sciences* **3**, 131–155.

Szpilrajn, E., 1930, Sur l'extension de l'ordre partiel, *Fundamenta Mathematicae* **16**, 386–389.

Tännsjö, T., 2002, Why we ought to accept the repugnant conclusion, *Utilitas* **14**, 339–359.

Thomson, W., 1983a, The fair division of a fixed supply among a growing population, *Mathematics of Operations Research* **8**, 319–326.

Thomson, W., 1983b, Problems of fair division and the egalitarian solution, *Journal of Economic Theory* **31**, 211–226.

Thomson, W., 1984, Monotonicity, stability, and egalitarianism, *Mathematical Social Sciences* **8**, 15–28.

Thomson, W., 1985, Axiomatic theory of bargaining with a variable population: a survey of recent results, in *Game Theoretic Models of Bargaining*, A. Roth, ed., Cambridge University Press, Cambridge, 233–258.

Thomson, W., 1986, Replication invariance of bargaining solutions, *International Journal of Game Theory* **15**, 59–63.

Thomson, W., 1990, The consistency principle, in *Game Theory and Applications*, T. Ichiishi, A. Neyman, and Y. Tauman, eds., Academic Press, New York, 187–215.

Thomson, W., 1996a, Discussion of Blackorby, Bossert, and Donaldson's paper, in *Social Choice Re-Examined, vol. 2*, K. Arrow, A. Sen, and K. Suzumura, eds., Macmillan, London, 163–166.

Thomson, W., 1996b, Consistent allocation rules, Working Paper 418, Rochester Center for Economic Research, University of Rochester.

Thomson, W., 2001, On the axiomatic method and its recent applications to game theory and resource allocation, *Social Choice and Welfare* **18**, 327–386.

Thomson, W., 2004, *Bargaining Theory: The Axiomatic Approach*, Academic Press, forthcoming.

Thomson, W. and T. Lensberg, 1989, *Axiomatic Theory of Bargaining with a Variable Number of Agents*, Cambridge University Press, Cambridge.

Tungodden, B., 1998, Social choices with independent norm levels, unpublished manuscript, Institute of Economics, Norwegian School of Economics and Business Administration.

United Nations, 1995, Review of population trends, policies and programmes: monitoring of multilateral population assistance, Department for Economic and Social Information and Policy Analysis, Population Information Network (POPIN) Gopher of the United Nations Population Division.

Uzawa, H., 1960, Preference and rational choice in the theory of consumption, in *Mathematical Methods in the Social Sciences, 1959*, K. Arrow, S. Karlin, and P. Suppes, eds., Stanford University Press, Stanford, 129–148.

Uzawa, H., 1971, Preference and rational choice in the theory of consumption, in *Preferences, Utility, and Demand*, J. Chipman, L. Hurwicz, M. Richter, and H. Sonnenschein, eds., Harcourt Brace Jovanovich, New York, 7–28.

von Neumann, J. and O. Morgenstern, 1944 (second ed. 1947), *Theory of Games and Economic Behavior*, Princeton University Press, Princeton.

Weymark, J., 1981, Generalized Gini inequality indices, *Mathematical Social Sciences* **1**, 409–430.

Weymark, J., 1991, A reconsideration of the Harsanyi-Sen debate on utilitarianism, in *Interpersonal Comparisons of Well-Being*, J. Elster and J. Roemer, eds., Cambridge University Press, Cambridge, 255–320.

Weymark, J., 1993, Harsanyi's social aggregation theorem and the weak Pareto principle, *Social Choice and Welfare* **10**, 209–222.

Weymark, J., 1994, Harsanyi's social aggregation theorem with alternative Pareto principles, in *Models and Measurement of Welfare and Inequality*, W. Eichhorn, ed., Springer, Berlin, 869–887.

Weymark, J., 1995, Further remarks on Harsanyi's social aggregation theorem and the weak Pareto principle, *Social Choice and Welfare* **12**, 87–92.

Weymark, J., 1998, Welfarism on economic domains, *Mathematical Social Sciences* **36**, 251–268.

Wold, H., 1943a, A synthesis of pure demand analysis I, *Skandinavisk Akguarietidskrift* **26**, 85–118.

Wold, H., 1943b, A synthesis of pure demand analysis II, *Skandinavisk Akguarietidskrift* **26**, 220–263.

Zhou, L., 1997a, Harsanyi's utilitarianism theorems: general societies, *Journal of Economic Theory* **72**, 198–207.

Zhou, L., 1997b, The Nash bargaining theory with non-convex problems, *Econometrica* **65**, 681–685.

Zoli, C., 2002, Variable population welfare and inequality orderings satisfying population replication principles, unpublished manuscript, School of Economics, University of Nottingham.

Author Index

Subject Index

Printed in the United States
By Bookmasters